BURT FRANKLIN: RESEARCH AND SOURCE WORKS SERIES #249
American Classics in History & Social Science Series #44

A

COLLECTION OF PAPERS

ON

# POLITICAL, LITERARY

AND

# MORAL SUBJECTS.

A

# COLLECTION OF PAPERS

ON

# POLITICAL, LITERARY

AND

# MORAL SUBJECTS.

BY NOAH WEBSTER, LL. D.

BURT FRANKLIN: RESEARCH AND SOURCE WORKS SERIES #249
American Classics in History & Social Science Series #44

BURT FRANKLIN
NEW YORK

Published By
BURT FRANKLIN
235 East 44th St.
New York, N.Y. 10017

AC
8
.W25
1968

ORIGINALLY PUBLISHED
NEW YORK: 1843
Reprinted 1968

Printed in U.S.A.

# ADVERTISEMENT.

THE observations on the Revolution in France, in this collection, were written and published in the year 1794, during the heat of the revolution, when I was frequently receiving fresh accounts of the ferocities of the violent reformers, exhibiting the appalling effects of popular factions.

The Essay on the Rights of Neutral Nations, owes its origin to the enormous outrages on the commerce of the United States, committed by the belligerent powers, during the French Revolution. It was published in New York in the year 1802. The principal points in it have a bearing on the *Right of Search;* a subject now agitated in this country, as it is in Great Britain and in France. An eminent jurist in Philadelphia, considers this essay as one of the best, if not the best work that has appeared on this subject. He mentions particularly the ground on which I have placed the jurisdiction of nations on the ocean. In the papers signed CURTIUS, the treaty of 1795 is vindicated on the principles of the law of nations, so called. In the essay on neutral rights, I give my own opinions.

A particular motive I have in this publication, is to record my testimony against the audacious practice of publishing misrepresentations, falsehood, and calumny, for party purposes. By this practice, the most virtuous, meritorious, and patriotic statesmen are vilified, and their influence impaired or destroyed; the harmony of our public councils is disturbed; and the co-operation of our citizens, in measures indispensable to our national prosperity, is prevented. In short, this practice frustrates the great object of a republican government, by subjecting our citizens to the sway of some petty oligarchy, changeable every fourth year. I have been a witness to the evil effects of this licentiousness, from the formation of the government, and I question whether any other age or nation has furnished an example of public calumnies of equal extent, and attended with equal injury to the morals and interests of the community.

# CONTENTS.

# MISCELLANEOUS PAPERS.

## CHAPTER I.

### REVOLUTION IN FRANCE.

#### INTRODUCTION.

MEN of all descriptions are frequently asking the questions, What will be the fate of France? What will be the consequences of the Revolution in France? Will France be conquered? and others of a like nature.

These questions are extremely interesting, as they respect every thing which concerns the happiness of men in the great societies of Europe and America; government, liberty, arts, science, agriculture, commerce, morality, religion.

It would be an evidence of daring presumption to attempt to open the volume of divine determinations on these momentous questions. But it is highly proper, at all times, to exercise our reason, in examining the connection between causes and their effects; and in predicting, with modesty, the probable consequences of known events.

It is conceived to be the duty of the historian and the statesman, not merely to collect accounts of battles, the slaughter of the human race, the sacking of cities, the seizure and confiscation of shipping, and other bloody and barbarous deeds, the work of savage man toward his fellow men; but to discover, if possible, the *causes* of great changes in the affairs of men; the *springs* of those important movements, which vary the aspect of government, the features of nations, and the very character of man.

The present efforts of the French nation, in resisting the forces of the combined powers, astonish even reflecting men. They far exceed every thing exhibited during the energetic reigns of Francis I. and Louis XIV. To ascertain the true principles from which have sprung the union and the vigor which have marked this amazing revolution, is a work of no small labor, and may be of great public utility.

#### JACOBIN SOCIETY.

It is conceived the first principle of combination in France, was the establishment of the Jacobin Society. The members of this association may not originally have foreseen the extent of the Revolution, or the full effect of their own institution. At the time it was formed, there may have been many persons in it, who were friends to the monarchy of France, under the control of a constitution, and an elective

1

legislative assembly. But the interest of the ancient court, the nobility and clergy, was then considerable, not only in Paris, but in every department of France. It was necessary, in the view of the leaders of the Republican party, to circumscribe or destroy the court influence by direct legislative acts; or to raise throughout France, a combination of republicans, who, by union and concert, might oppose it with success. The public mind was not ripe for the first expedient, the direct invasion of the privileged orders; the Republicans therefore, with a discernment that marks great talents, resorted to the last expedient, the institution of popular societies in every department of that extensive country. These societies are all moved by the mainspring of the machine, the Jacobin Society in Paris; and by the perfect concert observed in all their proceedings, they have been able to crush every other influence, and establish over France a government as singular in its kind, as it is absolute in its exercise.

### COMMISSIONERS.

In pursuance of the same principle of combination, though not cotemporary in its adoption, was the plan of conducting both civil and military operations in all parts of the Republic, by commissioners from the National Convention. It was found that, although the Jacobin Societies had a very extensive influence in seconding the views of the Republican party; yet this was the influence of opinion, and private exertion merely; an influence too small and indirect, to answer every purpose. These societies were voluntary associations, unclothed with any legal authority. To conduct the intended revolution, it was necessary there should be persons, in all parts of the country, vested with full powers to execute the decrees of the Convention, a majority of whom were Jacobins, and whose measures were only the resolutions of the Jacobin Society in Paris, clothed with the sanction of a constitutional form. To supply the defect of legal authority in the several popular societies, commissioners were deputed from the Convention, invested with the most absolute powers to watch over the civil and military officers employed in responsible stations, to detect conspiracies, to arrest suspected persons, and in short to control all the operations of that extensive country. These commissioners, being usually taken from the Jacobin Society at Paris, and having a constant communication with the Convention, which was ruled by them, were enabled to carry all their measures into full effect. A single club, by this curious artifice, gave law to France. An immense machine, by the most extraordinary contexture of its parts, was and is still, moved by a single spring.

To unclog this machine from all its incumbrances, and give vigor to its active operations, it was necessary to displace all its enemies. For this purpose, all suspected and disaffected persons were to be removed. Under pretense of guarding the public safety, and delivering the Republic from traitors, insidiously plotting its destruction, a Court was established, called the *Revolutionary Tribunal*, consisting of men devoted to the views of the Jacobins, and clothed with powers that made their enemies tremble. The summary jurisdiction, assumed or exercised by this tribunal, together with its executive instrument, the *guillotin*, have filled France with human blood, and swept away opposition.

The Commissioners in the several departments and municipalities have renewed the tyranny of the decemvirs of Rome. The writer is informed, that while they affect the pomp and the manners of Roman consuls, they exercise the powers of a dictator. The two Commissioners at Bourdeaux, imitating as far as possible the Roman habit, ride in a car or carriage drawn by eight horses, attended by a body of guards, resembling the pretorian bands, and preceded by lictors with their battle-axes.

The authority of all the commissioners is nearly dictatorial. They arrest, try and condemn, in a most summary manner. Not only difference of opinion, but moderation, and especially the possession of money, are unpardonable crimes, punishable with death, in the view of these delegates of dictatorial power.

By this *principle of combination*, has a party, originally small, been enabled to triumph over all opposition.

In the mean time, a numerous and ignorant populace were to be amused, united, won to their party, and fired with enthusiasm for liberty. These people, who little understand the principles of government, were to be rendered subservient to the views of the Republican party ; and as their reason could be little affected by arguments, their passions were to be roused by the objects of sense. As the most of them can not read, particular persons were employed in the towns and villages to read to them, the inflammatory writings which flowed from the Parisian presses. These readers collected the people in crowds, read to them such pieces against the king, queen, nobility and clergy, as were calculated to irritate their passions and inspire them with implacable hatred against these orders. They were taught to believe them all tyrants, traitors and oppressors. These public readers would also harangue extemporaneously on the same subjects : such artifices had a prodigious effect in changing the attachment of the people for their king and their priesthood, to the most violent aversion. This hatred soon discovered itself in the destruction of a great number of noblemen's chateaus ; the busts of ancient kings, pictures and other ensigns of the royal government. At the same time a number of patriotic songs were composed, as *Ca ira*, *Carmagnole*, and the *Marseillois hymn ;* which were soon spread over France, and have had a more extensive influence over the soldiers, seamen, and the peasantry of that country, in reconciling them to the hardships of war, and firing them with an enthusiasm for what they call *liberty*, than the world in general will believe ; an influence perhaps as powerful as that of all other causes combined.

Interrupted as our intercourse is with France, and agitated as the public mind must be with passing scenes, it can not be expected that we should obtain from that country a dispassionate and minute detail of causes and their consequences ; but I believe the facts I have mentioned will go far to account for the unprecedented union of the people of France, notwithstanding the operation of the usual causes of discord, and the influence of foreign gold very liberally exerted to disunite them, and perplex their measures. It has however been necessary for

the Convention to resort to the terrors of the guillotin, and of death
and the destruction of whole cities, to awe the spirit of opposition to
their system.  Very numerous and most terrible examples of punishment have had a powerful temporary effect, in subduing their internal
dissensions.  How far the people will bear oppression, is a point on
which we can not decide.

## NATIONAL TREASURY.

The measures taken by the Convention to prolong the resistance of
France, are no less singular, bold and decisive.  It was found that immense sums of money would be necessary to maintain the vast body
of men and military apparatus, requisite to oppose the combined forces
of more than one half of Europe.  To furnish the funds necessary for
this purpose, the Convention very early adopted the plan of issuing *assignats* or bills of credit, an expedient practiced with great success in
America during her late Revolution.  This paper however was issued
on safer ground than the American paper, as confiscated property to a
vast amount was pledged for its redemption.

It was found however that this paper would depreciate ; as the funds
pledged for its redemption were exhausted, or proved inadequate to the
enormous demands made upon the nation, in consequence of a great
augmentation of their military establishment, after opening the last
campaign.  To supply the deficiency, and to put it out of the power
of chance or enmity to drain the Republic of its specie, the Convention
adopted the following desperate expedients.  They exacted from moneyed men whatever specie they possessed, by way of loan.  This is
called *emprunt forcè ;* a forced loan.  And to make sure of this specie,
they contracted with certain bankers in Paris to advance twelve millions sterling of the money, paying them a large commission for the
risk and forbearance.  The amount of the specie to be thus brought
into the national treasury, may be twenty millions sterling.  This
measure, together with the proceeds of confiscations, has accumulated
a great proportion of the current specie of the country in the treasury.

Not satisfied with these measures, the Convention have taken possession of all the plate of the churches, which, in all Roman Catholic
countries, must be very considerable, but in France amounts to immense
value.  It is estimated by gentlemen well acquainted with this subject,
that this public plate which is carried to the mint, will amount to twenty
five millions sterling ; a sum nearly equal to the whole current specie
of that rich commerical country, England.

It was estimated by Mr. Neckar and others, just as the Revolution
commenced, that the current coin of France was at least eighty millions sterling ; a sum equal to one third, perhaps one half, of all the
specie of Europe.  Allowing large sums to have been carried out of
the country by emigrants, and some to be buried for safety, but taking
into the account the accession of twenty five millions coined from plate,
and we may estimate the amount of specie in possession of the Convention, to be from sixty to seventy millions sterling.

Having thus collected all the precious metals in that country, the
Convention, instead of using specie freely to furnish supplies for the

army, expend it with great economy. They hold it in reserve, for times and exigencies when all other expedients fail. At present they compel every person whatever, to take assignats for provision, clothing, and other articles, at a certain price fixed by a valuation. They seize whatever grain or other articles a man has, beyond an estimated supply for his own family, and pay him in paper at the stated price. In this manner they seem determined to make their paper answer every purpose as long as possible, and when this fails, they will still have specie enough at command, with the aid of some taxes, to prosecute the war for three or four years.

## PROBABLE EVENT OF THE WAR.

It may be doubtful whether the body of people will long sit easy, under such severe regulations. An enthusiasm for liberty will do much, the guillotin and an irresistible army will do more, toward preserving peace and order. But there is nothing dearer to a man than the liberty of making his own bargains ; and whether the forcible means employed to procure from people their produce or manufactures, will not at least check industry and limit the exertions of laborers to a bare supply of their own wants, is a point very problematical. But whatever may be the wants of France, there is little danger, while her specie is at the command of government, that her provisions will fail. Her rich soil will furnish the principal mass of food ; and should distress call for foreign supplies, her own shipping will supply her from abroad.

If these ideas are well founded, France is able to sustain a war of many years. She can supply men enough to resist the combined powers forever. Her natural population will forever repair her annual loss of men ; and the longer a war lasts, the more soldiers will she possess. The whole country will become an immense camp of disciplined veterans.

While policy, aided by the strong arm of absolute power, is thus furnishing France with the means of defense, what prospect have the combined powers of effecting their purposes ? France may defend herself until England is bankrupt, and Austria is beggared. Possibly England and Holland may sustain the war another campaign ; and more than this, they unquestionably will not. The states of Italy, which have been compelled to renounce their neutrality, will yield a cold, reluctant, feeble assistance, and embrace the first favorable moment to renounce the confederacy. Portugal is nothing in the contest. Spain, it is an equal chance, will be overrun and plundered by a French army, will itself be disabled and its riches only furnish the French with additional means of defense. Prussia has gained her principal object in obtaining a large division of Poland ; she now demands a considerable debt of the Empire, which the Diet is not well able to discharge. The Empress of Russia is encouraging the controversy, while she laughs at the combination and is adding to her dominions. Austria is powerful, but she is exhausting her resources ; and by reason of the distance which great part of her supplies are to be transported, her means must fail before those of France. Already the Emperor calls for voluntary aid from his subjects in Flanders. In this situation, where is the hope of conquering France !

It is more probable that France will not only resist all this force, but will retain strength sufficient to commence an offensive war, when the confederacy of her enemies shall be dissolved, and the resources of each exhausted. Her enemies will waste their strength in making France a garrison of disciplined soldiers, impregnable within, and terrible to surrounding nations. The moment the combination is broken, and the army now investing France disabled, half a million of hardy exasperated French warriors, inured to service, and fired with victory, will be let loose upon defenseless Europe ; and in their mad enthusiasm to destroy, not despotism merely, but all the works of elegance and art, they may renew the desolations of the sixth and seventh centuries. Already has France experienced a revolution in property, in manners, in opinions, in law, in government, that has not been equaled in the world since the conquests of Attila and Genseric. The ravages of Genghis Khan, of Tamerlane and the Saracens were extensive ; they were attended with slaughter and devastation. But the conquered nations only *changed masters* and remained *unchanged themselves*. The revolution in France is attended with a change of *manners*, *opinions* and *institutions*, infinitely more singular and important, than a change of masters or of government.

Of the two possible events, a conquest of France, and a total ultimate defeat of the combination against the Republic, I am free in declaring my opinion, that the *former* is *less probable* than the *latter*. And should victory finally declare for France, her armies may prove formidable to Europe. Italy and the Netherlands must inevitably fall under her dominion, unless prevented by a timely pacification.

Such being the origin and progress of this astonishing revolution, let us examine its probable effects.

### DEBTS.

The effects of war upon the hostile nations are always to exhaust their strength and resources, and incur heavy debts. Should France succeed in baffling her foes, an immense debt will be contracted, which must be paid, funded or expunged. An immediate payment is not to be expected ; it will be impracticable. It may be justly questioned, whether the best administration of her finances will, for many years, discharge the interest. Such a general war, which involves in it a diversion of laborers from their usual occupations, a destruction of manufacturing towns and villages, a limitation of commercial intercourse, and especially a loss of capital among all descriptions of citizens, must dry up the sources of revenue, and occasion a deficiency that will materially affect the credit of the nation. If therefore the government should be disposed to fund the national debt, its inability to pay the interest, must, for some years, cause a depreciation in the value of the receipts or evidences of that debt. This depreciation will renew the speculations of John Law's administration—or rather the scenes exhibited in America in 1790, 1791 and 1792. Should this be the case, immense fortunes will be made ; a new species of aristocrats, as they will be called, will arise out of the *equality* of *sans-culottism*, and unless a change of sentiment shall take place in the people, these new-fledged nabobs will be considered as noxious weeds in society, that are to be mown down with that political sythe, the all-leveling guillotin.

But the *funding of debts* is at present not an article in the national French creed. On the other hand, the revolutionists execrate the system that entails on posterity the debts of the present generation, and fills a country with negotiators and stock-jobbers. If then the nation *can not* pay the principal, and will not pay the interest, the remaining alternative is to *expunge* the whole debt.

We can not however suppose that the same administration of the government will continue for a long period. The probability is that when danger of external foes shall be removed, the nation will elect a new Convention of a very different complexion. Too many good citizens will be public creditors, to suffer the debts of the nation to be wiped away with a spunge. It is more probable that efforts will be made to discharge them; and as the proceeds of confiscations will be soon exhausted, and there are no wild lands in France, the government must resort to the usual modes of raising money, by customs, and taxes, with loans or anticipations of revenue. So that after all the fine philosophy of France, she will probably be obliged to submit to some of the old schemes of finance, which her wise legislators now execrate. We have therefore no great reason to apprehend that her government will be able to expunge her debts, nor can we suppose that absolute *freedom* from debt will constitute a part of her promised millennium of *reason* and *philosophy.*

## AGRICULTURE.

The important changes in the tenure of lands in France will produce the most distinguishable effects. The feudal system was calculated for no good purpose, except for defense among a barbarous people. It was every way formed to check the exertions of the great mass of people, whose labor, in all countries, is the principal source of wealth. That must always be a bad system of tenures which deprives the laboring man of the great stimulus to industry, the prospect of enjoying the reward of his labor. Such was the feudal system throughout Europe, and it is observable that agriculture and manufactures have made slow progress in every part of Europe where that system has been suffered to prevail in its ancient vigor. The principal cities of Italy and Germany first regained their freedom and revived industry. The abolition of military tenures in England may be considered as the epoch of her wealth and prosperity. Under the old government of France, the feudal system had lost much of its severity. There were many laboring men who enjoyed small freeholds; too small however for the purpose of improving in cultivation. But two thirds of the lands were leased to the peasantry, the landlord furnishing the stock of the farm, and receiving half the produce. This mode has ever been found less beneficial to a country, than leases on fixed rents in money.

But by the late revolution, a vast proportion of the lands will change hands; and much of them become freehold estate, subject to no rent,

or none that shall be oppressive.  The laboring people, becoming proprietors and cultivating for their own benefit, will feel all the motives
to labor that can influence the human heart in that particular.  The
mind, unfettered and prompted to action, will exert its faculties in various kinds of improvement; and when the distresses of war shall cease,
the French nation will push improvements in agriculture to a length
hitherto unknown in that country.  Previous to this however property
must be placed under the protection of law; and the laws must receive
an energy from a well-constituted executive power, that shall insure a
due execution.

### MANUFACTURES.

The same circumstances which will invigorate industry in one branch
of business, will extend their influence to every other.  For some years
indeed the desolating effects of war will be visible.  The destruction of
some manufacturing towns, the loss of capital, and the diversion of
laborers from their employment, will be severely felt for many years.
But the active genius of the French nation, unfettered from the imposing prejudices of former times, when it was held degrading to engage
in manual occupations, will surmount these difficulties; and the immense wealth of the emigrant nobles, the national domains, or other
property which had been monopolized and sequestered from employment, under ancient institutions, will be brought into action in every
branch of business.  After the ravages of war shall be repaired, a
greater mass of capital will be employed in useful arts, and rendered
productive.  All the plate of the churches, now converted into coin,
and immense sums formerly squandered by a profligate nobility, or
withheld from employment by cloistered monks, will he brought into
circulation, and become the means of encouraging industry.  Add to
these circumstances, the amazing increase of enterprise, which must
follow a revolution, that has awakened a nation from the slumbers of
ignorance and inaction, and roused into life the dormant faculties of its
citizens.

### COMMERCE.

Similar circumstances will forward the growth and extension of commerce.  France has long been respectable, for its commerce and its
navy.  But the increase of agriculture and manufactures, which will
necessarily follow the downfall of the feudal distinctions, and the more
general diffusion of property, will produce also a correspondent increase
of commerce.  This commerce will require the use of shipping, and the
late navigation law of France will recall to her some of the advantages of the carrying trade, heretofore enjoyed by the English and the
Dutch, and be the means of augmenting her navy.

### ARTS AND SCIENCE.

Free governments are the soil best fitted to produce improvements
in the arts and sciences.  All history testifies this.  France indeed, under her old government, had been distinguished for a cultivation of the
sciences, and many of the most useful and elegant arts.  In many re-

spects, the lover of philosophy was free, and full scope was given to human genius. In other respects, freedom of writing was restrained by the hand of power, and the bold writers of that nation were compelled to retire beyond the reach of it.

The universal freedom of writing, which we may expect to prevail, when the present storm subsides, will be among the most conspicuous blessings of that nation. The arts will receive new encouragement, and the sciences new luster, from the active genius of renovated France.

### RELIGION.

The progress of the revolution in France, with respect to morals and the religion of the nation, affords a most interesting spectacle to reflecting men. The hierarchy of Rome had established, over the minds of its votaries, a system of errors and superstition, that enslaved their opinions and plundered their purses. Long had nations been the victims of papal domination, and spiritual impositions. Accustomed from childhood to count their beads, to bow to the host, and chant *te deum*, men supposed the *ceremony* to be *devotion ;* while an artful priesthood availed themselves of their weakness and errors, to spunge from the deluded multitude, a great portion of the fruits of their honest labor.

For three centuries past, the reason of man has been removing the vail of error from his mind. In some countries, the vail has been rent asunder ; and human reason, aided and directed by revelation, has assumed its native dignity. But in France, science and education, while they had illuminated a portion of its inhabitants, had not dissipated the gloom that was spread over the mass of the nation. Inquisitive men had searched for truth, and astonished at the monstrous absurdities of the national religion, their minds, starting from the extreme of superstition, vibrated to the extreme of skepticism. Because they found religion clothed with a garb of fantastical human artifices, they rejected her as a creature of human invention, pronounced her ceremonies a farce, and derided her votaries. Hence sprung a race of literary men, denominated philosophers, who, under their illustrious champions, Voltaire and Rousseau, attempted, by secret undermining or open assault, to demolish the whole fabric of the national religion, and to erect upon its ruins, the throne of reason.

Before the present revolution commenced, this philosophy had spread among the literati of France ; and Paris exhibited then, what Italy does now, the two most irreconcilable extremes, of atheism and profound superstition ; the most scandalous vices mingled with the most scrupulous observance of religious rites ; the same persons retiring immediately from their mock devotions at Notre Dame, to the revels of prostitution.

In this situation of the moral and religious character of the French nation, began the revolution of 1789. The philosophical researches of Voltaire, Rousseau, and the Abbe Raynal, had long before unchained the minds of that part of the French nation who read ; a respectable class of men. These men understood the errors of their government and the nature of liberty. They were prepared to second the operation of those political causes, which hastened the crisis of a revolution. The first attentions of the reformers were occupied with the correction

of *political* evils, rather than those of *religion.* But when the first National Assembly came to examine the system of their government with
minute inspection, they found it a complicated machine, in which the
*ecclesiastical* state was so interwoven with the *political,* that it would
be impossible to retrench the corruptions of the one, without deranging
the whole fabric. It became necessary therefore (and the philosopher
rejoiced at the necessity) to take down the whole machine of despotism,
involving all the privileged orders in the proposed renovation.

The first Assembly proceeded as far as they durst, in laying their
hands upon the immense possessions of the clergy, and abolishing the
monastic institutions ; making provision, at the same time, for maintaining the clergy by granting them annual salaries, suited to their former
ranks in the church. This step was bold, and gave umbrage to many
of the higher dignitaries. But as the Assembly had the policy to augment the salaries of most of the inferior clergy, the curates or vicars,
who were the most numerous body, and had most influence over the
people, this measure instead of endangering, rather strengthened the
cause of the Revolution.

Upon the election of the second Assembly, a new scene was to be
presented. A party of violent republicans, not satisfied with the constitution of 1791, and resolved to exterminate monarchy, and with it all
the privileged orders, after a violent contest with their adversaries, the
Fuillans, in which the latter were defeated, assumed the government of
France ; and from the full establishment of the Jacobins, with a decided
majority in the Convention, we date many important changes in the customs and institutions of that country. The progress of these changes
in detail is left for the historian ; my limits confining me to sketches
only of these great events. In general, however, I may observe, that
the ruling party in France have waged an inveterate war with Christianity ; and have endeavored to efface all the monuments by which it
has been perpetuated. They have abolished not only the Sabbath, by
substituting *one* day in *ten* as a day of *rest* and *amusement* in lieu of *one*
day in *seven ;* but they have changed the mode of reckoning time, substituting the *foundation* of the Republic as the vulgar era, instead of the
Christian era. They have not indeed prohibited any man from believing what religion he pleases : but as far as their decrees can reach,
they have established, not *deism* only, but *atheism* and *materialism.*
For these assertions I have their own decrees. In their decree respecting burials, they say, they " acknowledge no other *doctrine,* except that
of national *sovereignty* and *omnipotence.*" If I understand this, it denies
the being of a God. They ordain, that deceased persons shall be carried to the place of burial, covered with a pall, on which shall be depict-
ed *sleep ;* under the shade of the trees in the field, a statue shall be erected, representing *sleep ;* and on the gate of the field, this inscription—
" death in an *everlasting sleep.*" This is an explicit denial of the immortality of the soul, and in effect the establishment of *materialism* by
law.*

---

* This was not an act of the Convention, but an order of the commissary Fouche,
at Nevers, in October, 1793. See Minerva, March 12, and April 8, 1794. See also
Life of Col. Trumbull, Appendix, p. 351.

The church of Notre Dame is converted into the *temple of reason;* a colossal monument is erected in honor of the day, when reason triumphed over what they call *fanaticism;* and festivals are ordained to celebrate the memorable epochs of important changes in the government and religion in France. A great number of the clergy have publicly renounced their profession, declaring their belief that their ancient religion was superstition and error, and that the only true religion is the practice of justice and moral virtue.

This account of the proceedings in France exhibits, in a luminous point of view, the singular contexture of the human mind ; *now* depressed with chimerical horrors ; demons, ghosts, and a God in terrors, armed with vengeance, and hurling nine tenths of mankind to the bottomless pit : *now*, elevated on the pinions of a subtil philosophy, men soar above all these bugbears ; revelation, piety, immortality, and all the Christian's hopes are rejected as phantoms ; the Supreme Jehovah is reasoned or ridiculed out of existence, and in his place is substituted the *omnipotence* of *national sovereignty.*

Vain men ! idle philosophy ! I will not attempt to expatiate on the pernicious effects of such mistaken and misdirected *reason.* A sorrowful prediction of woes that must fall upon the nation, thus set afloat on the wide ocean of doubt, and tossed between the ancient hopes of immortality, and the modern legislative assurance of *everlasting sleep* in annihilation, would be derided as the cant of bigotry ; the whining lamentations of interested priestcraft. But I will meet your philosophy upon your own ground ; and demonstrate, by the very decrees which demolish the ancient superstition, that you yourselves are the most bigoted men in existence.

It is the remark of a great philosopher, whose opinions I am sure *you* will respect, that the mind of man is subject to certain unaccountable terrors and apprehensions, proceeding from an unhappy situation of affairs, from ill health, or a melancholy disposition. This is the origin of superstition and priestcraft. The mind of man is also susceptible of an unaccountable elevation and presumption, arising from success, luxuriant health, strong spirits, or a bold confident disposition. This is the source of *enthusiasm.* Hume's Essays, Vol. I, p. 75.

I will not controvert this explanation of the two most remarkable principles in the mind. Nor will I wholly deny the conclusion he draws, that superstition is most favorable to *slavery*, and enthusiasm to *liberty.* But I will go further in this question than he did, and further than you will at first admit to be just—but it is a position warranted by all history and perpetual observation, that if superstition and enthusiasm are not essentially the same thing, they at least produce effects, in many respects, exactly similar. They always lead men into error.

*Superstition* and *enthusiasm* operate by different means and direct the mind to different objects ; but they agree in this respect, they imply or produce an *excessive improper attachment* to certain objects, usually objects of little *real* consequence. They are equally the humble votaries of some deity, though each has a different one and worships him in her own peculiar mode. From the only regular body of *deists* in the universe, as Mr. Hume calls the disciples of Confucius ; from the exalted philosophers of Greece and Rome, Plato, Pythagoras and Cicero ; or from the still more refined philosophers, the noble *disciples of reason*, the members of the National Convention of France, down to the lowest bigot that drones out a lifeless existence over his beads and his crucifix in some dark monastic cell, there is one single principle of the human mind operating steadily to produce these different characters : this principle is a strong, universal and irresistible disposition to attach itself to some object or some system of belief which shall be a kind of idol to be worshiped in preference to all others. The object only is varied ; the principle eternally the same. The principle springs from the passions of the mind, and can not be annihilated without extinguishing the passions ; which is impossible. When a *gloomy* mind clings to its priests or its altars, it is called *superstition*. When a bold mind and ardent spirits rise above groveling objects, and embrace spiritual delights, with raptures and transports, it is called *enthusiasm* or *fanaticism*. When a long series of reflection and reasoning has cooled or moderated the passions, the mind is governed less by *feeling* and more by *argument ;* the errors of *superstition* and *enthusiasm* are perceived and despised ; the mind fixes itself upon a *theory* of *imaginary truth*, between the extremes of error ; and this is pronounced *reason* and *philosophy*. That this *reason* is not *truth* itself, nor an infallible *standard of truth*, is obvious : for no two men agree what it is, what its nature, extent or limits. No matter ; *superstition* and *enthusiasm* are beat down ; *reason* is exalted upon a throne, temples are erected to the goddess, and festivals instituted to celebrate her coronation. Then begins the reign of passion ; the moment *reason* is seated upon her throne, the *passions* are called in to support her. *Pride* says, *I* have trampled down *superstition*, that foe to truth and happiness—*I* have exalted *reason* to the throne ; *I* am *right*—every thing else is *wrong*. Obey the goddess *reason*, is the great command ; and woe to the man that rejects her authority. *Reason* is indeed the *nominal* prince, but the passions are her ministers, and dictate her decrees. Thus what begins in calm philosophy, ends in a most *superstitious* attachment to a particular object of its own creation—the goddess *reason* is at last maintained by pride, obstinacy, bigotry, and to use a correct phrase, *a blind superstitious enthusiasm*.

The history of men is one tissue of facts, confirmatory of these observations. The Egyptians adored certain animals ; and to injure a cat in Egypt, was a crime no less enormous than to pull down a liberty cap, to use the Christian era, or wear abroad the robes of a priest in France ; it was sacrilege. When we are told by credible historians that the Egyptians, when a house was on fire, took more pains to save the *cats*, than the *house*, we stare and wonder how *men* could ever be so weak and stupid as to regard a cat as a sacred animal. But is not the cap of liberty now regarded with similar veneration ? Would not an insult offered to it be resented and call down the vengeance of its votaries ? How is this ? Why the answer is easy—the Egyptians venerated a cat and a cow, and our modern idolaters venerate a liberty cap. The passion of the Egyptians will be called *superstition* perhaps ; the passion of our people, *enthusiasm*. But it is the object that is changed, and not the principle. Our people are perpetually exclaiming, " *Liberty is the goddess we adore*," and a cap is the emblem of this goddess. Yet in fact, there is no more connection between *liberty* and a *cap*, than between the Egyptian deity Isis, and just notions of God; nor is it less an act of *superstition* to dance round a cap or a pole in honor of *liberty*, than it was in Egypt to sacrifice a bullock to Isis.

The Greeks were a learned nation; but they had their Delphic oracles, whose responses were regarded as inspiration. The Romans were more superstitious, and were governed in public and private affairs, by the appearances of the entrails of beasts, the flight of birds, and other omens. Both these nations were *superstitious ;* that is, they believed their fate to be connected with certain religious rites; they placed confidence in certain supposed deities or events; when in fact there was no connection at all between the cause and effect, but what existed in opinion. The Pythian god in Greece knew nothing of future events; the auspices in Rome had no connection with the fate of those who consulted them, but the people *believed* in those consultations, and according to the result, were inspired with confidence or depressed with apprehensions. There were philosophers indeed in those enlightened nations, who rejected the authority of their divinities. Cicero says, in his days, the Delphic oracle had become contemptible. Demosthenes declared publicly, the oracle had been gained over to the interest of Philip. These and many others were the deists of Greece and Rome; the Humes and Voltaires of antiquity. But they never had the courage or the inclination to abolish the religion of their countrymen—they treated the fabled divinities of their country with more respect than the Jacobin club has paid to the founder of Christianity. At the same time, while they indulged their fellow citizens in their own worship, they wrought out of their own imagination, some *airy deity*, some fine subtil theory of philosophy, which they *adored* with the *superstition of bigots.* It is idle, it is false, that these philosophers had refined their ideas above all *error* and *fanaticism*—they soared above the absurdities of material deities, the *lares* and *penates* of the vulgar; but they framed ethereal divinities, and spent their lives in paying homage to these fictions of imaginations.

In short, the only advantage they had over vulgar minds was, that common people were content to worship the gods of the country, already framed to their hands ; while the pride of each philosopher was busy in creating deities suited to his particular fancy.

When Christianity became the religion of Rome, many of the pagan rites were incorporated, and some of the temples and deities brought into use in the Christian religion. The use of incense or perfumes, holy water, lamps, and votive offerings in churches, are pagan ceremonies retained in the Romish church. In lieu of the images of heathen deities, Jupiter, Hercules or Bacchus, the Christians substituted the statues of saints, martyrs and heroes ; or else preserved the old images, giving them only a different dress. The Pantheon of ancient Rome was reconsecrated by Boniface IV. to the Virgin Mary, and all the saints.

What is all this ? the Christians pretended to abolish and exterminate pagan *superstition*—they only changed the name, and the objects to which veneration was to be paid.   Instead of worshiping and sacrificing to Bacchus, the new converts adored the figure of a saint.

The Roman had a celebrated festival, called *Saturnalia* in honor of *Saturn ;* this festival found its way into ancient Scandinavia, among our pagan ancestors, by whom it was new modeled or corrupted, being kept at the winter solstice.   The night on which it was kept was called *mother-night*, as that which produced all the rest ; and the festival was called *Iule* or *Yule*.   The Christians, not being able to abolish the feast, changed its object, gave it the name of Christmas, and kept it in honor of Jesus Christ, although the ancient name *yule* was retained in some parts of Scotland, till within a century.   (Mallet, North Antiq., Vol. I, 130.   Cowel, voc. Yule.)   What is the deduction from these facts ?   This certainly, that men have uniformly had a high veneration for some person or deity, real or imaginary ; the Romans for Saturn, the Goths for the *mother-night* of the year, and the Christians for the founder of their religion.   The Christians have the advantage over the pagans in appropriating the feast to a *nobler* object ; but the *passion* is the same, and the joy, the feasting, and the presents that have marked the festival, are nearly the same among pagans and Christians.

Let us then see whether the National Convention of France have succeeded in exterminating *superstition* and *fanaticism ;* and with them, their offspring, *persecution*.

They have indeed abolished the Christian Sabbath, because it was one of the institutions of superstition and the support of error, bigotry and priestcraft.   But with the absurdity and inconsistency that ever accompanies *fanaticism*, they have established a similar institution, under a different name ; instead of a *Christian* Sabbath once in *seven* days, they have ordained a *political* Sabbath once in *ten* days.   The object only is changed, while the uses of such a day are acknowledged by the Convention themselves ; and in spite of their *omnipotence*, the nation will appropriate that or some other day to nearly the same purposes.

They have abolished the Christian era, and substituted the epoch of the abolition of monarchy, or what is the same thing, *the foundation of the Republic*.   And what do they gain by this change ?   merely the trouble of introducing confusion and perplexity into their own mode of reckoning time, during the present generation, and into their negotiations with other powers.   The era itself is a thing of no kind of consequence ; it is not of the value of a straw ; but when this indifferent thing is established as a common point of reckoning time among a great number of surrounding nations, it becomes of great moment, and the change of it marks a contempt of *common utility* and a *superstitious* regard to the period of the Revolution, or rather the era of their own triumph over their opposers, that is equal to the ancient respect for the Delphic oracle, or the modern veneration for a papal bull. . The object only is changed ; the passion **is** the same.

They have also annihilated the national worship, **and** of course a great number of holidays.   But they have decreed **a most** magnificent and splendid festival, to be celebrated once in four **years**, in honor of the Republic.   What is this but a *superstitious* veneration for a new era, instead of the old ones ?   But what is singular in this institution is, that it is professedly copied from the celebration of the Olympic games in Greece. What then is become of the Convention's *reason* and *philosophy*, which was to buoy them above vulgar prejudices? Do they in this instance, exhibit proofs of exalted reason? Is it less a prejudice to venerate the Greek Olympiads, than the Christian Sabbath, or Christian era? Let Danton and Robespierre answer this question, or blush for their philosophy.

The Convention have also rejected the national faith, and sanctioned, with a decree, the doctrines of *deism* and *materialism*. This is another sublime effort of their Grecian philosophy to annihilate superstition and bigotry. But in the moment they are shunning Scylla, they are shipwrecked on Charybdis. It was not sufficient to destroy one faith; but they proceeded to establish another. They erect a statue to *sleep*, and on the gates of their burying fields, ordain this inscription, " Death in an everlasting Sleep." Laugh not, ye refined sages, at the poor ignorant Greeks, who, lost and bewildered in the mazes of doubt, with more honesty than yourselves, acknowledged their ignorance, and erected an altar to the *unknown God*. St. Paul informed that venerable body of sages, the Athenian Areopagus, that this was *superstition*; yet the inscription on the altar at Athens, and that on the gates of the burying places in France, proceeded from equal ignorance, and the devotion paid to the statue of sleep will be as blind, as headstrong, and as marked with superstition, as the worship of the *unknown God* in Athens.

The Convention, in their zeal for equalizing men, have with all their exalted reason, condescended to the puerility of legislating even upon *names*. That they should abolish titles of *distinction*, together with the privileges of the nobility and clergy, was natural; but that the common titles of mere *civility* and *respect* should be attacked was astonishing to indifferent spectators, who had expected their proceedings to be marked with dignity. The vulgar title of address, *Monsieur* and *Madame*, whatever might have been their original sense, had become mere names of civility, implying no distinction, and applied equally to all classes of people. They were literally terms of *equality* ; for when *A* addressed *B* with the appellation *Monsieur*, *B* answered him with the same address ; denoting an equality of standing and a mutuality of respect.

Yet these harmless titles, which had no more connection with government, than the chattering of birds, became the subject of grave legislative discussion, and the use of them was formally abolished. And what did the Convention substitute in their place? Why the awkward term *citizen*, which is in fact a *title of distinction*, denoting a man who is free of a city, and enjoys rights distinct from his fellow inhabitants ; or at least one that has a legal residence in a country, and in consequence of it, enjoys some rights or privileges, that are not common to all its people. In proof of this I need only suggest, that in the United States, and I believe in all other countries, certainly in France, legal provision is made for acquiring the rights of *citizenship*.* *Reflect*, ye philosophic legislators, and be ashamed of your contradictions.

---

* By the present constitution of France, citizenship is lost by naturalization in a foreign country. If Danton himself should come to America and be naturalized, he would no longer be a French *citizen*. *Mr.* is a mere title of civility, applicable to *all* men, in *all* places, and under *all* circumstances; the most *equalizing* title in the French or English language.

The Convention have also abolished the insignia of rank, civil and ecclesiastical. Even a priest can not wear his robes, except in the *temples*. But it was not sufficient to reduce all ancient orders; they established another distinction, which was represented by the *cockade of liberty*. Enthusiasm had only taken down one order, to put up another; and no sooner was the *order of liberty* instituted, than its members assumed an arrogant imperious behavior: they esteemed themselves better than their fellow citizens; the cockade became a badge of *despotism;* every one who would not join the order, and go to every excess in their measures, was denounced as a traitor, and a man must wear the national cockade, or be massacred. Yet there is not the smallest connection between a *cockade* and *liberty*, except what exists in the fanaticism of the order. It is superstition of the rankest kind; and precisely of the same nature as that which fired millions of bigots to rally under the banners of the cross, in the twelfth and thirteenth centuries, and march, under Peter the hermit, to recover the Holy Land from infidels. The *cross* in one case had the same effect in inspiring enthusiasm, that a cockade has in the other. Peter the hermit, and the Jacobins of France, equally acknowledged the principles and the passions of the human heart. To accomplish their purposes they made use of the same means; they addressed themselves to the passions of the multitude, and wrought them up into *enthusiasm.*

To complete the system of *reason* which is to prevail in France, in lieu of ancient errors and absurdities, all the statues of kings and queens, together with busts, medallions, and every ensign of royalty, nobility or priesthood, are ordered to be annihilated. Even the statue of Henry IV, on the New Bridge; a monument erected to the most patriotic prince that ever graced the royal diadem; who had projected a plan of universal peace in Europe, and who, had he not fallen prematurely by the hand of an assassin, would perhaps have done more for the happiness of society, than all the philosophers France ever produced; even *his* statue could not escape the philosophic rage for innovation. The statue is to be annihilated, and in its place, at the motion of David the painter, a colossal monument is decreed to be raised on the bridge, to transmit to posterity the victory of nations over kings, and of reason over *fanaticism.* Yes, philosophers, a noble victory this! But you forget that this very decree is the height of *political fanaticism.* The *monument* is changed with the object of fanaticism; and this is all the difference between *you* and the admirers of Henry IV, who erected the statue.

*Marat* also has a monument erected to his memory, in the Pantheon! And who was Marat? A Prussian by birth; by profession, a journalist, who lived by publishing libels on the moderate men who opposed the Jacobin club; by nature, a bloodthirsty wretch, the instigator of massacres, whose cruelty and baseness inspired a *woman* with courage to assassinate him. To such a pitch has the *fanaticism* of these philosophers carried them in this instance, that they have actually dispensed with the decree which denies the *honors of the Pantheon* to patriots, until they have been dead *ten* years, and in favor of his extraordinary merits, Marat was *deified* a few months after his death.

The refined imitators of the Greek philosophers have gone beyond their predecessors, in a stupid veneration for departed heroes; and if the present *fanaticism* should continue a few years, they will fill their new Pantheon with canonized Jacobins.

The same blind devotion to every thing ancient has led these superstitious reformers into the most ridiculous changes of names. *Church* is a relic of Christian bigotry—the name therefore is rejected, and in its place the Latin word *temple* is substituted. This in France is philosophical! But what is more extraordinary is, that in the moment when the modern calendar was abolished, and new divisions of time instituted, and even the harmless names of the months changed because the old calendar was the work of a pope and a relict of priestcraft: nay, at the time these wise and sublime reformers were abolishing, not only superstition, but even a belief in any *superior being;* they themselves sequestered a building for the express purpose of immortalizing men, and even gave it the Grecian name *Pantheon,* which signifies the *habitation of all the gods.* Such perpetual contradictions, such a series of puerile innovations, are without a parallel in the history of revolutions: and while these regenerators of a great nation believe themselves the devotees of *reason* and *philosophy,* and exult in their supereminent attainments, they appear to the surrounding world of indifferent spectators, as weak, as blind and as fanatical, as a caravan of Mohammedan pilgrims, wading through immense deserts of suffocating sands, to pay their respects to the tomb of the Prophet.

It is remarkable also, that with professions of the most boundless liberality of sentiment, and with an utter abhorrence of bigotry and tyranny, these philosophers have become the most implacable persecutors of *opinion.* They despise all religious *opinions;* they are indifferent what worship is adopted by individuals; at the same time, they are establishing atheism by law. They reject one system, to *enforce* another. This is not all; they pursue with unrelenting cruelty, all who differ from them on *political* subjects. The friends of a limited monarchy, to the constitution of 1791, to a federal government, however honest, fair and candid, all fall before the Jacobins. The Marquis La Fayette, that unimpeachable hero and patriot, fell a sacrifice to his *integrity.* He had sworn to maintain the constitution of 1791—he respected his oath—and was driven into exile and a dungeon. The Jacobins also swore to maintain that constitution—they perjured themselves—and now rule triumphant. Dumourier, the ablest general that has figured in France this century, after a series of unexampled victories, fell a sacrifice to Jacobin jealousy. The moment the Jacobin club felt their superiority, they commenced tyrants and persecutors; and from the execution of Mr. Delassart, the first victim of their vengeance, to that of Mr. Brissot and his adherents, a series of persecution for mere difference of opinion has been exhibited in France, that has never before been equaled. The Jacobins differ from the clergy of the dark ages in this—the clergy persecuted for heresy in *religion*—the Jacobins, for heresy in *politics.* The ruling faction is always orthodox—the minority always heterodox. Totally immaterial is it, what is the subject of controversy; or in what age or country the parties live. The object may change, but the imperious spirit of triumphant faction is always the same. It is only to revive the stale plea of *necessity;* the *state* or the *church* is in danger from *opinions;* then the rack, the stake or the guillotin *must* crush the heresy—the heretics *must* be exterminated.

It was the language of the pagan emperors who persecuted the Christians ; " these sectaries must be destroyed—their doctrines are fatal to our power." It was the language of the popes and cardinals, who instigated the persecution of the Hussites, Wickliffites, Lutherans and Calvinists ; " these reformers are heretics who are dangerous to the *true* church, they must be destroyed ; their doctrines must be exterminated ; it is the cause of God." It is the same language, which the barbarous followers of Mohammed employed and still employ to justify the enslaving of Christians. The same is the language of the British acts of Parliament, which lay all dissenters from the established church under severe restraints and disabilities. It is the present language of the court of inquisition in Spain and Portugal—it is the language of the Jacobin faction in France, with the change only of the word *liberty* for *church*. The mountain exclaim, " *liberty* is in danger from *traitors.*" But when we examine the proofs, nothing appears to warrant the charge, but the single circumstance that these dangerous men *belonged to another party ;* they were acknowledged republicans, but differed in opinion, as to the precise form of government, best calculated to secure liberty. Yet being Girondists, another party, they are wrong ; they are dangerous ; they must be exterminated. This is merely the result of faction ; for it is now, and probably will forever remain a mere speculative point, whether Danton or Brissot was right ; that is, whether a *federal* or an *indivisible* republic is the best form of government for France. But *power*, and *not argument* or *experience*, has decided the question for the present. It is the precise mode in which the Roman emperors decided Christianity to be dangerous—the precise mode in which the Chinese emperors reasoned to justify the expulsion of Christians from their dominions ; and a mode which a violent ruling faction always employs to silence opposition. As a temporary measure, it is always effectual : but I will venture to affirm, that such vindictive remedies for political and religious contentions are, in every instance, unwarrantable. In religious affairs, they proceed from bigotry, or a blind zeal for a particular creed. In political contests, an indiscriminate denunciation of opposers, and the infliction of death upon slight evidence, or mere suspicion, can proceed only from savage hearts, or the mad rancor of party and faction.

### MORALITY.

However necessary might be the revolution in France, and however noble the object, such great changes and a long war will have an effect on the moral character of the nation, which is deeply to be deplored. All wars have, if I may use a new but emphatic word, a *demoralizing\** tendency ; but the revolution in France, in addition to the usual influence of war, is attended with a total change in the minds of the people. They are released, not only from the ordinary restraints of law, but from all their former habits of thinking. From the fetters of a deba-

---

\* This is the first time this word was ever used in English. It is now common in the United States and in England.

sing religious system, the people are let loose in the wide field of mental licentiousness ; and as men naturally run from one extreme to another, the French will probably rush into the wildest vagaries of opinion, both in their political and moral creeds. The decree of the Convention authorizing divorces, upon the application of either party, alledging only unsuitableness of temper, hereby offering allurements to infidelity and domestic broils, is a singular proof of the little regard in which the morals of the nation are held by the ruling party. The efforts made by the Convention to exterminate every thing that looks like imposing restraint upon the passions, by the fear of a *supreme being* and *future punishments*, are a most extraordinary experiment in government, to ascertain whether nations can exist in peace, order and harmony, without any such restraints. It is an experiment to prove that impressions of a supreme being and a divine providence, which men have hitherto considered as *natural*, are the illusions of imagination ; the effect of a wrong education. It is an experiment to try whether *atheism* and *materialism*, as articles of national creed, will not render men more happy in society than a belief in a God, a Providence, and the immortality of the soul. The experiment is new ; it is bold ; it is astonishing.

In respect to manners also, the effects of the war in France must be deplorable. War, carried on between foreign nations, on the most humane principles, has a powerful tendency to *uncivilize* those who are immediately concerned in it. It lets loose the malignant passions of hatred and revenge, which in time of peace are laid under the restraints of law and good breeding. But in addition to the ordinary uncivilizing tendency of war, the present contest in France is carried on with the implacable fury of domestic rage, and the barbarity of assassination. Hostilities have raged in almost every part of that extensive republic, and have been inflamed by faction, insurrection and treason. The Parisians, aided by the Marseillois, massacred thousands on the 10th of August, and 2d and 3d of September, 1792 ; and great part of the victims of popular fury fell, merely because they were *suspected*, without the slightest proof of guilt. The like scenes were exhibited on a smaller scale at Lyons, and in some other parts of the country. The summary vengeance taken on the insurgents in various parts, and especially on the rebels at Lyons and Toulon, must have accustomed great bodies of people to scenes of cruelty, and rendered them unfeeling toward their enemies. But the sanguinary executions of persons condemned by the revolutionary tribunals at Paris, and in various cities of France, must have rendered the populace extremely ferocious. In many of the calamitous proceedings of the triumphant party in France, there has been displayed a rancor of malice and cruelty, that reminds of us savages ; and we can scarcely believe these things done by a nation unquestionably the most polite in the world. The facts however can not be denied ; and they illustrate my remarks, as to the effects of war on the moral character of men.

If these remarks then are just, it is to be supposed that the French nation, will for a few years, be so ferocious and licentious, as to render it extremely difficult to reduce them to a subordination to law. The *virulence* of party we know in America ; but in France, the spirits of men are still more exasperated against each other, and party rage will not, for a long time, be repressed without frequent bloodshed. If the odious distinction of whig and tory still exists in America, and frequently calls forth abuse, how much more will party spirit prevail in France during the present generation!

It then naturally occurs as a question, what will be the consequences of the abolition of Christianity, or the national worship of France ?

The general answer appears to me not difficult. Atheism and the most detestable principles will be the fashion of the present age ; but peace, education, and *returning reason*, will at length prevail over the wild ideas of the present race of philosophers, and the nation will embrace a rational religion.

The nation is now so totally demoralized by the current philosophy of the age, and the ferocious spirit of war and faction, that atheism is a creed perhaps most adapted to the blind and headstrong genius of the present generation. But I am yet one of the old fashioned philosophers, who believe that, however particular men under particular circumstances may reject all ideas of God and religion, yet that some impressions of a Supreme Being are as natural to men, as their passions and their appetites, and that *nations* will have some God to adore and some mode of worship. I believe some future legislature of France will be obliged to tread back some of the steps of the present Convention, with respect to the establishment of a chimerical *reason* in lieu of *religion*.

### GOVERNMENT.

I am of the same opinion respecting their constitution of government. France can not enjoy peace or liberty, without a government much more energetic than the present constitution would be, without the aid of danger without and a guillotin within. The moment France is freed from external foes and is left to itself, it will feel the imbecility of its government. France now resembles a man under the operation of spasms, who is capable of exerting an astonishing degree of unnatural muscular force ; but when the paroxysm subsides, languor and debility will succeed. This observation applies to its political force ; and when the war shall cease, the *military* will be strong, while the civil power is weak. The consequences of disbanding half a million of soldiers at once, I will not attempt to predict. Should any dissatisfaction prevail in the army at the moment of peace, on account of pay, provisions, or any other cause, the nation will have to contend with more formidable foes than the military *machines* of Austria and Prussia. Great caution and policy will be necessary in dispersing such a number of soldiers and bringing them back to habits of industry and order.

The seeds of *faction*, that enemy of government and freedom, are sown thick in the present constitution of France. The Executive Council, to be composed of *twenty-four* members, will be a hot-bed of party ; and party spirit is violent, malignant and *tyrannical*. The French could not have fallen upon a more effectual expedient to create and perpetuate *faction*, with its train of fatal evils, than to commit the execution of the laws to a number of hands ; for *faction is death to liberty*.

The republic of France is to keep an army in pay, in time of peace as well as war. This army will always be at the command of the executive. When the minister at war is a man of talents and a wicked heart, he may make use of the army for the purposes of crushing his competitors. A standing army in America is considered as an engine of despotism ; and however necessary it may be in the present state of Europe, it will or *may* prove dangerous to the freedom of France.

## REMARKS.

Let it not be thought that the writer of these sheets is an enemy to liberty or a republican government. Such an opinion is wholly unfounded. The writer is a native American ; born in an independent republic. He imbibed a love of liberty with his first ideas of government ; he fought for the independence of his country ; he wishes to see republican governments established over the earth, upon the ruins of despotism. He has not however imbibed the modern philosophy, that rejects all ancient institutions, civil, social, and religious, as the impositions of fraud ; the tyranny of cunning over ignorance, and of power over weakness. He is not yet convinced that men are capable of such perfection on earth, as to regulate all their actions by moral rectitude, without the restraints of religion and law. He does not believe with the French atheist, that the universe is composed solely of *matter* and *motion*, without a Supreme Intelligence ; nor that man is solely the creature of education. He believes that God, and not education, gives man his passions ; and that the business of education is to restrain and direct the passions to the purposes of social happiness. He believes that man will always have passions—that these passions will frequently urge him into vices—that religion has an excellent effect in repressing vices, in softening the manners of men, and consoling them under the pressure of calamities. He believes in short, that, notwithstanding all the fine philosophy of the modern reformers, a great part of mankind, necessitated to labor, and unaccustomed to read, or to the civilities of refined life, will have rough passions, that will always require the corrective force of law, to prevent them from violating the rights of others : of course, he believes government is necessary in society ; and that to render every man free, there must be energy enough in the executive, to restrain any man and any body of men from injuring the person or property of any individual in the society. But as many of the preceding remarks appear to be a severe reprehension of the ruling party in France, it is necessary to explain myself more freely on this subject.

The cause of the French nation is the noblest ever undertaken by men. It was necessary ; it was just. The feudal and the papal systems were tyrannical in the extreme ; they fettered and debased the mind ; they enslaved a great portion of Europe. While the legislators of France confined themselves to a correction of *real evils*, they were the most respectable of reformers : they commanded the attention, the applause and the admiration of surrounding nations. But when they descended to legislate upon *names*, *opinions* and *customs*, they could have no influence upon liberty or social rights, they became contemptible ; and when faction took the lead, when a difference of opinion on the form of government proper for France, or a mere adherence to a

solemn oath, became high treason punishable with death, the triumphant
faction inspired even the friends of the Revolution, with disgust and
horror.  *Liberty* is the cry of these men, while with the grimace of a
Cromwell, they deprive every man who will not go all the lengths of
their rash measures, of both *liberty* and *life*.  *A free republic* is their
perpetual cant ; yet to establish their own ideas of this free government,
they have formed and now exercise throughout France, a *military aristocracy*, the most bloody and despotic recorded in history.

But, say the friends of the Jacobins, " this severity is absolutely necessary to accomplish the Revolution."  No, this is not the truth.  It is
necessary to accomplish the views of the Jacobins ; but a revolution
was effected before the Jacobins had formed themselves into a consistent
body, and assumed the sovereign sway.  This first revolution did not
proceed far enough in changes of old institutions to satisfy the atheistical
part of the new Convention.  The first constitution had abolished the
distinction of orders—it had stripped the nobles and clergy of their
titles and rank—it had stripped the church of her possessions—it had
taken almost all power from the king—but it had left untouched the
two relics of monarchy most odious to little minds, the name of king
and his hereditary descent.  This furnished the violent members of the
Convention with a pretext for a further reform, in which, not royalty
alone, for this is a matter of little consequence, but even the customary
modes of speech, and the sublime truths of Christianity, have fallen
equally a prey to the regenerating enthusiasm of these profound philosophers.

What had *liberty* and *the rights of men* to do with this second revolution ?  If, on experiment, it had been found that the limited monarchy of the first constitution, which except its civil list, had scarcely
the powers of the executive of the United States, was productive of real
evils and real danger to the freedom of the government, the nation
would have seen the danger, and by general consent, in a peaceable
manner, and without the violence of party rage, monarchy would have
been abolished.  The progress of reason, information, and just notions
of government, was ripening the nation fast for an event of this kind.

Let us then separate the men from the cause ; and while we detest
the instrument, let us admire and applaud the *end* to be accomplished.
We see roses growing among thorns, and we know a Judas, in betraying his Lord, was a vile instrument of man's redemption.  I am an old
fashioned believer in a Divine Intelligence, that superintends the affairs
of this world, always producing order out of confusion.  So far as the
experience of three thousand years, and the present knowledge of men,
will furnish data for reasoning on political subjects, we may safely conclude that the affairs of France are in a state of vacillation, moving from
extreme to extreme by the impulse of violent causes ; and that in a few
years those causes will be removed, the vibration will cease, and the
legislature, tracing back some of the steps of their predecessors, will
take the middle path in government, religion, and morals, which has
ever been found practicable and safe.  *In medio tutissimus ibis*, is a
maxim that never yet deceived the *man*, the *legislator*, or the *philosopher*.

The revolution of France, like that of Rome, is fruitful in lessons of instruction, of which all enlightened nations should avail themselves, and which may be of great use to the United States of America. The most important truth suggested by the foregoing remarks is, that *party spirit* is the source of *faction*, and *faction* is *death to the existing* government. The history of the Jacobins is the most remarkable illustration of this truth. I will not undertake to say that there did not exist in France a necessity for a combination of private societies, because I do not know whether it was not necessary to exterminate the remains of royalty and nobility, before a free government could be established and rendered secure and permanent. On this point I am not qualified to judge. But that it was this league of Jacobins, combining the individuals of a party scattered over a vast extent of country, into a consistent body, moved by a single soul, that produced the second revolution in France, is a point of which there can be no question. Their opposers, the moderate party, impliedly acknowledged this truth, when they attempted to resist their force by the same means; and formed themselves into a society, called, from their place of meeting, *Fuillans*. But it was too late. The Jacobins were organized; they had already gained over the populace of Paris to their interest, and had, by caresses, and alarming their fears by the cry of despotism, won over a great part of the peasantry of the country. The Rubicon was passed; *party* had become *faction*; the Jacobins and the Fuillans were the Cæsar and the Pompey of France; one or the other must fall; the Jacobins were the most powerful; they employed a body of armed men to disperse their opposers; the Fuillans were crushed; and the Jacobins, like Cæsar, were seated on the throne. Admit the necessity of such a confederacy in France, or in any country where it is expedient and proper to overthrow the existing government; yet it becomes a more serious question, what is the use of such a combination of societies in the United States. When government is radically bad, it is meritorious to reform it; when there is no other expedient to rid a people of oppression, it is necessary to change the government; but when a people have freely and voluntarily chosen and instituted a constitution of government, which guaranties all their rights, and no corruption appears in the administration, there can be no necessity for a change; and if in any particular, it is thought to require amendment, a constitutional mode is provided, and there is no necessity for recurring to extraordinary expedients. In America therefore there can exist no necessity for private societies to watch over the government. Indeed to pretend that a government that has been in operation but five or six years, and which has hitherto produced nothing but public prosperity and private happiness, has need of associations in all parts of the country to guard its purity, is like a jealous husband who should deem it necessary, the day after his nuptials, to set a sentinel over his wife to secure her fidelity.

If the government of America wants a reform, the best mode of effecting this, is the constitutional mode. If it is become absolutely necessary to overthrow it, the most direct mode of doing it, is to organize a party for the purpose, by condensing its scattered forces into union and system.  But if the point is admitted, that the government does not require any essential alteration, which can not be effected in a legal way, it follows of course that the establishment of private societies is not necessary.  For the same reason that such societies were found useful in France, they ought to be avoided like a pestilence in America ; because a total renovation was judged necessary in that country, and such a total renovation is judged not necessary in America—because a *republican* government was *to be* established in that country ; and in this, it is *already established.*

As the tendency of such associations is probably not fully understood by most of the persons composing them in this country, and many of them are doubtless well-meaning citizens ; it may be useful to trace the progress of 'party spirit to *faction first*, and then of course to *tyranny.*

My first remark is, that contentions usually spring out of points which are *trifling, speculative*, or of *doubtful tendency.*  Among trifling causes I rank personal injuries.  It has frequently happened that an affront offered by one leading man in a state to another, has disquieted the whole state, and even caused a revolution.  The *real interest* of the people has nothing to do with private resentments, and ought never to be affected by them—yet nothing is more common.  And republics are more liable to suffer changes and convulsions, on account of personal quarrels, than any other species of government ; because the individuals, who have acquired the confidence of the people, can always fabricate some reasons for rousing their passions—some pretext of *public* good may be invented, when the man has his own passions to gratify— the minds of the populace are easily inflamed—and strong parties may be raised on the most frivolous occasions.  I have known an instance in America of a man's intriguing for and obtaining an election to an important trust, which he immediately resigned, and confessed he had done it solely to gratify his own will and mortify his enemies.  Yet had the man been disposed, he might have used his influence to strengthen a party, and give trouble to the state.

Another cause of violent parties is frequently a difference of opinion on *speculative* questions, or those whose real tendency to secure public happiness is *equivocal.*—When measures are obviously good, and clearly tend to advance public weal, there will seldom be much division of opinion on the propriety of adopting them.  All parties unite in pursuing the public interest, when it is clearly visible.  But when it is doubtful what will be the ultimate effect of a measure, men will differ in opinion, and probably the parties will be nearly equal.  It is on points of *private local* utility, or on those of doubtful tendency, that men split into parties.

My second remark is, that a contention between parties is usually violent in proportion to the trifling nature of the point in question ; or to the uncertainty of its tendency to promote public happiness.  When an object of great magnitude is in question, and its utility obvious, a *great* majority is usually found in its favor, and *vice versâ* ; and a large majority usually quiets all opposition.  But when a point is of less magnitude or less visible utility, the parties may be and often are *nearly equal.*  Then it becomes a trial of strength—each party acquires confidence from the very circumstance of *equality*—both become assured they are *right*—confidence inspires boldness and expectation of success—pride comes in aid of argument—the passions are inflamed—the *merits* of the cause become a subordinate consideration—victory is the object and not public good ; at length the question is decided by a small majority—success inspires one party with pride, and they assume the airs of conquerors ; disappointment sours the minds of the other—and thus the contest ends in creating violent passions, which are always ready to enlist into every other cause. Such is the progress of party spirit ; and a single question will often give rise to a party, that will continue for generations ; and the same men or their adherents will continue to divide on other questions, that have not the remotest connection with the first point of contention.

This observation gives rise to my third remark ; that nothing is more dangerous to the cause of *truth* and *liberty* than a party spirit. When men are once united, in whatever form, or upon whatever occasion, the union creates a partiality or friendship for each member of the party or society. A coalition for any purpose creates an attachment, and inspires a confidence in the individuals of the party, which does not die with the cause which united them ; but continues, and extends to every other object of social intercourse.

Thus we see men first united in some system of religious faith, generally agree in their *political* opinions. Natives of the same country, even in a foreign country, unite and form a separate private society. The Masons feel attached to each other, though in distant parts of the world.

The same may be said of Episcopalians, Quakers, Presbyterians, Roman Catholics, Federalists, and Antifederalists, mechanic societies, chambers of commerce, Jacobin and Democratic societies. It is altogether immaterial what circumstance first unites a number of men into a society ; whether they first rally round the church, a square and compass, a cross, or a cap ; the general effect is always the same ; while the union continues, the members of the association feel a particular confidence in each other, which leads them to believe each other's opinions, to catch each other's passions, and to act in concert on every question in which they are interested.

Hence arises what is called *bigotry* or *illiberality*. Persons who are united on any occasion, are more apt to believe the prevailing opinions of *their society*, than the prevailing opinions of another society. They examine their own creeds more fully, (and perhaps with a mind predisposed to believe them,) than they do the creeds of other societies. Hence the full persuasion in every society that theirs is *right* ; and if I am right, others of course are *wrong*. Perhaps therefore I am warranted in saying, there is a *species of bigotry* in every society on earth—and indeed in every man's own particular faith. While each man and each society is freely indulged in his own opinion, and that opinion is mere *speculation*, there is peace, harmony, and good understanding. But the moment a man or a society attempts to oppose the prevailing opinions of another man or society, even his arguments rouse passion ; it being difficult for two men of opposite creeds to dispute for any time, without becoming angry. And when one party attempts in practice to interfere with the opinions of another party, violence most generally succeeds.

These remarks are so consonant to experience and common observation, that I presume no man can deny them ; and if true, they deserve the serious attention of every good citizen of America.

The citizens of this extensive republic constitute a *nation*. As a nation, we feel all the. prejudices of a society. These national prejudices are probably necessary, in the present state of the world, to strengthen our government. They form a species of *political bigotry*, common to all nations, from which springs a *real allegiance*, never expressed, but always firm and unwavering. This passion, when corrected by candor, benevolence, and love of mankind, softens down into a steady principle, which forms the soul of a nation, *true patriotism.* Each nation of the world is then a *party* in the great society of the human race. When at peace, party spirit subsides, and mutual intercourse unites the parties. But when the interest of either is attacked, a war succeeds, and all the malignant and barbarous passions are called into exercise.

Admit national prejudices to be in a degree necessary ; let us see what other prejudices exist in the United States, which may prove pernicious to ourselves. The American nation is composed of fifteen subordinate states. I say *subordinate ;* for they are so in all national concerns. They are *sovereign* only in their internal police.

The states were erected out of British colonies; and it was the policy of Great Britain rather to foment, than to allay or eradicate colonial prejudices. She knew that such prejudices weakened the strength of the colonies, and kept them in subjection to the mother empire. Even the manners, the language and the food of the people in one colony, were made the subjects of ridicule by the inhabitants of another. Ridicule is accompanied or followed by a degree of contempt ; and hence sprung a dissocial turn of mind among the people of different colonies, which common interest and common danger have not yet converted into perfect harmony.

Since the Revolution, a jealousy between the states has sprung from the superior wealth, magnitude, or advantages of some, which the small states have apprehended would enable the large ones to swallow them up in some future time. This jealousy is mostly removed by the present constitution of the United States, which guaranties to each state its independence and a republican form of government. This guaranty is the best security of each.

Another source of apprehension has been, and still is, the danger of what is called *consolidation.* The states are constantly asserting their *sovereignty*, and publishing their fears that the national government will gradually absorb the state governments. Their jealousy on this head is alive, and alarmed at every breeze of air. I am clearly of opinion, that if peace and harmony can be preserved between the general and particular governments, the purity of our national government will depend much on the legislatures of the several states. They are the political guardians, whose interest is constantly impelling them to watch the progress of corruption in the general government. And they will always be the more attentive to their duty, as they entertain not only a jealousy of the general government, but a jealousy of each other.

But I differ from many people who fear a consolidation. So far as my knowledge of history and men will enable me to judge on this subject, I must think our danger mostly lies in the jealousy of the several states. Instead of a probable annihilation of the state governments, I apprehend great danger from the disuniting tendency of state jealousy, which may dismember the present confederacy. That the states have the power to do this, I have no doubt; and I consider our *union*, and consequently our *strength* and *prosperity*, as depending more on mutual *interest* and mutual *concession*, than on the *force* of the national constitution. Consolidation is with me a bugbear, a chimera, as idle and insignificant, as the medallion of a king. But from the disorganizing tendency of state jealousy, there appears to be a well founded apprehension of danger.

But the principal danger to which our government is exposed will probably arise from another quarter; the *spirit of party*, which is now taking the form of system. While a jealousy and opposition to the national constitution exist only in the legislatures of the several states, they will be restrained and moderated by the public dignity of those bodies, and by legal or constitutional forms of proceeding. Opposition thus tempered loses its terrors.

But opposition that is raised in private societies of men, which are self-created, unknown to the laws of the country, private in their proceedings, and perhaps violent in their passions, the moment it ceases to be insignificant, becomes formidable to the government and freedom. The very people who compose these societies, are not aware of the possible consequences that may flow from their associations. They are few of them persons of extensive historical knowledge; and they do not perceive, that under pretense of securing their rights and liberties, they are laying the foundation of factions which will probably end in the destruction of liberty and a free government. They do not consider, that when men become members of a political club, they lose their individual independence of mind; that they lose their impartiality of thinking and acting; and become the dupes of other men. The moment a man is attached to a club, his mind is not free : he receives a bias from the opinions of the party : a question indifferent to *him*, is no longer indifferent, when it materially affects a *brother* of the society. He is not left to act for himself; he is bound in honor to take part with the society—his pride and his prejudices, if at war with his opinion, will commonly obtain the victory ; and rather than incur the ridicule or censure of his associates, he will countenance their measures, at all hazards ; and thus an *independent freeman* is converted into a mere walking machine, a convenient *engine of party leaders*.

It is thus that private associations may always influence public measures ; and if they are formed for the express purpose of discussing political measures, they may prove pernicious to the existing government.

The society of Jesuits, formed at first without any intention of influencing government, became at last formidable to the civil power, wherever they were established, and the society was finally dissolved by the arm of power, on account of the danger of its intrigues. The society was at first small and insignificant; but its influence was increased and strengthened by such means as I have described, till a *small part* of the inhabitants of a country became dangerous to its government!

Private associations of men for the purposes of promoting arts, sciences, benevolence or charity are very laudable, and have been found beneficial in all countries.   But whenever such societies attempt to convert the private *attachment* of their members into an instrument of *political* warfare, they are, in all cases, hostile to government.   They are useful in pulling down bad governments; but they are dangerous to good government, and necessarily destroy *liberty* and *equality of rights* in a free country.   I say necessarily; for it must occur to any man of common reflection, that in a free country, each citizen, in his private capacity, has an *equal* right to a share of influence in directing public measures; but a society, combined for the purpose of augmenting and extending its influence, acquires an *undue proportion* of that general influence which is to direct the will of the state.   Each individual member of the state should have an *equal* voice in elections; but the individuals of a club have more than an equal voice, because they have the benefit of another influence; that of extensive *private attachments* which come in aid of each man's political opinion.   And just in proportion as the members of a club have an undue share of influence, in that proportion they abridge the rights of their fellow citizens.   Every club therefore formed for political purposes, is an *aristocracy* established over their brethren.   It has all the properties of an aristocracy, and all the effects of tyranny.   It is only substituting the influence of private attachments, in lieu of the influence of birth and property among the nobility of Europe; and the certain effect of private intrigue in lieu of the usurped power and rights of feudal lords; the effects are the same.   It is a literal truth, which can not be denied, evaded, or modified, that the *democratic clubs* in the United States, while running mad with the abhorrence of aristocratic influence, are attempting to establish precisely the same influence under a different name.   And if any thing will rescue this country from the jaws of faction, and prevent our free government from falling a prey, first to civil dissensions, and finally to some future Sylla and Marius, it must be either the good sense of a great majority of Americans, which will discourage private political associations, and render them contemptible; or the controlling power of the laws of the country, which in an early stage shall demolish all such institutions, and secure to each individual in the great political family *equal rights* and an *equal share of influence* in his individual capacity.

But let us admit that no fatal consequences to government and equal rights will ensue from these institutions, still their effects on social harmony are very pernicious, and already begin to appear.   A party spirit is hostile to all friendly intercourse: it inflames the passions; it sours the mind; it destroys good neighborhood; it warps the judgment in judicial determinations; it banishes candor and substitutes prejudice; it restrains the exercise of benevolent affections; and in proportion as it chills the warm affections of the soul, it undermines the whole system of moral virtue.   Were the councils of hell united to invent expedients for depriving men of the little portion of good they are destined to enjoy on this earth, the only measure they need to adopt for this purpose, would be, to introduce factions into the bosom of the country. It was faction that kept the states of Greece and Rome in perpetual perturbation; it was faction which was an incessant scourge of merit; it was faction which produced endless dissension and frequent civil wars; it was faction which converted a polite people into barbarous persecutors, as it has done in France; and which finally compelled the brave republicans of Rome to suffer a voluntary death, or to shelter themselves from the fury of contending parties, beneath the scepter of an emperor.

---

# APPENDIX.

### ON FACTION.

THE following short account of the disputes between Sylla and Marius in Rome, is too applicable to my purpose to be omitted.

Sylla and Marius were competitors for the command of the army destined to act against Mithridates in Asia. Sylla obtained the appointment. Marius, to revenge himself, and if possible displace his rival, had recourse to P. Sulpicius, a popular tribune of considerable talents, but daring and vicious. This man made interest with *the people*, sold the freedom of the city to strangers and freemen, with a view to strengthen his party, and proposed a number of popular laws, in direct violation of the Roman constitution—some of which artifices are exactly similar to those employed by the Jacobins in France and their disciples.

The consuls attempted to defeat these projects; but the tribune collected a multitude of the people, went to the senate house, and *commanded* the consuls to comply with their wishes. This is precisely the mode of proceeding adopted by the Jacobins in Paris.

The consuls refused; the populace drew their daggers; the son of the consul, Pompeius, was killed, but Sylla escaped. This answers to the manner in which the Jacobins destroyed their enemies, the Fuillans, by employing an armed body of ruffians.

Sylla however was brought back, and compelled to comply with the demands of the tribune. He was therefore left in possession of the consulship, and soon after joined the army. His colleague, Pompeius, was degraded, and Sulpicius obtained the laws he had proposed. Sylla was displaced, and Marius appointed to the command of the army. Just so the Jacobins proceeded, till they had filled all public offices with their own partisans.

Now the factions were ripe, and they ended as other factions end, in *repelling force with force*. Sylla would not resign his command to a faction. (La Fayette and Demourier had the spirit of Sylla, in like circumstances, but their troops would not support them.) He marched his army of thirty-five thousand men toward Rome. The city was in confusion. The senate, by order of Sulpicius and Marius, the Marat and Barrere of Rome, sent a deputation, forbidding the approach of

the army. The deputies were insulted by the soldiers. Other embassadors were dispatched by the senate, requesting Sylla not to proceed. He answered he would stay where he was; but he detached a
body of men to take possession of one of the gates of the city. The
people drove them back, but Sylla arrived in time to support them;
and he set fire to the adjacent houses. Marius resisted, and promised
freedom to the slaves that would join him. But he was forced to flee,
and Sylla, assembling the senate, proposed the banishment of Sulpicius,
Marius, and ten of their principal adherents. The edict was passed,
and Sylla set a price upon their head, and confiscated their estates.
Sulpicius was taken by the treachery of a slave and put to death. To
reward the slave, Sylla gave him his freedom, and then ordered him,
for the treachery, to be thrown from the Tarpeian rock—(the method
of rewarding and punishing modern traitors is much similar, giving
them a round sum of money and consigning them to infamy.)

Sylla convened the people, annulled the new laws of Sulpicius, created *three hundred* senators to strengthen his interest, and soon set out
for Asia with his army.

I can not detail the whole history of this business—suffice it to say,
this pitiful question, which of two able generals, (*either* of them fit for
the purpose, and not of a straw's value was it to the public which
gained the appointment,) should command the army in the Mithridatic
war, gave rise to two parties or factions, which pursued each other with
implacable enmity, till they brought their forces into the field, and an
action was fought, which cost the lives of *ten thousand* men.

Marius, the conqueror of the Cimbri, and savior of Rome, an exile,
took shipping, was cast away, taken by his foes, escaped, suffering
incredible hardships; finally arrived in Asia, where he was maltreated
—at last recalled by Cinna the consul, he returned to Italy, and em-
bodying a number of slaves, he entered Rome, and filled it with slaughter; his party putting to death every man, whose salutation Marius did
not return. Marius grew daily more bloodthirsty, and at last put to
death every person of whom he had the least suspicion. Who does
not see the guillotin in ancient Rome?

Marius soon after died; but his son headed an army and supported
his faction. Sylla, having defeated Mithridates and reduced him to
terms of peace, returned to Italy; fought the Marian party, and in two
actions, it is said, *twenty thousand* men were slain in each. Finally,
Sylla crushed his rival's party, and put to death the leaders, filling
Rome with slaughter, as Marius had done before him. Sylla's cruel
proscriptions fill the reader with horror. Nearly five thousand of the
best citizens of Rome were proscribed and massacred. Sylla's assassins roamed through Italy to find the adherents of Marius, and put
them to indiscriminate slaughter. When the senators appeared alarmed
at such outrages, Sylla answered them coolly, "Conscript fathers, 'it
is only a few seditious men, whom I have ordered to be punished'"—
precisely the language of the ruling faction in France, and precisely
the language of *party* in all countries.

It is remarkable also that the pretext for these violences is always
the same—"to rescue the state from tyranny—to destroy despotism—
to exterminate traitors." This was the perpetual cant of Sylla and

Marius, while they were butchering each other's adherents with merciless cruelty.  This was the pretense of Cromwell in England—and
it is the present language of the ruling men in France.  The state must
be saved, and to save it our party must prevail; *liberty* must be secured, but to secure it, we must be *absolute* in power, and of course
*liberty* is crushed.  A *republic* must be established; but to do this, a
few commissioners with *dictatorial* power, seconded by an irresistible
*military* force, must govern the country.  Our government shall be a
*republic, one and indivisible;* and to effect this, it is necessary to put
to death the representatives of one *half* the republic, that the *whole*
may be governed by the other *half.*  *Freedom of debate* is a *constitutional right;* but we must have a Paris mob to hiss down our enemies.

Sylla crushed his enemies, with the blood of nearly one hundred
thousand citizens and soldiers; and after he had thus delivered Rome
from *tyrants,* as he pretended, he ordered the *people* to elect him *perpetual dictator.*  He treated the people just as all *popular* leaders treat
them; first courting them with the cry of *liberty;* making them the
instruments of their own elevation; then trampling on them as *slaves.*
Just so in England, Cromwell destroyed the *tyranny* of Charles I, by
the cant of liberty and religion, then saddled the English with his own
*despotic* power.  Just so Danton and Barrere are now *dictators* in
France, without the name, but with all the powers; and who will succeed them, God only knows.

I beg the reader to consider these facts, as intended solely to set in
a strong point of light the danger of *faction.*  I will not say that the
tyranny and corruptions of the old governments in Europe, will not
warrant men in hazarding all possible *temporary* evils to effect a renovation.  I would with candor believe such violences, in some degree,
unavoidable.  But nothing short of most palpable corruption, the most
unequivocal proof of necessity, can warrant men in resorting to irregular bodies of the people for a redress of evils.  While law and constitution are adhered to, the remedy will always be safe.  But when
tumultuous meetings of people, unknown to the *laws,* and unrestrained
by legal modes of procedure, undertake to direct the *public will,* faction succeeds; and faction begets disorder, force, rancorous passions,
anarchy, tyranny, blood, and slaughter.

## NOTE 1.

### JACOBIN CLUB.

At the beginning of the late revolution in America, the people of
this country had recourse to a similar mode of combining all parts of
the continent into a *system of opposition* to the existing government.
In most of the colonies the British crown, by its officers, had considerable influence.  To resist this influence, the leaders found it necessary to call in the aid of the great body of the people; to rouse their
passions, inflammatory publications were circulated with great industry; and to *unite, condense,* and *direct* the opinions and passions of
an immense people, scattered over a great extent of territory, associations were formed under the denomination of committees of safety,

which had a correspondence with each other, and molded the proceedings of the people into uniformity and system. The first Congress grew out of the same system; and then followed union, concert, and energy in prosecuting the revolution.

It has been an inexplicable mystery to many very judicious men, how the Americans should have been brought to unite in opposing the usurped claims of Great Britain, when the *evils of slavery* were not in reality felt, but only expected by the people. In short, why such a number of illiterate men should be prevailed upon to resist tyranny in principle, and risk the evils of war, when the effects of the British claims were but slightly felt by the mass of the people. All parties however agree in ascribing this amazing union, to the *good sense* of the Americans.

The truth is, discernment and talents were necessary to form and direct the system; but the multitude were managed more by their passions than by their reason. The *committees of safety* were the *instruments of union ;* and the passions of the populace the instruments of action. The presses teemed with publications addressed to the passions; the horrors of slavery were presented to the imagination in striking colors; and the men who wrote intended, when they wrote, to exaggerate real facts for the purpose of rousing the passions of resentment and dread of evils, which reason told them, were not to be expected. These matters are now known. And it appears very clear from history and observation, that in a popular government, it is not difficult to inflame the passions of a people with *imaginary* as well as real evils. In Europe the people have real evils to extirpate. The passions of Americans are enlisting on one side or the other of the present contest in France. We feel no loss of personal liberty as yet, in consequence of the combination against France; but artful men address the passions of our citizens; they teach them to *fear*, that if France should be reduced, the combined powers will attack *liberty* in America. Cool men, who reflect upon the difficulties of such an attempt, consider all such apprehensions as groundless and idle. But two or three hundred men collected, might have their passions so wrought upon by an artful or noisy declaimer, as to believe the danger *real*. They then grow violent, and denounce as enemies, all who are cool or moderate enough to entertain no such fears. Thus two parties are formed on a mere imaginary evil, and when the parties are formed, some badge of distinction, a *button* or a *cockade* is assumed, to widen the breach, and create disaffection, suspicion, and hostile passions. All this is very visible in America; and because some men are too rational to be alarmed at chimeras, too temperate to commit themselves hastily, or too respectable not to despise little badges of distinction, the *livery of faction*, they are insulted as enemies to the rights of the people; and whenever opportunities offer, they fall a prey to the fury of popular passion. This is the triumph of *passion* over *reason*, of *violence* over *moderation*. Should the present controversy in Europe continue two or three years longer, I should not be surprised to see *party spirit* in America, which grew originally out of a mere speculative question, proceed to open hostility and bloodshed. People are easily made to believe their government is bad, or not so good as they might expect from *change;* they may be made to fear corruption, which they do not *see*, and which does not exist; and to risk real evils at the present moment, to guard against *possible* evils a century hence. All this may be done, if restless daring men will take pains to manage popular passions.

## NOTE 2.

It may seem strange that *moderation* should be deemed a crime; but it is a literal truth. In the sittings of the Jacobin Club, Dec. 26th, 1793, Robespierre was under the necessity of vindicating himself from the charge of being a *Moderate*, a *Fuillant*.

Nor is it less singular that some of the charges against their opposers should consist of mere trifles or suspicion, or were so indefinite as not to be capable of proof. One of the charges against Le Brun was, that he christened a daughter by the name of " Victoire Demourier Jamappe." This was done while Demourier was in full career of glory; yet his enemies, from this circumstance, deduced proof of Le Brun's conspiracy with Demourier. He was convicted of conspiring against the unity and indivisibility of the Republic; that is, of attempting to form a federal government in France.

## NOTE 3.

There is no instance of idolatrous worship recorded in history, that displays more *blind superstition*, than the celebration of the *festival of Reason*. The idol adored, is not the same as those worshiped by the ancient Druids, or modern Hindoos; but it is still an *idol*, and the pagan world can not furnish a more striking instance to prove that men will forever worship *something*, whether a cat, a bird, an oak, the sun, the moon, fire, or the *Temple of Reason*. Totally immaterial is it, what the idol is; the *deity of the day* has no connection with men's happiness, otherwise than as he is *visible;* he strikes the senses; he rouses the passions of the multitude; and they believe he is propitious to them—how or in what manner they never know or inquire. The oak of the Druids was just as good and powerful a deity, as the temple or altar of Reason. The oak inspired its votaries with *superstition* and *enthusiasm;* and that is precisely the effect of the French festival of Reason; for of all *fanatics* that ever existed, the French appear, in all that respects what they call *philosophy*, to be the *least rational*. The following is the account of the festival.

Paris, Nov. 12.

A grand festival dedicated to reason and truth, was yesterday celebrated in the *ci-devant* cathedral of Paris. In the middle of this church was erected a mount, and on it a very plain temple, the façade of which bore the following inscription: *A la Philosophie*. Before the gate of this temple was placed the Torch of Truth, in the summit of the mount, on the Altar of Reason, spreading light. The Convention and all the constituted authorities assisted at the ceremony.

Two rows of young girls dressed in white, each wearing a crown of oak leaves, crossed before the Altar of Reason, at the sound of republican music; each of the girls inclined before the torch, and ascended

the summit of the mountain.   Liberty then came out of the Temple of
Philosophy toward a throne made of grass, to receive the homage of
the Republicans of both sexes, who sung a hymn in her praise, extending their arms at the same time toward her.   Liberty descended afterward to return to the temple, and on re-entering it, she turned about,
casting a look of benevolence on her friends.   When she got in, every
one expressed with enthusiasm the sensations which the goddess excited in them, by songs of joy, and they swore never to cease to be faithful to her.

How little men see their own errors.   All this ceremony and parade
about *reason* and *liberty*, at a time when the governing faction were
wading to the altar through rivers of innocent blood; at a time when
the tyranny, imprisonments, and massacres of a century, are crowded
into a single year.

One absurdity more must be noticed.   The Jacobins have displayed
an implacable hatred of royalty and every thing that belongs to it.
Even devices of kingly origin on coins and rings have not escaped their
vengeance.   Yet these same people have borrowed the principal emblem of royalty themselves, to adorn this festival; and two rows of
young girls are furnished with *crowns* of oak leaves.

## NOTE 4.

### OF ARISTOCRACY.

There is not a word in the English or French language so much ban-
died about by designing men, and so little understood by their echoing
agents, as the word *aristocrat*.   A few days ago an honest man, by no
means the least informed, was asked if he knew the meaning of it; he
replied very ingenuously, " he did not understand it, but he supposed it
to be some *French* word."   Yet this word is used with great effect to
excite *party prejudices*.

*Aristocracy* in Europe denotes a distinction of men, by birth, titles,
property, or office.   In America this distinction does not exist with respect to hereditary titles or office; nor with respect to *birth* and *property*, any further than the minds of men, from nature or habit, are inclined to pay more than *ordinary respect* to persons who are born of
parents that have been distinguished for something eminent, and to persons who have large estates.   This propensity, whether *natural* or *ha-
bitual*, exists—no man can deny it; and this is all Mr. Adams, in his
defense, means by the words *well-born;* an expression that has rung a
thousand changes from New Hampshire to Georgia.   Yet the very de-
claimers who fill our ears with a perpetual din on this subject, are ex-
emplifying the truth of this *natural aristocracy*, in almost every negotiation of their lives.   The most noisy democrat in this country, who
feasts upon the words *liberty* and *equality*, can not put a son apprentice
to business, without searching for a respectable family to take him; nor
marry a son or daughter, without inquiring particularly into the family,
connections and fortune of the proposed partner.   It may be said, this
*propensity* to pay respect to such things is wrong and vicious; be it so—
the propensity exists—these things are true—they can not be contradict-

ed. And Mr. Adams, instead of advocating aristocracy and its exclusive privileges, makes it a main point in his defense, to explain the nature and tendency of this principle in men, and to point out cautions and expedients for guarding against its pernicious effects in government. His labors to check this spirit of aristocracy in America, entitle him to the character of a firm, intelligent republican.

If the word *aristocracy* is applicable to any thing in America, it is to that *personal influence* which men derive from offices, the merit of eminent services, age, talents, wealth, education, virtue, or whatever other circumstance attracts the attention of people. The distinguishing circumstances of nobility in Europe, are hereditary titles, estates and offices, which give the possessor some claims or rights above others. In this country, most of the circumstances which command particular respect, are personal, accidental or acquired, and none of them give the possessor any *claims* or *rights* over his fellow citizens. Yet the circumstances which do actually give this *personal influence*, which forms a kind of natural or customary aristocracy, exist universally among men, savage or civilized, in every country and under every form of government. The circumstances are either natural, or arise necessarily out of the state of society. Helvetius and other profound philosophers may write as much as they please, to prove man to be wholly the *creature of his own making*, the work of *education;* but facts occur every hour to common observation, to prove the theory false. The difference of intellectual faculties in man is visible almost as soon as he is born, and is more early and more distinctly marked than the difference of his features. And this natural difference of capacity originates a multitude of other differences in after life, which create *distinctions;* that is, they give rise to those circumstances of talents, wit, address, property and office, to which men invariably pay a kind of respect. This respect gives personal influence to the possessor, in some circle, either small or great, and this *personal influence* is the natural *aristocracy* of men, in all countries and in all governments. It exists among the native Indians; it has existed in every republic on earth: from the President of the United States, to the humble apple-dealer at the corner of Flymarket, every person enjoys a portion of this *personal influence* among his particular acquaintance. It exists in government, in churches, in towns, in parishes, in private societies and in families.

It is this *insensible aristocracy* of opinion and respect, that now forms the firmest band of union between the States. The long and eminent services of our worthy President, have filled all hearts with gratitude and respect; and by means of this gratitude and respect, and the confidence they inspire in his talents and integrity, he has a greater influence in America than any nobleman, perhaps than any prince, in Europe. This respect has hitherto restrained the violence of parties: whatever be the difference of opinion on subjects of government, all parties agree to confide in the President. This is the effect of his personal influence, and not a respect for the laws or constitution of the United States. Americans rally round the man, rather than round the *executive authority* of the Union. And it is a problem to be solved, after his leaving the office, what energy or force really exists in the executive authority itself.

If my ideas of natural aristocracy are just, the President of the United States is a most influential, and most useful aristocrat ; and long may America enjoy the blessings of such *aristocracy !*

A similar personal influence is observable in other men. In every state, in every town, there are some, who, by their talents, wealth, address, or old age and wisdom, acquire and preserve a superior share of influence in their districts. This influence may do good or hurt, as it is coupled with good or bad intentions. But that when confined to small districts, as towns and parishes, it has most generally a good effect, there is no doubt. An old respected citizen has a thousand opportunities of correcting the opinions, settling the quarrels, and restraining the passions of his neighbors. This personal influence in small districts is most remarkable in some parts of New England ; wherever it exists, peace and concord distinguish the neighborhood ; and where by any accident, it does not exist, society is distracted with quarrels and parties, which produce an uncommon depravity of morals.

One remark further. The people who contend most for *liberty* and *equality*, and who are most alarmed at aristocracy, are, in America, the greatest dupes of this aristocracy of personal *influence.* Federal men not only respect the President, but they make the constitution and laws of the United States their standard ; at least they aim to do it. On the other hand, their opposers rally round the standard of particular men. There are certain leading men in the antifederal interest, who have more absolute authority over the opinions of that party, than is possessed by any man in America, except the President of the United States. As the aristocracy of America consists in this personal influence, the men who in private associations have the most of this influence, are, in their sphere, the most complete aristocrats. And at this time, certain influential men in the democratic clubs, are the most influential aristocrats there are in America among private citizens.

While this personal influence is governed by good motives, or limited to small districts, it is not dangerous and may be useful. When it extends far, it may be useful or dangerous, according as it is directed by good or vicious men. . It is always to be watched—in public affairs, it is controlled by the laws ; in clubs and private citizens, it has no restraint but the consciences of men ; and it is to be watched with double vigilance, as its danger is in proportion to its extent.

## NOTE 5.

It is remarked that the Estates General in France, on their first assembling May 5, 1789, commenced their important labors with a solemn act of devotion. Preceded by the clergy and followed by the king, the representatives of the nation repaired to the temple of God, accompanied by an immense crowd, and offered up vows and prayers for success.

Contrast this with the late severe laws respecting the clergy, and the abolition of Christianity. Some of the Convention pretend to entertain a respect for *morality ;* yet as early as 1791, before they had proceeded to publish atheism as a national creed, one of the members in debate declared it " impossible for a society to exist without an immutable and eternal system of morality ;" and this declaration was followed with *repeated and loud bursts of laughter.* This is an instance selected from thousands to show their contempt of every thing that looks like the obligations of religion and morality.—(Moniteur, 15 November, 1791.)

### NOTE 6.

The following remarks of Mr. Neckar, who was in France and observed all the arts invented by the Jacobins to get command of the people, are too much in point to be omitted.

" It was an artful contrivance, the success of which was certain, to involve the constitution in two words, *liberty* and *equality.* Men of sense would perceive that between these ideas, and a just conception of a political institution, there was a vast distance. But the people are to be acted upon only by reducing things to a small compass ; it is by restricting their ideas to the narrow circle of their feelings, and absorbing their passions in a phrase, that we become their masters. This object accomplished, a watchword, or in its stead an outward token, a mark of distinction, the *color* or *fold of a ribin,* has greater effect than the wisdom of a Solon or the eloquence of a Demosthenes. Such are the multitude—such the description of the empire that may be obtained over them ; and criminal indeed are those who take advantage of their weakness, and practice arts to deceive them, rather than to render them happy by the sole authority of reason and morality."—(Neckar on Exec. Power, Vol. II, 269.)

The emissaries of the Jacobins are attempting to make themselves masters of the people in America by the same means—by clubs and a *button,* or other badge of distinction. Detestable is the artifice, and may confusion be the portion of the jesuitical incendiaries, who are thus secretly planting enmity and sedition in our peaceful country !

### NOTE 7.

Of the ferociousness of civil war, history furnishes innumerable proofs ; and the people of France are daily presenting new examples of the sanguinary spirit of all parties in that distracted country. The following official letter offers a specimen.

*Letter from the President and Members composing the Military Committee with the Army of the West, to the commonalty of Paris, dated Saumur, 6 Nivose, (Dec. 25.)*

" We have to communicate to you the interesting news of the total destruction of the banditti on the right bank of the Loire. There are here and there yet some small remains of these monsters in the interior part of La Vendee, but as our armies are no longer obliged to divide themselves, they will undoubtedly soon clear the whole country. Those who solicit the Convention to prevent the great measures of public welfare, and try to inspire them with a false compassion, are either traitors or egotists. If you had seen like me, what this fanatic herd is capable of ! Patriots thrown into the fire alive, others cut and chopped to pieces. Two days before the siege of Angers, in a country which was supposed to be all sacred to liberty, three hundred soldiers were

assassinated by these monsters, in the neighborhood of Chemeville, and nevertheless the evening before they had cried Vive la Republique! and declared that they sincerely repented of their errors : and in different parts of this unhappy country similar events have taken place.
(Signed)                                    FELIX & MILLIE."

It is surprising that men will be guilty of the most direct and palpable contradictions, and yet they will not see them—they can not be convinced of them.   The military committee call the insurgents a *banditti*, a *fanatic herd :* accuse them of throwing patriots into the fire alive, and chopping them to pieces.   Yet with the same breath, they declare the news of their total extirpation by shooting, drowning, and beheading them in cool blood.   Besides, who began these scenes of carnage ?   The patriots, so called ; the Jacobins and their adherents. The massacre of the 10th of August, and 2d and 3d of September, were the first scenes of the bloody drama that has been exhibiting for two years in that populous country.   In the first scenes of the tragedy several thousand men fell victims—many of them not even suspected of disaffection to the cause of liberty.   Who does not see the massacre of St. Bartholomew revived in all its horrors ?   Change but the names of Romanists and Protestants, to Jacobins and Royalists, and the same scene is presented.   The apparent motives are different, but analogous. The Romanists put to death the Protestants in 1572, because they opposed the power of the Romanists.   They opposed Catherine of Medicis, and the Duke of Guise ; and the latter, thinking them troublesome, pronounced them *traitors* and *heretics*—a scheme of universal assassination was formed, and the king, Charles IX, gave his assent to it. On that dreadful night, the sound of a bell was the *signal for rallying*, and the assassins were let loose upon the unsuspecting Protestants. Five thousand in Paris, and twenty-five or thirty thousand in France, fell victims to the savage fury of the *dogs of faction*.   All this was to *serve God and religion*.

Draw a parallel between this scene and the massacre of August and September, 1792.   The popular party suspected treason in their opposers.   Without trial or proof they must be exterminated.   A banditti is prepared, from Paris and Marseilles.   At midnight the bell gives the signal for rallying ; the populace collect and the bloody work is begun— the Swiss guards, all suspected persons, priests and prisoners fall a sacrifice, in the indiscriminate slaughter.   In these massacres, six or seven thousand persons are murdered—and for what ?   Why the old stale plea of necessity is called in to justify it ; and liberty in this case, as religion in the massacre of St. Bartholomew, is made the stalking horse to drive the trade of butchering their fellow men.   The truth is, religion in one case and liberty in the other directly forbid all such outrages.   It is *faction*.   Men are always the same ferocious animals, when guided by passion and loosed from the restraints of law.   Let parties grow warm— let their passions be inflamed—let them believe one man is the enemy of another—let opposition exasperate them—and it is only for some daring demagogue to cry, your religion, or your liberty is in danger—your enemies are *heretics* or *traitors*—they must be exterminated—and the murderous work begins, and seldom ends till one party crushes the other.

In all cases of this kind, without one solitary exception on record, faction ends in tyranny—the victorious party, even with the word liberty incessantly on their tongues, never failing to exercise over the defeated party the most cruel vengeful acts of domination.

This is a most interesting subject to Americans; as the seeds of faction, the bane of republics, seem to be sown by an industrious party in America, and God only knows what will be the fruit of these things. So strong is the impression on my mind, that the present situation of Europe, and our attachment to the French cause, require all the caution and vigilance of government and good sense, to save this country from running mad in theories of popular constitutions, and plunging itself into the evils of faction and anarchy, that I beg leave to subjoin the following facts and remarks on this subject.

The manner in which the reports to the National Convention mention the destruction of the rebels at La Vendee, many of them honest deluded country people, fills the reader with horror. " Our soldiers, hand to hand, cut them down in front of their cannon. Streets, roads, plains and marshes were encumbered with the dead; we marched over heaps of the slain." " This banditti, these monsters—this army of robbers is destroyed." " This war of rogues and peasants." " It would have done your heart good to see these soldiers of Jesus and Louis XVII, throwing themselves into the marshes, or obliged to surrender." " Five hundred rebels were brought in; they implored pardon, which was refused—they were all put to death." " Six hundred were brought to Acenis; eight hundred to Angers and a great number to Saumer—the representatives of the people would rid the earth of them by ordering them to be thrown into the Loire." " The late actions on the Vendee have cost the lives of forty thousand persons." " The civil war the last summer is supposed to have cost France two hundred thousand lives." These are the accounts we have received from France. " The rebels have been nearly all killed—the royalists have been all massacred—the prisoners are so numerous that the guillotin is not sufficient—I have taken the method," says Garrier, " of having them all shot to death." These are the words of the triumphant republicans. Nay, two brothers finding a third brother among the rebels, demanded he should be tried by the military committee.

But what exceeds all the descriptions of barbarity hitherto known in America, is the speech of Collot D'Herbois in the National Convention. " Jacobins! some persons wish to moderate the revolutionary movement; take care of it; never forget what Robespiere told you on this subject. Some persons wish to make you establish a committee of clemency. *No clemency!*—be always Jacobins and Mountaineers, and liberty shall be saved."

Such are the terrible effects of civil war, the offspring of faction. Foreign wars are conducted with more humanity: it is in civil wars only that men turn savages, and exult over the mangled carcases of their fathers, brethren and fellow citizens.

CONCLUSION.

Those who suppose France now in possession of a free government, are mistaken. At no period has France experienced a despotism so severe and bloody, as the present authority of the Convention, backed by a full treasury and more than a million of disciplined troops. This severe tyranny has imprisoned and executed more French citizens in eighteen months past, than had been thrown into the Bastile for three centuries, preceding its demolition.

Nor are the French now fighting for *internal* liberty; they are fighting against *external* foes; a vile league of tyrants that have unwarrantably attempted to control the internal affairs of France. God grant that they may be defeated, and severely chastised for their insolence!

It is this unprecedented league of princes that now gives union and energy to the French nation. It is perhaps the sole principle of union. When this combination shall be dissolved, and France left to *act only upon herself*, more than half the revolution will still remain to be effected. France will then have to conquer the *errors of her legislators* and the *passions of a turbulent populace.* She will find a defective constitution and feeble laws—she will find violent parties, strong prejudices, unbridled licentiousness to be subdued. Instead of one tyrant or a convention of tyrants, she will find a multitude of little tyrants in each of her forty-five thousand towns and villages. Anarchy, disorder and proscriptions will afflict her for some years; and probably the present Convention and their successors will be buried in the ruins of the present paper constitution of government.

But society can not exist without government. Experience and severe calamities will ultimately teach the French nation, that government immediately in the hands of the people, of citizens collected without law, and proceeding without order, is the most violent, irregular, capricious and dangerous species of despotism—a despotism, infinitely more terrible than the fixed steady tyranny of a monarch, as it may spring up in a moment, and unexpectedly spread devastation and ruin, at any time, in any place, and among any class of citizens. The tyranny of a monarch is the steady gale, which gives time to prepare for its ravages; it enables the seaman to clear his decks and hand his sails—the farmer to leave his field, to shut his doors and shelter himself and his herds from the impending storm. But popular despotism is a whirlwind, a tornado of passions; it collects in a moment; a calm clear sky is instantly darkened, and furious winds, bursting on their affrightened victims while helpless and unguarded, sweep away the fruits of their labor, and bury them in the ruins.

The French will learn this important truth, that the assembly of representatives, who are to govern twenty-six millions of people, is not to be a company of stage-players, whose speeches are to be regulated by the hisses and acclamations of a promiscuous collection of men in the galleries. They will learn that a Paris mob is not to govern France, and that the galleries of the Convention must be silenced, or France will be enslaved. In short the French people must learn that an enthusiasm, necessary to animate her citizens in time of war, will be a source of infinite disorder in time of peace ; that passions, essential to them when engaging a foreign enemy, will be fatal to their own government; that in lieu of private wills, the *laws* must govern ; and that parties must bend their .stubborn opinions to some conciliatory plan of government, on which a great majority of citizens can coalesce and harmonize. When all this is done, they must learn that the *executive* power must be vested in a *single hand*, call him monarch, doge, president, governor, or what they please ; and to secure *liberty*, the executive must have force and energy. They must also learn a truth, sanctioned by numerous experiments, that *legislative power, vested in two houses*, is exercised with more safety and effect, than when vested in a single assembly. The conclusion of the whole business will be, that civil war and the blood of half a million of citizens, will compel the nation to renounce the idle theories of upstart philosophers, and return to the plain substantial maxims of wisdom and experience. Then, and not before, will France enjoy liberty.

Americans! be not deluded. In seeking *liberty*, France has gone beyond her. You, my countrymen, if you love liberty, adhere to your constitution of government. The moment you quit that sheet-anchor, you are afloat among the surges of passion and the rocks of error ; threatened every moment with shipwreck. Heaven grant that while Europe is agitated with a violent tempest, in which palaces are shaken, and thrones tottering to their base, the republican government of America, in which *liberty* and the *rights of man* are embarked, fortunately anchored at an immense distance, on the margin of the gale, may be enabled to ride out the storm, and land us safely on the shores of peace and political tranquillity.

New York, 1794.

# CHAPTER II.

## THE RIGHTS OF NEUTRALS.

WITHIN the last two hundred years, many able pens have been employed, in ascertaining and defining the principles which do or ought to regulate the conduct of independent nations toward each other. These principles have been discussed under the various titles of the " Laws of Nations," " the Rights of War and Peace," " the Rights of Neutral and Belligerent Powers." In some of these principles, which are evidently founded on moral justice, all nations and all men are agreed; others of them, notwithstanding the labors of Grotius, Puffendorf, Burlemaqui, Vattel, and other learned authors, remain unsettled, and subject to be varied, enforced or annulled, by temporary stipulations in public treaties. Every war occasions the infraction of former treaties, and by varying the relative situation of nations, in regard to their commerce or connections, renders it necessary or convenient for princes and states to deny the validity of principles, which they themselves formerly contended for with fleets and armies, and had sanctioned by their express agreement in anterior conventions.

Among ancient barbarous nations, an almost unrestrained piracy preceded fair commerce. Not only goods, but the persons of men and women were the objects of plunder, the prizes of naval valor, in ancient Greece, Rome, and among the Baltic nations.[*] Nor was war on land excited by very different motives, or conducted on very different principles. Armies fought originally for superiority and spoil only; and it was not till the three hundred and forty-ninth year of Rome, that the soldiers of that commonwealth received wages in money— their only reward being the plunder of the vanquished.[†] Hence we are not to look solely to the ancients, for the principles of equity in national intercourse. The early state of nations was a state of war; men chose to plunder, rather than to earn their subsistence by labor. A martial life was their pride and glory; labor was drudgery beneath the honorable rank of a soldier, and reserved for the occupation of slaves and women.[‡] Hence we are to distrust the morality of maxims which derive their authority from nations governed by military principles and habits. We are not to suffer the imposing title of the " rights of war," to regulate entirely our opinions, concerning the fitness and propriety of those maxims. It has not been without the unceasing efforts of great and good men for many years, aided by the authority and influence of Christianity, that the practice of ferocious nations has been softened

[*] Polyb. 2, 2; Liv. lib. 9, 1; 30, 14; 31, 30; 7, 30; 9, 1. Justin. 43, 3. Mallet's North. Antiq. Ch. 13. In Scandinavia, the sea was called " the field of pirates."
[†] Liv. 4, 59; 6, 13; 7, 16, 24, 27.
[‡] Tacitus, de Mor. Germ. 14. Charlevoix, I, 380, 381. Garcillasso, 8. Colden's Hist. of Five Nations, I, 4.

down to that degree of mildness and equity, which now characterizes the laws of nations. And we are not certain, that further meliorations are not due to natural and social justice, as well as to the tranquillity of mankind. The questions that agitate modern commercial nations, relate principally to the *rights of neutrality ;* that is, to the claims of nations, not engaged in war, to carry on a free commerce with belligerent nations ; and also to secure to their flags the privilege of protecting every species of innocent property. Every war revives the question, " what is or is not the law of nations ?" a question that has divided nations and writers on maritime law ; has combined and armed powerful states and kingdoms in the defense of their respective decisions ; and has been in all cases determined by force, or conventions founded on necessity or policy.

To the United States, which an intervening ocean separates from the seat of the endless contentions of nations on the other continent, where claims are prosecuted and defended by the sword, where a treaty of peace is but a formal truce, intended to enable rival nations to recruit their armies, and replenish their coffers for fresh hostilities ; to an empire thus sequestered from the numerous territorial causes of war, and liable only to be drawn into the quarrels of European nations, by the necessity of defending its commercial rights ; a just determination of all questions relating to maritime law, is extremely interesting and important. If belligerent and neutral nations have appropriate and distinct rights, it is of consequence that they should be defined ; and as the United States have in their favor the chance of usually being neutral, when the maritime nations of Europe are at war, it is their interest to ascertain and preserve, unabridged, the *rights of neutrals.* What these rights are, seems not to be understood. When the northern powers, in 1780, confederated to establish the principle, that " free ships make free goods," the public sentiment in America, then at war with Great Britain, was decidedly in favor of the principle, and Congress explicitly recognized it. Great Britain, at that time, remonstrated against the establishment of the principle, calling it a " modern law" of nations ; but was not in a situation effectually to oppose the formidable confederacy by which it was maintained. The peace of 1783 superseded that league, and the intercourse between the powers was regulated by subsequent treaties.

The last war has revived a similar confederacy, formed for the purpose of maintaining the same principle in favor of neutral commerce. The naval power of Great Britain speedily and at one blow disarmed the confederacy of its terrors ; and the victory near Copenhagen compelled the northern kingdoms to adjust the controversy by convention. During this eventful crisis, it has been found convenient in the United States, to abandon the principles contended for by the Baltic nations, and to defend Great Britain, in asserting what is called the " ancient" law of nations. Where shall we look for the motives of this change of sentiment in America ? Were the venerable fathers of the Revolution under a cloud, with regard to this question, which recent illumination has dispersed ? Or, is the dereliction of the ground which they took, to be ascribed to the influence of changes in the political state of Europe, or to the condition of parties in the United States ?

Without attempting to answer these questions, I will examine the history of neutral rights, and endeavor to find the true grounds of the pretensions of both parties. It is only by a detail of historical facts, that we shall be able to understand the merits of the questions in dispute, and arrive to just conclusions respecting what is the "law of nations."

A writer in the Palladium* of Feb. 3, 1801, undertakes to make his readers believe that the "modern" law of nations, that "free ships make free goods," is a scheme of the French government, formed to cripple the power of Great Britain; that it is repugnant to the interests of neutrals themselves; that it deprives belligerent powers of the rights of war; that it is no law at all; and, in short, to use the jargon of the writer, it is a mere French humbug. He observes, "that nations at war have a *clear undoubted right*, as old as war itself, to seize their enemies' goods wherever they can find them on the high seas, that is, out of the jurisdiction of any friendly nation." The writer proceeds to fill half a column with a series of similar assertions, which will not be here recited; as a consideration of these and some other remarks in the same paper, will more properly *follow* an examination of facts on this subject.

It is justly observed by Grotius, *De jure Belli ac Pacis*, lib. 3, 5, that ancient history furnishes no evidence of any positive regulations made by princes or states, on the subject of the rights of neutral nations. All the light which antiquity affords, is derived from a few recorded instances of the *practice* of belligerent powers; a practice which seems to have been governed by no fixed principles, but dictated solely by arbitrary will. Grotius mentions the fact related by Polybius, of supplies furnished by the Romans to the "enemies" of the Carthaginians; but he has not stated all the circumstances, which were these :— After the close of the first Punic war, the troops of Carthage, which were mostly mercenaries drawn from Gaul, Liguria, and other remote countries, raised a mutiny on account of the non-payment of their wages. This mutiny proceeded to open rebellion, which menaced Carthage with ruin, and was not quelled without a three years' bloody war. During this civil war, many ships from Italy conveyed supplies to the rebels. The Roman state was then at peace with Carthage, and for aught that appears, this trade was carried on without the knowledge of the Roman government. The Carthaginians were incensed at the Roman merchants, and seizing them to the number of five hundred, threw them into prison. The Romans, says the historian, were offended at this proceeding of the Carthaginians, and immediately demanded the release of the prisoners, which was granted. This compliance so pleased the Romans, that they released the Carthaginian prisoners, which the late war had left in their possession, assisted the republic with their friendly offices, gave permission to their merchants to export any kind of commodities to Carthage, and prohibited them from carrying supplies to the rebels.—(Polyb. lib. 1, cap. 6.)

From this account, it is evident that no rules or laws existed between those nations, which regulated the conduct of neutral nations toward

---

* A newspaper printed in Boston.

powers at war; for although it appears that the furnishing of supplies to an enemy, was considered by the Carthaginians as an injury, yet the punishment of the traders by imprisonment was also considered by the Romans as an affront and a wrong. And the subsequent prohibition of such supplies, is a proof that no prior restraint was laid on that species of commerce. Either, therefore, no principles or rules, in regard to such commerce, were known and recognized as a " law of nations," or the punishment was left undefined. It is, however, to be observed, that this was a case of assistance given to revolters, in arms against their own country, and can furnish no authority for a case of war between two independent nations. A commerce, in the first case, might be highly improper and injurious, which, in the case of two sovereign states, would be perfectly legal. It is further to be observed, that the word, in the original,* denotes supplies of provisions or money, rather than warlike stores, though possibly it may comprehend every species of supply, except soldiers.†

Another instance of the practice of ancient princes, in regard to a trade with their enemies, is recorded by Plutarch in his life of Demetrius, and cited by Grotius. That prince undertook to deliver Athens from the tyrant Lachares, who had usurped the government. Whether he was solicited to this by the citizens, the historian does not inform us. As he approached the city, laying waste the adjacent country, with a view to cut off supplies of provisions, and reduce the city by famine, he took a ship laden with corn, bound to the port of Athens, and *hung both the merchant and the pilot.* This severity deterred others from carrying supplies to the place, and famine compelled the citizens to surrender themselves to the prince. In this case, Athens was besieged, or at least cut off from supplies; it therefore falls under the condition of a blockaded place, with which, it is agreed among writers and rulers, all commerce may be justly interdicted.‡ But the punishment inflicted on the merchant and pilot, is evidence that this act of Demetrius proceeded from the arbitrary will of a tyrant, and was not justified by any common principle of public law, known and recognized by nations.

It results from reason and natural justice, that a nation at peace, furnishing assistance to a nation at war, with the direct view of augmenting its military strength, becomes an associate in the war, and the enemy of the opposing nation. This principle is as old as history—recognized frequently in the contentions between the Grecian states, between the Romans and Philip of Macedon, and between all belligerent powers. But how far trade carried on by a nation at peace, with one party engaged in war, was considered as affording such aid, ancient history furnishes no means of determining. Livy, book 22, ch. 33, relates that the Romans, during the second Punic war, sent embassadors to the Ligurians, to expostulate with them, for aiding their enemies, the Carthaginians, with supplies and troops—" *opibus auxiliisque;*" but nothing further is said on the subject. Hannibal was then in Italy; the Romans were contending for their country and independence; and unquestiona-

---

* Choregemas.        † 1 Maccabees, ch. viii, v. 24—28.
‡ The limitations that morality ought to impose on this principle, will be hereafter considered.

bly had a right to prohibit every kind of intercourse with an enemy, in the heart of their country. Perhaps supplies furnished to an army directly, by a nation at peace, may be always considered as *intended* to augment the military force of an enemy, and render the supplying nation an associate in the war. When Mago, the Carthaginian, solicited the Gauls and Ligurians to join him and furnish him with supplies, the Gauls replied, that if they assisted him openly, the Roman armies would immediately invade their territory ; they could therefore render none but clandestine aid.—(Liv. 29, 5.)

No distinction is made, in the accounts of these transactions, between supplies of provisions, money and soldiers—all supplies being considered as associating the supplying nation with the belligerent party. At the same time, the cases are not analogous to most of those which occur between modern commercial nations. The examples noted by ancient authors, are those in which the aid was furnished directly to the military ; and if it was not so intended, it actually did immediately strengthen a hostile army. The case of the interruption of the usual commerce of a trading nation at peace, by a power at war, on the ground of disabling an enemy, by such interruption, and compelling him the sooner to seek terms of accommodation, has not occurred to my researches into the histories of ancient nations. The case of Demetrius, before mentioned, comes under the character of supplies furnished to a besieged or invested place. So that antiquity affords no precedent in point.

As the earliest histories of nations give us no clear light on the subject of neutral commerce, so the fragments of the celebrated Rhodian laws, which are extant—the equally celebrated laws of Oleron and Wisbuy, are silent on the subject. And we find no systems of regulations to have been adopted and practiced, by maritime states, till a period comparatively modern. Grotius mentions a work, in the Italian language, which contains the ordinances or constitutions of the Syrians, Cyprians, French, Spaniards, Venetians and Genoese, respecting this subject, and presents us with a summary, which will be hereafter recited.—(Lib. 3, annot.)

From the earliest treaties extant, and other authorities, it appears that commerce, when it first revived, after the desolating conquests of the northern barbarians, was subjected to severe restrictions. No merchant could resort to a foreign country to trade, without a special or general license from the prince ; and the first treaties between princes, in regard to trade, were little more than a reciprocal permission for their subjects to trade in each other's territories. In England, foreign merchants, as late as the fourteenth century, were liable for each other's debts, and even punishable for each other's crimes. In 1317, Edward II, at the request of Alphonsus, king of the two Castiles, granted safety and freedom of commerce to the merchants of Biscay, without being liable to be arrested or stopped for the debt of another Spaniard. In 1325, a similar privilege was extended to the Venetian merchants ; and as nations gradually emerged from barbarity, and learned the value of commerce, it became usual to insert, in public treaties, clauses exempting traders from the obligation to answer for the debts of others.—(Anderson's Com. Vol. I, p. 353, 377, 382.)

Previous to the date of Magna Charta, 1215, the kings of England, jealous of the enterprising spirit of foreigners, often issued orders prohibiting merchant-strangers from coming to England, except in time of public fairs, and then permitting them to stay only forty days. The forty-eighth article of Magna Charta abridged the royal prerogative, and granted free liberty for foreign traders, to come, to remain, and to buy and sell at pleasure. Yet a special permission to foreign merchants, to trade freely with a country, has been incorporated into almost all commercial treaties, from that day to the present. This will not appear extraordinary, when we consider that in the ninth and tenth centuries, and even in the eleventh, the Baltic and Mediterranean pirates infested all the western shore of Europe, so that not a river, a creek, or harbor, was safe from plunderers. To secure the fair trader from those robbers, was formed the great confederacy of the Hanse Towns, and other leagues; and hence it became necessary for every prince or state, to prohibit strangers from approaching their shores, under pretense of trade, without special permission. Even at a later period, every foreigner was liable to be seized, imprisoned, and subjected to a heavy ransom, to obtain his liberty.

The danger to a maritime state, from sudden attacks by sea, seems to have originated a claim to a limited dominion over the waters of the ocean, bordering on such state. And during the piracies of the middle ages, there was a stronger claim, if possible, to the exercise of such dominion, than that which now exists, in proportion as the danger was greater, and the means of naval defense less considerable. Nor was it the professed pirate alone, who was to be dreaded; but vessels were often seized as plunder, by the subjects of powers not at war, and by inhabitants not professed robbers. Ancient writings are full of complaints, from one prince to another, respecting such seizures.—(See the first volume of Anderson on Commerce, in a variety of passages.)

These remarks are intended to show, that the early state of man was a state of war and plunder; that no system of rules was ever adopted by general consent of nations, to regulate their commercial intercourse; but that all the modern rules and principles, respecting neutral commerce, have sprung from special ordinances of princes or particular treaties, or have been imposed by great powers on the weaker states, by compulsion. It will appear that some of these rules are supported by natural law or justice, and so far are to be considered as laws of nations. Others of them depend for their authority on special compact; and others are to be deemed direct violations of natural law or justice, and stand on no better foundations than the arbitrary will of powerful states.

The most clear and prominent rule respecting neutral commerce is, that a nation at peace shall not supply a belligerent with military stores. It seems to have been agreed by all writers and states, that this is a *law of nations*. Yet we shall perhaps find, that this principle derives its authority from arbitrary prohibitions or treaties; at least, history and the signification of the words by which goods of this sort are denominated, lead to this conclusion. It was an ancient practice for princes and generals to *prohibit* all persons from conveying arms, money, men and provisions, to their enemies, especially to armies and besieged gar-

risons.  It does not appear that they were guided, in such restraints, by
any law or authority but their arbitrary will ; and hence the inhuman
treatment which the traders received from Demetrius and the Carthaginians.  No distinction was made between the commodities supplied ;
every thing that could aid the enemy was *forbid*, provided the prince
or commander thought such restraint would aid him in reducing the
enemy.

The same practice prevailed among princes, after the settlement of
the northern nations in the southern countries of Europe.  In 1251,
the state of Genoa granted permission to the Florentines to trade, either
by sea or land, with the Genoese territories, provided they carried no
prohibited goods, nor *sailed with the enemies of the republic.*  In 1295,
the Emperor Adolph complained of the detention of some Hanse ships
in the English ports, laden with *corn* and *naval stores*, till security should
be given not to sail to French ports with such cargoes ; but King Edward silenced his complaints by convincing him that the goods were
*contraband.*  In 1305, Edward I. gave free license to the Flemings to
resort to England for the purposes of trade, provided they should not
supply his enemies, the Scots, with *arms* and *provisions.*  And in 1313,
the same prince, after many complaints to the Earl of Flanders, for
furnishing the Scots with *military stores* and *provisions*, seized all the
Flemish ships in the port of London.  Similar complaints for a like
practice were made in subsequent years.  The uneasiness sometimes
proceeded to open rupture, and gave rise to fresh agreements by treaty.—(See And. Commerce, Vol. I, under the respective years.)

In the year 1352, Edward III. complained to the republic of Genoa,
that the Genoese furnished his enemy, the French king, with galleys,
and expressed the hope that this practice would be restrained.  Here
we observe the English king undertook to consider *galleys* to be contraband ; that is, it was his sovereign will and pleasure so to consider
them, as he did all kinds of provisions, conveyed to the Scots by the
Flemings.  In 1357, the Doge of Venice obtained from the same Edward, passports for a certain number of " galleys laden with merchandise," to proceed without interruption to and from Flanders.  This was
on account of the war between England and France, and is further evidence that the English seized neutral vessels, even merchantmen, bound
to Flanders ; for otherwise such passports would not have been necessary.  These facts are additional evidence, that all questions relating to
contraband goods, depended on the arbitrary will and pleasure of the
belligerent prince.

That such prohibitions and seizures were considered as illegal, or unauthorized by any law of nations, or that the subjects of the prohibiting
prince were not governed by any precise rules in their captures, is also
evident from the indemnifications granted by the prohibiting prince, for
losses incurred by seizures.  Many instances are on record, and one in
1372, in which Edward III. stipulated to pay two thousand marks, for
losses incurred by the seizure of Genoese merchantmen—with a proviso,
however, that the Genoese should not " lend their ships nor men" to his
enemies, the Spaniards and French.  In this instance, the compensation
stipulated by Edward, seems to have been the price with which he purchased the neutrality of Genoa.  Yet in this same year, Edward found

means to engage a squadron of Genoese galleys, to *aid him against France.*

In the year 1373, we find another instance in which ordinary merchandise was seized by the English, as contraband. This consisted of woolens, wool, and other goods, laden on board of Florentine ships, bound from Bruges to Pisa, taken under pretext of being bound to Spain, then in enmity with England. And in 1375, we find a respectful letter written by the Doge of Venice, to Edward, requesting passports for five galleys bound to Flanders, whose Earl was then a vassal of France, the enemy of England. These are examples in which common merchandise was treated as contraband; but surely by no law, except the sovereign will of King Edward. To such a length was this despotic power exercised by the kings of England, that Henry IV, in 1399, granted, to a private subject, letters of marque and reprisal, directing his naval commanders to seize on all Dutch ships in English ports, and hold them until a private debt due from a merchant in Leyden to that subject, should be paid, with costs and charges.

In 1403, we find the General Assembly of the Hanse Towns, the city of Lubec, and the city of Hamburg, making complaints to Henry IV, that his subjects had seized their merchantmen and fishing vessels, under pretense of their carrying contraband goods. In short, the history of commerce is filled with similar complaints against the English, who assumed, in those early days, that dominion over the ocean, which they have maintained in modern times, and prescribed laws, at pleasure, to the smaller, and to the less commercial states on the Continent. On this subject, the learned and candid Anderson well observes, " We have but too much reason to suspect, that the complaints of weaker states against the depredations of stronger ones, though seldom redressed, were, at those times at least, generally well founded; and on the other hand, that the complaints and claims of the more powerful states, against the weaker ones, had often no better foundation than that of the lion in the fable."—(Vol. I, p. 533.)

During the flourishing condition of the Hanseatic confederacy, the insolence of power was often displayed by the ships belonging to the league; and especially in the beginning of the fifteenth century, when the ships of English merchants were often seized for trading to the Baltic, without any pretense of an illicit commerce, but merely from a spirit of jealousy. These injuries gave rise to many complaints, which were generally removed by negotiation. Similar instances of the seizure of the ships of nations in amity, merely from commercial rivalship and jealousy, and to prevent a competitor from enjoying a market which a nation wished to monopolize, were frequent in the infancy of modern commerce; and the injured state, in such cases, remonstrated, or resorted to reprisals for satisfaction.—(And. Com. Vol. I, p. 554, &c.)

In the year 1414, a treaty of truce between Henry V. of England, and the Duke of Bretagne, stipulated that no prizes taken from the English, by any power at war, should be carried in and sold in the ports belonging to the Duke; but prizes made by the English, were permitted to be carried in and sold by the captors; also, that the Duke's subjects should not assist the enemies of England, nor afford them encouragement, by *concealing their ships or goods.* This is the first treaty in which I have

found these stipulations, which are incorporated into most modern treaties of commerce. And it is observable that these stipulations are all
in favor of England, without an equivalent, or reciprocal concessions,
in favor of the Duke—another proof of the imperious tone assumed by
the princes of that country, which dictated maritime laws at pleasure.

In the year 1417, a truce between Henry V. and the Duke of Burgundy, on the part of Flanders, contains further stipulations, viz. " that so
long as war or reprisals shall last between England and Genoa, no Flem-
ing, nor the ships of any other nation, being in Flanders, shall lade any
merchandise on Genoese carracks, galleys or ships; otherwise they
will be in danger of forfeiture to King Henry, and his successors, if
found in them any where out of the ports of Flanders." It was also
stipulated mutually, that prizes taken from either party, should not be
sold in the ports of the other, and that the goods of an enemy should
not be imported into either country. So also the treaty between the
same parties in 1467.

These are the earliest records that I have found of a prohibition to
neutrals or nations at peace, to carry the goods of an enemy. The
clause above states, as a reason for the prohibition, that goods will be
" in danger of forfeiture to King Henry;" which seems to imply that no
certain rule or law, authorizing such forfeiture, then existed; but that
the King would confiscate the property, if he chose so to do. And it is
certain that belligerent nations made a practice of seizing their enemy's
ships and all the goods on board, without inquiring for the owners, long
before this period. This seems to have had its origin in the barbarous
*rights of war*, founded in violence and arbitrary will, and like other
similar rights, sanctioned by compact.

In 1421, a treaty of peace and alliance between England and the
Doge of Genoa, bears marks of more liberality in commerce; for it was
stipulated that the merchants of either contracting party should not be
hindered from freely trafficking with the enemies of the other; but *no
assistance by sea or land* should be given by one nation to the enemies
of the other. Here a distinction is made between *ordinary commerce*
and *military aid*—a distinction that was not often, if ever, made in treaties of an earlier date. And here we observe the beginning of a relaxation of the severe, rigorous, arbitrary, and barbarous customs and practices, in regard to trade, which originated in savage ferociousness and
piracy, or in the despotic will of haughty, uncivilized princes, who knew
not the value of trade, who considered every stranger as an enemy,*
and despised the occupation of a merchant.

Another striking proof that all regulations respecting trade were
originally founded on conventions, or prescribed by arbitrary will, is
the practice of princes, who often made commercial treaties, and observed them, permitting free trade with each other's countries, even
when they were at .war with each other. " This practice," says Ra-
pin, " was infinitely better than what has followed since, of making a

---

* Barbarians have usually considered all strangers as enemies. Hence *hostis* in
Latin, which originally denoted a *stranger*, became the appellation of an *enemy*.
This idea was too prevalent in Europe, during the middle ages, and was no small
obstacle to the progress of commerce.

prey of the merchants to their ruin." So necessary was commerce to
the belligerent states, that the rights of war, and the resentment of
princes, yielded to their demands for goods.

In the same manner, the *right of search* for prohibited goods was
derived from express stipulation. The first mention of this right, which
I have found, is in a treaty between Edward IV. of England, and the
Duchess of Burgundy, A. D. 1478, in which the parties yielded to each
other *the right of searching for goods prohibited to be exported from
their respective countries.*

In a treaty between Henry VII. of England, and the Archduke
Philip of the Netherlands, A. D. 1496, the tenth article stipulates,
that " the officers in either country, appointed for searching for contraband goods, shall perform it civilly, without spoiling them, or breaking
the chests, barrels, packs or sacks, under pain of a month's imprisonment. And when the searchers shall have opened them, they shall
assist in the shutting and mending of them, &c. Nor shall they compel the owners to sell or dispose of the same against their own incli-
nations."

Hitherto we find no regulations respecting the right of search for
enemies' goods on board of ships belonging to the contracting parties,
nor on board of neutral ships; nor respecting the right of search for
contraband goods destined for an enemy of one of the parties. The
article above recited relates solely to a search for goods prohibited to
be exported or imported, from or to the countries of the respective
parties in time of peace; and this was to be made by " officers in each
country," appointed for that purpose. As yet we hear nothing of a
right in the commanders of ships of war and privateers to stop and
search vessels at sea.

Nor do we find any stipulation or law of nations, prohibiting the
subjects of any neutral state whatever, or their own subjects, to carry
enemy's goods from an enemy's country to a neutral country. The
clauses in the treaties down to the foregoing date, restrain the subjects
of the contracting parties only, from importing enemy's goods into their
respective countries. Not a syllable do we find referring the obligation of these restraints to any law of nature or nations—much less authorizing an extension of restraints to the mere transportation of goods,
on the ground of their being the growth or manufacture of an enemy's
country.

In the splendid reign of Queen Elizabeth of England, we have a remarkable evidence of the opinion here advanced, that the rules of contraband trade never had any foundation, except compact, or despotic
power. In the war carried on by England and Holland against Spain,
during that queen's reign, the King of Spain fitted a large fleet for the
invasion of England, which project was disconcerted by the fleet under
Sir Francis Drake, in 1587. The Queen, being informed that immense
preparations were still making in Spain to invade England, (which
issued in producing the Armada,) published her proclamation, forbidding the Hanse Towns to supply her enemy Spain, with *corn and naval
provisions*, under pain of loss of ships and goods. The Dutch went
further, and prohibited all nations to carry to Spain *any goods or provisions whatever*. And in pursuance of these prohibitions, the English

fleet took, at the mouth of the Tagus, about sixty Hanseatic ships, " laden with wheat and warlike stores," which ships had sailed to the
north of the Orkneys to avoid seizure.  The cargoes were confiscated,
but the ships discharged.—(See And. Com. Vol. II, 229, Vol. IV, 23.)

We observe in this instance, that powerful nations, when much exasperated, or determined to subdue an enemy, can convert every species
of goods into contraband ; in short, that such nations make laws of
contraband *ad libitum.*

At the commencement of the war between Holland and the commonwealth of England in 1652, the Dutch persuaded the Danish court
to seize and detain in the Sound, an English fleet of merchantmen,
laden with naval stores—supposing by this act to distress England, their
enemy—and they published a placard, forbidding all persons to carry
such articles to England, under pain of confiscation.  But the States
General were obliged, on the adjustment of differences, to make restitution for the damages sustained by the seizure of the English ships by
the Danes.

In the seventeenth century, provisions continued to be considered in
treaties as contraband or not, according to the interest of the contracting parties.  In the treaty between England and Russia, in 1623, military stores alone are prohibited to be carried to the enemy ; but in the
eighth article of the treaty between England and Spain, in 1630, *provisions* are mentioned with naval and military stores, as prohibited.  In
a treaty between England and Denmark, in 1639, the parties stipulated not to supply the enemy of either with " warlike succors, either in
*money, provisions,* arms, ammunition, machines, guns, &c."

In the celebrated leagues between the States General of Holland and
the Hanse Towns, the one dated in 1613, and the other in 1615, whose
express object was to assure a perfect freedom of commerce and navigation in the northern seas, the contracting parties agreed not to supply an enemy with " *money,* troops, ships, ammunition, arms, *provisions,* and such other things," under pain of corporeal punishment, to
be inflicted on the offending subject.—(Postleth. Dict., Art. *Maritime
Affairs.*)

From this detail of facts, we find that the maritime powers of Europe, from the thirteenth to the seventeenth century, were governed by
no fixed principles, much less by any supposed law of nature or nations, in defining contraband goods.  On the other hand, powers at
war prohibited by proclamation, or restrained by seizure and confiscation, just what commodities, bound to an enemy, they saw fit ; and in
public treaties, princes and states stipulated to withhold from their enemies, and prohibited, whatever articles their interest, their convenience,
or the superior power of one party dictated.

It is remarkable also, that the original signification of the word *contraband,* confirms this conclusion.  It is composed of the two French
words *contre,* against, and *ban,* an edict or proclamation—it denotes
therefore goods *contrary to proclamation,* that is, *forbidden.*  Neither
in the meaning of the word, nor in the history of contraband, do we
find the least ground to refer its origin to natural right or justice.

The right of search, another subject of controversy, seems to have
been derived from the practice of examining foreign ships in port, to

prevent their lading with commodities prohibited to be exported. Thus in early times, *searchers* were appointed by princes in all their ports, whose business was to inspect the cargoes of all ships while loading ; and even down to the year 1668, treaties between states took notice of these officers, and regulated their conduct to prevent abuse and impositions. But anterior to the year 1632, no regulations were provided in treaties, as far as I can discover, concerning the searching of vessels at sea.* In the treaty between England and France, in 1632, the third article provides against damages to merchants by detention at sea, under pretense of searching for contraband goods. No more than three persons were permitted at one time, to enter a merchantman from a ship of war—and after search, they were not suffered to detain the ship nor " turn it out of its way."

The right of search seems incident to the right of prohibiting the transportation of goods. And it is probable, that as the practice of forbidding foreign nations to carry goods to an enemy was originally arbitrary, and authorized solely by the will of the sovereign who was at war, so the practice of searching vessels at sea for contraband goods was assumed by commanders of ships, or authorized by their sovereigns, long before it was sanctioned by treaty. Indeed there can be no rational doubt on this point, when it is considered that the first mention of this practice in treaties is, in clauses intended to regulate it and prevent its abuses. In most modern treaties, clauses are inserted for this purpose ; and after all possible precautions, no privilege is more liable to be abused by the imperious commanders of ships ; nor is there any abuse more difficult to be restrained by previous injunctions or subsequent punishment.

Having detailed a series of evidence, to prove that the principles of contraband were originally adopted in an arbitrary manner, and were afterward regulated by compact, or imposed upon weak nations by their stronger neighbors, and brought down the history of this subject to the middle of the seventeenth century, when treaties between commercial nations took nearly their present form, I proceed to show that the practice of prohibiting the carrying of goods to an enemy in time of war, has never been universally recognized as legal, but has in various instances been opposed by maritime nations.

The instance already related of the resentment of the Romans, when the Carthaginians captured their vessels bound with supplies to the revolted mercenaries, and imprisoned the traders, can not be relied on as an authority, because history has not recorded the reason of that resentment—whether it was solely for the *imprisonment* of the Roman traders, or for the seizure of the ships and provisions. It may however be fairly inferred, that it was principally the punishment which offended the Romans ; for it is related, that upon the release of the prisoners, the Romans were so much pleased, that they permitted their merchants to export all kinds of necessaries to Carthage, but " pro-

---

* I do not assert that no regulations of a prior date exist; for I have no collection of entire treaties, of a date anterior to the year 1600. And if any misstatement of facts should occur in these observations, it must be attributed to my want of such a collection.

hibited their carrying any to the enemy." Indeed no person can doubt, in this case, nor in the case of the prohibition of supplies to Hannibal's army while in Italy, that the restraint was perfectly reasonable, and consonant to natural and social justice.

As early as the year 1256, a commercial treaty between Hamburg and the Duke of Brabant, stipulated that commerce should not be intercepted, even in case of a war between the two sovereigns. Many similar facts are on record ; and though not directly in point, they prove that no natural or social law inhibits a free commerce between nations at war, or that its obligations may be superseded by the utility of such commerce. In short, the facts prove that there is nothing in a state of war, that necessarily renders it useful or expedient to prohibit a free trade ; and thus so far weaken the supposed foundation of the present regulations of nations, in regard to a trade with an enemy.

The celebrated fair of Leipsic, which has been a chief source of its greatness, is supposed to have had its origin in a similar privilege, granted to that city in 1268, by the Marquis of Landsperg ; permitting merchants of all nations to resort thither for traffick, even though he should be at war with their sovereigns.

In the year 1305, Robert, Earl of Flanders, in a letter to Edward V. of England, acknowledged the receipt of his license for Robert's subjects to resort and trade to England, on condition they should not supply his enemies, the Scots, with arms and provisions. He tells Edward he had forbid his subjects to give any aid to the Scots in their war against his majesty. But he subjoined that, " as his country had ever been supported by commerce, and was therefore free for all merchants to resort to it ; he therefore could not and ought not to prohibit the said Scots from coming, merely for commerce, to his country, as usual, with merchandise, which he was bound to defend from all oppression and wrong. He therefore requests the King to make his license absolute, and without restrictions." In 1319, the Earl gave a similar answer to King Edward II, but he went further, and declared that " he could not hinder the Scots from trading to Flanders, nor *his merchants from trading to Scotland*, as had been customary, since the contrary would bring ruin and desolation on his country." The same answer did Edward receive from the cities of Bruges and Ypres. And when the Flemish ships were seized for carrying on a trade to Scotland, the Earl remonstrated against the depredations on his commerce, as violent and unjustifiable. For thirty years, during the wars between England and Scotland, mutual complaints and recriminations passed between the three first Edwards and the Earls of Flanders, and the Hanse Towns ; the kings of England constantly claiming the right to restrain a neutral trade to Scotland, and the neutral cities and princes as constantly opposing the claim. These contentions often produced seizures and reprisals, and finally ended in negotiation and treaty. But it is remarkable that the princes and cities of Flanders and Brabant, expressed their sense of the seizures made by the English, by calling them *sea robberies*. So far were the laws of contraband, at that time, from being considered as founded on *natural right* or *justice*, or from being acknowledged as reasonable and justifiable, that the seizures under pretense of contraband, were denominated *piracy*, in the official communications between princes on the subject. And this is decisive evidence that many princes and states, in that period, considered any claim to interrupt a neutral trade with an enemy, as illegal and invalid, unless derived from express stipulations between the belligerent and the neutral.

In 1352, Edward III. complained to the republic of Genoa, that the Genoese supplied his enemy, the French king, with galleys, and *expressed his hopes that the government would prevent it in future.* This form of addressing the government of Genoa, is a strong evidence, that Edward himself considered his claim to restrain such supplies, as *doubtful* or *ill founded ;* for a prince of his character would not have *requested,* but *demanded,* what he was satisfied was his *right.*

In the year 1403, the General Assembly of the Hanse Towns, and the cities of Lubec and Hamburg, complained of seizures made by the Gascons, then the subjects of England, under pretense of contraband— another evidence that the claim to make seizures on that ground, was opposed as illegal.

In 1421, in a treaty between England and Genoa, the privilege of a free trade with the enemy of either party, was stipulated without restriction.

In a treaty between Henry IV. of England and the Duchess of Burgundy, in 1478, the armed ships of enemies are denominated *pirates,* and prohibited from entering the ports of either party. At least this is the sense in which Anderson understands the word, and the clause warrants the construction. Indeed, in a period when the prohibitions of neutral commerce were considered as illegal, unless authorized by compact, all seizures of ships in neutral trade, not warranted by such compact, must have been deemed *piratical ;* and it is clear from all history, that they were so considered.

We shall not be surprised at this view of the subject, if we consider that during the period under consideration, the land was infested with robberies, and the ocean with piracies. Nothing was more common, than for the ordinary merchantmen of every nation, to rob, if able, any ship whatever at sea ; and this practice gave to a clause, found in most ancient treaties, requiring the masters or owners of *all* ships, before their departure, to give ample security not to commit robbery, violence or murders on the high seas. In a memorable treaty of peace and commerce, between Henry VII. of England, and John, King of Denmark, A. D. 1490, the parties stipulate that " pirates and others warring at sea," shall not be received into the ports of either party— which stipulation evidently distinguishes between robbers at sea, who had no license or commission whatever, and ships authorized as traders or ships of war, that might commit robbery or violence. A subsequent part of the clause includes all such ships under the terms *pirates* and *sea robbers,* and ordains the same penalties for aiding and protecting them, without distinction.

The contradictory principles pursued by the same nation, in different years, and under different situations, confirm the opinions here advanced, concerning the origin of the laws of contraband. Grotius relates from Rhedanus, the Dutch historian, and Camden, the British antiquary, that Queen Elizabeth, in 1575, when a war raged between Holland and

Spain, sent two envoys to the Dutch, to inform them that the *English government would not submit* to have their vessels, bound to Spain, seized and detained by the Dutch.—(De Jure Belli, lib. 3, cap. 1, annot.)

Yet within fourteen years after, when Elizabeth herself was engaged in a war with Spain, she issued her proclamation, and sent letters to the German cities, actually forbidding them to send provisions to Spain. In this instance, which is far from being a solitary one, a sovereign refused to submit to restrictions, which she herself, when she found it convenient, imposed on others—an evidence that such prohibitions depended on the arbitrary will of princes, who regulated their public claims and pretended rights, by their interest and their power.

The haughty conduct of Elizabeth, however, on that occasion, and her capture of the Hanse ships in the Tagus, as before related, gave the Queen much trouble; for not only the Hanse cities, but the Emperor, and the government of Poland and Dantzic, remonstrated against the seizures, and finally an open rupture ensued between England and the Hanseatics.

In the year 1598, mutual complaints passed between the King of Denmark and Queen Elizabeth, respecting seizures of vessels. The Danes seized English ships, under pretense that certain goods had not been duly entered at the custom-house. The Queen remonstrated, and procured a remission of part of the confiscation. On the other hand, the Danish prince demanded redress for certain " piracies" committed by the English on his subjects : " for now," says Camden, " there began to grow controversies about such matters ;" meaning, the right of carrying contraband goods to an enemy. It is here observable, that the King of Denmark claimed a right to send goods of any kind to the enemy of England, and he calls the seizure and confiscation of his subjects' ships by the English, " piracies," and declares he can endure them no longer. This is no small proof that the laws of contraband were arbitrary, and did not command the assent of sovereigns, as laws of natural right or justice. Camden however mistakes in saying, " controversies about such matters then began ;" for we have seen the right of a belligerent to prohibit a neutral trade to an enemy disputed as early as the year 1305, almost three centuries anterior to the period under consideration.

Grotius, in the passage above cited, has compressed into a small compass, the ordinances and practice of the maritime nations of Europe, in regard to neutral commerce. When the ships and goods belong to an enemy, without controversy, both are the property of the captors. If the ship is neutral, and the merchandise the property of an enemy, the captor may send the ship into port, where the goods may be unladen and seized by the captor, but the ship must be discharged, and the owner receive his freight. If the ship belongs to an enemy, and its cargo to a neutral, both are lawful prize. But in the war between the Dutch and the Hanse Towns on the Baltic and Elbe, in 1438, the senate of Holland frequently determined that the goods of a friend on board the ships of an enemy, should *not* be lawful prize ; and this determination was afterward held by them to be law. In 1597, when the Dutch were at war with Spain, the King of Denmark sent envoys to Holland and the allies, vindicating a right to a free trade to Spain, their enemy.

The French almost always permitted a free trade to be carried on by neutrals to their enemy in time of war; so indulgent was the French government, that the enemy often covered his property under other names—which was attempted to be prevented by edicts in 1543 and 1584.

By those edicts, the French government permitted friendly nations to carry to any enemy, every species of merchandise except instruments of war; and even when these were seized, they were not confiscated, but paid for, at a just value. Indeed it is remarkable that the French princes were always liberal in regard to neutral commerce.

In 1613, the Hollanders and their allies agreed with the city of Lubec and its allies, not to furnish their enemies with *money, men, ships* or *provisions;* and in 1627, it was agreed between Denmark and Sweden, that the Danes should *hinder all trade* with Dantzic, then the enemy of Sweden, and should not permit any ships to pass the Sound with goods for her other enemies. For these engagements, however, the King of Denmark stipulated to receive a compensation in other advantages. These, says Grotius, are special conventions, from which nothing can be inferred to bind others.

But, continues our learned author, the Germans were not the only people who opposed the claims of Great Britain to interrupt all commerce with her enemy. The Polish government also remonstrated against the interruption of their trade to Spain, when at war with England, in 1597.

After the peace of Vervins between France and Spain, in 1598, Elizabeth, still continuing the war, requested the French to permit their ships, bound to Spain, to be searched for military apparatus; but *the French would not consent*, alledging that the English only sought a pretext to interrupt their commerce and plunder their ships. [This was in the reign of that able and generous prince, Henry IV. of France—a prince who perfectly well understood the laws of nations, and the true interests of his country. The application of Elizabeth to him for permission to search, and his refusal to grant it, are decisive evidences that neither of them understood the practice of searching, even for warlike stores, to be a *right;* on the contrary, they must have considered it as a special privilege, to be derived only from agreement, and a derogation from the common right of nations.]

In 1525, a league was formed between England and Holland, and their allies, in which it was agreed that other states, which had an interest in reducing the enormous power of Spain, should be solicited to prohibit all commerce between their respective countries and Spain; but if they should decline, then it was agreed to search their ships for military stores, but no further to detain the vessels, nor to injure the neutral, under the pretense of carrying such goods. In pursuance of this treaty, some Hamburg ships bound to Spain were taken, laden with military apparatus, which was 'confiscated, but the other goods were paid for. But the French resisted this practice, and when some of their ships, bound to Spain, were taken and confiscated, the government manifested its determination *not to submit* to such violence.

From these facts our author concludes, that public proclamation ought to be given by a nation, of an intention to interrupt the trade of a neutral; and he cites examples—but observes, that such notice is not always regarded. In 1458, such notice was given by the city of Dantzic to the city of Lubec, not to carry on commerce with her enemies; but no regard was paid to it. The Hollanders equally disregarded a notice given them by the Lubeckers, to abstain from a trade with the Danes, their enemies, in 1551. In a war between Sweden and Poland, the Hollanders utterly refused to permit the parties to interrupt their free trade.

From these authorities, we prove beyond controversy, that the practice of prohibiting neutral nations from carrying goods of any kind to an enemy, in the ordinary course of trade, *originated in arbitrary will, supported by superior power;* that no nation, until a very modern period of time, ever claimed the right thus to interrupt the trade of neutrals, on the ground of natural law, or general law of nations, sanctioned by common consent and practice; that the practice of princes and states on this subject, has been regulated entirely by temporary interests, despotic power, and mutual stipulations in conventions—of course has been variable and contradictory. It will be hereafter proved, that the present laws of contraband, as they are called, so far from being warranted by the principles of natural and social justice, are no more than the ancient practice of piracy, modified and meliorated by a few humane regulations.

From this detail of facts, regarding the prohibitions of neutral commerce by belligerent powers, from the earliest records of history to the period when commercial treaties began to take the form which they have since retained, I proceed to state the most material facts respecting the rules of contraband, as now understood and received by authors and nations.

The first treaty I have found, in which the articles deemed contraband are severally enumerated, is that between Charles II. of England, and the States General of the Netherlands, dated February, 1668. These articles are the warlike instruments used at that time, and nearly the same as those specified in more modern treaties. But it was expressly stipulated that all other merchandise should be free for one party at peace to carry to the enemy of the other party at war, except to places besieged, blocked up, or invested. And now, I believe for the first time, these nations determined to abolish the ancient custom of considering *provisions* as contraband, and stipulated that "corn, wheat, and other grain, pulse, oils, wines, salt, and generally any thing that belongs to the nourishment and sustenance of life," should not be prohibited. Here we see the modern refinement of manners, increasing humanity, and the true interest of commerce, triumphing over the barbarous maxims of antiquity, which authorized every species of plunder, and all possible means to distress and reduce an enemy. This period, in which the limits of contraband were narrowed, by excepting provisions from the list of articles, and in which precise stipulations were substituted for the arbitrary determination of princes and states, may be considered as an important epoch in the history of commerce.

Another considerable change in the intercourse of nations, was effected about the middle of the seventeenth century. This was an agreement to give full faith and credit to sea letters or passports, according to certain forms, in order to prevent the vexations practiced in searching for prohibited goods. The practice of searching vessels passing the Sound into and from the Baltic, was expressly abolished by treaty between Denmark and the States General in 1645, and it was declared that full faith should be given to the cocket, or custom-house clearance. The treaty of 1668, between England and the States General, declared also that entire credit should be given to a ship's passport, the form of which was annexed to the treaty—a form which has been retained in subsequent treaties. This stipulation was no inconsiderable acquisition to the merchants, as it exempted their ships from many losses and vexations, incident to the practice of detaining and searching ships at sea. The same treaty declared that neither the vessels of the parties, [nor the free goods contained in them,] should be confiscated, on account of carrying prohibited goods; but that goods laden on board of enemies' ships, should be subject to confiscation.

In the treaty of 1674, between the same powers, the same freedom of commerce was stipulated, and nearly the same articles declared to be prohibited. But the fourth article goes much further in the enumeration of the commodities which should *not* be deemed contraband. These articles are, " all kinds of cloth, and all other manufactures woven of any kind of wool, flax, silk, cotton, or any other materials; all sorts of clothing and vestments, together with the materials whereof they use to be made; gold and silver, as well coined as not coined; tin, iron, lead, copper and coals; also wheat, barley, and all other kinds of corn or pulse; tobacco, and all kinds of spices; salted and smoked flesh; salted and dried fish, butter and cheese, beer, oils, wines, sugars, all sorts of salt, and in general all provision which serves for the nourishment and sustenance of life; likewise all kinds of cotton, hemp, flax, and pitch and ropes, sails and anchors; also masts and planks, boards and beams, of what sort of wood soever, and all other materials requisite for building and repairing of ships"—all which were declared to be free goods, and with other free goods might be conveyed to an enemy, excepting to places seized, environed, or invested. Free goods, in the same ship with contraband, were not to be infected; and vessels carrying contraband goods, were not to be detained or turned out of their course, provided the master would surrender the prohibited goods to the captor. All the goods laden on board of an enemy's ship by the subjects of the parties, were declared to be confiscated; but all goods, except contraband, laden on board of the ships belonging to the subjects of the parties, were stipulated to be free, even though the goods belonged to an enemy.

To prevent all misconstructions, an explanatory declaration was signed by the same parties, on the 30th of December, 1675, in which it was agreed " that the true meaning and intention of the said articles is, and ought to be, that ships and vessels belonging to the subjects of either of the parties, can and might, from the time the said articles were concluded, not only pass, traffick and trade from a neutral port or place, to a place in enmity with the other party, or from a place in enmity to a neutral place; but also, from a port or place in enmity, to a port or place in enmity with the other party, whether the said places belong to one and the same prince or state or to several princes and states, with whom the other party is at war."

In the treaty concluded between England and France, in February, 1677, we find the stipulations respecting contraband to be the same, and nearly in the same words. The treaties with the Dutch were renewed by James II. in 1685, and by William III. in 1689. The treaty of Nimeguen, between France and Holland in 1678, contained precisely similar stipulations in regard to contraband goods, and neutral commerce.

Notwithstanding these treaties solemnly ratified, and renewed by successive princes, the formidable power of Lewis XIV, which alarmed surrounding nations, and occasioned the grand alliance with England, Germany, Spain, and Holland, to check the designs of that ambitious monarch, induced the King of England and the States General to form a new convention, *pro re nata*, dated August 12, 1689, in which it was agreed *to prohibit the commerce of all nations with France*, and to seize and confiscate the ships of any nation whatever, concerned in such commerce. This convention was notified to the several courts in Europe. Aware of the injustice of such a prohibition, the two powers formed a secret article, in which it was agreed, that " in case either party shall be incommoded or molested by reason of the execution of the present treaty, the parties do promise and oblige themselves to be guaranty for and to one another upon that account." It is evident that the parties expected such an unwarrantable exercise of power, interrupting the trade of all neutral nations, would be resented by neutral princes, and occasion an attack on one or both ; in which case the foregoing clause pledges the parties to defend each other. This illegal prohibition, it will be remarked, nearly resembles that of Queen Elizabeth, already related, and Sweden and Denmark entered into a league to oppose it and procure satisfaction.—(See Collection of Treaties, Vol. I, p. 6 ; London, 1772. Vattel, book iii, ch. 7, sec. 112.)

The treaty of Ryswick in 1697, which put an end to the war between France and England, contains one clause, in which the parties agree not to assist with " ships, ammunition, provisions or money," any *person* or *persons*, who should molest or disturb each other. This clause seems to be intended solely to restrain the King of France from affording any assistance to the Pretender.

The treaty of navigation and commerce concluded between Great Britain and France at Utrecht, March 31, 1713, contains such a full and clear explanation of what were understood to be the principles of free trade at that period, as to deserve a careful perusal. The seventeenth article is, in substance, as follows :

It shall be lawful for all and singular, the subjects of the Queen of Great Britain and of the most Christian King, to sail with their ships, with all manner of liberty and security, *no distinction being made who are the proprietors of the merchandise laden thereon*, from any port to the places of those who are now, or shall be hereafter at enmity with the King of Great Britain, or the most Christian King, &c., and to trade with the same liberty and security from the places, ports and havens of the enemies of both, or of either party, &c.—not only directly from the places of the enemy to neutral places, but from one place belonging to an enemy, to another place belonging to an enemy, whether they be under the jurisdiction of the same prince, or under several. And it is now stipulated concerning ships and goods, that *free ships shall also give a freedom to goods*, &c., and every thing found on board the ships belonging to the subjects of the parties, shall be deemed free and exempt, though belonging to the enemies of either party—contraband goods always excepted. And the same liberty is extended to *persons*, although enemies, and they are not to be taken out of the ships, unless they are soldiers and in actual service of the enemy.

The nineteenth article enumerates the contraband goods, which are instruments of war of all kinds. The enumerated commodities *not* contraband, are the same, and the article in nearly the same words, as the clause before recited from the treaty between England and the Dutch, in 1674. And it is remarkable that these treaties include nothing among instruments of war, unless actually wrought into a form proper for use ; and some part of naval stores, even in the form required for use, are excepted from the list of contraband, as ropes, cables, sails, pitch, anchors, planks, and masts.

By this treaty also, full credit was to be given to passports or sea letters, made out according to a form annexed ; and merchantmen, exhibiting these passports, *were not to be searched, molested, or compelled to quit their intended course*, unless contraband goods were found. Contraband goods only were subject to seizure and confiscation, without affecting the property of the ship or innocent goods. Goods laden on board of an enemy's ship, by the subjects of either party, were subjected to confiscation.

The treaty of navigation and commerce between Great Britain and Spain, dated November 28, 1713, contains stipulations respecting prohibited goods and neutral commerce, of precisely the same tenor.

In the defensive treaty between Great Britain and Sweden, dated January 21, 1720, the eighteenth article declares that, even in the case where one party should be at war, and the other not, but the neutral party should be required to furnish the auxiliary troops stipulated, till the neutral party might have a free trade with the enemy of the other, excepting only in goods " commonly called contraband, and declared to be such by the common consent of all nations."

The treaty of Aix la Chapelle, between Great Britain and France, dated October, 1748, made no alterations in regard to commerce ; it being merely a treaty of peace and friendship. But the treaty of Paris between the same powers, dated February 10, 1763, expressly renews, among others, the treaty of commerce signed at Utrecht in 1713, and confirms it in the fullest manner.

The treaty of navigation and commerce between Great Britain and Russia, concluded at Petersburg, June 20, 1766, places neutral commerce on the same principles as the treaty of Utrecht—making all goods free in free ships, except contraband articles ; and the list of these is much smaller than in other treaties, comprehending neither provisions, timber, nor any kind of naval stores.

These are the express stipulations in the commercial treaties made by Great Britain, with the principal maritime nations, from the year 1668 to 1766, and which were in force till the year 1780, the time when the northern powers confederated to defend the rights of neutral nations against the unwarrantable claims of Great Britain.

The stipulations in treaties therefore, which constituted the rules by which the maritime powers of Europe were bound to regulate their conduct toward neutrals, from 1668 to 1780, may be comprehended in the following summary :

I. A free trade for neutral vessels of either of the powers, to any nation at war with the other party, and an unlimited right to carry all goods not enumerated as contraband ; that is, free ships made free goods. Places besieged, invested, or blockaded, were excepted.

II. Contraband goods were declared to be warlike instruments only. Provisions, clothing, naval stores, and raw materials of most kinds, were declared to be free.

III. All merchandise, whether belonging to an enemy or neutral, if found in an enemy's ship, was confiscable ; but the goods of an enemy in the ships of a friend, were free.

IV. Neutrals were permitted to carry on the coasting and colonial trade of an enemy, without any restriction, except as to contraband goods.

V. The right of search was restricted to cases in which there was clear evidence or strong suspicion of contraband. Ships were to be provided with passports and certificates of lading, to which full credit was to be given, and if the certificate gave no evidence of contraband, the ship could not be detained, molested, or turned out of her intended course. If contraband goods were discovered, the hatches could not be opened, nor any chest, bale, or package broken, until brought on shore in the presence of the proper officers.

Thus stood the conventional code of maritime law, in Great Britain, France, Holland, and Spain, for more than one hundred years, preceding the date of the armed neutrality. I presume similar treaties existed among the Baltic nations, but I have seen none, except that of 1766, between Great Britain and Russia, and an extract from that between Great Britain and Sweden, in 1720.

It appears from these authorities, that the stipulations in the treaties recited, were intended to soften the rigor of more ancient and barbarous customs, and to limit the arbitrary practice of princes, in regard to neutral commerce. We have seen that princes and states, anterior to these conventions, usurped the power of restraining *all* commerce with their enemies. These conventions restricted the rightful exercise of that power to cases of prohibited goods. Before the date of these treaties, princes at war prohibited *all* goods to be conveyed to an enemy. These conventions restricted the right of prohibition to specific articles, which were the immediate instruments of war. The practice of searching ships, which was formerly arbitrary, and accompanied with every species of violence and abuse, was utterly abolished in all cases, except when the certificates of lading gave proof or strong suspicion that the ship concealed prohibited goods ; and in this case, the ship was not to be searched and plundered at sea, but conducted into port and unladen before proper officers.

So far the genius of humanity, and the pacific maxims of commerce, had triumphed over the ferocious manners of ancient nations, whose chief business was war, and whose sole objects were conquest and plunder.

But national engagements have, in no period of the world, been strong enough to bind the contracting parties. Not among martial barbarians alone, do we find a licentious spirit, incapable of being subdued by the maxims of social justice, and the obligations of compact; but in modern times, and among nations Christianized and civilized, we find the faith of the most solemn conventions, the most clear and explicit national contracts, yielding to a pretended necessity, or to temporary public expedience. It was not Queen Elizabeth alone, who, before the rules of contraband trade were defined and settled by treaties, assumed the power of inhibiting all neutral commerce to her enemy, Spain; but William III, in concert with the Dutch, in 1689, under pretext of a necessity of reducing the power of Lewis XIV, ventured, in the face of the principles deliberately recognized in treaties and solemnly confirmed by three successive princes, to interdict all nations from trading with France. Even in a later period, in the war commencing in 1755, the British government seized the Dutch ships carrying the property of the French, in direct violation of the principles which had been adopted in 1674, and which had been explicitly and solemnly recognized by the commercial treaty of Utrecht, in 1713. What is equally singular, the same government, in the treaty of Paris in 1763, revived the commercial treaty of Utrecht, and thus gave a new sanction to the principles of neutral trade, which, in the war then concluded, their government and their courts had violated or disregarded.—(See the several treaties; also And. on Commerce, Vol. III, p. 47.)

The foregoing facts and principles will be further elucidated, by a history of the armed neutrality of 1780, which forms a remarkable epoch in the annals of commerce.

The British writers, in their accounts of this confederacy, ascribed to it an attempt " to dictate a new code of maritime laws to mankind, in many respects essentially differing from those, which had, for several hundred years, been established amongst commercial nations," and to introduce " a bold innovation on the commercial law of nations." They declare the system to tend " directly to the destruction of that *sovereignty or pre-eminence on the ocean which had been so long claimed and maintained by Great Britain.*" They alledged it to have originated from " the jealousy entertained by the maritime powers of Europe, of the '*pre-eminence exercised by Great Britain on the sea.*'"—(And. Com. Vol. V, p. 362.)

How little foundation there is, for these charges against the confederated powers, let the following facts determine.

In the war between Great Britain and France, from 1755 to 1763, the British cruisers and ships of war seized Dutch ships, bound to France or carrying French goods, in contravention of the treaty of 1674, and the explanatory article of 1675. I have not a particular history of the controversy between Great Britain and the States General on the subject. So far as I am able to judge from a short statement in an English author, it appears that the British vindicated these seizures, on the ground of a different construction of the explanatory article annexed to the treaty of 1674; and on the ground of a secret article annexed to the same treaty. This article provides that " neither party shall give leave nor consent, that their subjects or inhabitants shall give any aid, favor, or counsel, directly or indirectly, by land or sea; nor shall furnish nor permit their subjects or inhabitants to furnish any ships, soldiers, seamen, victuals, money, instruments of war, &c. to the enemies of either party." So far as regards the victuals and money, this article contradicts the fourth article of the commercial treaty of 1674; and I am not sufficiently versed in the history of those times, to assign the reason. Certain it is, that Great Britain seized the Dutch ships, in cases which the Dutch held to be repugnant to the treaty, which occasioned numerous complaints from the Dutch government.

When the war broke out between Great Britain and the American colonies, the Americans obtained supplies from St. Eustatia, a neutral island belonging to the Dutch. In February, 1777, Sir Joseph Yorke, the English minister at the Hague, presented a spirited memorial to the States General, remonstrating against the allowance of that trade, and against the Dutch governor, Mr. Von Graaf. The Dutch government replied in friendly terms, and promised to recall the governor, which was done.

Toward the close of the year 1778, the merchants of Amsterdam, Rotterdam, and Dordrecht, presented to the States General three memorials, complaining of the seizures of their ships by the English, "when a bare inspection of their consignments and other papers, would sufficiently shew, that they were not laden with any sort of merchandise under the denomination of contraband goods." These seizures were alledged to be in violation of the treaty of 1674, and the explanatory convention of the following year. The States General remonstrated against this conduct, to the government of Great Britain, and were answered by Sir Joseph Yorke, who declared that "the interruption of the Dutch commerce was never exercised, but when the subjects of that republic were carrying *warlike* and *naval stores* to the enemies of Great Britain."

It will be observed that by this concession of the British minister, Great Britain had violated the treaty of 1674, for that expressly declares most of the articles, if not all, used in building and equipping fleets, to be free, and not contraband.—(See Art. 4, before recited.)

In July of the same year the French king issued an edict, expressly forbidding his subjects to stop or seize any neutral ship bound to or from an enemy's port; but reserving the right of revoking that edict, in case any foreign power should not agree to a similar regulation. A compliance was not expectable, and in January, 1779, the edict was revoked; but with an exception in favor of the city of Amsterdam, in consequence of its "patriotic exertions to persuade the republic to procure from the court of London the security of a free commerce, according to the rights of nations and treaties." This revocation produced a spirited remonstrance from the British minister to the States General, in which he charges the French king with a design to sow discord between the states of Holland, by granting exemptions to Amsterdam, and not to the other cities. He assures the Dutch that the British king will maintain the "legal trade" of the states, but must prohibit the transportation of "naval stores" to France, and in particular "timber," if escorted by men of war. On the 24th of July following, the French king issued another ordinance, exempting the whole province of Holland from the duties in his ports, from which the former edict had exempted Amsterdam.

From this abstract of facts, it is evident that Great Britain was determined, *per fas aut nefas*, to prevent as far as possible, the Dutch from furnishing France with supplies of naval stores. This consideration, together with a full conviction that the Dutch councils were greatly influenced by France, then at war with Great Britain, in favor of what she called her rebel colonies, induced the court of St. James to get rid of the commercial treaty of 1674, with the States General. The free commerce guarantied by that treaty had, in the former wars of Great Britain, been a serious obstacle to her views of maritime superiority. Instead of explaining away its provisions by arbitrary and forced constructions, and occasional violations of it, as convenience dictated, the British court determined to suspend its stipulations. For this purpose several pretexts were sought. One was, to make a demand upon the States General for the succors stipulated in the defensive treaties of 1678, as explained in that of 1717, to protect Great Britain from a predicted invasion from France. The Dutch did not comply, and this was held to be an infraction of the treaty. Another charge against the Dutch was, their harboring Paul Jones, declared by the British government to be a pirate, and demanded as such of the States General. Their High Mightinesses, however, declined interfering; alledging they could not take upon them to judge of the legality of Paul Jones's conduct; and that they only afforded him shelter from storms, without permitting him to unload and sell his prizes.

Another incident accelerated a rupture. The Dutch, to protect their trade to France, had ordered a convoy for their ships under Count Byland. The British government, having notice of it, ordered Commodore Fielding to intercept them, under pretense that the Dutch merchantmen were laden with naval stores. On meeting, the English commander requested permission to search the ships. The British writers alledge that this was refused—that in consequence, the British commodore sent his boats with express orders to search the fleet—these boats were fired on by order of the Dutch commander—the English then fired a shot ahead of the Dutch admiral, who returned a broadside. The English returned another, and the Dutch commander struck his colors.

This capture produced very violent complaints on the part of the Dutch. Sir Joseph Yorke, by order of his court, renewed the requisitions for the succors stipulated in the treaty; to which the States General replied that the demand should be laid before the several states, and an answer returned as soon as the course of deliberations would permit. This answer was considered by the British court as an evasion—and a manifesto, dated April 17, 1780, was immediately published, declaring that the British king considered the non-fulfillment of engagements on the part of the States General, as a desertion of the alliance; and therefore his Majesty suspended provisionally and till further order, "all the particular stipulations respecting the freedom of navigation and commerce, in time of war, subsisting between the two powers, and especially those contained in the marine treaty of 1674," and considered the States General from that time, as a *neutral power not privileged by treaty*.

From the whole history of these transactions, it is evident that Great Britain was determined no longer to be fettered by a compact, binding her to permit neutrals to enjoy a free commerce with her enemies. The States General, in their memorial to the King of Sweden, at the close of the year 1780, and their manifesto, dated in March, 1781, fully exculpate themselves from several of the charges which the British court had alledged against them. I shall not notice any part of the charges or defense, except what relates to a contraband trade. On this part of the subject, the States General alledge and maintain that the republic had a right, by the treaty of 1674, to export to France naval stores of all kinds—that the stipulations were clear and unequivocal, admitting of no doubt or misconstruction; but that Dutch vessels, sailing under the faith of the most solemn treaties, and not laden with any prohibited articles, were seized and detained—that the cabinet of St. James, knowing no other rule than an assumed right of *temporary convenience*, thought proper to appropriate the cargoes to the use of the crown, by a forcible purchase, and to employ them in the King's navy—that the subjects of Great Britain had fully enjoyed the advantages of this treaty, in the first and only case, wherein it pleased the court of London to remain neuter, whilst the republic was engaged in war. They declared further, that the attack on Count Byland was an outrageous and unprecedented insult to their flag.

Without giving full confidence to the assertions of the States General in their own favor, we have the authority of the British documents to prove, that the articles on board of the Dutch ships were naval stores, which, by the treaty of 1674, were expressly declared *not* to be contraband. This fact, in connection with the consideration, that it was the *particular stipulations respecting a free navigation and commerce*, in that treaty, which alone were suspended, leaves no room to question what has been before stated, that Great Britain, feeling her strength as a naval power, and finding the treaty some check on her unlimited views of superiority, determined to be no longer subject to its obligations. A free commerce gave her maritime rivals an equal advantage with herself; and therefore she resolved that commerce should *not* be free for her rivals. She had some regard for her own express agreements; but these were inconvenient in time of war, and therefore she *suspended their obligation*, without the assent of the other party; and placing, by an arbitrary act, the republic of Holland on the footing of any neutral nation, she could treat her rival, according to the *laws of nations*—which, on this subject, are just what a sovereign pleases to make them.

After this recapitulation of facts, we shall be at no loss to find the motives of the northern powers in confederating to preserve the freedom of navigation and commerce. It was obvious to those powers, from the conduct of Great Britain in the war of 1755, and more especially in the war commenced on account of the revolution in America, that the British court, either by evasions and forced constructions of treaties, or by annulling the clauses which regulated neutral trade, intended to enlarge the sphere of contraband goods, that they might be able, by interrupting the transportation of naval stores at pleasure, to check the growth of the maritime strength of their enemies. This was the policy which dictated the infraction or suspension of the old treaties, which had for more than a century made the ships of the contracting parties, when neutral, *free bottoms.* To effect this object, pretexts were not wanting; and it is very probable that the privileges guarantied to neutral nations had been abused. At the same time, a careful examination of facts will show, beyond a doubt, a predetermined and regular plan in the British cabinet of removing the restraints imposed on her power by commercial treaties, and substituting, in lieu of special stipulations, the indefinite obligations of what is called " the general law of nations." This policy, it was supposed, would, in time of war, be much for the benefit of the British nation ; because, as I have already proved, this " law of nations," so called, is nothing more than the various, arbitrary, and contradictory practices of sovereigns who knew no law, and were bound by no restraints ; and therefore might be set up as an authority to justify any prohibitions whatever of neutral commerce with her enemies. Such a pretended law of nations would be more convenient for a nation claiming the " sovereignty of the ocean," than the rules prescribed by treaties, which limited the exercise of power on the sea, and reduced the aspiring nation to the level with its rival neighbors. This view of the policy of Great Britain will show, the necessity of some effectual measures, on the part of the other maritime nations, to check the ambition of a formidable naval power, and insure to Europe the continuance of that liberal system of neutral commerce, which had been deliberately formed and repeatedly confirmed by all the great commercial nations. To repress any and every attempt to innovate on that system, was no less the policy than the duty of all commercial states. That the confederated powers of the north were actuated by such motives, is apparent from the history of the conduct of Great Britain toward neutrals, as well as from their own solemn declarations. And a bare inspection of the treaties which had existed between Great Britain and those powers for a long time—some of them for more than a century—and of the articles of the convention in 1780, will convince any man that the innovation was not on the part of the armed neutrality, but on the part of Great Britain.

The official declarations of the confederating powers, which were published at the time, are sufficient to convince any impartial man that their views were honorable, and supported by justice as well as a regard to their particular interests.

The Empress of Russia declared, in vindication of her conduct, that " her subjects were often molested in their navigation by the ships and privateers of the belligerent powers ; that the vexations offered to the liberty of commerce in general, and to that of Russia in particular, were of a nature to excite the attention of sovereigns and of all neutral nations ; and that she was under the necessity of freeing herself from those vexations, by all means compatible with her dignity and the welfare of her subjects ; that she was determined to protect the honor of her flag, and the security of commerce and navigation."

The declaration of the King of Denmark contains, in addition to similar sentiments, a number of excellent general principles, which ought to be recited. It states that his majesty had observed the most exact and perfect neutrality, with the most regular navigation and the most inviolable respect to treaties ; but neutral navigation had been too often molested, and the most innocent commerce of his subjects too frequently troubled—so that the King found himself " obliged to take proper measures to assure to himself and allies, the safety of navigation and commerce, and the maintenance of the inseparable rights of liberty and independence.  If the duties of neutrality are sacred, the law of nations has also its rights, avowed by all impartial powers, established by custom and founded in equity and reason.  *A nation independent and neuter, does not lose by the wars of others the rights which she had before the war, because peace exists between her and all the belligerent powers.  Without receiving or being obliged to follow the laws of either of them, she is allowed to follow, in all places, (contraband excepted,) the traffick which she would have a right to pursue if peace existed with all Europe as it exists with her.*  The King pretends to nothing beyond what the neutrality allows.  This is his rule and that of his people ; and the King can not accord to the principle, that *a power at war has a right to interrupt the commerce of his subjects.*"

The King of Sweden avowed similar sentiments in his manifesto, declaring that his subjects had claimed his protection, and that he had found it necessary to grant it ; that the declaration of the Empress of Russia was founded upon such just principles of the law of nations and subsisting treaties, that it was impossible to call them in question ; that the principles were accordant with the treaty of 1666 between Sweden and France ; that he will observe an exact neutrality, but will effectually protect the lawful commerce of his subjects.

The King of France declared, " that the freedom of commerce of neutral ships, restrained only in a very few cases, is the direct result of the law of nature, the safeguard of nations, the relief even of those who are afflicted by the calamities of war."

The King of Spain declared, that the principles of the confederacy " are founded in justice, equity, and moderation ; that the conduct of the English navy, both in the *last* and *present* war, a conduct wholly subversive of the received rules among neutral nations, had obliged his majesty to follow the example ; since *the English, paying no respect to a neutral flag, if laden with enemy's goods, even though the goods are not contraband,* there could be no reason why Spain should not make reprisals."  He mentions also that neutral vessels had furnished themselves with double papers, and used other artifices to prevent the capture of their vessels, which had occasioned captures and detentions innumerable.

These declarations, which were dated in the first months of the year 1780, were sent to the several courts of Europe.  Without giving full credit to every assertion of men pleading their own cause, we may at least yield as much credit to the declarations of the confederated powers, as to those of his Britannic majesty.  And on such terms of construction, the foregoing declarations prove, that Great Britain had unwarrantably disturbed the free navigation and trade of neutral powers, in direct violation of subsisting treaties.

What then are the principles of free commerce, which this league was intended to vindicate and maintain ?  The convention signed at Copenhagen, June 28th, 1780, expressly recognizes " a prohibition of contraband trade with the powers at war," and considers those articles only as contraband, which are declared to be so by subsisting treaties between the contracting parties and one or other of the belligerent nations. After declaring that their majesties, having laid down the general principles of natural rights, from which the liberty of commerce and navigation, and the rights of neuter nations are derived, are resolved not to depend any longer upon the arbitrary explication of those rights, which is generally *dictated by partial advantages and momentary interests*, the contracting parties agreed to the following articles :

1. That all neutral vessels shall be permitted to navigate from port to port, and on the coasts of the belligerent powers.

2. That the effects belonging to subjects of the belligerent powers shall be free on board of neutral ships and vessels, excepting only such articles as are stipulated to be deemed contraband.

3. In order to determine what is to be considered as a port blocked up, it is hereby declared, that that port only shall be deemed as such, into which no ships can enter without being exposed to an evident peril from the forces that attack the said port, and from the ships that shall have taken a station near enough for that purpose.

4. That neutral vessels shall only be liable to be stopped and seized for just and cogent reasons, and upon the most convincing proof, that justice shall be done to them without loss of time, and that the proceedings shall always be uniform, speedy, and according to the laws ; and that whenever any shall be found to have been stopped or to have suffered any damage without any sufficient cause, they shall not only be entitled to a sufficient compensation, but also to a complete satisfaction for the insult offered to the flag of their majesties.

These are the principles which the English call the " *modern law of nations*"—" *a new system of maritime laws*"—" *a bold innovation on the commercial law of nations.*" What is more singular and equally disgraceful to my countrymen, these principles have been received in America, on the faith of British writers, considered and understood as *new* or *modern*.

So far is this from being the fact, that the *two first and most material articles*, had been the law of most of the maritime powers, by express stipulations in all their commercial treaties, for more than one hundred years. They had been the express law of Great Britain from the year 1668, when these principles were incorporated into the treaty with the Dutch; which were more fully recognized in the treaty with the Dutch in 1674, in that with France in 1677, and in substance introduced into that with Russia in 1766. The same principles were fully expressed and recognized in the treaties of Utrecht in 1713, which were ratified and confirmed by the treaty of Paris in 1763. These treaties expressly declared that neutral ships should be free, and that free ships should make free goods, except contraband ; and that they might go from one port in enmity to another port in enmity, whether belonging to the same prince or to several—which words expressly guaranty the right of carrying on the coasting trade of a belligerent. And the Empress of Russia expressly founds this new convention on " primitive rights and laws," which belligerent nations can not invalidate, and on her treaty with England in 1766.

Instead, therefore, of attempting to introduce a new maritime code of laws, the northern powers, in 1780, confederated for the purpose of *restoring* and *vindicating* the old laws of trade which had been held obligatory on the parties for more than a hundred years—which had been observed with good faith by the Baltic nations—which had been occasionally violated by the Dutch, French, and Spaniards; but which Great Britain had not only infringed, but had made systematic efforts to abrogate or evade. The innovation had been made by Great Britain, by an attempt to extend the limits of contraband; by a claim to interrupt all property belonging to enemies in ships of friends, and to sacrifice the commerce of all nations for the sake of crippling her maritime rivals, and extending her own naval dominion.

The ninth article of the convention of 1780, declared, that the compact was to last during the war then existing; and that the engagements therein should form the basis for all future engagements and treaties, in case a future maritime war should disturb the tranquillity of Europe. To this convention acceded the northern powers, Russia, Sweden, Denmark, also Holland, France, Spain, and finally, the Emperor, King of Prussia, and the United States of America. This formidable confederacy could not fail to produce some effect on the court of Great Britain. Accordingly we find that court, the next year, making a concession not corresponding with the tone assumed on the first appearance of the league. The King of Denmark, in 1781, issued a declaration, " that the Baltic, being an inclosed sea, in which the ships of all nations might and ought to navigate in peace, and enjoy all the advantages of a public tranquillity, his majesty could not permit any of the ships or privateers of the belligerent powers to enter the said sea, with a view to commit hostilities against the subjects of any state whatever." It was added, that the two other northern powers had adopted and would support the prohibition. In consequence of which, his Britannic majesty issued instructions, charging the commanders of all ships and vessels, having letters of marque and reprisal, not to stop or detain any ships or vessels in the Baltic, for the purpose of making prize of them, but to let them proceed without interruption.

The strength and decided tone of the confederated powers, served to restrain the depredations of British armed ships on the commerce of neutral nations; and by rendering the contest with America hopeless, contributed to accelerate peace and the establishment of the independence of the United States. But these were not the only advantages. The union of all the maritime nations (except Portugal, which was under the immediate influence of Great Britain*) in defense of the long established principles of neutrality, served to awaken mankind from their delusions on that subject, provoke a spirit of inquiry into the natural right of independent states, and the benefits of a free trade—and finally, to establish the precedent of a firm resistance to the designs of Great Britain, which threatened to break down all the barriers which ancient treaties had erected, to protect the merchant from arbitrary seizures by the ships of belligerent nations. Indeed, something of this

---

* Portugal recognized the principles of the confederacy in February, 1783.

kind was necessary to prevent Europe from degenerating, in war, to the savage state of the year 1300 ; for by insisting on making prize of enemy's goods in friendly ships, as well as of the goods of a friend in the ships of an enemy—by insisting on the right to blockade nations, as well as islands, by the force of a proclamation—by insisting on a right of searching all ships for contraband goods, and detaining them or turning them hundreds of leagues out of their course—by prohibiting all coasting trade on an enemy's shores—by the assumption and exercise of these powers, a strong naval kingdom, engaged one half the time in war, might nearly destroy the commerce of the world. It would be literally a revival of the barbarous customs of the dark ages ; it would make plunder the object and the business of war, and constitute the greatest maritime power the chief pirate.

This important convention,* recognizing and establishing the freedom of navigation and commerce, as stipulated in former treaties, left the right of search undefined ; stipulating solely that neutral vessels should be liable to be stopped and seized for just and cogent reasons only, and upon the most convincing proof that justice should be done to them without loss of time. Nor did it contain any prohibition of searching vessels under convoy. It however recognized the principles relative to these points, which had been agreed to by Great Britain and Russia in the treaty of 1766, and in the treaties between Denmark and Great Britain, and Denmark and France.

In the treaty of commerce between Russia and Denmark, concluded in October, 1782, the principles of the armed neutrality were fully recognized, and the parties declared their determination to make them the unalterable rule of their conduct. In that treaty, it was agreed that vessels without convoy should submit to be searched, in the manner usually prescribed by treaties. But it was stipulated that merchant vessels under convoy of one or more ships of war, should not be subjected to search ; the word of the commanding officer being declared to be sufficient proof, that they contained no prohibited goods.

The same principle, that " free ships make free goods," is incorporated into the treaties between the United States and France, Holland, Sweden, and Prussia. And it is remarkable, that the very clauses containing the stipulations respecting a free trade, contraband, the manner of search, and the passports and certificates, are, in all these treaties, almost exact transcripts of similar clauses and articles in all the treaties between Great Britain, France, Holland, Sweden, Denmark, and Spain, from the year 1674 to the year 1786. The goods declared to be contraband and free, are nearly the same in all. Some small modifications are found in each, and especially the important stipulation, that the declaration of the commander of a convoy, that the ships under his protection contain no contraband goods, shall relieve them from the vexation of being searched, is found in our treaties with the States General, Sweden, and Prussia. In one particular the treaty with Prussia is singular—it declares that arms, ammunition, and other military stores, in the neutral vessels of either party, shall *not* be deemed con-

---

traband.   This is probably the first treaty which has, in modern times,
made all goods free, by *express stipulation*, as they undoubtedly are by
the laws of natural and social justice.

It is further to be observed, that although Great Britain had opposed
the armed neutrality, and in all her wars violated the freedom of
neutral commerce, yet in 1786, she formed a new treaty with France,
in which she again recognized all the essential principles of the maritime convention of 1780.   And in her definitive treaties with France
and Spain in 1783, she revived and confirmed the commercial treaties
of Utrecht, containing the same principles.   The only circumstance in
the system of the armed neutrality, that had a semblance of novelty,
was an attempt to extend the rights of a free trade to other nations, or
to render the principles general.   This was an offer to guaranty to all
neutrals, that their natural right to trade in any species of goods and
to any place whatever, should not be abridged by belligerent nations,
any further than the confederated powers had agreed, by treaty, to
suffer *their* natural rights to be abridged.

Such was the relative situation of Great Britain and the commercial
nations of Europe at the commencement of the revolution in France.
The principle that " free ships make free goods," had been adopted,
or revived and established by Great Britain, in all her new treaties, after
the peace of 1783.   The treaty of 1766, with Russia, was in force till
1780, and it is believed the old treaties with Sweden and Denmark were
also in force.   The treaty with France in 1786, and the definitive
treaty with Spain, had renewed the principle in its utmost extent.   I
do not find that Great Britain formed a new treaty of commerce with
the States General.   A treaty of defensive alliance was concluded in
April, 1788, the tenth article of which stipulates, that " until the two
powers conclude a treaty of commerce with each other, the subjects
of the republic shall be treated, in the kingdom of Great Britain and
Ireland, as the most favored nation."   If a treaty of commerce has
since been formed, I have no knowledge of it.   As the Dutch had been
the most active nation in trade, next to the English, and as they had,
under the old treaties, afforded the most ample supplies to the enemies
of Great Britain in time of war; as in consequence of this, the British
court had manifested a strong desire and even determination to come
to a rupture with the States General, for the purpose of annulling the
treaties which stipulated a free trade to their enemies, in Dutch ships
when neutral, it is presumable that the ministry would either wholly
decline a treaty of commerce with the Dutch, or at least, any engagements which should secure to them a freedom of trade, similar to that
guarantied by the treaty of 1674.

The revolution in France, as might have been expected, interrupted
all the friendly dispositions, which a free commerce tends to cherish
between nations.   In the novelty of the motives which led to it, the objects to which it was directed, the hostile passions it inspired, and the
sanguinary scenes which it exhibited, it was an event whose importance to the world could not be understood, nor its consequences to the
commercial and political state of Europe, duly estimated.   When the
French, however, manifested a determination to be restrained, in the
pursuit of their fancied republic, by no laws of morality, by no ties of

compact, and by no principles of natural and social justice, it was easy to see that surrounding nations, whose internal peace was threatened, and whose independence was attacked, would also transgress, in their own defense, all the ordinary rules and principles by which nations had been accustomed to regulate their mutual intercourse.

The war which has accompanied that revolution, was introduced with a remarkable proposition made by the French court to Great Britain, for the abolition of the practice of seizing merchants' vessels in time of war. The note presented by Mr. Chauvelin to Lord Grenville, and dated July 25, 1792, which was anterior to the death of the French king, proposes " to make navigation, and maritime commerce, and the goods of individuals, enjoy the same protection and the same liberty which the law of nations and the universal agreement of European powers secure to private property on land; in one word, to suppress that destructive practice, which, on occasion of quarrels between states and princes, interrupts on every sea the most necessary communications—renders abortive speculations, on which depends often the existence of nations foreign to these quarrels—which suspends the progress of human discoveries—which arms individual against individual, and delivers the goods of the peaceable merchant to pillage. The King does not consider it in relation to the particular interest of the French nation. His majesty knows that the advantages which it presents, must be much greater for a people essentially maritime, and whose relations of commerce and colonial possessions, extend, so to speak, from one pole to the other, than to a nation chiefly agricultural, like France. This is not, therefore, a combination dictated by that rivalship of power, nor by that mercantile rapacity, which have so long deluged Europe with blood; it is a great measure of beneficence, of justice, and humanity, which has been suggested by the general interest of nations, by morality, and by policy itself, well understood. Already in the treaty of navigation and commerce, of Sept. 26, 1786, France and Great Britain have renounced this odious traffick in every quarrel which should be foreign to them; and in the war which France is forced to maintain against Austria for the defense of her independence and her liberty, the two belligerent powers have spontaneously resolved to leave a free course to maritime commerce. Let this resolution, adopted by the two interested powers, become the basis of a new law among nations, which will strengthen the bonds which unite them, and diminish their motives of division and rupture."

Such is the substance of this remarkable proposition, which was never published, nor laid before Parliament, by order of the British ministry, nor was it ever answered. It was published by the convention of France.—(See State Papers, Vol. I, p. 198.)

After the execution of the King of France, war was speedily declared by the French convention, against Great Britain, February 1, 1793, and by Great Britain against France, on the 11th of the same month. On this occasion, as on all others, orders were issued to the ships of war and privateers of Great Britain, to seize French merchandise in the ships of neutrals. In pursuance of these orders, the American vessels were taken and plundered of French property; the United States not having any treaty with Great Britain, their vessels were treated according to what has been called the *general law of nations.* These depredations were soon represented to the French minister in the United States, who, on the 25th of July, 1793, remonstrated to our administration against the permission of such outrages. As our treaty with France had recognized the principle of free ships making free goods, and as we had no similar stipulation with Great Britain, the French were exposed to a particular hardship and inequality—their goods being liable to seizure, in American vessels, by the *general law of nations;* but their treaty with the United States restraining them from taking British goods from our vessels, while neuter.

Mr. Jefferson, then Secretary of State, in his reply to the representations of Mr. Genet, says, " I believe it can not be doubted, but that by the *general law of nations,* the goods of a friend, found in the vessel of an enemy, are free, and the goods of an enemy, found in the vessel of a friend, are lawful prize."—(Papers published by order of Congress, p. 55.)

I believe the facts and authorities already cited, abundantly prove that there is not, and never has been a *general law of nations* of this kind. It was the ancient barbarous custom for princes at war to seize all ships bound to an enemy's port, and confiscate them, without regard to the character of the owners. But this, so far from being a general law, assented to by nations on the ground of justice or right, that the practice, before the rules were settled by treaty, was always complained of, usually considered as piracy, and often resisted by war or reprisals. The ordinances of the French king in 1543 and 1584, allowed the captors to seize only contraband goods, in friendly ships, and not other merchandise, though belonging to an enemy.

The truth is, both principles, viz. that the goods of an enemy in the ships of a friend shall be free, and that the goods of a friend in the ships of an enemy shall be lawful prize, stand on the foundation of special conventions. The other principle, that the goods of an enemy in the ships of a friend, shall be lawful prize, stands on the ancient practice of barbarians, who seized on enemy's property as plunder, or prize, by the *rights of war*—a subject to be hereafter discussed.

Through the whole of his letter, the Secretary of State, however, considers this practice of seizing enemy's goods in friendly vessels, as founded on a *general law of nations,* and of as much validity as any principle of natural justice.* And Vattel seems so clear that the practice is derived from the undisputed rights of war, that he does not cite an authority in vindication of it.—(Book iii, ch. 7, p. 115.)

One passage in this letter of the Secretary, (or rather of the administration,) deserves notice. " England," says the Secretary, " has generally determined to adhere to the rigorous principle, (of the law of nations,) having in no instance, as far as I recollect, agreed to the modification of letting the property of the goods follow that of the vessel, except in the single one of her treaty with France." It is hardly credible that such a blunder should have escaped from our executive, considering the gentlemen who then composed his council. So far is it

---

*This state paper has been cited by British writers, to justify their construction of the law of nations.—(See Palladium, March 27, 1801.)

RIGHTS OF NEUTRALS.

75

from truth, that England had not agreed to the principle of " letting
the property of the goods follow that of the vessel," until her treaty
with France, which was concluded in 1786, that she had expressly stipulated the same principle in all her commercial treaties with the great
maritime nations of Europe, from the year 1668 to 1786. The very
article in the treaty with France, to which the Secretary alludes, was
an almost literal copy of a similar article in the commercial treaties
with France and Spain, concluded at Utrecht in 1713, and the substance of it taken from the treaties with the States General in 1668 and
1674. A similar article is found in her treaty with Russia. When
such a mistake in a plain historical fact occurs in the correspondence
of our government with a foreign minister, we are not to be surprised
that the gentlemen should take it for granted, on the authority of European writers, that the practice of taking enemy's property, wherever
found, is a *law of nations;* when in fact it is no more than the ancient
custom of piracy and plunder, continued with some modifications.*

While this subject was in discussion between our government and
the French minister, intelligence was received of a more serious invasion of the rights of neutral nations. The violent death of the French
king, and the obvious designs of the revolutionists in France to attack
the surrounding nations, either openly or by secretly spreading seditious principles among the people, justly alarmed all the governments
of Europe. To check the progress of their designs, bold and extraordinary measures were supposed to be necessary and justifiable. As
early as March 25th, 1793, a convention was formed by the British
and Russian courts, for mutually assisting each other, and distressing
France. For the latter purpose, it was agreed that the parties should
shut all their ports against French ships, and not permit the exportation
to France of military or naval stores, corn, grain, salt meat or other
provision; that they should take all other measures in their power to injure the commerce of France, and to unite all their efforts to prevent
neutrals from giving, on that occasion of common concern to every
civilized state, any protection whatever, directly or indirectly, to the
commerce or property of the French, on the sea or in the ports of
France. Between the date of this agreement and the first of September ensuing, similar conventions were concluded by Great Britain, with
the Emperor, the King of Prussia, the King of Sardinia, the King of
Naples, and the Queen of Portugal.—(See State Papers, Vol. I.)

In pursuance of this formidable project his Britannic majesty, on the
eighth of June, issued instructions to the commanders of ships of war
and privateers, to stop and detain vessels of neutral nations, bound to
France, with corn, flour or meal, and send them into British ports;

---

* The President, in his proclamation of neutrality, warned the citizens of the
United States against carrying to the nations at war any articles " which are
deemed contraband by the *modern usage of nations.*" And Mr. Pinckney, in a
note to Lord Grenville, represented that " the sense of a majority of the maritime
powers of Europe, had, *within the last twenty years,* been clearly expressed in favor
of the principle of free ships making free goods." The truth is, Great Britain had
agreed to the principle in most of her commercial treaties for one hundred and
eighteen years; and for the last twenty years, has been attempting to nullify the
principle.

where the cargoes might be purchased and the ships released, after payment of freight, or the masters of the vessels, on giving security, might be permitted to proceed to any port in amity with Great Britain. It was further ordered, that all vessels attempting to enter a blockaded port, should be seized and sent in for condemnation, with their cargoes, except the ships of Denmark and Sweden, which were only to be prevented from entering on the first attempt, but on the second attempt were to be seized and confiscated. From this order were excepted vessels which had sailed for the blockaded port, before the declaration of the blockade was known, unless after notice of the blockade they pursued their course to the same port.

This order occasioned, among all neutral nations, no less indignation than surprise. Mr. Pinckney, our minister at the court of St. James, remonstrated against it with great ability and spirit. Immediately on receiving a copy of the instructions, our government wrote to Mr. Pinckney, directing him to demand explanations on the subject. The letter of the Secretary of State, on that subject, is a highly valuable performance, both in regard to its style, its arguments and its eloquence. It alledges with great force and propriety, " that when two nations go to war, those who choose to live in peace, retain their natural right to pursue their agriculture, manufactures, and other ordinary vocations; to carry the produce of their industry, for exchange, to all nations, belligerent or neutral, as usual, without molestation; contraband goods, which are implements of war, being alone excepted; that corn, flour and meal, are not of the class of contraband, but articles of free commerce; that the culture of the soil, giving employment to such a portion of men, can not be suspended over the whole earth, whenever two nations go to war; that a state of war, between Great Britain and France, furnishes no legitimate right to either, to interrupt the agriculture of the United States, or the peaceable exchange of its produce with all nations; that no ground, acknowledged by the common reason of mankind, authorizes this act now, and unacknowledged ground may be taken at any time and at all times; that this practice is one to which no time, no circumstances prescribe any limits; it strikes at the root of our agriculture, that branch of industry which gives food, clothing and comfort to the great mass of the inhabitants of these states; that if any nation whatever has a right to shut all the ports of the earth against our produce, except her own and those of her friends, she may shut those also, and so confine us within our own limits. No nation can subscribe to such pretensions. The act also tends to draw us from a state of neutrality, an essential character of which is, that we furnish no aids to one party at war, which we are not willing to furnish to the other. If we permit corn to be sent to Great Britain, we are equally bound to permit it to be carried to France," &c.

Within five days after the date of this letter to Mr. Pinckney, the British minister, Mr. Hammond, inclosed to the Secretary of State a copy of the orders of June 8th, with his remarks, attempting to justify them. " It is laid down by the most modern writers, as the law of nations," says Mr. Hammond, " that all provisions are to be considered as contraband, and as such liable to confiscation, in the case where the depriving an enemy of these supplies, is one of the means intended to be employed for reducing him to reasonable terms of peace. The actual situation of France is notoriously such, as to lead to the employing this mode of distressing her, by the joint operations of the different powers engaged in the war." He even attempted to make the government of the United States believe, that this order did not go to the extent warrantable by the law of nations, as it prohibited corn and meal only, omitting all other provisions, and not subjecting the cargoes to confiscation, but only to a forced sale, or to a new destination.

Lord Grenville, also, in answer to the verbal remonstrances made by Mr. Pinckney, cited Vattel as an authority in vindicating the prohibition, urging the prospect of reducing the French to terms of accommodation. And what is remarkable, this flimsy pretext was offered by the ministry of a great nation, at the moment that the price of the prohibited articles was lower in France than in England, where there was no scarcity. A fact stated by Mr. Pinckney to Lord Grenville.

It is not to be concealed that this order of the British court was a direct infraction of the treaties subsisting between Great Britain and Sweden, which had expressly limited contraband goods to instruments of war. On the part of Russia also it was a direct violation of her treaties with several states, and an abandonment of the principles of the armed neutrality. It was a bold, insolent attack on all the rights of neutrals, like the similar prohibitions of Queen Elizabeth, and King William, in conjunction with the States General, which have already been mentioned. It is observable too, that when authorities are wanted to justify such an imperious and arbitrary contempt of right and justice, any and every general opinion, however equivocal or inapplicable to the case, if found in respectable treatises on the laws of nature and nations, is pressed into the service. A single line in Vattel, book iii, ch. 7, p. 112, enumerating among contraband goods, " even provisions, in certain junctures, when there are hopes of reducing the enemy by famine," has been tortured into a justification of this insulting prohibition. This authority extends no further than to places invested. It is impossible that any man of reading or sense, can suppose that the author intended to countenance the practice of declaring a nation in a state of siege or blockade, and then prohibiting all neutral trade with the country, much less an attempt to starve whole nations into subjection. A construction of this sort would prostrate all the commercial rights of nations at peace. Such a law of nations, if admitted, would subject all commerce to the arbitrary will of every government on earth. Not only Great Britain, but France, Spain, and even the smaller states, might pretend some cause of war with a neighbor, fit out a few armed ships, declare the country blockaded, and seize and confiscate every ship bound to its ports. The other nation, in retaliation, would take the same steps ; and the result would be, that the commerce of all countries would then be laid open, by this pretended law of nations, to a species of authorized piracy. Indeed the practice of Great Britain, for some years past, has reduced mankind nearly to this state of things ; for claiming this monstrous right of declaring ports, islands, and even whole nations, in a state of siege, by a simple proclamation, backed by half a dozen ships, she has proceeded to arrest all commerce with such places, in defiance of the power, and in contempt of the rights of neutral states.

Lord Grenville, in a note to Mr. Pinckney, dated July 31, 1793, goes so far as to alledge that the order of June 8th, "unavoidably resulted from that state of war in which the maritime countries of Europe were engaged." And to complete the enormous injustice of the measure, he tells him, that the steps adopted by his government, so far from being infractions of neutral rights, are more favorable than the law of nations on that subject, as established by the most modern and most approved writers upon it."

Are we then reduced to the necessity of submitting to surrender the privileges of commerce to the dicta of modern writers? Shall the belligerent nations, upon the authority of a sentence in Vattel, misunderstood and misapplied, undertake to justify a practice which subjects the citizens of a neutral, at least one half the time, to be plundered of their property on the ocean? And are the smaller nations thus to be victims of the ambition and tyranny of the great maritime powers, which are embroiled, a great part of the time, in hostile contentions? Are nations so degraded, so mean, so humbled, and lost to all sense of right and justice, as to consent to the establishment of a principle, which arms the subjects of the belligerent against the peaceable merchant, and compels the most pacific people to be robbed with impunity, or to resort to force and reprisals? Is there no limit to be prescribed to the inordinate claims of great naval powers? or must neutrals be always exposed to lose the fruits of their industry, at the pleasure of a powerful nation at war, which can blockade a continent with a proclamation, and turn pirate, under cover of a paragraph in Vattel? Surely it is the duty as well as interest of all civilized nations to associate, with a fixed and unalterable determination to repel such practices, and never to surrender the principles of a free commerce, but with their independence.

The consequences of the illegal and despotic restraint on neutral trade, imposed by the British orders of June 8th, were not limited to the loss and vexations occasioned by British cruisers. The French government, by way of retaliation, speedily issued similar orders to their privateers and ships of war; and neutral vessels laden with provisions, and enemy's goods in friendly ships, were seized and conducted into French ports. This order, so far as regarded the aggressors, was perfectly just; but as it regarded the American trade was unjust, in the highest degree; for in addition to the violation of the general rights of a neutral nation, it was a direct infraction of the treaty subsisting between the United States and France. Sensible of this injustice, or apprehensive that such a violent measure would check their growing influence in this country, and give their enemy an advantage, the rulers of France soon rescinded the order. But from the fluctuations of French councils, no stable measures could be expected. The order was again issued and extended to American vessels, which were seized and detained by both belligerent parties. (See Message from the President to the House of Representatives, Dec. 5, 1793.)

On the 6th of November, 1793, the British court issued a new order, for detaining and conducting into port for legal adjudication, all vessels laden with produce of any French colony, or carrying provisions or other supplies for the use of such colony. If any thing could have added to the injustice and tyranny of the former order, this was destined to fill up the sum of iniquity. Never was such a sweep made of American property at one time. In a few weeks, more than one hundred and fifty sail of shipping, with the cargoes, were seized and condemned in the West India islands. The manner of committing this robbery was as disgraceful to the British court, as the act itself was illegal; for the order was not published, but given to ships of war and privateers in a private manner—contrary to all the modern usages of civilized nations, and the maxims of honor. True indeed the British court consented, in the treaty of the following year, to make compensation to the suffering merchants; and in a few instances, the damages have been adjudged in their courts, and paid. This act of justice, while it *admits the injustice* of the order for seizing the vessels, has been but partially executed, and no equivalent indemnification has been made for the losses and vexations of the merchants.

The extreme and wanton injustice of the order of November 6th, could not fail to rouse the indignation of every neutral nation, and especially of the Americans. Even the court of Great Britain seemed to be alarmed at the effects of such rapaciousness, on the United States; and on the 8th day of January, 1794, revoked the order, and issued new instructions to their armed ships, which were a relaxation of the rigor of their former order, in regard to America. By the new orders, vessels laden with the produce of the French islands, bound directly to any port in Europe, were still liable to seizure, as were those whose cargoes belonged to French citizens. But vessels, with the produce of those islands, not owned by French citizens, and bound to the United States, were not included in the orders. Vessels attempting to enter any blockaded port in the French islands, were also made seizable, according to the tenor of the instructions of the 8th of June preceding.

This order was less unfavorable to the citizens of the United States; but the exemption of vessels bound to the United States and owned by our citizens, was no more than a particular exception from an outrageous and arbitrary violation of the rights of neutrals—a violation not authorized by even the practice of ancient kings. Neither law, treaty, nor usage, can be cited to apologize for seizing and confiscating goods, on the sole ground of their being the growth or manufacture of an enemy's country. Such a practice is not warranted even by the flimsy plea of reducing an enemy by distressing his commerce; for it is neutral merchants, and not the subjects of the enemy, who are distressed.

These unwarrantable steps of the British court, excited keen resentments in the United States, and the clamor for retaliation was so violent, as to call forth a proposition in Congress for sequestering British property in the United States. This measure was superseded by the appointment of an envoy for the purpose of negotiating a commercial treaty with Great Britain.

The treaty which was the result of this mission, and was concluded on the 19th of November, 1794, was in many respects valuable to the United States. It provided for a settlement of the eastern boundary of the United States, which was a desirable object. It provided for an adjustment of the differences which had long subsisted between the two countries, in regard to the recovery of many old debts due from American citizens to British merchants, and for a surrender to the United States of the western military posts, which had been held as a kind of security for those debts. These were great and interesting objects to both parties. No less important was the effect of this negotiation in suspending the violent proceedings of the American legislature, which menaced speedy hostilities, and thus securing to this country the benefits of the continuation of peace.

With regard to its effects on commerce, I shall give no opinion, except on the article respecting contraband goods, and in abandoning the principle that free ships make free goods. In these particulars, the treaty is extremely exceptionable. To the usual list of prohibited goods, it adds " timber for ship-building, tar, rosin, copper in sheets, sails, hemp and cordage, and generally whatever may serve directly to the equipment of vessels—unwrought iron and fir planks only excepted."—(Art. 18.)

On what principle these articles were admitted into the list of contraband, it is difficult to determine, unless to verify a clause in Vattel, which enumerates " naval stores and timber," together with " provisions," among goods which may be deemed contraband, " when there are hopes of reducing the enemy by famine." Surely some better authority, than an indefinite clause in a writer on general law, is necessary to justify a concession so novel, and so extremely prejudicial to the commerce of all neutrals, but especially to the United States, in one of which tar is a staple commodity, and in many of which ship timber is a material article of export.

In looking into the commercial treaties between Great Britain and other powers, we shall find that ship-timber, pitch, turpentine, sails, hemp, and other naval stores, are either not enumerated, or expressly excepted from the list, from the year 1674 to 1780. They are expressly excepted from the list in the treaty with the States General in 1674, which was ratified by three successive princes—expressly excepted in the treaty with France, signed at Utrecht in 1713—and not enumerated in the treaty of the same year with Spain, and of course excepted—not enumerated in the treaty with Russia in 1766, but excepted by a general clause—expressly excepted in the treaty with France in 1786—and by the definitive treaties in 1783, the commercial treaties of Utrecht, with France and Spain, were revived, and with them all the stipulations of Great Britain respecting contraband goods. I have not copies of all the commercial treaties of Great Britain with the smaller states ; but according to my inquiries, the treaty between the United States and Great Britain in 1794, is the *first* in which naval stores are stipulated to be prohibited, since the year 1674, except in an explanatory convention with Denmark in 1780.*

No man can be ignorant of the motive of the British court, for pressing these articles into the list of contraband. Strong circumstances, existing at the time, had no small influence ; but it is obvious that the insertion of such goods in the list, as well as the leaving enemy's prop-

---

* The only treaty, I believe, in which any of the maritime nations have admitted naval stores to be contraband, within a century, is that between France and Denmark in 1742.

erty liable to seizure in neutral ships, is part of a settled plan in that cabinet, for breaking down the barriers which nations had been erecting for more than a century, to restrain the arbitrary practice of belligerent powers in seizing and confiscating merchandise bound to their enemies—to mitigate the calamities of war, by limiting the number of confiscable goods—and finally, to secure to pacific nations some definite rights, and the privilege of pursuing the occupations necessary for their subsistence and welfare, without being a prey to the rapaciousness of every belligerent prince. For the honor of my country, and the essential interests of her commerce, I regret that the administration, in the very commencement of the national government, has consented to abandon ground, which the nations of Europe had, for more than a century, been struggling to obtain and to fortify. I have no hesitation in declaring, that no considerations of public danger can justify a commercial nation, in consenting to enlarge the field of contraband; nor can there be an apology for the renewal of the clause in the compact, by which our true interests and essential rights have been surrendered.[*]

From the conclusion of the British treaty to the year 1796, the commerce of the United States continued to be vexed by the belligerent nations, under various pretexts and various orders. The clause in that treaty, which admits that cases may exist in which provisions are lawfully prohibited, subjected the trade of the United States to great embarrassments and losses. And sorry I am to see it admitted in so many words, that provisions may become contraband, in some cases, "by the existing laws of nations." This is not a fact, in any case, except of a place besieged or blockaded. In no other case have modern nations *agreed* to consider provisions as prohibited; and the practice of forbidding such articles to be conveyed to an enemy, has been already proved to have no better authority than the piratical customs of ancient barbarians, or the arbitrary will of powerful princes, who adopted and enforced the principle, in defiance of the complaints, remonstrances, and feeble reprisals of the smaller states.

The French government, which, by embargoes and seizures, had harassed our trade from the year 1794, resorted in 1797 to a new pretext, and on the 2d of March passed a decree that every American vessel, not furnished with a *role d'equipage*, that is, with a list of her crew and passengers, with their names, places of birth and residence, or having a captain, supercargo, and one third of her crew English subjects, should be liable to capture and condemnation, as good prizes. The reason assigned for this order was, that many British vessels sailed under American colors, and many American vessels were navigated by British seamen, by which means the property of their enemy was covered under a neutral flag. Under this decree, a vast amount of American property was seized and illegally confiscated.

---

[*] The writer was one among many of the friends of the treaty, who supposed, at the time, that the extension of the list of contraband was authorized by the general law of nations. Further investigation has satisfied him of his mistake, and of the extreme danger of trusting to the opinions of modern elementary writers, without a careful inspection of original authors and documents.

To obtain correct ideas of the claims of the French government, to have American vessels furnished with this list of their crews and passengers, we must trace the history of passports and certificates.

It appears from the history of commerce, that when the rights of neutrality were neither understood nor respected, and when princes arbitrarily seized and confiscated all vessels bound to an enemy's port, that the seamen and passengers were considered as prisoners, or inhumanly abused. It must be further considered, that it was common for merchantmen to commit piracy on the high seas, plundering any vessels they could seize, and insulting the crews. Without a regard to this state of commerce, prior to the seventeenth century, our modern treaties can not be understood. It was these piratical and barbarous customs, then very common, not to say general in Europe, which gave origin to all the stipulations in modern treaties, respecting the good conduct of the masters and seamen, in the service or trade of the contracting parties. The stipulation that on a rupture between nations, the merchants should have some months to dispose of their effects, before they were compelled to quit the enemy's country, and that within that time they should not be liable to seizure, was occasioned by the ancient practice of seizing the persons and property of merchants, who were subjects of an enemy, as soon as war was proclaimed.

The stipulation that the subjects of the parties should not commit any hostility or piracy against each other, and the securities required of the masters of armed ships, were intended to restrain the savage practices of the ships of all nations on the ocean. These, and various other stipulations still found in modern treaties, are so many abridgments of the almost unrestrained license of treating alien merchants as enemies, and of robbing their ships at sea.

Among other vexations experienced by vessels at sea, was the practice of searching for prohibited merchandise in peace as well as war ; and in war, the searching for subjects of the enemy. The first regulation to lessen this evil, was to have searchers appointed by authority, and resident in the ports from which vessels departed, who were to examine the cargoes at the place of shipment, to prevent the exportation of prohibited goods ; and it was agreed in treaties that vessels in a foreign port, after being thus searched and taking a proper certificate, should not be liable to be stopped or examined in their voyage. The passport and certificate of lading, were originally intended to give to commanders of armed ships at sea, or to officers in a foreign port, a just account of all the articles of the cargo, and of the persons on board, whether seamen or passengers, to prevent the trouble of search and its attending vexations and abuses. The form of the passport now used is subjoined to the treaty between England and the States General, dated February 17, 1668, and without material alteration, has been used by all the maritime nations to this day.

It is one of the meliorations of the ancient custom of seizing and maltreating persons found on board of ships, that by modern treaties, no person, not even an enemy, shall be taken out of a neutral ship by the armed vessels of a belligerent nation, except he is *a soldier in actual service of the enemy*. This is an express stipulation in the twenty third article of the treaty between the United States and France. To render this article effectual, it is necessary, in time of war, that vessels of the neutral nation shall be furnished with such documents, as will enable the commanders of armed ships of the nation at war, to determine whether officers and crews of the neutral ship are, *bona fide*, the subjects of the neutral nation whose flag she bears, and whether there are on board any soldiers in the service of the enemy, who are liable to be seized as prisoners.

The passport, being annexed to the treaty by stipulation, necessarily becomes a part of it, and of equal validity. The form annexed to the treaty of 1778, with France, as it stands in our passports by order of government, is as follows :—

" To all who shall see these presents, greeting :

" Be it known that leave and permission have been granted to A. B. master or commander of the ship called ——, of the town of ——, of the burden of — tuns, now lying in the port of ——, and bound for ——, laden with ——, after that his ship has been visited, and before his departure, he shall make oath (or shall have made oath) before the proper officers, authorized for that purpose, that the said ship belongs to one or more of the citizens of the United States of America, *the act of which shall be put at the end of these presents*—and also that he will keep and cause to be observed by his crew, the maritime ordinances and regulations—and he shall enter (or deposit) a list, signed and attested by witnesses, containing the names and surnames, the places of birth and residence, of the persons composing the crew of the ship, and of all who shall embark on board, whom he shall not receive on board, without the knowledge and permission of the officers authorized for the purpose—and in every port where he shall enter with his ship, he shall show the present permission to the proper officers, and shall make to them a true report of all that passed during the voyage, and he shall carry the colors, arms, and ensigns of the United States during his said voyage."

[Attested by the collector of the port.]

Under this form, in the passports furnished by our government, is the certificate or attestation of the collector of the port, who declares, that the master of the ship has appeared before him and sworn that the ship is of the United States of America, and that no subject or citizen of the powers at war has any part or interest in the same, directly or indirectly.*

To understand this form, it is necessary to observe that it was originally intended to be a permission from the Lord High Admiral of England, or of France, &c.—the officer who had the supreme jurisdiction in marine affairs. In the old forms, annexed to the treaties of 1668, 1674, and 1713, it is so expressed, " We, Lord High Admiral of"—" Lewis, Count of Thoulouse, Admiral of France." The license or permission therefore is given on certain conditions, which are to be performed at the custom-house or office of admiralty in the port from

---

* There is a defect in the form of the passport as it stands in our treaty, and in the treaty of Utrecht. " Leave and permission have been granted to A. B."—but it is not expressed what the permission is granted for. After the words " laden with," should follow, *to sail to such a port*. These words are inserted in the more ancient forms, as in that of 1668.

which the ship is to depart.  We, the Lord High Admiral, or in our own case, the President of the United States, sends greeting—Be it known, that we have granted leave and permission to A. B. to sail from such a port to such a port, *after he shall have performed certain conditions at the custom-house.*  These conditions are, that the ship shall be visited or searched—that the master shall make oath that the ship belongs to one or more of the citizens of the United States, [the act or certificate of which oath is to be subjoined to the form]—that *he shall also make oath* that he will observe, and cause to be observed by his crew, the marine ordinances and regulations.

When these conditions are performed, the leave or permission to sail becomes absolute.  To render this transaction effectual, the officer of the customs must certify that these requisite conditions have been performed.

In the form of the certificate in our passports, there is a deviation from the precise words in the form of permission.  The latter requires the commander of the ship to swear that *she belongs to one or more of the citizens of the United States.*  In the certificate the words are, the master has declared upon oath that the vessel *is of the United States.*  And in the form of permission, it is required, that he shall make oath that he will keep and cause to be kept by his crew, the marine ordinances; but in the certificate no mention is made that this part of the oath has been taken.  Perhaps these variations from the form are not material; but in the old forms annexed to the treaties in 1674 and 1713, the form of the oath is subjoined, and is in general terms: " We ——, of the admiralty of ——, do certify that A. B. master of the ship named in the above passport, has taken the oath mentioned therein." Perhaps this general oath and attestation would be more eligible, as extending to all the provisions in the passport.

As to the list of the crew and passengers, opinions are not united. The French maintain that the ship of a neutral, in time of war, should carry papers to prove not only the property of the ship, and goods on board, but that she is not navigated by their enemies, and contains no soldiers in the service of her enemies.  The American government contends that the treaty requires no such *role d'equipage* to be on board, and that full credit ought to be given to the passport in its general form.

Considering the purposes for which the requirements in the passport were intended, there can be no question that our vessels ought, on the rupture between Great Britain and France, to have been furnished with such papers as would be good evidence that her crews and passengers were not liable to seizure, as persons in the service of the enemies of France.  All other persons being protected by treaty, it was proper and necessary for their safety, that their persons and characters should be so described, as not to expose them to be molested on suspicion. This was the more essential, as the Americans and English, speaking the same language, can not well be distinguished by foreigners; and American soldiers on board of an American ship, without due evidence of their nativity and residence, would have been liable to suspicion, and subject to vexations.  It is no excuse to say, that the French were lawless and paid no regard to papers—that was often true; but there were many instances in which respect was paid to proper documents. Besides, all governments should use every possible caution, in time of war, to guard their citizens and property. If they are negligent in furnishing the papers required by treaties, they can lay no claim to damages for injuries sustained.

Although the treaty, by express words, does not require a neutral ship to carry a *role d'equipage*, yet when we consider the purpose of inserting, in the passport, a demand that the master shall deposit a list of his crew and passengers in the custom-house, designating their names, places of birth and abode ; together with the last clause of the 23d article of the treaty, which protects all persons on board, except soldiers in actual service of the enemy, and leaves them to be seized as prisoners, there can be no doubt that the American vessels ought, within the spirit and obvious meaning of the treaty, to have been furnished with the list of all persons on board. Even without the specification of these particulars in the form of the passport, the 23d article of the treaty would have rendered such a list, duly certified, actually necessary to the safety of persons on board, who were not soldiers in the actual service of Great Britain. The prescribing of such a paper would have resulted from the treaty, as an executive duty, by way of precaution, to secure to innocent seamen and passengers the benefits of the treaty. It is a paper analogous to the certificate of lading, and designed to secure the *persons* on board from molestation, as the certificate secures the *goods*.

But the want of this paper was no more a just ground for confiscating American vessels and cargoes, than the want of Tom Thumb's Folio, or the Pilgrim's Progress. The passport, certificate of lading, and list of the crew and passengers, are papers intended to secure vessels at sea from the vexations of search and detention ; and are not absolutely essential to prove the neutrality of the property and persons. Any other papers, or any facts which afford satisfactory proof of neutral property, are sufficient, before an impartial tribunal, to protect the ship and cargo from condemnation. The decree of the French, therefore, subjecting vessels to confiscation for want of the *role*, was a flagrant breach of good faith, a direct infraction of the treaty, and an outrage on the rights of neutral commerce. Under this decree, however, a vast amount of American property was piratically seized, and condemned by the unprincipled tribunals of an unprincipled government. The want of the *role* was the pretext, and vessels furnished with it did often escape capture, while those which were destitute of it were seized and condemned.

The effect of the authorized depredations on our trade, were such as might have been expected. The commanders of ships, and especially of privateers, often lawless men, and urged by the hope of gain, soon found means to extend their captures to cases never contemplated by their sovereigns. The courts of admiralty in the West Indies, under the authority of profligate and needy judges, became partners in the nefarious work of plunder, and what was seized on flimsy or forged pretenses, was condemned without law ; while the privateersmen and the judge joined in dividing the spoil. In the mean time, piracy lifted her audacious front, and the sea swarmed with picaroons, consisting of

a banditti of negroes, mulattoes and outlaws, who, encouraged by impunity, proceeded to arm small vessels and boats without commissions,
and robbed the defenseless trade of our citizens.

Every occasion was seized, by the powers at war, to vex and destroy our trade. Wherever the Americans found a beneficial opening
for trade, the port was blockaded, or declared to be so; or their cargoes were seized, as being the growth or manufacture of the enemy
of a belligerent power. In this manner has our commerce suffered, in
consequence of the various instructions of the British and French governments to their armed ships; and most of the depredations, I am
sorry to say, have been committed under color of *pretended laws of nations*, on one part, or of the necessity and justice of resorting to the law
of retaliation, on the other.

After suffering innumerable losses and vexations from the belligerent
powers, the United States, by a new convention, obtained relief from
capture and condemnation by the citizens of France; and by spirited
remonstrances to the court of Great Britain, they obtained some restrictions to be imposed upon the cruisers of that power, and a new organization of her colonial courts of admiralty, which promises a diminution of depredations and abuses. But the British ministry have abandoned no part of their claim to interrupt, on emergencies of which they
are to judge, all the commerce of a neutral nation with their enemy,
*according to the laws of nations.* While they maintain this principle,
neutrals can enjoy no more than a temporary respite from vexations
and plunder. The claim of their armed ships and colonial courts, to
take and confiscate property in neutral vessels, because it had grown
or was made on their enemy's territory—a claim which had long
vexed our trade to the Spanish colonies—has been determined by the
admiralty court in England to be illegal. But whether neutrals shall
be permitted to carry that species of property, from the colonies to the
mother country of their enemy, is a question that the court has not yet
decided. May the genius of civilization deliver nations at peace, from
British constructions of the law of nations!

During these spoliations of American commerce, the northern powers of Europe were not able to escape similar injuries. Their trade
with France and Spain was occasionally interrupted, in violation of
their treaties with Great Britain; but nothing happened to threaten a
rupture, till a British squadron captured a Swedish convoy, for refusing
to permit the ships to be searched. This seizure, with some other differences, alarmed and roused the indignation, not of Sweden only, but
of all the Baltic nations; and contributed to revive the project of a
confederacy for the defense of neutral rights, similar to the armed
neutrality of 1780. As the French scrupled not to ascribe to the
intrigues and gold of the English, the coalition of powers against
France, as well as the intestine disturbances and civil wars, by which
their country has been afflicted; so the British retorted on every occasion, and ascribed to the intrigues of France, all the schemes of neighboring powers, that opposed their views of unlimited dominion on the
ocean. Charges like these answer the purpose of irritating the inhabitants of the two countries against each other, and keeping alive national
resentment; but a distant spectator has no concern with them. That

the French promoted and wished success to the confederacy, is true ; it was their policy to promote it, and it was consistent with the maxims which the monarchs of France had followed for several centuries.

But the Baltic nations had motives sufficient for attempting the confederacy, in the policy and necessity of securing to their commerce an exemption from arbitrary and illegal detentions and vexations. The league consisted of Russia, Sweden, and Denmark—to which also acceded the King of Prussia. As the principles of free commerce, which they associated to defend, are principally the same as those of the armed neutrality in 1780, already explained, it is not necessary to repeat an explanation of them. It is sufficient to say, that the confederacy was managed with far less ability than that of 1780, when the celebrated Catherine swayed the scepter of Russia. The spirit of Great Britain, seconded by the prompt and energetic measures of the ministry, and the daring enterprise of Admiral Nelson, dissipated, by the single battle of Copenhagen, all the hopes which neutral nations had entertained, of seeing the freedom of commerce established on the principles, by which Great Britain and all maritime nations had agreed to regulate their mutual intercourse, for more than a century preceding.

The victory near Copenhagen was followed by an armistice, and a negociation, which produced a new commercial treaty between Great Britain and Russia, dated June 17, 1801. By this treaty, Russia has secured in part the advantages contemplated by the confederacy. It is stipulated that ships of the neutral power, shall navigate freely to the ports and upon the coasts of the nations at war, agreeable to the tenor of all the old treaties. But by this convention, enemy's property is not protected on board of a neutral ship. This is an abandonment, on the part of Russia, of a principle which had been recognized in all preceding commercial treaties ; and it is a strong evidence of what has been before observed, that the British cabinet is aiming, with steady but persevering policy, to expunge from the political code of Europe, every stipulation which is supposed to abridge the privileges, permitted to a belligerent power by the pretended *laws of nations.*

By this convention, the list of contraband is not increased, and a state of blockade, one subject of contention, is defined, nearly as in old treaties. The right of search, a principal subject of dispute, is regulated in a manner more satisfactory than the former claim of Great Britain. It is permitted to ships of war only, and not to privateers ; and such precautions are to be observed, as to render the transaction less liable to abuse. It is also agreed that merchandise, the growth or manufacture of an enemy's country, shall not be considered as enemy's property, if acquired by the subjects of the neutral party, and transported on their account. This stipulation meets in part the evil of laying open to seizure enemy's property in neutral ships, as it is imposing upon the subjects of the neutral power the necessity of *purchasing* such property, instead of taking it on freight. But this regulation will produce another inconvenience of no small magnitude ; it will encourage innumerable fictitious sales to cover the property of an enemy ; and as it is extremely difficult to conceal these transactions from the eyes of clerks, seamen, boys and servants, who are liable to be tampered with, for the purpose of obtaining disclosures, all fraudulent or fictitious sales expose

the neutral to vexations without number, and hold out strong inducements to corruption and perjury.

Russia, from its interior situation, is principally concerned in the transportation of articles of its own growth and manufacture ; and therefore
less censurable, by its own subjects, for relinquishing privileges attached to the business of freighting.  But other nations, and especially the
United States, whose positions and advantages render them the natural
carriers of the produce of the West Indies to every part of Europe,
can not behold, without deep regret, any encroachment of the maritime
powers on the freedom of the carrying trade.  We however ought to
be silent on the subject, as our government has surrendered, to the im-
potent and undefined obligation of the general law of nations, the privilege of protecting by neutrality the goods of belligerent nations.  And
having abandoned the principle, in our treaty with Great Britain, with
what face shall we claim the benefits of it, in our future commercial
conventions with other nations?  No government can with propriety
consent to stipulate with us that free ships shall make free goods, since
this would secure the goods of their enemy in our ships, while it would
leave their own exposed to seizure and confiscation by Great Britain.
To such unequal terms, no commercial nation can agree, without de-
serting the essential interests of its subjects.

Having given a sketch of the principles and practice of nations in
regard to neutral commerce, I will proceed to examine the grounds of
the " general laws of nations," as they are called, respecting nations at
war.

The principle on which belligerent nations pretend to justify their interruption of the trade of neutrals to their enemies, is, that they have a
right to use all possible means to weaken the enemy, deprive him of resources for continuing the war, and thus reduce him to the necessity of
agreeing to terms of peace.  To obtain clear ideas of this question, it
is necessary then to examine what are called "the rights of war."

It is not necessary, in this place, to determine a question, agitated by
the theoretical writers, whether the natural state of mankind is a state
of war or of peace.  It is sufficient to observe that the first knowledge
we have of man, either from history or from discovering new islands
and countries, exhibits him in a state of hostility with his neighbors.  I
do not recollect an instance, that can be safely alledged to be an exception to this remark.  If therefore a state of war is not *natural*, it is acquired very early by savage tribes, and it is a melancholy truth, that
this state is continued through every stage of national progress.

The first objects of war among savages are, victory for the sake of
the reputation of superior bravery, or the spoil of the vanquished.—
(Liv. 7, 29.  Charlevoix I, 381.)  Then follows war for the sake of
territorial acquisitions, for commercial advantages, for revenge or satisfaction for injuries.  The savage tribes of North America were found
in a state of war, which was undertaken chiefly for the first object, that
of enjoying the reputation of the bravest warriors, and exercising an insulting dominion over tribes less powerful or courageous.

The next stage of society exhibits small clans or tribes of men, making war on each other for the sake of plunder, and this object, as it
was of early origin and long duration, impressed upon the practice and
customs of war many features which are retained to this day.

When nations engaged in war for the sake of plunder, the spoil was either the property of the soldiers who seized it, or of the prince or state. Similar was the distribution of the booty, obtained in wars undertaken for other causes. We have a remarkable instance, related in the thirty-first chapter of Numbers. The nation of Midian having been destroyed by the Israelites, the spoil was divided, one half among the soldiers who had performed the service, and the other half among the whole congregation. A fiftieth of the whole was reserved for the Levites, to be dedicated as an offering to the Lord. But it is observable that the officers and soldiers took a part of the prey to themselves, verse 53, which had not been thrown into the common stock, and of this they brought an oblation to the Lord. The males of the Midianites were all slain; the females and children were taken prisoners, and were considered as a *part of the prey*, verse 11. It is proper that the reader should note this circumstance, that not only the goods, but the persons of enemies were anciently considered and treated as spoil.

That individual officers and men, at the destruction of Midian, seized and appropriated a part of the spoil to themselves, is asserted in the chapter quoted; but either the practice of the children of Israel was not uniform, or was altered within a few years; for Achan was punished with merciless rigor, for taking and concealing a part of the plunder of Jericho, in disobedience to Joshua's orders. It is probable that the original practice was, for the soldiers to retain all the booty which they took, and that this practice was altered by the command of Moses or Joshua, who considered the prey as belonging to the whole congregation, but often gave it all to the soldiers. Thus the spoils of Jericho were all destroyed, except the silver, gold, and vessels of brass and iron, which were directed to be deposited in the treasury of the Lord. The spoils of Ai, on the other hand, were all given to the people.

Among the primitive Romans, the spoil, which was a principal object of their wars, was probably distributed among the soldiers, and this was their only reward, as I have already observed, till the 349th year of the city. That they claimed the whole plunder of the enemy's camp, appears from the resentment they showed against the senate and their general, who, on vanquishing the Volsci, A. U. C. 269, sold the spoil and deposited the money in the public treasury. The phrase which the historian uses, in relating the fact, "*militem prædâ fraudavêre*," (they defrauded the soldiery of the spoil,) is further evidence that by former practice, the soldiers had a just claim to the plunder, and considered the appropriation of it to public uses as a fraud or injury.—(Liv. 2, 42; 10, 46.)

A like sale of the plunder in the year 299, occasioned a similar uneasiness in the army; although it is expressly said to have been on account of the low state of the treasury. The tribunes made this appropriation of the spoil to the public, a ground of accusation against the consuls.—(Liv. 3, 31.)

That the question whether the spoil should belong to the republic or to the soldiers, was not clearly settled till a much later period, we see in Livy, 5, 20, when M. F. Camillus, the dictator, referred it to the senate to determine in what manner the booty of the city of Veji should be disposed of. After much debate, it was agreed that the soldiers should have it. But the free citizens taken captive were sold, and the

money placed in the treasury, which occasioned no small resentment in
the plebeians.   This was in the year 359.   In 361, a like appropriation
of the spoil of a vanquished enemy to the republic, was greatly resented by the soldiery ; but the stern virtue of Camillus, while it incurred
their hatred, inspired them with admiration and commanded obedience.
—(Liv. 5, 26.)

These facts prove that, in early times, the soldiers fought for plunder,
and claimed it as their right; and that they did not readily yield this
right to the claims of the public.   The claim of the state, however, was
finally established ; and it is now held to be the law of nations, that all
the goods of an enemy, when taken, belong to the prince or state of the
conquering party, by the " rights of war."

These facts, and others which are related concerning the mode of
warfare among uncivilized men, in every age and country, unfold the
true origin of the " right" of a conqueror to the property of his enemy.
This origin was, the ancient practice of making war for plunder—that
is, *public robbery*.   Savages prefer war and robbery to labor ; and the
practice of making war for the spoil of a neighboring tribe or clan, continuing age after age, as men were prompted by avarice, stimulated by
revenge, or fired with the love of glory, became universal ; and the barbarous custom was finally honored with the title of the " law of nations."

It is no inconsiderable evidence of the truth of this explication, that
the Latin word *prædo*, a robber, is from the same root as *præda*, prey or
spoil, indicating that national *plunderers* and *robbers* were originally
men of the same profession.   And indeed at this day, there is much less
difference between the two species of robbers, than a superficial view
of the subject would lead us to believe.   The moderns have erected
specious theories on the practice of plundering an enemy, and attempted to justify it, on the ground of the necessity of weakening his force
and disabling him from continuing the war.   This reasoning is, however, applicable only to the case of a just war, and is always false when
used to vindicate the unjust aggressor.   And with respect to almost
every modern nation, it is not true in fact, that the capture of merchandise on the ocean, or the interruption of supplies, destined to a party at
war, does really weaken him or deprive him of resources, so as materially to affect the progress or issue of the war.   This interruption of
supplies, therefore, is only the pretext for continuing the practice of plunder, which originated in open robbery ; a practice which multiplies seamen by holding out the prospect of gain, and thus contributes to augment the strength of a naval power.   But this practice stands on precisely the same ground as that of the ancients, who raised and supported armies by the spoil of their enemies.   It is in principle and fact,
public robbery.

We have thus traced the " law of nations," " that all the goods of a
vanquished enemy belong to the conqueror," to the savage practice of
making war for plunder.   The humanity of modern nations, which, in
this respect, are perhaps *half civilized*, has modified this law in a variety of particulars, which will be hereafter mentioned ; by which the calamities, naturally resulting from the rigorous application of the " rights
of war," are considerably mitigated.   But the principle is still laid down,
by all writers on the laws of nature and nations, in its utmost latitude ;

and what is singular, it is maintained chiefly on the authority of the practice of ancient barbarians, or tyrants, who acknowledged no law but their own will.

Let us then attend to another of these " laws of nations," that of en- slaving, or putting to death, prisoners of war. It is well known, that all ancient nations claimed the same right of sovereignty over the *persons* of their prisoners, as over their *goods;* and they either slew them, or sold them for slaves. And it is remarkable that the word *ser- vant* bears, in its derivation, the proof of these facts, being derived from the Latin word *servare,* to save. Hence *servus,* a servant, or slave, originally denoting one whose *life* was *saved,* when he was taken prisoner, indicated a practice of putting prisoners to death, which ava- rice and humanity abolished; substituting the practice of selling prison- ers at auction and depositing the money in the public treasury.—(See Liv. 5, 22 ; 10, 46 ; 23, 37. Grotius, lib. 3, 10.)

Such was the practice among the Romans and Greeks, who made war, not only to obtain goods and cattle, but men, who were equally valuable commodities in market. By these they enriched the public treasury, and furnished their citizens with slaves to perform all their la- bor, and this in late, and what is called *civilized* periods of their com- monwealths. The practice was essentially the same in principle, as that now subsisting on the coast of Africa, where the maritime tribes make war upon their neighbors, on purpose to obtain prisoners to sell to European traders.

This is another sample of the " rights of war," sanctioned by the practice of all savage nations, and not yet banished from the " laws of nations." It is still held that soldiers in a place taken by assault, may, by the " laws of war," be put to death, after the place is reduced, and the defenders have surrendered ; a relic of ancient barbarism that dis- graces our manners and our laws.

But the " rights of war" were not limited by the reduction of a prisoner to a slave ; they transferred to the purchaser or master, the power of the state over a prisoner; that is, the power of life and death ; and what was, if possible, worse, the posterity of a female slave were condemned to the same condition.—(See the authorities cited by Gro- tius, lib. 3. Burlemaqui, part iv, ch. 6 ; and the Roman code.)

This is not all. Even women and children were anciently compre- hended within these barbarous " rights of war," and were often con- demned to promiscuous slaughter. I say *often ;* for the humanity of the general sometimes interposed to save them ; but, as Grotius ob- serves, it was one of the " rights of war" to put them to death. See the authorities quoted by Grotius, lib. 3, 9. When Syphax was con- quered by Scipio, the general declared, that Syphax himself, his wife, his kingdom, his lands, his towns, his subjects, and all his property, be- come the prey of Romans.—(Liv. 30, 14.)

To complete this system of the " laws of war," it was the practice of belligerent nations to burn, ravage and destroy every useful thing in an enemy's country. In the wars between the Romans and Philip of Macedon, in Greece, in which the different states of Greece engaged on different sides, the Athenians, in a council of the Etolians, are in- troduced, as addressing to the council language of this kind : " Our country is ravaged and depopulated; but of this we do not complain. This devastation is the consequence of the ' rights of war,' and as it is proper to commit such hostile acts, so it is proper to submit to them. That our houses are burnt, our fields laid waste with fire, our citizens and their cattle seized as prey, is rather a misfortune than a subject of resentment." They then proceed to complain of the violation of tombs and temples, as the deed of barbarians.—(See Liv. 31, 30; 34, 57; 36, 24, 42.)

These customs and practices of savage nations constitute the ground-work of the modern " rights of war," which, without a recurrence to their origin, can not be perfectly understood. From this deplorable condition, when war was marked with useless cruelty and destruction, and followed by the slavery of the vanquished, humanity has been, for ages, striving to extricate mankind. Prisoners are no longer slain in cool blood, nor sold for slaves—but redeemed or exchanged. Women and children are not slain, unless by some barbarous nations, in towns taken by them. Rarely are fields ravaged and houses burnt, merely for the sake of destruction; nor is the soldier permitted to pillage, except on the field of battle, unless in some cases when towns or forts are taken by assault. In many cases, though not always, the defenders of a town, taken by storm, receive quarter; and in most cases, soldiers are forbidden to plunder individuals of their property, especially the peaceable husbandman and artisan.

It follows that the ancient " rights of war" have been found inconvenient, as well as inhuman; that they were not essential to a state of war, nor founded on natural justice, but arbitrary in their origin, and mischievous in their effects.

Similar remarks are applicable to the primitive state of navigation and commerce. The word *pirate*, derived from a Greek verb, signifying to *attempt*, to *risk* or *encounter danger*, originally denoted merely a *seaman* or marine soldier. In the civilized ages of Greece, however, the word came to denote a sea-robber. (See Liv. 37, 27, who uses the word in the sense of *prædo-maritimus*, which he had used, lib. 7, 25.) Under the Saxon kings of England, the word was used to denote a common seaman, or marine soldier; and the commander of these *pirates* was denominated *archipirata*, arch-pirate. King Alfred ordered long vessels to be built for the defense of the kingdom, and placing " pirates" on board, intrusted to them the protection of navigation. When Robert, Count of Normandy, attempted to land an army in England, he was repulsed by the " pirates" of King William. (See the laws, charters and authors, cited in Spelman's Glossary, Art. *Pirate*.) The word *archipirata* is once used by Livy, (lib. 37, 11,) for the commander of a small squadron of vessels, in the sense of our Admiral or Commodore.

Hence it appears, that the profession of a seaman was so commonly connected with lawless plundering on the ocean, in the middle ages, that the word itself lost its original meaning and came to denote solely a *sea-robber;* in the same manner as *villain*, a word originally denoting a laborer or servant, by the usual character of dishonesty attached to those classes of people in their humbled condition, under the feudal system, came to signify a man without integrity. To trace such chan-

ges in language, is to learn the history of man, and the connection between his occupation and his character.

These authorities are sufficient to prove the points intended—that
most of what are called the "rights of war," and many of what are
called the "laws of nations," had their origin in the uncontrolled passions of lawless barbarians. To the humanizing influence of the Christian religion, and to the refinements in society which have substituted
the arts of husbandry, manufactures and commerce, in lieu of the trade
of war and rapine, are modern nations indebted for the discontinuance
of many barbarous usages, which had been dignified as *laws and rights.**
But however we may boast of modern refinement, a careful comparison
of the present maxims of war, or laws of nations, with the principles
of natural right, or national justice, will convince a candid inquirer,
that nations, in regard to their intercourse with each other, especially
in war, are little more than half civilized.

If soldiers are not permitted to pillage without restraint, yet by the
present pretended laws of nations, the conquering prince or general
may impose contributions on an enemy's country, without any rule but
his own will. Writers attempt to justify this practice, on the ground of
a right in a conqueror to punish for a public injury, to procure damages,
or disable an enemy. But this principle is applicable only to a justifiable war, and is just as likely to operate in favor of the aggressor, as of
the injured party. Let the oppressed nations which have fallen under
the fangs of French republicans for seven years past, bear testimony to
the evils of vindictive contributions; and determine how far the present practice is a mitigation of the barbarous custom of general plunder.

If prisoners are not liable to be put to death or enslaved, by the present rules of war, yet an exception exists in favor of ancient barbarism,
in the cruel practice of butchering the garrisons of a fortress taken by
assault—a practice not warranted either by justice, necessity or utility.
Let the mangled bodies of the brave defenders of Fort Griswold, in
Connecticut; let the thousands of unresisting soldiers, and helpless
women and children, slaughtered after the capture of Ismail and Praga,
humble the pride of modern pretenders to refinement of manners, and
make them blush for the existence of the "rights of war."

And what have men gained, in modern days, in regard to the safety
and rights of commerce? It is true, the merchant and the master of
a ship is no longer a pirate, in time of peace; but in war, how little
short of general piracy must be the practice, if universally adopted,
under the pretended laws of nations? If princes and states adopt the
British principles, of arresting the trade of all nations with their enemies, when *they* shall judge it necessary to reduce them to terms of
peace; if they can direct a blockade to be formed by proclamation,
and by ordering a few ships to cruise along the coast of a nation or an
island; if they can take the property of a friend in the ships of an
enemy, and the goods of an enemy in the vessels of a friend; if they
can extend the constructions of the laws of contraband to cover every
species of merchandise, and prohibit all trade between an enemy's
country and her colonies; and if, after establishing these principles,

* Ward, on the Laws of Nations, Vol. I, 173, and Vol. II.

which are now actually maintained by Great Britain as the "laws of nations," war is to exist at least one half of the time ; in the name of humanity, what have neutral nations left that they can call their own ? Should these extravagant principles be universally admitted, the United States will find it not only expedient, but necessary to treat with belligerent nations, as with the Barbary states, and purchase temporary exemptions from plunder ; or arm the whole of their naval forces against them as against pirates ; or in time of war, haul up and dismantle their ships, and suspend all navigation, till the powers at war shall, in great condescension, permit neutral vessels to pass in safety. If the United States are capable of recognizing and submitting to the establishment of such principles, they merit degradation, and are prepared for a master.

The preceding historical sketches enable us to estimate the value of the observations found in the Palladium, during the months of February, March, April, and May last.

A writer in the paper of February 3, on the subject of "free ships make free goods," remarks that "the French call this the *modern* law of nations—in plain words, no law at all, but a pretty little humbug business, that they really wish and are no doubt interested to have other nations observe as a law."

The facts are directly the reverse. The English gave this rule the denomination of *modern* or *new*, to cast an odium upon it, as an *innovation ;* when in fact, as I have proved, it had been the maritime law of Europe for more than a century, and of Great Britain especially, by numerous conventions. The Russians, Swedes, and Danes, called it very justly, the *old* law of nations, and that was one of their reasons for confederating to maintain it, against the attempts of Great Britain to innovate, and establish the contrary principle.

The writer proceeds, "Nations at war have a clear, undoubted right, as old as war itself, to seize their enemy's goods, wherever they can find them on the high seas, that is to say, out of the jurisdiction of any friendly nation."

This principle, in the latitude here stated, is not true. It was indeed the practice of barbarous nations ; but without limitations, it is neither more nor less than the *right of robbery.* Among barbarians, no distinction was observed between a just and unjust war ; and with them, plunder on both sides was *right* and *honorable.* But among Christians, it is a disgrace to state the general proposition as a right. To say that a nation, invading another without cause, has a *right* to seize the goods of its citizens, in any place, is a mockery of common sense.

But the proposition, unmodified, is not true, even in defensive war. Nations do not defend themselves for plunder. They resist an enemy to preserve their independence, their tranquillity, their safety, and to obtain just satisfaction for injuries. Just so far as the shedding of blood and the seizure of goods is necessary to obtain these objects, so far they are justifiable acts, and belong to the "rights of war ;" but no further. Whenever, therefore, a belligerent power has defeated an aggressing and injuring enemy, and reduced him under his dominion, so that satisfaction and peace can be obtained, without further slaughter or plunder, all acts of hostility toward persons or goods become unjust, because they can proceed only from revenge. The laws of humanity are paramount to any laws of war, or positive institutions. Every act of violence, therefore, not *necessary* to defense, safety, and indemnification, is a tort. To defend our just rights and safety, is required by humanity; to push hostility beyond the means of securing these objects, is repugnant to humanity, and of course to modern right. In offensive war, therefore, the seizure of the goods of the invaded enemy, is always wrong; and in a defensive war, the seizure of the invader's goods is right only to a limited extent. In cases where both parties engage in war from inordinate ambition or other unjust cause, the seizure of property is of course wrong on both sides, and this is more generally the fact.—(Grotius, lib. 3, 12.)

But in regard to seizures on the ocean, an important question is to be discussed.

If the principle was just, that belligerent nations have a right to seize their enemy's goods, wherever they find them, on the territories of either of the parties, yet it is agreed by all writers and all men, that the parties have no right to enter on the territories of a neuter party, to seek the goods of their enemy. This is admitted to be true on land, with an exception however of an extreme case, where an enemy can not be attacked without violating neutral ground, as in the case of a fort situated on the verge of an enemy's country, adjoining the limits of friendly territory.—(See Vattel, book iii, ch. 7, sec. 120, 132. Burlemaqui, part iv, ch. 7 and 8. Liv. 28, 17.)

But this principle has never been extended to give the owners of neutral ships on the high seas, or their sovereigns, complete exclusive jurisdiction over them, in as ample manner as they possess the right and jurisdiction over houses and lands. Yet I venture to affirm that no good reason exists for the distinction.

It is incident to the very nature of property or ownership, that the owner has a power over the property, and a right to exercise it, in exclusion of every other person. It is equally incident to the very nature of sovereignty, that the supreme authority of the sovereign is to be exercised, in exclusion of every other person or power. On these principles, the territories of neutrals are held sacred in time of war, and no belligerent can step his foot on them, without permission of the sovereign, or infringing the rights of sovereignty. To suppose a qualified right in nations at war, to occupy neutral ground, upon pressing occasions, is to admit pretensions incompatible with sovereignty, and open a door for every species of abuse. I can not, therefore, assent to the exception above mentioned, that a belligerent may, on any occasion, lawfully enter on the territory of a neutral, without permission from the sovereign. Cases of this kind occur, and are sometimes overlooked, for the sake of peace; but they are to be considered as infractions of the *jus publicum;* not as precedents authorizing such trespasses.

Equally conclusive are the arguments in favor of the exclusive jurisdiction of neutrals over their own ships on the sea. It is admitted on all hands, that the ocean is the common highway of mankind; and that no nation can appropriate it to its own use, exclusively. The only right to a particular and exclusive jurisdiction on the ocean usually admitted, is within such limits along the shores of a country, as to enable the sovereign of the country to protect his subjects from injury and in-vasion. By usage and consent of nations, the waters within a marine league of the shore, are held to be within the exclusive jurisdiction of the sovereign of the country.

But there is another case in which a temporary exclusive jurisdiction over a particular part of the ocean, may be lawfully exercised. This is the case of a ship, which, while on the high seas, bears with it a complete ownership and jurisdiction over the place it occupies. The owner of the ship has an exclusive right to so much of the water as is necessary, for the time being, to give the ship a free, unmolested pas-sage ; and any master of another ship, who invades that portion of the water thus occupied or necessary for a free passage, or who in any manner annoys the occupant, is as much a trespasser, and subject to respond in damages, as a man who breaks his neighbor's inclosure on land.

Equally exclusive is the jurisdiction of the sovereign, over the ves-sels of his subjects on the high seas ; and in conformity with this prin-ciple, all injuries committed on board of a ship, in the remotest seas, are supposed to be committed in some county within the territorial do-minions of the sovereign, and actions for the same are triable only be-fore his tribunals.

These principles result from the very nature of society, of owner-ship, and of sovereignty. The practice, therefore, of stopping ships on the ocean, without permission of the owners, searching them, and taking out an enemy's goods, or turning them out of their course, so far from being a natural right of powers at war, is a direct violation of the *right of property and of sovereignty*. It is incompatible with the exclusive power of an owner over his own property, that a stranger should exercise a qualified or temporary right over that property. Nor can any such right exist, unless derived from the consent of the owner or his sovereign. Every pretense or claim to a right of search, being a claim in derogation of the exclusive rights of ownership and sove-reignty, must be derived from the assent of the party whose rights are abridged, or from usurpation.

It is said indeed, that " a nation at war resorts to the law of nature for its own preservation. In war we defend ourselves by annoying our enemy, by distressing his trade, cramping his enterprises, and depriving him in this way, also, of the sinews of his warfare against us. Neutrals have a right to trade, but not so good a right as nations at war to de-fend themselves ; for my preservation and existence is more precious than your convenience or profit."—(Palladium, No. 10.)

It is not a little strange, that in this period of the world men should utter such sophistry ; but it is more extraordinary that multitudes of men should be misled by it. It is *not* true that the interruption of neu-tral trade ever disables a belligerent nation, so as to shorten the dura-tion of war. If it was ever true that one party was reduced, by plun-der and ravages, to the condition of soliciting peace, it must have been in early ages, among small tribes, whose country might be overrun and desolated ; or among nations who have, and can have, no commerce. To suppose any of the maritime states of Europe can be deprived of the means of war, when it is impossible to blockade their whole coast, much less to arrest all intercourse by land, is the hight of absurdity. Examine the history of any of the wars of the last century, and state the instance in which any of those nations were compelled to ask for peace, by an interruption of supplies. Not one can be named. It is impossible so to guard an extensive coast, as to shut out ample supplies. Even in the wars between Great Britain and France, Great Britain, with a vast superiority on the ocean, has never been able to cripple her adversary, by arresting even military and naval stores. She can only induce a temporary scarcity, which, by enhancing the price, holds out a temptation to adventurers, which is irresistible and efficacious. Besides, the more commerce a nation has, the more vulnerable is she on the ocean, and as it is impracticable to extend protection to a navigation that covers the ocean, the commerce of one nation becomes the source from which the other is supplied. Thus, in the present war, with all the vigilance of Great Britain and her interdictions of trade, France has taken from her merchants, ten times the amount of property which the British ships have taken from the French. France is not crippled for want of military and naval stores, and if she wanted ten times the quantity of such stores, she might obtain them, by means of suitable encouragement. France wants officers and seamen—and these she can never have, until by a course of regulations steadily pursued, she shall become a more commercial nation.

But I will take broader ground, to defend the rights of neutrality. "Neutrals," says the writer, "have a right to trade, but not so good a right as nations at war to defend themselves." Here again we are assailed with a general rule, which, upon strict principle, can never be just unless when applied to the injured party. When applied to the aggressor, it must always be false; for neutrals have a good right to trade to any part of the world, but no nation has a right to attack its neighbor without cause. Much less has the *aggressor* a right to interrupt the trade of a nation at peace, under pretense of stopping supplies to her enemy; for this is to offer one crime in excuse for another.

With regard to an injured nation, it is true that she has a right to deprive the aggressor of all the *direct* means of annoyance. I say *direct* means; for provisions, clothing, all the implements of husbandry and manufactures, every thing that tends to preserve life or health, are *indirectly* the means of supporting war. But a remote possibility of the application or conversion of a commodity to the purposes of war, will not justify the interruption of the common business of mankind. Other nations must subsist as well as the belligerent.

But to determine the justice of arresting trade with an *aggressing* nation, two things are to be considered. First, the certainty that the interruption of trade will defeat his unjust intentions; and secondly, whether the right of the belligerent nation to intercept the trade of a neutral, is paramount to the right of the neutral to carry on such trade. With respect to the first consideration, it may be remarked in general, that, in no case, can the interdiction of trade essentially affect the general tenor or ultimate issue of a war. It is of use only in a case of actual siege or blockade, in which the right is never questioned.

The other consideration is of difficult decision. The facts on which it depends are not always obvious; and there is no arbitrator or com-

13

mon rule established, by which nations consent to be governed.  Extreme cases may exist, in which all men would readily acknowledge a rule of right.  For instance, a small nation hard pressed by a great power, and on the point of losing its independence, would be placed in a situation resembling that of a drowning man, who, to save himself, should sacrifice his comrade's property or even his life.  In such a case, the oppressed nation would have a right to resort to means which would be otherwise unlawful; and among these means, would be the interruption of supplies destined to the aggressor, provided such supplies could be directly applied to warlike purposes.  So also on the other hand, when the parties at war are great commercial powers, contending for distant possessions, and the independence of neither is at stake, those powers have no right to interrupt a commerce which can but remotely affect the issue of the contest, but which is essential to the support and comfort of a neutral nation.  For instance, the commerce of the Baltic nations consists very much in naval stores; their land is barren and unproductive; and the God of nature has kindly supplied the soil with timber, and the bowels of the earth with iron. The exchange of those commodities therefore which will not directly support life, for such as men require for clothing and subsistence, is not more clearly indicated by the necessities of the people, than by the original formation of the countries.  To alledge a right in other nations to arrest this exchange of their productions, so essential to the support and comfort of millions of inhabitants, whenever such nations choose to quarrel with each other, is to yield principles to crimes.  No law of nations can ever exist, which shall thus authorize a sacrifice of the great interests of whole nations to the contentions of others, and which shall make the productions of the barren, inhospitable soil of the north, the prey of the richer nations of the south, in whose disputes they have no concern.  Great Britain and France have been at war, about one half of the time, for five hundred years, probably much longer.  To establish a rule of nations, by which the chief means of subsistence, of wealth and strength, among whole nations of the north, are to be made lawful plunder one half the time, is to invert the moral and social system, to exalt the " rights of war" over the superior RIGHTS of HUMANITY, and to contradict the plainest dictates of natural justice.  The northern nations ought rather to risk extermination, than to surrender the rights of a free trade.

From these considerations, we see the fallacy of the remark, " that neutrals have not so good a right to trade, as nations have to defend themselves."  Men are apt to be misled by a mere turn of expression, or what is called *point*.  Since the days of Junius, nothing passes for a good style, or proof of genius in a writer, but *point*.  It is sometimes a beauty, but its frequent use is the quackery of style, a corruption no less fatal to true taste, than to sound reasoning.  It is one of the weapons by which modern philosophists are attacking old and well tried principles.  It is a species of style which takes the reader by surprise, and by the fascination of novelty, unexpected antithesis, or the harmony of words, entices his mind from the dominion of reason, and enlists it into the service of imagination.

It is not true, as a general remark, that the interruption of trade is necessary for the defense of nations at war. The instance does not happen in an age. It is only a *pretext* used by powerful nations, to cover their injustice and oppression—a thin disguise indeed, but sufficient to blind the eyes of superficial men, who *write* before they *read*, and *think* as they are directed by their party, or influenced by their wishes.

In general, the practice of privateering and the interruption of neutrals, has no apparent effect on war. It is a game in which the winnings and losses are nearly balanced—and the nations are neither enriched nor impoverished, to a degree that can affect their resources. It is a practice, however, immensely prejudicial to nations at peace, especially to those whose productions are most useful in war. It engenders a hostile, ferocious spirit on the ocean, where licentiousness is encouraged by the expectation of impunity; it makes the property of the industrious husbandman and merchant, the prey of the idle and needy adventurer; it alienates man from man; weakens the sense of moral obligation, and generates or exasperates national animosity.

Men, who write and prate about the "rights of belligerent nations," seem to consider *war* as the chief business of man. Look into the books on the laws of nations, and there see men vindicating the barbarous maxims of savage tribes, citing them as the ground of the *jus publicum;* and treating of war as a lawful trade or occupation, in which nations may engage with as little ceremony, as a company of merchants may fit out a ship to the South Seas. But when men shall cease to let fashion and prejudice guide their opinions, they will adopt the sound principles of the court of Denmark, which, in the declaration respecting the confederacy of the year 1780, has laid down the position, "That a nation, independent and neuter, does not lose by the wars of others, the rights which she had before the war, because the peace still exists between her and all the belligerent powers. Without receiving or being obliged to follow the laws of either of them, she is allowed to follow, in all places, contraband excepted, the traffick which she would have a right to do, if peace existed with all Europe, as it exists with her."

This is the broad principle of natural and political justice, derived from the very constitution of independent societies and the nature of sovereignty. A nation at war has no right over a nation at peace, which it had not before the war. To suppose a belligerent nation to have a right to abridge the rights of a nation at peace, is to admit the principle, that a nation at peace ceases to be an independent sovereignty, by the single act of the belligerent—or that one nation may restrain and limit the rights of another without its consent. It is therefore derogatory to the sovereignty of a state, that another power, by an *ex parte* act, as by a proclamation of war against a third nation, should be permitted to vary or modify the rights, which such state enjoyed before the proclamation. And hence it is that no nation at war can claim as a *natural right*, or as a *law of public justice*, the power of abridging the trade of a neutral, acknowledged to be her right in time of peace. Every admissible restriction of this sort must be derived from the consent of the neutral, that is, from convention; and every restriction not thus authorized, is usurpation and despotism.

The principle, that the necessity of defense justifies a belligerent in depriving its adversary of supplies, has no foundation in reason or law. The rule is void for uncertainty ; for it is not only uncertain when such necessity exists, but no standard or tribunal exists by which it can be made certain. It is a question which, from the want of a common arbiter, must be left to be decided by the parties interested ; and we know by events that, in every war, even for a point of honor, or a distant island, the plea of necessity is pressed into the service of the warring nations, to authorize depredations on peaceable nations.

There is therefore no possible rule for ascertaining the rights of belligerent and neutral nations, but compact. This principle had, by the treaties toward the close of the seventeenth and in the beginning of the eighteenth centuries, become established by the assent and practice of all the great maritime powers. It was Great Britain principally, which, previous to the year 1793, violated, and endeavored to abolish all the existing stipulations on this subject, so as to leave the commerce of neutrals open to arbitrary restriction and invasion. In 1793, as we have seen, all the maritime powers violated their own principles in their visionary project of reducing France to terms of compliance, by an entire interruption of trade.

There is another view of this subject which may, by some men, be deemed too speculative, but which no man of enlarged ideas can overlook or disregard. The very structure of the globe, the distribution of land and water, the various climates and their productions, afford the highest evidence, *a priori*, that the Creator intended men to have a free communication with each other, and to interchange the productions of the several climates. Had the globe been composed of earth only, the transportation of heavy commodities would have been limited to the extent of a few leagues. Had the oceans encircled the globe from east to west, within certain parallels of latitude, the intercourse between the climates, by far the most useful, would have been prevented. The superfluous commodities of the torrid zone, so useful and convenient for northern nations, and the produce of the frigid and temperate zones, so necessary to the inhabitants of the tropics, must have perished without use on their respective soils.

But the Creator of the universe has not subjected man to these inconveniences. Two oceans stretch from north to south, through every navigable latitude ; enabling man to convey with ease the produce of the tropics to the highest habitable regions, and return with the productions of the polar climates. It is this happy distribution of water, by which man, otherwise confined for subsistence and comfort to a narrow spot of earth, becomes the tenant of every climate, selecting from the fruits of the whole earth whatever his appetite may crave, or his health and his comfort demand. Nor is this all—the two continents, instead of extending from pole to pole, by which a communication between the different oceans would have been obstructed, run at one end only into innavigable regions, while on the south they terminate in temperate latitudes, leaving a safe navigation between the Atlantic, and the Indian and Pacific oceans. When to these arrangements we add the inland seas, lakes and rivers, distributed into various parts of the continents, almost superseding the use of land carriage ; when we consider the nature of the elements destined for the use of shipping, the heavier (water) to support, the lighter (air) to impel, the floating vehicles filled with goods and wealth ; the variableness of winds intended to accommodate voyages in different directions ; the tides to supply the defect of wind in rivers and narrow channels, and to float the stranded ship, whose weight defies the power of man,—let any person survey the vast apparatus and deny, if he dare, that commerce is the business of man, and that it was the original intention of his benevolent Creator, that the wants of nations should be supplied, their desires gratified, their interest advanced, their prejudices softened, their affections enlarged, their manners refined, and their knowledge extended, by an unlimited commercial intercourse.  To neglect these advantages is to spurn the gifts of heaven—to suffer ourselves to be stripped of them, at the will or caprice of belligerent nations, is to forfeit the rights assigned to the human race.

From the considerations therefore of the rights of sovereignty, the utility of a free commerce to the general welfare of mankind, and from the obvious indications of the Author of creation in the structure of the globe, we derive evidence of the most indisputable kind, that the interchange of commodities between nations, is a right of such extent as to claim universal respect.  This right can not be infringed for light, local or temporary causes, without violence and positive injustice.  Instead of saying that " neutrals have not so good a right to trade, as nations to defend themselves," the true proposition, grounded on fact and principle, is, *that neutrals have a better right to trade, than nations have to fight and plunder.*  In the first proposition, the premises are assumed, and contrary to fact—the defense and preservation of a state rarely, if ever, depend on the interruption of trade, and in the present condition of the world, the event must be so infrequent, that to establish a law on the necessity of such defense, would be to make the *exception* the basis of the *general rule.*  The general principles are, that nations have a sovereign right to direct and control their own trade—that one sovereign has no right to disturb a neighboring state in the exercise of this right, toward a third power—that commerce is the common concern of mankind, in which the subsistence, welfare and prosperity of every nation is involved—that the interest of a particular nation is an inferior consideration, which ought not to suspend or defeat the common occupation of mankind—much less ought a particular sovereign to exalt his own rights in war, over the general rights of humanity— and finally, it is incompatible with every idea of right or justice, to suffer a sovereign to hold the exclusive power of deciding when *his* rights may supersede the common rights of other states ; or in other words, *to make the case and apply the rule himself.*

The writer before cited remarks, " that it is not probably for the interest of humanity, to change the *old law* of nations."  The reason assigned is, that the distresses of war, if not restrained, will make the miserable people clamor for peace, and thus shorten the duration of war.

What shall we say to the refinement of modern days, when we behold the champions of free plunder stalk forth, and openly contend for the *policy* and even *humanity* of robbing nations at peace, for the good of nations at war ?   It is not sufficient for the subjects of the belligerent powers, to feel the inevitable distresses of war, and often for no good cause, but to gratify the ambition of a prince or of revolutionary fanatics; but we must consent to suffer these powers to spread the havoc among those who have no concern in the contest!   All trading nations must surrender their independence, and neutral merchants their property, for the benefit of the belligerent nations; who are thus to play the tyrant, for the sake of shortening the duration of their tyranny!   Arguments like these are very proper for the "small dealers" in public law.   Subjects never clamor government into peace, for want of means to continue the war, until success becomes hopeless.

The writer proceeds—"Experience affords no ground to think that this pretended *modern* law of nations, would operate in favor of America.   In a few years, she might be powerful at sea, and then it would be against her interest."   How against her interest?   By no other conceivable way, than by leaving neutral commerce open to be plundered by *our* ships, when we may be at war.   God forbid that the United States should ever *want* the means, or possess the *moral* power to exercise this license against neutrals.   Let them have naval strength to defend their own rights, but not to impair those of other powers.   It is easy to make general assertions, and readers are too apt to mistake an air of confidence for sound argument.   The fact is, that the rule of "free ships make free goods," always operates in favor of nations at peace, whether strong or weak; and for this reason, the United States, which *will* or *may be* always at peace, during the wars of Europe, have an immense interest in maintaining the rule.

But, says the writer, "A regulation so repugnant to the very nature of war, and the established mode of carrying it on, would be observed with reluctance by the weakest [weaker] nation, and not at all by the stronger.   The weaker would plead the example of England in seizing French goods on board of American ships, as an excuse for seizing English goods in American ships.   France has done this."   True, and this is the strongest of all reasons why we should not concede to *any* nation, the right of seizing enemy's property in our ships.   Is it not a most extraordinary, not to say insulting, species of sophistry, to alledge that *one* nation will not accede to a rule of justice, and therefore we ought to surrender it ?   It was a rule of nations in war, to put to death prisoners, to sell them, to mutilate them—so it was to seize travelers and merchants in a foreign country, even in peace, and make them pay enormous sums for their ransom—but would any man say, that if a great power will continue to exercise such barbarity, therefore all states ought to adhere to the practice, and establish it as a law of nations ?   Let us, for mercy's sake, defend the *principle*, though we may not be able to enforce the *practice*, of public justice.

It is true, that if one nation will continue the practice of barbarians in war, her enemies will resort to the same means.   And this is just; for retaliation is the only effectual weapon to punish the injustice of the oppressor.   France was perfectly right in regard to Great Britain, in adopting the rule toward neutrals which Great Britain had followed— all nations in war must do the same; and this is one of the most urgent reasons, why no nation should abandon the principles of free trade;

for every instance of concession fortifies the claim of the refractory, overbearing nation—it yields to an enemy, ground which is not easily recovered; and every step, in retreating from the principles of the northern confederacy, is an advance toward ancient piracy and barbarism.

It is extremely important that the question should be settled, whether the claims of Great Britain, or of all Europe combined against her, shall be admitted as the established law of nations. We are accustomed to hear most outrageous clamor against the French depredations on our trade; but let it be recollected, that every decree of the French government, authorizing the seizure of neutrals, was posterior to and in consequence of, the orders of the British cabinet, for the same purpose. The Spaniards are pursuing a similar practice, and with a few privateers pretend to blockade Gibraltar. These proceedings are in the nature of reprisals on Great Britain, and on the neutrals who countenance her arbitrary interruption of their trade. Every nation at war will adopt the like measures—the ocean will again become the " field of pirates," and peace will be expelled from the earth; for even nations disposed to be neutral, must become parties to every war in their own defense.

In the present state of things, treaties, always regarded with too little respect, are losing their efficacy; and from the inequality of their operation, will become a dead letter. France, in her treaty with the United States, in 1778, stipulated that free ships should make free goods—so that in her war with Great Britain, British goods were protected by the American flag. Great Britain would not consent to such a stipulation—of course, French goods in American ships were not protected. Will nations observe treaties in which advantages are not reciprocal? And who can blame them if they will not?

So by the British treaty with Russia, in 1766, and by that of 1801, naval stores are *not* contraband; but by our treaty with Great Britain, naval stores *are* contraband—of course, Russia can supply the enemy of Great Britain with naval stores, and the United States can not. How is it possible that treaties, with such unequal conditions, can be observed? For Russia to consent to make her staple commodities contraband, would be treason against her subjects and the intentions of heaven; and although the productions of the United States are more various, yet some of these productions are necessary in war; and it is the interest and the duty of our government never to consent to enlarge the usual list of prohibited goods.

A writer in the Palladium, with the signature of *Americanus*, has attempted, in a series of papers, beginning April 21, 1801, to maintain the impolicy of establishing the principles of the northern confederacy. In the very threshold of his essay, he lets us know that he is a party man, and intends to treat the subject on party principles. He tells us a work has been written at Paris, to exhibit the policy of France toward other nations; and that a copious extract from it, relative to maritime commerce, has appeared in the European journals, which makes it evident, that the northern league is entirely a French project, to unite all nations against the English, who alone can obstruct France in her designs to establish unrivaled power.

To a man who reads none but English publications, and who, will give more credit to them than to the official declarations of the powers of the north, the confederacy may be made to appear a " French project." The writer certainly allows a very small portion of wisdom and discernment to the courts of the Baltic nations, when he charges them with being persuaded by the French, to hazard a rupture with Great Britain. A little reading, with impartial views, and a careful examination of facts, connected with the nature of the Baltic commerce, will convince any man that the confederacy was dictated by the necessity of maintaining the *old* principles of free trade, against the alarming claims and encroachments of Great Britain. France is certainly very busy in aiding the project; but the league originated in sound principles of neutral policy, in which the Baltic trade is particularly concerned; and if the northern powers can not compel Great Britain to renounce her claims, and restore those old principles, they may surrender their independence at once, and become colonies of the British empire.

The practice of interweaving party views and temporary exigencies into the discussion of every question of general policy and the laws of nations, misleads men of the purest intentions. When reason enlists under the standard of wishes and prejudices, it is as likely to defend error as truth. Great Britain and France are the champions of the day; and every spectator of the contest wishes his favorite to use the means that will give him the victory.

Reason, impartiality, and general views, reject a decision formed on such a narrow basis. The interruption of a free trade and the claims of Great Britain, are not at all essential to her existence, as I have already observed; but if they were, the case would be an exception from ordinary events, and therefore not the foundation of a general rule. To reason from particulars to generals is always bad logic, and especially in a case in which the common welfare of nations is concerned.

Americanus offers a few remarks on the progress and termination of the armed neutrality of 1780, but has not given a correct view of the origin and principles of that confederacy. His sarcastic remarks on the concern which the French seem to have for the rights of neutrals, are wholly irrelevant to the question. No man believes either France or Great Britain has any concern for principles or the rights of other nations, when they interfere with their supposed interests. I lay out of the discussion all such extraneous considerations.

But the reasoning and assertions of *Americanus*, regarding the operation of the rule of *free ships make free goods*, on the commerce of neutrals in time of war, deserve examination. The first effect noticed is, that neutrals would lose the benefit of their neutrality, by transfers of the ships of belligerent nations to the citizens of neutral states. The only answer to this objection to the rule which it is necessary to make is, that either party might prevent this fraud—the neutral state would restrain the practice, for her own benefit, if the practice should operate against her; and the belligerent might, and justly, consider an open countenance given to it as a hostile act, associating the party with her enemy. We may leave the management of that business to the neutral nation or to individuals, who would not reduce their own profits, as

Americanus supposes, by encouraging fictitious sales. If neutral flags should be hoisted on board of ships belonging to belligerent nations, an examination would detect the fraud, and the ship would be seized. No regulations can elude the ingenuity of men, when exerted to secure their property ; but no fraud is more easily detected than that of carrying false colors. For more than a century most of the maritime powers have traded under their *old law of free ships free goods*, and without great inconvenience from the stratagems of false colors and fictitious transfers.

" But," says Americanus, " admit that this obstacle could be surmounted, and neutral vessels could protect property, this would be a benefit to the belligerent nations only, for neutral property is now as safe as laws can make it ; and if the property belongs to powers at war, the neutral is only the carrier, whose profit is a mere *pittance*. The neutral may now *carry* the goods of nations at war, subject indeed to be seized, [detained, conducted into port, harassed with admiralty proceedings, &c.] yet he *is entitled to his freight*. But if he owns the goods he can not be interrupted. This will operate as an inducement to *purchase*, instead of taking *freight*, and the profits of purchasing and selling are as much greater than those of freighting, as the gains of the Cornhill shopkeepers in Boston exceed those of their truckmen and porters."

In this train of reasoning, there is no small degree of fascination. In no way can we so easily reconcile a merchant to have his ships detained, vexed, and plundered, as to convince him that he makes a great profit by it.

If it was true, that to be purchasers rather than freighters, is highly advantageous to neutrals, it would still be hard to compel them to purchase, whether they are able and willing or not. This kind of compulsion would bear no small resemblance to that of French republicans, who generously offer to *force* nations to be *free*. But Americanus is as much mistaken in fact as in principle. Every merchant can inform the gentleman, that in all wars the freighting business is among the most profitable branches, as it is certainly the safest. The very great gains which he supposes our merchants have made in the present war, are, in a large proportion, derived from that source. The immense failures of the last six years have not been among *carriers*, but among *purchasers*.

In plain truth, it would be *best*, as it is the only *just* proceeding, to protect the property, whether owned by the neutral or the belligerent ; the merchant would then purchase goods, when he had capital or could find a market ; or in failure of these, he might take goods on freight. Such is the state of the question as it regards the merchant.

The administration of the United States, as well as the old Congress, have always considered the principles of the northern powers as highly valuable to this country. The Secretary of State, in his long and able letter to Mr. Pinckney, when in France, dated Jan. 16, 1797, speaking of the ill success of the armed neutrality, says, " this, no nation has more reason to regret than our own, as well because the principles in question respect some very valuable portions of our exports, as because our dispositions and our policy, preserving us in peace, such an extended liberty of commerce would prove highly advantageous to us, as carriers for the powers at war."

Americanus, having by a strain of sophistry arrived at the conclusion that the principle of *free ships, free goods*, if established, would " deprive neutrals of great advantages which they now enjoy"—a conclusion which he seems to think very obvious, but which all the wise heads of the confederated powers of Europe have not been able to see or understand—proceeds to make a remark which others have made, that it would be advantageous to inferior states only, and that the most powerful would oppose it, and always with success. To a man who believes that right and power are the same thing in *principle*, as Great Britain and France, at war, make them in *fact*, this kind of reasoning may pass for logic. If all contention for justice and national sovereignty is in vain, let small states, like the unresisting lamb under the hands of the shearer, consent to lie quiet and be *fleeced* without a murmur. Let the nations at war be the sole judges of what is the law of nations, and when to apply it ; and let the *ultima ratio regum* be the sole instrument of execution. With men who can coolly and deliberately advocate such principles, argument is useless.

Americanus, near the close of his essay, recapitulates the stale reason employed to justify an interdiction of trade with belligerents—the necessity and justice of disabling an enemy, by taking from him the means of prosecuting the war ; suggesting that the seizure of property on the seas is the least cruel, least offensive, and least odious method of effectually accomplishing this purpose.

The remarks in the preceding pages show, that in most cases this method has not the least effect. With respect to great maritime nations, with extensive coasts, numerous harbors, and a free intercourse with neutral nations by land, seizures on the ocean can never be effectual to disable or even to distress an enemy. If the experience of nations in the wars of the last fifty years does not convince men of information and reflection of that fact, they must be a prey to their own blindness. The captures of vessels by Great Britain and France, never shortened the wars between them a single week. If the reason alledged can ever be true, it must be in cases like the league of Cambray against Venice, when most or all the surrounding nations combine and invest a small state with enemies. And in such cases, the great powers being usually the aggressors, the interdiction of trade to the place, is to double the crime by robbing one innocent nation to injure another, and to aid the oppressor in subduing the oppressed.

But were it true that such maritime seizures could abridge the duration or lessen the calamities of war, still, such seizures of neutral property, being direct infractions of natural right, and encroachments on the sovereignty of nations, can never be lawfully exercised but in pursuance of special conventions. The right to carry on *ordinary* trade, even in implements of war, that is, *such trade as is usually carried on in time of peace*, can never be lawfully restrained by powers at war, unless authorized by treaty. The right to carry on such a trade is a natural right, resulting from the constitution of society, and the nature of sovereignty ; and is therefore paramount to any right incident to a state of war, which must be accidental, temporary, fluctuating, arbi-

trary, local, and consequently *subordinate* to the general and permanent rights of nations.

Americanus says that such seizures "violate no neutral territory."
This assertion must proceed from want of reflection, or from the habit
of considering ships at sea as a species of imperfect property. Reason
condemns the distinction between a right to property on sea and on
land. The right of an owner to his ship on the ocean, and of his sovereign to his jurisdiction over it, is in fact as complete and as exclusive,
as the right of an owner to his house, and of his sovereign to the jurisdiction over it, on neutral territory. In strict principle, a belligerent
has no more right to step his foot upon the deck of a neutral ship and
take out his enemy's goods, than he has to enter the territory and the
house of a neutral and plunder it of his enemy's property. The only
difference is in the habits of thinking, derived from the maxims of warring nations, which have been traced to the barbarous customs of antiquity. It is time to discard maxims, established when *power* was the
only measure of *right;* for venerable as may be deemed the *laws of
plunder*, from their early origin and long continuance, yet their authors
were *savages*, and their supporters have been *tyrants*.

Americanus closes his essay by very just strictures on the pretense
of the French to public morality and natural justice. It is true, that
such remarks have nothing to do with the subject under discussion. If
the French happen, for once, to be *right*, this is no reason why those
who hate them, should be wrong.

> " So much they scorn the crowd, that if the throng
> By chance go right, they purposely go wrong."

But there is one view of the subject before us, which is as interesting,
as it is just. The French revolutionists avow and pursue principles incompatible with the rights, the independence and the peace of other nations. They have attempted to undermine the allegiance of men to
their sovereigns ; they have solicited subjects to revolt, and have offered them their assistance.

They have attacked the foundation of civil society, by endeavoring
to root out from the human heart, all belief in revelation and in the
moral government of a Supreme Being ; and by weakening the influence of oaths and moral obligation. They have gone further ; they
have attempted, as they call it, to " conquer nations into liberty" ; assuming the right to destroy, modify and control their internal government. They have raised the nation in arms, to enforce these pretensions, conquering small states, annexing some of them to their own territory ; placing garrisons in others, which subsist on the vanquished inhabitants and eat out their substance, under pretext of *making them free;*
erecting in others new forms of government, presented by themselves,
and laying enormous contributions upon every country which their armies have penetrated. What will be the issue of these pretensions and
proceedings, on the moral and political condition of man, God only
knows.

But while I dread, as much as I abhor, these novel, tyrannical and
formidable claims of the French, to intermeddle with the concerns, violate the rights, and invade the independence of nations, I can not see,

with silent tranquillity, the equally unjust and tyrannical aggressions of
Great Britain, on the commerce of neutral powers. I consider her
claims to interdict all commerce with her enemies, or such part of it as
she deems expedient, on pretense of *necessity*, of the existence and degree of which she is the sole judge ; as unwarrantable as the pretensions
of France, to molest the states around her, under pretense of giving
them freedom. If a difference exists in the two cases, it is in *degree* and
not in *principle*. Each of those great powers makes the unjust pretensions of the other the pretext for maintaining its own, and if neither
party will recede from its claims, the war must be interminable, and
suspended only by treaties of short duration. Unfortunately, the claims
of Great Britain interfere more directly with the interests of the northern
powers, than those of France. Great Britain directly abridges their
commerce ; France does not directly attack their independence. The
consequence is, the northern powers are under strong inducements to
combine with France, to check the power of Great Britain. France
avails herself of this commercial interest, to strengthen her own power,
and divert the northern courts from any combination to arrest her progress in revolutionizing the contiguous parts of Europe. France attacks the rights of nations on land ; Great Britain on the ocean ; while
the Americans permit their wishes to enlist on one side or the other, as
they are prompted by new prejudices, or old attachments. To wish that
France may be restrained in her career, is the dictate of morality, of
justice, and humanity. But to abandon the most essential rights of nations on the ocean, were it necessary to restrain France on land, would
be a sacrifice without an equivalent ; it would be to prefer the particular interest, to the general ; the local, to the universal. When, however,
it is considered, that the invasion of neutral rights can not possibly affect
the issue of the contest, no good man can wish to see the claims of
Great Britain recognized as the law of nations. For Americans who
are affected by the contest, through the medium of their commerce, to
surrender the rights of a free trade, and defend the policy of Great Britain, is not only to consent to a prostitution of their independence, but
to become the panders of the crime.

The great question of the general rights of commerce ought not to be
decided by present exigencies. But since these are dragged into the
discussion, by the advocates of the claims of Great Britain, it may not
be improper to remark, that while any power openly maintains the right
to interdict the trade of neutrals, as she may judge time and circumstances render expedient, that power must naturally have all commercial
nations for her enemies. It is not simply the right of seizing enemy's
property in neutral ships, and of searching them at pleasure, which is
claimed by Great Britain ; but she undisguisedly maintains her right to
interrupt all trade with her enemy, when she may judge that such a
measure will reduce her enemy to terms of accommodation. She extends also her right to declare a place blockaded, and to intercept the
colonial trade of an enemy, as well as the produce of an enemy's country, to a degree that subjects the commerce of all nations to interruption
and plunder. And to crown this insulting system of maritime domination, she absolutely prohibits neutrals to trade with her enemy's ports
which she pretends to blockade, *while her own ships are licensed to*

*trade with these very ports.* Instead of blocking up ports to disable her enemy, she now declares them besieged, for the purpose of excluding neutrals, and giving the whole trade to her own subjects.* Such are consequences of the rights claimed and asserted by Great Britain, and such are the claims which Americans unblushingly defend!

Is it possible that such a nation should not be perpetually embroiled with her neighbors? Can maritime powers be her friends? If nations must submit to the lawless domination of one of the great rival powers, they ought at least to have the privilege of choosing their master.

The northern states of Europe are not and can not be the rivals of Great Britain on the ocean. No nations are more intimately connected by reciprocal wants. It is the policy therefore of Great Britain to cultivate the good will of all the Baltic powers. Yet she seems to pursue a directly different policy; she takes incredible pains to alienate the friendship of nations, on which she depends principally for naval stores. She seems to think it better to sacrifice their friendship and hazard their enmity, than yield to them the most indubitable rights. Whatever the narrow views of the moment may suggest, on the great scale of European politics, Great Britain loses more than she gains by her imperious demands. *She throws the northern powers into the interests of France;* she makes all commercial nations her enemies; she fosters enmities which would otherwise subside, and protracts every war in which she is engaged. To recede from her unreasonable claims, and permit inferior powers to enjoy their natural rights, would conciliate those powers, *detach them from the interest of her inveterate enemy and rival,* and by enabling them to supply her navy at all times with stores, and multiplying her markets, she would augment her own strength, while she would reduce the number and animosity of her enemies.

But whatever measures the court of Great Britain may pursue, the interest of all other nations points to their duty; they must defend their rights; and though compelled, for a time, to yield to the *power,* they must inflexibly resist the *claims* of Great Britain. The same is the duty of the nations adjacent to France. Depressed, for the moment, by the weight of her arms, submission is a duty; but time can never sanction her injustice, nor prescription give validity to her claims. Her principles are treason against civil society and national sovereignty; to admit their validity, is to become a partner in her guilt, and the common enemy of man.

Every friend of the rights and the peace of mankind, must acknowledge the services which Great Britain has rendered to Europe, by the firm and successful opposition she has presented to the extension of the power of France. But it is a fatal mistake to suppose that her depredations on neutral commerce are *necessary to that opposition.* The fact is directly the reverse, and her inadmissible claims weaken her comparative force, by increasing that of her enemy.

Her attempt to cut off all supplies to France, in conjunction with other powers, in 1793, and especially her secret order of November 6th, for seizing the defenseless trade of the United States, nearly completed

---

* See the letter of the Hon. Rufus King, American minister at the court of Great Britain, to Lord Hawksbury, March 13, 1801.

what an insidious French minister had begun—in driving the United States into the clutches of France. These unwarrantable orders renewed irritations which had subsided, and which it should have been the policy of Great Britain to moderate and allay. They were the very pretexts which the enemies of England desired, to justify all the predatory schemes of France. That France was bound by treaty not to plunder American ships, while England was not thus bound, was logic not suited to convince the government of France, or its friends in this country. Great Britain began to practice upon *her* law of nations; France found " nothing but disadvantage" in her treaty; renounced its obligations; let loose her privateers; and the lion and the tiger, while fighting with each other, united in devouring our unprotected commerce. Great Britain, it is alledged, has paid a little, and promised to pay more, by way of indemnification. But there is little in this to heal the wounds inflicted on our rights. If a man horsewhips his neighbor without cause, it is but little satisfaction that he offers to pay him damages, and then boasts of his *justice.* While Great Britain shall practice on her *jus publicum*, other nations will retaliate; and in the scramble for plunder, one gains about as much as another; the parties are not enriched, nor greatly distressed; neutrals are exasperated, and the flames of war extended. Such is the law of nations, according to the British ministry, and such the comment. These unwarrantable claims, and the practice upon them by Great Britain, with the attempts to justify them in this country, and the concessions made by our government in favor of those claims, have been extremely unpropitious to the federal interest.

A few remarks on the general principles which should be the basis of an intercourse between belligerent and neutral nations, shall close this discussion.

It has already been observed, that nations at war have no right to interfere in the customary occupations of nations at peace; on the obvious principle that all nations are equally sovereign, and one sovereign can not lose his rights by an act of another, without his own consent. A neutral does not consent to surrender any right to a belligerent, without an express convention for the purpose. If a nation in peace usually supplies another, even with instruments of war, she has the same right to continue the trade in war; it is her customary occupation, the means of subsisting her citizens, and not intended as a hostile act. Such is the law of natural justice. Nothing is *contraband* by *natural law*—the two ideas are imcompatible. Contraband, by its definition and origin, implies, what is prohibited by an express act of sovereign authority.

" Neutrals," says Vattel, " having no part in the quarrel of nations at war, are under no obligation to abandon their trade, that they may avoid furnishing them with the means of making war." Such is the law of justice resulting from the nature of sovereignty and equal rights.

On what principle then can a belligerent interfere with the business of a neutral? The general principle is an obvious one; but its details are difficult and perplexed. The general rule is, that a neutral nation may do every thing, in time of war, which does not make it a party in the contest, without being subject to be called in question by either party. An act of a neutral, evidently intended to supply one party with means, in preference to the other, is a hostile act, and associates the neutral with the party so supplied, as an enemy to the other party. Every act performed in the ordinary course of trade or business of any kind, not with a hostile intent, or with a view to assist one party in preference to another, is a lawful act, of which neither party can complain.

Among the ancient nations whose history is recorded, no precise rules were established, by which a neutral was deemed to become an associate with the party assisted. But it has been observed, that any supplies of provisions, as well as warlike stores, were arbitrarily considered as proof of a hostile disposition. When the Romans first invaded Asia, in their war with Antiochus, Æmilius, their naval commander, received intelligence that the Teji freely supplied the fleet of Antiochus with provisions, and had promised them five thousand measures of wine. He immediately changed his course and proceeded to their port, with a view to take the stores provided for his enemies, or " *ipsos pro hostibus habiturus*," (determined to consider them as enemies.) He landed and directed his troops to ravage the adjacent country. Envoys were immediately dispatched from the city, exculpating the citizens from any hostile act toward the Romans. The commander replied, that " they had supplied his enemy with provisions, and had promised him a large quantity of wine ; but if they would furnish similar supplies for *his* fleet, he would recall his men from plundering—if not, he should treat them as enemies."—(Liv. 37, 27, 28.)

The method taken by the Roman commander, to ascertain *quo animo* those people supplied his enemy, was the true mode ; that is, to require them to administer to his own fleet the same aids. If they consented, he was ready to consider them as impartial neutrals ; if not, he had a right to consider them as partners with his enemy.

This is unquestionably a true and sound principle, that a neutral, trading with each and every belligerent nation without reserve or preference, and impartially furnishing them with any commodities which can be spared, must be treated as a peaceable nation, and not incurring blame from either of the belligerent powers. Were nations to annul all prohibitions, and throw open the ports of nations at war to all neutrals, without distinctions of parties or cargoes, the operation of such free commerce would not essentially affect belligerent nations, nor the issue of their quarrels. They would be supplied more uniformly, and at a less price ; but in fact, present prohibitions and seizures never effectually interrupt supplies. Nations at war, in these days, always find supplies of provisions, naval and military stores.

The arbitrary customs and practices of nations, which formerly laid open all commerce to vexations by the parties at war, led to the scheme of obviating such inconveniences by positive institutions. The period in which this design was effected, as before observed, was the last forty years of the seventeenth century ; before which period, every belligerent sovereign took the liberty to prohibit trade with his enemies at pleasure. Such arbitrary proceedings, while some of the nations of Europe were almost always in war, produced seizures, confiscations, mutual complaints, recriminations, and reprisals without end. From this calamitous condition, when despotic will was law, and rights were undefined—when merchants were robbed and imprisoned, and sovereigns had no means of redress but reprisals, the benign policy of modern nations had, after long struggles and immense difficulties, extricated their commerce, by means of mutual stipulations in public treaties. This was a vast improvement in the political state of nations. Great Britain pretends that she finds " nothing but disadvantage" in such conventions, and is steadily pursuing the design of annulling their obligations, with a view of leaving sovereigns to regulate their conduct by the general " laws of nations." This is tantamount to an attempt to revive the savage state of man—to take off all restraint upon sovereigns at war—to leave the laws of nations, undefined, to be expounded by arbitrary will, according to exigencies, or by the ancient maxims of lawless and predatory barbarians.

But this systematic encroachment on natural rights—this abominable attempt to break down the few barriers which nations have erected against the barbarous maxims of despotic will, and to revive the ancient savage rules of warfare, ought to be resisted by every civilized nation. Natural law permits no abridgment of the sovereignty, nor interruption of the commerce of any nation, without its consent. This is the high prerogative of compact only, and wretched will be our condition, if we can not maintain the ground which has been gained by ancient treaties.

[Published in 1802.]

---

POSTSCRIPT.

The foregoing essay was sent to the press, before I had seen the pamphlet written by Mr. Jenkinson, now Lord Liverpool, in 1757, and republished in 1794. On perusing it, I find no occasion to alter my opinions or reasonings on the subject of the rights of neutral nations; but my opinions are greatly confirmed, by the weakness of many of his lordship's arguments.

His lordship asserts that " the right of protection must have for its foundation some law, which has force in that place where the right of protection is claimed. If neutral nations have any right to protect the property of the enemy, it must take its rise from those laws which are the established rules of conduct between nations, and particularly on that element where this right is supposed to be exerted. No civil or municipal institutions, and much less the privileges arising from them, can here take place; they have no force but under the dominion of those who agreed to their establishment."—Edit. 1794, p. 7. " The right which governments enjoy of protecting the property of the enemy, is a consequence of the right of dominion; unless therefore their dominion extends over the ocean, the right of property can not there take place."—pp. 8, 9. His lordship proceeds to state that dominion gives a right of enacting laws—that the laws of nations do not take effect under the special jurisdiction of nations; but that (on the ocean,) out of the verge of this particular jurisdiction, the laws and privileges which attend that dominion cease, and the general laws of nations have their force. The general inference from these principles is, that nations can not protect the property of the enemy of another, on the ocean, because such property is seizable by the laws of nations.

The whole of this reasoning is anticipated, and it is presumed amply refuted, in the preceding essay. The premises are assumed by his lordship, contrary to fact and principle. The ships of a nation are *not out of its jurisdiction* when on the high seas. On the other hand, the sovereignty or dominion is as complete, as within its territories on land. No offense, no trespass, no crime committed on board of a ship on the ocean, is triable by the laws of nations, (except piracy.) On the other hand, every crime and every controversy among the seamen, is cognizable alone before the tribunals of the nation to which the owner belongs. This fact proves the dominion to be *exclusive* and *complete*, as it is on land, within the territories of the nation. Pirates are the common enemies of nations; and the reason why all nations have a right to seize and try them, is that *all* have *complete* jurisdiction on the high seas. The right to the ocean is a *common* right and a *complete* right— *it is not imperfect*, nor subject to any participation of authority among nations. The sea is the common highway of nations—all have an equal right to the use or temporary occupancy—but the *place occupied for the moment*, is the *exclusive property* of the occupant. The same principle extends to the *laws* of the ocean. The jurisdiction, *perfect* and *complete*, accompanies the ship of every nation—the laws of that nation operate upon the property and the persons—and to the laws of each nation alone, are the persons on board of its ships amenable. And these rights of dominion can be impaired or abridged by no authority, except by mutual compact.—(Vattel, book i, ch. **23**; book ii, ch. **7, 9.**) The right of search, unless authorized by treaty, is no other than the *practice of violence*, established by the arbitrary usage of tyrannical princes or states, for their own convenience, but in direct opposition to morality and justice.

His lordship, in the whole of his argument, takes it for granted that by the *right of war*, all the goods and property of an enemy become subject to seizure and confiscation. This subject is also anticipated in the preceding pages, but a few remarks may be here added.

By the laws of *moral right and justice*, as now understood among civilized nations, the only *justifiable* reasons for seizing an enemy's goods, are for indemnification, when damage has been done, or that he may be *disabled from further injury, and compelled or induced to make peace*. These I believe to be the only reasons ever assigned for taking and destroying an enemy's property. There certainly can be no other *just* motives. Now I appeal to his lordship's own arguments, to *disprove* the right of belligerent nations to seize and apply to their own use, the property of an enemy, except for indemnification. His lordship, page 7, admits in so many words, that " governments succeed to no other rights, but such as their respective members enjoyed in a state of individuality;" that nations are to each other, as individuals in a state of nature, without a common judge and protector; and therefore have a right to protect themselves in the same manner. Granted. But if *A* makes an attack on *B* with a weapon, *B* has a right to arrest the stroke, and to seize the instrument; but the weapon *does not become the property of B*. The property is not changed. *B* can keep the weapon till the assailant is pacified, and himself delivered from the fear of his power. But this is no more than a sequestration, not a

change of property. There is not a case in which an individual aggressor forfeits his *natural* right to property, by using it for the annoyance of another. If such a forfeiture ever occurs, it must be by virtue of a municipal law. Damages alone are incurred by private injury,
and these are to be repaired; but all seizures beyond reparation, are
robbery.

If then, governments succeed to no rights not enjoyed by individuals,
they have no right to seize and appropriate the property of an enemy,
and this by his lordship's own statement. Upon this principle, nations
have a right only to seize and sequester such goods of an enemy, as
are the means of annoyance; but the danger being past, and the enemy reconciled, the goods ought to be restored. This is political morality, precisely analogous to the justice which is enforced by law among
individuals.

Should it be said that nations will not observe these maxims of morality, it is replied that such a remark is not relevant to the question.
The advocates of the laws of war and plunder, choose to rest their
cause on maxims of *right and justice*, and on this ground they are
combated. If they abandon this ground, and resort to expedience or
necessity, superior to morality, it will then be time enough to meet
them on that ground.

The right of seizure for the sake of indemnification, stands on better ground; and in cases of defensive war, is justifiable. But to show
how futile is this pretense, it is only necessary to remark, that if morality and justice had any influence in deciding the *rights of war*, an account of the goods and estate seized and conquered ought to be taken,
and the surplus, above the amount of damages, ought to be restored
upon pacification. Besides, the goods taken by privateers, are the
property of the owners, not of the state; nor are they applied to indemnify those who suffer damage. One individual suffers; another becomes rich. There is no adjustment of damages; government rarely
or never undertakes to pay the losses. So that although indemnification is the pretense, it is rarely or never procured by the plunder of an
enemy. It would be more honest and more honorable to avow the real
motives for war, which usually are ambition, revenge or the savage
passion for plunder, which modern delicacy affects to conceal but can
not extinguish.

"An individual then," says his lordship, "in a state of nature would
have had an undoubted right to protect his own person and property
against an attack—but if I am engaged in contention with another,
would he then have a right to protect him against me? Most certainly not; since he thereby would deprive me of a right which the
law of nature, for my own security, would in such case give me, of
seizing the property of this my enemy and destroying his person. If
he thought my conduct manifestly injurious, so as to call for general
resentment, he would, on that account, become my enemy himself;
but as he calls himself a neuter, to act in this manner against me,
would be no less absurd than unjust. Such therefore, and no more, is
the right of protection, which government enjoys at present in those
places, to which their own dominions do not extend. They have succeeded to the rights only of their respective members, and by consequence these only can they protect." p. 8.

No person denies, that a nation directly assisting another when at war, and with a view to add to its strength against an enemy, becomes an associate in the contest. But his lordship supposes that a neuter nation carrying the goods of a belligerent, deprives his enemy of a right given him by the law of nature of seizing his property and destroying his person. But the law of nature gives no such right of seizure and destruction, beyond what is necessary for defense and damages. It was a practice of barbarians to plunder, destroy and kill to the utmost—but this is not a law of nature, on the contrary it is as unnatural as it is cruel and immoral. And I have satisfactorily proved, that the plundering system, in modern days, has not the remotest influence on the issue of a war—it neither shortens its duration, nor contributes to the future security of the parties.

The writer takes it for granted, that it is necessary for the safety of a belligerent, to take his enemy's property, wherever he can find it: but this is utterly denied. This position, so generally conceded, is assumed in direct contradiction to fact and experience. The taking of a little property from the merchant, a subject of the enemy, is of no more consequence to the final issue of the war, than the color of his coat or the shape of his hat. If, in the case put by his lordship, of two persons fighting, a third person steps in and takes part, by striking or putting weapons into the hands of one of them, he makes himself a partner in the contest. But the persons who furnish food and clothing to them and their families, while they fight, do not become associates; because the duties of humanity and the ordinary business of life, are of paramount obligation.

Two persons, in a state of nature, if that state can be found, fighting for superiority or defense, can not, on that account, have any right to rob each other of things acquired by labor or other good title, and not directly necessary to maintain the contest. The goods of each, necessary for the use and conveniences of life, would still remain uninfected by the quarrel—the ownership of each would be unimpaired—and the ordinary trade of a third person, in those articles, would remain as legal and as little subject to justifiable violations, as when the parties were at peace. It is a fundamental principle, on which I rely with confidence, that no personal or political quarrel can affect the rights of a third person or of neutrals. Their right to trade in and to carry the goods of the parties at war, remains unimpaired. It is not in the power of the imagination to conceive a case, in which the rights and stipulations of A and B can be impaired by the sole act of C. The only plausible pretense on which a belligerent can claim to interrupt the commerce of a neutral in his enemy's goods, is, that a state of war gives him some title to such goods. But if the title is not actually changed and vested in the claiming power, by the state of war, it is an imperfect right, which becomes complete only by the possession. In this case, the sovereign must gain possession by a lawful act—but if he takes the property from a neutral nation, without its consent, he violates the sovereignty and independence of that nation, and commits a trespass. Such is the fact.

Lord Liverpool admits that an enemy's property is justly protected by a neutral nation within its exclusive jurisdiction; but declares that

this dominion extends not to the sea.  He says, on the ocean the law of
nations prevails, and all that pass thereon, are subject to it, without either privilege or exemption.—p. 10.  Astonishing assertions!  Who
has made this law of nations?  Who is the legislator, possessed of the
enormous power to abridge the rights of ownership on the ocean?  Who
has enacted that my *ship* is less my property than my *house*?  I challenge all the advocates of the plundering usages of nations, to point to
the origin of this distinction; to show me the law which declares that
my ship at the wharf is exclusively my property; and that two leagues
from land, the right is diminished, and the citizens of another nation
have participation with me, in the property.  Point me to the principle
of natural justice, which secures to a sovereign, at the wharf, an exclusive jurisdiction over a ship, and at two leagues' distance gives concur-
rent jurisdiction to another sovereign.

It will be said, the usages of nations are against me.  True; Demetrius hung the merchant who was carrying goods to his besieged enemies.  Here is precedent, will Lord Liverpool avail himself of it?  Go,
hang a Swede or an American, that is conveying goods to an enemy!
It was the universal usage of nations to plunder, burn and ravage, and
to murder or torment enemies; here is a precedent of vast authority!
Will my opposers plead it in their favor?  If precedent is authority,
there is not a crime nor a cruelty which the heart of man can invent or
his hand perpetrate, which will not be amply justified.  And to the
shame of civilized man, the precedents of tyrants and barbarians, in the
murderous work of destruction, are collected into volumes, and dignified
with the appellation of the " laws of nations!"

" Admit the freedom of neutral trade," says his lordship, " and it
becomes the interest of all commercial states to promote dissensions
among their neighbors; the quarrels of others would be their harvest."
But this remark supposes what is not true, that nations are intrigued into
war by the merchants of other states; for *they* are more directly interested in a free trade.  The reverse of the proposition is the truth; that
the right to seize an enemy's goods and interrupt neutrals, is a strong
temptation for nations to engage in war themselves.  And it is not a
little singular that his lordship should have overlooked the example of
Great Britain herself, who has more than once been impelled into a
war with Spain by the popular clamor, for the sake of plundering the
rich Spanish ships from America and the Indies.  Almost all the wars
of antiquity were waged for the sake of plunder; and the modern motives, however disguised, are not more honorable.  The wars between
Great Britain and France, are rendered popular by the hope of plunder.
It is time for mankind to awake from this delusion, and learn that the
laws of peace are more congenial with justice and morality, than the
laws of war; and that belligerent powers are not, by virtue of the savage laws of plunder, to trample on the sovereignty of neutral nations.

What is the foundation of the law of nations?  Morality and convention.  The principles of justice and utility among men, constitute morality; these principles, extended to nations, compose the laws by which
they ought to be governed.  Morality among individuals is enforced by
municipal laws; among nations it can not be enforced for want of a
common sovereign.  But the laws which do or ought to govern in both

cases, rest on precisely the same foundation, unless modified by special agreement.

I shall be told that the usages of nations are evidence of consent, and principles sanctioned by long usage have obtained the force of laws. But these usages, to constitute laws binding on a nation, must receive the assent of that nation. No usage, repugnant to justice and fundamental or natural rights, can be a law to a nation denying its obligation. Morality is binding on all men and states; practices, inconsistent with morality, have no authority over a nation, unless explicitly or tacitly recognized as law. The rights of flags and embassadors stand on political morality; without a sacred regard to their safety, no intercourse could take place between nations; controversies could not be adjusted, and war would be interminable. From the utility of these rights to society, their obligation is binding upon all sovereigns and states. These rights have been often violated by barbarous nations—the very nations whose usages, in regard to seizing the goods of enemies, now constitute the "laws of war." The violation of the safety of embassadors, is however reprobated by all civilized nations—but not more than the modern practice of robbing neutral ships of enemy's property, would be reprobated, were there a common sovereign over nations, to enforce a due respect to the rights of property, as well as of persons.

The idea of Lord Liverpool that the laws of nations only have force on the ocean, is extremely incorrect. They operate with as much force on land, within the territorial jurisdiction of nations, as the municipal institutions. Embassadors, envoys, consuls, and their suits, enjoy precisely the same immunities within the limits of a foreign country, as they do on the ocean; and for an obvious reason, that the laws of nations, which are the principles of morality and political justice, have the same binding force within as without, the particular jurisdiction of a sovereign. On the other hand, each nation has as complete jurisdiction over its property and subjects on the ocean, as within its territorial limits. The jurisdiction of a nation over the seamen of a ship at sea, belonging to its subject, is not held under any law of nations, established and operating on that element; it is derived from its own authority or right over that subject, and from its perfect right to the use of any portion of the ocean, not previously occupied. And this right of any and every nation to the use of the ocean, instead of being derived from the laws of nations, either expressed or implied, existed anterior to any usage or stipulation on the subject. It is a *natural* right of every nation, which no other state can abridge or modify, without its consent. From the common error on this subject, has proceeded the opinion that ships at sea, are less the property or less the castles of an owner, than his house on land. This error is extremely mischievous and ought to be subdued. Has a belligerent the right to enter the house of a neuter on land, and search for his enemy's goods? No, is the answer, and the principle is admitted by all parties. Is the property of a man in his ship less perfect than in his house? Is the jurisdiction of his sovereign less complete and exclusive over the ship on the ocean, than over the house on land? Let the political casuist define and prove the distinction.

But say my opposers, we admit *your* rights, provided you do not abridge *ours*. It is a settled maxim that a man must so use his own rights, as not to impair those of his neighbor. Admitted. But who shall determine the boundaries of our rights? Who shall fix the point where the use of my right *begins* to injure that of another? Shall this important decision be left to *one* of the parties? By no means. What then shall be done, when there is no common arbiter? The mind instinctively suggests the answer, THE POINT MUST BE FIXED BY CONVENTION. This is the answer dictated by justice and by truth. It is a principle which can be neither shaken by argument, nor evaded by sophistry.

This must be the final and important result of every candid investigation of this subject. Particular powers now claim, by virtue of the barbarous, irregular and capricious customs of princes and states, to prescribe the limits of the rights of neutral nations, without their consent. This is an *ex parte* business—we deny the right of the judge to decide, and the validity of the laws on which he pretends to found his decisions.

Every nation has a sovereign right to carry on commerce, not only in its own productions, but in the goods of every other nation, by its agreement or consent. The extent and manner of this intercourse are entirely at the disposal of the parties, whether in peace or war, and are not, in the remotest degree, subject to the control of a third power; unless in the case, where a nation by supplying one belligerent and refusing to supply the other, or by some other act, takes a part in the contest. By natural right, this freedom of trade extends to every species of goods and warlike apparatus, *so long as the supplies are furnished with impartiality to both the warring parties.* Any and every restriction of this natural right, must be by agreement and consent of the party restrained. Every attempt of a third power to restrain that right, is usurpation, and not the less unjust, because it can plead, in its favor, the usages of nations; for in regard to the customs of war, and of intercourse between states, prescription may be claimed in favor of every crime, every breach of morality, and every degree of violence. Once admit the claims of Great Britain to give laws to neutral commerce on the ocean, and the pretensions of France to conquer nations into liberty, and other states have very little left which they can call their own. May the United States never hold their rights, subject to such laws. Not to resist these claims would be to consent to national degradation; to admit their validity, would be to surrender the rights of sovereignty and independence.

# CHAPTER III.

## ON THE SUPPOSED CHANGE IN THE TEMPERATURE OF WINTER.*

It is a popular opinion that the temperature of the winter season, in northern latitudes, has suffered a material change, and become warmer in modern, than it was in ancient times. This opinion has been adopted and maintained by many writers of reputation; as the Abbé Du Bos, Buffon, Hume, Gibbon, Jefferson, Holyoke, Williams; indeed I know not whether any person, in this age, has ever questioned the fact.†

The arguments to prove that the winters, in ancient times, were far colder than at present, are the following. First, in regard to Palestine or Judea.

It is said that several passages in the Scriptures, written as early as the days of Moses and David, speak of snow, hail, ice, and hoar-frost, as common in those ages, where no such thing is now known. "He giveth snow like wool; he scattereth the hoar-frost like ashes. He casteth forth his ice like morsels; who can stand before his cold? The face of the deep was frozen," &c.

The passages in Job which mention snow, hail, ice and frost, are numerous. Dr. Williams supposes, with many others, that the book of Job was written by Moses; and that the descriptions refer to the land of Midian or Palestine, about the latitude of 30° or 31° north. He supposes also, that to produce solid ice on rivers, to answer to the descriptions, a degree of cold is necessary, corresponding with 25° by Fahrenheit. This he concludes to have been the extremity of cold, in the land of Midian, in the age of Moses.

The writings of David mention ice in the form of "morsels," or crystals, which Dr. Williams has observed to be congealed in a temperature of about 31° by Fahrenheit. On the strength of this single circumstance, he concludes that the climate, in about four hundred years, between Moses and David, had become warmer by six degrees.

I am really surprised to observe on what a slight foundation, a divine and philosopher has erected this theory. In the first place, we have no evidence that Moses wrote the book of Job; on the contrary, there is strong evidence that he was not the author.

Critics are not all agreed whether that book describes a series of facts, or is a species of dramatic composition, intended to represent the vicissitudes of life, and the human passions. Respectable and pious men are found on both sides of this question.

---

* Read before the Connecticut Academy of Arts and Sciences, 1799.
† Hume's Essays, Vol. I, 457, Ess. xi.—Gibbon's Hist. Vol. I, ch. ix.—Williams' Hist. of Vermont, p. 63, first ed., and appendix, No. 2.—Jefferson's Notes, query 7.—Memoirs of Amer. Acad. Vol. II, part i, 70.—Pelloutier's Hist. des Celtes, liv. xii.—Cyclopedia, by Rees, Art. *Climate.*

But it is not very material as to the present argument.   It is sufficient for my purpose, that the *scene* of that book is expressly laid in the land of Uz, near Chaldea, which is in that part of Arabia, called the Desert, extending from Syria and Judea, to Chaldea on the east, and the Euphrates on the north.*   Now, we have strong evidence that Moses was never in that country.   He was born in Egypt ; he afterward fled to Midian, then returned to Egypt, to deliver his countrymen from their bondage ; but was not permitted to go further north than Mount Nebo, in the land of Moab, over against Jericho, just upon the borders of Judea, and this but a short time before his death.

It is very evident that Moses had never before seen that country, because he was directed to ascend the mount, and take a view of the lands destined to be the residence of the Israelites—a circumstance that plainly indicates his former ignorance of the country, which could not have been the case, had he ever dwelt in Uz, to the north and east of Judea ; for in that case he must have passed through this country.

Nor is it at all probable that the writer of that book would lay the scene of it in a counry of which he was ignorant.   Every circumstance tends to prove that the writer knew the country, its climate and productions ; and the frequent mention of snow, ice and frost in Job is the highest evidence that the author had lived in a region where these substances were common and well known.   If we suppose the writer to have lived in Judea, or in the northern parts of Arabia Deserta, the situation of Uz, he must have seen snow and ice every winter ; but Moses probably had little or no knowledge of them.   In Midian and Egypt, where he had spent his days, they rarely occurred ; and in the five books, supposed to be of his writing, there are scarcely two or three references to snow or frost.   In the 31st chapter of Genesis, Jacob is represented as complaining to Laban that he had served him twenty years, enduring drouth by day and frost by night ; but this was in Padan-haran, to the northward of Jerusalem.   In Exodus, xvi, 14, the manna in the wilderness is compared to hoar-frost ; and in the 6th chapter, a leprous hand is compared to snow.   But in all the acknowledged writings of Moses, there is not the least evidence that ice was ever seen in Egypt, except in the time of the ten plagues, and in the form of hail.   The silence of those early records, on this point, is no small argument, that the climate of Egypt was then as warm as it is at this day.   Hail has been sometimes seen in that country, as it is in many other parts of the world where there is no weather cold enough to congeal water on the earth.†

Instead therefore of proving that snow and ice were formerly common in Midian and Palestine, the frequent mention of these substances in Job, is almost conclusive evidence that Moses was not the author. That book, which is an excellent description of human nature, was unquestionably written by some person, either in Uz, or in the northern parts of Judea, where ice, frost and snow were then, and are now, an-

---

* Sir William Jones has remarked, that the book of Job, from the language, must have been written by a man of Arabian extract.—(Asiatic Researches.) Bochart, from Hieronymus, observes that Job must have been well versed in Arabic.—(Geog. Sac., cap. 15.)

† See an account of a hail-storm in Africa—Hirtius Pansa de Bello Afric. 42.

nually seen on the mountains. " If I wash myself in snow water, and make my hands never so clean," says Job, chapter 9th; which is a description that would not answer for Egypt or Midian,* but answers well to the greatest part of Judea. " The sweet influences of Pleiades," mentioned in the 38th chapter, allude doubtless to the spring rains, which fell in Judea about the rising of that constellation, which, in Pliny's time, happened near the vernal equinox, but which, fifteen hundred years earlier, must, by the precession of the equinox, have happened about the first of March. This circumstance answers well to the climate of Syria, but not at all to that of Egypt, where the rising of that constellation was the most sickly and disagreeable time in the year. The former and latter rain, mentioned also in that book, indicate that it was descriptive of the climate of Syria and Judea; for the success of agriculture did then, as it does now, depend entirely on the autumnal and spring rains. This division of rainy seasons however did not exist in Egypt; it was used only in Syria and Italy, and perhaps in Greece. Every circumstance that occurs to my view, in regard to the book of Job, tends to prove that Moses could not have been the author; and most of the Jewish Rabbins have been of this opinion. Certain it is, from internal evidence, that the scene of it was laid in a country much colder than Midian, or the champaign country of Palestine; for Herodotus, in Euterpe, expressly declares that no ice was seen in Egypt; and, in another passage, that the climate is subject to no variations.

Let us then attend to the process by which Dr. Williams attempts to prove a change of climate in Palestine.

He *presumes* Moses wrote the book of Job—that the descriptions of ice and snow refer to the land of Midian and Palestine, and therefore that the winter, in those early ages, must have been severe enough to freeze solid ice, which, he says, requires a temperature of about 25° by Fahrenheit. He has no meteorological observations for Palestine, but presumes the climate to be nearly the same, as to heat, with that of Egypt. Mr. Niebuhr's observations in Grand Cairo in 1761–2, make the mean heat of January 57°, and of February 63°—the coldest weather therefore he supposes to be about 49° by Fahrenheit. Hence, if Palestine and Egypt have nearly a similar climate, he draws the conclusion that in modern days, " no ice or snow is ever seen in Palestine."

This inference is drawn from a very inaccurate view of the subject. The facts with regard to Palestine at this day, are these.

The whole country comprehended between Aleppo on the north, the Mediterranean on the west, and the barren plains of Arabia on the south and east, is divided into high hills, mountains and plains. Palestine on the south, is a level plain, and a very warm country. The thermometer in winter is seldom seen below 50°. If snow ever falls, it is speedily dissolved. In this mild climate, which extends along the Mediterranean shore, the orange, date, banana, and other delicate trees flourish, without injury from the winter's cold. Little fire is necessary for the inhabitants; instead of fire, which is sometimes wanted

* I speak of the Midian near the Arabic Gulf, where Moses lived, with his father-in-law; not of Midian on the borders of Judea.

during the cool rains of winter, the poor people shut up their cattle under the same roof with themselves, in a different apartment, and re-ceive heat enough from their bodies to make themselves comfortable. Such is the present climate of the plains.

But a great part of Syria and Judea consists of mountains, which are every winter covered with snow ; and often the earth is covered, for months, to the depth of several feet. The mountains from Aleppo to Jerusalem, are covered with snow every winter ; and when the snow melts, the Jordan overflows its banks. This happens in March ; but on some of the highest hills, as Mount Lebanon and Akkar, the snow is seen till the middle of summer. This was the fact in 1784, when Volney visited that country. See his Travels, from which these facts are extracted. This author further observes, that on the east of the mountains, the cold is more rigorous than on the sea-coast ; and at Aleppo, Antioch and Damascus, are several weeks of frost and snow every winter. The inhabitants of the mountains leave their habitations, which are buried in snow, in winter, and pass the season at Tripoli, on the sea-coast.*

The principal part of Judea, or the Holy Land, lies on the east side of the mountains, and experiences snow, frost and ice every winter. What shall we say then to the assertion of Dr. Williams, that in Pales-tine, " snow and ice are never seen" in modern days.

In Syria and Palestine, wheat and barley are sown in autumn, about the last week in October ; the time of the autumnal rains. Harvest, in the plains, is in April and May. On the mountains, it is in June and July. Spring crops are planted in March and April.†

Common winters therefore in Judea are mild in the plains, but cold on the hills. That country however is subject, like others, to severe winters, which prove destructive to men and vegetables. The poverty of the great body of the people, and the mildness of ordinary winters, prevent the same preparations to defend against cold, which are made in more northern latitudes. In 1741–2, the winter in Syria was very severe ; and that of 1756–7 sunk the mercury into the bulb, at Aleppo ; multitudes of vines were killed, as were olives that had stood fifty years. Many of the poorer people perished with cold. In winters like that, I presume, ice is formed in the mildest regions of Palestine.— (See Lond. Mag. 1764.)

That ordinary winters were far less severe, is obviously inferable from Exod. xxxv, 3. " Ye shall kindle no fire throughout your habitations upon the sabbath day"—an injunction which had reference to all sea-

---

* " Will a man leave the *snow of Lebanon*."—(Jer. xviii, 14.) Shaw, in his Travels, p. 362, says, Mount Libanus, in winter, is covered with snow ; and p. 363, that snow at Jerusalem, in February, causes great rejoicings. He mentions that snow fell at Cairo, Jan. 10, 1639.

† If the *byssus* of the ancient Egyptians was really cotton, as the commentators on Herodotus assert, then cotton must have been the produce of Egypt, from the earliest times, as the bandages in which mummies were wrapped, consisted of that article.—(Beloe's Herod. Euterpe, 86, note.)

When Ezra returned from the captivity, and set about reforming the abuses of marriage among the Jews, he assembled the men of Judah and Benjamin, on the 20th day of the 9th month, and it was a time of great *rain*. This was about the 10th or 12th of December.—(Ez. x, 9.)

sons of the year; and which could not have been given in a climate where fire was indispensable to the health and comfort of the inhabitants.

But the most positive evidence which can possibly exist to prove that the climate of Palestine has *not* suffered any increase of heat, for more than three thousand years, is the production of certain fruits in the days of David, which will not thrive in any but mild, warm countries; as pomegranates, olives and figs. The trees producing these fruits are so often mentioned in Scripture, that it would be idle to name the instances. They were in Judea in the time of Moses in the greatest abundance; for the spies sent to explore the country, returned with pomegranates and figs.—(Numb. xiii, 23.)

We know precisely the degree of heat necessary to bring these fruits to perfection; that is, a climate as mild as South Carolina and Georgia. Figs and olives grow well in Virginia, says Mr. Jefferson, but are liable to be killed by frost. We then ascertain beyond all controversy, that Palestine, in the days of Moses, was as warm a country as South Carolina and Georgia are in this age.

The palm-tree furnishes, also, a most clear and incontestible proof of the same fact. This tree will grow and bear fruit, says Pliny, in the maritime parts of Spain, but the dates have not the fine flavor of those which are produced in Judea. In Europe, for instance in Italy, they are barren. In Africa they come to perfection, but soon perish. " Judea vero inclyta est vel magis palmis," says that author ;—Judea is particularly renowned for palm-trees or dates.—(Lib. 13, cap. 4.)

These trees were not introduced and cultivated first in Judea by the Jews. The Israelites, when they migrated from Egypt, found palm-trees in the neighborhood of Jericho, and in the plains of Moab, in all their glory. Jericho is called the city of palm-trees, (Deut. xxxiv, 3 ;) and the word itself, in the Ethiopic, signifies a palm-tree.—(Ludolf's Lexicon, col. 37.)

No man will be skeptical enough to deny a uniformity in the laws of the vegetable economy. We have then *certain proof* that Palestine, more than three thousand years ago, was a milder climate than Italy, milder than the south of France, as mild as the coast of Africa, at that time, and milder than South Carolina at this day.

Another remarkable fact is decisive of this question. The Jewish month האביב *Abib*, was named from the ripeness of barley in Palestine and Egypt, at that season ; the word signifying fullness or ripeness from the *swelling* from the grain. *Abib* answers to the latter part of March and the beginning of April, which was the time of harvest in the earliest ages. Now this is the precise time of harvest in modern days.*

The facts above enumerated solve all questions as to the ancient climate of Judea and Egypt. Frost, snow, and ice were annually seen on the hills and mountains of Palestine, and were perfectly well known to writers among the Jews ; hence the justness of the descriptions in Job and other parts of the Old Testament. In hard winters, these phenomena must have been extended over the plains, along the banks of

---

* See Shaw's Travels, pp. 364, 430, folio. Niebuhr's Travels, sect. 28, ch. 3. Park. Lex., under אב.

Jordan ; and perhaps on the sea-coast.    But the plains in common years must have been very mild and warm.    All this is precisely the state of the climate in Palestine, in the present age.

Confirmatory and decisive of this inference is the fact, that from the earliest records of history, the inhabitants of Judea constructed their houses with flat roofs, as they do at this day, on which they not only amused themselves during the day, but erected altars, offered incense, and performed other pagan rites to the deities of the country ; and we have the express authority of the Scriptures to prove that as early as the days of Samuel, it was customary to sleep on the tops of the houses, as it is at this day.—(See Deut. xxii, 8 ; Josh. ii, 6 ; Judges xvi, 27 ; Jer. xix, 13 ; Zeph. i, 5 ; Dan. iv, 29 ; 1 Sam. ix, 25, 26.)

In winter, it was not unusual to kindle fires in Judea.    Thus we find Jehoiakim sat by a fire in the *ninth* month, Chisleu, which answers to a part of our November and December, (Jer. xxxvi, 22 ;) and Dr. Russel informs us that at Aleppo, they begin to kindle fires about the end of November.—(Nat. Hist. of Aleppo, p. 14.    Parkhurst, 330, under כסל.)

Dr. Williams proceeds to prove that the winters in Italy have, in about eighteen centuries, became warmer by seventeen degrees on Fahrenheit's scale.    His proofs are, that Virgil in many places of his Georgics, has given directions for securing cattle and sheep from the effects of snow and cold—that Virgil, Pliny, Juvenal and Ælian speak of ice, snow, and the freezing of rivers, as events common and annual.    But he observes, that in 1782–3, the mean temperature at Rome in January was 46°, and the mean of the greatest cold 42°, which is 17° less cold than what is necessary for the freezing of rivers.

The Abbé du Bos, Hume, and others alledge, in proof of the same doctrine, the following facts.    In the year of Rome 480, the winter was so severe as to kill the trees—the Tiber was frozen, and the ground was covered with snow for forty days.    Juvenal describes a superstitious woman as breaking the ice of the Tiber to perform her ablutions.

> " Hybernam fracta glacie descendet in amnem,
>   Ter matutino Tiberi mergetur."—(Sat. vi, 521.)

Horace also, says the Abbé, speaks of the streets of Rome as full of ice and snow.    These authors, it is alledged, speak of these as common events.    But, says the Abbé, " at present the Tiber no more freezes at Rome, than the Nile at Cairo."[*]

Dr. Holyoke mentions the description of the severe winter A. U. C. 536, in the second Punic war, when the siege of a town in Spain, near the present Barcelona, was obstructed by snow, which lay for thirty days to the depth of four feet.—(See Memoirs of Am. Acad. Vol. II, p. 70.)

From these representations, it is concluded that Italy has now a much more temperate climate than at and before the Christian era.    Let us examine this point.

Dr. Holyoke gives us the mean of the greatest cold at Rome, deduced from several years' observations, within the last half century ; which is 33°.46, a little above freezing point.    The greatest cold is

---

[*] I cite this from Hume, Ess. xi.

stated at 31°.  If we admit this statement to be correct, then Dr. Williams has stated the extreme cold in Rome almost nine degrees too high; of course we must deduct *nine* degrees from his seventeen degrees of alteration, in eighteen centuries, which is a very material difference.

This we must do, and more.  For Brydone, in the winter of 1769–70, found the greatest cold at Rome in January to be 27°, a degree capable of covering large rivers with a thin coat of ice.  That winter was perhaps colder than usual; but by no means of the severest kind.  At Naples, says Brydone, we had rainy weather; at Rome it was clear and *frosty.*  That winter then would at Rome produce all the phenomena of ice, frost, and snow, to answer the description of the Latin writers of the Augustan age.

If the mean temperature of the winter's cold at Rome is now about 33°, it is not more than eight degrees milder weather than in New England; for Dr. Holyoke found, by seven years' observations, that the mean winter temperature at Salem, in Massachusetts, is 25°.74.

I know not the position of the thermometer by which the observations at Rome were made.  But I would remark that, if those observations were made in the city, they do not represent the general temperature of Italy.  I found by numerous observations in New York, that ice as thick as glass in our windows, was uniformly made at a mile's distance from the city, when an accurate thermometer in the coldest positions *in* the city stood at 40°.  Such is the difference between the real temperature of an open country, and the artificial one of a city.  The same difference will not run through the observations of the whole year, but it will amount to two or three degrees.  I am inclined to believe this to be the source of great errors, in comparing meteorological observations in different countries.

If the ordinary winter temperature at Rome is near the freezing point, we are at no loss to account for the snow and ice of Italy in ancient times.  In all countries, and in every latitude, hills and mountains are cooler than plains.  This difference is according to the difference of altitude; but between Rome, in a plain, near the sea, and the Apennines, it can not be less than from six to ten degrees.  Thus while at Rome, and in Campania generally, the weather is mild, and exhibits little or no ice, the whole ridge of mountains between Tuscany and Naples, that region of Italy which furnished the pasturage, and for which the directions in Virgil's Georgics were intended, is covered with snow, and experiences severe frosts.  This was not only the fact in Virgil's time, but is so at this day.  Mr. Arthur Young, a distinguished agriculturist, traveled in Italy in November and December, 1789.  In passing the Apennines, between Florence and Bologna, the first days of December, he found the hills almost covered with snow; and the roads, on some declivities, a sheet of ice.  On the 26th of November, the weather was so severe as to freeze Cyprus wine, and milk burst the vessels that contained it.  In Lombardy, he found the peasantry at night, sitting in a passage between their cattle, in the stables, to keep themselves warm; a practice resembling that in Palestine, already mentioned.*

---

* Young's Tour, Vol. I, p. 516; Dub. 1793.

It is well known also, that the higher regions of Mount Etna in Sicily, a far milder climate than that of Italy, are perpetually covered with snow.

That the descriptions of ice and snow, in the Augustan age, allude principally to the hilly country, is very obvious from the writings of Virgil, Horace, and Pliny.

Virgil, in his first Georgic, speaks of the zephyrs dissolving the earth, and bringing moisture from the *whitened hills.*

Horace, in his ninth ode, mentions deep snow on Mount Soracte, in Etruria, about twenty-six miles north of Rome.

Pliny, in the nineteenth book of his Natural History, is more explicit on this subject. Speaking of the luxury of his days, he says, " Hi nives, illi glaciem potant ; pœnasque montium in voluptatem gulæ vertunt ;"—some drink snow, others ice ; and the evil or scourge of the mountains is converted into a gratification of the palate. This passage leaves no room to question, that the ice and snow used in Rome were ordinarily brought from the mountains, where they were considered as a calamity ; and the expression " pœnasque montium," clearly indicate that they were almost peculiar to the mountains.

Virgil directs the husbandman to plow in the first months in the year, and to pray for moist summers, and serene winters ; for, says the author, the *winter's dust* increases the crop. This passage is no inconsiderable proof that the earth in some parts of Italy was not usually covered with snow in winter.

The winters described by Livy, when the Tiber was covered with solid ice ; when the snow lay in the streets of Rome for forty days ; and in Spain, was four feet deep for thirty days ; when men, cattle, and trees perished, were singularly severe, like our modern winters of 1642, 1709, 1741, 1780, which happen but two or three times in a century. Any man will be convinced of this, who attends to the description of them in the original authors. I find they happen in modern days, as frequently as at any former period. Scarcely three or four such winters are described in the whole history of Rome, down to the age of Julius Cesar ; though many others happened, as may be collected from circumstances.

The severe winter of the year of Rome 354, is expressly declared by Livy to be a remarkable event. " *Insignis* annus hieme gelida ac nivosa fuit ; adeo ut viæ clausæ, Tiberis innavigabilis fuerit."—(Lib. 5, 13.) He calls it also " tristem hiemem ;" and it was followed by terrible pestilence. Nothing can be more clear, than that such a winter was an extraordinary occurrence. Without considering it in this light, the word " insignis" has no meaning ; and instead of proving the usual temperature of winter at Rome to have been severe, it is the strongest evidence to prove that the winters were *generally* mild, and the Tiber navigable in the winter months. Had this been a common winter, or any thing like it, it would not have been singled out by the historian as a subject of remark. This explanation is applicable to all the instances of cold winters, described by historians. Even the passage in Juvenal, if it proves any thing, confirms the opinion that the frost, in ·his days, was not ordinarily very severe. The circumstance of a woman's breaking the ice in the morning, to bathe in the Tiber, indicates that the ice was usually thin and easily broken; and by no means admits the supposition of ice a foot thick, like that which covers our rivers. It supposes a thickness of ice which is often seen on the Tiber at this day, frozen in the night, and dissolved the next day.

All the Roman writers speak of severe winters, by way of distinction. Virgil says, "sin duram metues hiemem"—if you apprehend a hard winter. And Horace attempts to dissuade Augustus from his design of resigning the empire, by describing the severe cold, snow, and hail of the winter, which he represents as prodigies, and evidences of the resentment of the gods. The winter to which he refers was probably of unusual severity. I apprehend the great source of error on this subject has been, that the moderns have taken for representations of ordinary winters, those which were intended for a few rare occurrences. Certain it is that the common winters of Italy were not severe, but mild. This I will demonstrate by a series of evidence, drawn from the phenomena of the natural world, which can not deceive us in regard to climate.

Pliny, in his Natural History, lib. 2, 47, has given us an account of the winds in Italy. Among other things, he informs us directly that the "spring opens the navigation of the seas, in the beginning of which Favonius, the west wind, mitigates the severity of winter, about the time when the sun enters the 25th degree of Aquarius. That time is the 6th day before the ides of February." This was the 8th day of the month, and this was accounted the beginning of spring. Virgil, in his third Georgic, confirms this declaration of Pliny, and speaks of the commencement of the rainy season, that is, the spring rains, about the last of January.

> " Cum frigidus olim
> Jam cadit, extremoque irrotat Aquarius anno"—

when cold Aquarius now sets and sprinkles his dews, at the close of the year. This refers to the old Roman year which ended the last of February, the month when Aquarius set. The name of this sign indicates that the season was *rainy ;* and the testimony of both these authors concurs, in proof that the winter was considered at an end, the beginning of February.

Aquilo, the northeast wind, began to blow about the setting of Pleiades or the seven stars, which was near the 3d of the ides of November, answering to the 10th day of the month.—(Pliny, lib. 2, 47.*) This was the introduction of cool weather. The Septentrio, or north wind from the Alps, was the coldest wind, and blew mostly in December and January.

Severe winter weather set in about the last week in December. The halcyon days were seven days before, and as many after, the winter solstice, when the kingfisher was said to tranquillize the sea. This period of mild or calm weather, seems to have resembled our " Indian

---

* By the precession of the equinoxes, that constellation now sets about three weeks later, or the first week in December. But our modern calendar corresponds nearly with the Julian calendar in Pliny's time. The name *Aquarius*, given by the Romans to the sign which the sun passes in the midst of winter, demonstrates that rain and not snow, predominated as the characteristic of that month.

summer," a period of fine weather that often happens just before winter. The fable of the halcyon days is no inconsiderable proof, that the winter did not set in with rigor till after the winter solstice.

But the best evidence of the true temperature of the climate of Italy, and the course of the seasons, is that which arises from the time of vegetation. This is infallible evidence.

Pliny relates, Nat. Hist. lib. 16, cap. 25, that spring began with the blowing of Favonius. This time is expressly fixed to have been the 8th of February. Pliny calls it the " genial breath of the world." This author informs us that some vegetables germinated on the first blowing of this wind. " Primo Favonio germinat cornus, proximus laurus, pauloque ante æquinoctium tilia, acer ;"—the cornelian cherry germinates on the first blowing of the west wind ; afterward the laurel, and a little before the equinox, the lime tree and the maple.

In the 5th chapter of the 18th book, he says, " some persons prefer planting gourds about the first of March, and cucumbers about the nones," or middle of the month. In the 34th chapter of the same book, he says, " Favonius begins the spring ; it opens the earth, being moderately cool and salubrious. It directs the husbandman to prune his vines, to take care of his corn, to plant trees, to graft apples, and tend his olives."

Spring radishes, says the same author, are to be sown after the ides of February ; but this plant, he adds, is so fond of cold weather, that in Germany it grows to the size of a *little boy*. Gardens are to be plowed, according to the same author, about the ides, the 13th of February.

Horace, book i, ode 4, expressly says, that spring begins by the favor of Favonius, when the cattle no longer seek their stalls, the husbandman his fireside, nor are the meadows any longer whitened with frost.—(Varro, de Re Rustica, lib. 1, 28.)

These facts indicate a moderate climate, like that of the Carolinas and Georgia in America ; and they could not be true of a climate where common winters were long and severe.

The real temperature of Italy is ascertained precisely by the olive and other plants, that we know will not bear severe frost, and will not thrive and come to perfection, but in warm climates.

The olive-tree has been known in Greece from time immemorial. (See Theophrast's History of Plants, lib. 4, 5, and notes.) At what time it was introduced into Italy, is not recorded. Fenestella, says Pliny, relates that in the age of Tarquinius Priscus, the olive was not known in Italy, Spain, or Africa. It was however cultivated in all parts of Italy, in Spain and Gaul, long before the Christian era.—(Plin. Nat. Hist. lib. 15, cap. 1.)

We have then the data to ascertain the ancient climate of Italy with great precision. In our country, olives will grow well in Virginia, but frosts are too frequent and severe to permit their cultivation, to any valuable purpose. In South Carolina, they are cultivated to advantage. Italy then has had, from very early ages, a climate as mild as that of South Carolina.

The fig seems to have been a native of Italy. Plutarch, in his life of Romulus, tells us that Romulus and Remus were found under a fig-tree, where they were nourished by a wolf. Whether this was true or not, it is certain that the Romans paid a particular veneration to a fig-tree that was in the forum,—" ob memoriam ejus, quæ nutrix fuit Rom-uli et Remi conditoris appellata," says Pliny, lib. 15, 18. If the fig-tree is a native of Italy, the climate could never have been colder than the Carolinas in America. This evidence is incontestable, and it totally overthrows the modern hypothesis of the severity of the winters in an-cient Italy. It is needless to swell this argument, by mentioning many other fruits, as dates, pomegranates and others, that will not thrive in cold climates.

The same plants grew and produced abundantly in Thessaly and Macedonia; although the ancients represented the latter as a cold coun-try. It was doubtless colder than Greece, perhaps colder than Italy; but certainly could not be much colder than the Carolinas in America.\*

The time of sowing corn in Italy, is a confirmation of what is here advanced. Virgil directs the husbandman to sow barley between the autumnal equinox and the winter solstice. Wheat was not to be sown till the last of October, and those who sowed earlier were disappointed of a good harvest.—(Georgic 1.) These facts all correspond with each other, and demonstrate that the climate of Italy was then mild, and nearly as mild as it is at present. The time of sowing wheat, it will be observed, was the same as in Palestine. Severe winters often occur now, as they did two thousand years ago. Several winters are on record within a few centuries, in which vines and trees perished with cold. The winter of 1709 killed trees in Italy; as did that of 1757 in Syria. I can name a number of such winters within three or four hundred years.

No longer ago than 1788–9, the winter was so severe in Europe, that the rivers in Estremadura in Spain, and in Alantajo in Portugal, two southern provinces, and of the mildest climate, were covered with ice; and the mountains of Asturia, Leon and Biscay were covered with deep snow, as late as the 6th of March. (See the gazettes of the year 1789.) It should be remarked that Barcelona, near which the Romans found snow four feet deep, as already related, is in the north-ern part of Spain.

Dr. Williams, as a further evidence of a mitigation of the cold in modern winters, mentions the present state of the climate round Con-stantinople and the Euxine Sea, compared with Ovid's description of it in his days. Ovid was banished to Tomos, near the Euxine, in lat. 44°, about the 7th year of the Christian era, and died there in the 15th year, or perhaps the 16th. He mentions that the Euxine was covered with ice, which was a highway for man and beast, and that wine was offered to him in a state of congelation. All this might be true at the time he was at Tomos, and even frequently true, without supposing the climate essentially different from what it is at present. But when Ovid asserts that the snow, in some places, was not dissolved during the sum-mer, we must understand him to refer to snow on the high mountains; for all history testifies that the country about the Euxine, and far north,

---

\* Herodotus, in Thalia, speaks of the seasons in Greece as " agreeable and tem-perate."—(Sect. 106.)

was, in Ovid's time, and long before, a fine grazing and corn country. Both Ovid and Virgil, when they speak of the Scythian country, as being always clothed with snow, must have intended the mountains; and we have the authority of Lady Montague, who traveled through the country along the Danube in 1717, that Mount Hæmus and Rodope are, in modern times, *always covered with snow.*—(Letter 25.)* These mountains are a degree and a half south of Tomos. Surely then we have no reason to think the climate has suffered any considerable alteration.

Dr. Williams mentions the year 401, when the Euxine was covered with ice for twenty days, as an evidence that the climate was formerly colder than at present; and notices the remark of Dr. Smith, in Phil. Trans., No. 152, that the Turks were greatly astonished at the appearance of ice at Constantinople in 1669; [Dr. Williams by mistake has 1667;] and he then adds, "In all the adjacent country, instead of frozen sea, frozen wine, and perpetual snow, they have now a fine moderate warm climate."

Here again Dr. Williams has run into the error before mentioned, of taking the accounts of a few *severe winters* as descriptions of the *ordinary winters.* The winter of 401, in the reign of Honorius, was during the approach of a comet, and was noted for its severity, as an *unusual* occurrence. Any person may observe this, who will consult the original histories. Three hundred and sixty years later, viz. in 762–3, a still more severe winter covered the Euxine with ice and snow of thirty cubits' thickness, which ice at the breaking up of winter, was impelled against the walls of Constantinople and beat down considerable portions of it.† This does not indicate any mitigation of the climate. A similar event happened in the reign of Achmet I, about the year 1613 or 1614, which marked a severe winter and no mitigation of the climate. The winter of 1669, when the Turks were astonished at ice in the Bosphorus, was also severe. These seasons are recorded as *rare occurrences*, and this was the fact in the fourth century, as well as in the seventeenth. Historians have taken no notice of ordinary seasons, either in ancient or modern times; but we are not to estimate the temperature of climates by a few cold winters.

Winters of severe cold still occur in Greece, fully answering to the descriptions of the winters of antiquity. Wheeler, in his Travels, says he was prevented from visiting Mount Hymettus, two miles from Athens, by the snows in February; and found woolen garments hardly sufficient to defend him from the cold of the valleys. The rivers of Thrace also were covered with ice.

Another proof of the decrease of cold, mentioned by Dr. Williams, is that in ancient times, the Alps were almost impassable in winter, on account of the snow and ice; whereas in modern days, they are crossed without uncommon sufferings. This statement is a most unfortunate one for the argument. It is but three years since the French troops suffered incredible hardships in crossing Mount Cenis into Italy, from most violent storms of snow; and the commander boasted in his dis-

---

* See Horace, book ii, ode 25, 26. Ovid, Metam. lib. 2, 222.
† Paul. Diac. lib. 22. Baronius, Vol. IX, 272. Hoveden, 231.

patches to the government, that the republican troops had surmounted obstacles that appeared too great for human efforts. The Alps are now, as in Hannibal's time, subject annually to severe cold, and violent snow storms; although the roads are doubtless better, and render a passage less difficult.

I am however surprised that the difficulties which Hannibal experienced from snow in crossing the Alps, should be mentioned in proof of the severity of the ancient winters; when it is expressly related by Livy, that no sooner had the army reached the foot of the mountains on the Italian side, than the horses and mules were turned out to graze, in a fine country and mild weather.* "Inferiora valles et apricos quosdam colles habent, rivosque prope silvas et jam humano cultu digniora loca. Ibi Jumenta in pabulum missa."—(Liv. lib. **21, 37.**) This was in November. Let us see then whether the climate of the Alps is mitigated.

In 1789, Arthur Young met with a snow storm and freezing weather in the plains of Sardinia on the 13th of December. The next day, the frost was severe, the snow deep, and ice five inches thick, near Alexandria. On the 21st he crossed Mount Cenis, on snow *ten feet deep.* On the 25th he reached Chamberry, and there was a thaw.—(See his Tour in France, Vol. I, 516, 527, 530, 537.) There is not a shadow of reason to suppose the least melioration of that climate within two thousand years.

The next series of facts to prove a great mitigation of the cold in winter, consists of what authors have recorded of ancient Gaul and Germany.

Diodorus Siculus, lib. 4, relates that "Gaul is infested with cold to an extreme degree. In cloudy weather, instead of rain, great snows fall; and in clear weather, it freezes so excessively, that the rivers are covered with bridges of their own substance, over which large armies pass with their baggage and loaded wagons. And there being many rivers in Gaul, the Rhone, the Rhine, &c., almost all of them are frozen over; and it is usual, in order to prevent falling, to cover the ice with chaff and straw."

"North of the Cevennes," says Strabo, "Gaul produces not figs and olives; and vines which have been planted, bear not grapes that will ripen."—(Lib. 4.)

"Colder than a Gallic winter," was used by Petronius as a proverbial expression, says Hume.—(Essays, Vol. I, 459.)

"The Rhine and the Danube," says Gibbon, "were frequently frozen, and capable of sustaining the most enormous weights. The barbarians often chose the winter to transport their armies and cavalry over a vast and solid bridge of ice. *Modern ages have not presented an instance of a like phenomenon.*"—(Vol. I, ch. 9.)

The last assertion of Gibbon is contrary to all historical evidence, and even to facts which took place during that author's life.

In opposition to Gibbon's assertion, I affirm then, that both the Rhine and the Danube have, within three centuries, been frequently covered

---

* The mountains were covered with snow, but the rivers of Italy were not covered with ice. The Po, the Ticino and the Trebia were crossed by bridges.

with ice sufficient to sustain the largest armies that ever issued from the north.

Dr. Williams has copied these remarks of Gibbon; and it is a most unfortunate circumstance for the author and the transcriber, that the very winter after Dr. Williams published his History of Vermont, the French troops crossed the Rhine into Holland *on the ice.* The rivers and canals were all converted into bridges in January, 1795.—(See the speech of citizen Paulus to the provisional convention, January 26; State Papers, Vol. III.) The cold was unusually severe; the event was an uncommon one; but it is one that happens in hard winters, a few of which occur every century.*

It appears by interrogatories made by the Stadtholder on the 18th of January, 1795, to his naval officers, that the Prince could not escape from Holland by any of the rivers of that country—the eastern and western Ems, the Elbe and the Weser, being obstructed by ice.—(State Papers, Vol. III.)

With respect to the other part of Gibbon's assertion, that the barbarians chose the winter season to make inroads into southern countries, because they could pass on the ice, I can readily believe this might have happened many times. From his acquaintance with the original historians, he was certainly well qualified to make the assertion. Some instances of this fact are recorded. I find in Cesar's History of the Gallic War no instance of this sort; but many instances of Roman armies and barbarians crossing the great rivers on bridges. Cesar was obliged to build bridges, at two or three different times, to throw his troops over the Rhine. Had the freezing of that river been an annual event, he would have taken the advantage of a bridge of ice.

That the Rhine did not freeze every winter, we have positive evidence, in the 4th book of the Gallic War. During the winter of the year 55 before the Christian era, two German nations attempted to invade Gaul, but were prevented by the want of boats. They employed a stratagem, and took possession of the boats belonging to the people or nation that inhabited the banks of that river, and by this means passed over, and subsisted for the remaining part of the winter, on the provisions they found on the other side. If the freezing of that river was a very common event, it is singular that Cesar, in all his wars in the adjacent countries, had not one occasion to mention the circumstance.

Cesar, in his 7th book of the Gallic War, mentions a winter campaign he made to quell an insurrection in the south of France. He was obliged to cross Mount Cebenna, now Cevennes, Languedoc, cutting a way through snow six feet deep. From this description of the snow, a superficial reader would draw the conclusion that the climate was intensely cold. Yet this was not the fact; for the river Loire, in the neighborhood, was not frozen so as to sustain troops; and in the siege of the town of Avaricus, Cesar relates that the town was protected by a river and a morass.

The truth is, the mountain where the snow was then six feet deep is high, and is annually covered with deep snow in this age; while the

---

* This event happened so opportunely for the purposes of the French, that even atheists were disposed to admit the existence of a God, for the purpose of arranging this event among the interpositions of heaven in their favor.

plains below enjoy a fine warm climate, that brings figs and olives to perfection. For these facts, I have the authority of Busching, (abridg. Vol. V,) and Arthur Young. Pinkerton describes the snows of these mountains in the following terms. "These mountains are in winter exposed to dreadful snowy hurricanes, called *acirs*, which, in a few hours, obliterate the ravins and even the precipices, and descending to the paths and streets, confine the inhabitants to their dwellings, till a communication can be opened with their neighbors, sometimes in the form of an arch under the vast mass of snow." This surely proves no moderation of the winters in France.

But let us attend to the vegetables which in the Augustan age flourished in Gaul. These, after all, are our safest guides.

Strabo says, Gaul produces not figs and olives north of the Cevennes; and grapes do not come to maturity.*

Diodorus Siculus goes further, and asserts that Gaul produces neither figs nor olives.—(Lib. 5.)

Strabo is correct, as to figs and olives; for they will not come to perfection, at this day, north of the Cevennes.

Diodorus Siculus is an author of less credit, and in the instance before us, we have proof of his inaccuracy.

Pliny, whose authority in this case must be indisputable, expressly mentions the wine made in Auvergne, Languedoc, Dauphiny, Burgundy, and French Compté. "Jam inventa vitis per se in vino picem resipiens Vinnensem agrum nobilitans, Arverno, Sequanoque, et Helvico generibus non pridem illustrata."—(Lib. 14, cap. 1.) This species of vine, he observes, was unknown ninety years before, in the age of Virgil; and consequently was not known to Diodorus Siculus, who was cotemporary with Virgil. Strabo lived somewhat later, and had more correct information. This wine constituted the glory of that part of France formerly inhabited by the Allobroges, now called Dauphiny and Viennois, extending on the east side of the Rhone, from the Lemanic lake to its mouth, and was highly valued at Rome.

Pliny expressly mentions a species of the olive which thrived in Gaul beyond the Alps. "Quæ nunc provenit trans Alpes, quoque, et in Gallias, Hispaniasque medias."—(Lib. 15, 1.)

Strabo says the olive will not produce fruit, to the north of the Cevennes.

It is remarkable that the limits of the olive region, here designated, are precisely those to which that tree is now confined. The line, beyond which olives will not produce fruit, as marked by Arthur Young, begins at the foot of the Pyrenees, in Rousillon, in the forty second degree of latitude, thence runs northeast, through Languedoc, to the southward of the Cevennes, crosses the Rhone at Montelimart, and pursues its direction, near Grenoble, towards Savoy, where it terminates.

---

* It is well known that there are many varieties of grapes, and some far less hardy than others. The Romans might attempt to propagate, in the north of France, some varieties which thrived well in the south, and in Italy, but which would not come to maturity in a climate eight or ten degrees farther north; and from some instances of failure, might conclude that no vines would come to perfection in that country. I believe there are many varieties now cultivated in Italy and Greece, which would not come to perfection in the north of France.

This district then includes part of Rousillon, part of Languedoc, most of Dauphiny, and all Provence. Olives grow and mature there precisely within the limits marked by Strabo and Pliny, and as far as we can judge, not a league further north than they did eighteen hundred years ago.

I am willing to rest the whole argument on this fact. It is possible that the clearing and cultivation of particular places, by removing moisture, may enable the moderns to raise particular plants, as the vine, for example, in those places, where the ancients could not. But I do not find, in history, any evidence that a change of climate generally has carried any of the delicate fruits into latitudes where they did not thrive in the earliest ages. If any climate has become warmer by seventeen degrees, it would admit plants to be removed northward about ten degrees of latitude. For instance, the mean temperature of South Carolina is 66° by Fahrenheit; that in Connecticut, is about 49°, precisely the difference supposed by Dr. Williams to have taken place in the climate of Italy. The difference between the latitudes of Carolina and Connecticut is about ten degrees. Ten degrees of latitude then give seventeen degrees difference of temperature. If then olives grew in the south of France, eighteen centuries ago, and the climate has become warmer by seventeen degrees, olives may have the same temperature now in 53° of latitude, that they formerly had in 43°. Of course they would thrive in Westphalia, Saxony and Prussia. Instead of which that tree is limited to Dauphiny and Languedoc, as it was at the Christian era.

The Roman writers speak of Gaul as a cold country. It certainly was colder than Italy, Greece, Africa, and Syria, the countries which were visited by the Romans, before they crossed the Alps. Accustomed to those mild climates, they were surprised at the rigorous winters of Gaul and Germany. They described the mountains of Thrace also, as covered with eternal snow; yet Thrace was a fine country, and vines flourished on the borders of the Hellespont. The mountains were cold in winter, in Italy, Gaul, and Thrace; but the growth of certain delicate plants, in those countries, is a better criterion of the real temperature of the climates, than the descriptions of poets and historians.

The winters in Gaul were colder than in England, according to the express testimony of Cæsar.—(Lib. 5.) So they are at this day. If the general temperature of Europe has moderated in eighteen hundred years, Britain, though an island, must have shared in the mitigation of cold. Yet we can not admit any considerable change on that island; for Tacitus, Life of Agricola, 12, expressly declares that it enjoyed a moderate climate in his days,—"Asperitas frigoris abest." The mean temperature of England now is about 48°. If the cold has moderated within eighteen centuries, as much as Dr. Williams supposes it has in other European countries, the climate formerly must have been intolerably cold, contrary to the testimony of Tacitus.

Another argument in favor of a great mitigation of cold in Europe, used by Buffon, and copied by Gibbon and Dr. Williams, is the retirement of the Rane* (deer) from the south of Europe, the Pyrenees and

---

* This is the true name of this animal, by an egregious corruption called rein-deer.

the forests of Germany, into the colder regions of Norway and Russia. Buffon asserts that this animal will not multiply and can not subsist, south of the Baltic.

I consider this argument as very fallacious. The rane seeks the forest, and flies before the ax of the cultivator, like the bear, the common deer, and the Indian of America. How can the deer subsist in open fields? We might as well expect a fish to live in air, as the rane in a country destitute of woods, and frequented by man. The Hyrcanian forest no longer exists; the husbandman has deprived that animal of his shelter, his food, his element. He does not like the company of man, and has abandoned the cultivated parts of Europe. It is just so with the common deer of North America, the bear, and other wild animals. The deer used to be found along our sea-coast, and on the neighboring islands; but for fifty miles from the shore, at this day, not a deer is to be found;* and in a century, not a bear nor a deer will be seen on the south of the lakes. But will any man ascribe this desertion of the country to their love of cold? Not at all. It is their love of the wild forest, and not of cold, which impels them to recede before the arts of cultivation. How could the rane subsist in an open, cultivated country, when it is well known that his favorite food is a species of lichen [rangiferinus] which grows only or chiefly on heaths and uncultivated hilly grounds? Instead of proving a change of climate, the retirement of the rane seems to have been the natural consequence of cultivation.†

But Gibbon's assertion that the Rhine and the Danube, in modern ages, have not been covered with ice, strong enough to sustain loaded carriages, must not pass uncontradicted. I know not what ages precisely, that author intended to include in the description of *modern*; but both the rivers mentioned have *often* sustained men and carriages on the ice within the *last two centuries*, as well as in preceding ages. In 821 and 994, history expressly mentions this to have been the fact. In 1233, the rivers in Italy sustained the heaviest loads on the ice; of course the Rhine and Danube must have done the same. The fact is also recorded of the year 1306; and in 1363 the Rhine was covered with solid ice for ten weeks. In 1402 the Baltic was passable on the ice for six weeks; and we may well suppose the Rhine and Danube were not open. I have no particular account of the effects of the rigorous cold of 1608, 1610, 1664, 1684, 1698, 1709, 1716, 1740, 1763, 1776, on those particular rivers; but the general accounts describe these and many other winters, during the last two centuries, as converting *all* rivers into highways for carriages, even as far south as Italy and Spain. But I have better proof of the fact. It is well known that the winters in England are *much milder* than in the same latitude on the continent. This is always the case, and an undeniable fact. Now I have accounts that the Thames at London has been covered with solid ice, equal to the support of the heaviest loads, not only in most of the

* These animals found shelter in the immense barren plain on Long Island; and are not yet driven from that spot by the hunters.

† King Alfred, in relating the story of Octher, who seems to have been a native of Sweden or Lapland, mentions six hundred ranes as a part of his wealth, and speaks of the animal as if he had never before heard of it.—(Alf. Oros. lib. 1.)

years mentioned, but in many others, during the last two centuries. From ten to fifteen or twenty rigorous winters occur, in every century, which convert most of the *small* rivers of Germany, France and England into highways ; and several winters, in every century, produce the same effect in all the *large* rivers.

No longer ago than 1717, when Lady Montague traveled from Vienna to Constantinople, in the midst of winter, the navigation of the Danube was interrupted by the ice. In a letter dated at Belgrade, Feb. 12, O. S. 1717, that lady says : " The weather is colder than I believe it ever was any where but in Greenland : we have a very large stove constantly kept hot, and yet the windows of the room are frozen on the inside." Between the date of that letter and the first of April, O. S. she pursued her journey to Adrianople, during which time, that is in March, she expressly says, " The Danube was now frozen over."— (See her Letter of April 1.)

This was not a winter of the greatest severity, though in England something colder than ordinary.—(See Short on Air, Vol. II, 20.) The preceding winter had converted all rivers into bridges, even in Italy. What shall we then say to the assertions of such celebrated men as Gibbon ? and what shall we think of the modern philosophy, erected on the authority of a few superficial inquiries ?

The climate at Constantinople is milder than on the Danube ; and in January, 1718, Lady Montague sat with her window open, enjoying a fine warm sun.—(Letter 38.) But this was an uncommon occurrence. In 1751, the people of Constantinople predicted the plague which raged terribly that year, from the *great snows of the preceding winter.*— (Chenier's Morocco, Vol. II, 275.) Indeed one single fact will demonstrate that the air at Constantinople is usually in winter below freezing point ; which is, that winter always puts an end to the ravages of the plague—an event that rarely, if ever, takes place there without frost. But Constantinople is subject also to severe frosts, in hard winters, like all other northern countries ; although the weather there, from the vicinity of the city to large bodies of water, is much less severe than in Hungary, Austria and Germany.

Men are led into numberless errors by drawing *general* conclusions from *particular* facts. " Lady Montague sat with her window open in January, 1718, and therefore there is little or no winter in Constantinople," is very bad logic. The farmers on Connecticut River plowed their lands, as I saw, in February, 1779 ; and the peaches blossomed in Pennsylvania. What then ? Are the winters all mild in America ? Not at all ; in the very next year, not only our rivers, but our bays, and the ocean itself, on our coast, were fast bound with ice.

In 1592, the drouth was so severe that the Thames was fordable at London. In 1388, the Rhine was fordable at Cologne ; and in 1473, the Danube was fordable in Hungary. Suppose in some future age, these facts. should be alledged as evidence of a wonderful increase of rains and moist weather, within the two last centuries ; would such conclusions be just ? Yet this is the reasoning which has principally supported the hypothesis of a modern diminution of cold in winter. Authors have mentioned and described the severe winters, while ordinary seasons have passed unnoticed ; and this is the source of a great error in philosophy.

But scanty as our materials are for a history of the seasons in antiquity, we have a direct authority that mild winters occurred in the latitude of Constantinople, more than two thousand years ago.

Hippocrates, during the plague in Athens, B. C. 430, resided on the
island of Thasus, which is in the Ægean Sea, near the coast of Thrace,
a cool country, and near the latitude 41°. This author has left a minute
description of the seasons for four years, with the current diseases.
The first of these winters was *mild like spring, with southerly winds.*
The second winter northerly winds prevailed, and great rains, attended
with snow. This seems to have been a *common* season. The third
winter, the weather was northerly, the cold severe, and the snow deep.
This seems to have been a hard winter, and if I am not deceived in the
chronology of events, this was within a few months of the appearance
of a comet, and the great eruption of Etna mentioned by Thucydides.
The fourth winter was mild, with southerly wind, except a period of
severe cold about the equinox, in March.

This authority is indisputable, that the winters in ancient times were,
as they are now, irregular and various ; and instead of being uniformly rigorous, some were mild as spring.

In later periods, I find occasional mention of mild winters, although
little notice has been taken of seasons, except when extraordinary for
cold. The winter of 802 was southerly, mild weather, followed by
the plague. Mild winters are also mentioned in 1186,* 1247, 1280,
1284, 1428, in some of which people wore summer clothes the whole
winter ; and in one instance harvest, in northern latitudes, was in May,
in consequence of the warm weather in the winter preceding. These
winters were antecedent to any great improvements in agriculture in
Europe.

It may not be improper here to introduce a fact related by Theophrast, of a change of temperature in Thessaly.

The river Peneus winds through a charming valley in Thessaly, and
between the mountains Olympus and Ossa, finds a passage to the
Ægean Sea. This passage, the ancients alledged, was opened by an
earthquake ; before which the valley was covered with stagnant water.
The draining of this valley is said to have rendered the country more
healthy, but at the same time, the air became colder. In proof of this,
authors alledge that olives, which before had flourished about Larissa,
would not endure the severity of the winters, after the valley was
drained, and vines were often frozen, which before was never known to
happen.—(See Anacharsis, Vol. III, p. 341.)

Whatever foundation may exist for this opinion, it seems the inhabitants had an idea that their climate had become *colder,* instead of
warmer ; and it is well known that places surrounded by water have a
milder climate, than others remote from water. This, by the way, is
the principal reason why Greece and Italy are more temperate than
other countries under the same parallels of latitude.

Let us now attend to the evidence of a mitigation of the cold of
American winters. The first proof adduced by Dr. Williams, is what
Kalm says, that on the first settlement of Philadelphia, the Delaware

---

* See my History of Pestilential Diseases, under the year 1186.

was commonly covered with ice about the middle of November, old style, corresponding with the last week of the month, in new style. But, says our author, " it is not now commonly covered with ice till the first week in January."—(Hist. Vermont, p. 58.)

Unfortunately for the argument, that river has been covered with ice for three years last past, not only by the middle of November, *old* style, but in one or two of the years, by the middle of that month, in *new* style.

Dr. Williams quotes Smith's History of New York, to prove his doctrine ; the page is not mentioned, but I suppose the passage to be a note in the margin of page 82, where the author says, " the climate of late is much altered, and this day, Feb. 14, 1756, three hundred recruits sailed from New York for the army at Albany, and last year a sloop went up the river a month earlier."

It is thus men are misled by founding general opinions on particular facts. The truth I find to be, that at the period mentioned, there were two or three winters in succession, the most mild that were recollected by the oldest men ; and all the world cried out, what a change of climate ! A few years however changed the common opinion, and a few such winters as 1780, 1784, 1796, 1797, 1798, and 1804, will leave very little room to believe in a change of climate.

Smith, however, when he wrote the foregoing note, was writing in the text of his history, that Governor Fletcher sailed from New York for Albany on February 13th or 14th, in 1693. This certainly was a rare event, but it should have made him doubtful at least of a change of climate. Another fact cited by Dr. Williams, is, that Baron Lahontau put to sea from Quebec in 1690, on the 20th of November, new style, the like of which had never been known in that place before. The St. Lawrence had been covered with ice on the 14th of November, but was cleared by a sudden thaw. Yet what conclusion can be drawn from the fact? Simply this, that the seasons then were sometimes very variable, as they are now. But Dr. Williams infers from this passage of history, that the St. Lawrence was, in former times, usually closed with ice by the middle of November ; whereas in modern days, he says, it is not frozen over till the latter end of December or beginning of January. But this inference is probably drawn from some mild winters. In one fourth of our winters, the Hudson, Delaware, and Connecticut, are closed with ice in the 42d and 43d degree of latitude, as early as the last week in November, or first week in December ; and it is against all probability that the St. Lawrence, in the 46th degree, continues open a month later.

In proof of his opinion, Dr. Williams cites a passage from Wood's Prospect, a work written in the early settlement of this country, which says, that the winters then began in December, and continued to February 21, (new style,) when the rivers and bays were unlocked by warm weather ; the duration of winter then was two months or ten weeks. This is mentioned to have been a very regular occurrence for ten or twelve years.

From this passage, the author concludes the bays about Boston, on the first settlement of New England, must have been " annually covered with ice," and that this bridge lasted through the winter months ;

whereas in these days, this is not a regular event, nor when frozen, does the ice continue so long. From data which he supposes sufficiently correct, he concludes that our climate has suffered a melioration in winter of ten or twelve degrees.

But we have here another instance of the fallacy of such general conclusions. In the first place Wood does not say that during the ten weeks of winter, the ice was never broken up by thaws, as it is in modern times; on the other hand, his expressions fairly intimate that such thaws were common; for he observes that about the 21st of February, the rivers and bays are unlocked, and " are never again frozen the same year." This expression doubtless alludes to the well known and common occurrence, that rivers, cleared of ice at an earlier period, were covered with ice again, in the same winter.

But that such thaws occurred, at that period, I have direct proof from Winthrop's Journal. In 1634, December 4th, old style, a violent snow storm was followed by a severe frost that covered Boston bay with ice in two days, but " it was free again before night." In the middle of January, a pinnace came to Boston from Port Royal; and about the end of the month, a boat coming from Deer's Island was detained at Bird's Island; and also others were detained at an island in the harbor by the ice, which was not sufficient to bear a man. After that the ice was firm for two or three weeks. This was no uncommon occurrence; a " January thaw" is a proverb handed down to us from our ancestors. That was a hard winter, yet many persons fell through the ice and were drowned.

But our ancestors had also mild winters, which made little or no ice in rivers or bays. Such was the winter of 1633–4, next preceding that last mentioned. Winthrop says expressly, " this winter was mild, little wind, and most south and southwest." The last of February, fell a deep snow, but the winter was at an end. This is decisive evidence that the winters have been from the first settlement of America variable, now mild, now severe, just as they are in the present age.

In 1635, Connecticut River was closed with ice November 15, old style, [26,] at Hartford, but at Saybrook not till December 10th, [21.] This was a severe winter.

A ship from Bristol entered Boston Bay in January, 1637, and by stress of weather was driven into Plymouth harbor.

In 1638, on the 13th of January, old style, [the 24th,] Boston harbor was open; for thirty men went down to Spectacle Island to cut wood. A snow storm arose in the following night; after that the wind was at northwest for two days, and then, says Governor Winthrop, " it froze so hard, as the bay was all frozen up, except a little channel." By this opening twelve of the men got to the Governor's garden; others escaped on the ice. Of this winter the Governor writes, " This was a very hard winter. The snow lay from November 4, [15th,] to March 23d, [April 3d,] one and an half yard deep about the Massachusetts," &c.—(See pages 146, 154.) Let it be observed, that in this " very hard winter," Boston harbor was open till the 24th of January.

*Note.*—In page 154, it is said this was in 1637. But it is immaterial.

The winter of 1641–2, was one of the most rigorous kind, like that of 1709, 1741, and 1780. It froze the bay at Boston as far out at sea as the eye could reach ; loaded sleds passed from Muddy River to Boston. All the rivers in Virginia, and even Chesapeak Bay, were covered with ice. These things are recorded by Governor Winthrop as *extraordinary occurrences*, such as passing on the ice from Pullen's Point and Muddy River to Boston—a proof that the several frosts supposed by Dr. Williams, were not annual events. And the Indians declared that a like winter had not happened in forty years preceding.

The next winter was milder than usual, and the winter following there was "little rain and no snow till March 3d."—(Winthrop, pp. 240, 269, 324.)

In an account of the natives of New England, written by Governor Winslow, and annexed to Dr. Belknap's second volume of American Biography, we have the following description of the climate of New England, in 1624 :—" For the temperature of the air, in almost three years' experience, I can scarce distinguish New England from Old England, in respect to heat and cold, frost, snow, rain, and wind."— " Experience teaches us that if the heat does exceed England, it is so little as must require better judgments to discern it. As for the winter, I rather think, *if there be a difference*, it is both sharper and longer in New England than Old ; yet the want of those comforts in one, which I have enjoyed in the other, may deceive my judgment also."—" The seed-time beginneth in the midst of April, and continueth good till the midst of May." This was written at Plymouth, a place whose heat in summer, and cold in winter, is moderated by the air from the sea. But the description does not warrant the idea of excessively cold winters. Seed-time was as early then as it is now.

In an account of the climate, soil, and produce of New England, written by the Rev. Mr. Higgeson, of Salem, in 1629, we have the following description of the seasons. " In the summer time, in the midst of July and August, it is a good deal hotter than in Old England ; and in winter, January and February are much colder, as they say ; but the spring and autumn are of a middle temper. In the winter season, for *two months*' space, the earth is commonly covered with snow, which is accompanied with sharp, biting frosts, something more sharp than in Old England, and therefore we are forced to make great fires." (Historical Collections, Vol. I, 117.)

This description answers well for the ordinary seasons in New England, at the close of the 18th century. The summers are hotter ; the winters colder than in England. A winter of eight weeks or two months' frost, may be considered as a medium winter, between our very mild and very severe winters.

From the same narrative, it appears that maiz thrived as well then as it does now, in the plantations about Salem, and produced the most abundant crops.

In a tract written in 1642, called " New England's First Fruits," the climate is thus represented, in answer to some objections that had been made to the project of settling the country. " True, it is sometimes cold, when the wind blows strong at northwest ; but *it holds not long together, and then it useth to be very moderate*."—(Hist. Col. Vol. I, 249.)

The writer mentions the purity and wholesomeness of the air, and the bright, clear, fair weather, which are preferable to the moist, foggy, cold air of Holland and England. This account of the seasons, answers well to the state of the weather in our days.

But I have a further remark to make on the passage cited from Wood's Prospect. This writer does not say that Boston Bay and Charles River were annually frozen for eight or ten weeks. His words, if rightly quoted, are, "For ten or a dozen years, the weather hath held himself to his day, unlocking *his icy bays and rivers*, which are never frozen again the same year." These words do not authorize Dr. Williams to suppose the writer meant Boston Bay and Charles River at Boston. He might have had in view more inland bays and rivers; and indeed he must have had; for it is proved by Winthrop's Journal, an unexceptionable authority, that Boston harbor was not always nor generally frozen in the midst of winter. If Wood then meant inland rivers and arms of the sea, his description is exactly true, at this day. I can aver, from thirty years' observation, that Connecticut River at Hartford is a bridge of ice, on an average, eight or ten weeks in a winter; rather more than less; that is, from the beginning or middle of December to the 20th of February. This is the precise time mentioned by Wood; and the passage, instead of favoring Dr. Williams' opinion, is direct evidence that there has been no sensible diminution of cold in America since its settlement.

In Winthrop's Journal I find a confirmation of this opinion. In page 23, there is a remark like that of Wood before cited, that " ever since the bay has been planted by the English, viz. *seven years*, it hath been observed, that at this day [February 10th, old style, 1631] the frost hath broken up every year." Fortunately we have in this Journal full proof that the remark was not intended to represent the breaking up of a bridge of ice over the bay of Boston or Charles River.

On the 22d day of December, O. S., Governor Winthrop writes thus : " Till this time there was for the most part, fair open weather, with gentle frosts in the night; but this day the wind came northwest very strong, and some snow withal, but so cold as some had their fingers frozen—three of the Governor's servants coming in a shallop from Mistick, were driven by the wind upon Noddle's Island."—(p. 21.) At this time then, the 3d of January, new style, there was no ice in Charles River.

On the 26th, the Governor writes, " The rivers are frozen up, and they of Charlestown could not come to the sermon at Boston, till the afternoon at high water." By this we are to understand that Charles River at the ferry was full of ice, which was removed by the flood tide, so that the river was passable in boats. This was on the 6th of January. On the 28th of December, O. S., [the 8th of January,] seven persons, says the Governor, set sail in a shallop, from Boston for Plymouth, and were cast away on Cape Cod. Boston harbor and bay must then have been open.—(See pp. 21, 22.)

On the 5th of February, O. S. [the 16th] arrived the ship Lyon, at Nantasket. On the 8th [the 19th] the Governor went aboard the Lyon, then lying by Long Island. On the 9th [20th] the Lyon came to anchor before Boston. On the 10th, O. S. [21st] says Governor Winthrop, " the frost broke up, and after that, though we had many storms and sharp frost, yet they continued not, neither were the waters frozen up as before." The Governor then remarks, that for seven years before, the frost had broken up on the same day of the month.— (See p. 23.)

This evidence is decisive to prove that the breaking up of the ice, was not said of the ice in Boston harbor; for the Governor went down to the ship Lyon, at Long Island, which is almost five miles from the town, and the ship came to anchor before Boston, *before the ice broke up.* Let it be noted also, that the severe frost in that year, set in about Christmas, and broke up on the 21st of February; of course it lasted about eight weeks, as in modern times.

It is obvious therefore that Gov. Winthrop and Mr. Wood, in the passages noted, speak of the breaking up of the rivers and frost in the country generally, and not of the ice in Boston harbor: and it is remarkable that the time mentioned is the same as that in which the winter of New England, in ordinary seasons, now breaks up, viz. about the 20th of February.

I will only observe further on this point, that in Winthrop's Journal, which comprehends the events of fourteen years, from the first settlement of Boston, from 1630 to 1644, we have positive evidence that Boston harbor was usually open, and that vessels entered and departed in the midst of winter. The freezing of the bay, in the extremely severe winter of 1642, and the passing of loads on the ice, are described as *rare occurrences;* and what is more explicit, Governor Winthrop declares, " the frost was so great and continual this winter, that all the bay was frozen over so much and so long, as the like, by the Indian relation, had not been these forty years." Yet this frost lasted only from the 18th of January to the 21st of February, old style, about five weeks.—(See p. 240.) This evidence is decisive of the question, and utterly disproves the opinion of a change of climate. On the 18th of January, O. S. 1644, Boston harbor was open.—(See p. 321.)

If Dr. Williams is unfortunate in his facts, he is still more so in his reasonings and deductions. The following is a specimen.

In 1782, the river between Boston and Charlestown was frozen, so that horses and sleighs passed over, for five or six days. The ice was permanent from February 2d to the 10th. During that time the lowest point of cold by Fahrenheit was 9°, the highest 28°, and the mean temperature 13°. From this statement the Doctor concludes, that the freezing of the bays mentioned by Wood about the year 1630, could not take place in a less degree of cold than 13°. He found from seven years' observations, that the mean temperature of December was, in these years, [from 1780 to 1788,] 29°.4; that of January, 22°.5, and that of February, 23°.9. Hence he concludes, that the change of temperature at Boston since the year 1630 must have been from " ten to twelve degrees."

I confess myself surprised that so intelligent a man should not have observed the fallacy of this reasoning. He takes the mean of *seven or eight severe cold* days in 1782, which covered Charles River with ice, for the standard by which to estimate the cold of 1630, and the mean of the *whole winter,* as the standard of cold in modern days, by which to compare it. This mode of reasoning is all fallacious. In the first place, it is not true that a mean degree of cold, answering to 13° by Fahrenheit, is necessary to keep Charles River covered with ice.  The effect would be produced with a much less degree of cold.  Let the mercury sink to 10° for five days, and a bridge of ice would be formed.  Then let the cold relax, and the mercury rise to 30° for five days.  The mean temperature of the whole ten days would be 20°.  Yet in this case probably, the ice would remain a solid bridge through the whole time, notwithstanding the rapid tides in that river.  And in fresh water, where there is no current, the bridge would remain a much longer time, and in much milder weather.  Indeed, I can prove that a river or pond of water may be covered with twelve inches of solid ice, when the *mean* temperature is not below freezing point.  But I will not rest the argument on calculations ; I appeal to facts.

In November, 1797, commenced a series of severe cold, although the beginning of the month was as mild as usual.  Towards the close of the month, the Hudson, Delaware and Connecticut were covered with solid ice ; yet the mean temperature of the whole month, at the Exchange at New York, was 38°.87 by Fahrenheit, almost seven degrees above the freezing point.  This fact exhibits the fallacy of the Doctor's conclusions.—(See p. 59, of his History of Vermont.)

In page 383, appendix, Dr. Williams states that in America, where the rivers are frozen to a firmness sufficient to sustain heavy loads, the " mean heat of the winter is from 15° to 20°."  This is a most egregious mistake, and contradicts his own observations of the weather between 1780 and 1788, as before stated.  The mean temperature of those seven winters was, by his own statement, 25°.2, and this corresponds nearly with the results of Dr. Holyoke's seven years' observations at Salem, which make the mean temperature of the three winter months 25°.76.  With this degree of cold, fresh-water rivers are annually covered, and held bound with solid ice.

To cover with ice salt streams, bays and arms of the sea, a greater degree of cold is requisite, and this degree occurs many times every century.

If then a mean temperature of 25° or 26° by Fahrenheit will keep the American rivers covered with ice for many weeks, we have further evidence that the Rhine and Danube, fresh-water rivers, must be frequently frozen in modern times.  Dr. Williams states the mean degree of cold at several places in Europe, as follows :

At Vienna, in 1779 and 1780, $\begin{cases} \text{January,} & 27°. \ 5 \\ \text{February,} & 33 \ .23 \end{cases}$

At Ratisbon, in 1781 and 1782, $\begin{cases} \text{January,} & 30 \ .52 \\ \text{February,} & 30 \ .76 \end{cases}$

At Manheim, in 1781 and 1782, $\begin{cases} \text{January,} & 35 \ .08 \\ \text{February,} & 35 \ .08 \end{cases}$

From these means he deduces the general mean of 31°.8 for January, and 33°.6 for February, which, he says, will accurately express the temperature of a German winter on those rivers.  Admit this conclusion, and what follows ?  The undeniable consequence that a German winter is almost as cold as a New England winter ; for the mean temperature of January in Vienna was 27°.5 ; the mean temperature of an American winter is 25°.76.  The difference is only *one degree and twenty nine hundredths*.  The difference between the general mean of

January above stated, 31°.8, and the general mean of America, 25°.76, is only 5°.32. If the vibrations of heat and cold are as great on the Rhine and Danube as in America, which is understood to be the fact, those rivers must be frozen every winter, although perhaps not sufficiently in a common winter to sustain loaded carriages. Certain it is that the cold at Manheim and Ratisbon is nearly equal to any thing experienced in New England. In the Memoirs of the American Academy, Part 1 of Vol. II, page 88, Dr. Holyoke has stated the greatest cold at Ratisbon, by a series of observations, to be 13°.45 below cipher by Fahrenheit, and the mean of the greatest colds, 2°.42 below cipher. At Manheim, the greatest cold was 8°.95 below 0, and the greatest mean of cold 1°.2 above 0. From all which it is obvious that no diminution of cold, equal to 16°, can have taken place since the Goths and Vandals invaded the Roman empire, as Dr. Williams supposes; for the cold which reduces the mercury by Fahrenheit's scale to 8° or 10° above cipher, if continued only two or three days, must cover the Rhine and Danube with solid ice.

Before I conclude this subject, it is proper to notice what Mr. Jefferson has written on the climate of Virginia.—(Notes, query 7.) "A change in our climate," says this author, " is taking place very sensibly. Both heats and colds are become much more moderate, within the memory even of the middle aged. Snows are less frequent and less deep. They do not often lie below the mountains more than one, two or three days, and very rarely a week. The elderly inform me, the earth used to be covered with snow about three months in every year. The rivers which then seldom failed to freeze over in the course of the winter, scarcely ever do so now. This change has produced an unfortunate fluctuation between heat and cold in the spring of the year, which is fatal to fruits."

What evidence there is of a diminution of heat in summer, I do not know; but I find abundant evidence that no such diminution has taken place. And that no very definite proof of the fact has appeared, is very obvious from the difference of opinion on the subject. Mr. Jefferson supposes a *diminution* of the heat of summer; Dr. Williams supposes a general *increase* of heat in our climate; and I leave them to adjust the difference between themselves.

Mr. Jefferson seems to have no authority for his opinions but the observations of elderly and middle aged people. But what shall we say to the following facts? Mr. Jefferson informs that in Virginia, the snow used to cover the earth about three months in every year. How shall we reconcile this account with the representation of the climate by Lord Delaware and Sir Thomas Gates, a few years after Virginia was first planted, A. D. 1611 or 1612? In that account it is expressly stated, that " the soil is favorable for the cultivation of vines, sugar-canes, oranges, lemons, almonds and rice—*the winters are so mild that the cattle can get their food abroad*, and swine can be fatted on wild fruits.— (See Purchas, Vol. V, 1758: Belknap's Biography, Vol. II, 39.)

If this description of the climate is just, the seasons in Virginia were then just what they are now. In ordinary winters, cattle and swine will get their living in the woods; but in severe winters, they are liable to perish.

Perhaps Mr. Jefferson's observations refer to the interior and mountainous parts of the state, where by the clearing of the lands, the winters may have become less steady, and the snows less durable ; but this is no proof of a general diminution of cold in the winter ; it proves only more variable weather. The description given by the first settlers about one hundred and ninety years ago, is decisive evidence that the general temperature of the climate was then the same as it is now ; and that in its rude state, Virginia produced the delicate tropical fruits, as far north as they can be cultivated at this day. Had there been a general increase of heat in our climate, the cultivation of the fig and the olive would have advanced northward to Pennsylvania or New England ; but instead of this, not a plant has advanced a single league since the first settlement of the country.

To the testimony of Lord Delaware and Sir Thomas Gates, may be added that of Beverly, who in his History of Virginia, written at the beginning of the last century, says, " The rivers and creeks were, in many places, covered with fowl during the winter"—which precludes the fact that they were covered with ice.—(p. 134.) " That elks, buffaloes, deer and other game," were hunted by the natives " in winter, when *the leaves were fallen, and so dry they would burn ;*" the Indians driving them into a crowd, by circular fires.—(p. 136.) In page 252, he alludes to the practice of letting cattle feed in the woods in winter, and charges his countrymen with ill husbandry, in not providing sufficiently for them all winter. In page 268 he says, the winters in Virginia are very short, continuing not above three or four months, of which thirty days are seldom unpleasant weather ; all the rest being blest with a clear air and a bright sun. However, sometimes the frost is very hard, but it *rarely lasts more than three or four days*, before the wind changes. The rains, except in the depth of winter, are extremely refreshing and agreeable.—(Lond. edit. 1722.)

It appears to me extremely unphilosophical to suppose any considerable change in the annual heat or cold of a particular country. We have no reason to suppose that the inclination of the earth's axis to the plane of its orbit has ever been varied ; but strong evidence to the contrary. If this inclination has always been the same, it follows that the quantity of the solar rays, falling annually on a particular country, must have always been the same. Should these data be admitted, we are led to conclude that the general temperature of every climate, from the creation to this day, has been the same, subject only to small annual variations, from the positions of the planets in regard to the earth, or the operations of the element of fire in the globe and its atmosphere.

The real truth seems to be, that when a country is covered with frost, the vibrations in the temperature of the air and of the earth near the surface, are less numerous and less considerable, than in an open country. Dr. Williams himself has furnished the data by which to determine this point. In 1791 he found an open field frozen to the depth of three feet five inches ; at the same time, in a forest, he found the temperature of the earth to be 39° by Fahrenheit, seven degrees above frost. This fact solves the question here discussed.

While a country is covered with trees, the face of the earth is never swept by violent winds ; the temperature of the air is more uniform, than in an open country; the earth is never frozen in winter, nor scorched with heat in summer; and snow that falls in November usually lies till March or April, although the earth below is not frozen, but gradually melts the snow and absorbs the water. On the other hand, an open country is exposed to violent winds, and frequent great changes of weather. The earth in winter is usually frozen into a solid mass from one to three feet thick; great snows alternate with heavy rains; the earth which is covered with snow to-day, is to-morrow left bare; and an iron surface of this week, is the next converted into soft mud. Hence probably as much snow falls in an open country as in a forest; or if the clearing of a country converts more of the vapor into water, yet it is liable also to more extreme cold, which preserves a balance in the temperature. That these are facts every man knows, who has observed the difference between the open country and the forest, in our old settlements; and Dr. Williams himself has given the results of meteorological observations which confirm them, and disprove the common theory of a moderation of cold. In page 50 of his history, he states the difference between the heat of the earth in an open field, and in the woods, during the summer; by which experiments it is demonstrated, that from the latter part of May to the close of August, the open country sustains about ten degrees of heat beyond that of the forest; the thermometer being sunk ten inches below the surface of the earth. At another time he found the winter temperature of the earth in the forest to be 39°, while in open field the earth was frozen. The vibrations therefore in the temperature of the earth, when cleared, are found to be much greater than when covered with wood. The differences, according to Dr. Williams, are as follows:

Winter temperature of the earth in the woods in Vermont, 39°.
"          "          of the open field at frost,          32°.

### Summer Temperature of the Earth.

|  |  | In an open field. | In the forest. | Difference. |
|---|---|---|---|---|
| May | 23, | 50° | 46° | 4° |
| " | 28, | 57 | 48 | 9 |
| June | 15, | 64 | 51 | 13 |
| " | 27, | 62 | 51 | 11 |
| July | 16, | 62 | 51 | 11 |
| " | 30, | 65½ | 55½ | 10 |
| August | 15, | 68 | 58 | 10 |
| " | 31, | 59½ | 55 | 4½ |
| Septem. | 15, | 59½ | 55 | 4½ |
| October | 1, | 59½ | 55 | 4½ |

From these observations, it results that in winter the earth of the forest is seven degrees warmer than the open field; and in summer it is on an average, from May 23 to August 31, 9¼° colder—and on an average, from May 23 to October 1, 8¼° colder. That is, the vibrations in the forest temperature of the earth are between 39° and 58°— only 19° of difference between winter and summer; while the vibrations in the temperature of the open country, are between 32°, or frost, and 68°—making a difference of 36° between winter and summer.

The vibrations of the temperature of the air are more considerable; but it is an unquestionable fact that they are much greater in an open country, than in a forest; and so far is it from truth, that the clearing and cultivation of our country has moderated the rigor of our cold weather, that the cold of our winters, though less steady, has been most sensibly increased. There is not a greater amount of cold during the winter, but the cold at times is more severe than before our country was cleared. The difference is so sensible, as to be a subject of popular remark among aged people.

Another effect of clearing the country, is to distribute the cold of the year more unequally: hence fruits are more exposed to spring frosts. This is a most serious inconvenience in Europe, and is becoming so in America. The reason of variable and late springs is obvious. While the earth is covered with wood, it is never frozen, but as soon as the snow is dissolved in spring, vegetation begins. In an open country, after the snow is melted, the earth is to be thawed; and the heat of the air for two or three weeks, is incessantly absorbed by the earth and water, while the frost is dissolving. Hence the heat of a warm day in spring is speedily absorbed, and cold succeeds. This alternation must continue till the earth is warmed. If the winter temperature of the earth in a forest is 39° and that of the open country 32°, we may easily conceive what an immense quantity of heat it must require to raise the temperature of the open field to that of the forest. It must demand nearly all the heat excited by the solar rays in April, so that in our open country, the earth is probably not warmer on the last of that month, than it was when a forest, on the first of the month.

It will be remarked that in discussing this question, I have admitted the fact assumed by my opposers, that there has been a clearing and cultivation of Palestine, since the settlement of the Jews in that country; and of Italy, since the days of Julius Cesar. But I must not quit the subject, without contradicting the fact assumed. The reverse is the truth.

When Joshua led the Israelites toward Palestine, that country was very populous, inhabited by various tribes of people, and containing large cities, whose enormous walls terrified the Israelites. Never has that country been so populous as in the few first centuries, after the Israelites took possession of it. The country, therefore, could not have been covered with wood, but every foot of cultivable land was occupied by husbandmen.

Equally true is it, that the countries on the north of Syria were as populous in the days of Darius, as at any subsequent period. It was the case also in Italy, which was more populous at the Christian era, than it has been for the last fifteen centuries. In all these countries, therefore, no clearing of the lands can have taken place, to influence the climates, within the period in which a moderation of cold is supposed. Germany, on the north of Italy, has been in a degree cleared; but the Rhetian Alps intervene between Italy and Germany; and the cold winds which affect Italy in winter, blow from those highlands, where the air is colder than in the less hilly country on the north. In every point, therefore, the hypothesis of a moderation of climate appears to be unsupported.

I would only further observe, that if the cold has abated ten or twelve degrees in our climate, within a century and a half, it must have been intolerable before that period. The mean temperature of Vermont now is about 43°. If we deduct 10° only for abatement of cold, the water in deep wells in Vermont, two hundred years ago, must have been of 33° of temperature, or nearly at the freezing point; in Canada it must have been at 32°, or the state of congelation. If we suppose the winter only to have changed, and deduct one half the supposed abatement, still the result forbids us to believe the hypothesis. If we suppose the heat of summer to have lessened in the same proportion, as just philosophy requires us to do, the summers formerly must have been intolerable; no animal could have subsisted under ten degrees of heat beyond our present summer temperature. On whichever side we turn our eyes, we meet with insurmountable difficulties.

From all I can discover, in regard to the seasons, in ancient and modern times, I see no reason to conclude with Dr. Williams, that the heat of the earth is increasing. It appears that all the alterations in a country, in consequence of clearing and cultivation, result only in making a different distribution of heat and cold, moisture and dry weather, among the several seasons. The clearing of lands opens them to the sun, their moisture is exhaled, they are more heated in summer, but more cold in winter near the surface; the temperature becomes unsteady, and the seasons irregular. This is the fact. A smaller degree of cold, if steady, will longer preserve snow and ice, than a greater degree, under frequent changes. Hence we solve the phenomenon, of more constant ice and snow in the early ages; which I believe to have been the case. It was not the *degree*, but the *steadiness* of the cold which produced this effect. Every forest in America exhibits this phenomenon. We have, in the cultivated districts, deep snow to-day, and none to-morrow; but the same quantity of snow falling in the woods, lies there till spring. The same fact, on a larger scale, is observed in the ice of our rivers. This will explain all the appearances of the seasons, in ancient and modern times, without resorting to the unphilosophical hypothesis of a general increase of heat.

------

# SUPPLEMENTARY REMARKS. *

WHEN the preceding dissertation was written, I had devoted very little time to an examination of the subject, and had read very few of the authorities cited to prove a moderation of cold in winter in modern times. Since that time, I have noted such passages in ancient authors, as have occurred to me, in the course of reading, with a view to ascertain, if possible, the real fact, whether the industry and improvements of men, by destroying forests and cultivating the earth, have occasioned a material alteration of climate.

------

* Written and read before the Academy in 1806.

Strabo, in the first book of his geography, cites from Homer, whom he calls the father of geography, a passage which describes the climate of the western part of Europe, where the poet places Elysium.—(See Odyssey, lib. 4.) This country, says the poet, experiences "no violent storms of snow, and little winter, but is perpetually refreshed by gentle zephyrs from the ocean." This description Strabo applies to Iberia, or Spain, and alledges that the *Fortunate* isles received their name from their vicinity to this happy climate. The description proves at least the opinion of the ancients respecting the climate of Spain and Portugal, and it corresponds with the present state of the climate.

Polybius, speaking of an invasion of Pelopennese by Philip of Macedonia, about the year before Christ 218, mentions the hardships which his army encountered, in passing Ligyrtus, a mountain of Arcadia, on his march to the siege of Psophis, by reason of *deep snow* which covered the mountain. But that the cold was not great, we have evidence in the same book, as the army, a few days afterward, passed over the river Erymanth, on a bridge, for it was not fordable.*—(Polyb. Megalop. Hist. lib. 4.)

In an account of the invasion of Sparta by Epaminondas, in the Travels of Anacharsis, the author remarks that the Theban general was making dispositions to pass the Eurotas, then swelled by the melting of snow, chap. 1, where is cited as authority, Plutarch's Life of Agesilaus.

From these passages, we conclude that snow fell in winter in Lacedemon, especially on the mountains, but was soon dissolved ; and hence Polybius observes of a river on the west of Psophis, that it was seldom fordable in winter. But I find no evidence in history that frost of any severity was ever experienced in Lacedemon or Attica. On the other hand, it is related from Plutarch, that when Epaminondas was in Arcadia with an army, in winter, he was invited by deputies from a neighboring city to take up his quarters in the city ; but he declined, assigning as a reason that if the Lacedemonians should see him and his men by the fire, they would take them to be ordinary men. He therefore chose to continue in camp, notwithstanding the rigor of the season, and continue their wrestling matches and military exercises.—(Anarch. chap. 5.) This anecdote indicates cool uncomfortable weather in that country in winter, but not severe cold, like that which freezes large rivers in America.

The author of Anacharsis relates from Columella, that the winter in every part of Beotia, is very cold, and at Thebes almost insupportable ; and that snow, wind and want of wood, rendered that part of Greece an unpleasing residence in winter.—(See chap. 34.) With what caution we ought to receive such general accounts of climate, may be understood from the fact, that in Thessaly, far north of Beotia, and in a mountainous country, vines and olives came to perfection, according to the testimony of the same writer, in the same chapter. Cold and heat are comparative ; and the degrees of them are not to be known from general assertions. Homer speaks of the wild fig-tree before the walls of Troy, a degree and a half of latitude north of Beotia.—(Iliad, lib. 6,

---

* Strabo, lib. 8, informs us that Arcadia is a mountainous region, some of the mountains being fifteen stadiums in altitude.

433.) And other ancient authors speak of the fig-tree, vines and olives growing in Macedonia, two degrees still further north.—(Anarch, chap. 65.) Pliny informs us that figs were produced at Mount Ida, near the site of Troy.—(Nat. Hist. lib. 15, cap. 18.) Theophrast informs us that figs grew in great abundance in Pontus, on the south shore of the Euxine.—(Hist. Plant. lib. 4, 6.) And Xenophon found, on his retreat with the ten thousand, figs and vines in abundance at Calpe, on the same shore, about eight hundred and seventy stadiums from Byzantium. —(See his account, lib. 6.) Pliny, in the book just cited, gives an account of a method of raising figs in Mœsia, the modern Bulgaria, in the forty fourth degree of north latitude, which was effected by covering small trees in winter with compost. These facts, and numberless others, which I have found in authors, furnish the most accurate test of the real state of the climate in Greece, Asia Minor, and the neighboring countries.

Joseph, in the fifth book of his Antiquities, ch. 5, relates that in the battle between the Canaanites and the Israelites, under Barak and Deborah, the Canaanites were exceedingly annoyed by a storm of rain and *hail*, which blew in their faces, and rendered their bows and slings almost useless; while the cold benumbed their fingers, so that they could not use their swords. This fact would seem to confirm the common opinion that, anciently, Palestine was far colder than at present. But we must not be misled by single facts. In the very next chapter, the historian, in relating the sufferings of his countrymen from the Midianites, informs us that their enemies invaded the country in time of harvest, and carried away or destroyed their corn for three years in succession; but permitted the Israelites to *plow their land in winter*, that they might furnish fruits of the earth for their plunderers. The latter fact entirely overthrows the opinion that anciently the winters were more rigorous than at present; for we see that it was customary to prepare the land for seed in winter, as it is at this day. A storm of hail or snow might happen occasionally in winter, as it does now in South Carolina and Georgia; but the frost of ordinary years was not sufficient to impede the agricultural operations of winter.

Appian relates that at the siege of Numantia in Spain, many Roman soldiers perished by cold and frequent hail storms, about one hundred and forty-five years before the Christian era. But Numantia was situated in the center and mountainous part of Spain, near the source of the Duro, where the laws of nature require us to suppose a considerable degree of cold in winter. Yet an anecdote related by Quinctilian, lib. 6, shows that in Tarracona, the country where Barcelona is now situated, the climate must have been as mild as at present. The people of Tarracona informed Augustus, that a palm-tree was growing from his altar. "From that I can judge," replied the prince, "how often you use fire upon it." This story implies that palm-trees grew in the north of Spain, and in the very latitude of Numantia, on the eastern coast, which is washed by the Mediterranean.

In the first chapter of the second book of Maccabees, the Jews of Jerusalem recommend to their brethren in Egypt, to keep the feast of tabernacles in the month Casleu, which answers to a part of November and December. This circumstance among others led Prideaux to pronounce the epistles of the Jews in this chapter to be spurious; for, says that learned author, the Jews could not, in the middle of winter, make such booths as in the feast of tabernacles; they could neither find green boughs enough, nor could they lie abroad in such booths.— (Connec., part ii, book 3.) This argument is undoubtedly founded on mistake; for in a country where the plowing and sowing of land were constantly carried on in winter, and where the palm-tree flourished in perfection, ordinary winters would not render the temporary lodging in booths very uncomfortable; nor could such a country be necessarily destitute of green boughs. Let it be added also, that in the second chapter of the Song of Solomon, we find the winter was a season of *rain*, and not of snow. " The winter is past; the rain is over and gone."

In opposition to Prideaux's opinion, and to the general hypothesis of the rigorous winters of antiquity, it may be remarked that in Greece, six degrees of latitude north of Judea, the theaters were not covered, but plays were acted in the open air.—(See Anarch., ch. 70, where Vitruvius, lib. 5, cap. 9, is cited as an authority.) The Roman theaters and amphitheaters were also without roofs. Indeed for centuries after theatrical representations were introduced at Rome, the theaters were temporary structures of wood, without seats, the spectators standing during the exhibition.—(Tacit. An., 14, 20.) It is evident also from a passage in Quinctilian, lib. 10, ch. 3, that the courts of justice were held in apartments without roofs; and so was the Areopagus in Athens.—(Acts xvii.)

Authors inform us that in the later ages of refinement at Athens, the stage, and a part of the theater occupied by the ladies, were covered; but the spectators in general had no covering but their clothes. Plays were indeed acted in Greece in the day time; but as they were acted at all seasons of the year, the open theaters forbid us to suppose the winters more rigorous and tempestuous formerly than in modern days.

The thin dress of the Romans and Greeks is another proof of the mildness of their climate. The Romans wore no garments answering to the modern breeches and stockings; their principal garments being the *tunica*, or close coat worn at home, and the *toga*, or loose gown without sleeves, worn in public; to which may be added the *trabea*, *paludamentum*, *chlamys* and *læna*, robes worn by men of distinction and military officers.—(Kennet, Antiq. Rom. II, 5, 7.) Hence the close garments which invested the lower limbs of the Celtic and Teutonic nations, were objects of notice among the Romans who traveled north of Italy. Ovid, among the curiosities of Thrace, the place of his exile, describes the skins and close *breeches* of the inhabitants.

" Pellibus et sutis arcent malè frigora bracchis."—(De Trist. lib. 3, 10.)*

And it is perfectly well known that this customary dress of the Gauls, gave rise to a distinctive appellation of the southwestern part of their country, which was called by the Romans *Gallia braccata*. The customary light dress of the Romans, which continued down to the ages

---

* This line is repeated, lib. 5, 7, with the change of *sutis* to *laxis*, loose breeches, or trowsers.

of wealth and luxury, and therefore can not be supposed to have been the effect of necessity, as it is among savage nations, furnishes strong evidence of the uniform mild temperature of ordinary winters in Italy.

Velleius Paterculus, lib. 11, cap. 105, mentions that the Roman troops, in the reign of Tiberius, kept their summer quarters till December in Germany, at the head of the Lippe, near the modern Paderborn, in Westphalia, and in the fifty-second degree of north latitude. This was favorable to the operations of the campaign, as the author remarks; and indicates a climate as temperate as in modern days. Yet at that time, the historian informs us, the Alps were almost impassable by reason of snow.

Xenophon, in his Anabasis or Expedition of Cyrus, has described the sufferings of the troops in their retreat through Armenia, four centuries before the Christian era, from great quantities of snow and severe frost. The snow in one place, he says, was a fathom in depth; and many horses and slaves, and some soldiers, died—others lost their limbs by the frost.—(Lib. 4.) Three days before the snow fell, the troops forded the Euphrates, with the water to their navel.

The troops of Lucullus experienced inconveniences from the same cause, in the same country, during the war against Mithridates. Plutarch informs us, in his life of that general, that before the winter solstice, the weather grew tempestuous, and great quantities of snow fell; that the soldiers, marching in the woods, were wet by snow which fell from the trees; but at the same time, he says, they were obliged to encamp at night in *wet* and *miry* places, so that it was not cold enough to freeze water. But we must not conclude from these facts, that the climate of that country is altered; for Chardin and Tournefort, in the seventeenth and eighteenth centuries, found the temperature of the winter precisely as described by Xenophon and Plutarch. Chardin informs us, that when he passed Caucasus, the snow was, in some places, ten feet deep; his guides wore snow-shoes, and in some places shoveled for him a path. At Tefflis, on the river Kur, it snowed all day, when he first arrived; and he repeatedly mentions that the mountains of Armenia and Georgia, which are in the fortieth, forty-first and forty-second degrees of north latitude, are never destitute of snow.—(See pages 166, 171, 241, 242, 247, 413; Lond. fol. 1686.)

Tournefort arrived at Erzeron, at the foot of a mountain near the head of the Euphrates, in the fortieth degree of latitude, on the 15th of June, and found the neighboring hills covered with snow. The nights were so cold that his fingers were too numb to write, until an hour after sunrise. The wheat harvest was in September.—(See his Travels, Vol. III, pp. 75, 81, 82, 94, 102, 107, &c.; Lond. 8vo. 1741.)

At Erivan, in the forty-first degree of latitude, says Chardin, the winter lasts long, so that it sometimes snows in April; the country produces wine in abundance, but the people are obliged to cover the vines in winter.—(p. 247.) From these authorities we may infer that the winter temperature of Armenia and Georgia has not abated within two thousand years.[*]

* Herodotus, lib. 1, relates that at Babylon, which was in a mild climate, far south of Armenia, the ancient inhabitants did not cultivate the vine, olive and fig;

It has been already remarked that snow formerly fell occasionally in Greece, even in the Peloponnese; and the most credible testimonies agree that Mount Ida, in Crete, was always clothed with snow.—(Plin. Nat. Hist. lib. 16, cap. 33. Theophrast, Hist. Plant. lib. 4, cap. 1.) Tournefort visited this isle in his voyage to the Levant, and testifies that the inhabitants of Canea fetch their snow, in summer, from the neighboring mountains; and he confirms the assertion of Theophrast and Pliny, that the cypress grows there among the snow. At the foot of these mountains grow figs, olives and other delicate fruits, as they did in the earliest ages.—(Tournefort, Let. 1.)

In Milo, says the same traveler, Let. 4, it never freezes, and *very rarely snows;* when it does, the snow melts in a quarter of an hour: the cold is not prejudicial to the olive trees, as it is in Provence and Languedoc, where the contexture of the bark is torn by the dilatation of the water which freezes in the pores.

When Tournefort visited Samos, in February, he found the cold severe on the mountains; and on the 23d of the month, some snow and a great deal of hail.—(Vol. II, Let. 3.)

On Mount Olympus, in Asia Minor, says the same author, nothing is to be seen but old snow in a very great quantity. This was in November. He also says, that a river which runs by Tocat, does much injury when swelled by rain or the melting of snow.—(Let. 9.)

The river Meles, which washes Smyrna, says Chandler in his Travels, ch. 20, swells into a torrent after heavy rains on the mountains, or the melting of snow. The houses in Smyrna, except those erected by Europeans, seldom have chimneys; but in cold weather, a pan of charcoals, under a table covered with a carpet, serves to warm the family. The same author mentions snow upon the summits of mountains, as he passed from Smyrna to Ephesus, Miletus and Laodicea, as late as March and April.—(See his Travels, 4to, Oxford, 1775, pp. 70, 80, 105, 164, 221, 224.)

The same author, Vol. II, p. 79, speaks of snow on the mountains of Attica. The Ilissus, he says, in summer is quite dry; and while he resided at Athens, he several times visited the river after snow had fallen on the mountains, in hopes to see it fill its banks. He observes also that the Cephissus is a small stream, and absorbed before it reaches the sea, except after the melting of snow, or a heavy rain. In describing the dress of the modern Greeks, he mentions in addition to their ordinary garments, a long vest, which they hang on their shoulders, lined with wool or fur for cold weather.—(Vol. II, pp. 110, 119.)

This author further states that when the mountains in Attica are covered with snow, the woodcocks descend into the plain; and if the ground continues frozen and the weather severe, they enter the gardens, and are so tame as sometimes to be taken by the hand.—(p. 127; see

---

but he insinuates that this neglect was owing to the peculiar fitness of the soil for corn. That it could not be on account of the climate, is certain; for the same author relates that the palm-tree was cultivated with success, and caprification was then practiced as in modern times. Herodotus also says, that palm wine was an article of merchandise, transported from Armenia down the Euphrates, in boats made of willows covered with skins.

also p. 163.) On his journey to Delphi, in the beginning of July, he found the summits of the mountains white with snow ; and Parnassus is covered with perennial snow.—(pp. 260, 270.) This confirms the account which Homer gives of the climate of Dodona, which he calls very cold.—(Iliad 11, 750.)

All these authorities prove beyond a question that the climate of Greece and Asia Minor, in modern days, corresponds well with the representations given of it in ancient history.*

There is a passage in Pliny, (Nat. Hist. lib. 2, 50,) which, after assigning reasons why there is no thunder in cold countries in winter,† expressly declares that the climate of Italy is always mild. " Mobilior aer mitiore hyeme, et æstate nimbosa, semper quodam modo vernat vel autumnat,"—always exhibiting the verdure of spring or the mildness of autumn. He says, chapter 47th of the same book, that the swallows appear by the 24th of February. This account corresponds with what has been before remarked, respecting the germination of plants in the same month.

There is a passage in Joseph, (Jewish War, lib. 3, ch. 10,) which describes the climate near the lake of Gennesareth, as remarkably mild and pleasant ; and after mentioning its fruitfulness in palm-trees, olives and figs, it is said that grapes and figs are supplied from the trees for ten months in the year. How incompatible is this description with the supposed rigor of the ancient winters in Judea !

Tacitus informs us, (Hist. lib. 3, 59,) that Vespasian's army, in passing the Apennines to quell a revolt in winter, suffered severe distresses from cold and snow. But we must recollect that the French army, but a few years past, suffered equally from the same causes, in the same country, on their march through the Neapolitan territories.

Pelloutier, in his History of the Celts, book i, ch. 12, asserts that in the time of the first Roman emperors, " On ne recueilloit encore dans les Gaules, ni vin, ni huile, ni d'autres fruits, et cela à cause de la rigueur du climat, et du froid excessif qui y regnoit." He admits indeed that in Germany were some cultivated fields, but not one fruit tree, as such could not sustain the rigor of the cold. The boldness and positiveness of this writer led me to recur to his authorities and examine them with care.

Strabo, a most diligent investigator and accurate geographer, in the very passage cited by Pelloutier, overthrows the assertion of the latter author. " Narbonensian Gaul," says Strabo, " produces the same fruits as Italy. Proceeding to the north and the Cevennes, the country produces the same fruits, the fig and olive only excepted."—(Book iv, sect. 2.) This account corresponds with that of Pliny, as I have in my

---

* There is a passage of Herodotus, in Euterpe, which indicates that snow sometimes fell in his native country, Halicarnassus ; for he asserts that a fall of snow must be followed in five days by rain. This remark represents the climate of that country nearly as it is at present.

† Herodotus, in Melpomene, mentions the same fact, in describing Scythia. This is known to be correct at this day. In northern climates, there is no thunder in winter; but in Italy and Greece, thunder is known only in winter or spring. This fact, corresponding with the statements of Herodotus and Pliny, proves the climates of Italy and Greece to be the same as in their days.

former dissertation stated at large; where it is proved that figs and olives grew, in the times of the first emperors, in the province of Narbonne, which comprehended the more modern Provence and Dauphiné, and that north of that region they will not now thrive, nor are they cultivated. But all parts of Gaul, says Strabo, will produce the fruits which grow in Italy, except the fig and the olive. Italy, it is agreed, produced figs, olives, and various kinds of wine. " Latium," says Strabo, lib. 5, " enjoys a mild climate and produces all kinds of fruits, [παμφορος,] excepting the marshy lands on the sea-coast, and some mountainous tracts; but even these produce abundant pasturage, many kinds of fruits, and even one excellent kind of wine."

Strabo, in his second book, makes very correct and judicious remarks on climate; stating that mountainous regions are colder than valleys and low plains. He mentions Bagadania, an elevated plain between Mount Taurus and Argea, which produced scarcely any fruit trees, although situated three thousand stadiums south of the Euxine, where, at Sinope, the country produced olives. This circumstance has not been sufficiently considered in estimating the descriptions of climates and seasons, in ancient authors. Strabo then observes, that upon the Boristhenes, now the Neiper, and in that part of Celtica which is *contiguous to the ocean*, the vine either will not grow or not produce fruit. Celtica was that part of Gaul which is comprehended between the Garonne and the Seine.—(Cesar, Com. lib. 1.) Now let it be remarked, that the vine is cultivated at this day, in the *maritime* part of France, to a very little distance north of the Loire, in the forty eighth degree of latitude, although in the interior country, it is cultivated with success to the fiftieth degree. Strabo's assertion therefore, with regard to Gaul, is almost literally verified by modern facts.*

Strabo then mentions the climate on the north of the Euxine, and the fact that, at the mouth of the Palus Mæotis, a general of Mithridates, with a body of horse, defeated the barbarians upon the ice, on the very spot, where in summer he defeated them in a naval engagement.

A fact of this sort is of no effect in settling the question respecting a change of climate, because we know not whether the water in the strait of the sea of Azof annually congeals in winter into firm and solid ice, or whether the fact mentioned was owing to an unusual occurrence, and related for that very reason. The circumstances naturally lead us to conclude that the ice in that year was stronger than usual, and that the winter was uncommonly severe.

Strabo then proceeds to state from Eratosthenes, the story of a brazen cup or vessel which had been burst by the freezing of water, and as an evidence of the fact, was preserved in the temple of Esculapius at Panticape, a town on the Cimmerian Bosphorus. He cites the inscription on the vessel, of which the following is a translation. " If any man disbelieves what events have taken place among us, let him view this vessel and learn the truth. This vessel has been deposited here by Stratius, the priest, not as a gift to the gods, but as an evidence of a *very rigorous winter*"—[χειμωνος μεγαλʊ.] The translator has

---

* See Young's Tour in France, Vol. II, ch. 3, and his map of the climate. Pausanias informs us that olives grew in Tithorea on Mount Parnassus, which is in the thirty ninth degree of latitude.—(Phocics, ch. 32.)

rendered these words by *immensi frigoris,* which would describe severe
cold in general.   But such mistakes of the meaning of original writers
are the sources of many false theories.   The Greek χειμων will not
justify this translation ; it signifies *winter*, and in connection with *great*,
evidently denotes, in this place, an *unusual winter.*   Strabo indeed
speaks of the freezing of the Cimmerian Bosphorus, in general terms,
and of large fishes being dug out of ice, where they had been caught
in nets ; and if this should on inquiry be found to be the fact now, we
ought not to be surprised, as that strait is in the latitude of Quebec.
Severe as the cold was, the Greeks opened a communication with the
nations on the north of the Euxine, and built cities on the coast, among
which were Panticape on the strait, and *Olbia* on the Boristhenes, near
the mouth of the Hypanis or Bog.   From what circumstance this town
received its name, I know not ; but it signifies *happy* or the pleasant
residence.—(Strabo, lib. 7.   D'Anville, Anc. Geog. ix.)

That Germany would not produce fruit trees, at the Christian era,
must not be believed ; for vines were cultivated in Gaul, as far north as
the territory of the Sequani, since called Burgundy and Frenche Compté.
And Strabo informs us, that a celebrated prince of the Getæ, after subduing some nations in Thrace and Pannonia, persuaded them to cut up
their *vines* and live *without wine.*—(Lib. 7.)   Yet Thrace, as well as
Germany, is represented by the Roman and Greek writers as oppressed
with intolerable cold.

That there is much  inaccuracy and  some  exaggeration in the descriptions which ancient writers have given of the winters north of the
Alps and the Danube, may be clearly proved by a comparison of these
accounts one with another.   Tacitus, a writer of great credit, says of
Germany, " Terra, etsi aliquanto specie differt, in universum tamen
aut silvis horrida, aut  paludibus fœda ;"—the country is *all* deformed
with woods and morasses.—(De Mor. Germ. 5.)   He observes that the
soil is " satis ferax"—sufficiently fruitful ; but " frugiferarum arborum
impatiens"—not fitted to  produce  fruit-bearing trees ; yet in a subsequent section, he informs us that the inhabitants eat " agrestia poma"—
wild or uncultivated apples ; and those who lived near the  Rhine, purchased wine—" Proximi ripæ et vinum mercantur."   If neither Gaul
nor Germany produced wine, where did  the  dwellers on the  Rhine
procure it ?

Tacitus informs us further, that the Germans cultivated land, chiefly
indeed by their servants, old  men and women, as the men  preferred
war to labor.   But they raised barley and other grain, not only for food,
but for drink ; for their chief liquor was a species of beer or ale, made
from fermented barley and other corn.   The lands were cultivated by
slaves, who lived upon the land, like tenants, and paid to their masters
a certain part of the produce.   How incompatible are these facts with
the assertion that the country was all covered with forest and morasses !
Nor is this account more compatible with the state of pasturage in Germany, which, as all authors agree, supported vast herds of cattle.

But to close all, Tacitus himself assigns reasons why Germany was
not well cultivated, without resorting to the asperity of its climate.   After stating that the inhabitants parceled out the fields among themselves,
*according to the rank of each individual,* (a fact in which we see the
germ of the feudal system,) and that the fields lay fallow every other

year, the author says, " Nec enim cum ubertate et amplitudine soli la-
bore contendunt, ut pomaria conserant, et prata separent, et hortos
rigent sola terræ seges imperatur." So that after charging the defect
of fruit trees in Germany to the severity of the winters, this grave writer informs us that it is to be ascribed to the *want of labor*. The people were warlike, impatient of labor, and not having known the pleas-
ures of luxury, they wanted only corn for subsistence. Here we have
the whole truth.

But the passages in Ovid and Virgil, describing a Thracian winter,
which I have before mentioned, require some consideration.—(Ovid de
Tristibus, lib. 3, el. 10.   Virgil, Georg. lib. 3, 355.)

Ovid employs the whole of the tenth elegy of his third book in describing the phenomena of a Scythian winter, as it appeared at Tomos,
a town built by the Greeks, near the south bank of the Danube, on the
Euxine. The passage is too long to be here transcribed ; but the principal phenomena of the winter were, violent storms, deep snow, and
frost so severe as to freeze wine in jars, and the Danube covered with
solid ice, sufficient to sustain horses and cattle with wagons, or whatever
might be the vehicles called *plaustra*. Virgil's description corresponds
in general with Ovid's ; and he adds that snow accumulated to the depth
of seven (ulnos) cubits, about ten or eleven feet ; that cattle perished
with cold ; and that deer, plunged in snow almost to the top of their
horns, were killed with knives, not being able to escape.

On these descriptions, I would offer the following observations :

1. Some allowance must be made for the license of the poet. Exaggeration is admitted into verse for the purpose of exhibiting strong images to the mind ; and when Virgil speaks of snow ten feet deep, it will
be obvious that he must have had in view snow-drifts, which often accu-
mulate to that highth, in the middle latitudes of the earth—taking, as
a poet naturally would, the most remarkable phenomenon as the subject
of representation ; or he must have intended to describe the piles of
everlasting snow upon the mountains ; or he must have described some
very extraordinary snows in severe winters. Every man will at once
perceive that no country would be habitable in winter, where the common depth of the snow should be ten feet upon a level. That the country of Thrace and Scythia, to the Tanais or Don, was inhabited by numerous tribes of men, who subsisted by hunting and pasturage, from
the earliest times, is an indisputable fact; and the numerous flocks of cattle and horses kept by the nomadic Scythians, long before the time of Virgil, is a powerful argument against the supposed severity of the winters
in their climate ; for they did not cultivate the earth to any considerable
degree, and if the winters were of six or eight months' duration, as ancient authors pretend, how was it possible for them to subsist their cattle ?

The " semper hyems, semper spirantes frigora cauri" of Virgil, must
therefore be intended for Mount Rhodope, which is still covered with
snow the whole year, or it must be a poetical fiction.*   In the same

---

* Virgil begins his description with the country about Rhodope, but a part of it
must refer to the polar regions, or be a poetical fiction.   Indeed the ancients had
but little knowledge of the country north of the Danube, and confounded various
climates in general descriptions.   Herodotus however informs us, that the land
along the Boristhenes was very fruitful in corn.   He also speaks of the *plowing*
Scythians.—(See his Melpomene, 52, 53.)

light must we view the representation Virgil gives of the mode of spending the winter in Scythia; where, he says, the inhabitants dug caves
for their residence, and warmed them by rolling *whole oaks and elms*
upon their fires. This and other parts of the description are evidently
too high colored. But most of the phenomena described by Virgil and
Ovid, are such as we observe in the northern parts of this country; and
such as occur in New England, in winters of uncommon severity. If
these were the ordinary phenomena of the cold in the countries along
the Danube, now comprehended in Bulgaria, Wallachia, Bessarabia and
Hungary; and if such phenomena do not now occur in ordinary years,
there must have been a change of climate. With regard to modern
winters in that region, I have very little information. It is certain, however, that the Danube still freezes; although my information does not
enable me to say to what degree.

2. My second observation is, that the freezing of wine does not imply
great severity of cold. Madeira congeals at 10° above cipher by Fahrenheit; and the lighter wines of Italy, Greece and Asia Minor, would
undoubtedly freeze with a less degree of cold.

3. The accounts which historians give, as well as Ovid, of the irrup-
tions of the barbarians into Thrace and Italy, in winter, by means of a
bridge of ice, and the drawing of their *plaustra* upon the ice and snow,
demonstrate that the snow was not of a depth beyond what is usual in
New England.

4. But we have, in Ovid's twelfth elegy, more certain data to judge
of the winters in Thrace. The poet after indulging his fancy in describing the gloomy scenes of a Thracian winter, assumes a more cheer-
ful air, and paints the beauties of the following spring. " Frigora jam
zephyri minuunt," says Ovid, at the equinox. He then observes that
the year past, the winter of Mæotis seemed longer than former winters.
Whether he means longer than former winters in the same country, or
whether, that being the first winter after his exile, the winter appeared
longer to him than it had done in Italy, is not quite certain. If the former, the winter was unusually long, and probably unusually cold; and
therefore not to be considered as a standard of the general temperature
of ancient winters. If we are to understand the passage in the latter
sense, the remark is rather trifling; for who could question that a winter
in Thrace, would not appear longer to any man than a winter in Italy;
and especially to a wretched exile, forced from his family, his country,
and all his former enjoyments?

But we must not pass unobserved the facts mentioned by the poet at
this time—the spring equinox.

Now the merry youth, says Ovid, gather violets, which the uncultivated earth produces; the meads are decorated with blossoms of various hue, and the woods resound with the melody of birds. To this he
adds that swallows appeared and built nests *sub trabibus.* If swallows
appeared in Thrace, immediately after the equinox, the spring must
then have been three or four weeks earlier than in New England; for
they do not appear here till late in April. The same fact is indicated
by the blossoming of plants. These representations of the poet appear
to be important in settling this question.

Several passages in the most respectable ancient authors, leave us no
room to question, that not only the Cimmerian Bosphorus, the Don and

Boristhenes, but that the Danube and Rhine were, in winter, covered with ice sufficient to bear the heaviest loads, and that armies often crossed them on the ice. These facts are directly asserted in the following passages.—(Herodotus in Melpomene, 28. Xiphilin's Epit. of Dion. Cassius, M. Ant. Herodian, lib. 6. Pausanias, lib. 8, cap. 28. Jornandes de Rebus Geticis, 55. Ammianus Marcellinus, lib. 31, cap. 10.) Herodotus speaks of the Euxine Sea and the Cimmerian Bosphorus. Ovid asserts the like fact of the Danube, and probably intended that part of the river which is near its mouth. Pausanias mentions the Hypanis, now the Bog; the Boristhenes, now the Neiper; the Ister, or Danube, and the Rhine. The other authors speak of the Danube and Rhine, near their sources in the south of Germany and Helvetia. These writers represent the freezing of these rivers as common events—at least they make no discrimination between winters; and Herodian, in the passage cited, says of the Rhine and Danube, φυσις μεν δη των ποταμων αυτη—*this is the nature of those rivers.* He speaks of these rivers as they were in the country which now comprehends the dominions of Austria, Bavaria and Swabia; for it was in those countries where the barbarians usually crossed the rivers to invade the Roman empire.

The ice however was not always sufficiently strong to sustain armies; for about the year before Christ 175, a body of Bastarnians, returning from an irruption into Dardania, attempted to cross the Danube on the ice and were almost all drowned.—(Baker's Livy, book 41.)

How frequently the Rhine and Danube, in the same countries, are covered with ice of similar strength in modern days, I know not, for unfortunately modern travelers furnish little information on the subject. Pelloutier, who has cited most of the authorities of antiquity on this subject, says, the freezing of the Rhine, the Danube, the Elbe, the Weser, and the Oder, in such a manner as to sustain armies, is now an extraordinary event, which happens scarcely once in ten years—" La chose arrivera à peine une fois dans dix ans."—(Hist. des Celts, lib. 1, ch. 12.) But Cluver says, " Danubius in Germania glaciem fert ;" the Danube in Germany bears or is covered with ice.—(Lib. 1, 12.)

Let it be remarked that at the battle of Austerlitz, Dec. 2, the Russian troops were said to have crossed a lake on the ice. Bonaparte, in his account of the action, represented that most of them fell through the ice and were drowned; but by the official Russian account, it appears that the troops passed over in safety.

Let it be further remarked that Cesar, in his history of his seven campaigns in Gaul, during which his troops were often disturbed in winter by insurrections of the inhabitants, which obliged them to leave their winter quarters and march great distances, though he often mentions the extreme hardships suffered by his troops in these marches, and particularly the difficulty of transporting baggage, has not mentioned the word *snow* [nivis] in a single instance, if my memory does not deceive me, except when speaking of the march over the Cevennes; and on these mountains, snow falls in modern days to a depth equal to that mentioned by Cesar.—(See Pinkerton's Geog., France.)

But whatever may be the fact with respect to the climate of Germany, there is positive evidence that the rivers in Greece and Italy did not freeze to any considerable degree at the Christian era.  Pausanias, after mentioning the freezing of the Danube and other northern rivers, describes the water of the rivers in Arcadia as fit for bathing even in winter.—(Lib. 8, 28.)  Herodian, speaking of the discontents (on account of the climate,) which prevailed among the troops of Commodus, who performed service on the Danube, and who complained that they had frozen water to drink, speaks of the rivers of Italy, by way of contrast, as cool flowing streams.—(Lib. 1.)  But our best authority is Ovid, who, after relating the fact that the " Sarmatic cattle draw carriages upon the Danube," declares, " Vix equidem credar"—I shall hardly be believed ; yet he adds, " when a witness has no motive to misrepresent facts, credit is due to his testimony."  Now if the freezing of rivers to such a degree as to sustain carriages and cattle appeared incredible to the inhabitants of Italy, to one of whom Ovid was writing, it amounts to full proof that the Italians had never seen such a phenomenon, in their own country.  This disproves utterly the degree of cold in ancient Italy, which modern writers have supposed, and confirms what I have before suggested, that the instance of the freezing of the Tiber mentioned by Livy, was an extraordinary event, which excited general surprise, like our winter of 1780.  Indeed, all the descriptions of the rigorous winters in Thrace, Germany and Gaul, being given by historians and poets who were accustomed to the mild climates of Greece and Italy, wear the features of exaggeration, which must have been impressed upon them by the astonishment of the writers.  These facts seem to decide the question, that the winters in Greece and Italy were, two thousand years ago, as mild as they are in this age ; and that if any change has ever taken place in those countries, it must have been anterior to the age of the writers mentioned.  Indeed Columella, de Re Rustica, lib. 1, 61, mentions the opinion of an author, that such a change had taken place ; and cites as a proof of it, the fact that vines and olives would thrive in countries where the cold, in preceding ages, had prevented their cultivation.  I am satisfied, however, that although the *draining* and *drying* of land is often necessary to the cultivation of particular fruits, yet most of what has been charged to *cold*, ought to be ascribed to the *indolence* or *military spirit* of savage men, who preferred war and hunting to agriculture.

In addition to what I have said, on the subject of the winters in America, I have a few remarks to cite from two writers of undoubted credit.

John Megapolensis, a Dutch clergyman, who resided at Albany, and wrote an account of the Mohawks, in 1644, a translation of which is in Hazard's Collection, Vol. I, 517, says of the climate, " the summers are pretty hot, and the winters very cold.  The summer continues till All Saints' Day, (Nov. 1,) but then the winter sets in, in the same manner as it commonly does in December, and freezes so much in one night that the ice will bear a man.  The freezing commonly continues *three months*—sometimes there comes a warm and pleasant day, yet the thaw does not continue ; but it freezes again till March, and then commonly the river begins to open, seldom in February."  According to this account, the winters have not moderated ; for the Hudson, at Albany, usually freezes early in December, and continues closed till March.  A common winter is of three months' duration.

Professor Kalm, who came to America in 1748, was very particular
in his inquiries on this subject ; and to the best information he could
obtain, he added his own observations.   He relates, Vol. I, p. 21, Lond.
1772, that at Newcastle, the Delaware seldom froze in winter so as to
obstruct navigation ; but at Philadelphia, that river was, almost every
winter, covered with ice, so as to interrupt navigation for some weeks
together.   In page 36 he says, the climate of Philadelphia was then
temperate ; the winter was not over severe, and its duration short ;
September and October were like August in Sweden, and the first days
in February frequently as pleasant as the end of April and beginning
of May in the middle of Sweden.

In page 38 he says, the only disadvantage which the trade of Philadelphia suffers, is the freezing of the river almost every winter for a
month or more.   In page 83 he states, that the winters he spent in the
country were none of the coldest, but common ones, and that during
his stay, the Delaware was not covered with ice strong enough to bear
a carriage.   In the next page, he adds, that the winters, though severe,
did not continue above two months, and at Philadelphia sometimes less.
Cherries were ripe about the 25th of May—(probably old style.)

In page 197, the author speaking of New York, states that the *harbor
is good, and never frozen except in extraordinary cold weather ;* but he
says, page 208, the winters at New York are much more severe than in
Pennsylvania.   He says afterward, that the ice *stands on the Hudson
several months,* by which he must mean the ice on that river in the
interior country.   January 21, 1749, people walked over the Delaware
at Philadelphia on the ice ; but no one ventured to ride over on horseback.   But in page 362, the author informs us, that the river was covered with ice soon after new year, and the ice became so strong that
people rode over on horseback : the ice continued to the 8th of February, when the river was cleared.

The old men, of whom Kalm made inquiries respecting a change in
the seasons, all agreed in the fact, that when the country was first settled, the weather was more uniform than it was in their time.   Most of
them were of opinion, that more snow fell when they were young ;
that the winters began earlier ; and that the springs were also earlier.
It was a saying among the old Swedes, that they had always grass at
Easter, whether early or late.

Mr. Norris, one of the first settlers of Philadelphia, and a merchant,
related, that in his younger years, the Delaware was usually covered
with ice by the middle of November, old style.   One old Swede, who
remembered the very severe winter of 1697-8, was of opinion, there
had been little change in the winters ; that there were as great storms
and as cold winters in his old age, as in his childhood.

Kalm, however, in his second volume, page 43, institutes a comparison between Old and New Sweden, as he terms the two countries, in
which he mentions, among the disadvantages of New Sweden, or Delaware and Pennsylvania, that the nights are darker than in Old Sweden,
where they are in part illuminated by snow and the *lumen boreale.*   In
this paragraph he says expressly, that the winters bring no permanent
snow in Pennsylvania, to make the nights clear and traveling safe.
The cold, he says, is often intense as in Old Sweden ; but the snow

which falls lies only a few days, and always goes off with a great deal of wet.

From a careful comparison of these facts, it appears that the weather, in modern winters, is more inconstant, than when the earth was covered with wood, at the first settlement of Europeans in the country ; that the warm weather of autumn extends further into the winter months, and the cold weather of winter and spring encroaches upon the sum-mer; that the wind being more variable, snow is less permanent, and perhaps the same remark may be applicable to the ice of the rivers. These effects seem to result necessarily from the greater quantity of heat accumulated in the earth in summer, since the ground has been cleared of wood, and exposed to the rays of the sun ; and to the greater depth of frost in the earth in winter, by the exposure of its uncovered surface to the cold atmosphere.

But we can hardly infer, from the facts that have yet been collected, that there is, in modern times, an actual diminution of the aggregate amount of cold in winter, on either continent.

# CHAPTER IV.

## ORIGIN OF THE FIRST BANK IN THE UNITED STATES.

THE Bank of North America, the first institution of the kind in the United States, originated in the efforts of the patriotic merchants and other citizens of Pennsylvania, to supply the wants of the army in 1780. The history of it is briefly this:

By means of the depreciation of the bills of credit issued by Congress, the want of funds to redeem them, and the want of power in Congress to levy taxes, the finances of the United States in 1780 were reduced to the most miserable and alarming condition. Confidence in the government was lost; the contractors for the army were without funds, and the troops without pay, provision, or clothing.

In this situation of affairs, Mr. Pelatiah Webster, an old, intelligent merchant of Philadelphia, whose practical knowledge of money concerns gave him great influence, and whose opinions were often consulted by the gentlemen in Congress, wrote and published a number of essays on free trade and finance, with a view to point out the defects of the systems which had been pursued, and the evils of deluging the country with paper, without possessing the means of redeeming it. His fifth essay, published in March, 1780, was intended to urge and enforce the necessity of taxing the people, to an amount that should meet the annual expenditures. These essays, by unfolding the nature of credit, and the natural operations of money and commerce, prepared the mind of our citizens, who were not generally versed in these interesting subjects, for an essential change in the system of public credit. But his principles were addressed to the patriotism of the legislatures of the several states—a virtue which had been often exercised, and was nearly exhausted. Congress, by a public act, fixed the depreciated value of the bills of credit at a fortieth of their nominal value, and struck new bills to the amount of ten millions of dollars, which were to be issued on the funds of the several states, bearing an interest of five per cent. and redeemable in gold and silver.

But the circumstances of the army were pressing, and admitted of no delay. During the session of the Assembly of Pennsylvania, in May, 1780, a letter was received by the Executive Council from Gen. Washington, and transmitted to the House. In this letter the General stated, that although he had confidence in the attachment of the army to the public cause, yet their distresses were such, from a want of every thing necessary or convenient, that he was apprehensive of a mutiny. The reading of the letter was followed by silence; marks of despondence were visible on the countenances of many of the members, and one of them at length ventured to utter the language of despair. Another attempted to dissipate the gloom, but a motion of adjournment suspended a consideration of the contents of the letter.

The substance of the contents of Gen. Washington's letter, was communicated to some patriotic citizens of Philadelphia, who immediately opened a subscription for the purpose of raising money to pay bounties to recruits.  A considerable sum in specie and bills of credit was subscribed.

While this subscription was on foot, advices were received of the surrender of Charleston to the British commander.  This misfortune increased the public distress, and the necessity for more powerful exertion to recruit and supply the army.  On the 17th of June, therefore, a meeting was held at the City Tavern, and a resolution passed to open a security subscription to the amount of three hundred thousand pounds, Pennsylvania currency, in specie ; the subscribers to execute bonds to the amount of their subscriptions, and to form a bank for supplying the army.  This was executed, and the former subscription discontinued. By means of this fund, which was called the Bank of Pennsylvania, the necessities of the army were relieved, during that campaign.

In the spring following, Mr. Robert Morris was appointed superintendent of finances : the eminent abilities and influence of that gentleman, were greatly useful to the United States, in rescuing their moneyed concerns from disorder, and restoring public credit ; and to him is due the honor of projecting that useful institution, the "Bank of North America," which was intended to be, and for a time actually was, a national bank.

On the 17th of May, 1781, the plan of a national bank was submitted to the consideration of Congress ; and on the 26th of the month, Congress resolved, " That they do approve of the plan of establishing a national bank in the United States, submitted to their consideration by Mr. Robert Morris, and that they will promote and support the same, by such ways and means, from time to time, as may appear necessary for the institution, and consistent with the public good."  They further resolved, that the company should be incorporated, as soon as the subscription should be filled, recommended to the states to permit no other banks to be established during the war, and to pass laws making it felony to counterfeit the notes ; and they made the notes receivable in payment of all taxes, duties, and debts, payable to the United States. These resolutions were published, and to these were subjoined some remarks of the projector, on the advantages of the proposed bank. The original subscription, amounting to four hundred thousand dollars, in shares of four hundred dollars each, was filled ; and the subscribers were incorporated by an ordinance of Congress, dated Dec. 21, 1781 ; and by an act of the legislature of Pennsylvania, dated April 1, 1782. To this institution, most of the subscribers to the private bank before mentioned, transferred their subscriptions ; or invested the specie value of their subscriptions in the purchase of shares.  Those who declined, were repaid their money by the superintendent of finance.*

The immense advantages of this institution to the credit and money operations of the United States, as well as to the merchants, could not

---

* Manuscript statement, by Robert Morris, Esq.  Dissertations on Government and the affairs of the Bank, &c. by Thomas Paine, Philadelphia, February, 1786. Original plan of the Bank of North America, by Robert Morris, superintendent of finance, 1781.

screen it from popular jealousy.  In 1785, petitions from a number of the inhabitants of Chester County were presented to the legislature, praying for a repeal of the act of incorporation, and the act for preventing and punishing the counterfeiting of the notes of the bank. Their objections to the bank were the most ill founded imaginable. The committee on these petitions reported, as their opinion, that the bank was incompatible with the public safety—that it had a direct tendency to *banish specie from the country, and to collect it all into the hands of the stockholders !*—that the great profits of the bank would tempt foreigners to vest money in its stocks, and thus draw away large sums for interest—that it would become an enormous engine of power, subject to foreign influence, and tend to reduce America back to a state of subordination and dependence on European powers—that it would destroy the equality which ought to prevail in a republic—that our government had nothing in it to counterbalance the influence it must create—in short, that the directors might in time govern Pennsylvania.*

Such were the absurd, weak, contradictory, and chimerical notions of the people respecting the bank.

---

* Minutes of the Assembly, March 21, 1785.

# CHAPTER V.

## LETTER FROM GENERAL WASHINGTON.

It has been controverted whether the capture of Gen. Cornwallis in 1781, was the result of a plan preconcerted between Gen. Washington and Count de Grasse ; or rather whether the arrival of the Count in the Chesapeak was predetermined and expected by Gen. Washington, and consequently all the preparations to attack New York a mere finess to deceive the enemy ; or whether the real intention was against New York, and the siege of Yorktown planned upon the unexpected arrival of the French fleet in the bay. The following letter will set the matter in its true light.

Mount Vernon, July 31, 1788.

Sir—I duly received your letter of the 14th inst., and can only an-swer you briefly and generally from memory ; that a combined opera-tion of the land and naval forces of France in America, for the year 1781, was preconcerted the year before ; that the point of attack was not absolutely agreed upon,* because it could not be foreknown where the enemy would be most susceptible of impression ; and because we (having the command of the water with sufficient means of conveyance) could transport ourselves to any spot with the greatest celerity ; that it was determined by me, nearly twelve months beforehand, at all haz-ards, to give out and cause it to be believed by the highest military as well as civil officers, that New York was the destined place of attack, for the important purpose of inducing the eastern and middle states to make greater exertions in furnishing specific supplies, than they other-wise would have done, as well as for the interesting purpose of render-ing the enemy less prepared elsewhere ; that by these means, and these alone, artillery, boats, stores, and provisions, were in seasonable prepa-ration to move with the utmost rapidity to any part of the continent ; for the difficulty consisted more in providing, than knowing how to apply the military apparatus ; that before the arrival of the Count de Grasse, it was the fixed determination *to strike the enemy in the most vulnerable quarter*, so as to ensure success with moral certainty, as our affairs were then in the most ruinous train imaginable ; that New York was thought to be beyond our effort, and consequently that the only hesitation that remained, was between an attack upon the British army in Virginia and that in Charleston : and finally, that by the intervention of several com-munications, and some incidents which can not be detailed in a letter, the hostile post in Virginia, from being a *provisional and strongly ex-pected*, became the *definitive and certain object* of the campaign.

---

* Because it would be easy for the Count de Grasse, in good time before his de-parture from the West Indies, to give notice, by express, at what place he could most conveniently first touch to receive advice.

I only add, that it never was in contemplation to attack New York, unless the garrison should first have been so far degarnished to carry on the southern operations, as to render our success in the siege of that place, as infallible as any future military event can ever be made.   For I repeat it, and dwell upon it again, some splendid advantage (whether upon a larger or smaller scale was almost immaterial) was so essentially necessary, to revive the expiring hopes and languid exertions of the country, at the crisis in question, that I never would have consented to embark in any enterprise, wherein, from the most rational plan and accurate calculations, the favorable issue should not have appeared as clear to my view as a ray of light.   The failure of an attempt against the posts of the enemy, could, in no other possible situation during the war, have been so fatal to our cause.

That much trouble was taken and finess used to misguide and bewilder Sir Henry Clinton, in regard to the real object, by fictitious communications, as well as by making a deceptive provision of ovens, forage, and boats, in his neighborhood, is certain.   Nor were less pains taken to deceive our own army ; for I had always conceived, where the imposition did not completely take place at home, it could never sufficiently succeed abroad.

Your desire of obtaining truth, is very laudable ; I wish I had more leisure to gratify it, as I am equally solicitous the undisguised verity should be known.   Many circumstances will unavoidably be misconceived and misrepresented.   Notwithstanding most of the papers, which may properly be deemed official, are preserved ; yet the knowledge of innumerable things, of a more delicate and secret nature, is confined to the perishable remembrance of some few of the present generation.

With esteem, I am sir,
Your most obedient humble servant,
G. WASHINGTON.

To N. Webster, Esq.

# CHAPTER VI.

CORRESPONDENCE WITH THE HON. JAS. MADISON,
ON THE ORIGIN OF THE CONSTITUTION.

*Letter from N. Webster to Mr. Madison.*

New Haven, August 20, 1804.

SIR—In the fall of Gen. Hamilton I feel, in common with my fellow citizens, that the United States have lost a very distinguished character, and I sincerely deplore the cause and the event. Yet I can not join the voice of his admirers to the full extent of praise. He had some failings which very much lessened his public usefulness; and I believe he has some credit which does not belong to him. On one important point I wish for information, which is the reason of my troubling you with this letter.

Dr. Mason, in his Eulogy, has asserted, p. 11, that Gen. Hamilton, with a view " to retrieve our affairs by establishing an efficient general government, consented to be a candidate for the legislature." The year is not mentioned, nor am I disposed to question the fact. He adds, " it is indubitable that the *original germ* out of which has grown up our unexampled prosperity, was in the *bosom of Hamilton.*" This may be true, that Gen. Hamilton very early perceived the necessity of a more efficient government than the old confederation; but was not the germ of such a government in the minds of many others? Dr. Mason adds that Gen. Washington accepted a seat in the convention at the persuasion of Gen. Hamilton. This may be true. Mr. Otis, in his Eulogy, has asserted that Gen. Hamilton in the convention at Annapolis "*first* suggested the proposal of attempting a radical change in the principles of our government." This may be true as it respects the proposal in the convention; but surely the proposal of a radical change was made long before. I published a pamphlet on the subject eighteen months before, and took the pains to carry it in person to Gen. Washington in May, 1785. At his house you read it in the ensuing summer. It is entitled " Sketches of American Policy." The remarks in the first three sketches are general, and some of them I now believe to be too visionary for practice; but the fourth sketch was intended expressly to urge, by all possible arguments, the necessity of a radical alteration in our system of general government, and an outline is there suggested. As a private man, young and unknown, I could do but little, but that little I did.

Who *first* suggested the proposition for the present government, I am not certain; but I have always understood and declared that you made the first proposal, and brought forward a resolve for the purpose, in the House of Delegates of Virginia, in the session of December, 1785. In this I am confident of being correct, for I was in Richmond at that time. If wrong, please to set me right.

Mr. Paine claims to be the first mover of the proposal for a national government, alledging that he suggested it to some friends in the year 1784 or 1785. Mr. Pelatiah Webster wrote a pamphlet on the subject of a different frame of government in 1784. Dr. Dwight, in a century sermon four years ago, suggested ideas similar to what Dr. Mason has published. This is a historical fact of some importance, and I think it ought to be known and authenticated during *your* life. No honest man can wish to have credit for what is not due to him, and what is due to him ought not to be withheld or bestowed on another. I must beg the favor of you to communicate to me the facts as far as you know them, not for the purpose of publication, but for the sake of enabling me to possess a true state of the facts, and correcting the errors of my neighbors.

I am reading, and am much pleased with, the first volume of the life of Gen. Washington. One or two errors have escaped the respectable author. In page 125, he has placed New Haven on Connecticut River, although thirty five or forty miles west of it.

In page 105 he has given an account from Hutchinson of the origin of representation in the General Court of Massachusetts; but the account is not perfectly correct. In the first volume of my " Elements of Useful Knowledge" in the office of state, p. 158, there is a brief but correct statement of that change, taken from the history written by Governor Winthrop, who was personally in the transaction; a valuable authority which I believe Chief Justice Marshall does not possess. It lay in manuscript till 1790, when I procured it to be copied and printed. It is now out of print, but is the safest guide of the historian for the first fourteen years after the settlement of Boston. I am the more anxious to have the causes of that event fully stated, as the facts repel a suggestion often made by French writers, that in the division of houses in our legislatures, we have been led by a disposition to imitate the parliament of Great Britain. It appears, however, that the first instance of it arose out of a state of things in Massachusetts, altogether extraneous to any such principle.

I have the honor, &c.

N. WEBSTER.

Hon. Jas. Madison.

*Reply to the foregoing.*

Washington, Oct. 12, 1804.

SIR—I received, during a visit to my farm, your letter of Aug. 20, and hoped that I should, in that situation, find leisure to give it as full an answer as my memory and my papers would warrant. An unforeseen pressure of public business, with a particular one of private business interesting to others as well as to myself, having disappointed me, I find myself under the necessity of substituting the few brief remarks which return to the occupations of this place, and the absence of my papers, will admit.

I had observed, as you have done, that a great number of loose assertions have at different times been made with respect to the origin of the reform in our system of federal government, and that this has particularly happened on the late occasion which so strongly excited the effusions of party and personal zeal for the fame of Gen. Hamilton.

The change in our government like most other important improvements ought to be ascribed rather to a series of causes than to any particular and sudden one, and to the participation of many, rather than to the efforts of a single agent. It is certain that the general idea of revising and enlarging the scope of the federal authority, so as to answer the necessary purposes of the Union, grew up in many minds, and by natural degrees, during the experienced inefficacy of the old confederation. The discernment of Gen. Hamilton must have rendered him an early patron of the idea. That the public attention was called to it by yourself at an early period is well known.

In common with others, I derived from my service in the old Congress during the latter stages of the Revolutionary war, a deep impression of the necessity of invigorating the federal authority. I carried this impression with me into the legislature of Virginia; where, in the year 1784, if my recollection does not fail me, Mr. Henry co-operated with me and others in certain resolutions calculated to strengthen the hands of Congress.

In 1785, I made a proposition with success in the legislature of the same state, for the appointment of commissioners to meet at Annapolis such commissioners as might be appointed by other states, in order to form some plan for investing Congress with the regulation and taxation of commerce. This I presume to be the proceeding which gave you the impression that the first proposal of the present constitution was then made. It is possible that something more might have been the subject of conversation, or may have been suggested in debate, but I am induced to believe that the meeting at Annapolis was all that was regularly proposed at that session. I would have consulted the journals of it, but they were either lost or mislaid.

Although the step taken by Virginia was followed by the greater number of the states, the attendance at Annapolis was both so tardy and so deficient, that nothing was done on the subject immediately committed to the meeting. The consultations took another turn. The expediency of a more radical reform than the commissioners had been authorized to undertake being felt by almost all of them, and each being fortified in his sentiments and expectations by those of others, and by the information gained as to the general preparation of the public mind, it was concluded to recommend to the states a meeting at Philadelphia, the ensuing year, of commissioners with authority to digest and propose a new and effectual system of government for the Union. The manner in which this idea rose into effect, makes it impossible to say with whom it more particularly originated. I do not even recollect the member who first proposed it to the body. I have an indistinct impression that it received its first formal suggestion from Mr. Abraham Clark of New Jersey. Mr. Hamilton was certainly the member who drafted the address.

The legislature of Virginia was the first I believe, that had an opportunity of taking up the recommendation, and the first that concurred in it. It was thought proper to express its concurrence in terms that would give the example as much weight and effect as possible; and with the same view to include in the deputation, the highest characters in the state, such as the governor and chancellor. The same policy led to the appointment of Gen. Washington, who was put at the head of it. It was not known at the time how far he would lend himself to the occasion. When the appointment was made known to him, he manifested a readiness to yield to the wishes of the legislature, but felt a scruple from his having signified to the Cincinnati, that he could not meet them at Philadelphia, near about the same time, for reasons equally applicable to the other occasion. Being in correspondence with him at the time and on the occasion, I pressed him to step over the difficulty. It is very probable that he might consult with others, particularly with Mr. Hamilton, and that their or his exhortations and arguments may have contributed more than mine to his final determination.

When the convention as recommended at Annapolis took place at Philadelphia, the deputies from Virginia supposed, that as that state had been first in the successive steps leading to a revision of the federal system, some introductory propositions might be expected from them. They accordingly entered into consultation on the subject, immediately on their arrival at Philadelphia, and having agreed among themselves on the outline of a plan, it was laid before the convention by Mr. Randolph, at that time governor of the state, as well as member of the convention. This project was the basis of its deliberations; and after passing through a variety of changes in its important as well as its lesser features, was developed and amended into the form finally agreed to.

I am afraid that this sketch will fall much short of the object of your letter. Under more favorable circumstances, I might have made it more particular. I have often had it in idea to make out from the materials in my hands, and within my reach, as minute a chronicle as I could, of the origin and progress of the last revolution in our government. I went through such a task with respect to the declaration of independence, and the old confederation, whilst a member of Congress in 1783; availing myself of all the circumstances to be gleaned from the public archives, and from some auxiliary sources. To trace in like manner a chronicle or rather a history of our present constitution, would in several points of view be still more curious and interesting; and fortunately the materials for it are far more extensive. Whether I shall ever be able to make such a contribution to the annals of our country, is rendered every day more and more uncertain.

I will only add that on the slight view which I have taken of the subject to which you have been pleased to invite my recollections, it is to be understood, that in confining myself so much to the proceedings of Virginia, and to the agency of a few individuals, no exclusion of other states or persons is to be implied, whose share in the transactions of the period may be unknown to me.

With great respect and esteem, I remain, sir,

Your most obedient servant,

Noah Webster, Esq.                  JAMES MADISON.

Montpelier, March 10, 1826.

DEAR SIR—In my letter of Oct. 12, 1804, answering an inquiry of yours of Aug. 20, it was stated that " in 1785, I made a proposition with success in the legislature, (of Virginia,) for the appointment of commissioners, to meet at Annapolis such commissioners as might be appointed by other states, in order to form some plan for investing Congress with the regulation and taxation of commerce." In looking over some of my papers having reference to that period, I find reason to believe that the impression, under which I made the statement, was erroneous ; and that the proposition, though probably growing out of efforts made by myself to convince the legislature of the necessity of investing Congress with such powers, was introduced by another member, more likely to have the ear of the legislature on the occasion, than one whose long and late service in Congress, might subject him to the suspicion of a bias in favor of that body. The journals of the session would ascertain the fact. But such has been the waste of the printed copies, that I have never been able to consult one.

I have no apology to make for the error committed by my memory, but my consciousness, when answering your inquiry, of the active part I took in making on the legislature the impressions from which the measure resulted, and the confounding of one proposition with another, as may have happened to your own recollection of what passed.

It was my wish to have set you right on a point to which your letter seemed to attach some little interest, as soon as I discovered the error into which I had fallen. But whilst I was endeavoring to learn the most direct address, the newspapers apprised me that you had embarked for Europe. Finding that your return may be daily looked for, I lose no time in giving the proper explanation. I avail myself of the occasion to express my hopes that your trip to Europe, has answered all your purposes in making it, and to tender you assurances of my sincere esteem and friendly respects.

JAMES MADISON.

Noah Webster, Esq.

# CHAPTER VII.

## ORIGIN OF THE COPY-RIGHT LAWS IN THE UNITED STATES.

THE origin and progress of laws, securing to authors the exclusive right of publishing and vending their literary works, constitute an article in the history of a country of no inconsiderable importance. The following are the most material facts respecting the origin of the laws on that subject in the United Staes.

In the year 1782, while the American army was lying on the bank of the Hudson, I kept a classical school in Goshen, Orange County, state of New York. I there compiled two small elementary books for teaching the English language. The country was then impoverished; intercourse with Great Britain was interrupted; school-books were scarce and hardly obtainable; and there was no certain prospect of peace.

In the autumn of that year, I rode to Philadelphia for the purpose of showing my manuscripts to gentlemen of influence, and obtaining a law for securing to authors the copy-right of their publications. As the legislatures of New Jersey and Pennsylvania were not then in session, the latter object could not be accomplished. On my way I called on Gov. Livingston then in Trenton, and inquired whether it was probable that a copy-right law could be obtained in New Jersey. The Governor replied that if I would wait till noon, he would consult his council, then in session, and give me an answer. At the time appointed I called again, when the Governor told me the council gave him very little encouragement.

In Princeton, I waited on the Rev. Samuel Stanhope Smith, then professor of theology in Nassau Hall, and afterward president of that institution, who examined my manuscripts, recommended the works, and expressed his opinion in favor of copy-right laws. The following is a copy of his opinion.

" Mr. Noah Webster having shown to me a plan of reforming the spelling book of Mr. Dilworth, associating with it an abridgment of Mr. Lowth's Grammar and other articles of knowledge, very proper for young persons in the country; and having shown to me a part of the execution; I do conceive that he proposes many useful improvements in a book of that kind; and that he has executed with judgment that part which he has already finished. Every attempt of this nature undoubtedly merits the encouragement of the public; because it is by such attempts that systems of education are gradually perfected in every country, and the elements of knowledge rendered more easy to be acquired. Men of industry or of talents in any way, have a right to the property of their productions; and it encourages invention and improvement to secure it to them by certain laws, as has been practiced in European countries with advantage and success. And it is my opinion that it can be of no evil consequence to the state, and may be of benefit to it, to vest, by a law, the sole right of publishing and vending such works in the authors of them.

SAMUEL S. SMITH."

Princeton, Sept. 27, 1782.

This paper was afterward signed by Archibald Gamble, of the University in Philadelphia.

In October following, I went to Hartford, with a view to petition the legislature of Connecticut, then in session in that place, for a law to secure to me the copy-right of my proposed book. The petition was presented, but too late in the session to obtain a hearing. I then returned to Goshen, and devoted the winter to a revision of my manuscripts, and the introduction of some improvements, which had been suggested by gentlemen in Princeton and Philadelphia.

In January, 1783, I prepared another memorial to be presented to the legislature of Connecticut, for the purpose of procuring a copy-right law, which memorial was committed to the care of John Canfield, Esq. But the necessity of it was superseded by the enactment of a general law upon the subject. This law was obtained by the petition of several literary gentlemen in that state.

In the same winter, I went to Kingston in Ulster County, New York, where the legislature was in session, with a view to present a petition for the like purpose. The necessity of such petition was prevented, by the prompt attention of General Schuyler to my request, through whose influence a bill was introduced into the senate, which, at the next session, became a law.

In the same winter, the legislature of Massachusetts enacted a copyright law; procured probably by the agency of the Rev. Timothy Dwight, then a member of the house of representatives.

As Congress, under the confederation, had no power to protect literary property, certain gentlemen, among whom was Joel Barlow, presented a memorial to that body, petitioning them to recommend to the several states, the enactment of such a law.

In May, 1783, on the report of Mr. Williamson, Mr. Izard and Mr. Madison, Congress passed a resolution, recommending to the several states to secure to authors or publishers of new books not before printed, the copy-right of such books for a term not less than fourteen years.— (Journals, Vol. IV, ed. 1823.)

In December, 1783, Governor Livingston informed me by letter that the legislature of New Jersey had passed a law agreeable to the recommendation of Congress.

In May, 1785, I undertook a journey to the middle and southern states, one object of which was to procure copy-right laws to be enacted. I proceeded to Charleston, but the legislature not being in session, I returned to Baltimore, where I spent the summer.

In November, I visited General Washington at his mansion; he gave me letters to Governor Harrison in Richmond, and to the speakers of both houses of the legislature. The law desired was passed for securing copy-rights.

In December, I visited Annapolis, where the legislature was in session ; and in February, I visited Dover, in Delaware, for the same purpose. On petition, the legislature of Delaware appointed a committee to prepare a bill for a copy-right law, just at the close of the session, but the enactment was deferred to the next session.

In the year 1790, Congress enacted their first copy-right law, which superseded all the state laws on the subject.

When I was in England, in 1825, I learned that the British parliament had, a few years before, enacted a new law on copy-rights, by which the rights of authors were much extended. This led me to attempt to procure a new law in the United States, giving a like extension to the rights of authors. My first attempt appears in the following letter.

*Extract from a letter to the Hon.* DANIEL WEBSTER, *dated September* 30, 1826.

There is another subject, sir, to which I take the liberty to invite your attention.

Since the celebrated decision, respecting copy-right, by the highest British tribunal, it seems to have been generally admitted that an author has not a permanent and exclusive right to the publication of his original works, at common law ; and that he must depend wholly on statutes for his enjoyment of that right. As I firmly believe this decision to be contrary to all our best established principles of *right* and *property ;* and as I have reason to think such a decision would not now be sanctioned by the authorities of this country, I sincerely desire that while you are a member of the House of Representatives in Congress, your talents may be exerted in placing this species of property on the same footing as all other property, as to exclusive right and permanence of possession.

Among all modes of acquiring property, or exclusive ownership, the act or operation of *creating* or *making* seems to have the first claim. If any thing can justly give a man an exclusive right to the occupancy and enjoyment of a thing, it must be the fact, that he *made* it. The right of a farmer and mechanic to the exclusive enjoyment and right of disposal of what they *make* or *produce*, is never questioned. What then can make a difference between the produce of *muscular strength* and the produce of the *intellect ?* If it should be said, that as the purchaser of a bushel of wheat has obtained not only the exclusive right to the use of it for food, but the right to sow it and make increase and profit by it, let it be replied, this is true ; but if he sows the wheat, he must sow it on his own ground or soil. The case is different with respect to the copy of a book, which a purchaser has obtained, for the copy-right is the *author's soil*, which the purchaser can not legally occupy.

Upon what principles, let me ask, can my fellow citizens declare that the productions of the farmer and the artisan shall be protected by common law, or the principles of natural and social right, without a special statute, and without paying a premium for the enjoyment of their property, while they declare that I have only a temporary right to the fruits of my labor, and even this can not be enjoyed without giving a premium ? Are such principles as these consistent with the established doctrines of property, and of moral right and wrong, among an enlightened peo-

ple ? Are such principles consistent with the high and honorable notions of justice and equal privileges, which our citizens claim to entertain
and to cherish, as characteristic of modern improvements in civil society ? How can the *recent origin* of a particular species of property
vary the principles of ownership ? I say nothing of the inexpedience
of such a policy, as it regards the discouragement of literary exertions.
Indeed I can probably say nothing on this subject, that you have not
said or thought; at least, I presume you have often contemplated this
subject in all its bearings.

The British parliament about ten or twelve years ago, passed a new
act on this subject, giving to authors and proprietors of new works, an
absolute right to the exclusive use of the copy-right for twenty eight
years, with some other provisions which I do not recollect; but the act
makes or continues the condition that the author or proprietor shall deposit *eleven copies* of the work in Stationer's Hall, for the benefit of certain public libraries. This premium will often amount to *fifty pounds
sterling* or more. An effort was made by publishers to obtain a repeal
of this provision; but it was opposed by the institutions which were to
receive the benefit, and the attempt failed.

I have a great interest in this question, and I think the interest of
science and literature in this question are, by no means, inconsiderable.

I sincerely wish our legislature would come at once to the line of right
and justice on this subject, and pass a new act, the preamble to which
shall admit the principle that an author has, by common law, or natural
justice, the sole and *permanent* right to make profit by his own labor,
and that his heirs and assigns shall enjoy the right, unclogged with conditions. The act thus admitting the right would prescribe only the *mode*
by which it shall be ascertained, secured and enjoyed, and violations of
the right punished; and perhaps make some provisions for the case of
attempts to elude the statute by slight alterations of books by mutilations
and transpositions.

Excuse me, sir, for the trouble I give you, and believe me with much
respect, your obedient servant,                                N. WEBSTER.
Hon. Daniel Webster.

*To this letter Mr. Webster returned the following answer.*

Boston, October 14, 1826.

DEAR SIR—I have received yours of the 30th of September, and shall
with your permission, lay it before the committee of the judiciary next
session, as that committee has in contemplation some important changes
in the law respecting copy-right. Your opinion, in the abstract, is certainly right and uncontrovertible. Authorship is, in its nature, ground
of property. Most people, I think, are as well satisfied, (or better)
with the reasoning of Mr. Justice Yates, as with that of Lord Mansfield,
in the great case of Miller and Taylor. But after all, property, in the
social state, must be the creature of law; and it is a question of expediency, high and general, not particular expediency, how and how far,
the rights of authorship should be protected. I confess frankly, that
I see, or think I see, objections to make it perpetual. At the same

time I am willing to extend it further than at present, and am fully
pursuaded that it ought to be relieved from all charges, such as depositing copies, &c.                        Yours,

D. WEBSTER.
Dr. N. Webster.

In the autumn of 1827, I applied to the Hon. Mr. Ingersoll, a representative from Connecticut, stating to him the facts of an extension of
copy-right in Great Britain, as also in France, and requesting him to
use his influence to have a bill for a new law brought forward in Congress.   Mr. Ingersoll very cheerfully complied.   On the 17th December, on the motion of Mr. Ingersoll, the House of Representatives "resolved, that the committee on the judiciary inquire into the expediency
of extending the time for which copy-rights may be hereafter secured
to authors, beyond the period now allowed by law ; and also of affording
further protection to authors against the publication of abridgments or
summaries of works, after the copy-rights thereof have been secured."
As the committee delayed several weeks to make a report, Mr. Ingersoll
conversed fully on the subject with one of the members, and addressed
a note to the committee, in which he stated the provision of the British
statute 34th, Geo. 3, enlarging the rights of authors, and the liberal provisions of the French laws on the subject.   He stated some of the defects of the old law of the United States, and urged the expediency
and justice of a more liberal law.

A petition signed by many respectable literary men, was, about this
time, presented to Congress, praying for the same object.   Some members of the committee were opposed to the measure ; but at length, on
the first of February, 1828, the committee reported a bill consisting of
three sections only, extending the term of copy-rights from fourteen to
twenty eight years, and securing the benefit of the act to authors who
had previously obtained a copy-right under the old law.

On the 21st of February, Mr. Verplanck submitted to the House of
Representatives an amendment to the bill reported by the committee,
entitled an "Amendment to a Bill to amend and consolidate the Acts
respecting Copy-Rights."   This amendment was printed by order of
the House.   It was intended to embrace all the material provisions of
the two former laws, and those of the bill reported by the judiciary
committee ; it contained also some additional improvements.   Nothing
further was done, and the bill and amendment died at the close of the
session.

At the next session (1829–30) the Hon. Mr. Ellsworth, a member
from Connecticut, was appointed one of the judiciary committee, of
which the Hon. Mr. Buchanan was chairman.   Before Mr. Ellsworth
left home, I applied to him to make efforts to procure the enactment of
a new copy-right law ; and sent a petition to Congress, praying for the
renewal of the copy-right of one of my books.   This petition, being
referred to the judiciary committee, brought the subject distinctly into
consideration.   After consultation, the committee authorized Mr. Ellsworth to prepare a bill for a general law on the subject.

In order to present the subject in its true light to the committee and
to Congress, Mr. Ellsworth wrote notes to the ministers of the principal

European nations, requesting information from each of them respecting the state of copy-rights in the nations they represented. From their answers, and an inspection of the laws of some of the governments, Mr. Ellsworth formed a report, stating the terms of time for which copy-rights are secured to authors in Great Britain, France, Russia, Sweden, Denmark, and certain states in Germany. He also formed a bill for a law intended to embrace all the material provisions of the old laws, with those of the bill reported by the former judiciary committee.

In this bill Mr. Ellsworth introduced some valuable provisions which had been omitted in the old laws, and in the bill and amendment offered at the former session. He also obtained from his friends some suggestions which enabled him to correct some errors and supply defects. This bill was approved by the judiciary committee, reported by Mr. Ellsworth, and printed by order of the House. But such was the pressure of business, and so little interest was felt in the bill, that no efforts of Mr. Ellsworth could bring it before the House at that session.

Finding the efforts of the friends of the bill in Congress to be unavailing to obtain a hearing, I determined in the winter of 1830–31 to visit Washington myself, and endeavor to accomplish the object. Accordingly I took lodgings at the seat of government, where I passed nine or ten weeks; and during this time, read a lecture in the Hall of the Representatives, which was well attended, and as my friends informed me, had no little effect in promoting the object of obtaining a law for securing copy-rights.

The difficulties which had prevented the bill from being brought forward now disappeared.

The bill, at the second reading in the House of Representatives, met with some opposition; but it was ably supported by Mr. Ellsworth, Mr. Verplanck and Mr. Huntington. It passed to a third reading by a large majority, and was ordered to be engrossed without opposition.

When the bill came before the Senate, it was referred to the judiciary committee. Mr. Rowan, the chairman, being absent, the committee requested the Hon. Daniel Webster to take the bill, examine it and report it, if he thought proper: he did so, and under all circumstances, deemed it expedient to report it without amendment. On the second reading Mr. Webster made a few explanatory remarks—no other person uttered a word on the subject; and it passed to a third reading by a unanimous vote. On the third reading, the Senate, on motion, dispensed with the reading, and it passed to be engrossed, without debate.

In my journeys to effect this object, and in my long attendance in Washington, I expended nearly a year of time. Of my expenses in money I have no account; but it is a satisfaction to me that a liberal statute for securing to authors the fruits of their labor has been obtained.

# CHAPTER VIII.

## VINDICATION OF THE TREATY OF AMITY, COMMERCE AND NAVIGATION, WITH GREAT BRITAIN.*

### No. I.

THE treaty between Great Britain and America has been a matter of great public expectation, and it has been rendered more interesting by the time and manner in which the negotiation originated.

Before the revolution in America, the people of the then colonies were under the government of Great Britain; they considered themselves as children of the same family; their trade was almost limited to the British dominions; the Americans had estates in Great Britain, and moneys in her funds; an extensive commerce had created innumerable debts and connections between the two countries, which could not be at once discharged and dissolved.

A long, expensive, and bloody war, to resist the unjust claims of the British parliament, attended with many instances of atrocious cruelty and perfidy on the part of the British governors and commanders, alienated the affections of the great body of Americans from the mother country. On the restoration of peace, however, and the acquisition of independence, the enmity of the Americans gradually subsided; and the usefulness of the commerce of England to these states, being every where experienced, soon revived the habits of friendly intercourse between America and Great Britain, which had been interrupted by the war—an intercourse which was not much affected by the controversies between the two governments on account of the inexecution of the treaty of peace. Almost as soon as the acceptance and organization of a constitution for the United States had given them a national capacity, it was the wish and desire of America to form a commercial treaty with Great Britain; and Mr. Jefferson, in a letter to Mr. Hammond, dated Nov. 29, 1791, requested to know whether he was authorized to enter into a negotiation for that purpose.

The circumstances which operated to defeat the attempts of our executive, and the controversies between the governments of the two countries, relative to the non-fulfillment of the treaty on one side and the other, are in every man's recollection; it is needless to mention them here. It is sufficient for my purpose, that the President was authorized by the public wishes, to negotiate a commercial treaty with Great Britain; and he is vested with full powers for this purpose by the constitution.

The uniform desire of Congress on this subject, is a complete answer to all cavils about the exertion of the President's constitutional powers.

---

* From the New York Minerva of 1795.

It was the nation, the United States, that requested and urged for a negotiation.

This also is an answer to the men who say the people of America supposed the appointment of Mr. Jay, as envoy extraordinary, was intended only to demand and procure a redress of wrongs, and indemnification for spoliations on our trade; and not for the negotiation of a commercial treaty. Whatever opinion people formed of the embassy, the instructions given to the envoy were in pursuance of constitutional powers; and if the people are surprised with a treaty of amity and commerce, before they expected it, this forms no objection to the treaty itself.

The time selected for this negotiation, and the exercise of the President's powers, at the critical moment when the public mind in America was in a violent flame, on account of the seizure of our vessels by British privateers, and when hostilities were expected between the two countries, however offensive to a party in America, are among the most fortunate circumstances of this whole business.

The sequestration bill, then before Congress, involved in it the events of peace or war. The bill, had it passed, would have been considered by Great Britain equivalent to issuing letters of marque and reprisal, and tantamount to a declaration of hostilities; and probably that act, had it been sanctioned by the several branches of the legislature, would have plunged us into the present most calamitous war.

Such a consequence was considered by the President as little less than inevitable. As a constituent branch of the legislature, and chief magistrate of the nation, he had a right to exert the powers he possessed—and if he thought the House of Representatives were rash in their measures, it was his *duty*, as the chief guardian of the public safety, to exert any of his constitutional powers for the purposes of arresting those measures. It was as much his right and his duty to interpose negotiation as a means of checking any measures that he deemed inconsistent with our national interest, if he judged that the best means, as it is to give his negative to a bill that has passed the other branches of the legislature, when he judges the bill unconstitutional or inexpedient.

The *right* of the President to interpose negotiation, at the time he did, can not be disputed. The *expediency* of the measure will perhaps never be admitted by its opposers; but every subsequent event has served to convince the friends of our present administration, that the measure was highly expedient, and the time well chosen.

That the President was right in resorting to a *peaceable demand* of indemnification for spoliations on our commerce, is capable of the highest proof. The law of nations makes it a duty, on the part of a nation thus injured, to make a peaceable requisition of damages or restoration of property, from the aggressing nation, before the commencement of hostilities.

Vattel, book iii, chap. 3, lays it down in the most unequivocal language, that an injured nation has no right to resort to force for satisfaction, until other means of obtaining it have proved fruitless.

In conformity with this principle of the law of nations, it is often stipulated by treaty, that letters of marque and reprisal shall not be granted by an injured nation, until means of redress have been sought in the ordinary course of justice. Of this tenor is the third article of the treaty of navigation and commerce between Great Britain and Spain, dated 1713.

It was in pursuance of this most salutary principle, that the President appointed an envoy extraordinary at the time he did ; and it was undoubtedly, in other respects, highly expedient; as no moment could be more eligible for a negotiation with England, than when she was engaged in an expensive and unsuccessful war ; a war that entrenches deeply on her resources, and demands a minute attention to her commercial interests.

But my opposers will say, " We admit the propriety of negotiation, before the commencement of hostilities ; but we contend that our envoy should have been restricted to a demand of the western posts, and indemnification for losses by illegal captures, and condemnation of our vessels and property. It was never understood that Mr. Jay had instructions to make a commercial treaty."

This objection amounts to nothing, and deserves no answer. The President had as good a right to authorize Mr. Jay to conclude a treaty of amity and commerce as any other man ; and he had the same right to choose one time as another.

Having made these preliminary remarks on the origin of this negotiation and treaty, I will proceed to answer such objections to the treaty as have come to my knowledge.

The daily invectives of newspaper paragraphists will be passed without notice. This is treating them as they deserve to be treated, and as they are in fact treated by the public.

A writer in a morning paper under the signature of *Decius*, appears to have assailed the treaty with more ingenuity than any other writer whose arguments I have read ; and it is probable that his writings comprise the amount and force of all the objections that are made to it. I shall therefore take his objections in the order they are published, and endeavor to prove them of little weight, or wholly unfounded.

The first remarks of this writer are aimed at the candor and integrity of the twenty members of the Senate, who, he insinuates, ratified the treaty from *motives of party spirit*. He does not indeed exempt the minority from the same censure of their conduct. But what refutes the insinuation is, the rejection of the twelfth article by the men thus criminated. Certainly the spirit of party was not the governing motive ; for party spirit is unconceding, and goes all lengths to carry its points. The rejection of that article, because it entrenches too much on our carrying trade, in the opinion of those gentlemen, is a proof that the *interest of commerce and the public good*, were the motives of their conduct in assenting to every other part of the treaty.

His next remark is leveled at the secrecy of the Senate, in conducting the debates on the treaty. " Is not this secrecy alone," says *Decius*, " a proof that the Senate conceived it disgraceful and prejudicial to the United States ?"

Let me ask that writer a candid question: Has not every treaty which we have made with other nations, been concluded and ratified in secret ? And is there one of those treaties disgraceful or prejudicial to our nation ? No objection was formerly made to these secret ratifica-

tions. Why should reasons now exist for opening the discussion of
treaties to the people, which did not exist in 1783 and 1785 ? The reason is obvious. Americans were formerly under no influence but that
of propriety; they acted themselves—now a party of them have deserted the principles which formerly guided our councils, and appear to
be ambitious only of finding opportunities to rail at all steady wisdom,
and to commit our interests to passion and party.

The secrecy of negotiations with foreign powers, through every
stage of the business, is dictated by sound policy. By making treaties
public before they are ratified, advantages would often be lost, and by
destroying confidence and freedom of communication, the business
would be often impeded or wholly defeated. Nothing marks the sense
of mankind on this subject, better than the practice of individuals, who
generally use secrecy in all important contracts of their own. This
common practice is a proof of its utility. Much more necessary is it
in treaties, which are national contracts or conventions.

Another remark of *Decius*, worthy of notice, is, that the " first impressions made by the treaty were unfavorable—all men and all *ranks*
[what ranks ? this writer has certainly forgotten one article of democracy—*equality*,] united in condemning it."

This remark has some foundation, and the fact is easily accounted
for. The first impressions on the minds of the public, were made by
an abstract of the treaty, which was published incorrectly, and there
are strong suspicions that it was done with the insidious view of exciting
improper impressions. The abstract was said to have been made from
memory. This can not be true. It is not in the power of man, after
the most careful perusal, to make out so large an abstract, without the
help of notes, of twenty-eight articles of a treaty, without intermixing
the articles in the sketch. The business must have been done with design; and it was inexcusable in any man to offer to the public a *sketch*,
much more an *incorrect* one, of so important an instrument.

These unfavorable impressions, however, answered the views of men
who perfectly well understood the importance of *prepossessing* the public mind. They excited a temporary clamor, and have perhaps made
a few weak friends to an expiring cause.

But the clamor of the moment subsided, on reading a correct copy of
the treaty—men all agreed it was not so bad as they expected. Still
many well-meaning people do not understand it; and every possible
effort is used to distort and misconstrue some passages of the treaty
which affect the commerce of the country.

The violent censure of the treaty which prevailed on its first publication, in skeleton, and the moderation of the clamor on further perusal of it, instead of being a proof that the treaty is in itself bad, is a
substantial argument in its favor; it is a proof that it bears examination;
and it is a proof, further, of what we should all regret, that the *passions*
of men outstrip their *judgment*.

Should the final result of the business prove to be, what I am confident it will be, a general conviction that the treaty is, on the whole, a
favorable one for the United States, and the most favorable of any
treaty we have yet formed; tne public will view with indignation, the
insidious attempts that have been made to excite a ferment, and oppo-

sition to its ratification, as well as to load with unmerited censure the able minister who conducted the negotiation.* Curtius.

## No. II.

The preamble of the treaty, says *Decius*, is not free from objections. It states that the differences between the countries are to be terminated " without reference to the merits of their complaints." *Decius* says, the merits of the controversy should never be lost sight of. But when this expression is explained, I believe every candid man will justify it in the present instance.

The *merits of the complaints*, in this instance, refer solely to the question, " which party first violated the treaty of peace." On the first opening of the negotiation between the ministers of the two countries, this became an important point of discussion. The American envoy alledged the first breach of the treaty to be on the part of Great Britain, and mentioned the carrying away of the negroes.

The English minister maintained that this was *not* a violation of the treaty. As this subject has occasioned as much altercation as any point between the two countries, and as the silence of the present treaty on that subject, is the ground of violent clamor, I will anticipate a consideration of this point, which would more properly fall under a subsequent article.

Whenever our ministers have urged the claim of restitution or compensation for the negroes, the British ministry have, invariably, answered them with the following remarks :

" The negroes carried from America by the British armies, were taken by the troops on their marches through the country, or came in, by proclamation, and put themselves under our protection.

" The clause of the treaty on which you ground your claim is in these words—' his Britannic majesty shall, with all convenient speed, and without causing any destruction, or carrying away *any negroes* or *other property* of the *American* inhabitants, withdraw all his armies,' &c.

" By the laws of the American states negroes are considered as *property* as much as cattle ; you claim them as *property* for the men who

---

* When the first number of Curtius appeared, a copy of it was sent to Mr. Jefferson, who immediately wrote to Mr. Madison a letter, dated Monticello, Sept. 21, 1795, from which the following are extracts.

" I send you by post one of the pieces, Curtius, lest it should not have come to you otherwise. It is evidently written by Hamilton, giving a first and general view of the subject, that the public mind might be kept a little in check, till he could resume the subject more at large from the beginning, under his second signature, Camillus. The piece called " The Features of the Treaty," I do not send, because you have seen it in the newspapers. It is said to be written by Coxe ; but I should rather suspect by Beckley. The antidote is certainly not strong enough for the poison of Curtius. If I had not been informed the present came from Beckley, I should have suspected it from Jay or Hamilton. I gave a copy or two, by way of experiment, to honest-hearted men of common understanding, and they were not able to parry the sophistry of Curtius. I have ceased therefore to give them. Hamilton is really a colossus to the anti-republican party. Without numbers, he is a host within himself. We have had only middling performances to oppose to him. In truth, when he comes forward, there is nobody but yourself who can meet him. For God's sake, take up your pen, and give a fundamental reply to Curtius and Camillus."—(Correspondence, Vol. III, 315.)

were their proprietors.  By the laws of war universally admitted, every species of movable property found and taken in an enemy's country, becomes the property of the captors.  By the seizure and possession of the negroes, the British armies became the rightful owners; the negroes were *booty*, as much as the horses and cattle taken by the same troops.

"Suppose an American boat loaded with goods, to be taken on one of your rivers in the time of war, would not that boat and goods be a fair prize?  Suppose a horse to stray into the British lines and be taken, would not that horse belong to the captors?  Could a claim be reasonably interposed for restitution or compensation in these cases?  Whether they were seduced or forced from the plantations, if they were *property*, that property, on their coming into possession of the British army, was changed, according to all the laws of war.

"The clause of the treaty contemplates negroes which were *American property* at the date of the stipulation.  'Negroes or *other* property' are the words.  But the negroes which our troops had taken in their marches, or which had put themselves under their protection, were not, at that time, the *property* of Americans.

"On this construction, which we hold to be the only rational one, that clause of the treaty will not maintain your claim.  The treaty may include slaves which were within the British lines, in possession of their American masters; but there is no pretense that such were carried away by the British troops.

"Besides, we can not surrender negroes which came into our lines on the faith of proclamations, without a violation of that faith; which can not be done.  We promised them freedom and protection—we gave them that freedom, and we must protect them."

Such is the substance of the minister's reply, to the claims of our envoy, which were repeatedly urged without success.  And the British ministry have invariably put the same construction on that clause of the treaty of peace.  Indeed it seems difficult to answer this reasoning.

Either the negroes were *slaves* and *property*, or they were not.  If they were slaves and property, as considered by the laws of most of the American states, the British had the same right to seize and carry them away as booty, as they had to seize and carry away horses and cattle; a right of war that was never disputed.  In this case, the property was changed the moment they came into the possession of the British armies, and at the date of the treaty, they were *not* American property, and consequently *not* included in the stipulation of the treaty.

If, on the other hand, the negroes were *freemen*, they had a right to put themselves under British protection, and we have no shadow of claim to restitution or compensation.

I am one who believe that no property can be obtained in human flesh, and any law authorizing the purchase and detention of a human being, as *property*, is, *ipso facto*, void.  Should this position be well founded, we have not a shadow of pretension to the negroes carried away by the British troops.

But the laws of many of the states do consider them as property; whether rightfully or wrongfully, is not now the question.  If we consider them as *property*, they are to be ranked among *personal* estates, for they certainly are not *real* estate.

Now Mr. Jefferson, the oracle of my antagonists, admits, in the fullest extent, the doctrine, that all personal estate is rightfully seizable by enemies in war.   The following are his words :—
" It can not be denied, that the state of war strictly admits a nation to seize the property of its enemies, found within its own limits, or taken in war, and in whatever form it exists—whether in action or possession."

In confirmation of this, he quotes Bynkershoek, l. 1, c. 7, who is clear and explicit on the subject.   See papers relative to Great Britain, published by order of Congress, p. 29.   This doctrine is the universal law of nations.

" As the towns and lands taken from the enemy, are called conquests, all *movable things* constitute the *booty*.   The booty belongs to the sovereign."—(Vattel, book iii, ch. 9.)

In the interpretation of treaties where there are two constructions, the one favorable, the other odious, that which is odious is always to be rejected : and what can be more odious than to construe this article of the treaty, so as to violate faith toward the wretched blacks, and render them back to the whips and scourges of slavery ?   At any rate, this point of the business the British ministry will not yield, as the first infraction of the treaty.

Then came the detention of the western posts, which our minister alledged to be a breach of the treaty, anterior to any violation on the part of the United States.   Here was introduced the correspondence between Mr. Jefferson and Mr. Hammond, and Mr. Jefferson's reasoning on the subject.   To this the British minister answered, by referring to dates of transactions.

The provisional articles between Great Britain and America were signed November 30, 1782, at Paris ; and notice of this was officially received by Sir Guy Carleton, April 5, 1783.   But the definitive treaty was not signed till September 3, 1783, and the ratifications were not finally exchanged till some time in 1784, though I do not know the day and the month.

A treaty is binding on a nation from the moment of signature ; but its ultimate validity depends on its passing through all the usual forms. According to the modern practice, the exchange of ratifications puts the seal to the validity of a treaty, and gives it an effect from the time of signature.

The British ministry state, that *ex gratia*, or as a matter of convenience to the nation, orders were given to Sir Guy Carleton to evacuate New York, immediately on signing the provisional articles in 1782. But they alledge they were not bound to do this, until they had been notified of the ratification of those articles by Congress, which could not have been till the middle of the year 1784.

The demand made by the Baron Steuben, by order of General Washington, of the surrender of the western posts, and the first demand made, was by his letter to General Haldimand, dated August 2, 1783. At this time the British minister could scarcely have heard whether Congress had agreed to the treaty or not ; much less could any orders have been sent to them from Canada for withdrawing the troops from the garrison.

Admitting this fact, that the British ministry were not *bound* by treaty to give orders for the troops to withdraw, until the treaty had gone through its usual forms, then the detention of the posts till long after they had been demanded by Baron Steuben, and perhaps as late as the demand of Colonel Hull in July, 1784, was justifiable and authorized by the practice of nations.

But long before this, Congress had declared the carrying away of the negroes an infraction of the treaty ; and in May, 1793, had sent orders to our foreign ministers to remonstrate against this measure and demand reparation.

The state of New York, so early as March 17, 1783, passed an act authorizing any citizen to bring actions of trespass against any person who had occupied or injured his estate, real or personal, within the power of the enemy. This was an express violation of the 6th article of the treaty, which declares that no person shall suffer any loss or damage, or any prosecution, on account of the part he had taken during the war. And Virginia, in December, 1783, passed an act, suspending executions on certain judgments, which materially affected British creditors. South Carolina in March, 1784, followed, and passed an act suspending all actions, both British and American, for nine months.

These legal impediments to the recovery of old British debts, determined the ministry *not* to surrender the posts, but to hold them as a security for these debts. And whatever clamor we may raise about this business, we may be assured that the western posts will never be delivered peaceably, until the payment of those debts has been amply secured.

I have been thus full in explaining what is meant by the *merits of complaints*, in the preamble of the treaty, to show, that our minister was justifiable in passing over the discussion of a point of extreme difficulty—a point which would have wasted time, and embarrassed, perhaps defeated, the negotiation. The question of the *first infraction* of the treaty of peace had been ably discussed before ; and at the close of the controversy, the parties were as remote from the probability of agreement as when they began.

Neither party would yield the point to his antagonist. The British ministry, it is evidently known, are determined never to admit the carrying away the negroes to be an infraction of the treaty, and they are equally determined not to surrender the western posts without a guaranty for the payment of old debts.

In this situation, was it not prudent and wise to pass over the first subjects of crimination, and proceed to an amicable adjustment of all differences, if it could be done, without attempting to decide who first infringed the treaty ? I am persuaded that every candid man who reads this explanation of the business, will be fully satisfied with the conduct of our envoy.

*Note.*—I generally use the word envoy or minister, in the singular, as referring to Mr. Jay, the principal in the negotiation. But it is proper to observe, once for all, that Mr. Jay, by order, communicated his instructions to Mr. Pinckney, consulted him on every point, and that the treaty and every article of it had the approbation of that gentleman.

CURTIUS.

## No. III.

The first article of the treaty contains words, of course, which deserve no notice.

*Art.* 2.—The first objection made to this article is the inexplicitness of it. It is said that the article should have defined from *what places* his majesty was to withdraw his troops.

The answer to this objection is, that there is not any dispute about the boundary line of the United States, except at the northeast extremity, on St. Croix River. The posts which we claim, are acknowledged to be in the United States. It is possible, that British officers at some of those places, as a pretext for some purposes of their own, may have pretended that they were on their own ground ; but I never heard it suggested that the ministry dispute the boundary line at or near any of the garrisoned places.

The time assigned for the evacuation is said to be too distant. But if we calculate, we shall find no ground for this objection. There was required time to exchange ratifications, and then for orders to be dispatched from England to the furthest post westward. If we allow a reasonable time for these transactions, it will require the whole period assigned by the treaty.

The jurisdiction of a military post will doubtless be considered, the reach of a cannon shot, or a league.

" Lastly," says *Decius,* " as the treaty of peace gave us these posts, what great benefit is obtained by this article ? Who would regard the second promise of a man, who had already, without an excuse, violated the first ?"

But *Decius* will please to remember, that there are two sides to a question—the legal impediments to a collection of old debts were an excuse for the detention of the posts which they deemed sufficient. If we comply with the sixth article, Great Britain will consequently comply with the second.

*Art.* 3.—Even this article of the treaty, which breaks down the barriers which have hitherto obstructed our trade to Canada, and opens a general intercourse upon most liberal principles, has not escaped criticism and censure. *Decius* says, the advantages in this article are on the side of Great Britain ; and the reason assigned is, that the extent of the United States is greater than that of the British territories. Now this is the very reason why the advantages of this article are in favor of the United States.

What is the present state of trade between Canada and the United States ? and what will its situation be under the treaty ? This is a fair way of determining the goodness of the treaty.

In the present state of things, almost all trade is prohibited on the part of Canada. Not a skin in the fur trade can be brought into the United States except by stealth. This prohibition makes the little trade in peltry, now actually carried on, very hazardous, and raises the article to a very high price. The peltry, it must be admitted, is almost *all* collected within the British territories ; the British have command of it by right ; and the removal of those garrisons to the other side of the lakes, without a removal of the prohibition on the peltry trade, would not have been of much advantage to the United States.  We have then every thing to gain by a free intercourse—the British, every thing to lose, so far as regards *that trade*.

*Decius* says, " the fur trade will probably fall altogether in the hands of British traders."  This is a most extraordinary supposition.  The truth is, the peltry trade now is all *in* their hands ; what we want is to get that *out* of their hands.  That is, we want to obtain a share of that trade on equal terms with British subjects.  This we have obtained by the article under consideration.  What right, what pretense have we to a monopoly of that trade ?  Do we expect that Great Britain would permit us, as *Decius* says, " to secure to ourselves the whole fur trade ?" To demand such a privilege on our part would be extravagant and ridiculous.

The trade by the third article of the treaty is placed on a fair and liberal footing.  Both parties are free to use all the rivers and lakes for the purpose of inland navigation, subject only to the common tolls and ferriages.  The exception of the limits of the Hudson's Bay Company is of no importance at present to the United States ; and the exception was a necessary consequence of the exclusive rights of that company.

*Decius* supposes there is a manifest inequality in permitting British traders to use all our ports and rivers, and in restricting the Americans from the same use of the ports of the British territories, and the rivers between the mouths thereof and the highest ports of entry.  But *Decius* will please to recollect, that this privilege enjoyed by British subjects, and the restriction of American subjects, are not created by the present treaty.  In this respect the parties are as they were before. American vessels have never been permitted to carry on the coasting trade of the British possessions in America ; and therefore we suffer no new abridgment of business by this article.  On the other hand, British vessels are *now* admitted into all our harbors, and to the highest port of entry for foreign vessels, so that this article gives no new privilege to such vessels.  But we have obtained by the treaty a *free inland trade with Canada*.  We can navigate all the rivers and lakes—we can go down the St. Lawrence to Quebec.  Articles are to be carried from the United States to Canada, and *vice versa*, subject to the lowest duties ever paid on these articles ; and peltry pays no duty at all.

This free intercourse will be highly advantageous to our citizens on the frontiers.  They will be deeply concerned in the fur trade, and we shall obtain furs much lower than formerly.  At the same time the inhabitants on our frontiers will find a market at Montreal or Quebec, and bring back in return such heavy articles as will come cheaper, through the St. Lawrence and the lakes, than through the Atlantic ports.

This trade is extremely wanted by our frontier settlements, which are every day increasing.  Their distance from the Atlantic lays them under heavy disadvantages, which the treaty before us alleviates as much as possible, by taking off all restrictions on inland trade.  And just in proportion to the number of people in the United States, who are to carry on and partake of that free trade, will be the benefits of this article of the treaty.

It should be considered further, that the citizens of the United States are taking up large tracts of land in Canada, and emigrating to that province. This business is encouraged by the British government. But while the people who settle in Canada, for the purposes of trade or agriculture, become subjects of Great Britain, they retain their attachment to the United States ; and from this circumstance important and beneficial consequences may hereafter be expected.

*Arts.* 4 and 5.—These articles have not been the subjects of much censure ; perhaps the mode prescribed for ascertaining doubtful points, relative to the boundary line of the United States, is as eligible as we could wish.

*Art.* 6.—This is a most important article. It involves in it the primary and principal causes of all the differences now existing between the two countries.

Before the war, most of the trade of Virginia, and a great portion of that of the states to the southward, was carried on by foreigners. I am well assured that it was esteemed in Virginia, disreputable for planters and their sons to engage in trade. This prejudice, which was, like a thousand follies adopted by Americans, introduced from Europe, and a remnant of the aristocracy of the feudal system, operated powerfully to keep trade in the hands of foreigners.

The British merchants availed themselves of the prejudice. They were the agents or factors for the planters, and gave extensive credit. The confidence created by this friendly intercourse, together with the prodigal habits of many planters, extended this credit to a very large amount.

The war necessarily suspended the payment of these debts. The treaty of peace provided that no lawful impediments should be interposed to prevent the recovery of those debts. The carrying away of the negroes by the British, when they left New York, exasperated the southern states ; they considered it as an infraction of the treaty, and as such, an excuse for violating it on their part. They passed laws which were impediments to the recovery of old debts. The British ministry, on their part, detained the western posts, as security for those debts, and damages sustained by the British merchants, in consequence of those legal impediments. Here the parties are at issue—here are differences between the two nations which can be settled only by the sword or amicable adjustment.

This is precisely the situation of the parties. Neither party will yield the point of *first infraction ;* and paper correspondence, to prove the point, has been exhausted, without giving any satisfaction to either. The issue then is, the alternative of *war* or *accommodation.* But if we enter into a war, will this settle the points in dispute ? Not at all. A ten years' war, and a waste of half the blood and treasure of the United States, would leave the controversy just where it now is—to be settled by negotiation. It is no answer to these remarks, to make outcries about British injustice. Admitting this in the fullest extent, that injustice is to be restrained only by the sword, or amicable agreement—we have our choice.

Is it not prudent and wise to make an effort to adjust all differences by a reference to equitable principles ? What better mode could be devised to settle differences so numerous, so complicated, as those which exist between the two countries, than by commissioners fairly and impartially appointed ? This is the mode which has been practiced for centuries, in like cases. In looking into collections of treaties, I find the same mode prescribed in all cases of difficult disputes between nations ; and the universal practice of resorting to this mode, is a proof that none better has yet been devised.

But it is said, " this mode of adjusting sums due to British creditors, is unjust toward those states which have interposed no lawful impediments in the way of recovering such debts ; as they must bear a part of the burden, and thus suffer for the delinquency of others."

This objection is susceptible of a very satisfactory answer. Our capacity, as a nation, arises from the union of the states under the constitution. All our intercourse with foreign nations is conducted by the United States, in that national capacity. Foreign nations can not negotiate with any of our individual states ; and the states are expressly prohibited, by our constitution, from entering into any treaty, compact, or agreement, with any foreign power.

The moment our union took place, the United States became, to a certain degree, responsible for acts done by states or individuals toward foreign nations. This responsibility results from the national capacity derived from the union.

Whatever hardships this may impose on particular states, it is a necessary consequence of the character we have assumed among the powers of the earth ; and indeed it is much more than counterbalanced by the protection and security derived from the same national capacity.

CURTIUS.

## No. IV.

*Art.* 7.—This article is said to be wholly exceptionable, because it places at too great a distance, compensation to which our citizens are entitled, for the most atrocious acts of piracy.

I will admit what my antagonists please to alledge against the injurious treatment of our vessels at sea by British privateers. I know that the right which the law of nations gives to powers at war, of stopping and examining neutral vessels, and seizing them when they have contraband goods on board, has been abused, and that great injuries and insolence have been suffered by our seamen ; and great losses have been incurred by our merchants by illegal detention and condemnation. My own feelings are keenly alive to such abuses, and I wish we had the means of vindicating our rights in a more ample manner.

But let me observe, that these injuries do not excite greater resentment in the breasts of Americans, than laws of our states, suspending the recovery of old debts, or making lands, goods and depreciated paper currency, a legal tender for these debts, awakened in the breasts of the British nation. As to every thing of this nature, anger, resentment and disgust are reciprocal : and ill usage alledged on one part, is retorted with ill usage in some other particular on the other part. There is no common tribunal to decide this question, Who has been guilty of the greatest outrage on faith and honesty ? We are satisfied that the charge belongs to Great Britain—*they* are as confident the blame is on our side. It is idle to waste time in criminating each other. Our interest and happiness, and those of Great Britain, demand an amicable accommodation, and to that point all our efforts should be directed.

The time which will be required to examine the claims of American merchants for losses, is certainly to be regretted. But how can this delay be prevented?

If we admit the right of powers at war to stop neutral vessels and examine them, do we not admit the right of ascertaining whether such vessels have contraband property on board or not? How shall this point be settled, where suspicion occurs? The papers of neutral vessels are not always to be relied on. We all know that subjects of nations at war, procure neutral vessels and neutral names to cover property of their own. This happens every day. We all know that contraband goods are often concealed in bales or casks of goods not contraband. We all know that masters, supercargoes and seamen, will evade direct answers, equivocate, and sometimes men are abandoned enough to perjure themselves in a court, to save property of their own or their friends.

What says the law of nations on this subject? Vattel, book iii, ch. 7, lays it down with great precision. "Without searching neutral ships at sea, the commerce of contraband goods can not be prevented. There is then a right of searching. At present a neutral ship refusing to be searched, would from that proceeding alone be condemned as lawful prize. But to avoid inconveniences, violence, and every other irregularity, the manner of the search is settled in the treaties of navigation and commerce. According to the present custom, credit is to be given to certificates and bills of lading, produced by the master of the ship, *unless any fraud appear in them, or there be very good reason to suspect their validity.*"

The mode of searching neutral vessels is regulated by our treaties with the States General, with Sweden and France, in which it is stipulated that credit shall be given to the ship's papers. But we have had no such treaty with Great Britain, and the treatment of our vessels depends on the law of nations, or the licentious will of the masters of privateers. Wherever there is suspicion of fraud in the papers, the vessels may be carried into port for examination and trial; and it is probable, this license has been carried to a most unwarrantable length, during the present war. The general expression, *cause of suspicion*, gives an almost unbounded latitude to those unprincipled men, who are usually engaged in the detestable business of privateering.

Such is the situation of our trade, in the present unhappy war. But making every allowance for ill usage, it must be admitted that great numbers of American vessels have, according to the laws of nations, been justly seized, and carried into port for trial. When this is the case, what mode of process must be had to determine what property is liable to confiscation, and what is not?

Our existing treaties with other nations admit the right of trial in the admiralty courts of the nation capturing the neutral vessels; and in these treaties, there are stipulations that bulk shall not be broke, until the cargo has been landed in presence of proper officers, and no part of the cargo sold, till legal process shall have been had, and sentence pronounced against the goods liable to condemnation.

Must not the same process be had in the British courts, though we have had no treaty with the nation? Where is the ground for maintaining a different doctrine?

We must then admit the principle, that American vessels seized and carried into port, with prohibited goods on board, or on suspicion of fraudulent papers, are subject to the usual legal process of British courts of admiralty. However hard this may appear, the effect flows directly from the state of war and the law of nations.

If we admit this principle, we admit all its consequences. If our vessels are liable to legal process, it is necessary that all the documents relative to the question of *legal capture or not*, should be produced and examined. And when we consider the distance from which many of these documents are to be procured, and the numerous cases that have arisen, who can say that final decisions can be had on the American claims in a moment? And in cases which involve equitable considerations, not proper for the decision of courts of law, what mode could be devised, more eligible for the claimants, than that of commissioners? Is the term of eighteen months too long for receiving claims? It appears to me the time is not unreasonably long; and even the length of the time is favorable for the claimants.

It is said that the British government ought to advance a sum on account, to be distributed among the sufferers. This suggestion seems to be grounded on an idea that has prevailed, that such a sum has been advanced by Great Britain to Denmark and Sweden—an opinion which, I have authority to say, is not well founded.

But to this measure there are insurmountable objections. The impracticability of doing even partial justice, before it is ascertained who are the objects of it, is merely chimerical.

Many of my countrymen are great sufferers, and I trust their just claims will be supported, and their just damages paid. But a summary trial might do great injustice—the innocent might suffer, and the guilty obtain reparation.

On the whole, the time and mode appear as eligible as justice and the nature of the cases will admit. With respect to the stipulation in the last clause of the seventh article, that engages payment for certain vessels taken by privateers within our jurisdiction or by vessels armed in our ports, I trust no man, who has a regard for honesty or national character, will ever object to it. I am one of those American citizens, that hold it as a duty for us to preserve a strict neutrality in the present war, and honorable in our government to make indemnification for every illegal proceeding of the nation and of individuals, toward foreign nations. Let him who demands justice, do justice himself. The amount of the sums to be paid, does not vary the principle, nor should it vary our conduct as a nation. I hope and trust the character of the United States will never be stained with a violation of faith and justice, even toward the corsairs of Barbary. Self-defense only will authorize any nation in arresting or withholding the property of individuals, even of an enemy nation. To withhold or to authorize the withholding of private property, contrary to law, is to degrade our nation to the rank of Algerines.

*Postscript to No. IV.*—To convince the public more fully of the little ground for objection, on account of delays in admiralty courts, adjusting differences between nations, I will make several extracts from the correspondence between our minister at Paris, and the French minister for foreign affairs. This correspondence was published in January, 1794, by order of Congress. It relates to the captures of our vessels by French privateers, under the decrees of the Convention of May 9, and July 27, 1793, in express violation of our treaty with France.

### Letter from Mr. Morris, October 12, 1793.

[TRANSLATION.]

Paris, October 12, 1793.

*The Minister Plenipotentiary of the United States of America to the Republic of France, to M. Deforgues, Minister of Foreign Affairs.*

SIR—I have the honor to send you herein inclosed, the copy of a letter which has been addressed to me by Citizen Postic, a lawyer residing at Morlaix. It appears that in the proceedings of which he has given an account, there are extraordinary irregularities ; and I think it my duty to inform you of them, as on the justice of tribunals often depends the salvation, and always the prosperity of a state.

I request of you at the same time, sir, to permit me to make two general observations on the whole of this business ; one of which applies to the organization, and the other to the proceedings, of the commercial tribunals. The referring of questions on sea prizes to these tribunals, appears to me dangerous, since they involve the interpretation of the treaties, and the application of the law of nations ; consequently of peace and of war. Now we may be permitted to entertain some doubt as to the knowledge of the judges, and we ought besides to fear, lest they may be interested, as owners of privateers, in the questions which are submitted to them.

But whatever may be the organization of the tribunals, it appears to me essential, sir, that in their proceedings they should receive all the claims which may be made to them ; that they should even invite without waiting for the authority of the persons interested, who are often at the distance of one thousand leagues. The jurisdiction of the tribunals within whose cognizance are the questions of prize, is *in rem.* They take possession of the things, and by that means render themselves responsible for it. Now as the tribunal, which is the depository of the thing, ought not to dispossess themselves of it, without a formal authoritative act of the true proprietor, it is their duty not only to admit, but also to seek proofs, which may establish to whom the property truly belongs. This is a double duty toward the neutral proprietor, and toward their own nation ; for every government which permits its citizens to fit out privateers, arms with the destructive sword of war, hands which are interested to extend its ravages, and renders itself responsible for the abuses which result from so dangerous a delegation of sovereignty. For the purpose of repossessing them, the admiralty tribunals have been established throughout the different nations of Europe. In these tribunals, the government furnishes the means of information, by the facility with which it admits therein every species of claim. It preserves, by appeals, the right of deciding, in the last resort, on the contests which shall therein arise ; and it gives the necessary time to enlighten its conscience on thorny questions, before the pronouncing of a sentence, which might extend or prolong the horrors of war.

These, sir, are the questions which experience has dictated to me. They daily make on me a more lively impression, on account of the claims addressed to me by my countrymen, of which I have communicated to you a very small part. I always send to the tribunals the injured persons, by giving them the most positive assurances that they will there obtain complete and prompt justice.

I have the honor to be, &c.

Gouv. Morris.

*Extract from the French Minister's answer to Mr. Morris, dated Paris, October* 14, 1793.

" These observations, sir, which you are too just not to appreciate, apply to the greater part of the claims, which you have addressed to me for some time. I have done, with respect to several of them, all that depended on me, in order to obtain in favor of your countrymen, an exception of the general measures, adopted with regard to neutral nations. I have used among others, all the means with which your letters furnished me, to have restored the ship Laurens; but I have met with insurmountable obstacles in the established laws, and in the opinion of the commercial tribunal at Havre. The tribunal has neglected nothing to render justice to the owners of this vessel. It has consented among other things, to have translated three hundred and sixty-one letters, merely to prove in the most authentic manner, the property of the cargo. The interested have, besides, avowed themselves that they had neglected an essential formality required by our laws.

" We hope that the government of the United States will attribute to their true cause, the abuses of which you complain, as well as other violations of which our cruisers may render themselves guilty, in the course of the present war. It must perceive how difficult it is to contain within just limits, the indignation of our marines, and in general of all the French patriots, against a people who speak the same language, and have the same habits, as the free Americans. The difficulty of distinguishing our allies from our enemies, has often been the cause of offenses committed on board your vessels; all that the administration could do, is to order indemnification to those who have suffered, and to punish the guilty."

Let any candid man view the whole of the transactions of England and France, and say whether, in proportion to the number of vessels captured, the delays and difficulties have been greater in England than in France.

N. B. Mr. Jefferson's letter on the right of nations at war, to seize enemy's property in neutral bottoms, will fall more properly under the eighth number of this discussion.                    Curtius.

## No. V.

*Art.* 8.—This article solely regards the mode of defraying the expenses of the commissioners, and supplying vacancies. No objection appears against it.

*Art.* 9.—This article gives the present holders of lands in the two countries the right of disposing of them, &c. without being considered as aliens.

In the first abstract of the treaty which was published, this article was erroneously stated, as extending to give the rights of citizens to any and all British subjects purchasing lands hereafter in the United States. The truth is, the article extends only to persons holding lands at the time the treaty was signed, and some provision of this kind was necessary.

To understand this article, it must be remembered, that the United States were settled from the British dominions, and till lately remained a part of the nation. Some persons in the United States now hold lands in England, which they inherit from branches of their families which are extinct in that country. Great numbers in the British dominions hold lands which they formerly enjoyed as inhabitants of the colonies, and which were not confiscated. Others have been compelled to take lands in payment of debts.

The circumstances of these two countries differ from those of all other countries. They were formerly *one country*, and linked together by a variety of individual interests. These private interests have been mostly created under one common government. They originated when the two countries were one in empire, and without any fault on the part of the persons interested. Was it not reasonable and just, that interests thus created should be secured by the provisions of a treaty which was to adjust all old differences ? Most certainly it was.

It has been said that this article infringes the rights of the states. As I have never seen any argument to prove this assertion, it will be sufficient to answer it by another assertion, and say it does *not.*

It is said also, that this article impairs the obligation of private contracts. As this is asserted without explanation or proof, it will be passed without notice.

The danger of aliens holding real estate in any country, is an idea that was propagated over Europe in feudal times, and modern writers on law have continued to transcribe the reasoning on that subject, from one generation to another, as they have on usury, intolerance, natural allegiance, and many other ancient errors, without allowing for the meliorated state of society and civil policy. The danger, however, is now a mere bugbear, and deserves no notice. Men may hold real estates, without the other privileges of citizens ; and it tends to promote commerce to admit foreigners to this privilege, under suitable restrictions. The only danger that now exists in an unlimited privilege of this kind is, that persons might possess themselves of large estates, and spend the income abroad, as is the case with the planters in the West Indies and the Irish nobility. Should this ever become an evil of extent, it will require legislative remedies.

But it is an important idea, which the United States should cherish, that men are never enemies to a free country. Men may scramble for offices, and oppose the administration of a government from selfish views ; but if foreigners find peace, liberty, and safety in our country, they will hardly give themselves the trouble of subjecting us to other governments. A liberality in our measures toward foreigners, strict justice and impartiality in our laws, will make all parties our friends, and this is one great object of the present treaty.

*Decius* attempts to make an invidious comparison between this article of the treaty and the eleventh article of our treaty with France, which, he says, is all in favor of the Americans, because it abolishes the *droit d'aubaine* in their favor, and gives the French nothing which the law of nations did not secure them before. To prove this he goes into a *common law* explanation of the terms used in the French treaty—*goods movable* and *immovable*. The words of the eleventh article of the treaty with France are—" The subjects and inhabitants of the United States shall not be reputed aubains in France—they may dispose of their goods, movable and immovable, by testament, donation, &c." *Immovable goods*, *Decius* says, mean chattels real, but not estates in fee, and quotes Sir Edward Coke and Blackstone. If *Decius* is a lawyer of great ingenuity, as he doubtless is, he ought to be very cautious to conceal his subtilties. His far-fetched arguments to make the French treaty a mere act of benevolence on the part of Louis XVI, and the present *treaty* a mere sacrifice on our part, will not, ultimately, succeed.

The explanation given by *Decius* to the terms *immovable goods* is unequivocally wrong. Does not *Decius* know that a treaty with France is not to be interpreted by the common law of England ? Does not he know that the terms *bona immobilia*, immovable goods, are borrowed from the *civil law*, that the civil law is the basis of almost every municipal constitution in Europe ? Does he not recollect that the municipal laws of France were derived from that source, and that terms used in that country are to be explained by the civil law ? Is not a treaty with France to be interpreted according to the legal import of the words in that country ? Let *Decius* then be apprised, that *bona immobilia* is a technical phrase as old as the civil law, and that it comprehended formerly and still comprehends, in most countries of Europe, real estate, that is, a freehold estate, and lands in fee, as well as chattels real. When used by writers on the law of nations, the phrase has that sense.

" Every state has the liberty of granting or refusing foreigners the power of possessing lands or other *immovable goods* within its territory."—(Vattel, book ii, ch. 8.) In the same page are these expressions : " If the sovereign does not permit aliens to possess immovables, no one has a right to complain of it, as the sovereign may refuse strangers the power of possessing immovables."—(So also in book iii, ch. 5, sec. 76.)

The foregoing paragraph relates to movable goods, but the rule is different with regard to *immovables*, to *estates in lands*, as they all in some measure belong to the nation, are part of its domain, &c., and the proprietor being always a subject of the country as possessor of a parcel of *land*, and *goods* of *this nature* do not cease to be the enemy's goods, though possessed by a neutral stranger. " Nevertheless, war being now carried on with so much moderation and indulgence, safeguards are allowed to *houses and lands* possessed by foreigners in an enemy's country. For the same reason, he who declares war does not confiscate the *immovable goods* possessed in his country by his enemy's subjects. In permitting them to purchase and possess *those goods*, he has, in this respect, admitted them into the number of his subjects. But the income may be sequestrated, for hindering the remittance of it to the enemy's country."

Bynkershoek (Quest. Jur. Pub. 1, c. 7) uses the word *immobilia* in the same sense, and lays down the doctrine above quoted from Vattel. But the most direct authority in point, is from Domat's Civil Law, preliminary book, title 3, sec. 1. The following passage is express: " Immovables are all the parts of the surface of the earth, in what manner soever they are distinguished, whether into places for buildings, or into woods, meadows, arable lands, vineyards, orchards, or otherwise, and to whomsoever they belong."

In sect. 2, of the same title, Domat expressly enumerates lands, whether *allodial* or charged with quit-rents, among *immovables.** As this writer was a French civilian, he doubtless used the word in its technical sense, as understood in France, and by this sense must our treaty with France be interpreted. Indeed, whatever may be the opinion of lawyers here, I have no doubt, that by the eleventh article of that treaty, French citizens are fully entitled to hold real estate in the United States, and American citizens in France.

In all our other treaties, the article in question restricts the subjects of the two countries, to the enjoyment of *personal estate or effects*, in the jurisdiction each of the other. Most nations retain the old feudal jealousy respecting foreigners possessing lands in their countries. But the liberality of France, in her treaty with America, ought to be an example to all nations ; and the United States, of all countries on earth, ought to reject all such remains of feudal prejudice. I trust the explanation before given of the terms *immovable goods*, will be satisfactory ; and will evince the truth of what was advanced by the writer of " Candid Remarks on the Treaty," that the 11th article of our treaty with France amounts to a *total abolition of alienism*, between the two countries.

Unless *Decius* succeeds better hereafter in " detecting fallacies," he may as well let his pen rest, or employ it more to his own reputation. His writings on the subject, so far as they have hitherto appeared, are little more than a series of misrepresentation.                              CURTIUS.

## No. VI.—By JAMES KENT.

The 10th article of the treaty provides that " neither the debts due from individuals of the one nation to individuals of the other, nor shares nor moneys which they may have in the public funds, or in the public banks, shall ever in any event of war or national differences be sequestered or confiscated." The faithful observance of the restriction contained in this article is so much for our interest as well as honor, that we should naturally have concluded, the most determined enemies to any good understanding with Great Britain, would at least have passed it by in silence. But so strong are the prejudices of a certain party amongst us, or so virulent their passions, that they have given to almost every paragraph in the treaty an equal condemnation. Decius has complained of this article as being, like many others, exclusively advantageous to England, and as arresting from our government a lawful and powerful weapon of war. I am greatly mistaken, however, if it is not completely defensible against every part of this accusation.

* It deserves remark, that the French word *biens*, goods, comprehends estate in land. This sense is borrowed from the civil law.

It is true that by the law of nations, as existing a century ago, the debts owing from one nation to another were legal objects of sequestration in war. " But at present (to use the language of Vattel, book iii, ch. 5, sec. 77) in regard to the advantage and safety of commerce, all the sovereigns of Europe have departed from this rigor. And as this *custom has been generally received*, he who should act contrary to it would *injure the public faith;* for strangers trusted his subjects only from a firm persuasion that the *general custom* would be observed. The state does not so much as touch the sums which it owes to the enemy. Every where, in case of a war, funds credited to the public, are exempt from confiscation and seizure." This clear explanation of the modern law of nations, as far as it relates to the public funds, is also to be found in a report of the English judges in the year 1753, in answer to the Prussian memorial ; a report of much authority, which Vattel does not scruple to call an excellent piece on the law of nations. " It will not be easy," say the judges, " to find an instance where a prince has thought fit to make reprisals upon a debt due from himself to private men. There is a confidence that this will not be done. A private man sends money to a prince upon the faith of an engagement of honor, because a prince can not be compelled, like other men, in an adverse way, by a court of justice. So scrupulously did England, France and Spain adhere to this public faith, that even during the war, they suffered no inquiry to be made whether any part of the public debts was due to subjects of the enemy, though it is certain many English had money in the French funds, and many French had money in ours."

But these principles have received sanction from a source, which the adversaries of the article will be disposed to admit as of still greater authority and respectability, I mean from the proceedings and decision of the French convention. It appears from Paris papers which in April last were translated and republished in the *Aurora*, that in the sitting of the Convention, Dec. 29, 1794, after the house had passed to the order of the day, " Johannot read the following articles of the projected decree, which were as follows—(here follow five articles.)

" *Art.* 6.—The decree concerning the sequestration of the property of the subjects of the powers at war with the republic is annulled. Such sums as have been paid by French citizens into the treasury in consequence of those decrees, will be reimbursed." This article occasioned some debate. Gaston was against it. Cambon observed, that the law of sequestration was extorted from the Convention by the faction of Fabre d'Eglantine and Danton, but ought you to return the property of the Spanish to the despot of Madrid ? Thiriot agreed with Cambon. Colombel desired the assembly to annul only the sequestration of the sums due for commercial relations. Ramel showed that the law of sequestration had been urged by the foreigners themselves and stockjobbers, *that it had prepared the ruin of commerce, and broken off, against the rights of nations, the obligations of merchants in different states;* though the powers at war with the republic should not repeal the sequestration of French property, it is our duty to set the example. The sixth article was maintained as reported."

I have thought it not useless to give a brief sketch of this very interesting proceeding in the French convention, because it not only estab-

lishes what I contend to be the law of nations, but exposes the injury
and injustice of departing from this part of it even in the midst of the
most violent war. And it ought to be remarked to the honor of our
country, that during the course of our revolution, notwithstanding the
warm resentments it called forth, we never attempted to annul the British debts, but finally agreed to the fourth article of the treaty of peace,
" that creditors on either side should meet with no lawful impediment
to the recovery of all bona fide debts heretofore contracted." So also
in the Amsterdam and Antwerp loans, we expressly stipulated, that they
should not be impaired on the event of a future war between the two
countries.

I think it will be evident from the authorities which I have adduced,
that the sequestration and confiscation of debts and public stock, are
not *now* the customary and admissible weapons of war. The ancient
maxims on this head are justly and generally exploded by civilized nations, and the interests of commerce in this, as in many other instances,
have happily set bounds to the intemperance of Gothic rage. In stipulating to a formal renunciation of this mode of warfare, we have done
no more than what we were bound to do by the acknowledged dictates
of good faith. We have renounced a weapon which our own sense of
right and policy had before forbidden us to use. If however it should
be supposed that occasions may sometimes arise in which it would be
expedient, for the purpose of more effectually wounding our enemies, to
attack public or private contracts, then let me ask, what difficulty has
the treaty thrown in the way? The same fierceness of character which
would lead us to violate the received maxims of war and national duty,
would readily set aside the moral obligation of this article. Its only
effect arises from laying down in the rational season of peace, the rule
of conduct in war, and by superadding an express, to the implied, sanction of good faith.

But it is alledged that this article has no actual reciprocity, because
all the debts are due from us either as a nation or as individuals, and
that our citizens hold no British stock, and have few or no demands upon their subjects. If, however, this species of confiscation be really repugnant to the present usage of nations, and is unjust and impolitic, the
renunciation was equally fit and proper, whether it was mutual or not,
and in proportion to the means we had of using this mode of warfare,
does the sacrifice redound to our credit and character. But the truth is,
that the beneficial operation of this article is principally on our side.
It is much more satisfactory and necessary to us, than it is to Great
Britain, because it tends directly to foster and strengthen the credit of
the United States, both public and private, a circumstance of the utmost
moment to our prosperity as an infant nation.

It is by force of public credit, that our government has attained to its
present stability, and has so many competent means of acting with efficacy whenever the public exigencies require it. Credit, as a good
judge of our interest has observed, is *the invigorating principle of this
country.* Any addition to it, however small, will give much greater
power of self-defense, than the little perfidious and exploded resources
of confiscating debts or violating the pledged negotiability, and sacred-
ness of public stock. Nor is private credit of much less utility in a

country which has so little capital, in proportion to the extent and variety of the demands for it. We have immense territories of waste land to clear and settle ; and abundance of raw materials for nourishing the manufacturing and mechanic arts ; but to answer these ends, requires an unceasing supply of capital, or credit, which in most cases is its eligible substitute. In short there are no people upon earth who have so many inducements as the United States, to declare unequivocally to the world, that the claims of their creditors shall always be deemed sacred in peace and in war.

After taking such a full view of the subject, we can not withhold our astonishment that Mr. Burr and Mr. Tazewell, should each of them, in the Senate, by formal propositions of amendment, single out this article, among others, as a proper object of censure and repeal. There is one more objection to this article, which merits some attention for its singularity ; and because it places in a strong light, the extreme jealousy or predetermination to condemn, with which every part of the treaty has been read. It is apprehended or rather pretended to be, that the king of Great Britain will engross all the shares of our several American banks, and thereby obtain the entire control of them and fill them with British directors. It is just as rational to suppose that he will buy up all our goods and chattels, and thereby put a total stop to agriculture and manufactures. If the king of Great Britain is disposed to expend his money for the disturbance of our government, there are much more effective methods of doing it than by the indirect means of our banks. Such an apprehension is ridiculous in the extreme, and can not surely impose on the most credulous mind, especially when it is known that the several bank charters expressly provide that *all the directors shall be American citizens*, and that no stockholder shall be entitled to vote for a director unless he either *attends in person or resides within the United States.*

We have now finished an examination of the first ten articles of the treaty, and which form the permanent part ; for the commercial articles which follow being of more difficult adjustment, and their effect not being so easily ascertained by theory as experience, were wisely limited to a short period. It has often been asked, and with an air of conscious triumph, what single equivalent have we got for so many and great concessions on our part ? Let us review for a moment the ground we have gone over, and see if an answer can not be given which will satisfy all the real friends to the interest of our country.

We have gained all the western posts without bloodshed—we have obtained a promise of complete indemnity for all unlawful spoliations on our trade, as soon as an impartial tribunal shall have ascertained the amount of our losses—we have obtained a liberal and permanent commerce between our frontiers and the whole frontier of the British provinces in America, and we have by these means removed the principal sources of national complaint against Great Britain, and secured to our country the continuance of the blessings of peace. And what have we conceded on our part ? We have promised to pay such losses only as British creditors have suffered in their debts, by occasion of legal impediments in this country, as soon as an impartial tribunal shall have ascertained the amount of such losses, and to pay for such British vessels only as we have suffered, without using the means in our power to prevent it, to be captured within our territory, contrary to the law of nations. And we have also allowed a liberal and permanent commerce between Canada and our interior possessions. These are the material parts of the permanent treaty, and it appears that both nations have conceded, in those instances, what in justice and equity they ought to have done, and to have manifested a mutual disposition to forget past animosity, and to live upon friendly terms hereafter.                CURTIUS.

## No. VII.—By JAMES KENT.

In examining the commercial part of the treaty, we are not to inquire, as we have heretofore done, into matter of strict right. Arrangements of commerce must depend upon the good will and pleasure of the contracting parties. They are things of imperfect obligation only, and can not be peremptorily demanded. Every nation will accommodate so far, and so far only, as suits her interests or policy, and it will always be a question to be determined in sound discretion by other powers, how far *their* interest or policy will admit of a connection, on such terms as can be obtained. Commercial propositions may be granted, acceded to, or rejected by either party, without affording to the other any just cause of war. It is therefore a matter for consideration, how far the remaining articles of the treaty are admissible or not, upon the principles of public expediency.

Although the 12th article may now very properly be left out of discussion, yet since it is the fashion to reprobate it in the most unqualified terms, and to use it as an instrument for inflaming the public passions, as well as to carry disgrace to the other parts of the work, it may not be amiss to give it some examination.

It is well known that every European nation has endeavored, more or less, to monopolize to itself the commerce of its colonies, and upon that account prohibited the ships of foreign nations from trading to them, and has prohibited them from importing European goods from any foreign nation. This has been the case with Denmark, Holland, France, Spain, Portugal, and Great Britain, although the manner in which this monopoly has been exercised in those different nations, has been very different. Great Britain has been as much distinguished as any of her neighbors during a century past, for a pertinacious adherence to the monopoly system, and it has become one of the riveted maxims of her policy, to regard the exclusive enjoyment of her colony trade, as an essential nursery of seamen, and a constant support of her naval power. So late as the year 1783, Lord Sheffield gave his sanction to this ancient doctrine, and said that it would be impolitic in Great Britain to admit American vessels into the British West India islands, and we see with what great allowance we ought to compare the privileges conceded in this article, with the theory of an unlimited commerce.

The French convention, during their present revolution, have recognized and adopted the English policy. This appears from the eloquent report of Barrere, upon their navigation act, which is intended for perpetuity, and is declared to be the basis of their policy and commerce. The act ordains, that no commodities shall be imported into France but in French vessels, or in those of the country which produced the commodity ; and that foreign vessels shall not transport from one French port to another, any commodities of the growth or manufacture of France or her colonies. And, notwithstanding the necessities of the war may have induced the French to a temporary departure from this act, we may be assured, the principles advanced in the report are too generally and powerfully felt, not to induce them to adhere to it on the return of peace, as the sure basis of their maritime strength. " The prohibitions of a navigation act," says Barrere, " should be as extensive as they could be made, for without them it would be a mere illusory measure. The English," continues he, " from whom we borrow this system, have given it that extension, and, indeed, they are to be applauded for it."

When we consider the value that is attached to the carrying trade, in the opinion of the European nations, we have no reason to be disappointed that Mr. Jay could not get access to the British islands on better terms. It was to have been wished that he could have got the admission of vessels of any burden into this trade, but this was undoubtedly beyond his power. While Great Britain consented to admit us to trade to her islands in our own bottoms, we may be assured she was determined to do it in such a manner as not materially to affect her carrying trade, the source of her security and greatness. This must have been the reason with her for restricting our vessels to seventy tuns and under, (and indeed it is understood that the treaty was kept open for some time on the part of Mr. Jay, while he was endeavoring to extend this clause,) and from carrying any melasses, sugar, coffee, cocoa or cotton, either from her islands in vessels of the United States, to any where but this country. It will be asked why Great Britain should wish to restrain us from carrying any of these articles to Europe, provided they are not the growth of her islands ? The answer is, that nothing short of a total prohibition, would in her opinion, effectually secure her carrying trade, since her own and foreign sugar or coffee would not easily be distinguished, and any modification would have opened a wide door to elude the whole intent of the restraint, would have rendered the whole prohibition, to use the words of Barrere, *a mere illusory measure.*

It is not my intention to vindicate either the justness or liberality of this policy on the part of Great Britain. It is sufficient to say that it appears to have been her inflexible policy, and to which she thought herself bound in duty to adhere. The only question is, whether there was any reasonable prospect at present of our obtaining better terms ; and if not, whether it was not upon the whole for our interest to accept of the trade upon those terms ? This may yet be a doubtful point, though I acknowledge a considerable objection to the 12th article as it now stands, that is, the prohibition to carry melasses, sugar, cotton, &c. to Europe, is so general as to include those articles even of our own production. This prohibition, with respect to coffee and sugar in particular, it is said, would be very inconvenient to us during the present war, though in time of peace it would be of no consequence. The 12th article does not prohibit us from exporting any of those articles from the other West India islands to any part of the world. We are only restricted from exporting them from the British West India islands, (ex-

cept to the United States,) in order to preserve to the English their carrying trade, and from the United States in order to preserve the other
restraint from evasion.

It ought not to be forgotten, that this article was limited to two years
from the conclusion of the present war, and then the contracting parties
were to endeavor to regulate this trade, with a view to their mutual advantage, and *the extension of commerce;* and if they should not agree
on new arrangements, all the articles of the treaty, except the first ten,
were to fall to the ground. At the end of the two years we should
most probably have entered on the negotiation with much less difficulty
than at present. The British West Indies would have been for some
time accustomed to the benefits of our trade, and have got into the
habit of placing their dependence as well as their affections upon it ;
while the mother country would have been a little familiarized to our
trade with her colonies, and her jealousies and prejudices would probably have greatly diminished with regard to it. We should have renewed the discussion with all those advantages which we now want, and
the chance is, that the intercourse would not only have been continued,
but have been attended with a favorable enlargement. And if eventu-
ally the negotiation should have failed and left only the ten first articles
of the treaty remaining, yet those articles, as we noticed in the last
number, are well worthy of the mission, since they restore tranquillity
and justice to our country.

The 13th article of the treaty relates to our commerce with the British East Indies, and all the advantages which are conceded to us by this
article, are without the smallest pretended equivalent on our part. The
privileges of this article are not denied by those who have been most
distinguished for their indiscriminate condemnation of the whole treaty.
*Decius* complains, however, that our commerce was on a better footing
before, by the mere permission of the British government. It is sufficient to observe, in answer to this, that the same permission can still
be continued : there is nothing in this article which prohibits the India
coasting trade. It would have been unnecessary, for such prohibition
existed before. The article barely declares, that none of its privileges
shall be construed to extend to the coasting trade. In other respects it
leaves that trade just as it found it, under the precarious pleasure of the
British government. But prior to this article, our whole intercourse
with British East India was a matter of favor, and surely it is a very
important consideration that we can now claim it as a matter of right.
Mr. Jefferson, in his report on the privileges and restrictions of our
commerce in foreign countries, seems to have thought very differently
from *Decius*, on the subject of a precarious trade. He considered a
commerce depending on the sole discretion of a foreign power, as a
real inconvenience. "The disadvantage (he observes) of a tenure
which may be suddenly discontinued, was experienced by our merchants on a late occasion. The embarrassments of the moment were
great, and the possibility of their renewal lays our commerce to England under a species of discouragement. The distinction is too remarkable not to be noticed, that our navigation is excluded from the
security of fixed laws, while that security is given to the navigation of
others."

These remarks of Mr. Jefferson are solid ; and they outweigh a thousand town-meeting resolves. *Without this treaty our trade to every British port can be interdicted by a nod of the British executive.* But by this treaty, our commerce to England and the East Indies, which now rests on the will of the ministry or the colonial government, is placed on the footing of permanent right. In this respect we gain an immense advantage—an advantage that we do not enjoy to the same extent with any other nation upon earth.

The commercial concessions on the part of Great Britain, which we have been just reviewing, are not only equal, but superior to those which are to be met with in the commercial treaties between her and other powers for more than a century past.

The treaty between Great Britain and Spain in 1667, and which for its advantages in matters of trade was confirmed in 1713, takes special care to limit the commerce of the two nations to the territories, provinces and islands, *to which trade and commerce had before been accustomed.* And yet two years afterward his Catholic majesty, as an evidence of his inclination to cultivate friendship, does indeed allow the English to gather salt in the isle of Tortugas, *because they had enjoyed that liberty in the reign of Charles II.*

In the treaty of commerce and navigation between Great Britain and Russia, which was made in the year 1766, the friendly privileges of trade between the two powers, were confined to such places *where leave is granted to the subjects of other nations.* In the same spirit of jealousy and colony monopoly, which appears but too prevalent throughout Europe, Russia takes care in her treaty of amity and commerce with Denmark, in the year 1782, to except from the commercial grant, her ports of the Black and Caspian Seas, and all her other possessions in Asia ; and the king of Denmark, on his part, excepts also his possessions in America, and elsewhere out of Europe. Nay, in the more recent treaty between France and England in 1786, and which was made with the express view of promoting a more liberal intercourse, the trade is limited to each other's territories *situated in Europe.*

Nor have our own treaties of commerce with the powers of Europe been more favored in this respect. In the treaty with France, on which so much unqualified applause has been bestowed by the enemies of the instrument under consideration, there is no very extensive admission to her colonial possessions. France indeed grants us as a matter of favor, one or more free ports in Europe, and *the free ports which have been and are open in the French islands in America.* And in our treaty of commerce with Holland, we expressly stipulate to leave to the Dutch the *peaceable enjoyment of their rights in the countries, islands, and seas in the East and West Indies, without any hindrance or molestation.* This is, indeed, stipulating for the perpetuity of their monopoly. On the other hand, Great Britain, by the 13th article of the present treaty, gives us a free and liberal admission into all her territories in the East Indies ; an immense country, which contains more than twenty millions of inhabitants, is guarded by an army of above seventy thousand men, and yields an annual revenue of more than eight millions sterling. And the only restriction to which we bind ourselves in return, is not to carry *her* East India commodities to any country but America, where they shall be unladen—a restriction which Britain could very reasonably ask as a security to her carrying trade.

I can not but conclude, that every reasonable man will see in this article, some evidence of a spirit of accommodation on the part of Great Britain, and much proof of influence and ability in our negotiator.

CURTIUS.

## No. VIII.

*Art.* 14.—This article admits Americans to a free trade to the British dominions in Europe, and British subjects to the same free trade in the United States.

One would think this article so reciprocal as to admit of no ground of censure.  But even this article has not given us an equivalent in the opinion of some men, who contend, that as British vessels are excluded from *no port* in the United States, so American vessels ought to be excluded from no port in the *British territories.*

*Decius* says, " we can only go to a small part of the British dominions, viz. to those in Europe ;" and he should have added, we are admitted there only by proclamation from year to year.

But does *Decius* value a commercial country by its geographical dimensions ?   Do these constitute the greatness or smallness of commercial privileges ?   This certainly is a new doctrine ; and the chicanery of such insinuations deserves reprobation by every honest man.

No matter what is the size of Great Britain—admit that it does not comprehend more land than the state of New York has, in a *republican humor*, sold to an individual ; this is nothing to the point.   The trade of that spot of earth, is at least double, not to say treble, the trade of the United States.   By admitting American citizens to a free participation of this commerce, we have more than an equivalent for a free admission of British vessels into all the ports of the United States.

The reflection of *Decius*, that our " envoy has, in this place, brought the principles of inequality into conspicuous action, as if anxious to circumscribe our commerce, and that he loses no opportunity of imposing restrictions on it," has not a shadow of foundation—it is the fabrication of a most malignant mind.   The whole article is founded on most equal and reciprocal principles, so far as regards Great Britain, independent of her colonies : but in proportion to the extent of the manufactures and exports of that country, it is most advantageous to America.

It is said we are not admitted into all the British colonies.   True ; but such admission would be a concession to us without an equivalent, for we have no colonies to exchange the benefit.

Let us contrast this article with the privileges obtained by the treaty with France, negotiated by the " venerable Franklin."   By the 30th article of that treaty, " The most Christian majesty will grant the subjects of the United States *one or more free ports in Europe,* and the free ports which have been and are open in the French islands."   Since the revolution, necessity has compelled the Convention to open all the ports in France : but which nation was most liberal in times of peace, or most jealous of its trade ?

Great Britain opens *all* her ports in Europe—all her ports in the East Indies—and all her ports in the West Indies, to vessels of small burden, restricting only the direct carrying trade from her colonies to Europe. France opened one or more ports in Europe, some of her ports in the West Indies, and not one in the East Indies.

This is a fair statement of the advantages of trade with the two countries, as we enjoyed them with France before the revolution, and as we should enjoy them by the present treaty with Great Britain ; and let any man decide, which treaty is the most liberal, in respect to opening the ports of the two countries and their colonies. The advantage is infinitely on the side of the present treaty with Great Britain.

*Art.* 15.—This article stipulates that each nation shall be treated by the other, on the footing of the most favored nation. So far the article corresponds exactly with all our other treaties : viz. with France, Sweden, Holland and Prussia. The second clause of the article, reserving to Great Britain the right of imposing duties on our tunnage, equal to what we impose on British tunnage in our ports, concedes nothing but what Great Britain now enjoys ; that is, the right of treating our trade as we treat hers. And the agreement in the last clause, that the United States will not for a certain period increase the duties on British tunnage, is a restriction that can not injure our trade.

Indeed no objection seems to be made to this article, except that it binds the United States to treat Great Britain as well as we treat other nations. This, with men of party spirit, who suffer their passions to lead their opinions, is a most unpardonable crime.

I trust, however, that the government of America will regulate its measures, even toward Great Britain, with justice and impartiality. I am persuaded it is not only most honorable, but most expedient ; and that justice and a spirit of accommodation will procure more advantages than a revengeful, retaliating, hostile disposition.

The 16th article, respecting consuls, is probably not objectionable.

*Art.* 17.—This is one of the articles which has excited the most violent clamors. Indeed we can not but observe, that such articles as may affect the French, are reprobated with more warmth than those which affect solely the interests of the United States. It would seem by the zeal discovered on this occasion, that this treaty ought first to have consulted the wants and wishes of France ; and the interests of the United States ought to have been only a *secondary* consideration. There is certainly a precept of high authority, " that we should love our neighbor as ourselves ;" but I know of no rule that requires one nation to love another *better* than itself.

I am disposed to treat the French nation with the utmost impartiality, justice and friendship ; and in our compacts with their enemies, we ought to make no sacrifices of their interest, and yield no points to their enemies, which the necessity of the case and the essential interests of our own country do not require.

By this maxim let the articles which may affect France be fairly examined.

The great objection to the 17th article is, that it " has solemnly relinquished a point, which to us was of more value than the amount of all the depredations on our trade, the sums due to us for negroes, and losses by detention of our posts." Now, what is the point relinquished ? The answer is, nothing which was our own ; nothing which we could command ; nothing which the British nation did not enjoy before.

The article stipulates, that vessels captured on suspicion of having enemies' property on board, or of carrying contraband articles to an enemy, shall be brought into the nearest or most convenient port, and if any property of an enemy is found on board, that part only which belongs to the enemy shall be made prize.  This is said to be a relinquishment of an important point on our part.  This is a gross misrepresentation.

Relinquishment implies an abandonment of something possessed.  If we never had a right to prevent the capture of our vessels, on suspicion of having enemies' property on board, and to prevent the seizure of that property, then we have not relinquished it.  But that right, with respect to nations not in treaty with us, we never possessed; we, therefore, have yielded nothing that we before enjoyed.

By the law of nations, any neutral vessel may be stopped and searched, and any property of an enemy found on board, may be seized.  This law can not be altered but by consent of the contracting parties.

This being the true state of things, what has the article of the treaty stipulated?  Observe the terms.  It is not said the property of an enemy *may* be taken—but, taking the right for granted, it says, the *enemy's property*, *only*, *shall* be made prize.

The article further stipulates, and this was obviously the main purpose of inserting it in the treaty, that the vessel shall be suffered to proceed with the rest of her cargo, without impediment—that there shall be no delay in deciding on such cases and in the payment or recovery of indemnification by the owners or by the masters of the vessels.

In short, the whole amount of the article is, that the practice of stopping and examining ships for enemy's property—a practice authorized by the law of nations—a practice which Great Britain will not resign, and which we can not persuade or compel her to resign—that this practice shall be rendered as little inconvenient to our trade as possible.  The article was intended to restrain, as far as possible, the abuses of this practice by licentious privateers.

There are many men, who, without any rule of conduct prescribed to them, would behave with unbounded licentiousness; but if a national compact is before their eyes, they will respect the rules prescribed.  So far, therefore, as the article goes, it can do no harm; but it may and often will do good.

But to exhibit this thing in still stronger light, I will give the whole of Mr. Jefferson's letter on the subject.  It is an answer to a remonstrance from Mr. Genet to the President, respecting the seizure of French property on board of American vessels, dated July 9, 1793.  It is the very point in question, and as the reasoning of Mr. Jefferson is in the present case unanswerable, it is proper the public should have the letter entire.

Philadelphia, July 24th, 1793.

*Mr. Jefferson, Secretary of State, to Mr. Genet, Minister Plenipotentiary of France.*

Sir—Your favor of the 9th inst. covered the information of Silvat Ducamp, Pierre Nouvel, Chouquet de Savarence, Gaston de Nogere,

and G. Beustier, that being on their passage from the French West Indies to the United States, with slaves and merchandise of their property, these vessels were stopped by British armed vessels, and their
property taken out as lawful prize.

I believe it can not be doubted, but that by the general law of nations,
the goods of a friend found in the vessels of an enemy, are free, and
the goods of an enemy, found in the vessel of a friend, are lawful prize.
Upon this principle, I presume, the British armed vessels have taken
the property of French citizens found in our vessels, in the cases above
mentioned, and I confess I should be at a loss on what principle to reclaim it.    It is true, that sundry nations, desirous of avoiding the inconvenience of having their vessels stopped at sea, ransacked, carried into
port, detained, under pretense of having enemy's goods on board, have,
in many instances, introduced by their special treaties, another principle
between them, that enemy bottoms shall make enemy goods, and friendly bottoms, friendly goods ; a principle much less embarrassing to commerce, and equal to all parties in point of gain and loss ; but this is altogether the effect of particular treaty, controlling, in special cases, the
general principle of the law of nations, and therefore taking effect between such nations only as have so agreed to control it.    England has
generally determined to adhere to the rigorous principle, having, in no
instance, as far as I recollect, agreed to the modification of letting the
property of the goods follow that of the vessel, except in the single one
of her treaty with France.    We have adopted this modification in our
treaties with France, the United Netherlands, and Prussia ; and therefore, as to them, our vessels cover the goods of their enemies, and we
lose our goods when in the vessels of their enemies.    Accordingly, you
will be pleased to recollect, that in the late case of Holland and Mackie,
citizens of the United States, who had laden a cargo of flour on board a
British vessel, which was taken by the French frigate Ambuscade, and
brought into this port ; when I reclaimed the cargo, it was only on the
ground that they were ignorant of the declaration of war when it was
shipped.

You observed, however, that the 14th article of our treaty had provided that ignorance should not be pleaded beyond two months after the
declaration of war, which term had elapsed, in this case, by some few
days ; and finding that to be the truth, though their real ignorance was
equally true, I declined the reclamation, as it never was in my view to
reclaim the cargo, nor in yours to offer to restore it, by questioning
the rule established in our treaty, that enemy bottoms make enemy
goods.    With England, Spain, Portugal and Austria, we have no treaties ; therefore we have nothing to oppose to their acting according to
the general law of nations, that enemy goods are lawful prize, though
found in the bottoms of a friend.    Nor do I see that France can suffer,
on the whole, for though she loses her goods in our vessels, when found
therein by England, Spain, Portugal or Austria, yet she gains our goods
when found in the vessels of England, Spain, Portugal, Austria, the United Netherlands or Prussia ; and I believe I may safely affirm, that we
have more goods afloat in the vessels of these six nations, than France
has afloat in our vessels, and consequently, that France is the gainer, and
we the loser, by the principle of our treaty ; indeed we are losers in

every direction of that principle ; for when it works in our favor, it is
to save the goods of our friends ; when it works against us, it is to lose
our own ; and we shall continue to lose while the rule is only partially
established.   When we shall have established it with all nations, we
shall be in a condition neither to gain nor lose, but shall be less exposed
to vexatious searches at sea.   To this condition we are endeavoring to
advance ; but as it depends on the will of other nations, as well as our
own, we can only obtain it when they shall be ready to concur.

I can not, therefore, but flatter myself, that on revising the cases of
Ducamp and others, you will perceive, that their losses result from the
state of war, which has permitted their enemies to take their goods,
though found in our vessels, and consequently, from circumstances over
which we have no control.

The rudeness to their persons practiced by their enemies, is certainly
not favorable to the character of the latter.   We feel for it as much as
for the extension of it to our own citizens, their companions, and find
in it a motive for requiring measures to be taken, which may prevent
repetitions of it.*           I have the honor to be, &c.

TH. JEFFERSON.

I beg the reader to note the following clause of the foregoing letter :
" To this condition we are endeavoring to advance ; but as it depends
on the *will of other nations*, as well as our own, we can only obtain it
when *they* shall be ready to concur."

I will close with remarking, that by our treaty with France, it is expressly stipulated, that *free* ships should make *free* goods.   The Convention, however, in 1793, ordered vessels, laden with provisions, to be
carried into their ports, in violation of that treaty.   They afterward revoked the decree with respect to American vessels.   They afterward
extended the decree to American vessels, in defiance of the treaty.   A
few months ago, they relented, confessed they had ill-treated their allies,
and annulled the decree a second time.   A statement of these facts
was made by the President to Congress, Dec. 5, 1793.   See his address
of that date, prefixed to the correspondence between Mr. Jefferson and
Mr. Hammond.

Such unsteadiness in public measures operates peculiarly to the prejudice of trade.   The merchant, if he knows enemy's property is liable
to seizure, may avoid risk by declining to take it on board.   But when
a nation is changing its regulations on this head, the merchant is exposed
to vexations, without the power of avoiding the evil.        CURTIUS.

No. IX.

*Art.* 18.—This is one of the articles in the treaty which gives great
offense.   The objections to it are—" that it enumerates among contraband goods, timber for ship-building, tar and rosin, copper in sheets,
sails, hemp and cordage, and generally whatever may serve directly to
the equipment of vessels, unwrought iron and fir planks only excepted ;
and that it admits provisions in certain cases to be contraband," contra-

---

* In opposition to the principles stated in this letter, see the *Essay on the Rights
of Neutrals* in the preceding pages.

ry to all other treaties, and even contrary to the treaty of 1786, between Great Britain and France.

I frankly acknowledge that no part of the treaty is more vulnerable than this : no part can furnish more substantial grounds of complaint. This article proceeds from a strict adherence on the part of Great Britain, to the law of nations, which favors her superiority as a great maritime power ; and its defense rests on the inability of our envoy to procure a relaxation of those laws.

The time for negotiating this article was unfavorable, as in most other respects it was favorable. Great Britain, always anxious to preserve her naval strength, the great and only bulwark of the nation, is now engaged in a most inveterate war with France, a war on which her very existence depends, and at this time, will not yield one clause of the law of nations, to abridge her own power of crippling the naval force of her enemy. This is a fixed point ; and our envoy could only admit the article in that form.

There were but two alternatives, both of which would result in the *same consequences to our trade.* This idea is an important one. If the article had been rejected by our minister, Great Britain actually *exercises* the right by the general law of nations, to consider all those articles contraband, and to declare them such, when she judges that by these means she can reduce her enemy. If the article was received, it could give no greater latitude to Great Britain than she enjoyed before. Whichever alternative our envoy might choose, our trade must be subject to the exercise of the same right and to the same embarrassments.

If the right of treating all the articles mentioned as contraband, results from the law of nations, and if Great Britain will not abandon that right, is it not better, in a treaty of a temporary nature, to accede to the right, and enumerate the articles which are liable to seizure and confiscation, that our merchants may know the law, and avoid losses, than to suffer that right to stand on the law of nations, which is less known, and which might expose our citizens to heavy losses ?

Every liberal man must wish to see the field of confiscations in war narrowed as much as possible ; but if we can not circumscribe that field, is it not of great importance to our citizens, to mark out the ground with distinct lines, that every man may distinguish it and shun the danger ? Every rational person will say *it is ;* and this is the effect of this article of the treaty.

I know it has been contended that timber and provisions are not, by the law of nations, contraband. But Vattel, a modern French writer, of the highest authority, includes them among contraband goods. His words are, " commodities particularly used in war, and the importation of which to an enemy is prohibited, are called contraband goods. Such are arms, military and naval stores, timber, horses, and even provisions, in certain junctures, when there are hopes of reducing the enemy by famine."—(Book iii, ch. 7, sec. 112.)

The words naval stores, include cordage, hemp, tar, rosin, and every thing that serves for the equipment of ships of war. In the treaty of 1786, Great Britain and France had excepted naval stores and provisions from the list of contraband articles. That treaty is annulled by the present war. But naval stores are generally considered by Great Britain as contraband by the general law of nations. The right to consider them so can be abridged only by treaty ; and Great Britain, at this moment, will consent to no such abridgment.

Some people say, it is better to let this point rest on the law of nations, than to admit it in a treaty. This is merely a matter of expedience ; but if the safety of the merchant's property is consulted, it is unquestionably better to have the contraband articles enumerated.

The stipulations in the second and third clause of the 18th article, are in favor of neutral vessels. The agreement, that when provisions are regarded as contraband, they shall be paid for to their full value, with a mercantile profit, freight, and demurrage, is a rule of direction to the captors, that may prove favorable to a neutral trade, subject to be embarrassed by powers at war. And the provision of the last clause, that neutral vessels entering a blockaded port, not knowing it to be blockaded, shall not be seized and confiscated for the first attempt, is equally salutary and favorable.

*Art.* 19.—This article provides against the ill usage which the subjects of neutral powers are liable to receive from the commanders of ships of war and privateers. This article is common in treaties—it is in nearly the same words as in all our other treaties with foreign nations. But it will be of much more use between Great Britain and America, as it will operate as a prohibition against impressing American seamen on board of English ships. It has been objected to the treaty, that no provision of this kind is included in it. But the 19th article is a direct prohibition of this practice.

On account of a sameness of language, it is desirable that some effectual mode might be devised to distinguish American from British seamen. It might be of importance that American seamen should be provided with certificates of their citizenship, under the seal of some public officer. This doubtless deserves the attention of our executive, perhaps of Congress, as not only British commanders, but French also, have mistaken American seamen for British, and our citizens are thus exposed to injustice from both parties.

It has been objected that the bonds required of the commanders of privateers to indemnify persons injured, are not large enough—the sums being limited to £1500 sterling for small privateers, and £3000 sterling* in case the privateer carries more than one hundred and fifty men. It is sufficient to say, in answer to this, that few cases can occur, where damages to a greater amount will be incurred ; and where the bonds do not secure the damages, a complaint to government will ensure any further claims founded in justice.

It may be observed, that this clause of the article is copied nearly from a similar one in the treaty of 1786, between Great Britain and France. The sums limited by that treaty are the same ; and will probably be found equal to all necessary purposes.

The last clause obliges judges of admiralty, in case any sentence of condemnation has been pronounced against vessels or goods, to deliver

---

* The sums of £1500 and £3000, are the same as specified in treaties for more than a century.

on demand authentic copies of the proceedings to the master, he paying the legal fees.  A stipulation of this kind was necessary, as instances of delay and refusal of such copies have been experienced by our
citizens during the present war.

The 20th article is usual in all treaties.  It makes provision for guarding property from pirates, or restoring it to its proper owners—a provision of mutual benefit to the contracting parties, and liable to no objection.                                                        CURTIUS.

## No. X.

*Art.* 21.—This article prohibits the subjects of the contracting parties, to commit acts of hostility against each other—to accept commissions from a foreign prince or state, enemies to the other party—to enlist them into military service, &c. and declares that the laws against
such offenses shall be punctually executed.  The law of the United
States, passed in June, 1794, enacts the penalty of a fine, not exceeding $2000, and imprisonment for the foregoing offenses.

The same article of the treaty makes it piracy to accept a foreign
commission or letter of marque, for arming any privateer to act against
the other party.  This is prohibited also by the same law of the United
States, under a penalty of imprisonment, at the discretion of the court,
and a fine not exceeding $5000.

When the treaty first appeared, this article excited much acrimony.
It was considered as pointed at the military maneuvers of a late French
minister, who had attempted to excite Americans to war against the
Spanish settlements, and to privateering against Great Britain.  It was
supposed to restrain the right of *expatriation ;* a doctrine first propagated by the same Frenchman, to evade the law of nations, and a doctrine which never would have entered the heads of our citizens, had
it not been taught by that artful sophist.  In giving their decided
opinion against this article of the treaty, many rash men found themselves in a dilemma, when they were informed that the article was in
our treaty with France.

So eager were the people of a certain faction to condemn the whole
treaty, that they would not give themselves time to be informed whether
it was right or wrong.  But when they came to be told that they were
restrained from taking foreign commissions to act against a power at
peace with the United States, by the acknowledged laws of nations, by
an express statute of the United States, and by an article in all our
other treaties, they began to blush for their haste in giving opinions on
what they did not understand.  No article in the treaty is more requisite
for the peace of our nation, and none more conformable to the principles of justice between governments.

Vattel says, " A nation ought not to suffer the citizens to do an injury
to the subjects of another state, much less to offend the state itself.  If
you let loose the reins of your subjects against foreign nations, these
will behave in the same manner to you ; and instead of that friendly
intercourse which nature has established between all men, we should
see nothing but one nation robbing another."—(Book ii, ch. 6.)

" I account associates of an enemy, those who assist him in his war
without being obliged to it by treaty."—(Book iii, ch. 6.)

A nation is not accountable for every act of an individual citizen; but if a state or nation openly permits the citizens to take part with the enemies of a third nation, that third nation has a right to consider that state as making a common cause with its enemies, and to declare war against i of course. The peace of neutral nations depends on the prohibitions of this article of the treaty.

It has been objected to this article, that it is unconstitutional as it creates the crime of piracy, when the power of defining piracy is vested in Congress. But the act of Congress before mentioned, admits the right of the President and Senate to define piracy in treaties; as the ninth section enacts, "that nothing in the act shall be construed to prevent the prosecution or punishment of treason or *a piracy defined by a treaty*, or other law of the United States."

Nothing marks the partiality of a certain faction more distinctly than their objections to this article. We have had a similar article in our treaty with France more than seventeen years; and in our treaties with Sweden, Prussia, and the States General, more than ten years, and not a syllable of objection was lisped against the principle. People did not generally know that such an article existed. But the moment our government treats Great Britain with the same measure of justice as we had before observed toward other nations, our Jacobins begin to clamor.

It is this popular partiality for France, this disposition to favor every thing French, at the expense of every principle of justice and equity, which occasions all the difficulty our executive has encountered in preserving our peace, and in accommodating our differences with Great Britain. Nay more; this partiality displayed on all occasions, and to a degree highly improper for a neutral nation, has been a principal cause of the abusive treatment our seamen have received from British privateers.

It is agreed on all hands that our interest as a nation is supereminently concerned in preserving peace. But how can peace be secured unless we treat the powers at war with impartiality and justice? Vattel observes, " A neutral nation desirous safely to enjoy the conveniencies of that state, is in all things to shew an exact impartiality between the parties at war; for should one nation favor another to its detriment, that nation can not complain if the other treats it as an adherent and confederate of his enemy."

Our people have indeed a fine apology for showing a preference to France—that of favoring liberty and republicanism. So far as the French fight for national independence against the combined powers, they are engaged in a just and necessary war, and the wishes of all Americans must be with them. But people who think France has a republican government, or any other free government, are egregiously mistaken. Nor is there as great a prospect of her establishing a republic, as there is that she is doomed to despotism, or to be split into a multitude of small factious democracies perpetually at war with each other.

People are, therefore, in every view, unjustifiable in aiding any of the powers at war, in a manner not warranted by the laws of neutrality. As we value our own government, and the prosperity of the country, we are to avoid every act which can commit a breach on our public peace.  It is rashness and madness to combine our interest with any European power in such a manner as to be drawn into their political contentions.  The pretense of aiding the *cause of liberty* is a mere artifice to catch our passions.  If the nations of Europe can not defend their liberties, we can not be answerable for their ill success.  We aid them best by our peace and our industry.

The 22d article of the treaty stipulates, that in case of injuries or damage on one side or the other, neither party will authorize reprisals, until a statement of the same, verified by proof, shall be presented to the other, and satisfaction demanded.  This stipulation is in exact conformity with the law of nations, and is supported by principles of policy and justice.

The provisions in the 23d article are well adapted to advance the intentions of the contracting parties, and are reciprocally beneficial.  The permission of American vessels to enter prohibited ports in case of distress, is a concession conformable to the laws of hospitality.

The objection to the clause which enjoins a respect to be paid to officers according to their commissions, can be raised only by men who are destitute of the civility which enjoins that respect.

The 24th article prohibits foreign privateers with commissions, from a prince or state in enmity with either nation, to arm or sell prizes in the ports of the parties.

The 25th article makes it lawful for the ships of war and privateers of either party to enter the ports of the other, without being liable to be searched, seized, or detained, or to pay admiralty fees.

These stipulations are also in our treaty with France ; and no well grounded objection has been made to them.  Some superficial people have supposed that they clash with our treaty with France.  But there is an express declaration that these stipulations shall not be construed to operate contrary to former existing treaties.  And if no such caution had been taken, the treaty with Great Britain could not have operated to the prejudice of France : for it is an express law of nations, " That a sovereign (or state) already bound by a treaty, can not make others contrary to the first.  The things about which he has entered into engagements, are no longer at his disposal.  If it happens that a posterior treaty is found, in some point, to contradict one that is more ancient, the *new treaty is null with respect to that point.*  This relates to treaties with different powers."—(Vattel, book ii, ch. 12, sec. 165.)

So far the fears of people are totally groundless.  But the following clause has excited acrimonious remarks.  " The two parties agree that while they continue in amity, neither of them will in future make a treaty that shall be inconsistent with this and the preceding article." What can be the objection to this clause ?  The laws of nations, and the rules of moral justice, forbid a state to make a subsequent treaty to infringe a prior one.  No nation can do it.  The passage just quoted from Vattel is expressly to this purpose : and the clause has done nothing more than convert a moral obligation into a contract, a law of nations into a conventional law between the parties.  Stipulations of this kind, like statutes in affirming of common law, add the sanction of a positive contract to an implied one.  No new obligation is created ; an agreement of this sort may be considered as strengthening the old one.

The 26th article provides, that in case of war, merchants may continue to reside in the respective dominions, behaving peaceably—and in case their conduct shall render them suspected, the term of twelve months is allowed to settle their accounts and remove their families and effects. This is a favorable provision, and highly necessary, between countries so extensively connected in commerce. The term of twelve months for removal, is longer than is usually allowed; the term generally assigned in treaties is six or nine months.

To the two last articles, I presume no objections are made.

CURTIUS.

## No. XI.

Thus having attempted to remove every objection of consequence that has been urged against the treaty, I will lay before the public a general view of our trade with the different countries of Europe, Asia and the West Indies.

It has been stated by the opposers of the treaty that the commercial arrangements want reciprocity—that we concede much, and gain nothing which we did not before enjoy.

With respect to the inland trade to Canada, the converse of the proposition is the truth. The United States *gain* a free trade to Canada, on equal terms with British subjects, which we did not before enjoy. British subjects gain little or nothing by the stipulation, which they did not before enjoy. In this part of the treaty, the advantage is on the side of the United States.

With respect to our foreign commerce, it depends on the will of nations over whom we have no control. All nations claim the right of admitting ships and goods into their ports, or prohibiting them at pleasure; or of burdening our commerce with heavy duties. This right is absolute, and when we obtain any privilege in their trade, it is by way of grant or concession. The United States have the same right as to their own ports; but they have not seen fit to exclude the ships of any nation from a free participation of their trade.

The maritime powers of Europe find a navy so necessary to their safety, amidst the contending interests of the different nations, that every measure is taken to multiply their seamen, and increase their shipping. Great Britain is the nation most interested in this system. From her insular situation, a navy is her only defense—to man a navy, she must raise seamen—to secure a supply of seamen she must extend her commerce and her carrying trade as far as possible.

In pursuance of this system of defense, originated her navigation act, in 1660, which restricts her trade to British vessels, and manned mostly with British seamen. That act has been in operation from its first passing to the present day; and to prevent temporary or local inconveniences, from a rigid execution, the parliament have empowered the king and council to dispense with it on occasion, and open the ports of Great Britain, or her colonies, at such times and to such nations, as necessities may require.

All the nations of Europe have laws respecting their trade, which operate more or less to encourage their own commerce, and lay that of their neighbors to their own dominions under restrictions.

A view of the privileges and restrictions of commerce, was offered to Congress, Dec. 16, 1793, by Mr. Jefferson, which, though not sufficiently correct or comprehensive, throws much light on the subject. These general facts will be sufficient for my purpose in this place.

The admission of our vessels into the British dominions in Europe, rests now on an annual proclamation of the king and council. Although interest and expedience may operate to continue the privilege of entering those ports at all times, and with vessels of any burden, yet the tenure of the privilege is precarious.

By the present treaty, this precarious privilege becomes a right, which can not be abridged by the executive of the English nation. This is an advantage ; and Mr. Jefferson, in his report, admits it to be such. It was an objection he urged against our former state of commerce to Great Britain, that it was precarious. That objection by the treaty is removed.

With respect to her colonial possessions, Great Britain has observed the jealous policy common to all the nations of Europe. The ships of all nations are excluded from her colonies, unless it may be a port in the West Indies, where the Spaniards are permitted to enter with logwood.

In opening her West Indies to American vessels of seventy tuns burden, and her East India ports to American vessels of any burden, she has conceded a privilege, which she grants to no other nation on earth. The sacrifice of the carrying trade on the part of the United States, to obtain admission into the English West Indies, is deemed more than equivalent, and that stipulation will fall to the ground. But the direct trade to the British East Indies, is generally admitted to be highly beneficial.

Let us contrast these advantages in trade with those we enjoy with other nations.

Our navigation to Spain and Portugal is free : but many of our exports are prohibited, as tobacco, and rice and whale oils to Portugal. The American trade, however, to Spain and Portugal is highly advantageous in a number of articles. But both these countries prohibit all intercourse with their colonial possessions. The ports of Sweden and Denmark are open ; but the duties paid on most of the American productions amount to a prohibition.

Our navigation to the United Netherlands is free ; but some of the most material articles of our country, as beef, pork and bread-stuff, are prohibited, as well as by Great Britain. We can have no intercourse with their possessions in the East Indies.

France, before the war, guarantied to the United States one or more free ports in Europe, and such ports in the West Indies as were free. In general, her West Indies were open by an arret of the king. Even the coasting trade in France was principally carried on by foreign vessels.

The revolution has sensibly varied the whole scene of commerce. Necessity has opened all French ports to neutral nations. But a navigation act, similar to that of Great Britain, was decreed September 2, 1793, to take place January 1, 1794. This, with a long spirited report of Barrere, was transmitted to Congress, and published by their order

in February, 1794. This act is suspended only on account of the necessities of France, her commerce being wholly dependent on neutral
bottoms. The moment this act shall take place, we shall be cut off
from all right to the trade of France, except what is guarantied by
treaty, that is, *one or more free ports ;* and such privileges as we shall
be able to obtain by future stipulations. The decree is in these words :

### Act of Navigation, of the French Republic.

The National Convention, after having heard the report of their committees of marine, of commerce, and of public safety, considering that
the French nation has the incontestible right of securing by every method, the prosperity of her agriculture, commerce and industry ; that nothing has a more direct tendency to this end than a navigation act ; and
that in the solemn declaration of this act she only makes use of the same
right which she acknowledges to belong to all other nations, decrees as
follows :

*Art.* 1. That no foreign commodities, productions or merchandise,
shall be imported but directly by French vessels, or those belonging to
the inhabitants of the country of which they are the growth, produce or
manufacture, or to the inhabitants of the country of the ordinary ports
of sale and first exportation ; the officers and three fourths of the crew
of a foreign vessel being of the country whose flag the vessel bears ;
the whole on pain of confiscation of the vessel and cargo, and a fine of
three thousand livres, jointly and severally against the owners, consign-
ees, and agents of the vessel and cargo, the captain and lieutenant of
the vessel.

2. That foreign vessels shall not transport from one French port to
another French port, any commodities, productions or merchandises of
the growth, produce or manufactures of France, the colonies or possessions of France, under the penalties declared in article 1st.

3. That after the 10th of August next, no vessel shall be reputed
French, nor enjoy the privileges of a French vessel, unless such vessel
shall have been built in the colonies or possessions of France, or declared a good prize taken from an enemy, or confiscated for contravention
of the laws of France, and unless the officers and three fourths of the
crew are Frenchmen.

On the whole, it is demonstrated that no country on earth yields more
extensive privileges to the American merchant, than Great Britain. It
is also equally demonstrable that Great Britain yields more privileges
in her trade with the United States than she grants to any other nation.

It has been objected to several articles of the treaty, that they are *not
reciprocal,* because from the circumstances of the two countries, British
subjects will be principally benefited. Thus the 9th and 10th articles
are said to yield advantages to Great Britain, without *an equivalent,* because her subjects hold large tracts of land in the United States, and
have debts due them to a great amount : whereas American subjects
hold little or no land, and have no debts or moneys, in Great Britain.

Objections of this kind must proceed from a peevish captious disposition. It may just as well be objected, that we should have no trade with
Great Britain at all, because her exports to this country exceed her im-

ports from it—or because her dominions contain double the number of people, that are in the United States. Nay, it may just as well be said that every man has not an *equal right* to a highway, because some use the highway ten times as much as others.

In all conventions between states, an *equality in principle constitutes an equivalent.* If an article of any treaty gives to both parties a right of doing the same things, and under the same advantages, that article is reciprocal, though one of the parties never makes use of the right.

Thus in our treaty with France, we permit French armed vessels to bring their prizes into the ports of the United States. The French also permit the American vessels to carry their prizes into French ports. The French are in a condition to use the privilege and do use it every day. We are not at war, and do not use the privilege. But will any man say, that article of the treaty is not *mutual?* Will any man deny that we have an *equivalent* for the right conceded to France? Just so with respect to our commerce with England or any other power. Suppose a nation to have but a single port for shipping and commerce, and the United States to have a thousand. Each party agrees to open all their ports, and admit the other to a free trade; will it be denied that this is reciprocal? Certainly not. It is *equality in the principle*, not in the amount or extent of its operation, which constitutes *reciprocity*. If people are disposed to cavil at *inequalities of condition*, as well as of *principle*, they may find as many causes of discontent, in all other treaties, as in this with Great Britain.

The truth is, when our other treaties were formed, Americans had confidence in the constituted authorities of our country. They believed men, who had made commerce, treaties, and the laws of nations, a study and matter of contemplation, were best capable of negotiating treaties. They trusted to the men appointed for this purpose. The great mass of people are not competent to decide what is, or is not for our public interests, in complicated negotiations and national compacts; and unless they repose confidence in public characters, we shall forever be embroiled with factions.                                    CURTIUS.

## No. XII.

Having in the preceding papers, answered such objections to the treaty, as appear to have any weight, I will close this vindication, by addressing to my fellow citizens, some considerations of a more general nature.

It was the public opinion the last year, and it is an opinion still maintained among one description of Americans, that Great Britain has been so humbled by France, that she will consent to make great sacrifices for the purpose of securing peace and commerce with this country. It is also believed by many people, that the kingdom is upon the point of an internal revolution: and that holding in our hands the power of sequestrating the debts of her citizens, we may command, at all times, peace and favorable treatment. All these opinions, though unquestionably erroneous, have contributed to raise the public expectation, respecting the success of the treaty, to an unwarrantable pitch.

With respect to the humble condition of Great Britain, where are the proofs? That her land forces were defeated and cut to pieces, the last campaign, is undeniable; and there is no question that any combat by land, would be decided in favor of France. The numbers, the discipline, and the enthusiasm of the French forces on land render them irresistible. But the best troops and the best discipline, without other resources, will not maintain the greatness of a state or kingdom, for any length of time.

France now supports her armies mostly upon her conquered countries. Her finances are exhausted ; and what is, if possible, a more serious calamity, her internal dissensions debilitate her force, distract her councils, and disconcert her operations.

The plan of Robespierre was a system of despair. By putting every thing in requisition, the persons of men, their goods, provisions, and money, the whole force of France was collected to a point, and the whole energy of that force was exerted to defeat the most formidable combination ever raised against the independence of a nation.

This measure was perhaps indispensable in the crisis when it was adopted. But unfortunately violent exertions in the body politic, as well as in the human body, are ever followed by debility and languor. The system of requisitions and the maximum, were calculated to destroy the capital of a country, which, in all cases, ought to be left untouched, as a source of further productions. The interest or income only of a country can be safely used for national purposes ; and when a state is compelled to seize the capital stock, though its exertions may be great, they must certainly be of short duration.

But this is not the only calamity incurred by the system of terror. To enforce such an arbitrary system, recourse must be had to violent punishment for refusals to comply with it ; and the summary mode of condemning, as well as the sanguinary process of executing, tend to excite all the malicious and revengeful passions of men. The guillotin of France has left every deadly and rancorous passion, waiting only for a favorable moment for vengeance. The surviving friends of those who fell victims to the system of terror, will not easily forget or forgive the injuries they suffered ; and thus that terrible despotism, which for a few months compelled all men to unite to defeat foreign foes and to crush internal insurrections ; that system has spread over France the seeds of faction and dissension, which will afflict the country and weaken all its exertions for at least a generation to come. Thus the last season, the victories of France by land, astonished all nations, and spread dismay through Europe, while her frigates scoured the ocean, and marred the commerce of her enemies. But the present season, her armies and her fleet are inactive, her resources fail, and all is debility and languor.

Great Britain, on the other hand, though her army was destroyed in the Netherlands, retains all her activity and resources. Her territories have not been the seat of war ; her land has been under full cultivation, her manufactures have been carried on as usual, her goods are exported nearly as cheap, and in nearly the same quantities, as in time of peace ; her government retains its vigor, and her fleet, notwithstanding a scarcity of seamen, still rides mistress of the ocean. The commerce of Great Britain, though a little impaired, still exceeds that of any other country ; and the government has not been compelled to distress her trade to man her navy. Were there a pressing necessity for so violent a step, that country, by stripping her merchantmen for a time, would bring upon the ocean a fleet superior to any that has ever ap-

peared under one command.   But Great Britain has not yet been compelled to adopt this ruinous expedient ; she has not materially impaired
her commerce by impressing seamen—she has not entrenched upon
the capital stock of her husbandmen and manufacturers.   Her debt
has indeed been augmented ; but still immense sums of money are offered, and the only question with government is, whose money shall be
received on loan, for the competitors are numerous.   Such is the moneyed capital of that country, and such the resources, that Great Britain
will probably be able to carry on the war longer than any other power.

Nor is the idea of an approaching revolution well founded.   Ireland
may perhaps give trouble ; but the government of England has seldom
ever been supported by a more numerous and powerful majority of the
people.   The private associations in England and Scotland, gave some
uneasiness for a time ; but the moment government called for a suspension of the *habeas corpus* act, it was granted, and the executive dissipated all private societies, with their plans of revolution.   The ease
with which this whole business was conducted, certainly does not mark
either fear or weakness in the administration of the government of
Great Britain.

Where, then, is the ground for supposing Great Britain in a distressed state of humiliation, compelling her to make sacrifices to the United
States ?   On the contrary, Great Britain at this moment, maintains as
commanding an attitude among the powers of the earth as at any former period.   All the hopes of Americans, founded on an opinion of
the depressed state of that nation, are wholly delusory.   Nor can we
expect any thing from the generosity or good will of the British or any
other nation.   National generosity is a mere phantom of the imagination.   It is to the interest, or, at most, to the justice of a nation we must
address ourselves ; and no nation will make concessions beyond what
these require.   We are not in a situation to *command* any foreign nation, to *enforce* our claims, or to *compel* the exercise of justice.

If our sanguine enthusiasts are mistaken totally as to the present
power of Great Britain, they are equally so as to the force and effect
of sequestration.   The injustice of attacking private debts for national
wrongs, is generally admitted ; but many people contend that it may
be necessary at times to resort to this measure, as the only effectual
weapon in our power to terrify Great Britain, a perfidious nation, into
a sense of justice.

It is surprising how such reasoners mistake the real and certain effects of such a step.   Any man who will give himself time to reflect
on the pride of nations, and especially of the English nation, must be
convinced that the use of this weapon, instead of inducing concessions
on the part of Great Britain, would excite every hostile feeling, not
only in the government, but in the very creditors whose debts should
be sequestered.   Such a violation of all good faith, such an attack upon
commercial confidence, as the sequestration of private debts to avenge
national injuries, would put it out of our power to accommodate differences but by the sword.   It would provoke a war of double fury ; and
the very man whose debts should be detained, would be the first to encourage and the last to abandon the contest.

All the high raised expectations of our citizens of obtaining from
Great Britain in her present state, humiliating concessions which her

pride would forbid her to yield in time of peace, are supported by not one circumstance of rational probability. People who dwell on such prospects of success are grossly deceived, both as to facts, and as to the character of the English nation.

But Judge Rutledge of South Carolina, has, on this subject, uttered the silliest expressions that ever fell from human lips. " England," says he, " is hoping for peace on whatever terms France may grant it: she is reduced to the last gasp, and were America to seize her by the throat, she would expire in agonies at her feet."

A man must be little less than insane, to utter such absurd ideas, especially at a moment when Great Britain possesses more actual resources, the sinews of war, than all the other powers at war, even France included. And no man but an insolvent debtor, who hates his creditor, because he has injured him, would wish to see a great agricultural, manufacturing, and commercial nation *expiring in agonies.* Whatever be the injuries Great Britain has done this country, it is not for the interest of mankind, that she should be blotted out of existence. In no country on earth do the American merchants find more good faith, fair dealing, and convenient credit, than among British merchants—no creditors are more indulgent to debtors than the British—and no country on earth finds extensive credit more useful than the United States.

Whatever be the resentments of our citizens toward Great Britain, they may rest assured of one fact, and it is of no small moment to some of the United States, that the treatment Americans will receive from that country will be *more friendly*, when the conduct of American debtors is more *just.*

Another objection to the treaty, or to any treaty with Great Britain, is, that it begets an unnatural alliance between a monarchy and a republic. This is clearly the most trifling objection ever offered, and is beneath a serious answer. And those who make it, ought to blush at their inconsistency, especially as these very men are rejoicing at the late treaty between France and the monarch of Prussia, and earnestly expecting every day, to hear of a treaty between France and Spain.

On the whole, let me ask my fellow citizens what sacrifices we may make by the treaty ? We have old inveterate disputes with Great Britain, which must be terminated. War or accommodation are the alternatives. If we wish a war, we waste the blood and treasure of America, without an object; for at the close of the war, the old disputes will remain, and new ones be originated. Instead of bettering our condition, we render it infinitely worse by hostilities.

Is it not wise, therefore, to compromise these differences ? And though considerable time and expense, perhaps some sacrifices of just claims, should be incurred on our part, yet between these evils, and the continuance of inveterate enmity and hostile views, on which side does the balance lie ? Every reflecting man must say, *on the side of accommodation and peace.*

The commercial part of the treaty is of a temporary nature ; and even if some sacrifices were to be made, these will not come in competition with the other great and important objects of the treaty. But it is not true that any material sacrifice is made in the commercial part of this compact. We do not cede *one material privilege* which Great Britain does not enjoy by the laws of nations or the laws of the United

States.  I am bold in the assertion, and call on my opposers to name the part in which such sacrifice is made.  On the other hand some *material concessions* on the part of Great Britain, are made to the United States by the treaty.

It is said, Great Britain may enter with her ships into *all* the ports of the United States.  True ; but she enjoys that privilege *without* this treaty.  She gains nothing in this respect except that she changes a *precarious privilege* for a *right ;* just as we do, in the trade to the British *European* dominions.

It is said, we bind ourselves not to increase the duties on British tunnage and goods imported in her ships beyond what we lay on those of other nations.  True ; we agree on this head, to treat Great Britain as well as the most favored nation.  If this is a concession on our part, it can not be a *material sacrifice*, for we have an equivalent in this, that Great Britain stipulates the same thing to the United States.

It is said, *we cede* to Great Britain the right of increasing duties on our tunnage to equal our present duties on hers and on goods imported in British bottoms.  Nothing can be more puerile than such an allegation.  In this respect we *cede* nothing.  Great Britain had that right before the treaty ; and her right is precisely the same as before.

It has been said, we *cede* to Great Britain the right of seizing our vessels and taking the enemy's property ; and that we have *made* naval stores and provisions contraband by treaty.  These charges have been proved *not true*.  Great Britain enjoys these rights by the *law of nations*, independent of all treaties.

We have therefore made very few sacrifices in this part of the treaty ; but we have gained something.  We have obtained a permanence of trade to Great Britain.  We have gained a free trade to Canada and the British East Indies, without any considerable concessions, and what is more, we have preserved the *blessings of peace*.

Why then, my fellow citizens, will you not leave the management of this treaty where the constitution has placed it ?  What ground have you to suppose, that the President, our late envoy and the majority of the Senate, have, in a moment and on this single occasion, deserted the interest of our country ?  What reason have you to believe that old tried patriots have renounced the uniform principles of their lives, and turned apostates ?  Is there a shadow of reason to believe, that men grown gray in the service of their country, whose patriotism and virtue were never suspected, have now in the evening of life, and at the close of all their active . public scenes, commenced traitors ?  You can not believe insinuations of this kind.  The suggestion of British gold and undue influence, is the work of dark malicious hearts, detested by all good men, and discredited by the very children in the streets.

No, my countrymen, you have been deceived.  Your passions have been taken by surprise ; you have been precipitated into rash opinions, and violent measures, by a set of men who are the foes of our present free and happy government and its administration.  You may be assured, there is a confederation of characters, from New Hampshire to Georgia, arrayed in opposition, either to the constitution of the United States, to its administration, or to particular men in office.  The opposition of the principal men in this confederacy can be traced to some known causes, originally of a personal nature.  Disappointment in application for some office, or the failure of some favorite scheme in their political system, has converted many of the friends of our late revolution, into determined opposers of the general system of the present adminis-tration. These men will never be contented till they can displace the present officers of government, and introduce themselves, their friends, and their measures, into our councils. You may rest assured, that most of the ferment raised against the treaty, originated with men of this description.

This confederacy was formed and is still maintained and strengthen-ed, by spreading jealousies and suspicions among the people, who though honest in their views, are very liable to be misled by artful men. One of the most successful weapons ever wielded by this coalition of disap-pointed men, is furnished them by the present war in Europe. The combination of powers against France, which we all reprobate, is said to be a combination against *liberty in general*, and if France should fail of success, it is said we shall be the next object of attack.

This is a mere suggestion of our restless men, to alarm your fears, and drive you, if possible, from your neutral ground into hostilities. The suggestion was first made by the late French minister, whose mis-sion to this country was for the *express purpose of flattering*, *intriguing*, *or forcing you into the war.* His instructions are clear and explicit on this point.

That minister was displaced, and his views counteracted by the firm-ness of our President, seconded by the northern states. But the party which originally rallied under that man, still exists, and forms a league, co-extensive with the United States, connected in all its parts and acting by a single impulse.

Thus, in the infancy of our empire, the bane of all republics is al-ready diffused over our country, and poisons the whole body politic. Faction is a disease which has proved fatal to all popular governments; but in America it has assumed an aspect more formidable than in any other country. In ancient republics, popular commotions were sudden things, excited by the emergencies of the moment, bursting instantly on the existing government, producing a revolution, banishing a tyrant who was powerful, or a patriot who was popular, and an object of jealousy to some ambitious competitor.

But in America, faction has assumed consistency and system—it is a *conspiracy perpetually existing*—an opposition organized and disci-plined, for the purposes of defeating the regular exercise of the con-stitutional powers of our government, whenever a measure does not please the secret leaders of the confederacy.

My countrymen, be watchful of the progress of the associations, formed on the plan of the Jacobin society in France. That society was a powerful instrument in the work of demolishing the monarchy; but on the ruins of monarchy, it raised the most frightful despotism recorded in history. Leagued with sister societies in every village and city of France, the Jacobins governed the Convention, Paris and all France for a long time, and filled it with blood, confiscation and ruin. So terrible was the tyranny of these associations, that the Convention were compelled to prohibit their meetings; but so numerous are the members, and so active the spirit of revenge, that two or three insurrections have been raised by the Jacobins in Paris, blood has been shed in various parts by that faction, they have been in possession of Toulon, a civil war is often excited, and it seems yet doubtful whether the *national representatives, or private unauthorized clubs* shall govern France.

My countrymen, you are threatened with a similar evil.    Under the pretended mask of *patriotism and watching over our liberties*, private associations are formed and extending their influence over our country. The popular societies of France did the same.    The cry of *patriotism* was forever on their tongue ; but when they became strong enough, they ruled with a rod of iron.    Fire, sword and the guillotin were instruments of their administration.

Be not deceived into a belief that our citizens are incapable of similar outrages.    Violent men may be found in every country, and already are the heads of our government denounced as traitors ; already is our country threatened with blood and civil war.    If men who regard their rights, and who believe the constitution and laws alone to be the guaranty of those rights, do not unite and show a formidable countenance against all irregular opposition to those laws, our whole country will be speedily subject to a confederacy of men, a small minority indeed, but bold, though secret in their machinations, indefatigable in their measures, and determined on success.

It is not the treaty alone which is opposed ; this is a convenient instrument for them to wield ; but the causes of opposition lie deeper. The treaty is not altogether satisfactory ; but if carried into effect, it will not be followed with any dangerous consequences, except what will be created by its opposers.    If left to go peaceably into operation, it would have no general effect on business which people at large could feel—agriculture would still flourish ; trade would be carried on as usual with little variation ; national disputes would be in a train of adjustment, and peace and tranquillity would reign throughout our happy land.    But if the opposers of the treaty can possibly embroil our country in civil war, it will be effected.    From such a frightful calamity, may your good sense, my fellow citizens, preserve us !

Should the treaty not be ratified, and should the consequences be foreign war, the *people, not the government of America*, must be answerable for all its melancholy consequences.

No period of our political life has been more critical, or deserving of more temper on the part of the people, and of more prudence and firmness on the part of our executive.

One party wishes to *draw closer our alliance with France*, even at the hazard of war with all the world.    Our government and its supporters wish for perfect neutrality toward all the powers at war—they wish for strict justice and impartiality to be preserved toward all parties, and they wish for friendly intercourse with all—in fine, they wish for uninterrupted peace.

When parties are thus marshaled, it behooves all good men to determine on which side they will range themselves.    One or the other must prevail ; and on the final prevalence of one or the other of these parties, are suspended the peace, prosperity and happiness of the United States.                                                         CURTIUS.

# CHAPTER IX.

## ORIGIN OF AMHERST COLLEGE IN MASSACHUSETTS.

THE origin and history of the literary institutions of a nation, serve, in no small degree, to illustrate the character of the nation, and their improvements in arts, sciences and manners. To future generations then, correct accounts of the origin and progress of such institutions will form most interesting portions of national history. Such an account of the origin of Amherst College, in the state of Massachusetts, will be the more interesting, as the circumstances attending its foundation, were in some respects peculiar.

In the month of July or August, 1812, a subscription for establishing an Academy in Amherst, was set on foot by Hezekiah W. Strong, Esq. By means of this subscription and subsequent additions to it, a brick edifice was erected, and instructors were procured for the education of youth of both sexes. Success attended this establishment; and at the session of the legislature of the state, in the winter of 1816, an act of incorporation was obtained, dated February 13th. The trustees named in this act were David Parsons, Nathan Perkins, Samuel F. Dickinson, Hezekiah W. Strong, Rufus Cowles, Calvin Merrill, Noah Webster, John Woodbridge, James Taylor, Nathaniel Smith, Josiah Dwight, Rufus Graves, Winthrop Bailey, Experience Porter and Elijah Gridley.

At the annual meeting of the board of trustees, on the 18th of November, 1817, a project, formed by Rufus Graves, Esq., was adopted for increasing the usefulness of the Academy, by raising a fund for the gratuitous education of pious young men. For this purpose, the trustees adopted the following resolve and preamble.

" Taking into consideration the local situation of this Academy, its growing importance and flattering prospects, the following resolution, with the preamble, was unanimously adopted by the board of trustees.

" Whereas it hath pleased the Disposer of events to cause an Academy to be established in this place, the primary objects of which are to improve the hearts, as well as to cultivate the minds of youth; to inculcate the doctrines and precepts of sound morality and evangelical piety, as well as to instruct in the principles of science and useful literature : And whereas in pursuance of these principles, under the guidance of a propitious Providence, this institution has succeeded beyond the most sanguine expectation, and animating hopes are cherished of its future growth and progress, and it has therefore become an object of the highest consideration with this board, to place the institution in the most eligible circumstances, for great and increasing benefits to the present and succeeding generations, by obtaining a large and an accumulating permanent fund, in order to afford its instructions gratuitously to indigent young men of promising talents and hopeful piety, who shall manifest a desire to obtain a liberal education with the sole view to the

Christian ministry, and who, on a reasonable probation, shall be adjudged worthy of the benefactions of the seminary : And whereas in order to the realizing of the benefits aforesaid, it becomes requisite that the principal instructor at least, should be made permanent : And whereas, also, the institution having been located in an elevated and healthy situation, in the center of an extensive and wealthy population of regular moral habits, where the means of living are as cheap and as easily obtained, as in any part of this commonwealth, and completely insulated from any institution embracing similar principles, it presents to the community no ordinary prospects, promising extensive, increasing and lasting blessings to the church and to the world : Therefore, We, the trustees aforesaid, feeling ourselves under the weight of the most impressive responsibility to the Author of all good, faithfully and assiduously to avail ourselves of every advantage of this auspicious situation, as well as sacredly to discharge the trust reposed in us by the commonwealth, and by every mean in our power to carry into complete effect the objects contemplated in our act of incorporation, and expressed in the foregoing preamble : Encouraged by the past, and animated with the prospects of the future, humbly and devoutly relying on the Divine assistance in all our endeavors to promote the cause of truth, and train up the rising generation in science and virtue—

" Do hereby resolve, as an important object of this board, to establish in this institution for the purposes aforesaid, a professorship of languages, with a permanent salary equal to the importance and dignity of such an office ; and that Rufus Graves, Joshua Crosby, John Fiske, Nathaniel Smith and Samuel F. Dickinson be a committee to solicit donations, contributions, grants and bequests, to establish a fund for that and the other benevolent objects of the institution ; and the veracity of the said board is hereby pledged for the faithful appropriation of any benefactions according to the will of the donor."

The committee named in the foregoing resolve formed a constitution and system of by-laws for raising and managing a permanent fund, as the basis of a classical institution for the education of indigent young men of piety and talents for the Christian ministry ; and reported the same to the board of trustees at their meeting on the 18th day of August, 1818. The board unanimously accepted the report, approved the doings of the committee, and authorized the committee to take such measures and communicate with such persons and corporations as they might judge expedient and conducive to the great objects connected with their appointment. The Rev. Nathan Perkins and the Rev. Edwards Whipple were added to the committee.

The committee, before this report was made, had solicited subscriptions to constitute a fund for the support of a professorship of languages, according to the first project, but without success. They found that the establishment of a single professorship for the purposes mentioned in the project was too limited an object to induce men to subscribe. To engage public patronage, it was found necessary to form a plan for the education of young men for the ministry on a more extensive scale. These considerations determined them to frame and report the constitution and by-laws above mentioned.

*A Constitution and System of By-Laws, for the raising and managing a permanent Charitable Fund, as the basis of an Institution in Amherst, in the county of Hampshire, for the Classical Education of indigent young men of piety and talents, for the Christian ministry.**

Taking into consideration the deplorable condition of a large portion of our race who are enveloped in the most profound ignorance, cruel superstition, and gross idolatry ; and many of them in a savage state without a written language : together with vast multitudes in Christian countries, of which our own affords a lamentable specimen, who are dispersed over extensive territories as sheep without a shepherd :—

Impressed with the most fervent commiseration for our destitute brethren, and urged by the command of our divine Savior to preach the gospel to every creature ; we have resolved to consecrate to the Author of all good, for the honor of his name, and the benefit of our race, a portion of the treasure or inheritance which He has been pleased to intrust to our stewardship, in the firm belief that " it is more blessed to give than to receive."

Under the conviction that the education of pious young men of the first talents in community, is the most sure method of relieving our brethren, by civilizing and evangelizing the world ; and that a classical institution judiciously located, and richly endowed with a large and increasing charitable fund, in co-operation with theological seminaries and education societies, will be the most eligible way of effecting it :

Therefore, we, the undersigned, have solemnly, deliberately, and prayerfully made, constituted and ratified, and by these presents, and for the foregoing weighty considerations, do make, constitute and ratify, the following constitution and system of by-laws, together with the preceding preamble, as the basis of such a fund, and for the raising and managing of the same.

*Art.* 1. In contemplating the felicitous state of society, which is predicted in the scriptures of truth, and the rapid approach of such a state, which the auspices of the present day clearly indicate ; and desiring to add our feeble efforts to the various exertions of the Christian community, for effecting so glorious an event ; we have associated together for the express purpose of founding an institution upon the genuine principles of charity and benevolence, for the instruction of youth in all the branches of literature and science usually taught in colleges ; to be located in the town of Amherst, in the county of Hampshire, and incorporated with the Academy in that place, and with Williams College also, should it continue to be thought expedient to remove that seminary to said county of Hampshire, and to locate it in the town of Amherst, and to be called ———

*Art.* 2. In order to effect the benevolent object aforesaid, we whose names are hereunto subscribed, severally and solemnly promise to pay to the trustees of Amherst Academy for the time being, or to their successors in office, the sums annexed to our respective names, for the purpose of raising a permanent fund, of the amount of at least fifty

---

* This constitution was prepared by Rufus Graves, Esq.

thousand dollars, as the basis of a fund for the proposed institution, the interest of which to be appropriated in manner herein after provided, to the increasing said fund, and for the classical, or academic and collegiate education of indigent young men of promising talents and hopeful piety, who may desire such an education, with the sole view to the Christian ministry, and whose talents, piety, and assiduity, upon a suitable probation, shall entitle them to the patronage and assistance of the institution.

Provided nevertheless, and with a view to remove all doubt relative to the success of said object; that in case the sums subscribed to this instrument, in the course of one year from the date hereof, shall not amount to the full sum of fifty thousand dollars, then the whole, or any part thereof, shall be void according to the will of any subscriber or subscribers, he or they giving to the trustees aforesaid, three months' notice of his or their desire of such avoidance; and his or their obligation, or obligations shall be returned, or his or their money, as the case may be, shall be refunded; provided, however, that the said notice be given as aforesaid, within three months next after the expiration of the said one year from date.

*Art.* 3. The aforesaid sum of fifty thousand dollars, together with any other sums that may be subscribed to this instrument, or any sums which may be added to it by gift, grant, or bequest, not otherwise particularly appropriated by the donor, shall be denominated the Charitable Fund of the Classical Institution at Amherst, and is consecrated to the education of indigent young men of piety and talents as aforesaid, for the Christian ministry, in said institution. The interest and other avails of said fund, shall be forever appropriated as follows, viz. five sixths thereof to the purposes aforesaid, namely, the classical education of indigent, pious young men; the other sixth part shall be added to the principal as it shall accrue, for its perpetual increase.

The principal of the fund shall be sacred and intangible, not subject to be diminished by any exigency, the act of God excepted, but shall be perpetually augmenting, by donations, subscriptions, grants, legacies, and bequests, and by the addition of one sixth part of the interest and other avails, as aforesaid.

*Art.* 4. The property of said fund, unless it be in productive real estate, shall as soon as convenient be vested in the funds of this commonwealth, in the funds of the United States, or in some other safe public fund; or be secured by real estate; and retained in as productive a situation as may be, consistently with perfect safety.

*Art.* 5. Until the aforesaid contemplated classical institution, of which the said fund is to be the basis or main pillar, is formed, established and incorporated a body politic, and organized for operation, *the property of said fund and the management thereof, shall be vested in the Board of Trustees of Amherst Academy; so however, as to be in perfect conformity to the provisions of this constitution,* and not repugnant to the constitution of this commonwealth. At the accomplishment of which, meaning the establishment, incorporation, and organization of said institution as aforesaid, the trustees of said Academy shall, without loss of time, transfer, set off, acquit or convey to, give possession of, and pay over to the board of trustees of said institution, the whole of the property of said fund, whether real, personal or mixed, in possession or reversion ; together with the titles and evidences of the same, with the obligations, records, files, et cætera ; in whom and their successors in office, the property of said fund and the management and appropriation thereof, according to the provisions of this constitution, and system of by-laws, is hereby, and shall be forever vested.

Whatever, in the safe keeping, skillful management, and faithful appropriation of the aforesaid fund is made binding on one of the said boards of trustees, in whom the same is or shall be vested, in the one case, is and shall be equally binding on the other.

*Art.* 6. For the greater safety, and more prompt and easy management of so important a concern, there shall be appointed as is herein after provided, a board of overseers, consisting of at least seven in number, a skillful financier, and an able auditor.

*Art.* 7. It shall be the duty of the trustees of said Academy, or of said institution, as the case may be, to appoint, either from their own board, their treasurer excepted who shall be ineligible, or from the public at large, a skillful financier, who shall be sworn to the faithful discharge of the duties of his office, and under sufficient bonds to said board for the security of his trust ; and subject to be removed at their discretion whenever the interest of the institution shall require it.

It shall be the duty of the said trustees also, to examine all candidates for the charities of the institution ; to put them upon such probation as shall be deemed sufficient to determine their qualifications for admission as beneficiaries ; and to apply the avails of the fund, either in whole or in part, to the assistance of those who may upon the issue of such examination or probation be admitted ; or who may be admitted from similar institutions, or from education societies : to keep a correct record of the amount of said fund, the situation and estimated value of each part and parcel thereof which may be in real estate, the rate of rent, at which each may be leased, and the time when due ; if in other estate, the places of its deposit, the security upon which its safety depends, and the average rate per centum of interest which it may produce ; the progressive increase of the whole fund, with the ways and means by which it is effected ; the amount received into their treasury in interest, rent, and otherwise, and of their disbursements ; together with a detail of all their proceedings, a list of all vouchers, and a summary of the accounts, vouchers and reports of the financier : to preserve on file all papers that may directly or indirectly relate to the said fund, or to the management thereof ; and to make a detailed report of the same annually, with a digest of their plan of operation for the ensuing year, to the board of overseers at their annual visitation ; exhibiting at the same time, and at other times, also, if requested, to the said board, or to the said auditor, their books of record, their files, the books and files of the financier, and any other evidence it may be in their power to furnish. It shall be the duty of the said trustees, likewise, to keep an annual account current of all the losses and gains, receipts and expenditures of said fund, to which shall be brought up all unliquidated and unsettled accounts, arrearages, or surplusages of former years ; and ready to be submitted to said auditor for his inspection, at least five days next preceding the annual commencement, or meeting of said board of trustees, who is authorized to call for all necessary vouchers to the same, whether written or unwritten.   It shall be the duty of the said trustees, also, annually, immediately preceding their annual meeting, to cause a manuscript copy of their records for the then past year, and also a copy of their files for the same period, to be taken and attested by their secretary, and ready to be delivered to the said board of overseers for safe keeping, as a security against their loss by fire or any other casualty.

*Art.* 8.  It shall be the duty of the financier to receive all moneys and other personal property from the subscribers, promisors, obligors, donors, and executors or trustees of legators to said fund, and without loss of time to place the same in the most productive situation, according to the provisions in the fourth article of this constitution ; and to receive possession of, and to farm let any real estate which may have been, or which at any time hereafter may be presented to said fund, by gift, grant or bequest, or which may in any other way become the property of said fund ; and to purchase insurance of any property of said fund, which may be in danger from fire or from any other unforeseen occurrence.   It shall be his duty also, diligently and skillfully to manage the prudentials of the said fund, carefully guard against contingent losses, and lose no time in shifting or securing the property when in danger ; to receive the interest and rents of the fund as they become due, and without delay place one sixth part of the amount in some safe and productive department of the fund, and deposit the other five sixths in the treasury of said Academy or institution, as the case may be, and take triplicate receipts for the same, of the treasurer thereof ; one to keep for his own security, one to deposit with the secretary of said board of trustees, and the other with the said auditor.

It shall be his duty likewise to keep an accurate account of the whole fund, its original amount, and progressive increase ; of its amount at the end of each year successively, computed immediately preceding the annual meeting ; of the amount of each department thereof, where and how secured ; the rate per centum of interest at which each may lie, and the time when due ; the rate of rent at which each part, parcel and tenement is leased, and the time when due ; the amount of interest and rent added to the principal of the fund, and the amount of money deposited in the treasury of said Academy or institution ; and to report the whole to said board of trustees, with such remarks and suggestions as he may choose to submit relative to any particular system of finance· he may deem necessary to be pursued in future, and to lodge the same, together with his account current, with the treasurer of said board, at least seven days previously to the annual meeting of said board, that the necessary adjustments may be made, the account current and report of said board completed, the requisite vouchers arranged, and ready to be submitted to the inspection of the said auditor of accounts, and board of overseers, at the respective times appointed for that purpose.   It shall be the duty of the said financier also to be present at all meetings of the said auditor and board of overseers, for the examination of the accounts and state of the fund, and to present his books, files, and vouchers for their inspection, and to offer for their consideration any information relative thereto, which it may be in his power to afford.   It shall be his duty, likewise, in case of his resignation or being succeeded in office, to deliver to the said board of trustees, or on their order to his successor in office, the whole of the property of said fund, with all the titles and evidences of the same, together with all his books, papers, and files, that may directly or indirectly relate to the fund or the management thereof; and in case of his death, his executor or administrator shall do the same.

*Art.* 9. The financier shall be paid from the avails of the said fund, a reasonable sum for his services and responsibility; and all other necessary expenses that may accrue in the management and appropriation of the fund, or the avails thereof, shall be paid in like manner.

*Art.* 10. The board of overseers, who are hereby constituted the guardians of said fund, shall be appointed and perpetuated in manner following, viz. Four shall be appointed by the four highest subscribers to the aforesaid fifty thousand dollar fund, each shall appoint one; the other three shall be elected by a majority of votes of the remaining subscribers to said fund, who may assemble for that purpose. Said elections to be made, as soon as convenient after the filling of said subscription. The said board shall perpetuate their existence as such, by filling their own vacancies in the following manner, viz. No seat shall be suffered to be vacant for more than six months. Vacancies occasioned by death, resignation, removal, incapacity by age or otherwise, of which incapacity the said board shall always be competent to determine, shall be filled by a majority of votes of the members present at any annual or special meeting, regularly notified for that or other purposes. Should the said board, from neglect, or by any fortuitous circumstances whatever, be reduced to two members, or even to one, they or he as the case may be, shall be competent to fill the vacancies to the number sufficient to constitute a quorum, and the said board thus filled, shall elect the remainder. And in case the said board shall at any future period become extinct, the governor and council of this commonwealth are hereby authorized and requested to appoint a new board, with all the rights, powers and immunities of the former one. In all meetings of the said board of overseers, for the transaction of business, except in the matter of filling vacancies, four members shall be necessary to constitute a quorum. And to prevent the sudden disorganization of the said board at any time, so as to interrupt business; all resignations shall be made in writing to the board when in session, and if convenient, handed in by the member himself, that the vacancy may be immediately filled. But, the resignation shall not be accepted, so as to disqualify the member so offering his resignation from acting with the board, in all matters pending before them, till another shall be elected in his stead, and has signified his acceptance.

*Art.* 11. It shall be the duty of the board of overseers, as the guardians of said fund, to appoint annually, or to appoint and continue in office during their pleasure, either from their own body, or from community at large, an able auditor of accounts, who shall be sworn to the faithful and impartial discharge of the duties of his office; and to certify to said board of trustees every such appointment.

It shall be their duty also, to visit the said institution at its annual commencement, or the board of trustees in whom the property and management of said fund are vested, at their annual meeting in each year successively forever; to receive and diligently and impartially examine their report, which should always contain a correct statement of the nature and amount of the original fund, the evidences of the property, how situated, where deposited and how secured; its progressive increase from year to year, and the ways and means by which effected, with the aggregate amount at the date of each annual report; the amount of interest and rent, the avails of the fund, or of donations and subscriptions made in aid of said fund, received into their treasury, with the amount of their disbursements; together with a list of the beneficiaries receiving support in whole, or in part from said fund, and the amount of assistance afforded to each; to receive also, and examine the report of the said auditor, and to inspect the records, files and vouchers of the trustees and financier aforesaid. It shall be their duty likewise, scrupulously and impartially to examine and compare all the documents, carefully attend to the oral representations of the officers and trustees aforesaid explanatory thereof, and in view of all the facts to decide, whether the said fund has been skillfully managed, and whether the avails thereof have been sacredly and economically applied according to the will of the donors, as is provided in this constitution and system of by-laws; and whether the financial system pursued, or proposed to be pursued in future, is consistent with the spirit of this instrument. The sacred nature of the trust reposed in the said board of overseers, as the representatives of the rights of the dead, as well as of the living, urges upon them the imperious duty of investigating every subject relative to their important trust, so as to enable them to approve or disapprove of the management of any part of the concern; to point out any errors they may have observed, or any improvements which they conceive may be made; to detect any violation of rights, breach of trust, or abuse of powers; any perversion of the fund, or misappropriation of the avails thereof, and to suggest the same to the said trustees with a view to produce a reform. Should the circumstances be such in any case, as to force a conviction, that the constitution and laws had been violated, and the sacred deposit perverted; should the trustees aforesaid, to whose fidelity it had been intrusted, disavow the facts, and persist in the vindication of the purity of their motives, and the wisdom of their measures; and should the reasons offered in justification thereof, be insufficient to satisfy the said board of overseers, and to remove those impressions; they the said board of overseers shall enter their protest in writing, specifying the grounds of their conviction as aforesaid; which together with the reasons offered by the said board of trustees in their justification, shall be entered on the records of both boards. And the question shall be submitted to the honorable justices of the supreme judicial court of this commonwealth, whose decision shall be final; and shall be entered on the records of both of the said boards. Any similar or other questions of rights, powers or amenability shall be submitted in the same way. It shall be the duty of the said board of overseers to keep a fair and correct record of all their proceedings, relative to the execution of their important trust; to record or preserve on file the annual reports of the said board of trustees, and the reports of the said auditor; to receive and safely preserve the manuscript copies of the records, and the copies of the files of the board of trustees, which shall be annually furnished and attested by the secretary thereof, and delivered at the annual visitation, that the whole of the records of the institution may be safely preserved in the archives of both boards.  And in case of the loss, or destruction of the records and files of either of the said boards, by fire or otherwise, the secretary or recording officer of the other, shall lose no time in furnishing attested copies of the whole to supply the deficiency.

It shall be the duty of the said board of overseers, annually, or whenever in their opinion the interest of the institution, or the public good requires it, to publish a correct report of the state of said fund, its progressive increase, growing importance and extensive utility.

*Art*. 12. It shall be the duty of said auditor to attend at said institution a sufficient length of time within the five days next preceding the annual commencement, or annual meeting of said board of trustees, to receive and audit all the accounts of said board relative to the management of said fund, examining all books, files, vouchers and oral testimony which it may be in their power to afford illustrative of the same ; and to make a detailed report of the state in which he finds them, to the said board of overseers at their annual visitation.  It shall be his duty also, to attend to the duties of his office at other times, in the interval, if the exigencies of the institution or fund shall require it.  He shall also keep a correct record of all his proceedings from year to year ; and in case of his resignation, or being succeeded in office, shall lodge the same with the said board of overseers.

*Art*. 13. It being the design of the founders of this establishment, that its benefits should be handed down inviolate to all succeeding generations, and considering the inadequacy of human forethought to provide for every exigence that may occur in the course of long experience, we the undersigned agree, that this constitution and system of by-laws, may be altered or amended, by the board of trustees of said institution, and the board of overseers of said fund, so however, as not to deviate from the original object of civilizing and evangelizing the world, by the classical education of indigent young men of piety and talents ; but, it shall not be altered or amended, except from the most weighty considerations, and by the concurrence of both the said boards, each holding a negative upon the other ; nor without the majority of two thirds of the members of the said board of trustees, and five sevenths of the members of the said board of overseers.

A proposition for amendment may originate in either of said boards, but it shall not be proposed to the other, till it has been fairly and deliberately discussed where it originated, and passed by the majority assigned as above to the said board.  It shall then be sent to the other board for concurrence, where it shall undergo a like discussion, and if concurred in by the majority assigned also to that board, it shall become a part of this constitution, otherwise not.

*Art*. 14. In order to prevent the loss or destruction of this constitution, by any wicked design, by fire, or by the ravages of time, it shall be the duty of the trustees of the said institution, as soon as the aforesaid sum of fifty thousand dollars shall be hereunto subscribed, to cause triplicate copies of the same, together with the names of the subscribers and the sum subscribed annexed to each name, to be taken, fairly written on vellum, one of which to be preserved in the archives of said institution, one in the archives of the said board of overseers, and the other in the archives of this commonwealth.   And in case of the loss or destruction of either of said copies, its deficiency shall be immediately supplied by an attested copy from one of the others.

May 23, 1818.

It will be seen by the vote of the trustees on the 18th of August, above cited, by which the committee were authorized to " communicate with such persons and corporations as they might judge expedient," that the trustees of the Academy had been apprised of the contemplated design of the trustees of Williams College, to remove that institution to some town in one of the counties which formerly constituted the old county of Hampshire.   A committee of the trustees of that college had visited Amherst for the purpose of inquiring into the situation and advantages of the town for being the seat of that college ; and under the authority of the vote of August 18 above cited, two gentlemen from the board of trustees of Amherst Academy had waited upon the trustees of Williams College the first week in September, and presented to them a copy of the said vote, and a copy of the constitution above cited.   The board of trustees of Williams College returned the papers to the committee without any answer.   This silence of the board of trustees of Williams College, was considered by the trustees of Amherst Academy as a declining to accede to any proposal for uniting that college with the proposed institution in Amherst.

On the tenth day of September, soon after the committee had returned from Williamstown, the board of trustees of Amherst Academy resolved, " that in the opinion of this board, it is expedient to invite a convention of clergy and laity to approve and patronize the charitable literary institution contemplated by this board, for the education of pious indigent young men for the gospel ministry."

" Resolved, that this convention be composed of the congregational and presbyterian clergy of the several parishes in the counties of Hampshire, Franklin, and Hampden, and the western section of the county of Worcester, with their delegates, together with one delegate from each vacant parish, and the subscribers to the fund."

Noah Webster, Esq., the Rev. John Fiske, and Rufus Graves, Esq. were appointed a committee to prepare a circular for convoking the convention, and managing the concerns of the corporation before that body.   The following is a copy of the circular addressed to the clergy.

*To the Rev. ———.*

Sir—The trustees of Amherst Academy have, for some time past, contemplated the establishment of a charitable institution, for the purpose of educating pious indigent young men for the Gospel ministry. The interests of Zion in our own country, and the conversion of the heathen, present powerful motives for the union of all good men in combined and vigorous exertions to multiply the number of well educated ministers of the Gospel, to supply missionaries and furnish destitute churches and people in our own extensive republic.   Impelled by their own conviction of the importance of this object, and urged by the advice and solicitations of many respectable Christian friends, both of the clergy and laity, they have adopted the resolution to attempt the establishment of such a seminary. For this purpose they have formed a constitution for a charitable fund, to be the basis of such an institution, and have made such progress in procuring donations, as to afford most animating encouragement of success. The disposition of the public to encourage and support such an institution, appears to be favorable, beyond our most sanguine expectations. As it is proposed to instruct young men in all the branches of literature and science usually taught in colleges, the magnitude of the object renders it, in our opinion, important that such an institution should embrace the interests and unite the hearts of good men, in a territory of considerable extent.

For this reason we have judged it expedient to invite to a concurrence and combined effort, the settled ministers of the Gospel, within the three counties of Hampshire, Hampden, and Franklin, and of the towns in the western part of the county of Worcester ; each minister to be attended by a lay delegate, to be chosen or appointed in such manner as he shall deem expedient. A delegate will also be invited from each vacant parish. It is requested that the clergy and delegates should meet in convention with the subscribers to the fund, at the church in the west parish in Amherst, in the county of Hampshire, on Tuesday, the twenty ninth day of September instant, at nine o'clock, A. M ; then and there to deliberate on this important subject, equally interesting to the present and future generations.

If, sir, you concur with us in opinion respecting the importance of such an institution in this district of country, and are disposed to lend to it the aid of your influence, we request your attendance, with a delegate, at the time and place above named.

By order of the Board of Trustees,

NOAH WEBSTER, ⎫
JOHN FISKE, ⎬ *Committee.*
RUFUS GRAVES, ⎭

Amherst, Sept. 11, 1818.

On the twenty ninth day of September, 1818, the proposed convention was formed in the church in the West Parish of Amherst. It was composed of the following gentlemen.

### HAMPSHIRE COUNTY.

#### *Ministers and Delegates.*

*Amherst,* (1*st Parish.*)—Rev. David Parsons, Hez. W. Strong, Esq.
" (2*d Parish.*)—Rev. Nathan Perkins, Dea. Nathan Franklin.
*Belchertown.*—Rev. Experience Porter, Col. Henry Dwight.
*Cummington.*—Mr. Amos Cobb.
*Easthampton.*—Rev. P. Williston, Dea. Thaddeus Clapp.
*Enfield.*—Rev. Joshua Crosby, Mr. Rufus Powers.
*Granby.*—Rev. E. Gridley, Dea. John Stebbins.
*Goshen.*—Oliver Taylor, Esq.
*Hadley.*—Rev. John Woodbridge, Samuel Porter, Esq.
*Hatfield.*—Rev. Joseph Lyman, D. D., Col. Jos. Billings.
*Northampton.*—Rev. S. Williams, Hon. Joseph Lyman.

*Ware.*—Rev. L. Ware, Dea. Eli Snow.
*Pelham.*—Rev. Winthrop Bailey, Dea. Abia Southworth.
*Southampton.*—Rev. Vinson Gould, Maj. John Lymán.
*Westhampton.*—Rev. E. Hale, Dr. William Hooker.
*Williamsburg.*—Rev. Henry Lord.
Rev. Dan Huntington of Hadley attended.

### FRANKLIN COUNTY.

*Buckland.*—Rev. J. Spalding, Mr. Alpheus Brooks.
*Conway.*—Rev. J. Emerson, Capt. John Williams.
*Gill.*—Rev. J. W. Cannon, Col. Seth S. Rowland.
*Greenfield.*—Rev. S. Woodbridge, Mr. Quintus Allen.
*Poll Parish.*—George Grennell, Esq.
*Deerfield, Poll Parish.*—Rev. Mr. Rice, Dea. Elisha Clary.
*Hawley.*—Rev. J. Grout.
*Heath.*—Rev. Mr. Miller, Roger Leavitt, Esq.
*Leverett.*—Rev. J. Wright, Mr. Erastus Field.
*Montague.*—Rev. A. Gates, Mr. Martin Root.
*Shelburne.*—Rev. Theoph. Packard, Mr. Elisha Smead.
*Shutesbury.*—Rev. J. Taylor, Mr. Samuel Clark.
*Sunderland.*—Rev. James Taylor, Mr. Benj. Graves.
*Whately.*—Rev. R. Wells, Dea. John White.

### HAMPDEN COUNTY.

*Blanford.*—Rev. J. Keep.
*Granville.*—Rev. T. M. Cooley.
    "    *2d Parish.*—Rev. J. Baker, Mr. Hezekiah Robinson.
*Palmer.*—Rev. S. Colton.
*Westfield.*—Rev. T. Knapp.

### WORCESTER COUNTY.

*Sturbridge.*—Rev. O. Lane, Mr. Eli Wheeler.
*Southbridge.*—Rev. J. Park, Mr. John Morse.
*New Braintree.*—Rev. J. Fiske.
*North Brookfield.*—Rev. T. Snell, Mr. Moses Bond.

The convention chose the Rev. Joseph Lyman, D. D., president, and Col. Joseph Billings and George Grennell, secretaries.

The meeting was introduced by prayer by the president. The proposed constitution and by-laws for the government of the proposed institution was read by N. Webster.

After some discussion, the convention voted to appoint a committee of twelve, to take the subject into consideration and make report. The following persons were elected committee :—

Rev. Theophilus Packard, Roger Leavitt, Esq., Hon. Joseph Lyman, Rev. Timothy M. Cooley, Rev. Thomas Snell, Rev. Dan Huntington, Elisha Billings, Esq., Rev. Enoch Hale, Rev. Moses Miller, Rev. John Keep, Rev. Otis Lane, Rev. Vinson Gould.

In the afternoon a sermon was delivered before the convention by the Rev. Joseph Lyman, D. D., who received a vote of thanks for the same.

On Wednesday the 30th of September, the committee reported to the convention, as follows :

Your committee, sensible of the confidence reposed in them by the convention, and of the obligation under which they act, have taken the subject proposed into serious and careful consideration, have examined it in its several bearings and relations, and beg leave to report :

The plan of a literary institution founded on the general principles of charity and benevolence, to give a classical or collegiate education to indigent pious young men of talents, while it proposes the ordinary advantages to others, is peculiarly suited to the exigencies of the day, and calculated to answer extensively benevolent purposes, in relation both to the church and to the world.

This plan proposes a literary institution of a peculiar character, in no way hostile to any other in our country—an institution in its very nature and tendency suited to receive aid and encouragement from other charitable institutions, and at the same time to impart aid and influence to every other system of benevolent exertion, now in operation to spread the gospel, and extend the empire of divine grace.

The written constitution, submitted to this convention, is obviously the fruit of much judicious reflection and mature consideration. Already has it received the sanction of a considerable number of benevolent individuals, who, after deliberate examination, have subscribed the instrument as donors. Your committee, according to their ability and opportunity, have examined and approved said constitution, as a legal instrument. In their opinion, it is executed with skill and judgment, guarding, in the most satisfactory and effectual manner, the faithful and appropriate application of the property consecrated by the donors. And while the general object is to benefit our own and other countries by the education of indigent young men of hopeful piety and talents, the instrument is so formed, as to leave open a door for a union of interests with Williams College, upon fair and honorable principles, should the guardians of that institution deem it useful and expedient to remove their charge and form the connection.

That an institution of this description, designed to diffuse its blessings, with increasing influence, to the end of time, should be judiciously located, can not be reasonably questioned ; nor can it be reasonably doubted, that Hampshire County presents one of the most eligible places for the purpose in the United States. Thus would it be established in the central part of Massachusetts proper, naturally excite an extensive interest, and hopefully secure the patronage of the state. Here it would stand in the heart of New England, and almost equally distant from six other colleges ; in an extensive section of country salubrious, fertile and populous, where industry and moral order, together with a disposition to cultivate science and literature, habitually prevail ; where ministers and churches are generally united and harmonious, and where the numerous streams of benevolent charity, flowing into the treasury of the Lord, afford ample assurance that an institution of this description would be cordially embraced, extensively patronized and liberally supported.

Having compared a number of pleasant towns in this vicinity, in relation to advantages and disadvantages, in either of which an institution of this sort would be undoubtedly cherished and liberally aided with great cordiality, they are of opinion,

1st. That an institution might flourish as located in the constitution, and at the same time, are convinced, that it might flourish to a greater extent, were it to have the advantage of that union, which would result from its location by a disinterested committee appointed by the convention.

2d. In this general view of the subject submitted to their consideration, the committee cordially approve the object of a religious and classical institution on a charitable foundation, in the town of Amherst, and recommend to the convention to give it their united and individual patronage.

3d. They also recommend that suitable measures be adopted by the trustees of Amherst Academy, for the establishment of a college in connection with the charitable institution, possessing all the advantages of other colleges in the commonwealth.

4th. That it is expected by this convention that in order to satisfy the public, the people of the town of Amherst show themselves worthy of such an important privilege by affording seasonable and liberal aid toward erecting college buildings.

5th. They also recommend that such preparations and arrangements be made, as will accommodate students at the institution, as soon as possible.

With these resolutions and recommendations, your committee express their fervent wish that the great object may be kept in distinct view in this body, that there may be union and harmony of feelings and deliberations, and that it will please our God and Savior to succeed the endeavors of his servants, and render the contemplated institution a rich blessing to the church of this generation, and to the most distant posterity.   Adopted unanimously by the committee.

A true copy.

Attest,    JOSEPH BILLINGS, *Secretary.*

After a full discussion, the preamble of the report was approved and accepted.   On motion of Mr. Grout the first article of the report was rejected.   The second article was amended by inserting " in the town of Amherst" after *foundation.*   The third article was amended by inserting, " by the trustees of Amherst Academy," after the word *adopted ;* and the fourth article was amended as above recited, and then the whole report was adopted by a large majority of votes.

At a special meeting of the board of trustees of Amherst Academy, October 26, 1818, the board appointed the Rev. John Fiske, Noah Webster, and Nathaniel Smith, Esquires, a committee to confer with the board of trustees of Williams College at their session to be held in Williamstown on the second Tuesday of November then next, to communicate to them the result of the late convention in Amherst, and to make suitable statements and explanations, respecting the same.

In pursuance of this appointment, the committee repaired to Williamstown, at the proper time, and presented to the board of trustees of Williams College a copy of the proceedings and resolutions of the convention, and also made to the board such verbal representations of facts, as they supposed to be useful and proper.

To these communications no answer was given.  But at this meeting, the board of trustees of Williams College resolved that it was expedient to remove the college, on certain conditions, and as a preliminary measure, they appointed the Hon. James Kent, Chancellor of the State of New York, the Hon. Nathaniel Smith, one of the Judges of the Superior Court of Connecticut, and the Rev. Seth Payson, D. D. of Rindge in New Hampshire, to determine the place to which the college should be removed.

In consequence of this determination of the board of trustees of Williams College, the trustees of Amherst Academy at their annual meeting, November 17, 1818, appointed Noah Webster, Esq., the Rev. John Fiske, the Rev. Edwards Whipple, the Rev. Joshua Crosby and Nathaniel Smith, Esq., to be a committee to attend upon the committee appointed to locate Williams College, to represent to them the claims of the town of Amherst to be the seat of the college, including the funds procured by the trustees of the Academy for a charitable institution, the recommendation of the convention of clergy and lay delegates in convention in September last, the conveniences of geographical position, and all other facts and circumstances that might affect a decision of the question.

At this meeting of the board, the secretary, Rufus Graves, Esq. reported that the subscriptions to the charitable fund, and the value of the six acres of land given by Col. Elijah Dickinson for the site of the buildings of the institution, amounted to twenty five thousand and five hundred dollars.

On account of the lateness of the season, when the locating committee received their appointment, their meeting on the business of their appointment was deferred till the following spring.  In May, 1819, the committee met, and took a view of several towns in Franklin and Hampshire counties, and of Amherst, among the others.

The committee of the trustees of Amherst Academy, appointed to attend upon the locating committee, and present to them the claims of Amherst, waited upon them at Northampton, and read to them the following observations, which had been previously prepared.

In designating the situation of Williams College, we suppose the most important considerations are—

1. The conveniences of the situation for accommodating the people of the five western counties of Massachusetts.

2. The salubrity of the climate and pleasantness of the country.

3. The cheapness of subsistence, including provisions and fuel.

4. The advantages for literary and moral improvement in this and in future ages.

1. In the first particular, the town of Amherst has, in our apprehension, a decided advantage over every other town in the counties on the river.

The territory to be particularly accommodated by this college, comprehends the counties of Berkshire, Hampshire, Hampden, Franklin, and Worcester.  Many persons in Middlesex and Norfolk counties take a particular interest in this institution.  The hill in the center of the west road in Amherst, on which the church stands, is within about two miles of the geometrical center of this territory ; taking Pittsfield on the west, and the town of Worcester on the east, as the two extremes. It is equally central between the limits of the commonwealth on the north and south. In addition to this fact, it may be observed that it is almost equally distant from the university of Cambridge, the college in Providence, and the college in New Haven; the distance from each being about eighty five miles. It is.a hundred miles from Union College, in Schenectady, N. Y., from Dartmouth College, in Hanover, N. H., and a greater distance from Middlebury College, in Vermont.

The roads leading to and from this town are as good as any roads in the country, excepting perhaps a mile or two on the mountain, the road leading to South Hadley and Granby, which is not so well made and in as good repair as the other country roads. But this road, with the usual labor bestowed on public highways, will be as good as others, and furnish an easier passage over the mountain than the river road, as the hills are not so long and difficult. It is important also to state, that in the spring of the year it often happens that the river road from South Hadley is impassable for days or weeks by means of a flood in Connecticut River.

2. In regard to the salubrity of the climate, no great advantage, we believe, can be pleaded in favor of any town in the river counties, as the climate is every where healthy. But in all the particulars which constitute salubrity and pleasantness of situation, Amherst presents advantages, which, in no respect, are exceeded in any town, and in some respects are unrivaled. The land on the hill before mentioned is so elevated as to command an uninterrupted view of the plains on the banks of Connecticut River, and of a great extent of country west of the river. With a radius of thirty miles in length, an arch may be described, which will comprehend about thirty townships, extending from the south line of Hampden County, into Franklin County on the north, all of which fall within a single view ; and it is said by gentlemen well acquainted with these three counties, that the church of the first parish in Amherst may be seen from twenty seven towns.

The scenery presented to the eye at this spot is highly beautiful. The range of mountains on the south and southwest, the hills on the east, the more distant cliffs on the north, the great variety of slopes and vales which diversify the scenery, and the vast extent of prospect on the west and northwest, offer to the eye of a spectator one of the most picturesque landscapes which New England affords.

Nor are the advantages of this situation calculated only to gratify the eye ; they furnish also means of health, particularly useful to students. It is to be observed that this hill presents an open prospect to the *west*, giving the advantage of an uninterrupted current of wind from that quarter, from which the wind usually blows in summer, when refreshing breezes are most necessary for men of study. In winter, the temperature of the air appears, by thermometrical observations, to be no colder than it is at Northampton and in other towns on the river. But if it were, it would be no material inconvenience, as we can always moderate cold at pleasure in warm rooms, but we have no power to moderate extreme heat, which is far more inconvenient to the student, by its debilitating effects, except by availing ourselves of a fresh current of air. And while this hill in Amherst offers the best advantages for this purpose, it is remarkably defended from the unpleasant effects of easterly winds by a range of hills on the east of the town.   It may be asserted with truth, that the easterly winds in this town are not ordinarily of half the strength which they are on the sea-coast.   It may be added, that the water found in this hill is abundant and of the best kind.

3.  In regard to the expenses of subsistence, Amherst offers as favorable a location as can be found in the three river counties.   The land is generally good, and well cultivated by sober, industrious farmers, who can supply the officers and students with provisions of every kind, at as low prices as they can be afforded in any other town.   The town and the lands adjacent in other towns, abound with wood, and fuel may be obtained at all times, on as favorable terms, as in any town proper for such an institution.   And we apprehend, that both provisions and fuel and all the necessary expenses of subsistence for officers and students, must necessarily be lower in Amherst than in the shire town of either of the counties.   Being merely an agricultural town, the expenses of living will be less liable to be enhanced by the artificial refinements of more gay and fashionable life.

4.  In regard to the advantages for moral and literary improvement in this and future ages, we conceive that no situation can be found in the three counties, which is more eligible than the town of Amherst.

It is agreed by all good judges of the subject, that a literary institution ought not to be situated in a large or populous town.   The particular extent of population which is best suited to accommodate a college, without exposing the persons attached to it to unnecessary or exorbitant expenses, and the students in particular to the danger of evil examples and of extravagance in dress and other expenses, may not be easily defined, and respecting these points, there may be a difference of opinion.   In our opinion, a college should not be located in a town which *does*, or hereafter probably will consist of a population, which shall invite and maintain the more fashionable expenses and amusements of the higher classes of society in this country ; and which of course must be infected with the vices which necessarily prevail among the lower orders which must always form a part of a numerous population in any town of fashionable resort.   We are not to be governed in our opinions on this subject by the present state of the towns in this country.   We are to look forward to the state of them in future ages.   From facts which have already taken place, we may form a tolerably correct judgment of the facts that will hereafter take place.

The town of Amherst must, from its position, forever be an agricultural town.   It can be neither a shire town, nor a commercial or manufacturing town.   From its situation with regard to Connecticut River, and the neighboring towns, it can not be the center of a great commerce, and its streams of water will never support great manufacturing establishments.   Its inhabitants must be chiefly laboring farmers, who, dispersed over the town and occupied in their own pursuits, can have no particular connection with the students ; of course no enmity will probably bring them into collision, and produce those quarrels and riots which have frequently disturbed the peace of some other colleges.

If it should be said that such a town affords less advantages for improving the manners of the students, we reply, that some well-bred gentlemen will always be attached to such a seminary, and others may reside in the neighborhood. But the design of the college is to teach the arts and sciences, and to cultivate the mind, rather than to polish the manners. One fourth part of the year consists of vacations, in which the students may visit their friends and mingle with the world; but in term-time we are persuaded, from observation and experience, that the less intercourse they have with the world, the more advantageously will they cultivate both the head and the heart. And it may well be suggested, that the situation of the colleges and universities of Europe, in cities and large towns, has been a principal cause of the depravity and infidelity which are so prevalent among the higher orders of society in that quarter of the world, and whose baleful influence has been extended to the higher classes of society in this country.

From all the considerations above recited, and from every view which we have been able to take of this subject, we are compelled to believe the town of Amherst offers the most eligible situation for a college. In all respects, the situation is as favorable as that of any other town; and in several particulars it possesses advantages which are not to be found in any other town in the three counties.

To the considerations already enumerated, we would subjoin a few other observations.

It is well known, or must be admitted, that the cheapness of a collegiate education in this country is not merely favorable to an extension of it, but absolutely necessary. The great body of people in New England consists of men of moderate estates, who are utterly unable to give their sons an expensive education. Already are the expenses of a four years' education, in some of our colleges in or near large towns, so great, that if there were no colleges in the country where education is less expensive, a large portion of young men, who now receive a college education, would be utterly precluded from that advantage. Great numbers of men can afford two hundred or two hundred and fifty dollars a year, who can not afford four or five hundred. Now let it be considered that the larger part of the men who constitute those most useful classes—ministers of the Gospel, and instructors of youth in colleges, academies and other seminaries of learning, are the sons of the yeomanry of the country; men of small estates, who, if they educate their sons at all, must educate them in the cheapest manner that the country affords. A course of liberal education is already so expensive in some of our colleges, that were there no other means of obtaining an education, the country here would be deprived of the necessary supplies of ministers and teachers.

This is not all. It is well known that the vast western and southern states, now rapidly settling, depend chiefly on New England for ministers of the Gospel and teachers of seminaries, and the wants of the settlements can not be fully supplied. This is then a matter of vast moment, that in all the plans of education adopted in New England, all possible facilities should be given to the multiplication of men intended for literary, moral, and religious instructors. To this purpose it is an essential prerequisite that the means of education should be as easy and as accessible as possible to the pious and well disposed sons of our yeomanry. This consideration derives additional importance from the circumstance that great numbers of young men destined for these employments are educated by charitable contributions.

We deem it very important that the charitable fund of fifty thousand dollars should be united in operation with Williams College ; for the following reasons :

1. Because the money will produce much more effect, united with the College, than it will if unconnected with it, as one set of instructors will answer for both.

2. Because the tuition of the beneficiaries on this fund will aid the College as effectually as the proper fund of the College.  Twenty beneficiaries paying twenty dollars each for tuition annually, or $400, are equal to a fund of $6,667, and more, in the same proportion.

3. Because any attempt to remove the location of this fund will destroy it, and the Christian public will lose the benefit of it.

4. Because the two institutions, if located in different towns, will not only produce less effect, but may be in collision.

5. Because the convention of clergy and laity at Amherst last September manifested a desire that the two institutions should be united.

6. Because one sixth part of the interest of the charity fund is reserved as an accumulating fund, on the principle of compound interest. Of course, the means of supporting and enlarging the usefulness of Williams College will be continually increasing.

7. Because experience and facts prove that funds for charitable religious purposes in this country, are more easily augmented than the funds of a mere literary institution.  Such is the disposition of pious and well disposed people in the present age, to encourage the education of pious youth and to spread the Gospel, that multitudes will make donations for these purposes, who will not give their money to a mere classical institution.  Hence we infer that a connection of the College with this charity fund will essentially promote its prosperity.

N. Webster,
John Fiske,         } Committee of the Trustees
Edwards Whipple,  } of Amherst Academy.
Nathaniel Smith,

The foregoing were the most material arguments and statements presented to the locating committee, in favor of removing the college to Amherst.  The committee, however, were unanimous in naming Northampton as the most suitable place for the institution.

The trustees of Amherst Academy, on the 18th day of November, 1818, appointed Noah Webster, Esq., the Rev. John Fiske, the Rev. Edwards Whipple, the Rev. Nathan Perkins, the Rev. Joshua Crosby, the Rev. James Taylor, the Rev. Winthrop Bailey, Nathaniel Smith, Samuel F. Dickinson, and Rufus Graves, Esquires, a committee to solicit subscriptions to the charitable fund, and also *for the foundation and support of a college* to be connected with the same, as recommended by the convention.  But in consequence of the proceedings of the corporation of Williams College, in resolving to remove that institution, and in appointing a committee to locate it, the trustees of Amherst Academy suspended further measures in relation to the foundation of a college, until the event of an application of the corporation of Williams College to the legislature, for an act authorizing such removal, should be known. They made no opposition to that application, and took no measure to defeat it.

At a meeting of the board of trustees of Amherst Academy, July 6, 1819, a committee appointed to examine the subscriptions to the charity fund, reported that the money and other property subscribed amounted, at a fair estimate, to fifty-one thousand four hundred and four dollars.

On the 23d day of June, 1819, the trustees of Williams College published a printed address to the public, assigning their reasons for proposing to remove that institution, and soliciting donations to increase the funds, and promote its prosperity in its proposed location at North-ampton. One paragraph in the address is in the following words.

" The trustees, highly approving the object of the charitable institu-tion at Amherst, and the benevolence which has influenced so many to unite in contributing to the very important object of educating poor and pious young men for the ministry, are particularly desirous that that should be so united with the college at Northampton, and the college with that, that contributions to either should be conducive to the good of both, and so form an institution which would receive the united pat-ronage of all the friends of literature, science, and religion."

A copy of this address was sent to the trustees of Amherst Academy, inclosed in a letter from the president, the Rev. Zephaniah Swift Moore, dated July 1, 1819.

To this letter and address the trustees of Amherst Academy return-ed the following answer. The vote directing it to be sent, is dated August 18, 1819.

*To the Rev. Zephaniah Swift Moore, president of the board of trustees of Williams College.*

REV. SIR,—The trustees of Amherst Academy have received your letter dated July 1, addressed to the president of the board, inclosing the address of the trustees of Williams College, on the subject of its removal, and have given the subject of it their deliberate consideration. In answer to the queries contained in your letter, we would remark that, in our opinion, a union between the college and the charitable in-stitution in Amherst, would be conducive to the interest of literature, science, and religion, in the western section of Massachusetts. The constitution of the charitable fund opened the door for that union, and nothing on our part, we believe, has been wanting to accomplish the object. We entertain the most friendly disposition toward Williams College, and shall rejoice in its prosperity, although we see not at pres-ent, how a union between the college and the charitable institution can be effected ; yet if a plan could be devised for that purpose, not incom-patible with the constitution of the fund, it would meet our most cordial approbation.          In behalf of the board of trustees,

DAVID PARSONS, President.

RUFUS GRAVES, *Secretary.*

The corporation of Williams College made an application to the legislature of Massachusetts in the winter of the year 1819–20, for an act authorizing them to remove the college to Northampton ; but it failed of success.   In consequence of this failure, the trustees of Amherst Academy judged that the way was open for them to proceed in their original design, and put in operation the charity fund intrusted to their care.   Therefore on the 15th day of March, 1820, they resolved, " that this board consider it their duty to proceed directly to carry into effect the provisions of the constitution for the classical education of indigent pious young men, and the financier is hereby directed to proceed with as little delay as possible to effect a settlement with subscribers, to procure notes and obligations for the whole amount of the subscriptions, and also to solicit further subscriptions from benevolent persons, in aid of this great charity, and for erecting the necessary buildings."

At the same meeting the Rev. Experience Porter, Hezekiah W. Strong, and Samuel F. Dickinson, were appointed a committee to form the plan of a building for the use of the charity institution, to estimate the expense and make report, and also to solicit subscriptions for erecting said building.   At the same meeting they directed the secretary to notify the subscribers to the fund to meet at the academy in Amherst, on the second Wednesday of May then next, for the purpose of choosing overseers of the fund, agreeable to the provisions of the constitution.

This meeting was not held at that time, and the appointment of overseers did not take place till August following.

At a meeting of the board of trustees, May 10, 1820, the committee appointed to form the plan of a building, as before mentioned, was discharged, and the following vote was passed.

" *Voted*, That Samuel F. Dickinson, Hezekiah W. Strong, and Nathaniel Smith, Esquires, Dr. Rufus Cowles and Lieut. Enos Baker, be a committee to secure a good and sufficient title to the ten acres of land conditionally conveyed to the trustees of this academy, as the site of said institution, by the late Col. Elijah Dickinson, and for the special benefit of the charity fund ; to digest the plan of a suitable building for said institution, to procure subscriptions, donations or contributions for defraying the expense thereof; to prepare the ground, and erect the same as soon as the necessary means can be furnished ; the location to be made with the advice and consent of the prudential committee."

At this meeting it was resolved further, that " great and combined exertions of the Christian public are necessary to give due effect to the charitable institution," and the Rev. Joshua Crosby, Jonathan Grout, James Taylor, Edwards Whipple, John Fiske, and Joseph Vaill, were appointed agents to make applications for additional funds, and for contributions to aid in erecting suitable buildings for the accommodation of students.

The committee proceeded to execute the trust committed to them, secured a title to the land, marked out the ground for the site of a building of a hundred feet in length, and invited the inhabitants of Amherst, friendly to the design, to contribute labor and materials, with provisions for the workmen.   With this request, the inhabitants of Amherst, friendly to the institution, and a few from Pelham and Leverett, most cheerfully complied.   The stones for the foundation were brought chiefly from Pelham, by gratuitous labor, and provisions for the workmen were furnished by voluntary contributions.

The foundation of the building being nearly completed, the board of trustees met on the 8th day of August, 1820.   Present, Noah Webster, Esq., vice president, Rev. James Taylor, Rev. Joshua Crosby, Rev. Daniel A. Clark, Nathaniel Smith, Esq., Samuel F. Dickinson, Esq., Rufus Graves, Esq.

The session was opened by prayer by the Rev. Mr. Crosby, and this was ordered to be the constant practice in future.

At 2 o'clock, P. M., on the 9th day of August, 1820, the board met after an adjournment, and " voted that this board will proceed immediately to lay the corner-stone of the edifice for the charitable institution, and that the Rev. Joshua Crosby be requested to open the ceremony with prayer ; that the Rev. David Parsons, president of the board, be requested to perform the ceremony of laying the corner-stone ; and that Noah Webster, Esq., vice president, be requested to close the ceremonies at the foundation, with an address.   Voted, also, that after the ceremonies, the Rev. Daniel A. Clark be requested to preach a sermon, and that the Rev. E. Porter and the Rev. J. Grout, be requested to assist in the other exercises."

In pursuance of this vote, the trustees proceeded to the place, and the president of the board, with appropriate remarks, laid the corner-stone at the northwestern corner of the building, in the presence of a numerous audience.   After which, the vice president, standing on the same corner-stone, delivered the following address.

*To the benefactors of the Institution to be founded in this place,—*

We are assembled this day to lay the corner-stone of an edifice, designed for the accommodation of the beneficiaries, who may be placed on the fund which your benevolence has constituted for their education in classical literature and the sciences.   This act and the ceremonies of the day will witness to you the sincere intentions, and ardent desire of the board of trustees of Amherst Academy, to carry into effect the design of the liberal charity which you have consecrated to the advancement of the Christian church.   That they have not sooner commenced the execution of the trust reposed in them, by the constitution of the fund, is to be ascribed wholly to considerations of prudence and expedience, arising out of circumstances over which they had no control. If, however, this delay has contributed to strengthen the cause, by removing obstacles and illuminating the path of duty, we are confident that the patrons of the institution will justify the board, in this exercise of their discretion.

The object of this institution, that of educating for the gospel ministry young men in indigent circumstances, but of hopeful piety and promising talents, is one of the noblest which can occupy the attention and claim the contributions of the Christian public.   It is to second the efforts of the apostles themselves, in extending and establishing the Redeemer's empire—the empire of truth.   It is to aid in the important work of raising the human race from ignorance and debasement; to enlighten their minds ; to exalt their character ; and to teach them the way to happiness and to glory.   Too long have men been engaged in the barbarous works of multiplying the miseries of human life.   Too long have their exertions and resources been devoted to war and plunder ; to the destruction of lives and property ; to the ravage of cities ; to the unnatural, the monstrous employment of enslaving and degrading their own species.  Blessed be *our* lot !  We live to see a new era in the history of man—an era when reason and religion begin to resume their sway, and to impress the heavenly truth, that the appropriate business of men, is to imitate the Savior ; to serve their God ; and bless their fellow men.

Such an institution, with an appropriate destination, in which the views and hopes, the liberality and prayers of an extensive Christian community, may be concentrated, seems to be a desideratum in our country ; and it is believed, will command the respect, and receive the patronage of the public.  The place selected for the seat of this seminary, is believed to be peculiarly well adapted to secure its prosperity. It is to be situated in a populous country, abounding with provisions ; in a climate remarkable for its salubrity ; in a village where no peculiar circumstances exist to invite dissipation and extravagant expenditures ; surrounded by a well cultivated territory, inhabited by people, whose moral, religious and literary habits, dispose them to cherish the cultivation of the mind, and the propagation of evangelical truth, while the extensive prospect and diversified scenery, presented to the eye from this elevation, is adapted by nature and by art, to delight the student, and to furnish, to piety, perpetual sources of contemplation and improvement.

In such a situation, and under the patronage of a religious community, can this institution fail of success ?  Small, indeed, are its beginnings, and feeble the human instruments by which it is to be raised and supported.  And more, it encounters opposition.  But opposition to a good cause must stimulate exertion, and contribute to ultimate success.  And why should it be opposed ?  It has no competitor, it interferes essentially with no other seminary, for none exists of a similar character.  Will not New England supply it with students ?  Let the numerous applications to the education societies, beyond their means, furnish the answer.  Are not well educated ministers of the gospel wanted, in great numbers, to repair the waste places of our old settlements ; to supply a numerous destitute population in the new states, and to carry the gospel to millions of the human race, who are perishing in ignorance and barbarism ?  Let the continual and pressing demands on our theological institutions, answer this question.

But can the means be found to erect the necessary buildings, and to endow the institution with funds that shall raise it to reputation and usefulness ?  Let the doubts on this subject be dissipated by considering the success which has hitherto attended every benevolent institution, designed to enlarge the bounds of the Redeemer's kingdom.  The great Head of the church who commanded his disciples to preach the gospel to every creature, who promised to be with them, to the end of the world, can not forsake his own cause, nor be unfaithful to his promise. If this institution is commenced with pious motives, and adapted to advance the moral and religious interests of men, it is the duty of Christians to lend their aid to its establishment and support, in humble confidence that a blessing will attend their sacrifices and their labors.  No sordid views should infect the prosecution of the plan ; no selfish passions, no local interests, should be permitted to interrupt the union and coöperation of the friends of Christ. Minds, elevated with evangelical hopes and views, will discard, as base and dishonorable, all reference to personal or local advantages, and consider this institution as intended to embrace, in its effects, the whole community of man.

And should success attend this establishment, how delightful to the friend of religion must be the thought, that he has thrown his mite into this treasury of the Lord! With what satisfaction will the sons of its benefactors hereafter hear it related, that a missionary, educated by their fathers' charity, has planted a church of Christ on the burning sands of Africa, or in the cheerless wilds of Siberia—that he has been the instrument of converting a family, a province, perhaps a kingdom of pagans, and bringing them within the pale of the Christian church! Who that duly appreciates the influence of the gospel in civilizing the savage, and in preventing or restraining the disorders of civilized society, can hesitate a moment, even on motives of temporal advantage, to enrol his name among the benefactors of such an institution! No, my friends; the man who loves peace and security *in this life*, must lend his aid to the propagation of the *gospel*, and contribute to give efficacy to its *principles*. The gospel only can convert swords into plowshares and spears into pruning hooks—the gospel only can supersede the necessity of bolts and bars—the gospel only can dispeople the state prison and the penitentiary!

Let us then take courage! The design is unquestionably good, and its success must be certain. Small efforts combined and continued, can not fail to produce the desired effect, and realize the hopes of its founders. Prudence and integrity will subdue opposition, and invite coöperation; perseverance will bring to our aid new accessions of strength, and a thousand small streams of charity from unexpected sources, will flow into the common current of benevolence which is to water and refresh this nursery of gospel ministers. This institution will grow and flourish, and become auxiliary to a thousand associations which Christian philanthropy has formed, to reclaim and evangelize the miserable children of Adam. Charity will nourish, protect and augment what charity has begun; and the prayers of piety will invite blessings on this humble effort to diffuse the gospel of peace.

May the great Head of the church, to whose service this edifice is to be consecrated, multiply the benefactors of the institution, and crown their charities with his loving kindness and tender mercy! And may the benefits of their benevolence, in diffusing truth, and exterminating idolatry and sin, be as extensive as the human family, and as durable as time!

After the address, the trustees and the spectators repaired immediately to the church, where the Rev. Mr. Clark delivered an appropriate discourse from 2 Kings, vi, 1—3, which was published with the title, "A plea for a miserable world."

On the following day, the trustees directed the secretary to notify Henry Gray, Esq., of Boston, Gen. Salem Town, Jr., of Charlton, the Rev. Theophilus Packard, of Shelburne, the Rev. Thomas Snell, of North Brookfield, the Rev. Luther Sheldon, of Easton, the Rev. Heman Humphrey, of Pittsfield, and Hezekiah W. Strong, Esq., of Amherst, of their election by the subscribers to the charity fund, to be overseers of that fund.

The trustees also voted that their thanks be given to Noah Webster, Esq., for his address, and to the Rev. Mr. Clark, for his sermon, and requested a copy of each for publication.

At this meeting also the trustees voted to request a number of respectable gentlemen residing in different parts of the United States, to act with the board as correspondents, in promoting the interest of the institution. More than twenty were named for this purpose ; but it is not known that this measure produced any valuable effect.

At the same meeting Dr. David Parsons resigned his seat in the board of trustees, and Noah Webster, Esq., was elected president of the board.

At a meeting of the board of trustees, September 7, 1820, a committee was appointed to correspond with the American Education Society, on the subject of the terms on which the board might co-operate with that society in the education of their beneficiaries.

At a meeting of the board, November 8th, 1820, the trustees appointed John Leland, Esq. as their agent to receive all donations made for the benefit of the charity institution, other than those made to the permanent fund. They passed a vote also authorizing the prudential committee to receive into the Academy, as beneficiaries from education societies or elsewhere, charity students not exceeding twenty.

At this meeting also the trustees resolved to establish in the charity institution three professorships, one in mathematics and natural philosophy, one in rhetoric and one in the learned languages. A committee was appointed to solicit and obtain the necessary funds to support them.

Notwithstanding the building committee had no funds for erecting the building, not even a cent, except what were to be derived from gratuities in labor, materials and provisions, yet they prosecuted the work with untiring diligence. Repeatedly, during the progress of the work, their means were exhausted, and they were obliged to notify the president of the board that they could proceed no further without aid. On these occasions, the president called together the trustees or a number of them, who, by subscriptions of their own and by renewed solicitations for voluntary contributions, enabled the committee to prosecute the work. And such were the exertions of the board, of the committee and of the friends of the institution, that on the *ninetieth day* from the laying of the corner-stone, the roof-timbers were erected on the building.

At the meeting of the board in November, the trustees voted their thanks to the building committee, to the inhabitants of the town of Amherst and of the neighboring towns, and to all who had aided in the great work, for their noble exertions and generous liberality in contributing labor, materials, money and provisions toward erecting a building for the charity institution.*

But the interior of the building was not yet finished ; and at a meeting of the board, February 13, 1821, a committee of four persons, Rev. Mr. Porter, Rev. Mr. Clark, Rev. Mr. Whipple and Rev. Mr. Vaill,

---

* Occasional contributions from individuals in Hadley and Belchertown were received.

were appointed as agents to make application to evangelical associations to combine their efforts to carry into effect the design of this institution ; to form societies and to invite the aid of societies already formed for charitable purposes, and in short, to procure donations for enlarging the funds and maintaining the professorships.

At this meeting the Rev. Heman Humphrey, of Pittsfield, was requested to deliver a discourse before the trustees of Amherst Academy at their meeting in May, then next ; and the Rev. Luther Sheldon was appointed his substitute.

At a meeting of the trustees of Amherst Academy on the 8th day of May, 1821, it was

" Voted, unanimously, that the Rev. Zephaniah Swift Moore, be and he is hereby elected president of the charity institution in this town."

" Voted, that the permanent salary of the president of this institution for his services as president and professor of theology and of moral philosophy, shall be twelve hundred dollars, and that he be entitled to the usual perquisites."

The trustees at the same meeting determined to build a house for the president, provided they could procure donations of money, materials and labor. Also that the first term of study in the charity institution should commence on the third Wednesday in September, then next. They also voted an address of thanks to the Rev. Heman Humphrey, for his very appropriate and useful sermon delivered on the 9th instant.

At this meeting, also, the trustees passed a vote prohibiting the students from drinking ardent spirits or wine, or any liquor of which ardent spirits or wine should be the principal ingredient, at any inn, tavern or shop, or to keep ardent spirits or wine in their rooms, or at any time to indulge in them, under the penalty of admonition for the first offense, and for the second offense of admonition or expulsion, according to the nature and aggravation of the offense, at the discretion of the prudential committee.

On the 9th of May, 1821, the votes of the board of trustees appointing the Rev. Z. S. Moore president of the charity institution, and granting him a permanent salary, were sent by the president of the board to that gentleman at Williamstown. To these communications President Moore returned the following answer.

*To the President and Trustees of Amherst Academy.*

GENTLEMEN—I received from the president of your board, a copy of your vote of the 8th May, 1821, appointing me to preside over the charity institution in Amherst, and other votes relating to the same subject, attested by the secretary. I have attended to the subject with earnest desire, so far as I know my own heart, that my decision might be such as God would approve. Previous to receiving any notice of your appointment, I had made up my mind to resign my offices in this college at the next commencement. Providence had clearly made it consistent with my duty to leave then, if not sooner. I have ascertained, so far as I have had opportunity, the opinion of those who are the friends of evangelical truth, with respect to the necessity, prospects and usefulness of such an institution as that contemplated at Amherst. I have much reason to believe there is extensively an agreement on this subject. In my own opinion, no object has higher claims on the charity and benevolent efforts of the Christian community, than the education of pious young men for the gospel ministry. This classical education should be thorough, and I should be wholly averse to becoming united with any institution which professes to give a classical education inferior to that given in any of the colleges in New England. On this subject I am assured your opinion is the same as my own, and that you are determined that the course of study in the institution to which you have invited me, shall not be inferior to that in the colleges in New England. I am also assured that you will make provision for the admission of those who are not indigent, and may wish to obtain a classical education in the institution.

After such deliberation, and such attention to the subject as I supposed its importance demanded, I have concluded to accept your appointment to the presidency of the charity institution in Amherst, and I do hereby manifest my acceptance of the same.

I shall resign my offices in this college at the next commencement, if not sooner, after which I shall consider myself devoted to the interests of the institution intrusted to your care.

May God continue to bless your efforts to build up an institution, which, I trust, he designs, in his wise and gracious providence, to make eminently useful in promoting the interests of literature and science, and particularly in promoting the interests of the Redeemer's kingdom, which, by his sure promise, is one day to be extended, with all its blessings of peace, pardon and salvation to all the nations that dwell on the face of the earth. I am, gentlemen, very respectfully yours,

ZEPH. SWIFT MOORE.

Williams College, June 12, 1821.

On the same day President Moore addressed a letter to Noah Webster, Esq. president of the board of trustees of Amherst Academy, in which he states, among other things, the doubts he had entertained respecting the expediency of his accepting the appointment. " I think," he wrote, " I have decided right. I know it will require much effort to make the institution in Amherst what it ought to be. There will probably be many difficulties to encounter. But the object is an important one, and merits the efforts and self-denial and the prayers of all the friends of Zion."

On the thirteenth day of June, 1821, the trustees of Amherst Academy elected the Rev. Gamaliel S. Olds, to be professor of mathematics and natural philosophy, in the collegiate charity institution ; and Joseph Estabrook to be professor of the Greek and Latin languages.

At the same meeting, the board voted that persons wishing to avail themselves of the charity fund, as beneficiaries, should be under the patronage of some education society or other respectable association, which should furnish to each beneficiary a part of his support, amounting at least to one dollar a week, for which he was to be furnished with board and tuition. They required also that every applicant should produce, to the examining committee, satisfactory evidence of his indigence, piety and promising talents.

The trustees voted also that the preparatory studies or qualifications of candidates for admission to the collegiate institution, and the course of studies to be pursued during the four years of membership, should be the same as those established in Yale College.

At this session of the board, it was determined that the president and professors of the collegiate charity institution should be inaugurated, and the college edifice dedicated, with suitable religious services, on the Tuesday next preceding the third Wednesday of September next, and that Professor Stuart, of Andover, be invited to preach the dedication sermon. In case of his declining, the committee were authorized to request the Rev. Mr. Osgood of Springfield to perform that service.

At a meeting of the board of trustees, August 6, 1821, the Rev. Jonas King was elected to be professor of oriental languages in the collegiate institution. [Mr. King soon after went to Greece, and declined accepting the appointment.]

At a meeting of the board of trustees, September 18, 1821, the Rev. Zephaniah S. Moore, D. D., Rev. Thomas Snell, and Rev. Daniel A. Clark were appointed a committee to report a confession of faith to be subscribed by the president and professors of the collegiate institution, previous to their entering on the duties of their respective offices.* This service was performed.

The trustees then proceeded to the inauguration of the president, and Professor Estabrook; Professor Olds not being present. The ceremonies were performed in the parish church, and were introduced by the following observations of Noah Webster, president of the board of trustees.

"A number of charitable citizens of this state, having by donations constituted a fund for the education of pious young men for the gospel ministry, and having committed that fund to the management of the board of trustees of the academy in this town, until an act of incorporation shall be obtained, the board, in pursuance of their powers and in execution of their trust, have erected a college edifice, for the accommodation of students, and have appointed a president and professors, qualified to give them a classical education. And in conformity to the recommendation of a respectable number of the clergy and laity of this and the neighboring counties, convened in this town in September, 1818, the board propose to annex to this institution a college, for the education of young men who have the means of defraying their expenses.

As it is the duty of men, on all occasions, to acknowledge their dependence on divine aid for success in their lawful enterprises; so it is peculiarly proper that an undertaking which has, for its special object, the promotion of the Christian religion, should be commended to the favor and protection of the great Head of the church. To his service is the charity fund consecrated by the donors, and to him is the edifice now erected to be, at this time solemnly dedicated."

Then followed prayer by the Rev. Mr. Crosby of Enfield, Mass., and a sermon by the Rev. Dr. Leland of Charleston, S. C., who was on a

---

* The rule, requiring the president and professors to subscribe a confession of faith, has been long since repealed.

visit to his father, then resident in Amherst—Prof. Stuart having, for special reasons, declined to preach on that occasion; and the Rev. Mr. Osgood not being present.

The president of the board of trustees then proceeded:—" The board of trustees have elected the Rev. Zephaniah Swift Moore, to be president of the collegiate institution in this town, and the president is *ex officio* professor of theology and moral philosophy. They have also elected the Rev. Gamaliel S. Olds, to be professor of mathematics and natural philosophy, and Mr. Joseph Estabrook to be professor of the Greek and Latin languages in the same institution. Mr. Olds is not present, but he has accepted his appointment." Then addressing Dr. Moore, the president asked him whether he then publicly manifested his acceptance of the office of president of the collegiate institution in Amherst. Dr. Moore answered in the affirmative. The president then asked Mr. Estabrook whether he publicly manifested his acceptance of the office of professor of the Greek and Latin languages in the collegiate institution. Mr. Estabrook answered in the affirmative.

The confession of faith was then read and the gentlemen assented to it. The president of the board then proceeded:—" Then in behalf of the board of trustees and by their authority, I publicly announce that you, Zephaniah Swift Moore, are constituted president of the collegiate institution in this town, and by the same authority, you are invested with the power of superintending, instructing and governing the students according to your best discretion, and according to the statutes and regulations that are or may be established for these purposes. And I further declare that you, Joseph Estabrook, are, by the same authority, constituted professor of the Greek and Latin languages in the same seminary, with power to assist the president in the instruction of the students, and in the government and discipline of the institution.

" Sensible of the difficulties which will attend a faithful and discreet discharge of your arduous duties; feeling their own responsibility, and solicitous to promote the best interests of the seminary; the board of trustees will cheerfully coöperate with you, gentlemen, in such measures as circumstances may demand or prudence dictate, for giving effect to the regulations prescribed; and will assist in devising the best means for elevating the character and extending the usefulness of the institution.

" Most devoutly and affectionately, dear sirs, do we commend you to the holy guidance and protection of the Supreme Head of the church, to whose service this institution is consecrated. Most earnestly do we pray that the blessing of heaven may accompany your labors, and crown them with success. Under your pious care, diligent instruction, and prudent government, may this infant seminary commend itself to the affections and respect of the community; while the fostering patronage of the Christian public, shall raise it to distinction among the literary institutions of the American republic.

" By your precepts and example, may virtue be honored and piety encouraged among the youth of the seminary; while every species of immorality shall be discountenanced and repressed. May your instructions enlarge the sphere of intellectual improvement, and circumscribe the dominion of error. In yonder edifice may the youth of America, be richly furnished with the science and erudition which shall qualify them for eminent usefulness in church and state.   There may they be instructed in the principles of our holy religion, and armed with forti- tude and grace, to defend and  maintain its doctrines in  their apostolic purity.   And while your labors contribute to exalt the moral, religious and literary character of your own country, may there issue from this seminary some beams of the light of civilization and of heavenly truth, to illuminate the ' dark places of the earth which are full of the habita- tions of cruelty.'   Here may a flame of  holy zeal be enkindled in the breasts of young Christians, which shall glow with inextinguishable ardor, and animate them with courage to hazard all temporal enjoyments and life itself, in bearing the message of redeeming love to an ignorant and guilty world.   And when your labors on earth shall have ceased, may it be your everlasting joy, that you have been the instruments of pre- paring many souls to join that great multitude which no man can num- ber, whose blissful employment it shall be to ascribe salvation to him that sitteth on the throne and to the lamb forever."

On the  following day, Sept. 19, Noah Webster resigned his seat in the board of trustees, and Dr. Moore was elected a member and presi- dent of the board, to supply his place.

# CHAPTER X.

## AN ADDRESS BEFORE THE AGRICULTURAL SOCIE-
## TY IN NORTHAMPTON, OCTOBER 14, 1818.

In the history of the creation, we are informed that " God made every plant of the field, before it was in the earth, and every herb of the
field, before it grew ; for Jehovah God had not caused it to rain on the
earth, and there *was not a man to till the ground :*" but after man was
created, God planted a garden in Eden, and there he placed the man,
" *to dress it, and to keep it.*" From these passages of sacred history,
we learn, that antecedent to the apostasy, and by divine appointment,
agriculture was assigned to man as his proper occupation.

In conformity with the divine purpose, in this destination of man, the
upper stratum of the earth, was, by the Creator, fitted for the production of plants. The soil, which covers the greatest part of the globe,
though diversified in its constituent materials, its qualities, depth, and
consistence, is generally composed of very fine particles, which render
it permeable by water, and capable of containing the greatest quantity
of it : at the same time, though so friable, as to be easily pulverized by
instruments of husbandry, and so loose as to be pervious to the roots
of plants ; it is sufficiently compact to sustain herbs, shrubs, and even
trees, in an erect position.

As the cultivation of the earth was the first business assigned to man,
so of all his temporal concerns, it is the most important and necessary ;
for the productions of the earth furnish almost all the materials of food
and clothing. Observations on the savage life will inform us, how small
a population the spontaneous produce of the earth will support. Even
the rude natives of America, few and scattered as they are, depend on
tillage for a part of their means of subsistence ; and the wild animals,
which supply no small portion of their food and clothing, derive their
nourishment from the productions of the earth. The produce of seas,
rivers, and lakes, whatever may be the amount, must always constitute
a small comparative portion of the food of a well peopled country, and
no part of the food of domestic animals.

Agriculture then is essential to the support of a dense population. It
supplies food for men and their domestic animals, and the materials of
manufactures ; and the surplus, beyond the necessary consumption of
a country, furnishes the means of commerce, and becomes a source of
wealth. Hence, the more productive the earth is rendered by cultivation, the more inhabitants and domestic animals may be subsisted on a
given extent of territory ; and the greater is the wealth and strength of
a nation.

Nor is the cultivation of the earth less favorable to the health and
longevity of the human species. As a general remark, it may be affirmed, that the labors of the husbandman are better adapted, than any
other labor or employment, to give strength and firmness to all parts of

the human body, by calling into action and keeping in motion the various limbs and muscles, without an undue pressure on any particular part; thus promoting equally the circulation of the blood and the various secretions essential to health. Excess of labor will, in this, as in every other occupation, impair health, and shorten life or render it uncomfortable; but in general, the greatest portion of sound health, and the most robust men, the strength and defense of a nation, are found among the cultivators of the earth.

Equally well adapted is the business of the farmer to enlarge and invigorate the intellectual faculties, and to generate a spirit of independence favorable to civil and political liberty. This is particularly the fact in a country where the cultivators are proprietors of the soil. Immense is the difference in the exertion and improvement of the mental faculties, between those who labor for themselves, and those who labor for others. The very ownership of property tends to expand the mind, and give it a tone of firmness and independence; while the prospect of increasing the value of property, and enjoying the fruits of labor, calls into action more vigorous exertion, more enterprise, and more invention. At the same time, the possession of the title to land attaches a man to the country in which he is a freeholder, and binds him to the government and laws by which his person and his property are protected.

Nor ought we to forget, in this enumeration of the advantages of agriculture, that this employment is peculiarly suited to the preservation of morals in a community. The sequestered situation of the husbandman, occupied daily on his farm, remote from scenes of vice and dissipation, secures him, in a great degree, from the contagion of evil examples, and from many temptations to vice, which large associations of people present, to seduce men from their duty. And if the agricultural state of society does not exhibit more positive virtue and excellence than any other, it supplies fewer instances of atrocious crimes and deep depravity. Nor is it less true, that this state of society presents peculiar advantages and powerful inducements to the cultivation of pious affections. The farmer, after all his industry and good management, must depend entirely on Divine Providence for a harvest. He must feel, every day and every hour, that by his own power and skill, he can no more produce a blade of grass or a single corn, than he can create a world; and this consciousness of his dependence on the Supreme Being, can not fail to generate, in a mind not absolutely brutish, a spirit of humility and submission to his Maker—a spirit of unceasing reverence, piety, and gratitude. When the husbandman considers further, that his labors are continually liable to be frustrated by excessive rains, floods, and drouth; by untimely frost, blasting, and mildew; by destructive storms and devouring insects; calamities which, by no human efforts, can be averted or controlled; with what face can he deny the providence or spurn the government of his Maker? How can he fail to acknowledge his own imbecility and dependence, and place all his trust on that Being who alone can crown his labors with success?

But the ingenuous mind is not to be influenced solely by the dread of calamities. It will find, in the works of nature and Providence, irresistible motives to admire the power, the wisdom, and the benevolence of the Supreme Being. Who can examine the wonderful laws of the vegetable economy, the curious and infinitely diversified structure of plants, without being led to "look through nature up to nature's God," and to form exalted views of Divine power and wisdom? Who can cast his eyes on spacious fields robed with verdure and adorned with flowers—some, presenting the promise of a rich harvest of fruits—others, expanding their beauties to delight the eye and regale the senses of man, or to supply insects with nectarious food—and thousands of others, which, from our ignorance of their uses, are destined to "waste their sweetness on the desert air"—who can view this rich provision of all that can charm the eye, and delight the mind of man, without admiring the goodness of the benevolent Author? Hard and insensible must be the heart that is not softened by gratitude for all the blessings lavished on the human race, and humbled by regret that man should ever forget his glorious Benefactor.

Notwithstanding agriculture is confessedly the first and most important occupation in society, it is among the last which have engaged the attention of scientific men. Princes have been employed in extending their power and dominions ; nobles and men of distinction have been occupied in the pursuit of pleasure or of military skill and glory ; while the culture of the earth has been left to the care and toils of the humble peasant, to mercenaries and slaves. To this neglect are chiefly to be ascribed the frequent famines which afflicted the nations of Europe anterior to the last century. But within the last seventy or eighty years, men of science and property have been engaged in agricultural improvements, particularly in Great Britain ; and the effect of their exertions has been to increase the value of lands, and to furnish subsistence and augmented wealth to a more numerous population.

In this country, improvements in agriculture are of still later origin ; and I well remember the time when no farmer thought of restoring fertility to an impoverished soil by the aid of the grasses. The Revolution first disengaged the minds of our countrymen from the shackles of custom, and gave a spring to industry and enterprise. The first effect of the independence of the United States, was visible in the extension of commerce, but it soon appeared in every branch of industry. The removal of the restrictions of the British laws of trade, opened a wide field for commercial enterprise, which, by finding new markets for the productions of the earth, presented to the farmer new inducements to supply the demand. The wars which arose out of the revolution in France, threw into the power of our merchants an uncommonly lucrative commerce that absorbed a large amount of capital. This capital was, in a few years, greatly augmented. A large portion of this capital, has, by the event of general peace, been liberated from commercial employment, and may now be devoted to agriculture and manufactures. And fortunately there appears to be an increasing disposition in capitalists to turn their property into these channels. Of this fact, the recent formation of numerous societies for these objects, and the attention of men of wealth and distinction to agricultural pursuits, are honorable and cheering testimonies. As the society which I have the honor to address was not the last in its institution, it may be presumed it will not be the most languid in the prosecution of its objects.

The great design of this and of similar institutions, is, to ascertain the best mode of tilling the earth ; that mode which shall enable the farmer to obtain the greatest quantity of produce, upon a given extent of land, with the least expense and labor. This end is to be accomplished partly by science, but chiefly by experiments. A perfect knowledge of the nature of soils, and the fitness of each to produce a particular species of grain, would aid the scientific farmer in his practice. But a chimical analysis of soils is beyond the reach of most husbandmen ; and if it were not, the knowledge derived from it would be a less safe ground of practice than experiment ; as the effect of soil would be liable to be varied by the situation of the land, by the seasons, and other extraneous causes. Experience and observation will furnish the farmer with the facts most necessary to guide him in his rural economy. He will find that wheat, rye, and maiz or American corn, on wet, cold, heavy land, will frustrate his hopes ; that oats and barley will bear more moisture than the grains just mentioned ; but that land of this kind is best fitted for mowing and grazing. He will also find that the warmest lands on plains and moderate elevations, are best fitted for tillage, and the colder lands on mountains, are most properly appropriated to the feeding of cattle. He will find that although water is essential to the growth of plants, being the principal instrument of conveying to them nutrition, yet that a superabundance of that fluid, no less than a deficiency, is injurious. He will observe that soils possess different capacities for retaining water—that sand and silicious soils are too loose—and that clay is too compact when dry, and too adhesive when wet ; and he will adapt his mode of tillage to the modification of these qualities. Experience will teach him that a soil of loose texture should be laid as smooth as possible, by harrowing and rolling, as a smooth, compact surface retards evaporation—that, on the contrary, a moist, heavy soil should be thrown into narrow lands or ridges, for the purpose of casting off the water, and exposing, to the rays of the sun, a greater extent of surface. Nothing can be more injudicious than to drag down to a smooth surface a wet, cold, argillaceous soil, especially for a crop of American corn or potatoes. For these crops, the land should be left in the furrow as loose and uneven as possible. The more smooth the surface, the longer the land retains water, the less pervious is it to the heat of the sun, and the more compact does it become by the weight of falling rains. In our climate, land in the spring is usually too wet and cold for the rapid growth of corn ; and as a general fact, our crops suffer more from an excess than from a deficiency of water. In preparing land for maiz, therefore, the judicious farmer will leave his land in furrow, or in ridges ; as in this form it warms sooner, is more easily tilled, and the harrow, at hoeing, will perform double the work in pulverizing the earth and covering weeds. Even sward land, according to my own experience, should be managed in the same manner. The sod, well turned over by the plow, should not be broken or disturbed, till the first, and generally not till the second hoeing. The decomposition of the vegetable matter will keep the land sufficiently light and mellow, and the process of decomposition is rather retarded than accelerated, by an earlier use of the harrow or plow. Indeed dragging or cross plowing too early, turns back a part of the sod, rendering the land more grassy and difficult to till ; and often it disturbs the worms which lie harmless, feeding on the grass beneath, and compels them to seek the tender corn for food. I have known several fields of corn nearly ruined by breaking the turf and disturbing the worms at the first hoeing.

A primary object in rural economy, and one to which every farmer must direct particular attention, is to replenish the earth with the proper nutriment of plants. Our ancestors found the earth covered with a rich vegetable mold, the remains of decomposed leaves and plants, which, for a series of years, produced abundant crops, and precluded the necessity of making or preserving manures. This circumstance generated a habit of negligence, in providing manure, the effects of which are still visible, in every part of the country. If we were to inquire, who, in this respect, is without fault, it might be difficult to find the man who would venture to throw the first stone. About our houses and barns, in the highways and in the fields, we every where see proofs of this negligence. But nothing is more certain, than that land will be exhausted, and agriculture decline, unless the soil is regularly supplied with as much nutrition as the crops draw from it. To devise the means of furnishing adequate supplies of manure, is a most important object, and calls for a contribution of all the knowledge and experience of the members of this society, and for all the information derivable from other sources.

In general, it may be observed that almost every animal and vegetable substance furnishes a portion of the food of plants ; and every such substance, not more valuable for some other purpose, should be converted to this use. Great improvements may be made, in making and collecting manure, by so constructing stables, sties and barn-yards, as to save the excretions of domestic animals, and by mixing them with other manuring substances.

Ashes, leached and unleached, are well known to be a valuable manure—and their effect is particularly remarkable in producing clover on dry land.

Lime or calcarious earth, is considered as a manure of value upon some kinds of soil ; but probably it has been little used within the limits of this society. It must remain for future experience to determine its efficacy, and the kind of soil to which it may be usefully applied.

Marine shells, beds of which give inexhaustible fertility to certain tracts of land on the sea-shore, are not within our reach—and the like remark is applicable to fish, muscles, and sea-weed.

Marl is a manure of great value; but I am not informed whether any considerable beds of it have been found in this region. The discovery of such beds is however an object too interesting to escape the attention of this society.

Gypsum is a very efficacious manure, on some kinds of soil, and for some species of plants. Its real value however has not been ascertained in all cases, by accurate experiments ; and on some crops its value is probably overrated. A series of experiments on different soils, conducted with skill and care, and the results ascertained by weight and measure, would throw important light on this subject, and direct the husbandman to a more successful application of this manure.

There is one resource for restoring fertility to an impoverished soil, which is within every farmer's power—this is the seeding of land with some kind of grass. It is a striking evidence of the wisdom and goodness of the Creator, that those species of plants which either grow spontaneously in the greatest abundance, or are produced with the most ease by cultivation, as herbage for cattle, should also be well adapted to fertilize the earth, and prepare it for producing grain, the food of man. The sowing of grass-seed and a rotation of crops, are among the most important improvements in agriculture, introduced during the last century. The beneficial effects of this practice are now so well understood, that the man who suffers his land to rest unseeded, after a crop, for the purpose of recruiting its strength by a spontaneous growth of weeds and grass, may be considered as neglecting one of the most obvious advantages which Providence has offered to his industry.

In the preparation and management of the manure of barn-yards, and of compost, it is important to provide shelter to secure them from waste. In the common practice of suffering the substances to lie spread, and exposed to a burning sun and to washing rains during the summer, it is probable that one half of the nutritious matter is lost. The substances, in a state of decomposition, should be sheltered from rains and the direct action of the sun, or, if this can not be done, they should be collected into large piles, and covered with earth, weeds or straw.

In rural economy, it is of no small moment to attend to the destruction of weeds. The more perfectly free from weeds land can be kept, the larger and better will be the crops; as weeds deprive grain of a part of the nutrition of the soil, and prevent the action of the sun, which is necessary to elaborate the juices, separate the water from the nutritious matter, and bring the fruit to perfection. Noxious plants therefore should be effectually subdued; and such as spring up among corn and potatoes, after the plow and hoe can be used with safety, should be extirpated by the hand, before their seeds are ripened. And what shall we say of the farmer who suffers a rank, luxuriant growth of briers and weeds to stand unmolested about his house and barn, and on the borders of his garden and fields? The best mode of subduing and extirpating weeds, is a subject that demands particular attention— nor is it less important to check the introduction and spread of any new plant that is noxious to the growth of grass and grain. The Canada thistle, one of the most pernicious and troublesome weeds, and of very difficult extirpation, has spread over the northern parts of New England, and is extending itself into the southern. It is now seen in the counties of Franklin and Hampshire, and in the town of Windsor in Connecticut; the seeds being conveyed from the north in grass-seed and in oats or other fodder for horses. Its seeds are feathered, and wafted to a distance by the wind; and it propagates itself by lateral or horizontal roots. My own experience teaches that it is barely possible to eradicate this plant, and if the farmers have a just sense of their true interest, they will attack it on its first appearance, and check its propagation.

The variety of the species of grass and roots which grow well in this climate, precludes the probability of a general failure of provisions and fodder; and the experience of nearly two centuries authorizes the belief that the inhabitants of New England are little exposed to famine. But let it be considered that our seasons are extremely variable, and that the revolution of a few years exhibits all the varieties of wet and dry, warm, cool, and temperate summers. Our crops are also exposed to destruction from winter-killing, insects and unseasonable frost. We know by observation that some species of grain thrive best in one kind of season; others, in another; cool, temperate and moderately dry weather is far most favorable to wheat, rye, oats and barley; but warm summers are necessary to ripen maiz or American corn. As we are unable, when we sow and plant, to foresee what the general character of the summer is to be, prudence dictates that we should commit to the earth every year a due proportion of the seed of every species of grain and roots, on which we depend for the subsistence of men and cattle. By this practice we multiply the chances of securing a good crop from one or more of the kinds. The failure of one species of grain, in a particular season, is no good reason for neglecting to attempt to raise it the next year. Indeed, in such a variable climate, such failure rather increases the probability of a good crop the succeeding year. After the loss of American corn by frost in 1816, a great cry was raised against the cultivation of that species of grain in New England, and with no inconsiderable effect; for a less quantity of it has been planted the last two years, and more land has been appropriated to the raising of other species of grain, and of potatoes. The present year has shown the impropriety of this change of practice; for potatoes and several kinds of grain have produced a light crop, and the season has been favorable to maiz. The inference from these facts is that we should not suffer a particular instance of ill success, to influence our general course of husbandry.

In the course of agricultural improvement, the art of draining wet lands, which is now in its infancy in this country, will demand the attention of farmers. Land abounding with springs may often be much improved by draining. Valleys or depressions of land between hills, often contain a body of alluvial soil, swept by rains from the adjacent declivities, enriched by deposits of vegetable mold, which have been accumulating for ages. These when freed from a superabundance of water, and exposed to the influence of the sun, will often be found most excellent land for grazing or tillage.

For the security of crops, good fences are indispensable; and most of the towns within this district abound with materials for this purpose. The hilly country is generally furnished with stone; and many towns have a supply of chestnut, an invaluable timber for fencing. The towns adjacent to the river, when other materials fail or become too expensive, will find a resource in the cultivation of the thorn.

This subject naturally suggests the importance of attending to the preservation and increase of wood and timber. Perhaps in no particular are the people of this country less provident than in the continual destruction of these articles, without attempting to supply the waste. They seem not to consider that the labor of a few weeks only is suffi-

cient to prostrate a forest; but that the growth of an age is necessary
to replace it.  In a large part of New England, good timber and wood
for fuel are already scarce; and with an increasing population, and
growing manufactures, in a cold climate, what is to be the situation of
the inhabitants, a century hence without more care and economy !  Let
every owner of land consider that even now a forest of pine, oak,
chestnut, ash and maple, adds a great value to his farm; and that this
value will increase or diminish, according to his care in the management of his wood-land.

In the cultivation of fruit trees, there is in this region of country,
great room for improvement; both in the pruning and cultivation of
such trees as we have, and in supplying better species of fruit.  It is
painful to see valuable orchards in a state of decay, merely for want of
culture; and equally to be regretted that so little attention is paid to
the selection of good fruit, especially durable and pleasant fruit for winter's use.  The trouble and expense of procuring the best species, are
very inconsiderable, and furnish no just apology for the neglect.  Apples and pears are cultivated in all parts of New England, and the trees
are durable.  Peaches thrive well, in this neighborhood, but the produce is precarious, and the tree short-lived; yet it is easily replaced,
as it bears fruit the fourth or fifth year from the seed.  The quince
thrives well, and seldom fails to yield fruit.  The plum-tree grows well,
but is subject to premature decay from the bursting of the bark, and a
consequent excrescence.  This has been ascribed to the puncture of an
insect, and the excrescence often contains a small worm.  But this is
not always the fact; and it may justly be questioned, whether the puncture of any insect would produce such an effect.  It is most probably a
disease, for which no effectual remedy has yet been discovered.  But
the most favorable position for this tree, according to my observation,
is in a moist, strong soil, and in the coldest situation that can be found,
as on the north side of a building or hedge.  Cherries of all kinds may
be cultivated to advantage.

To the cultivation of the more rare and delicious fruits, there is an
objection, arising out of the moral state of society, which ought not to
pass unnoticed.  Many persons neglect to plant some of the best kinds
of fruit-trees, and, in some instances, such trees have been hewn down,
because the fruit is subject to be stolen.  The fact can not be denied;
and it is evidence of a defect of morals reproachful to the character of
the country.  Apples are in such abundance, that the taking of a few,
from a neighbor's orchard, without his knowledge or consent, has not
been treated as theft.  This indulgence has perhaps contributed to induce the practice of plundering gardens and orchards of more rare, and
on account of their scarcity, more valued fruits.  But surely men, in a
Christian country, must know, and are able to make their children and
apprentices understand, that in the eye of reason and of law, and in the
view of Heaven, it is as really the crime of theft, to take fruit from another's inclosure, without his consent, as to take money from his chest.
If the youth of this country do not thus understand the fact, it is important that the instructions of the desk, the discipline of parents and guardians, and the penalties of law, should be combined, to impress upon
their minds, this salutary lesson of morality.

Another object, interesting to the community, and especially to the agriculturist, is the improvement of domestic animals. This is to be effected, not so much, I apprehend, by importing and raising varieties of a larger size, as by selecting for propagation those of the best shape and qualities, from the species we now possess, and by giving them all the perfection of which they are susceptible. Among individuals of the same species, there is a great difference in the form and qualities which render them profitable to the owner; both in the males for labor, in the females for dairy, and in both for slaughter. The improvement of domestic animals of all kinds must depend chiefly on selecting the best of the species for propagation, and in supplying them with a sufficiency of good fodder, and suitable shelter from inclemencies of the weather. And it deserves to be well considered, whether it is not ill-timed economy to turn off young cattle with cold lodgings in winter, and a scanty supply of coarse fodder. When young animals have been stinted in their food for two or three years, and their growth checked, when it should be most rapid and vigorous, is it rational to suppose that better feeding will afterward give to them their full expansion of body and strength of limbs? If the expense of good feeding is somewhat greater, will not the owner be amply repaid in the increased value of the animals? And what is the difference in the taxes paid on cattle of a poor quality, and on those of more value, and of a higher price in the market?

The horses generally used in this part of New England are of an inferior breed, and of low price; but probably for use on farms, they are preferable to those of a larger size and more beauty, which can hardly be supposed to perform services equal to the additional price of purchase, and expense of keeping. But it deserves to be considered, whether for the saddle, for the carriage and for market, it would not be eligible to introduce and encourage the propagation of a handsomer breed.

Of sheep and swine we probably possess the best species; but doubtless improvements may be made in the mode of feeding and fattening them with the least expense.

In regard to the importance of manufactures, the encouragement of which is one object of this association, there can be only one opinion. Every country should, as far as possible, not only produce the materials of the clothing, utensils and furniture consumed by its inhabitants, but should work those materials into the form required for use. No nation should depend on foreign countries for essential articles; as supplies of such articles are liable to be interrupted in time of war; and as they draw from the country, the profits of its agriculture. The more completely a country is supplied with every article of consumption, by the labor of its own citizens, the more independent it must be, and the more sources of wealth does it retain in its own power. In many respects, the present state of our manufactures is highly gratifying; and in particular with respect to the articles of prime use and necessity made in families. In New England, most of the clothes of coarse fabric are manufactured in families, and chiefly by the industry of females, the value of whose labor, in this respect, is not easily estimated. To such an extent are these domestic manufactures carried,

that in some towns, and probably in many, not a piece of coarse foreign
cloth is consumed by the inhabitants.   Nor are these domestic labors
limited to the manufacture of cloths for wearing apparel ; they extend
to many other articles.

In the manufacture of the finer cloths, our country is making rapid
advances ; and already such cloths enter advantageously into competition with superfine imported cloths.   The manufacture of cotton, which,
at the close of the late war, suffered extreme depression, is again revi-
ving, but under many disadvantages.   Many of the most necessary
utensils and articles of clothing and furniture, are made, in New England, not only for home consumption, but for exportation ; such as hats,
shoes, saddlery and cabinet-work.   We are supplied also from our own
manufactories with axes, hoes, sythes and various castings ; and it may
be well to consider, whether the manufacture of saws, screws, cutlery
and some other utensils of iron, might not be introduced or extended
by due encouragement.   On this subject, a detail of particulars can not
be expected in this address ; but I will take the liberty to offer a few
remarks on the obstacles that impede the progress of manufactures in
the United States.

It may be admitted, without an improper indulgence of national vanity, that our citizens are not deficient in ingenuity or dexterity ; and skill,
in any kind of work, they may and will acquire, whenever suitable encouragement is offered to call their ingenuity into exercise.   Most of
the raw materials, which enter into the manufacture of essential articles, are produced or found in our own country, and others are within
our reach.   Under these advantages, however, our manufacturing establishments have to contend with a serious obstacle in the high price of
labor, more especially in the making of articles of fine texture.   The
use of machinery, and the employment of females and children, supply,
in part, a remedy for this evil ; and government lends its aid by protecting duties.   Still, it must be difficult for a country, in which a dollar will
purchase only one or two days' labor, to sustain a competition in manufactures, with a country in which a dollar will purchase four, five, or
six days' labor.   The great obstacle, then, to the success of manufactures in the United States, is the depreciated value of money—an evil
which also materially affects our commerce.

Since the American revolution money has lost nearly half its former
value.   In the ordinary intercourse of our citizens with each other, this
evil is less sensibly felt ; for the prices of provision and labor have
advanced nearly in the same proportion.   When the farmer gives to
the laborer a bushel of rye for a day's work, it makes no difference to
the parties whether the *nominal* value of the rye and the labor is fifty
cents or a dollar—the *real* value is the same in both cases.   The advance of *price* is no evidence of an advance in *value ;* and if rye were
to rise to ten dollars a bushel, and labor to ten dollars a day, the relative condition of the farmer and the laborer would be the same—neither party would gain or loose by the advance.   But the case is different
with the exporting merchant and manufacturer, who send their produce
or wares to countries in which silver and gold have not suffered a depreciation.   The merchant gives more than he formerly did for the
produce of this country, but he obtains no higher prices for it abroad.

The manufacturer pays a higher price for labor and provisions at home, but his wares bring no higher prices in foreign markets. In this case, the depreciation of money in our country is a clear deduction from the profits of our commerce. So in regard to articles manufactured for home consumption, the manufacturer can make no profit, unless he can afford his wares at as low prices as those of imported wares of a like kind—and this can not always be done, on account of the high prices of labor and provisions in this country.

The principal source of this evil is to be sought in the number of our banking institutions, and the amount of notes which they issue. In the history of commerce, perhaps no parallel instance can be found, of such unceasing demands for the privilege of banking, and of such improvident compliances with these demands, without any regard to the pernicious effects of an undue augmentation of the circulating medium, as have been witnessed in the United States. Upon an application for a new banking corporation, the only question with legislatures seems to be, whether it will accommodate the petitioners. The far more important questions, whether the money in circulation is not sufficient for the purposes of trade, and whether an augmentation will not depreciate its value, and thus affect existing contracts, as well as the trade and manufactures of the country, appear not to occupy a moment's attention. The injuries resulting from this inattention to political economy, are far more extensive than a superficial view of the subject would lead men to suppose. A salary settled on a clergyman thirty or forty years ago, and then probably no more than sufficient to maintain his family, will now purchase little more than half of the commodities, and especially of our home productions, which it would at the time of the contract. The property of a widow or an orphan, vested in stock thirty years ago, has already lost nearly one half its value. Innumerable losses of this and of similar kinds, always result from a depreciation of the current money of a country. Men are apt to suppose that an increase of *nominal* value is an increase of wealth, which is often a great mistake. The value of money or of estate is determined only by what it will purchase. If five thousand dollars forty years ago would purchase as much labor, and as many of the necessary goods and provisions of life, as ten thousand dollars will now, then the farm which was estimated at five thousand dollars forty years ago, was worth as much as the farm now estimated at ten thousand. The owner of the former was as rich as the owner of the latter. The increased price of lands within the period mentioned, is owing to two causes ; real improvements in agriculture, and a depreciation of money. That part of the value which proceeds from improvements, is an increase of *real* wealth—that which proceeds from depreciation of money, is merely *nominal*.

The present depreciated state of our currency, is one of the greatest political evils now experienced in the United States ; an evil which can be corrected only by more just and enlarged views of the operations of money than the councils of the several states appear at present to possess. But without entering into discussions which pertain to legislation, let individuals and associations of men employ their time and faculties, in devising and executing plans of improvement, in directing and invigorating industry, and augmenting the wealth and resources of the country. In almost every branch of business there is ample room for improvement, and those are the real benefactors of the community, who direct their time and means to multiply the sources of public prosperity.

But let it not be imagined that valuable improvements can be effected in a moment, or without encountering serious obstacles. Those who know the immense power of habit in governing the conduct of the great mass of mankind, will prepare themselves to contend with numerous discouragements. Men are not easily convinced of the errors of their practice ; and when convinced, they will not always surrender their wills to their conviction. Add to this that sloth, negligence, and inattention, often render the progress of improvement extremely slow. The potatoe, a native of America, was first cultivated in Europe. Nearly a century and a half had elapsed, after its discovery, before it was introduced into New England, and probably men are still living who never saw it in their youth. The late Count Rumford was the first to introduce it into Bavaria, and to this day it is not universally cultivated in Europe. Yet beyond a question, this esculent root is one of the most profitable and useful articles which the farmer can raise ; particularly necessary to the peasantry of Europe ; and one of the best temporal blessings which man has received from his Maker.

This is a single instance, selected from a multitude which might be mentioned, of the disposition of men to rest satisfied with their present practice and attainments, and of the reluctance with which they meet every attempt to introduce a change, even for the better. Nor is this disposition confined to unlettered people ; it is often found in men of erudition and science, and serves to continue, from age to age, the most palpable errors in opinions and practice.

But the slow progress of improvement, and the difficulties that attend it, are no good reason why it should not be attempted. The rational powers of men are talents entrusted to them by their Creator for the purpose of use and improvement—and we are not authorized to keep them in a napkin. In regard to improvements in agriculture and the arts, we are to consider that private interest will operate as a stimulus to efforts, and that well directed and persevering efforts will ultimately be crowned with success.

In reviewing the history of the human race, it is melancholy to observe how large a portion of men have devoted their talents and their property to illegitimate purposes. My friends, what have been the principal objects of pursuit among men of wealth and distinction, in every nation and in every period of the world ? In the rude ages of society, tribes of men have almost always been making war upon each other for dominion and plunder. Disdaining the cultivation of the earth, as an employment fit only for women and slaves, they have considered that glory was to be acquired only in the field of battle, and property to be sought in depredations on their neighbors. And whatever modifications may have been introduced into the modes of warfare, by refinement and the union of men in kingdoms and empires, war still wears its savage character. It almost always springs from savage principles—the love of power or glory, and the love of plunder. And what a large proportion of the population of every kingdom and state is constantly employed in manufacturing and using instruments of destruction! What an enormous amount of money is annually appropriated to purchase arms and provision, and to hire men to destroy lives and property—to slaughter, impoverish, subdue or enslave those who are brethren of the same family! Yes, men, rational beings, the offspring of a common father, possessed of the same powers and rights, entitled to the same privileges and blessings, capable of the same enjoyments, and destined to the same end, are often exerting their utmost powers, and wasting their substance, to inflict misery on their own species! Is this the business assigned to man by his Creator?

And what is the state of civil society in peace, and among men not personally engaged in the work of havoc and desolation? Is not the pursuit of pleasure, power, and distinction, the principal employment? And when men have acquired riches, wrung perhaps from the toils and oppression of their fellow men, and are able to riot in luxury, and

> " Roll the thundering chariot o'er the ground,"

to what purposes has their wealth been applied? How large a portion of it has been squandered on the most contemptible sports and the most degrading vices! See a prince, a nobleman, a gentleman—for none but gentlemen are entitled to the privilege—see him mounted on his steed, with a pack of hounds, leaping ditches, and hedges, and five-barred gates, in pursuit of a stag or a hare! Yes, a man, a rational being, and a company of dogs, chasing a little timorous, helpless animal! The hungry savage must seek his food among the wild beasts; but what sort of sport is this for a civilized man?

Go to the cock-pit, and see gentlemen of education and property, spending their time and money in the very rational entertainment of seeing one fowl spur and tear to pieces another. Is this the business of man?

Go to the race-ground, and behold whole counties collected to see which of two horses can run a few feet or a few inches further than the other in a given time, and note the sums of money laid upon the issue of the mighty contest! Is this the business of man, and the proper use of money?

Go to the circus, and behold an immense concourse of rational beings, assembled to see a man ride round in a circle, standing on two horses, or standing on one leg, or leaping upon a horse at full speed! Is this the business of man?

Go to the gaming table; behold a circle of gentlemen, and of ladies too, intensely employed, for hours together, to win money from each other, by dexterity or by fraud—or see the bold adventurer stake his fortune and the subsistence of his family on the cast of a die, or a stroke of the mace! Is this the proper employment of rational beings, and the legitimate use of money?

Then go to the theater, and witness the proud distinction of a player—the bursts of applause bestowed on the man who can most exactly dress and speak and act and laugh and strut like the person he represents—who can best mimick a prince, a fop, or a clown! Is this the proper employment of man?

To complete a view of human folly, go to a bull-baiting—yes, a bull-baiting in a civilized, a Christian country! And what is the entertainment, and who the spectators? Why princes and nobles, gentlemen and ladies, assembled by thousands, to see a rational being tease and fight a bull!

What sort of employments are these for intellectual beings? What is the loss of time and the expense of money, in these diversions? Sufficient perhaps every year to convert a wilderness into a garden, or to Christianize a whole empire of pagans!

My friends, men have wandered from the path of their duty—they have abandoned the employment assigned to them by their Maker. Let men of wealth and distinction resume their proper employment, and instead of leaving the cultivation of the earth to peasants and slaves, let them devote their time and their capital to agriculture; let them enrich their country by their improvements, and dignify the occupation by their influence and example.

The proper business of man is to enlarge the powers of his mind by knowledge, and refine it by the culture of moral habits; to increase the means of subsistence and comfort; to supply the wants and alleviate the distresses of his brethren; to cherish the virtues and restrain the vices of society; to multiply the rational enjoyments of life; to diffuse the means of education, and the blessings of religion; and to extend his benevolence and charities to the whole human family. In a word, the duty, the whole business of man is to yield obedience to his Maker; and just in proportion to that obedience, will be the private happiness, and the public prosperity of a nation.

## CHAPTER XI.

### A LETTER TO THE HONORABLE DANIEL WEBSTER.

(PUBLISHED IN PHILADELPHIA IN 1837.)

*To the Honorable Daniel Webster,—*

SIR—In your public addresses or speeches, and in those of other gentlemen of high political distinction, I have often seen an opinion expressed like this—That *intelligence* and *virtue* are the basis of a republican government, or that intelligence and virtue in the people are necessary to the preservation and support of a republican government. These words, *intelligence* and *virtue*, are very comprehensive in their uses or application, and perhaps too indefinite to furnish the premises for the inference deduced from them. Men may be very intelligent in some departments of literature, arts and science; but very ignorant of branches of learning in other departments. By intelligence, as applicable to political affairs, it may be presumed that those who use the term, intend it to imply a correct knowledge of the constitution and laws of the country, and of the several rights and duties of the citizens.

But, sir, the opinion that intelligence in the people of a country will preserve a republican government, must depend, for its accuracy, on the fact of an intimate, or necessary connection between *knowledge* and *principle.* It must suppose that men who *know* what is right, will *do* what is right: for if this is not the general fact, then intelligence will not preserve a just administration, nor maintain the constitution and laws. But from what evidence can we infer that men who *know* what is right will *do* what is right? In what history of mankind, political or ecclesiastical, are the facts recorded, which authorize the presumption, much less the belief, that correct action will proceed from correct knowledge? Such an effect would imply the absence of all depravity in the hearts of men; a supposition which not only revelation, but all history forbids us to admit.

Let me ask, sir, whether the Greeks, and particularly the Athenians, were not an intelligent people? Were they not intelligent when they banished the ablest statesmen and generals, and the purest patriots of their state? Was their intelligence sufficient to insure, at all times, a just administration of the laws? In short, if intelligence could preserve a republic, why were not the Grecian republics preserved?

Then let us turn our attention to the Roman state. Were not Sylla and Marius intelligent men, when they rent the commonwealth with faction, and deluged Rome with blood? Were not Cæsar and Anthony and Lepidus, and Crassus and Brutus and Octavianus, intelligent men? Did not the Roman commonwealth fall into ruins in the most enlightened period of its existence? And were not the immediate instruments of its overthrow some of the most intelligent men that the pagan world has produced?

Then look at France during the revolution, when there was no settled government to control reason.  Were not the leading men of the parties intelligent men ?—men who cut off the heads of their opponents, with as little ceremony as they would tread a worm under their feet, and for the *sake of liberty*.  When one party was crushed, the others cried out, the *republic or liberty is safe*.  When another party fell under the guillotin, then the triumphant party shouted, *liberty is safe*. But after all, the republic was *not* saved ; and all parties at last were glad to find peace and security under a throne.

Intelligence alone then has not yet saved any republic.  But intelligence, it is said, must be accompanied with *virtue*, and these united are to give duration to a republic.

Now, sir, what is this *virtue ?* what does it mean in the sentiment or opinion above cited ?  What did Montesquieu intend by *virtue*, when he wrote about its influence in preserving a republic ?—(Spirit of Laws, *passim.*)

The virtue of a Roman citizen consisted in personal bravery, and in devotion to the defense and extent of the commonwealth.  In particular men there existed a strong sense of right or political duty, which may take rank as a moral virtue.  But such instances were rare, and most rare in the decline of the commonwealth, when the citizens were most intelligent.  But in general, the virtue of the Romans was a passionate attachment to the commonwealth, for the grandeur of which they fought and conquered, till they had brought the civilized world to the feet of the republic.  This *virtue* extended the dominion, but did not secure the existence of the republic.

If by *virtue* is intended the observance of the common social duties, this may proceed from a respect for custom, and a regard to reputation ; and either, with or without better principles, is a useful practice.

But such virtue as this will not save a republic, unless based on better principles than a regard to custom or to reputation.  The reason is obvious ; such morality will often, not to say generally, yield to selfishness ; that is, to the ambition of obtaining power and wealth.  When strongly tempted by private interest, men often find the means of enlisting reason in its service ; and invent excuses for disregarding the *public good*, which *ought* to be, and for the preservation of republican government *must be*, the ruling motive of citizens.

The *virtue* which is necessary to preserve a just administration and render a government stable, is *Christian virtue*, which consists in the uniform practice of moral and religious duties, in conformity with the laws both of God and man.  This virtue must be based on a reverence for the authority of God, which shall counteract and control ambition and selfish views, and subject them to the precepts of divine authority. The effect of such a virtue would be, to bring the citizens of a state to vote and act for the *good of the state*, whether that should coincide with their private interest or not.  But when or where has this virtue been possessed by all the citizens, or even by a majority of the citizens of a state ?  History does not authorize us to believe that such virtue has ever existed in the body of citizens in any community ; or to presume that such a community will ever exist.

If such virtue as this can be introduced into a community, the opinion that intelligence and virtue will preserve a republic, may be well founded. But with respect to intelligence, it may be questioned whether such a portion of it can be imparted to the mass of citizens as will secure the public from the most injurious, if not fatal, mistakes. And as to genuine virtue, based on divine authority, are we authorized to expect this to exist, unless in a millennial state?

But if a correct understanding of the public interest would, in any case, secure a pure administration, under wise and impartial rulers, how is it possible to prevent deception and mistake among the people? The press must be free, and if free, it will often be used as the instrument of deception. How is this evil to be prevented? If it can not be prevented, then the use of intelligence is defeated.

It appears to me, sir, that there are radical errors in the opinions of our citizens in regard to the principles on which a republican government is to be founded, and the means by which it is to be supported. The constitutions of government in the United States commence with a declaration of certain abstract principles, or general and indefinite propositions; as that all men are *born free and equal*, or all men *are created equal*. But as universal propositions, can they be true? In what sense are men *born free?* If they are born under a despotic government, they are not born *free*. But in any government, children are born, subject to the control of their parents, and this by the express ordinance of the Creator. No man will question the right or the expedience of parental government; it is for the benefit of the child that he should *not* be free, till he has acquired strength to procure his own subsistence, and knowledge or wisdom to direct his voluntary actions.

The general proposition then, that *all* men are *born free*, is the reverse of the truth, for *no person is born free*, in the general acceptation of the word *free*.

In what sense then are men born *equal?* Is it true that all men are furnished with equal force of constitution, or physical strength? Is it true that all men are endowed by the Creator with equal intellectual powers? No person will contend for an affirmative answer to these questions. Men are not formed with equal powers of body or mind; and if they were, the race would be an exception from all other works of the Creator, in which a prominent feature is diversities without end, even in the same genus and species.

Equally indefinite is the proposition, that all men are entitled to the enjoyment of *life* and *liberty*. They are entitled to life, unless it has been forfeited; but even life is to be enjoyed, upon the conditions prescribed by law, for the enjoyment of life must be in consistency only with the public safety. The enjoyment of liberty is subject to a like restriction. No society can exist without restricting the liberty of every member by the laws or will of the community; for it is a first principle of the social state, that every member must so use his own liberty, as not to injure or impair the rights of another.

It would seem then to be clearly proved, that the general principles assumed by the framers of our government, are too indefinite to be the basis of constitutional provision. The natural freedom of men must be restrained by regulations which are essential to the public safety,

and to that of every individual. This freedom is *civil* liberty, that is,
the liberty which the law permits each citizen to enjoy. Even in a
savage state, the liberty of each individual must be under some restraint, or no individual can be safe.

The principle then which must be the basis of a good constitution, is,
that every member of the community or state is entitled to all the freedom which the laws permit, and which is compatible with the public
safety. This is the right of every citizen ; and in the possession of this
right, every man is *equal*.

It is believed, however, that the loose, undefined sense in which the
words *free* and *equal* are used in some of the American constitutions,
has been and will be a source of immense evil to this country. Illiterate men will mistake the just limitation of the words, and unprincipled
men will give them a latitude of construction incompatible with the
peace of society.

There is, in my apprehension, a common mistake in this country, in
regard to the nature of democratic and republican governments. It
seems to be held as a truth not to be questioned, that a republican government is of course a *free* government, or a government which, by
the very fact that it springs from the people, will certainly secure to
the citizens the enjoyment of their rights.

That a proper democracy, in which the whole body of citizens constitute the legislature, is a turbulent government, is a fact too well
established by historical evidence to be disputed. But it seems to be
generally understood, that a government by representatives of the people, is not subject to the same evil ; and that such a government will
not abuse its powers and oppress the people. In short, it is generally
believed that, in a republic, liberty is safe.

One reason for this general belief may be, that the history of the
nations in the old world, and particularly in Asia, has, from time immemorial, exhibited monarchs as tyrants. It seems to be taken for
granted that all monarchies, all kingly governments, are tyrannies.

This, as a general fact in past ages, may be admitted. But connected with this subject, there are some popular errors which ought to
be corrected.

1. The tyranny of a monarch depends on his disposition. If one
man has the sole power of making laws, the government is arbitrary in
form, but the administration of it may be mild or tyrannical, at the
pleasure of the prince. And it often happens that a monarch administers the government in such a manner as to do equal justice, and
secure to all his subjects their rights or all the liberty which they desire.

2. In modern Europe, in nations civilized, and in which a great portion of the citizens are educated men, cultivating arts and science, and
carrying on trade and manufactures, monarchs can not exercise tyrannical power. In such nations, the public sense of rights, to which the
citizens are entitled, restrains kings from acts of oppression. This
improved state of society, which began with the revival of learning,
arts and commerce, in the thirteenth or fourteenth century, for ever
precludes the possibility of the establishment and continuance of tyrannical governments in the western portion of Europe. Men, understanding the principles of freedom, and possessing property, can not be reduced to the vassalage of former ages.

3. The kingdoms of France and England are not, in the true sense of the word, *monarchies*. Their governments are a mixture or union of aristocracy and republicanism. The kings are hereditary executive magistrates, but they have not the power to make a single law, and of course can not exercise arbitrary government over the citizens. In this respect, the kings are as essentially restrained from acts of tyranny, as the president of the United States. The house of peers is an aristocratical body, possessing powers of government by virtue of title or rank ; but the commons, elected by the people, are a republican body. These houses are complete checks upon each other, by which the rights of both are secured ; and both are a complete check upon the king.

Now the great source of mistake in this country is, that monarchies have generally been characterized by arbitrary and oppressive government ; and particularly in rude ages and uncivilized countries, where the mass of the population have had neither learning nor property. This fact being well known, and incessantly proclaimed by our patriotic conductors of the revolution, has produced in the minds of American citizens, an extreme odium against all monarchies, leading them to make royal government and tyranny synonymous terms, and impressing the belief or opinion, that a sure remedy and the only remedy for the evil, is to be found in a republican form of government.

Both these opinions, carried to the extent, are incorrect. The governments in the civilized parts of Europe, with kings at the head of them, are not tyrannies. So far from it, that the citizens in those countries consider themselves as free as they wish to be, and perfectly well protected in their rights. I leave out of this representation the oppression which the people of England suffer from old establishments and monopolies, which had their origin in ages of ignorance ; for these are, in many cases, extremely oppressive. But to the form of the government, to royalty, and to the general administration of the laws, the people have no objection. On the other hand, they are strongly attached to them, and would by no means exchange the form of the government for any other.

Equally incorrect is the opinion, that a republican government is of course a free government, or one that of course will secure to the citizens all their just rights. So far is this from being true, that democracies and republics may be, and have often been, as tyrannical as monarchies.

The principle that our statesmen have universally adopted and proclaimed, that the people in a state or community are the only legitimate source of power, is just ; all government ought to have its origin in the will of those who are to be governed. But in the application of this principle, our theorists and statesmen have overlooked, or not sufficiently regarded one important fact, that in framing a constitution, it is as necessary to guard against the *tyranny of the people*, as it is to guard against the *tyranny of kings and nobles*.

How could those distinguished men overlook the fact, that *all* men are made with like passions ; that men of all classes, whether kings, nobles, priests, or working men, have the same love of power and property, the same ambition, the same selfishness, the same jealousies ;

in short, the same disposition to rise above their fellows, by advancement in wealth and power, and the same depravity or want of good principles to control their passions ?   All history testifies that the people, when they possess uncontrolled power, often use that power as tyrannically as kings and nobles.   Their tyranny, if not as steady, is usually more violent and inexorable than that of kings, as their passions are under less restraint from honor, education, or responsibility, and exasperated or stimulated by numbers.

From an inattention to this truth, that all men would be kings if they could, and tyrants if they durst, our patriotic fathers, while they have fortified the constitution against the introduction of kings and nobles, have not sufficiently guarded it against an abuse of power by the people.   Hence the frequent outbreakings of popular tyranny ; the people, or portions of them, rising in multitudes, above all law, and violating the rights of property, and personal safety.

In connection with this subject, we may advert to a remarkable example of the influence of names or words, on the mass of people who have not discriminating or just views of men, and of the nature and tendency of political measures.   The use of the word *republican* has, by its own magic, revolutionized public sentiment in this country.   So popular is a republican government in this country, that the man who aims at office, or the printer who aims at extensive patronage, takes the name of a *republican*, as a sure passport to his object.   This practice proceeds in general from honest views ; but in the demagogue, it is often assumed to cover the most dangerous designs.   The name, however, has its effect, and an artful popular man may, with this passport, travel to a throne, before the mass of a nation discover his views. Among a people jealous of power, the only way by which an ambitious man can gain *superior* and *unequal* power, is to make the people believe him to be the friend of *equal* rights and *equal* power.

It is admitted, on all hands, that the senate in the American constitutions, was designed not only to give to legislative proceedings a more full discussion of important questions, but to check and control any violent, rash, and precipitate measures of the more numerous branch of the legislature.   This purpose it has often accomplished.   But there appears to be a defect in the mode of constituting this body, which may frustrate the design.   This defect is in the election of senators by the same constituents as the representatives in the other branch.   Now, the way to render the senate an inefficient check upon the house of representatives, is to bring the body of constituents to have the same views of public men and measures, and they will elect men of similar views to both houses.   In this case, there is no check of one house upon the other.   In many cases of legislation, this would be no evil. But in times of party violence, the want of this check, or the loss of the proper balance in the constitution, may endanger the very existence of the government ; or when this consequence does not follow, it may derange the operations of the government, by giving to the executive an improper exercise of power, and utterly defeating the purposes of impeachment.

The most obvious method of preserving a proper balance in the constitution, and creating an effectual check of one branch upon the other, is to place the election of the two branches in different hands.   In this country, where there are no distinct orders or ranks of men, and none can be admitted, this constitution of the two houses by different electors, may be the only mode of securing the separate independent action of the two branches.

The people of the United States do not consist of two distinct orders of men, nobles and commonalty, as is the case in England.   But the distinction of rich and poor does exist, and must always exist ;  no human power or device can prevent it.   This distinction produces jealousies, different interests and rivalship, which, if not effectually controlled by the government, may agitate the state or even overthrow it.   Both classes of citizens are to be protected in their rights, and each class must have power to defend its own rights against the invasions of the other.   The poorer class must be as effectually secured against the powers of the rich, as the rich are against the turbulence of the populace.   How this object is to be effected in this country, where there is no distinction of rank, is a problem not easily solved.   But it *must* be solved ;  the two classes must be equally secured in their rights, and each have a complete check upon every attempt of the other to invade its rights ;  or there can be neither harmony nor durable tranquillity in the state.

This great object of making each class of men so independent of the other in government, as to allay jealousy and party strife, and settle every question of rivalship by the peaceable process of discussion and voting, must be accomplished by constitutional provisions.   It must not be left for each party to seek its share of power and influence by intrigue, corruption, or the influence of the press.   This mode will excite perpetual feuds, engender evil passions, and incessantly agitate the public mind.   The mode of preventing all such strife and agitation, must be by definite constitutional provisions.

To effect this object, the most simple process would be to separate the electors into two classes, the qualifications of one of which shall be superior age, and the possession of a certain amount of property ; while the other class of voters shall comprehend those who have not the same qualifications.   These two classes may be independent of each other in elections, and their representatives compose different houses, each with a negative upon the acts of the other.

Some provision of this kind will probably be found indispensable to the due protection of the rights of the different classes of citizens ; and universal suffrage, without some such provision, will destroy that equality of rights which our constitution was intended to maintain.

To understand the operation of universal suffrage, we must consider that there are two kinds of rights to be secured by government—the *rights of person* and the *rights of property*.   The *rights of person* are *equal*, in all classes of men.   The protection of the person of the poor man is of as high a nature, and of as much importance in a code of laws, as the protection of the person of the rich man ; and the one must be as well guarded by the constitution and laws as the other.   In this respect, both classes of men have an equal interest in the government.

Not so with regard to the rights of property. The man who has half a million dollars in property, and pays five hundred or a thousand dollars annually to support the government and laws which *protect the poor man* as well as the rich, has a much higher interest in the government, than the man who has little or no property, and pays *nothing for the protection of his own person* and the property of others. Without some provision recognizing this distinction, and giving to men of property the means of securing it, and regulating the disposal of it, without being wholly subject to the power of those who have little or no property, universal suffrage may become the instrument of injustice to the most enormous extent. What can be more absurd and more inconsistent with a republican government, whose principle is the security of *equal rights*, than that the owners of property should not have the right to govern it ; or that those who have no property or the least share of it, should have the power to control the property of others! A constitution based on such a principle, must sooner or later produce consequences fatal to just rights. And it is of no use to the poor: for in the protection of *personal rights* all men have an equal interest, and the rich have the same motives to protect the rights of the poor, as they have to protect their own. But it is otherwise with regard to the *rights of property*, which the poor have not the same motives to protect, as those have who own it; and nineteen twentieths of the laws of all commercial states respect property.

The constitution of the executive department of government involves questions of the highest concern.

From the principle that the people or great body of citizens in a free state are the sources of all legitimate power in government, it is understood that in them resides the right of selecting, not only the men who mature the laws, but the men who are to execute them. The government of some of the New England colonies, from their first institution, recognized this right, and it is now recognized in the constitution of the United States, as also by all the state constitutions.

On the assumed principle, that the electors in a great nation *can know* and will *do* what is right or expedient in every case of exercising the elective franchise, this provision in a republican government is just and wise. But the premises here supposed have not been found to exist in all the experiments of elective governments; and the factions which have been generated by competitions for the high office of chief magistrate, have produced such tremendous evils, that most nations have a settled conviction that it is better to trust to hereditary succession for a chief magistrate, than to a popular election. The history of Poland furnishes valuable materials for judging correctly on this subject.

The people of this country are making the experiment of electing their chief magistrates and most of their executive officers. The result of this experiment is not finally determined; and prudence requires that we should not confidently predict what the issue will be.

In the mean time, it may not be improper to suggest some thoughts on the subject, with a view to call public attention to the evils which exist, and to the remedy.

The first suggestion is, that in a country of such extent as the United States, it is difficult, not to say impracticable, for the whole body of electors to have a sufficient knowledge of the candidates to form an accurate estimate of their respective characters, and be enabled to select the most suitable person.  The difficulty is increased tenfold, by the representations given of their characters by the friends and the opposers of the different candidates, through the medium of the press.

The second suggestion is, that a great mass of people are and always must be very incompetent judges of the qualifications necessary for the chief magistrate of a great nation.  The populace are often influenced by the splendid achievements more than by the solid talents of the candidates ; yet a man may gain a great victory on land or water, without the most ordinary qualifications for a chief magistrate.

The third suggestion is, that when party spirit is violent, the people imbibe such strong prejudices as to disqualify them for exercising a temperate, unbiassed judgment.

There is a great defect in the constitution of the United States, which, if permitted to exist, will ultimately shake the government to its center.  This defect is, the want of some effectual provision to prevent candidates from seeking the office of chief magistrate by corrupt and illegal means.  So long as the President has the bestowment of most of the offices, and the power of removal from office, at pleasure, the most daring and unprincipled intriguer for the office has the best chance of success.  It is hardly to be conceived how wide the avenues of corruption and undue influence are laid open by the possession of these powers.  These avenues must be closed, or the most important feature in a republican government, the right of election, will be defaced, annihilated, or converted into an instrument of ruin.

There is perhaps no mistake as to the proper mode of constituting and maintaining a republic, which is so menacing to the purity and stability of our institutions, as that of vesting the right of electing executive and judicial officers in the people ; and the more frequent the elections, the more dangerous will be the exercise of this right.  There appears to be no method of weakening the execution of the laws, so effectual, as to make executive and judicial officers dependent for their offices on annual elections by the people.  When a law is popular, and all men concur in the propriety of its execution, the law will be executed.  The murderer, the robber, and the thief will be punished, by universal consent.  But when a law bears hard upon any portion of citizens, the officers will often wink at violations rather than risk the loss of their re-election.  If there are exceptions to this remark, yet it will generally prove to be true.

The independence of the judiciary has been a theme of eulogy ever since it was secured to the judges of the higher courts in Great Britain.  It is said to have been established with a view to secure impartial decisions, in opposition to the influence of the crown.  Be it so ; but it is equally necessary to raise the judges above the influence of the citizens in a republican government.  It is even more necessary, as the danger of losing the office by offending the electors, occurs more frequently and steadily in a government like ours, than the danger of losing the office in Great Britain does by offending the king.  And it is surprising that the obvious good effects of this independence in judges, in securing unbiased decisions, have not induced our legislators to extend the same independence to inferior courts, and to many executive officers.

It is a mistake, and a most mischievous one, to suppose that annual or frequent elections are the proper correctives of mal-administration in judges and executive officers. The proper correctives are impeachment or other punishment; not the popular odium against an officer which may be excited without just cause, and even by the most meritorious acts of the officer in the faithful discharge of his duty.

The proper rule in our governments appears to be this. The citizens composing the state, being the sources of power, should be the constituents of the legislature ; but the legislature, or a council designated for the purpose, should be the appointing power, and also the impeaching or punishing power. This is the fact now in regard to many officers in our state governments. The appointing power should not be invested in a single magistrate elected by the people, unless some provision can be made to restrain him effectually from using the power to secure his election. And how is this to be done ?

The office of president is a prize of too much magnitude not to excite perpetual dissensions ; and if the contentions for the office of chief magistrate, do not ultimately overthrow our constitution, it will be a miracle. It is desirable, however, that the experiment should be fully tried, to determine whether our government, with this feature, can be rendered permanent.

A mode of electing the president *may* be devised which shall preclude the possibility of his using undue influence to obtain the office. But the practicability of introducing such a mode is questionable.

There are errors of opinion on the subject of republican government, so long cherished, and so interwoven with the habits of thinking among our citizens, that reasoning will not remove or correct them. The opinion that the rich are the enemies and oppressors of the poor, industriously propagated by designing men for their selfish purposes; and the opinion that all incorporated companies are aristocratic in their tendency, are among the false and most pernicious doctrines that ever cursed a nation.*

Equally injurious to the public interest is the attempt to excite jealousies against learning and the seminaries in which young men are to be qualified for the professions and for the higher offices of govern-

---

* It is often said, by intelligent men, too, that the rich capitalists are drones in society, living on the industry of the working bees. How can men utter such sentiments ?

In this country, as a general fact, the rich are the men who gain their property by their own active diligence, economy, and good judgment, or it has been gained by these virtues of their ancestors. Are reproach and disgrace to be the reward of these virtues ?

But the rich do *not* live on the labors of the poor; they live on the fruits of their own industry and good management, or those of their ancestors. More than this; the rich are the men who furnish the means of great public improvements, either by their own investments, or by loans to government. Such means can not be furnished by the poor.

But further, the rich are the *support* of the poor, by giving them employment, which they can not otherwise obtain. The rich and the poor are, in a great degree, dependent on each other; and the most direct mode of distressing the poor, is first to destroy the business and the prosperity of the rich.

ment. This war against superior attainments in science, and against large possessions of property, is a most suicidal attempt to destroy the dignity of the state, degrade our public character, and check the spirit of improvement. The effect is, to raise to the higher offices, men wholly incompetent to discharge their duties with honor and advantage. To these dispositions we may ascribe the derangement of our financial concerns, and the disturbance of the usual course of business, producing unparalleled distresses in the community. The extensive and complicated operations of finance, in a great commercial nation, can be managed only by men of long practical experience and observation. Men of narrow views, scanty information, and strong prejudices, can not regulate commerce and finance. Very few of our public characters are competent to this task.

Another most pernicious opinion prevails, that the legislator is to follow the wishes of his particular constituents, called the *people*. This opinion, reduced to practice, changes the legislator into a mere agent or attorney of the district in which he is elected. This is to invert the whole order of things in legislation. The man who is chosen to the legislature by a city, town, or county, is not elected to make laws for that particular district, but for the whole state. He then becomes the representative of the state, and is bound by his duty and his oath, to act for the interests of the whole state. He is not to be governed by the wishes or opinions of a particular district, but by a view of all the interests of the several parts of the state. Probably no rule of public duty is more frequently violated than this.

In addition to this consideration, it must be observed, that in most cases, a man's constituents in a particular district, have not the means of forming correct opinions, and are as likely to be wrong as right. Examples are continually presented to us of candidates for election pledging themselves if elected to vote for or against a particular measure, when the opinions of their constituents are mere prejudices, instilled into their minds by false reasoning and misrepresentations, and the measures they expect their representative to advocate, operate directly against their own interest.

This practice of looking to the *people* for direction destroys the independence of the representative, and must often reduce him to a mere machine, obliging him to act in direct opposition to his own views of what is right and expedient.

The object of assembling representatives from all parts of a state, is to collect a knowledge of all the interests of the whole community ; to unite the counsels of intelligent men, and from the concentrated wisdom of the whole, to adopt measures which shall promote the general welfare. The practice of taking the opinions or wishes of a particular part of the state, as the binding rule of action, may and often does defeat the object of collecting the wisdom of the whole. It is an inversion of the proper order of legislation, in which wisdom should be drawn from the collected views of the whole state, and not from the partial views of a portion.*

* The doctrine of instructions seems to spring from an opinion, that a delegate to Congress or to any legislative body, is the representative only of his immediate constituents. This is a great error. A delegate to Congress, chosen in Maine,

Another very common error is, to consider offices as created for the benefit of individuals, rather than for the state. From this mistake proceeds the demand of rotation in office. In this particular men do not make an important, but just distinction, between legislative offices and offices in the other departments of government. Legislators may be changed frequently, without inconvenience or prejudice to the public. It is not necessary nor expedient to change every year, for experience in legislation is highly useful. But a part of the legislative body may be changed every year, often to advantage.

But to subject executive, ministerial, and judicial offices to frequent changes, for the sake of distributing the salaries and emoluments among numbers, is a most injurious practice. It often displaces officers who are dependent on the salaries or fees for the support of their families, and who are thus deprived of means of living, when there is no pretense of unfaithfulness, and when the incumbent is better qualified to discharge the duties of the office than any other man.

But this demand of rotation in executive offices is fruitful of evils to the community. It promotes that scrambling for office, in which all the worst passions of men are called into action; in which characters are vilified, neighborhoods disturbed, and the harmony of society is violated.

It is for the peace of society, for the interest of the incumbents in office, and for the good of the community, that all executive and judicial officers should hold their offices during good behavior. No man should be removed from office, merely to make a vacancy for another man. It is a species of injustice to faithful officers, which ought to be reprobated by every good citizen.

Much less ought faithful officers to be removed on account of their political opinions. The practice of constraining men to vote for a particular candidate, under the penalty of losing his means of subsistence, is one of the wickedest and meanest practices that ever disgraced a representative government. It is intolerance, as detestable in principle as the punishment of the rack, to compel men to support a religious establishment. It is to compel men to violate their consciences, and assume the garb of hypocrites. It is a practice that destroys the independence of citizens, and actually makes them the slaves of a

---

whether senator or representative, is, in the enactment of laws, as much the representative of Ohio or Georgia as he is of Maine. He is supposed to bring into the national council a knowledge of the particular interests of Maine, for communicating the proper information to the council; every delegate from the several states does the same; but in the determination of the mind respecting the proper vote to be given on any proposed measure, every delegate is bound to take into consideration the interests of every state, and to determine his vote by a regard to the general interest. If he is governed solely by a regard to the interests of his particular constituents, or by their instructions, when these are at variance with the general interest, he violates his duty and the spirit of the constitution.

Equally erroneous is the practice of *pledges*, by which a man promises to vote for a particular measure, in order to secure his election. This practice obliges a man to do, what he has no right to do, and what his constituents would have no right to do, were they to go to the legislature in person; that is, form a decision on a question of public interest, before he enters the council, where alone the decision should be formed. It is a practice that requires a judgment before the trial. These errors produce all manner of injustice and confusion in legislation.

party. And it is one of the most extraordinary instances of self-deception, which is exhibited in human life, that men, professing to be the warmest friends of a republican government, and of equal rights, should subject their fellow citizens to this species of injustice, and triumph in the practice.

The doctrine that the *spoils belong to the victors*, originated in savagism. The original state of savages is a state of war for plunder, and the ancient barbarians of the north of Europe avowed the object for which they invaded more civilized nations. " Quum illi se in armis jus ferre, et omnia fortium virorum esse, ferociter dicerent."—(Livy, 5, 36.) The Gauls declared that they bore right on the point of their swords, and that every thing belongs to the brave.

Now what is the difference in principle between the Gauls who fought to rob their enemies of their cattle and their lands, and a political party that contends by all means, moral and immoral, for victory in election, to strip their opposers, and engross all the emoluments of the government? And how can men claim to be republicans, who perpetually struggle to deprive their opposers of the equal benefits of government, and engross the whole for themselves and their adherents? A practice of this kind is a species of tyranny, which tarnishes the honor of the state, corrupts the citizens, and agitates the community with endless contentions and animosity.

But other principles of a still more alarming tendency begin to prevail. One is, that there can be no such thing as *vested rights*, but that all grants of a legislature may be revoked by a subsequent legislature at pleasure.

This principle seems to have had its origin in the opinions of Mr. Jefferson, which are found in his published letters.—(See Vol. III, pp. 27, 426, and Vol. IV, pp. 196, 275, 396.)

The general principle adopted by Mr. Jefferson is that *the earth belongs in usufruct to the living ;* that the dead have neither power nor rights over it ; that no man can by natural right oblige the lands he occupied, or the persons who succeeded him in that ocupation, to the payment of debts contracted by him, for if he could, he might, during his own life, eat up the usufruct of the lands for several generations to come, and then the lands would belong to the dead, and not to the living ; that what is true of every member of the society individually, is true of them all collectively ; since the rights of the whole can be no more than the sum of the rights of the individuals ; that each generation may be considered as a distinct nation, with a right, by the will of its majority, to bind themselves, but none to bind the succeeding generation ; that the period of a generation is thirty four years ; that a majority of a generation therefore will be dead at the end of eighteen years and eight months ; and that at nineteen years from the date of a contract, the majority of contractors (the generation) are dead and their contract with them. Mr. Jefferson then supposes a case in which a majority of a generation borrow a sum of money equal to the fee simple value of a state, and consume it in eating, drinking or quarreling and fighting. From this he infers, that in nineteen years, when the majority are dead, there is an end of the debt.

This theory seems to have been suggested by a consideration of the evil of an enormous national debt, like that of Great Britain; and the alarm which the writer felt, lest the United States should be involved in a like calamity. At any rate, it is the most extraordinary instance of false premises and fallacious reasoning that ever entered the head of an enthusiast.

What is a generation? A multitude of individuals, old and young, unconnected by any legal or political tie which can constitute them a person in law, or a corporation, and of course incapable of contracting debts or expending money, as a body; in short, incapable of doing any act as a body. A generation can neither make a law nor repeal it.

And what sort of social right is that which an individual has to purchase or sell lands and contract debts, when the mere fact of the death of the majority of the society, an event over which he can have no control, dissolves the contract, and expunges the debt? And how is the fact, at any time, to be ascertained, that a majority are dead? A man who can seriously reason in this manner is worthy of a straight jacket.

But the case of a state or its legislature stands on different principles. A state is a perpetual corporation; all the members of it are united by consent or compact in one body, constituting a person in law, capable of enacting laws, and repealing them, and of contracting and paying debts. This corporation never dies; and the powers it had the last year, or twenty or a hundred years ago, are the same powers which it possesses this year. The act of the state, fifty years ago, is the act of the state this year; and a contract made fifty years ago, binding the state *then*, continues to bind the same state *now*. A change of the members of the corporation makes no change in the being or powers of the body.

These principles, known and established by every government on earth, show in what cases one legislature can repeal or amend the act of a former legislature.

The legislature is the *acting state;* it is the only *form of the state* in which it can act at all. A convention is a legislature elected for a particular purpose; and for that purpose, the framing of a constitution, organizing the several departments of the government, it may be convenient to consider it as a body having powers superior to those of an ordinary legislature, and particularly when the constitution is ratified by the whole body of the citizens, acting as individuals.

But in ordinary cases of legislation, the legislature is the supreme power of the *state* in the only form in which it can act, as a state.

This body then has always the same powers, and the legislature of this year may repeal a law enacted the last year. The reason is, that a *law* is the will of the state, acting on *itself* or *on its own members*, and the body that repeals a law is the same body that enacted it.

But in the case of charters granted or debts contracted, there are *two parties*, the state and the individuals to whom a grant or a promise is made; there are *two wills* concerned, both of which are essential to the act. In this case *one party* has no better right to annul a grant or violate a promise, than one private person has to annul a covenant which he has made with another. Nor does it make any difference, whether the state acts by an ordinary legislature or by a convention, for, in both

cases, the state is the *same party*.    A change of representation no more
alters the *identity* of *the party* to a contract, than a man changing his
coat makes him another man.

It is not unusual for a state, in granting charters, to reserve the right
of repealing the act—a reservation which shows that legislatures have
always considered a grant without such reservation as not repealable.
Indeed all the principles of justice and right, in regard to the contracts
of individuals with each other, are applicable to grants and contracts of
states.

The citizen or citizens who accept a charter, with a clause of reservation as above stated, accept the grant on the condition specified, and
no injury is done by the legislature in taking back the grant.

The doctrine that there can be no vested rights subverts the foundation of society; and a country, adopting and acting on that doctrine,
would soon be depopulated, or compelled to submit to be governed by
a military force.

Many of our public evils have evidently proceeded from false opinions, propagated by some of the founders of our government.   Their
ideas of a free government were not always correct.   Mr. Jefferson,
and many other distinguished men, believed, that men can govern themselves without a master; meaning, probably, without a king.   True,
but they can not govern themselves without a controlling power, a force
of some kind or other that shall be sufficient to keep them in subjection.
If the citizens of a state will voluntarily create such a power, they can
be governed; if they will not, they can not be governed; that is, there
can be no regular administration of just laws without a coercive power.
If men will not have a king, they must have laws and magistrates,
armed with power to bring them all into obedience.   If this is not the
fact, there is no free government.

We hear it constantly proclaimed, that men may be governed by
reason.   Why then have they never before been governed by reason?
Why do not men govern their social actions without law?   Why do not
parties in controversy settle their private disputes by the dictates of
their reason?   Why are courts, consisting of men uninterested in the
controversies of individuals, established to decide upon questions of
private rights?   If men are capable of governing themselves by reason, why have all democratic and republican governments come to ruin?
Why have they not been permanent?

Corruption, it will be said, has ruined them.   True; and this is con-
ceding the whole question.   It is the depravity of man which has ruined
all former free governments, and *which will ruin ours*.

We have already had terrible examples of the manner in which men
govern themselves without a master, that is, not only without a king,
but without a competent force of law.   And it is not a little singular,
that when the citizens of Baltimore had suffered immensely by popular
violence, they had no remedy except to organize a military force of
volunteers for their protection.   What is more worthy of notice, they
gave the command to one who had, all his life, been devoted to democratic principles, and who thus became the *master* of the people, who
were supposed to be able to govern themselves *without a master*.

The truth is, many of our leading political men, during and after the Revolution, were visionary enthusiasts, who had read history without profit, or due application of historical facts. Their ideas were crude, and utterly at variance with the truth of history, and with all experience. They seem to have supposed, that to obtain liberty, and establish a free government, nothing was necessary but to get rid of kings, nobles, and priests; never considering that the same principles of human nature, and the same disposition to tyrannize, exist in all other men, and that the people, when they have the power, will abuse it, and be as tyrannical as kings. This mistake has led to deplorable consequences; one of which is, that people mistake the nature of tyranny or oppression, supposing that the sovereign people may do that which a king can not do without oppression. One judge has publicly declared, that if a small number of persons are guilty of violating law, they may be indicted; but if a great multitude outrage law and rights, they can not be indicted or punished. It is painful to the friends of a republic that such a monstrous doctrine should be uttered by any man whose duty is to carry laws into effect.

We continually hear eulogies on the happy condition of the citizens of the United States; resulting from the freedom of our government. These eulogies, to a certain extent, are well founded. Our active, industrious, and enterprising citizens, possessing a vast extent of fertile land, growing and profitable manufactures, and a commerce that reaches every spot on the globe, enjoy blessings beyond those of any other country. But, on the other hand, we are subjected to injustice and tyranny in a thousand ways. For thirty years past, party spirit has produced a constant series of oppression; the triumphant party using its power to deprive the defeated party of its rights. The proscriptions inflicted on men in office for holding political principles different from the dominant party, are among the most detestable acts of tyranny.

The infringements of the most solemn treaties, the palpable violations of the constitution, and the usurpation of unconstitutional powers by the executive, exhibit most woful departures from the genuine principles of a free government. And it may be questioned, whether any kingdom in the civilized part of Europe has suffered so many violations of public and private rights, as the people of the United States have suffered within thirty years, without an attempt to punish their oppressors.

And now we read, in our public prints, repeated complaints of misrule, and outbreakings of popular violence; and the writers seem to be surprised at such events. They do not consider, that these outrages are the *natural*, not to say *necessary*, consequences of the doctrines which *they themselves*, in many cases, have been preaching or eulogizing ever since the constitution was formed. Such men are beginning to learn that men must have something to govern them besides *reason*.

Most persons seem to think that the election of a good president will remedy all our evils. This is a vain hope; a temporary alleviation is all that is to be expected from the best chief magistrate that the United States can find. There are defects in our form of government, and errors in popular opinions, that no administration can rectify; and until such defects are amended, and such errors corrected, we shall continue to be a divided, distracted community; incessantly agitated by violent factions; each in its turn triumphing and oppressing the other.

One thing is certain, that the election of the chief magistrate must be conducted in some way that shall effectually prevent intriguing for the office. If this can not be effected, the constitution, for securing a just administration and equal rights, is not worth a straw.

Another thing is equally certain, that unless executive and judicial officers can be placed beyond the influence of popular caprice, many of them at least will be time-servers, the laws will be feebly executed, and impartiality will be banished from our tribunals of justice.

Must we, then, despair of the republic? No, sir, not yet. The people of this country are republican in principle; and will not abandon the hope that a republican government may be sustained. But, sir, that hope *must* be abandoned, unless the great men of our country will lay aside their party strife, and unite in some vigorous effort to amend the defects of our constitution. The leading men, sir, must cease to expend their breath in speeches about banks and monopolies and metallic currency, and mount up to the source of our public evils. There only can be applied the catholicon which shall be efficacious in restoring to the confederacy health and soundness.          MARCELLUS.

# CHAPTER XII.

## ANSWER TO His Exc. JOHN BROOKS, GOVERNOR OF THE COMMONWEALTH OF MASSACHUSETTS.

(FROM THE COLUMBIAN CENTINEL OF JUNE 5, 1819.)

MR. WEBSTER, of Amherst, of the committee on the subject, reported the following Answer to the Governor's Speech; which was unanimously accepted, and the committee directed to present it.

*May it please your Excellency,—*

In meeting your Excellency, on your re-election to the office of chief magistrate of the commonwealth, and uniting with the other branches of the government, in deliberations on the means of promoting the public prosperity, the house of representatives most sincerely concur with your Excellency, in acknowledging the goodness of that Almighty Being, from whom are primarily derived all the blessings of peace, plenty, general health, good order and freedom. And it is with great satisfaction that we see a gentleman, whose patriotism and valor, in early life, contributed to defend the rights and establish the independence of his country, called by his fellow citizens, to preside over the administration of the laws in this commonwealth; and by the influence of venerable years and mature experience, recommending the cultivation of those virtues, and the encouragement of those institutions, which are adapted to give stability to republican government—to secure the rights, and elevate the character of freemen. Duly appreciating the importance of the privileges which the people of this commonwealth enjoy, under the constitution of the state, and of the United States, we can not be insensible to the high responsibility resting on us, to exert our best endeavors to guard the interests of the state, and to advance the prosperity of its citizens.

We rejoice that the people of this commonwealth have had the opportunity to form, and have now the happiness to enjoy, a republican constitution of government. We rejoice that man, doomed in former ages and in other countries, to be the victim of conquest and vassalage, has, in this part of the globe, resumed his natural rights, and vindicated his claim to govern himself. We admire the fortitude, the patience, and the sufferings of our venerable ancestors, who selected, settled, and defended this sequestered continent, as a secure retreat from the evils of the European world, no less than we reverence the intelligence, the virtue, and the piety from which we have derived institutions and systems of laws, probably more nearly perfect than any which have before fallen to the lot of man. But we perfectly accord in sentiment with your Excellency, that without intelligence and virtue in the people, from whom springs all legitimate government, there can be no rational expectation that these invaluable privileges can be long preserved; and we feel that we should betray the trust reposed in us by our constituents, if we should neglect to cherish the principles, guard the rights, and improve the institutions, civil, religious, and literary, which we inherit from our ancestors and from the founders of our constitution.

In accordance with the opinion of your Excellency, the house of representatives number the early instruction and discipline of youth, among the most efficacious means of promoting the happiness and improving the condition of society. Habits of early subordination, just views of moral obligation, and reverence of the Supreme Being, have, in our apprehension, the most powerful tendency to restrain the progress of vice, and extend the dominion of virtue. It is obvious from experience, no less than from the declaration of inspired truth, that the training of children in the path of integrity and virtue, is the best method to secure their future rectitude of conduct, their reputation, their influence, and their usefulness. We hold it to be a truth that ought to be impressed on the heart of every parent and guardian, and too important not to be repeated on every suitable occasion, that the rudiments of the public character of a nation or people, are unfolded in families and seminaries of learning. Families, the elementary associations of man, which spring from the divine institution of marriage, constitute the germs of all human society; and from the instructions and discipline of families and primary schools, the minds of youth receive a direction, which, in a great degree, gives to them their future character as members of a community.

Under these impressions, the house of representatives hold it to be their indispensable duty, as it is their highest interest, to encourage every practicable measure that may be suggested or devised, to carry into effect the requisitions of the constitution respecting the education of youth. To form plans for diffusing literary and moral improvement among the indigent classes of citizens, in connection with religious instruction, will be no less our pleasure, than it is a duty which we owe to society. To draw from the obscure retreats of poverty, the miserable victims of ignorance and vice; to enlighten their minds; to extirpate corrupt principles; to reform their evil habits; and to raise them from debasement to the rank of intelligent, industrious, and useful members of the community, will never cease to be an object of deep solicitude with a wise legislature; and we trust that no opportunity will be neglected by the house of representatives, to lend their influence to any measure calculated to promote this object.

The increase of pauperism is an evil to be deeply regretted. In this commonwealth, where property is diffused among all classes of people, and the means of subsistence are not difficult to be obtained, this evil is probably less alarming than in Europe. Yet in this state, the evil is too obvious not to be perceived, and to awaken apprehensions; and the view which your Excellency has presented to us, of the pauperism of some European countries, in connection with ignorance and crimes, can not fail to impress on our minds the importance of attending to every scheme that human wisdom can devise, to arrest its progress in this commonwealth. In regard to the most efficacious mode of preventing crimes, by early instruction and discipline, forming the minds of youth to habits of moral order and industry, we entirely coincide with your Excellency; and we shall not fail to improve every suggestion that may be offered, and promote every salutary measure that may be devised, to prevent an accumulation of the evils which spring from ignorance, indolence and vice.

The house of representatives are highly gratified to learn from your Excellency, that the great penitentiary at Charlestown and the hospital for the insane, are in a prosperous condition; and that both institutions justify the expectation, that they will prove extensively beneficial to the community. And while we would express our full confidence in the judicious arrangements and economical management of those to whom these institutions are intrusted, we would manifest a readiness to give to them any aid which the demands of justice and humanity may require, and which may not be incompatible with the resources of the commonwealth.

NOTE, 1843.—The opinion, that intelligence and virtue are the support of a republic, seems to have acquired among us the authority of an axiom. It was borrowed, at least in part, from the writings of Montesquieu on the Roman republic. In common with my fellow citizens, I may have often repeated the opinion, supposing it to be true as an abstract proposition, but without examining the ground on which alone it can be maintained as a practical truth.

In order to support a popular government by moral influence, the citizens of a state must have a degree of intelligence which will enable them, under all circumstances, to *understand* the true interest of the state, and the proper measures to sustain it; and this degree of intelligence must be supported by a high degree of moral principle, which shall, under all circumstances, be sufficient to control the selfishness of the citizens, and induce them to *unite* in measures to promote the public good, even when adverse to private interest. Nothing short of such intelligence and virtue, always active and of sufficient energy to combine the operations of the citizens, could effect the object.

Now a community or state, in which the citizens possess these requisites, can not be supposed to exist on earth, without a preternatural change in the character of the human race. No such community has ever existed; and we have no reason to suppose such a community will ever exist.

Human learning, whatever advantages it may confer on individuals and a state, never corrects the dispositions and passions of the human mind, from which proceed the disorders and corruptions of government. On the other hand, it may increase the evil by enlarging the power, multiplying the motives, and augmenting the means of doing mischief. Men are not governed by knowledge, but by their passions, their habits, their prejudices, and especially by their interests. Knowledge and reason are useful to selfish men, when they coincide with interest; but when they are at variance with it, their influence is rejected, or they are, or may be, perverted and employed to justify measures dictated by interest, whatever may be the moral character of such measures.

The abstract opinion therefore, that intelligence and virtue are the support of a republic, is adapted to deceive us with fallacious hopes.

# CHAPTER XIII.

## A LETTER TO THE REV. SAMUEL LEE, PROFESSOR OF ARABIC IN THE UNIVERSITY OF CAMBRIDGE.

Cambridge, Dec. 20th, 1824.

REV. AND DEAR SIR—As I have crossed the Atlantic for the purpose of completing and publishing a dictionary of our language, it would be very gratifying to me and to my countrymen, and I think by no means useless in England, to settle, by the united opinions of learned men, some points in pronunciation, orthography, and construction, in which the practice of good writers and speakers is not uniform, either in England or the United States. The English language is the language of the United States; and it is desirable that as far as the people have the same things and the same ideas, the words to express them should remain the same. The diversities of language among men may be considered as a curse, and certainly one of the greatest evils that commerce, religion, and the social interests of men have to encounter.

The English language will prevail over the whole of North America, from the latitude of 25° or 30° north, to the utmost limit of population toward the north pole; and, according to the regular laws of population, it must, within two centuries, be spoken by three hundred millions of people on that continent. If we take into view the English population in New Holland, and other lands in the south and east, we may fairly suppose that in two centuries the English will be the language of one third or two fifths of all the inhabitants of the globe.

Besides this, the English language is to be the instrument of propagating sciences, arts, and the Christian religion, to an extent probably exceeding that of any other language. It is therefore important that its principles should be adjusted, and uniformity of spelling and pronunciation established and preserved, as far as the nature of a living language will admit. In regard to the great body of the language, its principles are now settled by usage, and are uniform in this country and in the United States. But there are many points in which respectable men are not agreed, and it is the sincere desire of my fellow citizens that such a diversity may no longer exist. If a delegation of gentlemen from the two universities of Oxford and Cambridge could be induced to meet and consult on this subject, either in Oxford, or Cambridge, or in London, I would meet them with pleasure, and lay before them such points of difference in the practice of the two countries, as it is desirable to adjust, and the gentlemen would consider any other points that they might think it expedient to determine. I would also lay before them some thoughts on a plan for correcting the evils of our irregular orthography, without the use of any new letters.

I know that the decisions of such a collection of unauthorized individuals would not be considered as binding on the community, and it might be thought assuming. But the gentlemen would disavow any intention of imposing their opinions on the public as authoritative—they would offer simply their opinions, and the public would still be at liberty to receive or reject them. But whatever cavils might be made at first, those who know the influence of men of distinguished erudition on public opinion, in cases of a literary nature, will have no question respecting the ultimate success of such a project. That my countrymen would generally receive the decisions and follow them, I have no doubt.

I sincerely wish, sir, that this proposition may be transmitted to some gentleman of your acquaintance in Oxford, and that you would converse with the masters and professors of this university on the subject.

I am, sir, with great respect, your obedient servant,

N. WEBSTER.

Rev. SAMUEL LEE, D. D.

A copy of this letter was sent to Oxford, but no answer was returned.

## CHAPTER XIV.

REPLY TO A LETTER OF DAVID McCLURE, ESQ., ON
THE SUBJECT OF THE PROPER COURSE OF STUDY
IN THE GIRARD COLLEGE, PHILADELPHIA.

New Haven, Oct. 25, 1836.

DEAR SIR—I have received and perused the system of education for
the Girard College for Orphans, which you have been so good as to
send me, and for which please to accept my thanks.

In regard to the merits of the system, on which you request my opinions, I will make a few remarks, although I do not think myself so well
qualified to judge of it as many gentlemen who have been in the employment of instruction in our higher seminaries.

The mode you propose for instructing children in the French and
Spanish languages, is nearly the same as I have always supposed to be
the best, if not the only mode of making pupils perfectly masters of a
foreign language. An accurate pronunciation and familiarity with a
language can not easily be acquired, except in youth, when the organs
of speech are pliable, and by practice, as we learn our vernacular language.

In regard to your system in general, I can only say, that it appears
to be judiciously constructed, and well adapted for the purpose of making thorough scholars. If on trial it should be found susceptible of improvement, experience will direct to the proper amendments. One
remark, however, I take the liberty to make. I do not suppose an exact conformity to a particular course of studies to be essential to a
thorough education. One course may be preferable to another, but
there seems to be " no royal way to geometry ;" *close and persevering
application only* will make good scholars, and this will accomplish the
object, without an adherence to any precise order of studies.

As by Mr. Girard's will, there can not be in the college any instruction in the Christian religion, I shall take the liberty to make a few remarks on that subject.*

In my view, the Christian religion is the *most important and one of
the first things* in which *all* children, under a free government, ought
to be instructed. In this institution it is of more importance, as the
pupils will be orphans, and may be destitute of parental instruction.

No truth is more evident to my mind, than that the Christian religion
must be the basis of any government intended to secure the rights and
privileges of a free people. The opinion that *human reason*, left without the constant control of divine laws and commands, will preserve a

---

* The clause in Mr. Girard's will is in the following words : " I enjoin and require that no ecclesiastic, missionary, or minister, of any sect whatever, shall ever
hold or exercise any station or duty whatever in the said College ; nor shall any
such person be admitted for any purpose, or as a visitor, within the premises appropriated to the purposes of said College."

just administration, secure freedom, and other rights, restrain men from violations of laws and constitutions, and give duration to a popular government, is as chimerical as the most extravagant ideas that enter the head of a maniac. The history of the whole world refutes the opinion; the Bible refutes it; our own melancholy experience refutes it.

When I speak of the Christian religion as the basis of government, I do not mean an ecclesiastical establishment, a creed, or rites, forms, and ceremonies, or any compulsion of conscience. I mean primitive Christianity, in its simplicity, as taught by Christ and his apostles; consisting in a belief in the being, perfections, and moral government of God; in the revelation of his will to men, as their supreme rule of action; in man's accountability to God for his conduct in this life; and in the indispensable obligation of all men to yield entire obedience to God's commands in the moral law and in the Gospel. This belief and this practice may consist with different forms of church government, which, not being essential to Christianity, need not enter into any system of education.

Where will you find any code of laws, among civilized men, in which the commands and prohibitions are not founded on Christian principles? I need not specify the prohibition of murder, robbery, theft, trespass; but commercial and social regulations are all derived from those principles, or intended to enforce them. The laws of contracts and bills of exchange are founded on the principles of *justice*, the basis of all security of rights in society. The laws of insurance are founded on the Christian principle of *benevolence*, and intended to protect men from want and distress. The provisions of law for the relief of the poor are in pursuance of Christian principles. Every wise code of laws must embrace the main principles of the religion of Christ.

Now the most efficient support of human laws is, the full belief that the subjects of such laws are accountable to higher authority than human tribunals. The halter and the penitentiary may restrain many men from overt criminal acts; but it is the *fear of God and a reverence for his authority and commands*, which alone can control and subdue the will, when tempted by ambition and interest to violate the laws. Whatever superficial observers may think, it is beyond a question, that the small band of real Christians in Protestant countries has more influence in securing order and peace in society than all the civil officers of government. Just in proportion as the influence of such men is impaired, is the increase of crimes and outrages upon the rights of individuals and upon the public peace.

It has been a misfortune to the citizens of this country, that, from their abhorrence of the ecclesiastical tyranny of certain orders of the clergy in Europe, they have contracted strong prejudices against the clergy in this country, who have neither rank nor temporal power, and whose influence is derived solely from their personal attainments and worth, and their official services.

The clergy in this country are generally men of learning and of good principles. They have been uniformly and preëminently the friends of education and civil liberty. The learned clergy among the first settlers of New England had great influence in founding the first genuine republican governments ever formed, and which, with all the faults and

defects of the men and their laws, were the *best* republican governments on earth.  At this moment the people of this country are indebted  chiefly to their  institutions for the  rights and  privileges which
are enjoyed.

During the Revolution the clergy were very useful in supporting the
courage and fortitude of our citizens, and in restraining their intemperate passions.  They have uniformly been the supporters of law and
order, and to them is popular education, in this country, more indebted than to any other class of men.  That such men should be precluded from any concern in the  education of youth in a literary institution, is a reproach to a Christian country.

It may be said that the clergy are bigoted men, and often engaged in
controversy.   But other classes of men are liable to the same imputa-
tion ; and nothing in the character of clergymen furnishes a good reason for proscribing their aid in the education of youth.   Clergymen
differ chiefly on speculative points in religion ; in the fundamental
points to which my description of religion is limited, they are probably
*all united ;* and in support of them they would join in solid phalanx to
resist the inroads of licentiousness.

The foundation of all free government and of all social order, must
be laid in families, and in the discipline of youth.  Young persons
must not only be furnished with *knowledge*, but they must be accustomed to subordination, and subjected to the authority and influence of
good principles.   It will avail little that youths are made to *understand*
truth and correct principles, unless they are accustomed to submit to be
governed by them.  The speculative principles of natural religion will
have little effect, or none at all, unless the pupil is made to yield obedience
to the practical laws of Christian  morality ; and the practice of yielding such obedience  must be familiar, and wrought into habit in early
life, or the instruction of teachers will, for the most part, be lost on
their pupils.  To give efficacy to such a course of education, the pupil
must believe himself to be accountable for his actions to the Supreme
Being, as well as to human laws ; for, without such belief, no dependence can be had upon his fidelity to the  laws, when urged to violate
them by strong passions, or by the powerful temptations of present advantage.  The  experience of the whole world evinces that all the restraints of religion and law are often  insufficient to control  the selfish
and malignant passions of men.  Any system of education, therefore,
which limits instruction to the arts and sciences, and rejects the aids of
religion in forming the characters of citizens, is essentially defective.

In giving this view of my opinions, I am aware that I expose myself
to the obloquy of modern philosophers.  But this I disregard ; for I
have, in support of my opinions, the experience of the whole civilized
world, as well as the proofs presented by inspired truth, from the beginning to the end of the Bible ; that book which the benevolent Creator has furnished for the express purpose of guiding human reason in
the path of safety, and the *only book* which can remedy, or essentially
mitigate, the evils of a licentious world.

From a full conviction of these truths, I firmly believe, that without
material changes in the principles now prevalent in the United States,
our republican government is destined to be of short duration.

An attempt to conduct the affairs of a free government with wisdom and impartiality, and to preserve the just rights of all classes of citizens, without the guidance of Divine precepts, will certainly end in disappointment. God is the supreme moral Governor of the world he has made, and as he himself governs with perfect rectitude, he requires his rational creatures to govern themselves in like manner. If men will not submit to be controlled by *His* laws, he will punish them by the evils resulting from *their own* disobedience.

Be pleased, sir, to accept the respects of your obedient servant,

N. WEBSTER.

## CHAPTER XV.

### LETTER TO A YOUNG GENTLEMAN COMMENCING HIS EDUCATION.

My Dear Friend—As you are now commencing a course of classical education, and need the guidance of those who have preceded you in the same course, you can not but receive with kindness, and treat with attention, the remarks of a friend, whose affection for you, excites in him a deep solicitude for your future reputation and happiness. I feel the more desirous to furnish you with some hints for the direction of your studies, for I have experienced the want of such helps myself; no small portion of my life having been spent in correcting the errors of my early education.

It has been often remarked, that men are the creatures of habit. The rudiments of knowledge we receive by tradition; and our first actions are, in a good degree, modeled by imitation. Nor ought it to be otherwise. The respect which young persons feel for their parents, superiors and predecessors is no less the dictate of reason, than the requirement of heaven; and the propensity to imitation, is no less natural, than it may be useful. These principles however, like many others, when pursued or indulged to an extreme, produce evil effects; as they often lead the young to embrace error as well as truth. Some degree of confidence in the opinions of those whom we respect, is always a duty—in the first stages of life, our confidence in parents must be implicit, and our obedience to their will complete and unreserved. In later stages of life, as the intellectual faculties expand and the reasoning power gains strength, implicit confidence in the opinions even of the most distinguished men, ceases to be a duty. We are to regard their opinions only as *probably* correct; but refer the ultimate decision of this point to evidence to be collected from our own reasonings or researches. All men are liable to err; and a knowledge of this fact should excite in us constant solicitude to obtain satisfactory reasons for every opinion we embrace.

As men are furnished with powers of reason, it is obviously the design of the Creator, that reason should be employed as their guide, in every stage of life. But reason, without cultivation, without experience and without the aids of revelation, is a miserable guide; it often errs from ignorance, and more often from the impulse of passion. The first questions a rational being should ask himself, are, *Who made me? Why was I made? What is my duty?* The proper answers to these questions, and the practical results, constitute, my dear friend, the whole business of life.

Now reason, unaided by revelation, can not answer these questions. The experience of the pagan world has long since determined this point. Revelation alone furnishes satisfactory information on these subjects. Let it then be the first study that occupies your mind, to learn from the Scriptures the character and will of your Maker; the end or purpose for which he gave you being and intellectual powers, and the duties he requires you to perform. In all that regards faith and practice, the Scriptures furnish the principles, precepts and rules, by which you are to be guided. Your reputation among men; your own tranquillity of mind in this life; and all rational hope of future happiness, depend on an exact conformity of conduct to the commands of God revealed in the sacred oracles.

The duties of men are summarily comprised in the Ten Commandments, consisting of two tables; one comprehending the duties which we owe immediately to God—the other, the duties we owe to our fellow men. Christ himself has reduced these commandments under two general precepts, which enjoin upon us, to love the Lord our God with all our heart, with all our soul, with all our mind and with all our strength—and to love our neighbor as ourselves. On these two commandments hang all the law and the prophets; that is, they comprehend the substance of all the doctrines and precepts of the Bible, or the whole of religion.

The first duty of man then is to love and reverence the Supreme Being. The fear of God is the beginning of wisdom or religion. But the love of God implies some knowledge of his character and attributes—and these are to be learned partly by a view of his stupendous works in creation, but chiefly from the revelations of himself recorded in the Scriptures. The great constituent of love to the Supreme Being is however an entire complacency in his character and attributes, and unqualified approbation of his law, as a rule of life. Such complacency and approbation can exist only in a holy heart—a heart that delights in moral excellence. But wherever they exist, they produce a correspondent purity of life. The natural effect then of a real conformity of *heart* to the first and great commandment, which enjoins supreme love to God, is, to produce conformity of *life* to the injunction of the second command, to love our neighbor as ourselves.

In applying the commands of God to practice, be careful to give to them the full intended latitude of meaning. The love of God comprehends the love of all his attributes—the love of his *justice* in condemning and punishing sin, as well as of his *mercy* in forgiving and saving penitent sinners—the love of his *sovereignty* as well as of his *grace.* The divine character is an entire thing; and there can be no genuine love to the Supreme Being which does not embrace his whole character. When in obedience to the third commandment of the decalogue, you would avoid profane swearing, you are to remember that this alone is not a full compliance with the prohibition, which comprehends all irreverent words or actions, and whatever tends to cast contempt on the Supreme Being, or on his word and ordinances.

When you abstain from secular employments, on the Sabbath, and attend public worship, you must not suppose that you fully comply with the requisitions of the fourth commandment, unless you devote the whole day to religious improvement. If you spend any part of the day in convivial entertainment, in reading novels, plays, history, geography or travels, you undoubtedly violate the letter as well as the spirit of that command.

The command to honor your father and mother comprehends not only due respect and obedience to your parents; but all due respect to other superiors. The distinction of age, is one established by God himself, and is perhaps the only difference of rank in society, which is of divine origin. It is a distinction of the utmost importance to society, it can not be destroyed, and it ought not to be forgotten. Hence filial respect has ever been esteemed one of the most amiable virtues. Let your respect for your parents, and others who are of like age or standing in society, be sincere, cordial and uniform; and let the feelings of your heart be manifest in your exterior deportment. Never forget the deference due to their age, nor treat them with a familiarity that is incompatible with that deference. Even the customary forms of address should not be overlooked, or neglected; for in doing honor to age, you honor a divine command, and secure to yourself a source of permanent consolation. It will afford you particular satisfaction, when your parents are consigned to the tomb.

In obedience to the sixth command you are not merely to avoid direct homicide, but you are to avoid every thing that may indirectly or consequentially impair your own health, or injure that of others. Intemperance or excessive indulgence of passion and appetite which gradually weakens the constitution, falls within the prohibition of this commandment; as does every known unnecessary exposure of the body to extreme hardship.

From your education and principles, it is presumed that there is little need of cautioning you against a violation of the eighth commandment, by a felonious taking of the property of another, in a manner to incur the penalties of human laws. But the prohibition covers much broader ground—it extends to every species of fraud or deception by which the property of another is taken or withheld from him. If in receiving or paying money, a mistake throws into your hands a sum of money beyond what is your right, it is a violation of the eighth command to retain that sum in your own hands, let it be never so small. You are under the same moral obligation to return the surplus money to the rightful owner, as you are not to take a like sum from him by theft.

In like manner, in trade, the man who by deception gets a dollar more for an article, than the purchaser would have given, had he not been deceived, is in the view of God as guilty as if he had taken that dollar from the purchaser's chest.

The man who by an artifice conceals the defects of his goods, or gives them a false appearance, and thus deceives the purchaser, is guilty of fraud; and any money that he may get by this deception, is taken as wrongfully as if taken by theft.

The farmer who brings his produce to market, and sells it in a bad state, knowing it to be defective and concealing the defect, or giving a false representation of it, is guilty of fraud, and falls within the purview of the eighth command.

The man who adulterates his drugs, and sells them as genuine, certainly violates the eighth command, and *may* violate the sixth.

The wine seller and the distiller who mix and adulterate their liquors, and sell them for what they are not, are guilty of fraud, and in a greater or less degree fall within the prohibition of the eighth command;

and by using poisonous substances in such adulteration, they may incur the guilt of the sixth.

The methods by which this command is violated in the ordinary commerce of life, are literally innumerable—and if judgment should be laid to the line, who could stand ?

Be very careful then to resist every temptation to deception and fraud. Let every transaction with your fellow men be just and honorable. This is required no less by your own reputation, than by the law of God ; for *deception* in every form is *meanness.*

Nor would I have you more careful of your neighbor's property than of his good name, which is dearer to him than his property. Say nothing of your neighbor falsely ; and never publish his faults, unless to circumscribe their influence, or prevent an injury to other men.

Let it then be the first study of your early years, to learn in what consists *real worth* or *dignity of character.* To ascertain this important point, consider the character and attributes of the Supreme Being. As God is the only perfect being in the universe, his character, consisting of all that is good and great, must be the model of all human excellence ; and his laws must of course be the only rules of conduct by which his rational creatures can reach any portion of like excellence. In the very nature of things then a man is exalted in proportion to his conformity to the divine standard of worth ; and degraded in proportion to his want of conformity to that standard. Nothing can be *really honorable* and *dignified,* which is not in *exact accordance with rectitude.* Let this be imprinted on your mind as the first principle of moral science. A violation of human laws implies *meanness* as well as *wickedness ;* it impairs the reputation and lessens the moral worth of the offender—much more does a transgression of the divine law, imply want of dignity and self-respect, as well as contempt for the Supreme Lawgiver—it sinks a man in his own estimation, and debases him in the opinion of his fellow men.

Nothing can be more false than the opinion that *honor* can exist without *moral rectitude.* Every violation of moral duty is *meanness* as well as *crime*—for it implies a disposition to offend or treat with contempt the greatest and best being in the universe, or a disposition to injure a fellow citizen, or both ; and a disposition in one being to injure another, implies a want of that benevolence and love of justice which are essential to greatness of mind, which regards primarily the common welfare and happiness of moral beings.

Real honor then consists in a disposition to promote the best interests of the human family—that is, in an exact conformity of heart and life to the divine precepts. Whatever voluntary conduct in man impairs human happiness or introduces disorder into society, manifests a defect of character, a destitution of honorable principles.

One of the first efforts of an ingenuous mind, is to disabuse itself of the prejudice, that the *laws of honor* may *require* or *justify* what the *laws of God* and *man forbid.* Amidst the corrupt maxims of fashionable life, no young man is safe, whose mind is not elevated to that pitch of moral heroism, which enables him to combat successfully with vicious principles disguised under the garb of *honor.* The laws of honor, so called, are derived from pagans and barbarians ; they hang

on half civilized men, as the tawdry trappings of savage ancestors—
they deform the manners and debase the character of the age. To
weak minds, less under the influence of principle than of fashion, they
present fascinations not easily resisted. But let it be deeply impressed
on your mind, that no person is duly fortified against their enticements,
who is not convinced, and who does not habitually act from the conviction that *moral principles and practice are essential to the character of
a gentleman.* Whatever may be a man's external deportment, his politeness, or his hospitality, if he will seduce my wife, my sister, or my
daughter; if he will take my money from me at the gaming table, or
my life in a duel, he is destitute of the *first requisites of a gentleman—
justice, humanity, benevolence, and real dignity of mind.* Under a
polished exterior, he conceals the heart of a barbarian.

On the subject of dueling, I would further observe, that the practice,
far from exhibiting unequivocal proof of true courage, evinces, in my
view, the most disgraceful cowardice. It proves a man to be more
afraid of the scorn of perverted minds, than of the wrath of heaven,
or the vengeance of the law—more afraid of incurring the contempt of
unprincipled men, than of forfeiting the favor of the most perfect judge
of right and wrong, and of the most virtuous of his fellow citizens—
more afraid of a temporary stigma on his own reputation, than of
sacrificing all his obligations to his family and friends, and of plunging
his parents, his wife, his children, and his brethren in the deepest distress—nay, if married, more afraid of popular odium incurred by
manly rectitude, than of violating his solemn marriage vows, which
have pledged his veracity and his honor, to provide for his consort, and
to cherish her with tenderness. This species of cowardice, this miserable, this mean obsequiousness to popular prejudice, is evidence of a
degraded mind, and an indelible stain on the human character.

There is another view of this subject which ought not to be overlooked. Duels almost always originate in a defect of true politeness—
and a challenge accepted, is presumptive evidence that the parties are
*not* gentlemen, in the sense in which the word should always be understood, and in which alone it can be *correctly* used. A real gentleman
never voluntarily gives offense; and if he offends without design, he
instantly acknowledges his error. The offended party, if a real gentleman, will as promptly accept this acknowledgment. If the parties
disagree as to the nature and aggravation of the offense, and the value
of the atonement offered, if they are really gentlemen, they will readily submit the decision of the question to an impartial friend, and rest
satisfied with his decision. In nine cases of ten, perhaps in every case
of an appeal to arms, to obtain satisfaction for injuries or affronts, it
may be clearly seen by the impartial world, that the affair has proceeded from a defect of *real honor* and *good breeding* in one party or in
both. Instead therefore of vindicating their honor by arms, they manifest to the world that they are destitute of the genuine principles of
good breeding, and of the real magnanimity which is characteristic of
gentlemen.

In selecting books for reading, be careful to choose such as furnish
the best helps to improvement in morals, literature, arts and science;
preferring profit to pleasure, and instruction to amusement. A small

portion of time may be devoted to such reading as tends to relax the
mind, and to such bodily amusements as serve to invigorate muscular
strength and the vital functions.  But the greatest part of life is to be
employed in useful labors, and in various indispensable duties, private,
social, and public.  Man has but little time to spare for the gratification
of the senses and the imagination.  I would therefore caution you
against the fascinations of plays, novels, romances, and that species of
descriptive writing which is employed to embellish common objects,
without much enlarging the bounds of knowledge, or to paint imaginary
scenes, which only excite curiosity, and a temporary interest, and then
vanish in empty air.

The readers of books may be comprehended in two classes—those
who read chiefly for amusement, and those who read for instruction.
The first, and far the most numerous class, give their money and their
time for private gratification; the second employ both for the acquisition of knowledge which they expect to apply to some useful purpose.
The first gain subjects of conversation and social entertainment; the
second acquire the means of public usefulness and of private elevation
of character.  The readers of the first class are so numerous, and the
thirst for novelty so insatiable, that the country must be deluged with
tales and fiction; and if you suffer yourself to be hurried along with
the current of popular reading, not only your *time*, but your *mind* will
be dissipated; your native faculties, instead of growing into masculine
vigor, will languish into imbecility.  Bacon and Newton did not read
tales and novels; their great minds were nourished with very different
aliment.

Theatrical entertainments have strong attractions, especially for the
young and the thoughtless.  They are vindicated as a rational and in-
structive amusement, and men of sober judgment and sound morals
sometimes attend them—not however, I believe, with the expectation of
gaining useful knowledge; but for the purpose of being entertained
with seeing the powers of the actors.  They are pleased to see one man
imitate another, and the more exact the imitation, the more are they
delighted.  The representation of elevated characters has a show of
dignity; the low scenes are mere vulgar buffoonery.  Very few plays,
however, are free from sentiments which are offensive to moral purity.
Many of them abound with ribaldry and vulgarity, too gross for exhibition before persons of delicacy and refined manners.  Before I can
believe the stage to be a school of virtue, I must demand proof that a
single profligate has ever been reformed, or a single man or woman
made a Christian by its influence.  And let me ask, what sort of entertainment is that in which a thin partition only separates the nobleman
from his lackey, and the duchess from her kitchen-maid; in which the
gentleman and the lady associate at the same board with the footman,
the oyster-man, and the woman of the town, and all partake of the
same fare!  With what sentiments must superior beings look down on
this motley school of morality?

In forming your connections in society, be careful to select for your
companions young men of good breeding, and of virtuous principles
and habits.  The company of the profligate and irreligious is to be
shunned as poison.  You can not always avoid some intercourse with

men of dissolute lives; but you can always select, for your intimate associates, men of good principles and unimpeachable character. Never maintain a familiar intercourse with the profane, the lewd, the intemperate, the gamester, or the scoffer at religion. Toward men of such character, the common civilities of life are to be observed—beyond these, nothing is required of men who reverence the divine precepts, and who desire to "keep themselves unspotted from the world."

I would advise you never to become a member of any association, the object of which is concealed. If times and circumstances, in any country and at any period of the world, have rendered such associations necessary for the protection of person or property, or for the reformation of public abuses, no longer tolerable, such circumstances do not exist in this country. Secret societies or clubs, may have innocent and even good objects in view; but concealment always exposes them to suspicion; and it seems incompatible with true dignity of character to expose one's self voluntarily to such suspicions. A good man, a man of truly philanthropic principles, will always direct his views to valuable objects of public or private utility, and these require no secrecy. Associations for intellectual improvement, for executing useful undertakings, and for combining and giving effect to exertions of benevolence, are highly laudable. But always bear in mind this important fact, that men are all members of one great family, and benevolence should know no bounds, but the limits of this family. It should therefore be our aim not to attempt to narrow the limits of benevolence which God himself has prescribed. It may well be questioned, whether, as society is now constituted, the partialities of men, originating in distinctions, national and local, political and religious, do not contract the benevolent principles of our nature, within much narrower limits than is consistent with Christian morality. No philanthropist can see, without pain, nations and states, parties and religious sects, perpetually struggling to secure, each to itself, some exclusive or superior advantages in property, power or influence, and often by means base and dishonorable. This conduct usually originates in pride or selfish views, as unfriendly to social happiness, as they are repugnant to the will of our common father. Whether in politics or religion, this is an odious trait in the human character.

When we consider that men are all brethren of the same family, all created with similar capacities, and vested with the same natural rights; and in this country all enjoying equal civil and religious rights, under the protection of law; all equally entitled to security and public privileges; all placed under the same moral discipline, and all destined to the same end—how disgusting is it to see one party or one sect arrogating to itself superior merit, or proud distinction, and saying to others, "*stand by thyself—come not near me, for I am holier than thou!*" Yet such is the language of parties; often in religion—always in government. When the fundamental principles of government or our holy religion are assaulted, good men must unite to defend them. But the most numerous and most violent parties that trouble society, spring from private ambition and interest, when no principles are in jeopardy —or from an undue attachment to speculative opinions in politics, or to the externals of religion; and in such parties, the human character is displayed in all its depravity and degradation. In the tranquil condition of affairs in this country, when our citizens enjoy all the privileges which good men can desire, and more than many can enjoy without abuse, a disposition to exalt one class of citizens and to depress another, is a foul reproach to men—a fouler reproach to Christians.

Never, my dear friend, degrade yourself by an unhallowed alliance with a political party that assumes the right of controlling all public affairs, to the exclusion of other citizens who have equal rights and equal property to defend, and equal claims to a share in the management of that property. The attempts and often successful attempts, in this country, to exclude one class of citizens from any control in legislation over the property which their industry has acquired, and which bears its proportion of the burdens of government, is as rude an assault on liberty, as ever disgraced the annals of despotism. Accustom yourself from your youth to consider all men as your brethren, and know no distinction between fellow citizens, except that which they make themselves, by their *virtues* or their *vices ;* by their *worth* or their *meanness.*

A republican form of government is evidently the most rational form that men have devised for the protection of person and property, and for securing liberty. But hitherto no means have been devised to guard this form of government from abuse and corruption. Men in republics are as wicked, and as selfish as in monarchies, and with far more power to introduce disorders, both into legislation and into the administration of the laws. In republics, the influence of selfish and ambitious men over the weak, the ignorant and unsuspecting, has its full range of operation ; and sooner or later, this influence will place in office incompetent men, or men who will sacrifice principle to personal emolument or aggrandizement. The corruption of the electors is the first step toward the ruin of republics ; and when the sources of power are corrupted, the evil hardly admits of a remedy.

It seems to be a political axiom, that republics should be founded on an equality of rights, or so constructed as to preserve that equality. But with all the declamation which is heard on this subject, this equality of rights seems not to be understood ; the very terms want definition. That all men have an equal right to the protection of their persons, their reputation and their property, is undeniable. But it may be asked, has a man who has no property to defend, and none to support the expenses of government, an *equal right* to legislate upon property, as a man who has property to guard and to apply to the support and defense of his country ? May it not be true in a republic, that a *majority* of the citizens may possess a *minority* of the property, and may it not happen that the *minor* interest may govern the *major interest ?* And in this case, what becomes of the *equality of rights,* on which we profess to found a republican government ? When the sober, industrious citizen, who, by his toil and economy, collects a moderate estate, brings up a family in good habits, and pays his taxes to government, finds that his property and virtue give him no influence or advantage as a member of the government, over the idle penniless lounger, who earns little and spends that little in vice, paying nothing to government, what attachment can this good citizen feel to the government ? What confidence can he place in its administration ? What expectation can he entertain of its durability ? And what sort of government is that in which the *owners* of the country do not govern it ?

Melancholy as this view of the subject is, you are the subject and the citizen of a republic, and in these characters, duties will devolve on you of no ordinary magnitude. As a *subject*, yield an entire obedience to the laws and established institutions of society. Never for the paltry consideration of interest, resort to deception, concealment or equivocation, to evade your proper share in the burdens of government. As a *citizen*, exercise your rights with integrity and unshaken independence of mind. An obsequious elector, who temporizes with party, and yields to every varying breeze of popular opinion, is a most contemptible character.

In selecting men for office, let principle be your guide. Regard not the particular sect or denomination of the candidate—look to his character as a man of known principle, of tried integrity, and undoubted ability for the office.

It is alledged by men of loose principles, or defective views on the subject, that religion and morality are not necessary or important qualifications for political stations. But the Scriptures teach a different doctrine. They direct that rulers should be men *who rule in the fear of God, able men, such as fear God, men of truth, hating covetousness.* But if we had no divine instruction on the subject, our own interest would demand of us a strict observance of the principle of these injunctions. And it is to the neglect of this rule of conduct in our citizens, that we must ascribe the multiplied frauds, breaches of trust, peculations and embezzlements of public property which astonish even ourselves; which tarnish the character of our country ; which disgrace a republican government ; and which will tend to reconcile men to monarchy in other countries and even in our own.

When a citizen gives his suffrage to a man of known immorality, he abuses his trust ; he sacrifices not only his own interest, but that of his neighbor ; he betrays the interest of his country. Nor is it of slight importance, that men elected to office should be *able* men, men of talents equal to their stations, men of mature age, experience, and judgment ; men of firmness and impartiality. This is particularly true with regard to men who constitute tribunals of justice—the main bulwark of our rights—the citadel that maintains the last struggle of freedom against the inroads of corruption and tyranny. In this citadel should be stationed no raw, inexperienced soldier, no weak temporizing defender, who will obsequiously bend to power, or parley with corruption.

One of the surest tests of a man's real worth, is the esteem and confidence of those who have long known him, and his conduct in domestic and social life. It may be held as generally true, that respect spontaneously attaches itself to real worth ; and the man of respectable virtues, never has occasion to run after respect. Whenever a man is known to seek promotion by intrigue, by temporizing, or by resorting to the haunts of vulgarity and vice for support, it may be inferred, with moral certainty, that he is not a man of real respectability, nor is he entitled to public confidence. As a general rule, it may be affirmed, that the man who *never intrigues* for office, may be most safely *intrusted* with office ; for the same noble qualities, his pride, or his integrity and sense of dignity, which make him disdain the mean arts of flattery and intrigue, will restrain him from debasing himself by betraying his trust. Such a man can not desire promotion, unless he receives it from the respectable part of the community ; for he considers no other promotion to be honorable.

Both in government and religion, form your opinions with deliberation, and when you have settled your opinions, adhere to them with firmness. Particularly would I commend to you this course in adopting your religious creed. And when you have attached yourself to any system, from deliberate conviction, do not rashly and for light causes, abandon it. When satisfied that you have embraced an error, conscience will direct you to renounce it. But let not a temporary inconvenience, a slight, or a fit of discontent for a trifling cause, induce you to forsake the denomination with which you have been united. Such change evidences want of principle or want of firmness and stability, neither of which is compatible with true dignity of character.

# CHAPTER XVI.

## FORM OF ASSOCIATION FOR YOUNG MEN.

WE, firmly believing the revealed will of God, as delivered in the Scriptures, to be the standard of moral rectitude, and moral rectitude to be the only basis of true honor and dignity of character, do associate for the purpose of giving efficacy to these principles, and for discountenancing, as far as our influence may extend, the operation of principles which tend to render vice respectable or diminish its infamy.

We assume it to be an incontrovertible truth that the character of the Supreme Being is the only perfect model of excellence ; that a conformity to this character in man, as far as it is practicable, is the only foundation of human excellence. These principles being admitted, the converse of them must also be admitted, that every crime and vice, that is, every deviation from the laws of God, is a defect of honor or dignity in the human character ; in other words, must partake of meanness.

In pursuance of these principles, we hold ourselves bound to regulate our own conduct and opinions by the revealed will of God, and to consider every known departure from the rules which he has prescribed, as disreputable. We shall therefore consider every person, giving or accepting a challenge to fight a duel, and all persons acting as seconds, as forfeiting a character which entitles men to respect. In like manner, we must consider lewdness, intemperance, seduction, gaming, violations of holy time, fraud, overreaching in trade, falsehood, deception, or other vice, however common or sanctioned by fashion, as despoiling character of its honor and respectability, rendering those who practice them unworthy of our esteem, and disqualifying them for intimacy in social fellowship.

In all our intercourse with our fellow men, we hold ourselves pledged to observe the strictest integrity. Whether in trade or in mechanical employments, all orders for goods or work, sent from customers at a distance, shall be executed with the same fidelity as if our customers were present.

Deeming the character of the female sex to have a most important bearing on the education of youth and on the moral habits of society, we pledge ourselves to treat the sex with the utmost delicacy and respect, and in all practicable ways to defend and preserve their reputation, exalt their character, and extend the influence of those amiable virtues which tend to restrain licentious manners.

As all citizens of this free country have equal rights, and are equally entitled to any advantages or promotion which they may obtain by honest industry, and the lawful exertions of talents, we shall deem it dishonorable and unjust to take any advantage over our fellow citizens by secret associations, combinations or stratagem, and we pledge ourselves never to unite with any fraternity whose objects are concealed from the public.

The integrity of rulers being a chief guaranty for the faithful enactment and administration of laws, and religion the best guaranty for integrity and fidelity in rulers, we hold ourselves bound, both in conscience, and by a regard to expedience and political wisdom, to consider a sincere respect for religion, and its institutions, as indispensable qualifications in legislative, executive and judicial officers ; and we shall ever frown on attempts to elevate to such offices men of licentious morals, and of known contempt for religion.

Believing men to be made for active employments and for usefulness, and a life of idleness or devotion to pleasure and amusements to be immoral in itself and pernicious to society, we pledge ourselves to give no countenance or support to persons whose occupation is to furnish amusements which tend to demoralize society.

# CHAPTER XVII.

## MODES OF TEACHING THE ENGLISH LANGUAGE.

EDUCATION, in the most comprehensive sense of the word, consists in the instruction of the young and the ignorant in what is necessary or useful for them to know, in order to be qualified to procure their subsistence, to correct their evil propensities, to direct their minds to the proper objects, and to form their moral, social and religious characters. In short, the objects of education are to furnish pupils with the best means of providing for themselves; of being useful in all the relations of life; and prepared for a future state of happiness. But the remarks now proposed to be made by the writer, will be restricted to the modes of acquiring knowledge in seminaries of learning.

In the business of teaching, there is one general rule which is applicable to instruction in every department of science and literature; this is to begin with the most simple elements, and proceed step by step from that which is easy to that which is more difficult. In this procedure, the most important point is to make the pupil perfectly master of one step or degree, before he proceeds to the next.

In learning the English language, the first thing is to make the pupil perfectly acquainted with the letters of the alphabet. While he is learning the shape and the name of each letter, he should learn to repeat the letters in the alphabetical order, and commit them to memory in this order, so as to be able to repeat them without the least hesitation. The reason is, that every person through life has frequent occasions to use the letters in this order, in seeking words in a dictionary, in consulting indexes, in arranging documents, &c. Hence the extreme impropriety of dividing the alphabet into sections, and arranging the letters in any other order than the alphabetical. Let a child form a habit of repeating letters of the alphabet in any other order than the alphabetical, and he will be liable to be embarrassed with it all his life. These observations are also applicable to learning the days of the week in their order; as also the months of the year, and the books of the Old and New Testaments.

From single letters, the pupil should proceed to combinations of two letters, and learn perfectly the pronunciation of each combination; then proceed to combinations of three letters; and this without much regard to the signification of words. The opinion that a pupil should never pronounce a word which he does not understand, is a great error; as it makes it necessary that a knowledge of spelling should proceed no faster than that of definition. A more absurd opinion, and one more directly opposed to the laws of the human mind, was never broached.

If it should be objected that the learning of the alphabet is difficult, let the importance of the practice be the answer; take more time; one great fault in teaching is going too fast, learning the first rudiments imperfectly, and thus retarding future progress.

There are various modes of teaching, all of which may effect the object; but there are some mistakes which are very common, and deserve notice.

1. The first error I shall notice is, the practice of beginning to teach children *when too young*. It is a common opinion that the sooner a child is put to his books, the greater the amount of knowledge which he may obtain in a given number of years. My own observations do not confirm this opinion, but the reverse. A child that begins to learn the letters of the alphabet at *four* years old, will be as far advanced at *five* as one that begins at *three*. A child that begins at *three*, will be two or three years learning to read well; but one that begins at *five*, may be taught to read well in *six or eight weeks*. Experiment has proved the fact.

2. The like mistake is made in putting children to difficult studies at *too early an age*. A child of five or six years of age is put to the study of geography, arithmetic, or history; his progress is slow; he learns a little and that imperfectly; and thus he spends a winter or two to very little purpose. The same child at nine or ten years of age will learn as much in *two months*, as he will at *five* or *six* years of age in *two winters*—and understand and retain what he learns much better.

3. Another mistake is in attempting to instruct young people in *too many things at once*. The most important point perhaps in a system of instructions, as in every kind of business is, *to do one thing at a time*. Mr. Locke mentions this as a primary rule to be observed in teaching. When the greatest merchant in Holland was asked how he could transact such an immense business, he replied—*By doing one thing at a time*.

This rule is not observed in our schools. The reverse is the fact, to the great detriment of education. Children are put to several studies the same day; they learn a little of one thing, and then a little of another; they learn nothing perfectly; and a great part of what they do learn is soon forgotten.

Children should first learn perfectly the letters, and their sounds in combination in the more easy syllables; and these should be so familiar that they can pronounce them correctly at sight without hesitation. When this is accomplished, pupils should proceed to *words*, monosyllables. If the words are what are called household words, as words in daily use, they probably understand their meaning, and if not, the teacher may explain them. This, however, is not very important, in this stage of instruction; as it is the spelling and pronunciation which they are now learning.

In this stage of instruction, are first seen the benefits of *classification* in elementary books. Words of like formation are to be pronounced alike. Similarity of sounds aids the memory. In this and in the following stage of instruction, the pupils should be taught in classes; and *every one* in the class should be directed to spell *every word* in the lesson, and then to pronounce *every* word. This repetition should be continued till *every child* can spell and pronounce correctly *every word* in the lesson without the smallest hesitation. Such repetition will fasten the true spelling and pronunciation upon the mind of every child; and this process occasionally repeated *in reviews* will accomplish the object.

From monosyllables the pupil will proceed to dissyllables.  In this stage, a knowledge of *accent* is to be added to that of spelling and the pronunciation of letters.  The pupil is to be taught what *accent* is, and pronounce every word in the lesson with its proper accent.  The whole class should be taught to repeat, pronounce, and spell every word in the lesson.

In a proper classification of words, those of like termination should be arranged in the same lessons or columns.  In many classes of words of like termination, the accent is uniformly on the same syllyble ; that is, at the same distance from the termination.  Suppose the pupil is to spell words of three syllables ending in *ity;* as in *amity, dignity, lenity ;* he is to be informed that all words with a similar ending have the accent on the last syllable but two, (the antepenult.)  When, by repeating and spelling a lesson of these words, he is made familiar with the pronunciation, he may be put to words of more syllables with the same termination, and the accent on the same syllables, as in *ability, deformity, mutability, immutability, infallibility.*  From practice in these classes, he will learn to accent and pronounce correctly every word in the language, having a like termination.

In like manner, the pupil will learn that all words ending in *tion* and *sion,* have the accent on the last syllable but one, (the penult ;) that all words ending in *ology* and *ography,* have the accent on the last syllable but two, as in *doxology, orthography, &c.*

In order to break ill habits in children, and teach them a full enunciation of letters, a distinct articulation of syllables, and the proper accent, classes of pupils should be made to repeat columns of words, first of one formation and then of another.*

This is the business of the first year of learning ; it is to learn *letters, syllables* and *words, pronunciation* and *accent ;* and these should be so familiar that a child can pronounce every common word, correctly, as soon as it is presented to his eye.  When this is accomplished, the child is in a state of improvement, which enables him to enter upon *reading understandingly.*  When he is no longer perplexed with hesitation about the *pronunciation,* he proceeds with advantage to the tasks of *gaining ideas,* and learning definitions.  *One thing at a time. Words* are to be *first learned,* for they are the *instruments* of subsequent acquisition.  The practice of learning language word by word, without classification, must be a slow method.  It is a peculiar advantage in learning English, that great numbers of the words admit of classification—an advantage that does not occur in some other languages.

The common method of putting *beginners* to read easy, familiar lessons, which they understand, is very judicious.  But after they are more advanced, and can read without hesitating, their reading lessons should be of a different character ; containing no puerile phrases ; no baby language.

And here it may be suggested that many persons question the usefulness of pictures in elementary books.  A teacher in the South rep-

---

* The spelling book does more to form the language of a nation than all other books.

robates the practice of using pictures ; parents remark that their children contract such a habit of looking at pictures, that they will not read books without them ; teachers remark that children employ most of their time in looking at pictures, turning over the leaves and wearing them out, or soiling them.   If to some extent pictures are useful, it is very certain, that the practice of filling books with pictures is carried to excess ; they increase expense without an equivalent advantage, and it may be questioned whether pictorial books have not done as much harm as good.   Gentlemen observe that they have very much promoted superficial learning.

It may be added that many of the pictures in school-books are not representations *of the life* of real objects ; but *fictitious* representations formed by a painter or the engraver.   This fact may not be generally known.

In regard to books for reading in seminaries of learning, it is important that most of these should be selected for *important facts* and *sound principles ; not for amusement.*   Among these, the history and geography of our country should have a prominent place.

In reading for the purpose of learning *facts* and *important truth,* children should not be permitted to run over many pages at a lesson. A class of eight or ten pupils should read a paragraph or short section, every pupil of the class repeating the same, till each can read it well, observing the emphasis and pauses.   When each can do this, then let the teacher ask each what the section contains ; what are the facts stated, and take care that all understand the words used.*   Definitions are best learned by explaining words in connection.

The proper mode of impressing facts and truths on the mind of youth, is, by *repetition ;* and by competition in classes, to fix the attention of each pupil upon the subjects presented to them.   A careless perusal of several pages of a book does not answer the purpose.   By attempting too much at once, the principal design is frustrated.

This is a prominent evil in most of our schools.   There is too much hurry, and too heavy burdens are imposed on the tender minds of youth. Hence the imperfect knowledge of the elements of language ; children are urged forward to geography, history, arithmetic, &c. before they have learned to spell one half of our common words.

This is a great error.   In the method here proposed of *learning one thing at a time,* and *that perfectly,* before the pupil proceeds to another thing, he may be made as good a scholar in *five* or *six winters,* as in the usual mode he can be made in *ten winters.*

Most of the foregoing remarks are as applicable to the instruction of youth in Latin, Greek, and other languages, and in the sciences, as they are to instruction in our own language.

---

* A list of questions is often inserted in books for schools, as in History.   The expedience of this is questioned, as it encourages negligence and inattention in the teacher.

## CHAPTER XVIII.

### ORIGIN OF THE HARTFORD CONVENTION IN 1814.

Few transactions of the federalists, during the early periods of our government, excited so much the angry passions of their opposers, as the Hartford Convention, (so called,) during the presidency of Mr. Madison. As I was present at the first meeting of the gentlemen who suggested such a convention; as I was a member of the House of Representatives in Massachusetts, when the resolve was passed for appointing the delegates, and advocated that resolve; and further, as I have copies of the documents, which no other person may have preserved, it seems to be incumbent on me to present to the public the real facts in regard to the origin of the measure, which have been vilely falsified and misrepresented.

After the war of 1812 had continued two years, our public affairs were reduced to a deplorable condition. The troops of the United States, intended for defending our sea-coast, had been withdrawn to carry on the war in Canada; a British squadron was stationed in the Sound to prevent the escape of a frigate from the harbor of New London, and to intercept our coasting trade; one town in Maine was in possession of the British forces; the banks south of New England had all suspended the payment of specie; our shipping lay in our harbors embargoed, dismantled, and perishing; the treasury of the United States was exhausted to the last cent; and a general gloom was spread over the country.

In this condition of affairs, a number of gentlemen in Northampton in Massachusetts, after consultation, determined to invite some of the principal inhabitants of the three counties on the river, formerly composing the old county of Hampshire, to meet and consider whether any measures could be taken to arrest the continuance of the war, and provide for the public safety. In pursuance of this determination, a circular letter was addressed to several gentlemen in the three counties, requesting them to meet at Northampton. The following is a copy of the letter.

Northampton, January 5, 1814.

Sir—In consequence of the alarming state of our public affairs, and the doubts which have existed, as to the correct course to be pursued by the friends of peace, it has been thought advisable by a number of gentlemen in the vicinity, who have conversed together upon the subject, that a meeting should be called of some few of the most discreet and intelligent inhabitants of the old county of Hampshire, for the purpose of a free and dispassionate discussion touching our public concerns. The legislature will soon be in session, and would probably be gratified with a knowledge of the feelings and wishes of the people; and should the gentlemen who may be assembled recommend any course to be pursued by our fellow citizens, for the more distinct expression of the public sentiment, it is necessary the proposed meeting should be called at an early day.

We have therefore ventured to propose that it should be held at Col. Chapman's in this town, on Wednesday, the nineteenth day of January current, at 12 o'clock in the forenoon, and earnestly request your attendance at the above time and place, for the purpose before stated.

With much respect, I am, sir, your obedient servant,

JOSEPH LYMAN.

In compliance with the request in this letter, several gentlemen met at Northampton, on the day appointed, and after a free conversation on the subject of public affairs, agreed to send to the several towns in the three counties on the river, the following circular address.

SIR—The multiplied evils in which the United States have been involved by the measures of the late and present administration, are subjects of general complaint, and in the opinion of our wisest statesmen, call for some effectual remedy. His excellency, the governor of the commonwealth, in his address to the General Court, at the last and present session, has stated, in temperate but clear and decided language, his opinion of the injustice of the present war, and intimated that measures ought to be adopted by the legislature to bring it to a speedy close. He also calls the attention of the legislature to some measures of the general government, which are believed to be unconstitutional. In all the measures of the general government, the people of the United States have a common concern; but there are some laws and regulations which call more particularly for the attention of the northern states, and are deeply interesting to the people of this commonwealth. Feeling this interest, as it respects the present and future generations, a number of gentlemen from various towns in the old county of Hampshire, have met and conferred on the subject, and upon full conviction that the evils we suffer are not wholly of a temporary nature, springing from the war, but some of them of a permanent character, resulting from a perverse construction of the constitution of the United States, we have thought it a duty we owe to our country, to invite the attention of the good people of the counties of Hampshire, Hampden, and Franklin, to the radical causes of these evils.

We know indeed that a negotiation for peace has been recently set on foot, and peace will remove many public evils. It is an event we ardently desire. But when we consider how often the people of the country have been disappointed in their expectations of peace, and of wise measures; and when we consider the terms which our administration has hitherto demanded, some of which it is certain can not be obtained, and some of which, in the opinion of able statesmen, ought not to be insisted on, we confess our hopes of a speedy peace are not very sanguine.

But still a very serious question occurs, whether, without an amendment of the federal constitution, the northern and commercial states can enjoy the advantages to which their wealth, strength, and white population justly entitle them. By means of the representation of slaves, the southern states have an influence in our national councils, altogether disproportioned to their wealth, strength, and resources; and we presume it to be a fact capable of demonstration, that for about twenty years past, the United States have been governed by a representation of about two fifths of the actual property of the country.

In addition to this, the creation of new states in the south, and out of the original limits of the United States, has increased the southern interest, which has appeared so hostile to the peace and commercial prosperity of the northern states. This power, assumed by Congress, of bringing into the Union new states, not comprehended within the territory of the United States, at the time of the federal compact, is deemed arbitrary, unjust, and dangerous, and a direct infringement of the constitution. This is a power which may hereafter be extended, and the evil will not cease with the establishment of peace. We would ask then, ought the northern states to acquiesce in the exercise of this power? To what consequences would it lead? How can the people of the northern states answer to themselves and to their posterity, for an acquiescence in the exercise of this power, that augments an influence already destructive of our prosperity, and will, in time, annihilate the best interests of the northern people?

There are other measures of the general government, which, we apprehend, ought to excite serious alarm. The power assumed to lay a permanent embargo appears not to be constitutional, but an encroachment on the rights of our citizens, which calls for decided opposition. It is a power, we believe, never before exercised by a commercial nation; and how can the northern states, which are habitually commercial, and whose active foreign trade is so necessarily connected with the interest of the farmer and mechanic, sleep in tranquillity under such a violent infringement of their rights? But this is not all. The late act imposing an embargo, is subversive of the first principles of civil liberty. The trade coast-wise between different ports in the *same state*, is arbitrarily and unconstitutionally prohibited; and the subordinate officers of government are vested with powers altogether inconsistent with our republican institutions. It arms the President and his agents with complete control of persons and property, and authorizes the employment of military force to carry its extraordinary provisions into execution.

We forbear to enumerate all the measures of the federal government, which we consider as violations of the constitution, and encroachments upon the rights of the people, and which bear particularly hard upon the commercial people of the north. But we would invite our fellow citizens to consider whether peace will remedy our public evils, without some amendments of the constitution, which shall secure to the northern states their due weight and influence in our national councils.

The northern states acceded to the representation of slaves, as a matter of compromise, upon the express stipulation in the constitution, that they should be protected in the enjoyment of their commercial rights. These stipulations have been repeatedly violated; and it can not be expected that the northern states should be willing to bear their proportion of the burdens of the federal government, without enjoying the benefits stipulated.

If our fellow citizens should concur with us in opinion, we would suggest whether it would not be expedient for the people in town meetings, to address memorials to the General Court, at their present session, petitioning that honorable body to propose a convention of all the northern and commercial states, by delegates to be appointed by their respective legislatures, to consult upon measures in concert, for procuring such alterations in the federal constitution, as will give to the northern states a due proportion of representation, and secure them from the future exercise of powers injurious to their commercial interests ; or if the General Court shall see fit, that they should pursue such other course, as they, in their wisdom, shall deem best calculated to effect the objects.

The measure is of such magnitude that we apprehend a concert of states will be useful, and even necessary to procure the amendments proposed ; and should the people of the several states concur in this opinion, it would be expedient to act on the subject without delay.

We request you, sir, to consult with your friends on the subject, and if it should be thought advisable, to lay this communication before the people of your town. In behalf, and by direction of the gentlemen assembled,      JOSEPH LYMAN, *Chairman.*

In compliance with the request and suggestions in this circular, many town meetings were held, and with great unanimity addresses and memorials were voted to be presented to the General Court, stating the sufferings of the country in consequence of the embargo, the war, and arbitrary restrictions on our coasting trade, with the violations of our constitutional rights, and requesting the legislature to take measures for obtaining redress, either by a convention of delegates from the northern and commercial states, or by such other measures as they should judge to be expedient.

These addresses and memorials were transmitted to the General Court, then in session ; but as commissioners had been sent to Europe for the purpose of negotiating a treaty of peace, it was judged advisable not to have any action upon them, till the result of the negotiation should be known. But during the following summer, no news of peace arrived ; and the distresses of the country increasing, and the sea-coast remaining defenseless, Gov. Strong summoned a special meeting of the legislature in October, in which the petitions of the towns were taken into consideration, and a resolve was passed, appointing delegates to a convention to be held in Hartford. The subsequent history of that convention is known by their report.

This measure of resorting to a convention for the purpose of arresting the evils of a bad administration, roused the jealousy of the advocates of the war, and called forth the bitterest invectives. The convention was represented as a treasonable combination, originating in Boston, for the purpose of dissolving the Union. But citizens of Boston had no concern in originating the proposal for a convention ; it was wholly the project of the people in old Hampshire County ; as respectable and patriotic republicans as ever trod the soil of a free country. The citizens who first assembled in Northampton, convened under the authority of the *bill of rights*, which declares, that the people have a right to meet in a peaceable manner and consult for the public safety. The citizens had the same right then to meet in convention, as they have now ; the distresses of the country demanded extraordinary measures for redress ; the thought of dissolving the Union never entered the head of any of the projectors, or of the members of the convention ; the gentlemen who composed it, for talents and patriotism, have never been surpassed by any assembly in the United States ; and beyond a question, the appointment of the Hartford Convention had a very favorable effect in hastening the conclusion of a treaty of peace.

All the reports which have been circulated respecting the evil designs of that convention, I know to be the foulest misrepresentations. Indeed, respecting the views of the disciples of Washington and the supporters of his policy, many, and probably most of the people of the United States, in this generation, are made to believe far more falsehood than truth. I speak of facts within my personal knowledge. We may well say with the prophet, " Truth is fallen in the street, and equity can not enter." Party spirit produces an unholy zeal to depreciate one class of men for the purpose of exalting another. It becomes rampant in propagating slander, which engenders contempt for personal worth and superior excellence ; it blunts the sensibility of men to injured reputation ; impairs a sense of honor ; banishes the charities of life ; debases the moral sense of the community ; weakens the motives which prompt men to aim at high attainments and patriotic achievements ; degrades national character, and exposes it to the scorn of the civilized world.

## CHAPTER XIX.

### A BRIEF HISTORY OF POLITICAL PARTIES IN THE UNITED STATES.

The origin of the two great political parties which have agitated the United States for half a century ; the causes which have produced and sustained them ; and their injurious effects upon public measures—are subjects of deep interest to the citizens of our confederacy. As it has fallen to my lot to be well acquainted with the origin and history of these parties, it may be interesting to the present generation, most of whom have been born since they originated, to see a brief narrative of facts relating to their origin, their respective motives and measures of policy, and to their influence in disturbing public harmony, embarrassing our national councils, and interrupting the prosperity of the country.

The claims of Great Britain to govern the people of this country, when in a colonial state ; to tax them at pleasure, and impose restrictions on their trade, roused an opposition which resulted in open resistance by force, and which terminated in a revolution. As the inhabitants of the colonies were generally attached to their father-land, small causes could not have induced them to withdraw from it, by dissolving all connection with its government. But the stamp act and other acts of the British Parliament which our fathers deemed unconstitutional and oppressive, gradually produced a conviction in the minds of the more intelligent citizens of this country, that it was necessary to resist the British claims at all hazards.

In order to prepare the minds of our citizens for such a resistance, our leading statesmen deemed it necessary to attempt to detach the affections of the people from the British government and nation, by presenting to their view the corruptions of that government, as well as the consequences of their claim to "bind the colonies in all cases whatsoever." Among other things they insisted much on the oppressiveness of the *excise* laws of Great Britain, and on the injustice and corrupt use of *pensions*. These articles are specified for the purpose of showing the effects which the writings of the fathers of the Revolution afterward had on the measures of our own government. The declamations against the oppressive operation of the excise laws of Great Britain, excited, in this country, an extreme popular odium against that mode of taxation ; and this odium directed against the duties of excise, laid by Congress upon distilled spirits, was among the most powerful causes of the insurrection in Pennsylvania. The arguments which our writers had used against the oppressive laws of Great Britain, to alienate our citizens from the British government, were turned with effect against a similar law of our own government.

Still more general and violent was the opposition in this country to *pensions*. It was represented, and probably with truth, that the administration in England used the power of granting pensions for corrupt

purposes. Yet the practice of bestowing pensions on old public servants, civil and military, when they retired from office, was and is a
noble feature in the British government. But popular opinion, in this
country, made little or no distinction between pensions; they were all
condemned as unjust, and the continual clamors against them served
the purpose of increasing the alienation of our citizens from the British government. The prejudices thus excited against the practice of
granting pensions, were, at the close of the revolutionary war, directed against the grant of half-pay to the officers of the American
army, and its substitute, the grant of five years' full pay, to indemnify
them for the losses they sustained by receiving in payment a depreciated currency.

Hence in the first organization of our government under the present
constitution, Congress granted pensions only to certain disabled officers
or the widows of officers; neglecting to pension most of those who
had assisted in achieving our independence, who descended into their
graves without an indemnification for their losses.

An extreme jealousy of the powers of the government, which had
been excited and fastened on the minds of the American people by
an opposition to the claims of the British Parliament, began very early
to be manifested in this country by popular resolutions against an undue
extension of the powers of our own government. An example of this
jealousy occurred in the county of Fairfax in Virginia, before the definitive treaty of 1783 was signed.

On the 30th of May, 1783, the representatives of that county in the
house of delegates, received instructions from their constituents on several subjects. Among other things, they were instructed to oppose all
attempts of Congress to obtain a perpetual revenue. The people, giving instructions, considered the requisition of Congress on the states for
revenue, as exhibiting strong proofs of a lust of power. They expressed a decided opposition to the proposal of Congress, Oct. 10, 1780, for
appropriating the proceeds of unappropriated lands that might be ceded
to the United States. They also recommended to their representatives in the legislature, to endeavor to obtain an instruction from the
general assembly to the Virginia delegation in Congress, against sending
embassadors to the courts of Europe; on the ground that, in the circumstances then existing, the United States were unable to defray the
expense. They added that such appointments could hardly fail of producing dangerous combinations, factions and cabals in the great council
of America; and from the great distance, and the difficulty of knowing
and examining their conduct, they argued that there was danger that
some of the persons sent might be corrupted and *pensioned*, by the
courts near which they might reside. They supposed that consuls
would be sufficient to answer every good purpose.

Not long after appeared, in the northern states, a public opposition
to the resolve of Congress, granting to the officers of the revolutionary
army five years' extra pay, to make good their losses by the depreciation of continental bills. It must be remarked that Congress, to make
good such losses, had at first passed a resolve to grant the officers half
pay for life. This grant alarmed the people, who considered it as the
beginning of that odious practice of *pensioning*, which existed in Great

Britain ; and such was the clamor excited by it, that Congress substituted for it the grant of five years' full pay, which was generally called the *commutation.*

The commutation however did not satisfy the people.   On the 4th of July, 1783, a popular meeting was held in Amenia, in Duchess County, N. Y., in which it was resolved that the officers of the late army were, neither in justice nor equity entitled to half-pay or to five years' full pay, for the following reasons :

1.  Because when they entered the service, neither Congress nor the state engaged to them any such thing, and that, if in the hour of distress with Congress, the officers availed themselves of a promise for the same, neither the honor nor the justice of the state was pledged to fulfill it.

2.  Because the depreciation of their pay had been fully made up, while most of the citizens had equally suffered by depreciation of the currency.

3.  Because they judged it unjust to make an odious and partial distinction between officers and privates.

4.  Because the state had engaged to the officers a generous bounty in the best lands in the state.

5.  Because such *pensions* would lay a foundation to enslave a free state.

6.  Because it would make an undue discrimination between the service of the line and of the militia.   And

Lastly, because such *pensions* would endanger the making so many drones in the state hive.

On the 15th of July, 1783, a town meeting was held in Torrington, in Connecticut, in which the justice of the five years' pay to the officers was called in question.   The meeting resolved, that although they had the highest opinion of the merits of the officers, and admitted that strict justice ought to be awarded to them ; yet that many of them had found employment in the army, when they had lost other employment ; that many of them had enriched themselves ; that men who had entered the army poor, had returned in affluence ; that it was doubtful whether Congress had the power to make a grant of extra compensation to the officers ; they believed not ; that such a grant was not a charge of the war ; that deranged officers were to receive a *pension ;* that officers continuing in the army were to receive a *pension ;* that *pensions* were always agreeable to men in office, but destructive to the community. Such was the substance of their objections.   Several other towns held meetings and passed similar resolves on this subject.

On the 21st of August, a town meeting was held in Killingworth, in which the grant to the officers was boldly denounced.   It was resolved, that Congress had no power to make such a grant, and that the states were not bound to make it good.   The meeting closed by the appointment of a committee to correspond with the other towns on the subject.

Major William Judd, of Farmington, who had been an officer in the army, was designated by his brother officers, to procure for them the certificates or securities, to which they were entitled under the resolve of Congress.   He repaired to the seat of government, and petitioned Congress to adjust the claims of the officers, that the balances might be received.   On the 22d of March, 1783, Congress passed a resolution for the purpose. Major Judd received the securities, and was on his return, when on Sabbath evening, August 3d, the time when he was expected to arrive in Farmington, the populace collected with a view to seize the securities, to prevent them from being delivered to the officers. He had notice of their design and avoided them. The next morning, the populace assembled at his house, but the Major could not be found. Disappointed of their object, they resolved themselves into a town meeting. In this proceeding, they anticipated the town meeting which had been previously warned to be held the next day.

In this meeting, the most respectable people of the town attended, and an unanimous vote was passed, condemning, " in terms of the highest resentment," the conduct of Major Judd, declaring that it tended to the subversion of the rights of the people, and merited the severest reprehension of the town. They then appointed a committee to serve Major Judd with a copy of the vote. The subject of commutation was then discussed, and the grant of Congress was denounced as unjust, impolitic, oppressive to the people, subversive of the principles of a republican government, and a dangerous precedent.

The meeting then appointed a committee to correspond with the committees of other towns, with power to propose a convention of delegates to consult on the means of counteracting the effect and operation of the commutation.

On the 23d of August, a committee consisting of Thomas Seymour, Hugh Ledlie, George Smith, Seth Collins and Daniel Pitkin, of Hartford, John Robbins of Wethersfield, and Wait Goodrich of Glastenbury, notified that a meeting or 'general convention of delegates of towns should be held at Middletown, on the first Wednesday of September then next, to consider what ought to be done upon the subject of the commutation, in order to some constitutional mode of redress.

On the 16th of September following, the town of Hartford gave instructions to their representatives, in the legislature, Thomas Seymour and George Pitkin. In these instructions, the representatives were expressly directed strenuously to oppose all encroachments of the American Congress on the sovereignty and jurisdiction of the separate states, and every assumption of power not expressly vested in them by the confederation ; to thoroughly investigate the question whether Congress had power to grant half pay for life to the officers of the army, or five years' full pay, as an equivalent ; to use their utmost endeavors that the vacant lands in the United States might be ceded and appropriated for the general benefit of the United States. They recommended to them to use their influence to obtain an instruction from the General Assembly to the Connecticut delegation in Congress against sending embassadors to the courts of Europe ; it being an expense, which in the existing circumstances, they deemed unnecessary and insupportable ; and finally the gentlemen were instructed to exert themselves, that *placemen* and *pensioners* and every other superfluous officer of state should be discontinued and removed.

The proposed convention met in Middletown on the 3d day of September, but a majority of the towns not being represented, they adjourned to meet again on the 30th of the month. In their proceedings, they recommended to the freemen to instruct their representatives, early to set on foot, at the next session of the Assembly, a candid and thorough inquiry into the extent of the powers of Congress ; and if it should be found that Congress, in granting the commutation to the officers, had exceeded their powers, then the most effectual constitutional means were to be used to relieve the people from that burden.

In this convention an attempt was made to effect an entire change in the council or senate of the state ; all the members who had assisted in conducting the country through the war were to be displaced ; a nomination of other men was made ; but the printers in Connecticut declining to print it, it was sent to New York, printed and privately circulated.

To aid the attempt to change the members of the council, the most ridiculous tales were circulated to render them odious.  One story, aimed particularly at the Hon. Oliver Wolcott of Litchfield, the father of the late Gov. Wolcott, was propagated with great industry and no little success in Litchfield County ; viz. that this gentleman had said, " we shall never have good times, till a poor man is obliged to live on sheep's head and pluck."  This ridiculous falsehood was so far believed, in that county, that Mr. Wolcott came near to lose his election to the next legislature.  The same or a similar story was circulated respecting the Huntington family in Norwich.  This miserable artifice however did not succeed, and the former councilors were re-elected.

At the second meeting of the convention at Middletown on the 30th of September, about fifty towns were represented, which, at that time, were a majority of the towns in the state.  Nothing however of importance was done, except to address a petition or remonstrance to the General Assembly on the subject of the commutation.  They adjourned to meet again on the 16th of December following.

At the meeting in December, the convention issued a recommendation to the people of the state to peruse a pamphlet published by Judge Burke of South Carolina, against the establishment of the society of the Cincinnati, by the officers of the late army.  This society was considered by many persons as the germ of an order of nobility ; and so violent was the popular jealousy respecting it, that a general meeting of the society was afterward held in Philadelphia, in which Gen. Washington presided, and the more objectionable articles of their constitution were expunged.

This convention adjourned to meet at the same place on the third Tuesday of March then next.  They met accordingly on the 16th of the month and framed an address to the good people of Connecticut, in which they urged their objections to the resolve of Congress, granting extra pay to the officers, and also against the society of the Cincinnati. In the closing paragraph, the convention stated that as the Cincinnati had adjourned to meet in July then next, they thought best to adjourn the convention till August ; but they never afterward assembled.  The able discussions of the subject, during the winter of 1783–4, had convinced a majority of citizens that the resolve of Congress was expedient, and that opposition to the measure was wrong, and would be ineffectual. At the election in April, a large majority of the towns elected representatives who supported the measures of Congress ; and at the session of the Assembly in May following, an act was passed granting power to

Congress to lay an impost of five per cent. on imported goods, for the purpose of raising a revenue.

Thus ended this formidable opposition to the acts of Congress, which, for several months, threatened a revolution or entire change of rulers in this state.*

This opposition to the measures of Congress gave rise to the democratic party in Connecticut. It proceeded from honest motives, an extreme jealousy of power in the hands of rulers; a jealousy which had been manifested by the colonists from the first settlements in America; a jealousy which had resisted all the efforts of the British government to bring New England under a general governor, to be appointed by the crown; a jealousy which had been fanned into a flame by the stamp act, and which finally determined the colonists to resist the British claims by force.

The party thus formed on the question of the right of Congress to grant extra pay to the officers, constituted about one third or one fourth of the citizens. On the question of ratifying the constitution in 1788, the votes of the convention were one hundred and twenty-eight in the affirmative, and forty in the negative. And this was nearly the proportion for several years, till new questions arose in the administration of the government under the constitution of the United States.

And in this place I will take the liberty to correct a common error in popular opinion, in regard to the parties at the time the constitution was formed. It is well known that the friends and supporters of the ratification were denominated *Federalists;* and the opposers *anti-federalists.* It has often been alledged, in recent times, that the *federalists* were in favor of a *consolidation* of the several states, which should reduce them to the condition of mere corporations under the general government. But this is a mistake; the federalists were never the advocates of a consolidation; they were opposed to it. The mistake arose from the fact that the opposers of the ratification were apprehensive that the

---

* It may be remarked, that of the discontents among the people on account of this resolve of Congress, we have no history. The subject of the convention in Connecticut is not mentioned in Marshall's History of the Life of Washington; it is not mentioned in most of the histories for schools now used, and except a brief account in my History of the United States, this portion of the history of Connecticut is all a blank to the present generation.

The popular discontents respecting the commutation of half pay, appeared in Massachusetts. In February, 1784, a committee of the towns of Wrentham and Medway, with the advice of the selectmen of the towns of Franklin and Billingham, sent a letter to the selectmen of Boston, and to all the towns in the county of Suffolk, to take into consideration the commutation, and also the act of Massachusetts, granting an impost to raise a revenue to Congress, without proper restrictions. The committee further voted to desire the several towns in Suffolk, to choose a delegate or delegates, to meet at the house of Mrs. Woodward, innholder in Dedham, on the third Wednesday in March, to take into consideration these subjects and advise to some measures for the redress of grievances.

A town meeting was held in Boston; the letter from the committee of Wrentham and Medway was laid before the meeting, and the subjects debated. On the 15th day of March, the town, by their clerk, William Cooper, returned an answer, expressing their disapprobation of the county meeting proposed, and of any attempt to oppose the resolves of Congress. This letter, it is believed, prevented any further proceedings of towns on this subject.

These letters are published at large in the Connecticut Courant of March 30, 1784.

powers vested in Congress were too extensive, and that the *effect would be* to destroy the sovereignty of the states, and result in a consolidation. But at the time when the subject of ratification was under discussion, the anti-federal or democratic part of our citizens never charged the federalists with the *design* to effect a consolidation. This is a modern calumny.

It is a remarkable fact that the democratic party, with few or no exceptions, opposed the ratification of the constitution; and beyond a question, had that opposition succeeded, anarchy or civil war would have been the consequence. The federalists *made* the frame of government, and with immense efforts, procured it to be ratified, in opposition to nearly one half of the citizens of the United States, headed by some of the ablest men in the Union.

During the first session of Congress, the same parties existed, and arranged themselves on different sides of several important questions which occupied the deliberations of that body. The democratic party opposed the funding of the public debt of the United States, and the assumption of the state debts; those important measures which were necessary to do justice to the creditors, and revive the credit and the languishing commerce of the United States. The genius of Hamilton, and the wisdom and firmness of Washington and his federal supporters, overcame the opposition; the public debts were funded, courts were established, and the government in all its departments was organized.

One of the objections to the funding of the debts, arose from the apprehension that the United States would contract a permanent debt, like that which oppresses the British nation. Mr. Jefferson's mind was filled with this terrific phantom. It is strange that a single glance at the immense resources of this country, should not have dissipated all such apprehensions.

Another objection to the funding of the public debts, arose from the depreciated value of the evidences of those debts, which had sunk to one-eighth of the nominal sum, and to a great extent, had been sold at that value. It was considered unjust that the purchasers of those securities, who had given for them only one-eighth of their original value, should have them funded at par; and Mr. Madison introduced into the House of Representatives a proposition for a discrimination, which should give to the original holders of the securities a part of their original value. This project was defeated.

It may be here remarked how erroneously the opposers of the constitution reasoned in regard to its operation and effects. One of the strongest objections to the constitution, proceeded from an apprehension that the federal government would reduce the states to mere corporations; in other words, would produce a consolidation. Events have shown that the danger is on the other side, and that we have most cause of fear that the states will be too strong for the federal government.

Soon after the government was organized, and business began to be prosperous, a new cause of party contention arose from an effort of Mr. Jefferson and his friends to divert the trade of this country from Great Britain to France. The pretext for this change was the restrictions which Great Britain laid on the commerce of this country. To prove that Great Britain imposed higher duties on our exports to that country and her colonies, and subjected our trade to more severe restrictions than France laid upon our commerce to that kingdom and her colonies, Mr. Jefferson sent to Congress a lengthy report on the privileges and restrictions of our trade in the several countries of Europe. Soon after this report, Mr. Madison introduced into the House of Representatives a series of resolutions, adapted to carry into effect the purpose of Mr. Jefferson, and encourage a trade with France, in preference to that with Great Britain. These resolutions occasioned animated debates, but they were ultimately negatived.

In these efforts of Mr. Jefferson and his friends to change the course of our trade, it was easy to discover the strong predilection of that party for a connection with France. Popular feeling also was on the side of France. The people of this country had not forgotten their sufferings from the British armies, and particularly the cruelties practiced on American prisoners, during the Revolution. On the other hand, the assistance rendered to the United States by France, in support of independence, had conciliated the favor and friendship of our citizens for that country. In addition to these circumstances, Mr. Jefferson's long residence in France, in the character of American minister, and the coincidence of his principles with those of the most eminent French authors and philosophers, had produced in him a strong predilection for that nation; while he entertained the bitterest enmity to Great Britain. Of this he has left abundant evidence in his published letters.

Through the instrumentality of these means, the democratic party became, in some measure, identified with the partisans of France. Subsequent events strengthened this union.

It is well known that after the treaty of peace with Great Britain in 1783, the government of that country refused to deliver, to the United States, the forts on our northern frontier, until the British merchants had received payment of the debts due to them from our citizens, for goods sold to them before the Revolution. At the same time, citizens of the southern states demanded, from the British government, compensation for the slaves which the British armies had carried away at the close of the war. The controversy between the two governments, on these subjects, was violent, obstinate, and extremely embarrassing to the President. This controversy was adjusted by the treaty negotiated by Mr. Jay. The British government agreed to pay for the slaves, and the United States stipulated to pay the debts due from our citizens to British merchants.

But new causes of controversy arose. The revolution in France, which had just put an end to the monarchy, had alarmed the kings of the neighboring nations, and they combined to check the progress of French principles; or at least to prevent them from overturning their thrones. One of the methods adopted by Great Britain to distress France, was to prevent neutral nations from supplying that country with provisions for food, as well as munitions of war. The British statesmen knew the predilection of American citizens for France, and for a republican government, which they supposed the French would establish. It was therefore the policy of Great Britain to prevent the United States from joining France in her contest with the combined powers. This was probably one motive which induced the British gov-

ernment to issue an order of council, directing their ships to capture
American vessels, and conduct them into her ports for adjudication.
In consequence of this order, the ocean was swept of American ves-
sels.  These captures raised a spirit of universal indignation in the
United States, and very much strengthened the democratic party.

Other causes contributed to the same effect.  After the death of the
King of France, and the commencement of the republican form of
government, the French rulers began to entertain the project of revolutionizing Europe by overthrowing monarchies.  This project they
supposed to be so congenial to the opinions of the Americans, that they
expected our government would readily unite with France, in resisting
the combination of kings to defeat the purpose.  With a view to bring
the United States into alliance with France, Mr. Genet was dispatched,
as minister to this country, authorized to induce our government to join
France in defending herself against the combined powers, and in extending republican principles and forms of government.

Mr. Genet landed at Charleston, in South Carolina, and without presenting his credentials to the President, he proceeded to constitute
French consuls to be judges of admiralty, with authority to condemn
British vessels taken as prizes, and sent into port by French privateers
fitted out in American harbors.  He also commissioned men to be military officers for raising troops to invade the Spanish possessions on our
southern border.  On his way to the north, he promoted the formation
of democratic societies to support him in attempts to draw this country
into an alliance with France.  These societies held meetings, and
passed violent resolutions in favor of French principles.  The democratic society in Kentucky assumed a high tone in demanding the free
right to enter and navigate the Mississippi, the mouth of which was
within the Spanish territories.  They charged our government with
neglect of their interests in not procuring a free navigation of that river.
Their claim to such freedom was reasonable, but the right to it was to
be obtained by negotiation, and their charges against the executive of
the United States of neglecting to obtain it were not to be justified.

The conduct of the French minister gave great offense to our citizens
and to the executive.  He evidently supposed that his influence, favored
by a predilection of our citizens for a republican form of government,
and supported by the democratic societies, was sufficient to control the
measures of our government.  Hence when President Washington issued a proclamation recommending neutrality, and manifested a firm
determination to oppose the designs of France, Mr. Genet *appealed to
the people.*  This bold and rash declaration ruined his cause.  The
President was not a man to surrender his authority to a foreign minister,
and he demanded his recall.

In the midst of the most perplexing difficulties, with a popular French
minister intriguing to draw this country into an alliance with France, in
her war with the combined powers, and boldly usurping rights of sovereignty in the United States ; compelled to struggle with the opposition
of some of his cabinet, and with many popular leaders of the democratic party, acting in concert with the French minister, President
Washington stood as firm as a rock ; and to his popularity chiefly was
this country indebted for its escape from a connection with France,

which would have involved the fate of this country with hers, in the most obstinate contest ever witnessed in Europe.

But the democratic party in this country had now become identified with the French partisans in the United States. To show how intimately these parties were united in views, and how much dependence the French had on the leaders of the democratic party in this country, I will relate an anecdote.

In the month of August, 1793, I was in New York at the house of a Mr. Bradley in Maiden Lane, where Mr. Genet and his suit were lodging. While sitting at dinner, I related the news which had just been received, that a British vessel had arrived in the harbor of Boston, a prize to a French privateer, and that the marshal of the district had taken possession of the vessel, by order of our government, to prevent her from being condemned by the French consular court of admiralty. On hearing this fact, Mr. Paschal, a secretary of Mr. Genet, immediately remarked that *General Washington was making war on the French nation.* He spoke in French, not knowing that any person at table, except his countrymen, understood him. Mr. Genet immediately said that our government was bringing this country back under the power of Great Britain. This remark excited my spirit to reply bluntly, that our government could no more bring us again under the dominion of Great Britain, than they could remove Catskill mountains, or words to that effect. I asked him if he thought Gen. Washington, Mr. Jefferson, and Mr. Hamilton were fools. Mr. Genet replied instantly, " Mr. Jefferson is no fool."

I informed Mr. Wolcott, controller of the treasury, of this conversation, and he, after advising with some members of the cabinet, wrote to me, requesting me to send him an affidavit of the facts. This was done, and the affidavit is among the papers of the late Governor Wolcott.

The policy of President Washington was pacific ; he knew the interests of his country required the continuance of peace, and to this object he devoted all his authority, and directed all his measures. To effect an adjustment of controversies with Great Britain, he nominated Mr. Jay, as special envoy to negotiate a treaty with the government of that kingdom, and this embassy was successful. The great questions respecting the surrender of the northern forts by Great Britain, and the claims of British merchants for debts due from our citizens, were settled.

This event frustrated the project and hopes of the democratic party in this country, of forming an alliance with France in her revolutionary struggle. Their disappointment was manifested by continued ebullitions of the bitterest opposition to Mr. Jay's treaty.* Never was the rancor of party spirit exhibited with more force, than in the writings which filled the opposition prints on that occasion. A specimen of that rancor is furnished by a paragraph published in Davis's Gazette, in Richmond, Virginia. It was in these words :—

" Notice is hereby given, that in case the treaty entered into by that d—d arch traitor, J—n J—y, with the British tyrant, should be ratified,

* " I join with you in thinking the treaty an execrable thing."—*Jefferson's Letter to E. Rutledge*, Vol. III, p. 317.

a petition will be presented to the General Assembly of Virginia, at their next session, praying that the said state may recede from the Union, and be left under the government and protection of one hundred thousand free and independent Virginians."

" P. S. As it is the wish of the people of the said state to enter into a treaty of amity, and commerce, and navigation, with any other state or 'states of the present Union, *who* are averse to returning again under the galling yoke of Great Britain, the printers of the (at present) United States are requested to publish the above notification."

Notwithstanding the violent opposition made to this treaty by the democratic party, and by many of the federal party, President Washington, after long deliberation, set his signature to its ratification. The event proved how erroneous was popular opinion in regard to the merits of that treaty ; for in its operation, it proved to be highly favorable to the commercial interests of this country, and the expiration of certain articles at the end of ten years, was deeply regretted.

But the adjustment of our controversy with Great Britain did not put an end to our troubles. The inveterate contest between France and the combined powers continued, with a bitterness that set at defiance all the established rules of international law by which the rights of neutral nations had been protected. Great Britain, for the purpose of crippling France, issued orders for blockading French ports ; and in retaliation, the French government issued orders for blockading British ports. Thus our commerce was subjected to interruption by the cruisers of both nations ; our ships were taken and condemned by both, and scarcely to this day have our merchants been indemnified for their losses.

Another cause of continual irritation, was the orders of the British government for impressing seamen on board of American ships. These orders did not extend to the impressment of native Americans, but of British born subjects, in American service. By the laws or established usages of Great Britain, a British subject can not alienate his allegiance to the British crown. Hence naturalization of subjects in the United States gives no protection to British subjects in American ships. In executing these orders, it sometimes happened that native Americans were impressed from our ships. This was justly considered an outrageous injury ; and to compel Great Britain to relinquish this practice, was a principal reason for declaring war against that nation in 1812.

During the whole period of President Washington's administration, and amid the most perplexing difficulties, that great man maintained the most rigid impartiality toward the belligerent nations ; his integrity, firmness, justice, and love of his country, remained unshaken. But his prudence could not shield him from incessant abusive attacks in the democratic papers. He was charged with partiality to Great Britain, and his cabinet with enmity to republican principles. He bore the calumnious charges with astonishing magnanimity ; but his sensibility was at times so wounded that he vented complaints. "I wonder," said he, " why I am so much abused ; I do as well as I can."

We have a specimen of the charges of the democratic party against President Washington's administration, in a letter of Mr. Jefferson to his Italian friend, Mazzei, who had resided some time in this country.

The letter was written in April, 1796, some months after the ratifica-tion of the treaty negotiated by Mr. Jay. The copy from which was made the first translation published in this country, was a version in French, printed in the Moniteur of January 15, 1797, to which were attached severe animadversions on the conduct of our government to-ward France, charging it with the basest ingratitude. The paper con-taining this letter was put into my hands in April, 1797, by Mr. Epaph-ras Jones of Hartford, who had just returned from France. I was then the editor of two papers in New York—the Minerva, afterward the Commercial Advertiser, and the Herald, afterward the Spectator. The letter of Mazzei attracting my attention, I translated it and published it in my papers.

On the appearance of this letter in Philadelphia, it attracted the no-tice of the public, and particularly of the members of the cabinet. Mr. Jefferson did not deny the authenticity of the letter, but he alledg-ed that it had been altered or incorrectly translated. On comparing the published copy with that which has been since published in the cor-respondence of Mr. Jefferson with his friends, (Vol. III, p. 327,) it ap-pears that there is no material difference except in a misprint of the word *form* instead of *forms*. This misprint would make the writer, Mr. Jefferson, charge his political opposers with attempting to give us the *form* of the British government, instead of the *forms* or ceremonies of the British court, which he alledged to be his meaning. The fact of Mr. Jefferson's denial of the correctness of the published copy, induced Col. Pickering to write to me in New York, requesting me to send to him the French original. I complied with this request, and the letter in the original, with a translation, was published in the Gazette of the United States. The French paper, the Moniteur, was then returned to me, and as I was under an obligation to deliver it to Mr. Jones, I had the precaution to make a correct copy of the original French, and to procure it to be attested, as a true copy, by Mr. afterward Chief Jus-tice Kent. This copy is now in my possession, and I will give it in the original and in plain English.

Florence, le 1er Janvier.

*Lettre de M. Jefferson, ci-devant Ministre des Etats Unis en France, et Secretaire au department des affaires etrangères, a un citoyen de Virginie.*

Cette lettre litteralment traduite, est addressée a M. Mazzei, auteur des Recherches Historiques et Politiques sur les Etats Unis d'Amerique, demeurant en Toscane.

"Notre etat politique a prodigieusement changé, depuis que vous nous avez quitté. Au lieu de ce noble amour de la liberté et de ce gouvernement republicain, qui nous ont fait passer triomphans a travers les dangers de la guerre, un parti Anglican-monarchico-aristocratique s'est elevé. Son object avoué est de nous imposer la substance, comme il nous a deja donné les formes de gouvernement Britannique ; cepend-ant le corps principal de nos citoyens reste fidele aux principes repub-licains. Tous les proprietaires foncieres sont pour ces principes, ainsi qu'une grande masse d'hommes a talens. Nous avons contre nous re-publicains le pouvoir executif, le pouvoir judiciaire, deux des trois branches de la legislature, tous les officiers du gouvernement, tous ceux qui aspirent a l'être, tous les hommes timides qui preferent le calme du despotisme a la mer orageuse de la liberté, les marchands Bretons, et les Americaines qui trafiquent avec des capitaux Bretons, les speculateurs, les gens interesses dans la banque et dans les fonds publics, etablissements inventès dans des vues de corruption, et pour nous assimuler au modele Britannique dans ses parties pourries.

" Je vous donnerais la fievre, si je vous nommais les apostats qui ont embrassé ces héresies, des hommes qui etaient des Solomons dans le conseil, et des Samsons dans les combats, mais dont la chevelure a eté coupée par la catin Angleterre.

" On voudrait nous ravir cette liberté que nous avons gagnée par tant de travaux et de dangers.  Mais nous la conserverons ; notre masse de poids et de richesse est trop grand pour que nous ayons a craindre qu'on tente d'employer la force contre nous.  Il suffit que nous nous reveillions, et que nous rompions les liens lilliputiens dont il nous ont garottes pendant le premier sommeil qui a succédé a nos travaux.  Il suffit que nous arretions les progress de ce système d'ingratitude et injustice envers la France, de que on voudrait nous aliener pour nous rendre a la influence Britannique, etc."

A true copy from a French paper, entitled " Gazette Nationale, ou le Moniteur Universel," 6 Pluviose, l'an 5 de Republique.

JAMES KENT.

New York, May 22, 1797.

Florence, 6th of January.

*Letter of Mr. Jefferson, formerly Minister of the United States in France, and Secretary in the department of foreign affairs, to a citizen of Virginia.*

This letter, literally translated, is addressed to Mr. Mazzei, author of Historical and Political Researches on the United States of America, resident in Tuscany.

" Our political state has been prodigiously altered since you have left us.  Instead of that noble love of liberty and of republican government, which enabled us to pass triumphantly through the dangers of the war, an Anglican, monarchical, aristocratical party has arisen.  Their avowed object is to impose on us the substance, as they have already given us the forms of the British government.  Nevertheless, the principal body of our citizens remains faithful to republican principles.  All our landholders are in favor of those principles ; so also the great mass of men of talents.  We republicans have against us the executive power, the judiciary power, two of the three branches of the legislature ; all the officers of the government ; all those who aspire to offices ; all timid men who prefer the calm of despotism to the stormy sea of liberty ; the British merchants and Americans who trade with British capitals ; the speculators, the people who are interested in the banks and in the public funds ; establishments invented for the purpose of corruption, and to assimilate us to the British model in its corrupt parts.

" I should give you a fever, if I should name to you the apostates who have embraced these heresies, the men who were Solomons in council, and Samsons in combat, but whose locks have been shorn by the harlot England.

"These men would ravish from us that liberty which we gained by so many labors and dangers. But we shall preserve it; our mass of weight and of wealth is too great to suffer us to fear that our opposers will employ force against us. It is enough that we are awake, and that we shall break the lilliputian ties with which they have bound us, during the first slumber which succeeded our toils. It is sufficient that we arrest the progress of that system of ingratitude and injustice toward France, from which they would alienate us, to subject us to British influence, etc."

To this letter were subjoined the following remarks in the Moniteur.

["This interesting letter from one of the most virtuous and enlightened citizens of the United States, explains the conduct of the Americans in regard to France. It is certain that of all the neutral and friendly powers, there is none from which France had a right to expect more interest and succors than from the United States. She is their true mother country, since she has offered to them their liberty and independence. Ungrateful children, instead of abandoning her, they ought to have armed in her defense. But if imperious circumstances had prevented them from openly declaring for the republic of France, they ought at least to have made demonstrations and excited apprehensions in England, that at some moment or other they should declare themselves. This fear alone would have been sufficient to force the cabinet of England to make peace. It is clear that a war with the United States would strike a terrible blow at the commerce of the English, would give them uneasiness for the preservation of their possessions on the American continent, and deprive them of the means of conquering the Dutch and French colonies.

"Equally ungrateful and impolitic, the Congress hastens to encourage the English, that they might pursue in tranquillity their war of extermination against France, and to invade the colonies and the commerce of England. They sent to London a minister, Mr. Jay, known by his attachment to England, and his personal relations to Lord Grenville, and he concluded suddenly a treaty of commerce which united them with Great Britain, more than a treaty of alliance.

"Such a treaty, under all the peculiar circumstances, and by the consequences which it must produce, is an act of hostility against France. The French government in short has testified the resentment of the French nation, by breaking off communication with an ungrateful and faithless ally, until she shall return to a more just and benevolent conduct. Justice and sound policy equally approve this measure of the French government. There is no doubt it will give rise, in the United States, to discussions which may afford a triumph to the party of good republicans, the friends of France.

"Some writers, in disapprobation of this wise and necessary measure of the Directory, maintain that in the United States, the French have for partisans only certain demagogues who aim to overthrow the existing government. But their impudent falsehoods convince no one, and prove only what is too evident, that they use the liberty of the press to serve the enemies of France."]

The charges against President Washington and his supporters, the federalists, so boldly affirmed in this letter, I *know* to be the foulest misrepresentations that ever characterized political enmity. I was well acquainted with the leading men in the cabinet and in our public councils at that time ; with several of them I had had an intimate acquaintance for ten, twenty or thirty years ; and I *know*, as well as one man can know the opinions of others, that there was no Anglican, monarchical, aristocratical party among them ; and that the banks and the public funds were *not* contrivances invented for the purposes of corruption, and for assimilating us to the British government in its corrupt parts. The men who composed the councils of the country, under President Washington, were all republicans in principle, men of the firmest integrity, and as sound patriots as ever honored a free country. The funding of the public debts was a measure dictated by a high sense of justice to the public creditors, and by the soundest policy, as were all the laws and measures of the first Congress under the present constitution. It was this policy which, being pursued by Washington and his successors, revived the credit and the commerce of the United States, and gave them an exalted name among the nations of the earth. There was not a man in Washington's cabinet, and I believe not in the federal party, who wished to extend the measures of the government beyond the legitimate limits of the constitution.

The charge of a predilection for monarchy among the leading men of the federal party, was however continually repeated in the public prints ; and as this charge had no small influence in alienating the minds of honest citizens from the administration of Washington, it deserves a more particular notice.

The person most generally charged with being a monarchist, was Gen. Hamilton. This charge is unfounded ; that gentleman never advocated the establishment of a monarchy in the United States. He believed that the mixed kind of government in Great Britain, formed the best constitution that had ever been devised. If that form of government is not the best that men can devise, yet the success of that government in raising the British nation to power and wealth, and in giving stability to public measures, may well justify Mr. Hamilton's opinion.

But Mr. Hamilton knew and declared that a monarchy could not be established in the United States ; and it is proof of great ignorance or of great hypocrisy, for men of this generation, the younglings of yesterday, to charge the federalists of a former generation with the design to erect a monarchy in this country. It was a principle then acknowledged, that a nation consisting mostly of independent landholders would never consent to yield the powers of government to a single man. Mr. Hamilton, well versed in the history of republics, and foreseeing evils like those which this country has experienced, and is now suffering, wished to incorporate into the constitution, the most effectual guards against corruption and factions. But the highest toned propositions which he made, for this purpose, in the convention which framed the constitution, were, that the president, the senate, and judges of the supreme court, should hold their offices during their good behavior, and the house of representatives should be elected by the people, to serve three years.

Events have shown how well Mr. Hamilton understood the character of a popular government. Nor was he singular in his opinions. Intelligent and reflecting men, at that period, generally entertained similar opinions ; and our past history furnishes woful evidence to verify them. That such was the fact, may appear from the following remarks of a disciple of Washington, published forty years ago.

" Nothing is so fatal to truth and tranquillity, as party spirit ; it is rash, imperious, unyielding, unforgiving. Blind to truth and deaf to argument, it sees no merit in an enemy ; no demerit in a friend. Urged by the passion or convenience of the moment, it rushes impetuously to the attainment of its object, regardless of events, and forgetting that its own example may be drawn into precedent, and under a change of parties, prove a two-edged sword as fatal to friends as foes.

" To a man versed in the history of nations, the condition of parties in the United States presents nothing new, but the men and the forms of proceeding. The general principles, views, and passions displayed, are the same as have characterized parties in all ages and countries. Individuals of aspiring minds, who have been mortified by neglect, or irritated by the agitations of successless competition ; men who can neither bear an equal nor yield to a superior, have the address to enlist into their service, the credulous and illiterate multitude. To oppose them, men of principle unite and form a party ; public measures are proposed or attacked with zeal ; opposition begets obstinacy ; argument is resisted by will ; mutual concessions are either not proposed or are rejected ; and laws passed under such circumstances are either soon repealed, or are ineffectual in their operation.

" Parties thus arrayed against each other, often lose sight of the original points of difference, or magnify trifling differences into matters of vast concern to the public. Zeal is inflamed to enthusiasm ; a regard to truth is extinguished in the desire of victory ; and moderation yields to the apprehension of defeat. Then begins the reign of corruption ; each party determines to triumph ; and neither constitution nor law, religion ·nor morality, reputation nor conscience, can raise effectual barriers to restrain their passions and pursuits.

" In this warfare of parties, the adherents to each voluntarily put themselves under a favorite leader, and take a popular name. Thus organized, each party rallies under the *name* and the *leader*, with the *esprit du corps* for the moving principle ; forgetting the origin, or ignorant of the motives of the association. The leader is stimulated by pride ; his adherents, by the sound of his name, or by the appellation of the party, which is neither understood nor intelligible. A white rose, a red rose, a cockade ; round-head or cavalier, whig or tory, federalist or democrat, or other insignificant appellation, becomes the rallying point for a headstrong populace, prepared for violence.

" In the effervescence of popular passions, the leader who has gained the confidence of a party must feed the hopes and gratify the expectations of his adherents. Applying to faction the military maxim of M. Porcius Cato, ' Bellum seipsum alit,' war feeds or sustains itself— a victorious leader supplies the wants and secures the attachment of his followers by dividing among them the spoils of the vanquished. Then commences the reign of persecution and revenge. The man who mounts into office on popular confidence, may rise with impunity above the constitution of his country, and trample on the rights of the people.  Under the specious titles of a *republican* and *friend of the people*, he may exercise the despotism of a Frederick.  The men who flatter the people become their masters ; and the party, which, while a minority, will lick the dust to gain the ascendency, becomes in power, violent, vindictive, and tyrannical."

These opinions, when first published in 1802, may be considered as *predictions*.  What are they now but *history ?*

The slanderous charges against the leading federalists continued to be repeated, until a majority of the people of the United States were brought to believe them ; then followed a change of the administration. From the time when the anti-federal party assumed the more popular appellation of *republican*, which was soon after the arrival of the French minister in 1793, that epithet became a powerful instrument in the process of making proselytes to the party.  The influence of *names* on the mass of mankind, was never more distinctly exhibited, than in the increase of the democratic party in the United States.  The popu- larity of the denomination of the *republican party*, was more than a match for the popularity of Washington's character and services, and contributed to overthrow his administration.  The misrepresentations which effected this change, impressed falsehood upon the minds of a great portion of the citizens of the United States, and particularly of the western states.  These falsehoods are often repeated and republish- ed, to the prejudice of the soundest republicans, and firmest friends of our beloved country.  So entirely perverted is public opinion, that the term *federalist*, the honored appellation of Washington, of the mem- bers of his cabinet, and of the whole party which framed the constitu- tion, put it in operation, and saved the country from anarchy or civil war, or from both, is now used as a term of reproach.

The incessant attacks on General Washington and his adherents, for several years, succeeded at length in rendering that great and good man so unpopular, that it is doubtful whether, if he had been a can- didate for election at the expiration of his second term of office, he would have received a majority of votes for president.  But at the close of that term, he declined a re-election, and retired.

On the very day when General Washington became a private citizen, there appeared in the Aurora, the leading democratic paper in Phila- delphia, the following article.

" ' Now lettest thou thy servant depart in peace, for mine eyes have seen thy salvation,' was the pious ejaculation of a man who beheld a flood of happiness rushing on mankind.  If there ever was a time that would license its reiteration, the time has now arrived, for the man who is the source of misfortunes to our country, is this day reduced to a level with his fellow citizens, and is no longer possessed of power to multiply evils on the United States.  If there was ever a period for re- joicing, this is the moment.  Every heart in unison with the peace and happiness of the people, ought to beat high with exultation, that the name of Washington from this day ceases to give currency to political iniquity, and to legalize corruption ; a new era that promises much to the people ; for public measures must now stand on their own merits ;

and nefarious projects can be no longer supported by a name. When a retrospect is taken of the Washington administration for eight years, it is a subject of the greatest astonishment, that a single individual could have cankered the principles of republicanism in an enlightened people, and should have carried his designs against public liberty so far as to put in jeopardy its very existence. Such however are the facts; and with them staring us in the face, this day ought to be a day of jubilee in the United States."—*Aurora, March* 4, 1797.

Who can read or hear this infamous libel on Washington and his administration, without indignation and amazement?

President Washington, in his last message to Congress, recommended the formation of a navy competent to defend our commerce and our sea-coast. Mr. Adams, his successor, countenanced the same proposition. But this project was strenuously opposed by the democratic party, more particularly by members of Congress from the southern states. A few frigates and other smaller vessels of force had been built, with a special reference to the protection of our seamen and our commerce against the Algerines; but an increase of naval force was violently opposed. One member of Congress said openly, that if our little navy was on fire, and he could extinguish the fire by spitting, he would not spit.

This opposition to a naval force was subdued by the brilliant victories of our frigates in the war of 1812. To the honor of the candid Monroe, it ought to be related that at the first session of Congress after those victories, he acknowledged his error in opposing the establishment of a navy, and avowed his purpose of supporting it. From that time the opposition to the establishment of a navy ceased. Certain it is, that if the commerce and sea-coast of the United States ever need defense from an enemy, the most economical and most effectual means of defense must be on the ocean.

Mr. Adams, in administering the government, pursued, with some exceptions, the general course of policy which President Washington had adopted. But during his administration, an attempt was made to check the flood of slander with which our government had been for many years assailed; and further, to counteract the influence of spies, who were supposed to swarm in the country. For these purposes, Congress passed two laws, called the alien and sedition laws. These acts raised a violent clamor; they were denounced as unconstitutional; and the ablest men in Virginia employed their pens in composing most pointed resolutions in opposition to these laws. So far do those resolutions proceed in arguing in favor of state rights, that their authority was cited in vindication of the efforts of South Carolina to resist certain measures of Congress; efforts which threatened a nullification of the confederacy.

With regard to the sedition law it may be remarked, that this act of Congress created no new offense. The publication of malicious falsehood, to the injury of government, was and is a crime at common law; and some of the judges of the Supreme Court of the United States have pronounced this law of Congress to be constitutional. But though constitutional, it was probably not expedient; for a law of that kind can not, in this country, be enforced. When political parties of nearly equal strength, are arrayed against each other, any law restricting the licentiousness of the press, will be denounced as unconstitutional. The publication of falsehood can not be restrained by law. The sedition law expired by its own limitation.

In regard to the alien law, it may be stated, that laws of a similar tenor have existed in all civilized countries. A state of enmity and war between nations has led the governments to employ spies or secret emissaries in an enemy's country, to detect schemes of hostile policy, or to seduce citizens of such country into their interest. At the time when Congress enacted the alien law, and for years previous, it was believed that emissaries of foreign nations were employed to gain our citizens to promote their views, and seduce them into a connection with some of the belligerent powers of Europe. Certain it is that party spirit, in this country, was greatly exasperated by agents of the French government in the United States.

During the heat of the French revolution, I superintended the publication of two newspapers in New York; of course I was carefully watched by the partisans of France, as these papers were established for the purpose of vindicating and supporting the policy of President Washington, which those partisans alledged to be unfriendly to the French interest. When conversing with gentlemen in the coffee-house, I sometimes turned round suddenly and found a Frenchman just behind me, standing with his ear as near me as convenient, listening to the conversation.

The alien law was justified by the general policy and usage of all nations, and by peculiar circumstances then existing in this country. With regard to alien enemies, such a law now exists in our statute book, and it was executed by President Madison, during the war of 1812, upon Mr. Stuart, the English consul residing in New London.*

The division of the citizens of the United States into two political parties originated in principle or honest views; at least with a great portion of those citizens; but when formed these parties were converted into the instruments of personal ambition.

The principal cause of the parties now existing in this country, and one which will endure as long as the constitution, is the election of the chief magistrate. The power of the president to appoint most of the officers of government, and to remove them at pleasure, gives to him, and to the candidates for that office, almost unlimited influence, and means of corruption; and we are not to suppose that such means will be neglected. While these powers are vested in that magistrate, our country will never cease to be harassed with scrambling for offices, and violent political agitations. And if corruption is used, it is the corruption of the citizens on whom depends the election of the president; and the chief magistrate, elected by a party, will usually or always be the president of a party, rather than of the nation.

Parties, to some extent, will exist in all free governments; but in this country, the constitution, the fundamental form of government, is

---

* It may be noticed that the celebrated orator and patriot, Patrick Henry of Virginia, approved the alien and sedition laws, as good measures.—*Wirt's life of that gentleman, p. 271, ed.* 1841.

adapted to call them into existence, and perpetuate them. The powers of the president for appointing and removing officers, are sources of endless contentions in election ; contentions which will produce every species of corruption, sometimes violence, and always instability of public measures. With these provisions in the constitution, such evils can no more be prevented by prohibitions and penalties, than the laws of gravity can be suspended by human power. In this assertion, I am warranted by the whole tenor of the divine oracles, in the description of the character of man ; by the history of mankind from Adam to this day, every chapter of which verifies the Scriptures ; and by the observations of every man who has lived half a century. The reason is obvious ; government is restraint ; but our constitution, instead of restraining the selfishness and ambition of men, those unconquerable passions which occasion the principal political disorders, presents the most powerful motives to excite them into action. The emoluments of office operate as bounties to excite and encourage factions.

These are some of the principal causes which rend our nation into irreconcilable parties, frustrating all efforts at union, and with the collision of interests growing out of the different circumstances of the states, defeat all attempts to establish a permanent system of laws and measures of general utility, which are demanded by all our national interests.

Thus it happens that some of the provisions of the constitution, intended to be the principal means of securing popular rights, on republican principles, become the instruments of interminable discord.

The limitation of the tenure of the presidential office to one term may mitigate the evils, but will not wholly remove the cause. Nor will changes of men have the desired effect. If the United States are ever to enjoy tranquillity, with general contentment of the citizens, and with a wise and stable system of public measures, while the president is elective, two things are indispensable : the first is, that the candidates for that office shall be deprived, utterly deprived of the power of intriguing for the office : the second is, the establishment of a senate on such principles as to secure their entire independence, that they may effectually check the proceedings of the other branch of the legislature. The independence of each branch of the government is the sheet anchor of constitutional liberty.

There are other causes of public evils in our nation which are more obstinate and formidable than an injudicious mode of electing a chief magistrate. There are, among all classes and all parties of our citizens, erroneous opinions respecting the principles of republican government, which are at variance with experience, and forbid us to expect, that while these prevail, we can ever have a wise, efficient, peaceful, and stable government. These errors are deeply rooted in this country ; they will not yield to argument ; they must be left to experiment, and can be corrected only by disappointment and suffering. In the mean time, the general character and operations of the government will be essentially the same as at present. Occasionally the correction of a mistake may produce a temporary alleviation of distress, a kind of lucid interval in national disorders, but no radical cure.

If the citizens of this country expect redress from arguments and appeals to the people; from incessant complaints of illegal proceedings in elections and legislation; from bitter criminations and recriminations of parties; from the influence of the press; from education in schools, and discussions on morality; or if they expect that the triumphs of either party, with splendid dinners, long speeches, and boisterous hurrahs over dinner tables, will unite discordant opinions and interests, restrain selfishness, ambition, and corruption, subdue the spirit of insubordination, the contempt of law and constitution now prevalent, and subject the mass of people to the influence of truth, by correcting their errors, and detaching them from their seducers,—they unquestionably indulge a most fatal illusion.

A discussion of the great causes of our political and commercial disorders, is not within my design. On one subject, however, I must take the liberty to make a few remarks.

The citizens of the United States profess to constitute a *Christian* nation; but they have attempted to establish a government solely by the help of *human reason*. Our constitution recognizes no Supreme Being, and expresses no dependence on Divine aid for support and success. In this respect, the framers of the constitution are rebuked, not only by the Scriptures, but by heathen sages. Says Cicero, "I never thought any religion to be despised. I have always considered the foundation of our state to be laid in religious institutions, and that without the favor of Heaven, the republic would never have arrived to its present flourishing condition."*

But what say the sacred writers? "Take ye wise men and understanding, and known among your tribes, and I will make them rulers over you." "Thou shalt provide out of all the people, able men, such as fear God, men of truth, hating covetousness, and place such over them, to be rulers of thousands, rulers of hundreds, rulers of fifties, and rulers of tens." "He that ruleth over men must be just, ruling in the fear of God."†

Such are the directions of inspired truth; but in the selection of men to make and execute the laws, is any regard paid to these commands? Even if we had no divine precepts on the subject, every intelligent man might know that the characters here described are the only suitable persons to be intrusted with government.

Human reason is imperfect, subject to error and perversion from a thousand causes, proceeding from ignorance, from prejudice, from interest, from deception. To aid men in the proper use of this faculty, and in the exercise of the intellectual powers, the Creator has furnished them with laws and precepts of positive authority, and binding on the conscience. The observation of these laws is essential to the safety and happiness of human society in all relations, domestic, civil, and political. It is not possible to deviate from the divine precepts, either in the choice of rulers, or in the administration of laws, without exposing society to evils. In electing to office men wholly incompetent or vicious, our citizens depart from divine precepts, renounce divine author-

* De Nat. Deorum, lib. 3.
† Deut. i, 13; Ex. xviii, 21; 2 Sam. xxiii, 3.

ity, and become responsible for all the evil consequences of their reliance on their own reason.  It is an eternal truth, that when the wicked bear rule, the people mourn.

The institution of the Sabbath was designed by the Creator for most important purposes; and the proper observance of it would do more to preserve peace and order in society, than the prohibitions and penalties of law.  But the desecration of this day is sanctioned by the government in the transportation of the mails.  Thus we are at war with the principles of public tranquillity; at war with our duty; at war with our interest; at war with heaven.

It is certain that a government thus formed, and thus administered, can not be a good government; it is not possible.  It is the irreversible decree of heaven, that in all governments founded by human wisdom, and conducted only by human reason, corruption and disorders must ultimately compel men to resort to physical force for the execution of law and the preservation of public peace.  These facts and principles may be considered as unalterable, so long as the throne of the Almighty and his moral government remain unshaken.

# CHAPTER XX.

## STATE OF ENGLISH PHILOLOGY.

### COMMON VERSION OF THE BIBLE.

In the first verse of Deuteronomy, it is said that Moses spake to the children of Israel on this side of Jordan, [the east side,] over against the *Red Sea*. This is an erroneous translation, which, as Calmet observes, sadly confuses geography. The Hebrew word *Suf* here used, is the same word as is used to denote the Red Sea in other passages of the Scriptures, but in all those other passages, it is followed by the Hebrew word for *sea;* in this verse in Deuteronomy, the word for *sea* is not inserted. The Israelites, at this time, were on the east side of Jordan, in the land of Moab, over against the Dead Sea, or Asphaltic Lake. The word *Suf* signifies sea-weed, and it is remarkable that it is still found in the Swedish language with the same signification. The Israelites then were *not* over against the Red Sea, or Arabian Gulf; and the present translation tends to mislead or confound young readers.

In Genesis ii, 13, the river Gihon is said to encompass the whole land of Ethiopia; but the Gihon was one of the rivers of Paradise, in Asia, and of course it was impossible that this river could encompass Ethiopia in Africa, for in such a case, the Gihon must have crossed the Arabian Gulf. The Hebrew word for Ethiopia is *Cush;* and perhaps no error of the translators appointed by King James is more palpable than their conversion of *Cush*, in this and other passages, into *Ethiopia;* following the Septuagint instead of the Hebrew. Ethiopia is a word of Greek formation, not found in the Hebrew, nor is any place of that name found in Asia. Yet Josephus actually decides that the Gihon was the Nile. There is however no difficulty in correcting this error. The *Cush* here mentioned was a territory on a branch of the river Tigris in Persia, the inhabitants of which are called by Pliny, *Cossei;* the country is called in 2 Kings xvii, 24, 30, *Cuthah;* the Hebrew word *Cush* being written in Chaldee *Cuth*.

In Daniel vi, 24, there is a mistake in orthography which makes bad English, and obscures the sense of the passage. When the accusers of Daniel were cast into the den of lions, it is said the lions had the mastery of them *or* ever they came to the bottom of the den. The word *or* should be *ere*, before.

In Psalm lxxvii, 2, is this clause of the verse, " My sore ran in the night." In the margin we find the Hebrew word for *sore* is the name of the *hand*. It is difficult to understand why the hand should *run* in the night; unless the translators supposed the Hebrew word would authorize them to suppose a *running sore* on the hand was intended. The Hebrew verb *nagar* here used signifies indeed to *flow;* but it signifies also to *spread* or *extend*, for *flowing* always implies *spreading* or *extending*. The translation should be, *my hand was stretched out* or *spread*, and so is the version in the French copy of the Bible, published by the Bible Society ; in the Italian copy by Diodati ; in the Latin translation annexed to Vander Hooght's Hebrew Bible, by Smith ; in the version of Jerome ; and so is the clause translated by Parkhurst and by Gesenius.

In several passages of the Old Testament, the word *ancients* is the version of two different Hebrew words, one of which signifies old men or persons, *seniores ;* the other, men of former ages, *antiqui.* As in present usage, the English word *ancients* refers almost exclusively to men of former ages, *antiqui,* I have made the distinction in my copy of the Bible, and when the Hebrew word refers to *seniores,* I have rendered it, *elders.*

In Matthew v, 21, 27, 33, there is, in the common version, this passage : " Ye have heard that it was said *by* them of old time." This is evidently a wrong translation ; instead of the word *by*, the word *to* should be used. So is the passage rendered in all the versions in my possession, except in the English. For proof of this, the learned reader may turn to the Greek, Rom. ix, 26 ; Gal. iii, 16 ; Rev. vi, 11 ; in which the same Greek verb is followed by *to.*

In Matthew xxiii, 24, the word *at* should be *out :* " Who strain *out* a gnat." Every boy in our grammar schools knows that the Greek verb used here signifies to *filter.* Christ did not refer to extraordinary efforts in swallowing a gnat, but to the purifying of liquor by filtering it. The use of *at* is evidently an oversight or misprint, for in the first version of the Bible by Tyndale, the word *out* is used. All the versions of the New Testament in my possession, six in number and in different languages, are correct, except the English. It is surprising that such an obvious mistake should remain uncorrected for more than two centuries.

In John viii, 6, the translators have inserted the words, " As though he heard them not," which have no authority in the original. In no copy of the Bible, do I find these words, except in the English.

In Psalm xix, 1, occur the words *handy work*—" The firmament showeth his *handy work.*" *Handy* implies skill derived from use or experience, and the word is not applicable to the Supreme Being. Dr. Jenks, in his Commentary, justly observes, that there is no warrant for these words in the original. The Hebrew is, the *work of his hands.* But there is another objection to the use of these words : there is no such legitimate compound as *handy work* in our language. The true word in the Saxon original is *hand-work.*

In Acts xii, 4, the word *Easter* is inserted for *Passover.* How could the translators make such a mistake ? The apostles celebrated the Jewish Passover, not Easter.

In Acts vii, 59, there is a most extraordinary interpolation in this clause, " They stoned Stephen calling upon *God,* and saying Lord Jesus receive my spirit." The word *God* is not in the original ; and the insertion of the word makes Stephen guilty of an inconsistency, as his prayer was to Christ. This erroneous interpolation is noticed by Dick in his Theology, Vol. I, 331, Greenough's edition. In all the editions of the Bible in my possession, except our common version, this passage is correct: "They stoned Stephen invoking or praying, and saying Lord Jesus receive my spirit."

In 1 Cor. iv, 4, there is a mistake in the use of the word *by* instead of *against :* "I know nothing *by* myself," ought to be "I know nothing *against* myself ;" that is, I am not conscious of having done any thing wrong.

In Romans viii, 21, the word *because* should be *that :* "By reason of him who hath subjected the same in hope *that* the creature itself shall be delivered." There should be no mark of a pause after *hope* in verse 20th; the pause and the following word *because* render the passage obscure, or rather unintelligible. This mistake is the consequence of classing the Greek *oti* with conjunctions ; a mistake still retained in our Greek grammars and lexicons, to the reproach of our literature.

There is a similar mistake and owing to the same cause, in Luke i, 45 : "Blessed is she that believed, *for* there will be a performance." In this passage, instead of *for* should be *that :* "Blessed is she that believed *that* there will be a performance." This correction appears in the lexicon of Schrevelius, written more than a hundred years ago. See *oti* in that work.

In Colossians iii, 7, there is a mistranslation in all the versions in my possession. "In which ye also walked formerly, when ye lived *in them.*" By this rendering, *in them* must refer to the vices specified in verse fifth. This is tautology, for to *walk* in vices or crimes, and to *live in them*, must mean the same thing. But the apostle undoubtedly meant, by the words *en autois*, to refer to the *children of disobedience*, the wicked perpetrators of the vices, and therefore the Greek words should be rendered *with* them or *among* them.—(See Rosenmuller and Macknight.)

The language of the Bible consists chiefly of Saxon words, as they were used when the first version was made by Tyndale, more than three hundred years ago. The most of these words continue in use, and constitute our present popular language. But the first translator was a native of the north of England, and seems to have used mostly the Scottish dialect. To this circumstance perhaps may be ascribed the common use of the auxiliary *shall* in the Scottish sense, which differs from the English, and as Bishop Lowth observes, *shall* in the version of the Scriptures is often used in the sense of *will.* Hence we must often understand *shall* as equivalent to *will* in modern English, or we must understand passages of the Scriptures as expressing what was never intended. *Shall* in the second and third person expresses a command, promise, determination, or threatening. For example, we say to a child or to a servant you *shall* have a suit of clothes ; you *shall* have a certain sum for a month's service. This is a promise of the father or master. We say to persons under our authority, you *shall* perform such a service ; he or she *shall* do what I command. This expresses a determination of the speaker, and amounts to a command. We say such a child or servant *shall* be punished for a fault. This is a threatening. Such is the use of *shall* in these forms of speech ; every person, old or young, understands this language as here explained ; and no person customarily speaking or hearing genuine English, ever understands *shall*, in such phrases, in any other sense. It is language used by superiors to inferiors; but never by inferiors to superiors.

Now such language can not be used in speaking of the Supreme Being, without a violation of the reverence which man owes to his sovereign. But such use is often found in the common version of the Scriptures. "The Lord *shall* reward the doer of evil according to his wickedness." 2 Sam. iii, 39. In this passage David did not intend to command or promise what the Lord would do, but merely to *foretell*, and *shall* is improperly used. The Lord *will* reward, is the sense. How very irreverent it appears to say, God *shall* give Pharaoh an answer of peace; our God *shall* fight for us! So in the following passages, "the brother *shall* deliver up the brother to death;" "the children *shall* rise up against their parents;" "ye *shall* be hated by all men;" *shall* is very improperly used for *will*, as Christ intended only to *foretell*, and not to threaten, promise or command. In no modern writings is *shall* thus used by good English authors; nor would such use be tolerated.

Equally improper is the use of *should* for *would*, in passages like the following: "If he were on earth, he *should* not be a priest." "For he knew who *should* betray him." These are not good English; *should* ought to be *would*.

It is probable that the use of *which* for *who*, respecting persons; of *shall* for *will*, and of *should* for *would*, has introduced into the common version, a thousand instances of bad English.

*God speed* are either from the Saxon, in which *good* is spelled *god*, and then the word *good* should be used, *good speed*, which would be correct English; or these were the initial words of some proverbial phrase, *God speed you*. Whatever the truth may be, the words as now written ought to be rejected, for they are neither grammar nor sense. It is painful to hear them uttered, as they often are, in a proverbial phrase.

There are many words used in the common version which were well inserted when the translation was made, but having in present usage lost their former signification, they do not, to ordinary readers, express the true sense of the Scriptures. Some of them are wholly obsolete; others are in use, but expressing a different sense from that which the original languages express. Thus *prevent, conversation, carriage, cunning*, never express in the Bible the sense in which they are now understood.

It is often said that the present version of the Bible is the standard of correct English, and useful in preserving it. This seems to me a great mistake; there being no book now in common use, the language of which is so ungrammatical as that of this version. This language is, for the most part, our popular language; and if properly corrected, would be a fine specimen of our Saxon or native tongue. But to be made a model of grammatical English, it must be purified from its numerous errors. This is the more necessary, as our young theologians sometimes use bad English, in imitating the language of the Scriptures. Especially ought the version to be purified from words which express a sense directly the reverse of that which was intended to be expressed. No man can be excused for writing or saying *yes*, when he means *no*;

especially in a solemn document. Neither time nor usage can justify the use of *disannul* and *unloose*, in the version of the Scriptures, when the true sense of the word of God is *annul* and *loose*.

There is a great fault in the present version, in retaining indelicate words and phrases, introduced when the inhabitants of England were rude and unrefined. It appears to me inexcusable, if not immoral, to suffer words to remain in the version, which our manners do not permit to be uttered in company. Doubtless the Hebrew original was not offensive to the Israelites, not being at variance with their opinions and manners. Very different is the case with us. How can we justify the retaining, in the sacred oracles, of language which no decent person can repeat in company, or in the pulpit, and which, if uttered before his family, or in a company of females, would expose a person to be turned out of doors.

Most of the ideas now expressed in objectionable terms, may be expressed in language which would not give offense, or cause a blush in any mixed company, at the present day.

*Obsolete words and ungrammatical phrases, in the common version of the Scriptures.*

*Which* for *who*, referring to persons. This impropriety runs through the version.

*Leasing* for *falsehood*, is wholly obsolete. Ps. iv.

*Trow* for *think*, *suppose* or *trust*, is obsolete. Luke xvii, 9.

*Wist*, *wit*, *wot*, for *know* or *knew*, are obsolete.

*Deal* for *part*, as a *tenth deal*, is obsolete. Ex. xxix.

*Cunning* for *skillful*, is obsolete. Ex. xxvi.

*Surety* for *certainly*, is obsolete. " Of a surety," for *surely*, is not now good English.

*Folk* for *persons* or *people*, is obsolete. Gen. xxxiii, 15.

*Kinsfolk* for *kindred*, is obsolete. Luke ii, 44.

*Evening tide* for *evening*, is obsolete. Gen. xix, 1.

*Trade* for *employment* or *occupation*, is improper. Gen. xlvi, 32, 34.

*Usury* has now a different sense from that in which it is used in the version.

*Let* for *hinder*, is obsolete. Rom. i, 13; 2 Thess. ii, 7.

*Chapiter* for *capital*, is obsolete. Ex. xxxvi, 38.

*Fenced* for *fortified*, is obsolete. Num. xxxii, 17.

*Bid* for *invite*, is obsolete. Matth. xxii, 9.

*Coast* for *border* of inland territory, is obsolete. Ex. x, 14.

*Meat* for *food* in general, is obsolete. Gen. i, 29.

*Carriage* for *baggage*, is wholly obsolete. Judges xviii, 21.

*Entreated* for *treated*, is obsolete. Gen. xii, 16.

*Hay* for *herbage* or *green plants*, is improper. Prov. xxvii, 25.

*Fray* for *terrify* or *drive away*, is obsolete. Deut. xxviii, 26.

*Give suck*, is obsolete or intolerable. Matth. xxiv, 19.

*Discover*, in many passages, should be *uncover*, *disclose*, *reveal*, or *lay bare*. Micah i, 6; Is. iii, 17.

*Conversation*, in the version, never signifies mutual discourse. Ps. xxxvii, 14.

*Prevent*, in the version, never has the sense in which it is now used.

*Bushel.* There is now no such vessel in use. Matth. v, 15.

*Offend*, in the version, has a different sense from that in which it is now generally used and understood.

*Instantly* for *earnestly*, is now improper. Luke vii, 4.

*Strange* for *foreign*, is, in many passages, improper. Ezra x, 8.

*Ship* for *boat*, is very improper. Matth. viii, 24.

*Hell* is often used for *grave*, or the invisible world, and not for a place of torment.

*Devil* is often used most improperly for *demon*. *Devils*, in the plural, is improper, for there is but one devil mentioned in the original Scriptures.

*Convinceth* for *convicteth*, is improper. John viii, 46.

*An hungered* is not good English. Matth. iv, 2.

*Cast out* for *reject*, is improper. John vi, 37.

*Thrust out* for *excluded*, is improper. Luke xiii, 28. How can persons be *thrust out* before they have entered?

*Minished* for *diminished*, is not a word in use. Ps. cvii, 39.

*Straitest* for *strictest*, is obsolete. Acts xxvi, 5.

*Provoke* for *incite*, is not proper. 1 Chron. xxi, 1.

*Demand* is sometimes used improperly for *ask, inquire,* or *request.* Job xlii, 4.

*Take no thought* for *be not anxious*, is not proper. Matth. vi, 25.

*God speed* is neither grammar nor sense.

*God forbid* is a phrase not authorized by the original languages, and sometimes is highly improper. "Hath God cast away his people? *God forbid.*" Here the phrase is applied to a *past* event. "God forbid that God hath cast away his people." Rom. xi, 1.

*Beast*, in several passages in Revelation, is a bad translation.

### ENGLISH AUTHORS.

It is often remarked by foreigners, that the anomalies in the English language render it of very difficult acquisition, and they express much surprise that the English nation should have neglected to reduce it to more regularity. Other nations have not been thus negligent of their languages, but have taken great pains to give them a regular orthography and construction.

This charge of neglect is too well founded, and is reproachful to English literature. The difficulty of learning our language, is not only experienced by our own children, but it is a serious obstacle to the diffusion of it in foreign countries, to the progress of science, and to the success of the gospel among heathen nations.

It may seem strange, but it is true, that the elements of our language are imperfectly understood by those who write expressly for teaching it. I have never yet seen in any British book, a just exposition of the English alphabet, nor any accurate description of articulation. John Walker took great pains to make a book for teaching orthoepy; but see what work he makes in describing and naming consonants.

*B* is flat, *p* is sharp; *v* is flat, *f* is sharp; *d* is flat, *t* is sharp; *z* is flat, *s* is sharp; *th* in *the* is flat, in *eth* is sharp; *g* is flat, *k* is sharp; *ng* is dento-guttural or nasal; *g* in *go* is hard, in *ginger* is soft. The gutturals are *k, g, q,* and *c* hard.

Now the epithets *flat* and *sharp*, *hard* and *soft*, do not describe the quality or uses of the letters ; these might just as well be called *round* and *square*. The difference between *b* and *p* is simply that *b* does not represent so close an articulation of the lips as *p ;* but both represent the same articulation. The same is true of *d* and *t*. The difference between *f* and *v*, is that *f* indicates a mere aspiration without sound ; *v* an aspiration with sound. The same is the case with *s* and *z*, and with *th* in *think* and in *that*. *G* indicates a close articulation in *go*, and in *ginger* its sound is compound, like that of *j*. There is no guttural letter or sound in the English language.

Walker's miserable account of the English alphabet, furnishes the compilers of spelling books in this country with nearly all they choose to write on the subject. Some of them give a part of Walker's erroneous description of the letters ; others nothing. To supply this defect, I have given a more correct account of the alphabet, in the introduction to the recent edition of the American Dictionary, in two volumes octavo, Vol. I, page 71 ; but a more full exposition, particularly of the consonants, in the analysis prefixed to an improved edition of my Elementary Spelling Book.

Walker, in the introduction to his Dictionary, speaks of the doubling of consonants to produce another syllable, as in *mar, marry*. In accordance with this opinion, he informs us that the word *singer* does not finish the *g* like *finger ;* and that *longer, stronger*, have *g* hard and perfectly heard, as in *finger, linger*. In reliance on this opinion, compilers of spelling books in this country tell us that *anguish* is pronounced as if the first syllable ended with *g*, as in *ang-guish ; languid* is pronounced *lang-guid*. In some words the sound of *g* is doubled, as in *angry*, pronounced *ang-gry*.

In pursuance of this principle, *linger* is directed to be pronounced *ling-gur*. Walker writes it in the same manner ; Jameson writes it *ling-ger ;* Jones and Sheridan write it *ling-gur*. All the modern writers, as far as I know, agree in this principle, that an additional consonant is necessary to produce another syllable, as in the examples given by Walker, *mar, marry*.

Now any person may in a moment detect the error of this principle, by pronouncing in the customary manner, *mar-y* and *mar-ry*, for both are pronounced in precisely the same manner. In no case of this kind is there more than one articulation ; the second consonant being entirely useless. So far is it from the truth, that a second consonant is necessary in the second syllable, that it is impossible to pronounce it without stopping at *mar*, removing the tongue from its position, then replacing it for a second articulation. In *ban-ner* we articulate *n* with the end of the tongue against the gum of the upper teeth ; but this is done but once. To pronounce the two consonants *n, n*, we must utter *ban*, then remove the tongue from the gum, and replace it to represent the second *n*. This fact was well understood by the old grammarians, for Johnson, in No. 88 of the Rambler, mentions the decision of the Hebrew grammarians to this effect.

In the case of *ng*, the truth is that these letters always represent one and the same articulation ; the only difference being in the *closeness of the pressure* of the organs. In *singer*, the pressure of the tongue against the roof of the mouth is slight ; in *finger*, the pressure is more close ; but contrary to the declaration of Walker, the letter *g*, to use his words, *is finished* in both cases, and completely finished. A moderate pressure gives the sound of *ng* in *singer ;* a closer pressure gives the sound in *finger*, *linger ;* and the most close articulation gives the sound of *nk*, as in *link*. This degree of pressure stops all sound, while the pressure in *singer* and *finger*, suffers a nasal sound to be uttered ; though in *finger* it is slight.

This exposition refutes the opinion expressed in many of our spelling books, that *n* has a nasal sound before *k*, *q*, and *x*, as in *ink*, *lynx*, *puncto*. It is all a mistake ; *bank* is not pronounced *bangk*. Men who utter a nasal sound in *ink*, *bank*, and similar words, must have a very inaccurate ear, and a very bad pronunciation. Walker's mistake, in this respect, is mischievous.

The reason for doubling consonants, in a multitude of words, was to prevent a mispronunciation of the first vowel. Had *dinner*, *tanner*, been written with a single *n*, as in the words *dine*, *tan*, that is *diner*, *taner*, the learner would be apt to give the first vowel its long sound, as in *di-ner*, *ta-ner*. This introduction of a second consonant, when not authorized by the etymology, was arbitrary, though its effect in preventing a wrong pronunciation is obvious. The practice, however, was not carried through the language ; and we have *habit*, *tenure*, *limit*, *merit*, *melon*, and a large portion of words in which the orthography retains a single consonant, in conformity with that of the original languages from which they are derived, yet the first vowel is short.

But let us attend to the consequences of the mistake of English writers on this point. Supposing a second consonant to be necessary to form a second syllable, the orthoepists in expressing the pronunciation, write two consonants instead of *one*. Thus Walker writes *morral* to express *moral*, *litteral* for *literal*, *tennor* for *tenor*, *anggur* for *anger*, *nativvete* for *nativity*, *ballance* for *balance*. All the orthoepists do the same, to some extent ; but there is no uniformity in their works ; nor does any good reason appear, why the *v* should be doubled in *nativity*, and the *d* not doubled in *rapidity*. The truth is, all these writers mistook the fact, and wrote without rule, or in opposition to principle, introducing thousands of consonants which are needless, as they express or represent nothing.

In my books for teaching the English language, I have made such a division of syllables, that two short rules expressed in two or three lines, determine or show the accented syllable and the sound of the vowel which it contains, in a great proportion of all the words in the language. In this scheme my rules lead to a correct pronunciation, without the use of a single additional consonant, in any regularly formed word.

There is another fault which runs through all the English dictionaries, in which syllables are separated for expressing the pronunciation ; this is the neglect to keep the original word distinct from its affix, or other additional syllables in its derivatives. This can not always be done to advantage, especially in elementary books for young learners, on account of some change of the word in spelling, or for other reasons.

*Ar-ri-val* is a better spelling for a young pupil, than *ar-riv-al*. So *a-ba-ted* for *a-bat-ed*.

But in many cases, the division of syllables should present the original word distinct from additional syllables, that the mode of spelling the original may be uniform, and that the manner in which the derivative is formed may be visible.

The following specimens from English books, will illustrate my observations.

Ab-sur-di-ty for ab-surd-i-ty ; ac-cep-ter for ac-cept-er ; ban-dage for band-age ; bon-dage for bond-age ; de-pen-dence for de-pend-ence ; de-fen-dant for de-fend-ant ; doc-to-ral for doc-tor-al ; doc-tri-nal for doc-trin-al ; dog-mat-i-cal for dog-mat-ic-al ; do-mes-ti-cate for do-mes-tic-ate ; for-mal for form-al ; im-por-ta-tion for im-port-a-tion ; in-fan-try for in-fant-ry ; mus-ki-ness for musk-i-ness ; meth-o-dist for meth-od-ist ; par-en-tage for par-ent-age. Even Lowth wrote correspon-ding for correspond-ing.

Having in early life been instructed in all the irregularities of English orthography, many of them were introduced into my first publications. In my later publications, I have taken great pains to banish them. But in most or all the American elementary books, the compilers have paid little regard to this subject.

The fault of most consequence in Walker's dictionary is the wrong notation of sounds, which tends to lead the inquirer to an erroneous pronunciation. He gives to *a* in *last, mask*, and to a class of words in which *a* is followed by *s*, the same sound it has in *fancy* and *man*. This is called by Jones, a later writer, a *mincing, modern affectation*. He gives to *oo* in *look* and *took*, the same sound as in *booth, tool*. In these examples, Walker directs to a pronunciation which, if it is heard at all, is local, but utterly at variance with general usage in Great Britain, as well as in this country.

To the letters *ch* in *bench, branch*, Walker gives the sound of *sh, bensh, bransh*. This is contrary to the notation of other orthoepists, and to all good usage.

To the short *i* and *y* unaccented, especially to *y* at the end of words, Walker gives the long sound of *e* ; as in *asperity, artillery, article, vanity*, which then are to be pronounced *aspereetee, artilleeree, arteecle, vaneetee*, which Jones denominates *ludicrous ;* but it is more, it is wrong, contrary to all good usage, and absolutely ridiculous.

Walker's pronunciation of *nk*, in *bank*, as if written *bangk*, is not merely wrong, but it manifests an incorrect ear or perception of sounds.

Walker's conversion of *t* before *e* into *ch* in *bounteous, beauteous, plenteous*, which he pronounces *bouncheous, beaucheous, plencheous*, is wrong even to ridiculousness ; it is contrary to all good usage in England as well as in the United States. Equally wrong is his *frontyeer* for *frontier*.

On Walker's notation of *d* and *t* before *u*, hear what Jameson, a later and more correct orthoepist, writes. " The letter *d*, in certain situations, especially before the vowels *i* and *u*, when carelessly pronounced, is apt to slide into the sound of *j*. This, which in fact arises from a slovenly enunciation, is, by Walker, laid down as the strict rule ; *adu-lation* is to be pronounced *adjulation, compendium* is *compenjeum, in-*

*gredient* is *ingrejent.* This, in a passage read or spoken with solemnity, would be *intolerable.* In like manner, the syllable *tu,* in the words *congratulation, flatulent, natural,* &c. will, even when most carefully spoken, receive a sufficient degree of the aspirate, without following Walker's direction to pronounce them *congratshulashun, flatshulence, natshural.*"

This pronunciation is said to have had its origin in the sound or pronunciation of *u,* which Jameson alledges to be *yu.* This name begins with a consonant, and we use it in *unit, union, unanimous, failure,* and a few other words; but this is not its proper pronunciation, in the great mass of words in the language; it is an exception, and a corruption. The proper sound of *u* occurs in *duty, tumult, mutiny, tribunal, fury.* This sound is not *yu* nor *eu,* although it is diphthongal. The attempt to give to *u* this pronunciation, *yu,* in a vast number of words, where it is utterly improper, has introduced more corruptions than any other event since the Norman conquest.

Knowles writes that Walker's pronunciation in these examples is absolute vulgarity and absurdity. Yet these intolerable dandyisms are now taught in this country, and especially in our principal cities.

Nothing is of more consequence in a language than to preserve uniformity in the use of the letters of the alphabet. Every change of their proper sounds is to be reprobated and rejected. Let *d* and *t* have their usual sound.

Among all English orthoepists, there is a mistake which claims notice; this is, that *t* and *c* before *i* in certain words have the sound of *sh,* as in *ocean, ingratiate,* pronounced *oshean, ingrashiate.* But the sound of *sh* in such words does not proceed from *c* or *t* alone; it results from the combination of *c* and *t* with the following vowel. The effect of this mistake is, to make, in many words, a syllable too much. In customary practice, *ingratiate, negotiate* are pronounced in three syllables; never in four. And Walker contradicts his own rule; for he pronounces *ocean, social, saponaceous,* in this manner, *oshun, soshal, saponashus.*

To show how ill-adapted the notation of Walker is to express the real pronunciation of words, take the example of words of four syllables ending in *ary,* as *momentary, secretary.* The vowel *a,* in words of this class, is, by several of the English orthoepists, marked for the sound of the short *a* in *at, fat.* Then the last two syllables are to be pronounced precisely like the verb *tarry.* Now if any public speaker should pronounce them in this manner, *momentarry, secretarry,* he would be derided. The truth is that the real pronunciation is, by all men of every class, *momenterry, secreterry;* and so are these words marked to be pronounced by Sheridan. But this mistake has led into error all the compilers of spelling books in this country, who follow Walker's notation.

If such erroneous notations are strictly followed in our schools, the effect is mischievous; and if they are not followed, they are useless, as well as troublesome. Indeed the attempt to mark the sounds of most unaccented syllables must be useless; for such slight, obscure sounds can not be represented on paper. Besides it is useless for another reason; the pronunciation is learned from usage by the ear, and can not be altered by directions in a book.  The notation of thirty or forty slight sounds, incapable of definition, or of discrimination, except by the ear, is a useless incumbrance in any elementary book.  In addition to these considerations, it may be stated that the notations of sounds in the English books differ in more than a thousand words ; ten times as many as the differences in pronunciation among men of education, either in this country or in Great Britain.

The attempt to teach pupils a difference in the sound of *a* in *parent* and in *fair ;* a difference of sound in *branch* and *last ;* a sound of *a* intermediate between the sound of that letter in *bar, far,* and in *man ;* and between the sound of *e* in *mercy* and *merry,* is perplexing without profit. There is no intermediate sound of *a* in *far* and in *man ;* the sounds in these words are distinct ; the pretended intermediate sound is a mistake ; and the slight difference of the sound of *e* in *merry* and *mercy,* is better learned by usage than by rule.  The fastidiousness of men who attempt to teach these distinctions does more harm than good.

### FALSE ORTHOGRAPHY AND ILL-FORMED WORDS.

No fact in philology presents, in a stronger light, the extreme negligence of English writers, than the introduction into the language, and continued use of words of no legitimate origin.  Any writer may make a mistake through ignorance or by oversight ; but that a nation should suffer the most palpable blunders and vulgar errors, to be continued in use, age after age, is a fact which would be incredible, if we had not the evidence before our eyes.  We have examples in the words *disannul* and *unloose,* which are nonsense ; yet *disannul* occurs in *six* passages of the common version of the Scriptures, and *unloose* in *three ;* and they have stood there from the first translation by Tyndale, more than three hundred years.  What is equally surprising, the word *disannul* occurs in the writings of Lord Bacon, in the works of Robert Hall, and in seven passages of Dick's Theology ; the writings of the last two authors being recent publications.  These are instances of the carelessness of men of the first reputation for scholarship ; for the words mentioned are just as improper as *disruin, unkill* and *undestroy.*

The prefix *un* in English gives a negative sense ; but in some words, it has no effect, for when prefixed, the principal word remains unchanged.  This is the case with *unto,* which by the prefix must signify *not to,* a signification directly contrary to what it is used to denote. This compound word is not in the Saxon, and hence it is never used by the common people, unless it is taken from books.  It is an improper compound, which is now rejected by writers, and ought to be rejected from the version of the Scriptures, and from the language.

The same remarks are applicable to the use of *un* in *unless ;* but *un* can not be rejected from this word, for the use of *less,* in its original application, can not now be revived.

*Wiseacre* is a most extraordinary instance of vulgar corruption received into use.  How *wise* can be applicable to a quantity of land, is a question that must have often puzzled inquirers.  The true word is *wise-sayer,* (German, *weis sager.*)

*Country-dance* for *contra-dance* is an error still used both in Great Britain and the United States. It is found in dictionaries and in the writings of respectable authors. It is not merely bad spelling, but bad spelling that leads to a mistake of its signification.

*Furlough* for *furlow* is another mistake or blunder that tends to mislead a reader. We have the word from the Dutch *verlof* or Danish *forlov*, which signify, *leave to depart, leave of absence,* the precise signification of the word; but our spelling introduces the word *lough*, a lake, which makes the word etymologically nonsense.

*Comptroller* for *controller* is another example of blundering in English writers, very extraordinary, for a bare inspection of the French original (*contre* and *rolle*) might have corrected the mistake. A *comptroller* is a *computer* or *counter* of rolls or records, instead of what it was intended to express, an officer to check the accounts of another officer. Were it not for the mischief such a mistake does, it would be laughable enough to see Congress, and other legislative bodies using this word, and adhering to the practice when they may or do know it to be wrong. The formers of the word might as well have written *cogroller* or *comptstroller.* It is not a little ridiculous for a nation to write one word when they intend to express the signification of another, and continue the practice from age to age; especially when the writing of the letter *n* instead of *mp* would correct the error, and restore the purity of the language. Now see the effect of this mistake. In the laws and resolves of Congress, and in those of the state of New York, we see the word *comptroller ;* in Pennsylvania, the word is written correctly, *controller ;* in Connecticut, it is sometimes written in one way and sometimes in the other. In this case, it is just as easy to be right as wrong; and how desirable is it that men, who claim to be intelligent, should prefer correctness to mistake, and uniformity to diversity.

*Redoubt* and *redoubtable,* instead of *redout* and *redoutable,* are mistakes which were introduced by gross carelessness; for any man might have corrected them by simply opening a French dictionary. What a wretched blunderer must a man have been, to suppose these words to have a connection with the English word *doubt !*

*Handicraft* and *handy-work* for *hand-craft* and *hand-work* are easily accounted for. The mistakes in writing undoubtedly proceeded from a vulgar corruption of the pronunciation. The mischief is, these mistakes lead to the opinion, that the first part of the words is the adjective *handy,* which is not true.

*Farther* and *farthest* present another example of inexcusable negligence in English writers; for a moment's reflection might convince any English scholar that there is no such word in English as *farth,* from which the comparative and superlative forms of the word can be derived. Dr. Johnson noticed this impropriety in his dictionary ninety years ago. The true words, *further, furthest,* from *forth,* are uniformly used in the common version of the Scriptures, and no other word ought to be used.

There is a grammar published in Philadelphia, in which *farther* and *farthest* are given as the comparative and superlative of *far,* and such a book is recommended to use in schools!! Such is the state of scholarship in our country.

Why is *hainous* from the French *haineux*, written in English *hein-
ous* ?   We pronounce it right ; why spell it wrong, introduce an
anomaly, and perplex the learner ?   It is just as easy to be regular
and right, as it is to be irregular and wrong.

Why do the English, in pronunciation, change *humor* into an abominable vulgarism, *yumor* ?

The French *suite*, when we give it the sense of a set of clothes, or
of rooms, or of cards, we write and pronounce as an English word,
*suit*.   Why, when it signifies a *retinue*, do men write it as a French
word, *suite*, and pronounce it *sweet* ?   How ridiculous is it to have two
modes of writing and pronouncing the same word, to express its different applications !   Jameson has rejected the French spelling, as I
have done.

We have *lanch* from the French *lancer* ; why then is *u* introduced
into the word ?

The passion of the English for the French language, or their ignorance of their mother tongue, has introduced several changes from right
to wrong in spelling.   Thus the Saxon *mold*, which some of the best
English writers formerly wrote correctly, has been changed to *mould*,
evidently from the French.

The word *tun*, a cask and a weight, a genuine Saxon word, which
was retained in writing down to the reign of Henry VIII, or later, has
given way to *ton*, from the French *tonne ;* and this change confounds
it with *ton*, from the Latin *tonus*.

In like manner *mode* in grammar, regularly formed from the Latin
*modus*, has given way to *mood*, which spelling is identical with *mood*,
temper or state of the mind, a word of Saxon original.   I follow Bishop
Lowth, who writes it correctly, *mode*.

The Saxon *ecg*, *hege*, or *hegge*, *leger*, *wecg*, and the French *loge*,
are now written *edge*, *hedge*, *ledge*, *wedge*, *lodge*.   The letter *d* was
introduced to prevent a mispronunciation, or to present to the eye the
correct pronunciation of the words.   The same reason requires the *d*
in *alledge* and *ledger ;* for if the etymological spelling is retained,
*allege*, *leger*, the true pronunciation may be readily mistaken.   Writers
err very often in consequence of not understanding the rules which
have been long established.

Why is the letter *e* retained in *height*, when it is not in the original
word *high*.   Why not reject *e*, and write *hight* and *highth* ?

Why is *calcarious* written *calcareous*, contrary to the rule observed
in every other word from a like Latin original ?

When the discoveries of Lavoisier rendered a new word convenient,
and he with his associates formed *oxyd*, regularly from the Greek,
why did the English change the word to *oxide*, departing from a rule
invariably observed in other words, by which the Greek *upsilon* is represented by the English *y* ?   And why add *e* final, when no reason
required it ?   I am glad to see that Ure has restored the letter *y* in *oxyd*,
and wish he had omitted the final *e*, which has no claim to the place.

I am glad also to see that Ure has adopted the true spelling of such
words as *sulphureted*, in which one *t* only is to be used.

Why in mineralogy has the word *gang*, so written in the Teutonic,
been changed into the barbarous *gangue* ?

The English, after hunting for ages for the origin of *chimistry*, resorting by conjecture to different Greek words, and writing it *chymistry* and *chemistry*, both wrong, may now write the word correctly by the change of one letter, which would be in conformity to the spelling in all other European languages. But no; they continue to write it in both the erroneous modes; some with *e* and some with *y*; and in this country, the false spelling *chemistry* is beginning to corrupt the pronunciation.

The English lexicographers, ignorant of the origin of *camphor*, adopted the popular or vulgar spelling, *camphire*, and this finds its way into American books.

How it happened that the English jurists adopted the practice of writing *thoro*, in the phrase *a mensa et thoro*, I can not conceive, as there is no such Latin word as *thoro*, *thorus*; the Latin is *torus*.

The English, for the American *sleigh*, write *sledge*, and use it to express what we write *sled*, which Jameson acknowledges to be correct. The English word, when we have occasion to use it, should be translated into *sled*.

*Plow* and *to plow*, the noun and the verb, should be written in the same manner; they are the same word. So also *practice* and *to practice*; why write *practise*, any more than *notise* from *notice*?

The word *sythe* ought to be written without the letter *c*; *vise*, an instrument, should be written with *s*, not *vice*. *Ax* should be written without the final *e*, as should *deposit*. *Embassador* should be written with the same initial letter as *embassy*, and so it is always printed in Blackstone's Commentaries.

*Melasses*, from the Italian *melassa*, should be written with *e*, as it is always written by Edwards, in his History of the West Indies.

*Zink* should be written with *k*, as it is always written in the languages from which it is derived, the German, Danish, and Swedish; and for another reason, we want the adjective *zinky*, as written by Kirwan, and this could not be formed from *zinc*.

*Build* should be written *bild*, as it is in the German; we pronounce the word right and spell it wrong; the letter *u* does not belong to the original word, and like many other useless letters, serves only to perplex the learner.

*Sluice* is a wrong spelling; it should be *sluse*, as it is contracted from the Latin *exclusus*.

Mistakes in etymology sometimes lead into mistakes of history, and of institutions and customs. Such is the mistake of the British writers on the feudal system, in considering the word *fee*, emolument, and *fee*, a tenure of land, to be the same word, or of the same origin. Hence the writers infer that a *fee* of land, or *feud*, was given to the original owners, as a *reward* for *past* services. This is a great error, which renders the feudal system an absurdity, in requiring a forfeiture of the fee, for failing to perform *future* services. The truth is, *fee*, a tenure of land, has not the remotest connection in origin, with *fee*, an emolument; the latter being from the Saxon *feah*, cattle, which were used for payment, before our ancestors had money; and *fee*, a tenure of land, is an abbreviation of the Latin *fides*. A *feud* is land granted *in trust*, for the performance of certain services in *future*. No person can question this origin, who will look into the Italian language. The word and the feudal system were introduced into England from the south of Europe, not from the north. Hence the word *fee*, a tenure of land, is not found in any language in the north of Europe.

When foreign words are introduced into the English language, we should, in imitation of the Greeks and Romans, make the word to conform to English rules in spelling and in termination. This practice has been pursued in very many words; in others it has been neglected; and this neglect has made the English a strange compound of French and English. For example, *aiddecamp* has become a naturalized English word, for which we have no substitute. Then let it be pronounced as an English word, and have an English plural, *aiddecamps*.

It is on this principle, I have carried through the language, the English spelling of *center, meter, miter, scepter, sepulcher;* for the rule had been long established in *disaster, disorder, enter, encounter, tiger, chamber*, and many other words. Hence I write *maneuver*, and also make *rendezvous* a regular English verb. The French *menagerie* is a common and a useful word, and I have made it English, writing it *men′agery*, with an English accent and pronunciation, in accordance with *baptistery, cemetery, presbytery*.

Words of French origin, which have been long used in their French dress, and which can not be reduced to the English form, without taking an offensive appearance, are left unaltered.

Such a word as *daguerreotype* ought not to be naturalized in English; and especially as we have two elegant words, *heliography* and *photography*, to express the same ideas.

In common practice, a diversity of spelling has been introduced into English books, from the differences in their orthography in the languages, Latin or French, from which different writers derive them. This is the fact with *indorse, insure, inclose*, which are written also *endorse, ensure, enclose*. I have adopted the former spelling.

Of this class of words we have many ending in *ise* or *ize*. I have, in this class, followed the French spelling, in words which we have directly from the French language; as *devise, revise, merchandise, surprise*. But all terminations from the Latin or Greek *izo*, I write *ize*, as *temporize, civilize*. When the original word ends in a vowel, the letter *t* is prefixed to *ize*, as in *stigmatize, anathematize;* but when the original ends with a consonant, the termination *ize* only is to be added. Hence *systematize* is ill-formed; it should be *systemize*.

All words of the same analogy should be written alike, unless for some peculiar reason. Thus if *author, successor*, are written without *u* in the last syllable, *honor, favor, candor*, and others of a like formation, should be written in the same manner. The want of uniformity is perplexing to learners, and it was a great fault of Dr. Johnson to neglect it.

The word *amongst* is not a legitimate word, but a corruption. It should be always written *among*.

*Afterwards, onwards, towards, upwards*, are of ancient origin; but the final letter *s* is useless, and I have rejected it.

English authors have not always attended to analogies or rules, in their decisions on accentuation. Hence they accent *catholicism* on the second syllable. But the rule is, that the termination *ism* never changes the accent of the word to which it is added. This word then is to be pronounced *cath'olicism*, with the accent on the first syllable, as in *cath'olic*.—(See my Elementary Spelling Book, page 132.)

So also *imbecile*, pronounced by the English orthoepists *imbes'sil*, should have the accent on the first syllable, as it is in analogy with *juvenile, puerile, volatile.*

So also *detinue*, in analogy with *avenue, revenue, retinue*, should have the accent on the first syllable, not as the English books have it marked, *detin'ue*. Our practice in pronouncing it *det'inue* is correct.

*Whilst* for *while* is also a corruption, and I have rejected it.

In closing my remarks on false or irregular orthography, I would suggest that American printers, if they would unite in attempting corrections, would accomplish the object in a very short time. To prove how much influence printers have on this subject, I would state that within my memory they have banished the use of the long *s* in printed books; they have corrected the spelling of *household, falsehood*, in which the *s* and *h* were formerly united, forming *houshold, falshood ;* and this has been done without any rule given them, or any previous concert.

### GRAMMAR.

It is a remarkable fact that a correct English grammar is yet a desideratum in Great Britain. All the English grammars follow the old classification of the parts of speech, and the division and names of the tenses, though very ill adapted to represent the real distinctions of time.

The first rule of our grammars is, " that the article is a word prefixed to nouns to point them out and to show how far their signification extends. In English there are two articles, *a* and *the ; a* becomes *an* before a vowel, *y* and *w* excepted, and before a silent *h* preceding a vowel. *A* is used in a vague sense, to point out one thing of the kind, in other respects indeterminate."

Now it so happens, that in a strict sense, there is no article in the English language. *A* is not the original word, but *an ;* and this for the ease of utterance, loses *n* before a consonant, and *a* takes the place of *an.* The truth then is, *an* or *ane* is the Saxon spelling of *one*, the Latin *unus ;* the same word differently written ; and instead of being an article, attached to a word and making a part of it, is an adjective denoting *one*, and nothing more.

It is said that *an* or *a* is indeterminate, or indefinite, that is, it is used before words indeterminate in their signification, referring to one thing of the kind, but not determining which thing. This is not true, as a universal fact ; for *an* or *a* is used indifferently before any noun, definite or indefinite. In the sentence " bring me *an* orange from the basket," *an* refers to any one of a number indefinitely ; but the same is the case with *two, three* and every numerical word in the language. Bring me *two* oranges, any two ; bring me *three* oranges from a basket, any three, and so on to any number.

But in other phrases and sentences, *an* or *a* refers to nouns as definite as possible. " Boston stands on *a* peninsula." Is *peninsula* here indeterminate ? " New York stands on *an* island." Is *island* here indefinite, one of a number, but uncertain which ? " Him hath God exalted to be *a* prince and *a* savior." Are these nouns indefinite ? " But ye are *a* chosen generation, *a* royal priesthood, *a* holy nation, *a* peculiar people." Are these nouns indeterminate ? " There stood up one in the council, *a* pharisee, named Gamaliel, *a* doctor of the law." Are these nouns, *a* pharisee, *a* doctor of the law, indeterminate ?

In the first rule of our grammars then there are three errors ; *an* is not an article, but an adjective, like *one, two, three, four ;* it precedes any noun, definite or indefinite ; *a* does not become *an* before a vowel, but the reverse is the truth ; *an* is original and becomes *a* before a consonant. Yet this rule has stood in our grammars for ages, and our children are daily instructed in all these positive errors.

Johnson writes, " *an* has an indefinite signification, and means *one* with some reference to more." True ; every number has reference to more. He says also, " that *an* or *a* can be joined with a singular." True ; how can *one* be plural ? He says also, " *A* has a peculiar signification, denoting *proportion* of one thing to another." Thus we say, " the landlord has a hundred a year." But this is an elliptical sentence. " The landlord has a hundred pounds in *one* year, or for the rent of *one* year." But we may say also, " the landlord has two hundred pounds for *two* years' rent, or he has a hundred pounds for *two* years' rent, or a thousand pounds for *ten* years' rent ;" and in these sentences *two* and *ten* have a *proportion* to the sums mentioned, as truly as *a* to *one* hundred ; the only difference being, the last sentences are not elliptical. But Johnson's remark is copied into an American dictionary.

To an ignorance of the real character of *an* must be ascribed the use of *an* and *one* together ; as in the phrase such *a one*, or such *an one*. " Such *an one* caught up to the third heaven." " I have had such *a one* made."—(Jefferson, I, 442.) This is in signification precisely the same as *such one one*, and nothing more. We might just as well use the Latin *duo* with *two*, such *duo two*, such *tres three*. The Germans and the French give this word the same names ; they call it an *article* and an *adjective*, but they never use the word twice together, *solch ein ein, tel un un ;* this is an absurdity or blunder peculiar to the English.

Our grammars present us with six tenses of verbs ; but do not allow the definite tenses a place. Yet the combination of auxiliaries and participles in *ing*, forms tenses as certainly as such auxiliaries and participles in *ed*. *I was writing* is as clearly a *tense* as *I have written ;* and the definite tenses in the English language constitute a peculiar excellence, by expressing time with exactness,—an excellence that gives it a superiority over all other modern languages.

In the classification of the parts of speech there are mistakes which render it impossible to analyze many sentences. *If* and *though* are called conjunctions ; but this is not true : they are no more conjunctions than *come* and *go*, or *allow, suppose, admit*. " *If* it shall be fair weather to-morrow, we shall ride." What property of a conjunction, in this sentence, has *if ?* " But I pursue, *if that* I may apprehend." *If* being a conjunction, what is *that ?* How is the sentence to be analyzed ?

*Though* also is said to be a conjunction. Then let the following sentence be analyzed : " But *though that* we or an angel from heaven preach any other gospel." This sentence is found in an old version of the Bible, and is a correct sentence. Then according to our grammars, *but* is a conjunction, *though* is a conjunction ; and what is *that*, and how governed ? In the original form of such sentences, *that* always followed *if* and *though ;* but *that* is now omitted, and the sentence is elliptical.

The truth is, *if* is as certainly a verb, as if it had never been abbreviated and were now written *give ; though* is as really a verb as it would be if not defective ; and the sense of these words when used is the same as it would be if they were called verbs. On no other principle can the sentences in which they occur be correctly understood and resolved.*

*Both* is also called a conjunction. "Burke and Fox were *both* great men." Is *both* in this sentence a conjunction ? What would the Latin *ambo* be in a like construction ?

*Because* is also classed with conjunctions. "We see they could not enter in *because of unbelief*." Let this sentence be resolved upon the principle that *because* is a conjunction. Look into Tyndale's version of the New Testament, and you will see the two words are separate—*be cause*, that is *by cause*. *Because* is no more a conjunction than *by reason*.

*Notwithstanding* is also classed with conjunctions, and *provided* has puzzled our lexicographers and grammarians, who seem at a loss how to dispose of it. Hence the following mistakes of very distinguished writers :

"When human sacrifices are enforced and applauded in one nation, this is not because of their cruelty, but *notwithstanding of their cruelty.*"—Chalmers.

"They are willing to retain the Christian religion, *providing* it continue inefficient."—Robert Hall.

These sentences are little better than nonsense. But let the sentences be resolved on my principles. This is not because of their cruelty, but *notwithstanding their cruelty ;* that is, *their cruelty not opposing,* or in our modern practice, *in opposition to their cruelty ; crudelitate non obstante,* the clause independent or absolute.

They are willing to retain the Christian religion, *provided it shall continue inefficient ;* that fact, *it shall continue inefficient, being provided*—the clause independent.

*That,* when it refers to a sentence, is also classed with conjunctions ; and so are the corresponding words in Greek and Latin, *oti* and *quod.*

---

* The following extracts are from the pen of a president of one of our colleges :
1. Suppose a parent *allows* his child to mingle in society.
2. Suppose the child honestly *desires* religious instruction.
3. If the child *come* to me and *ask* for it.
4. Suppose a child of full age—*came* to me.
5. The law gives the parent the power of prevention, if he *choose* to use it; but if he *does* not use it, and the child *comes* to me to perform this religious service.

*If* and *suppose* are, in these examples, perfectly equivalent. Now substitute *suppose* for *if* in the third example. "*Suppose* the child *come* to me and *ask* for it." "Suppose a parent *allow* his child to mingle in society."

In the fifth example, *if* is followed by *choose,* and *does,* and *comes,* in different modes.

All these discrepancies and improprieties occur within the compass of twenty lines.

This is the most pernicious error that has infected grammar for fifteen hundred years. In consequence of this mistake, Jerome, in his version of the Scriptures, has filled his work with erroneous translations, such as the following: "Think not *because* or *since* I am come to destroy the law and the prophets." "Ye have heard *because* it was said to the ancients." "And then will I profess to them, *because* I never knew you." "Believe ye *because* I am able to do this?"—and so on throughout the New Testament. The same mistake is adopted in a version of the New Testament by Montanus, published with an excellent copy of the Greek Testament by Leusden.

These mistakes in the version of Jerome are corrected in the Douay edition of the Bible, and in the Rheims New Testament. But there are two or three mistakes in our common version of the New Testament, which are the consequence of classing the English *that* with conjunctions.—(See Luke i, 45, and Romans viii, 21, which have been before mentioned.)

Horne Tooke has mentioned this mistake, and correctly explained the use of *that* when referring to sentences; but with astonishing inconsistency he calls it a *conjunction*.

GRAMMATICAL ERRORS IN THE COMMON VERSION OF THE SCRIPTURES, AND IN THE WRITINGS OF THE MOST EMINENT BRITISH AND AMERICAN AUTHORS.

### *Mistakes in the use of the tenses.*

For they feared the people, lest they should *have been* stoned. [Should be.]—Acts. v, 26.

The chief captain, fearing lest Paul should *have been* pulled in pieces of them. [Should be pulled in pieces *by* them.]—Acts xxiii, 10.

We were willing to *have imparted* to you, not the gospel of God only, but also our own souls. [We were willing to impart.]—1 Thess. ii, 8.

Whom I would have retained with me, that in thy stead he *might have ministered* to me, in the bonds of the gospel. [Might minister.]—Philemon, 13.

On the morrow, because he would *have known* the certainty why he was accused by the Jews. [Would know.]—Acts xxii, 30.

Nothing but the expectation of this could have engaged him to *have undertaken* this voyage. [To undertake.]—Jefferson's Works, vol. i, 253.

The merchants were certainly disposed to *have consented* to accommodation. [To consent.]—Id. vol. ii, 22.

I expected to *have sent* also a coin. [To send.]—Id. vol. ii, 91.

I intended to *have written*. [To write.]—Id. vol. ii, 303.

See also vol. iii, 400, 460, and vol. iv, 23, 207, 231.

We can not think that they would all have dared to *have claimed* their admission. [To claim.]—Milner's Church History, ch. ix.

Upon these particular attractions—I intended to *have touched* in the present lecture. [To touch.]—Good's Book of Nature, p. 46.

It furnished us with a great laugh at the catastrophe, when it would really have been decent to *have been* a little sorrowful. [To be.]—Mem. of Hannah More, London, 1776.

I intended to *have sent* this away. [To send.]—Id. 1783.

It was so dismally cold, I should not have been sorry to *have staid* in town. [To stay.]—Id. 1789.

I intended to *have answered* your little shabby letter immediately. [To answer.]—Id. 1789.

If I had not been sensible that an intrusion on your time would *have been* [would be] a breaking in upon what was dedicated to piety and virtue, I could not so long have forborne to *have troubled* [to trouble] you with a letter.—Id. Mrs. Montague, 1791.

They were restrained from publishing it by the evils which they found they might *have suffered* on that account. [Might suffer.]—Macknight, note, Rom. i.

When I transcribed this prayer, it was my purpose to *have made* this book a collection. [To make.]—Johnson's Works, p. 682, Dearb. ed.

It would have been gratifying to *have witnessed* its effects. [To witness.]—Reed and Matheson, i, 281.

I might sooner have gathered materials for a letter, had I not hoped to *have been* reminded of my promise. [To be.]—Johnson's Adventurer, No. 53.

I would fain have fallen aslsep again to *have closed* my vision. [To close.]—Addison's Spect., No. 3. See Nos. 5 and 223.

We hoped to *have seen*. [To see.]—Id. No. 50.

If it had been found impracticable to *have devised* models of a more perfect structure. [To devise.]—Hamilton, Federalist, No. 9.

He had thus as good a right to give this advice to the guardian, as he would have had to *have given* [to give] it to the world.—Webster's Speeches, vol. i, 162.

John Huss appears to have expected that he should *have been* allowed to preach before the council. [Should be allowed.]—Milner's Church History, iv, 185.

Not one of the preceding passages is good English. In this sentence, " *I intended to have written*," the verb *intended* expresses the *time* when the person had the *intention*, and at that time, the purposed writing was *future ;* but to *have written* expresses an act *then past*.

This fault occurs in almost all authors ; it is an every day occurrence in public prints and periodicals. Several examples occur in the common version of the Scriptures, which have remained uncorrected for two or three hundred years.

*Other mistakes.*

They supposed it *had been* a spirit. [To be.]—Mark vi, 49. They will find it difficult to call a single man to remembrance, who appeared to know that life *was* short. [Is short.]—Johnson's Rambler, No. 71.

The prevalent opinion was that the soul *survived* the body. [Survives.]—Campbell's Gospels, p. 306.

She observed—that she *was done* with this world. [Had done.]—Mem. of H. More, 1792.

This latter fault is so common in some of the states, as to be admitted into books for Sabbath schools.

*Would* we not judge in the same manner. [Should we not.]—Campbell's Gospels, p. 93.

He had offered himself a sacrifice for the sins of men, *was* risen from the dead for our justification, and in sight of his disciples *was* just *ascended* up to heaven. [Had risen, and had ascended.]—Milner's Ch. Hist., ch. 1.

The days *were* not expired.   [Had.]—1 Sam. xviii, **26.**

After the year *was* expired.   [Had.]—Esther i, 5 ; Ezek. xliii, **27** ; Acts vii, 30.

*Was* expired.   [Had.]—Roscoe, Leo X, I, 84.

If she *is* returned to her father's house.   [Has returned.]—Lev. xxii, **13.**

*Is* counsel perished—[Has.]   *Is* their wisdom vanished.   [Has.]— Jer. xlix, 7.

Inclined to pine for that which *is* irrecoverably *vanished.*   [Has.]— Rambler, No. 17.

Heshbon *is perished.*   [Has.]—Numbers xxi, 30 ; 2 Sam. i, 17 ; Job xxx, 2.

I *am* lately *returned.*   [Have.]—Jefferson, vol. ii, **18.**

Flavia *is* departed.   [Has.]—Rambler, No. 17.

Demochares *was* arrived.   [Had.]—Rambler, No. 101 ; see 163, 198.

Workmen *were arrived.*   [Had.]—Mitford's Greece, vol. v, **111** ; Butler's Analogy, 138, 37 ; Murphy's Tacitus, vol. i, 76.

*Are* now *ceased.*   [Have.]—Butler's Analogy, 193.

The sixty days *were* not *elapsed.*   [Had not.]—Murphy's Tacitus, vol. i, 171.

The first transports of new felicity *are subsided.*   [Have.]—Rambler, No. 72.

Ours *were* either *fled* or imprisoned.   [Had fled or were imprisoned.] —Hume's Hist., vol. ii.

They *were arrived.*   [Had.]—Gibbon, vol. i, 2.

This use of *intransitive* verbs in a *passive* form is common in England ; though infrequent in the United States.   It is evidently a departure from the original idiom of the Saxon, for it is rarely heard among our yeomanry.   The English seem to have borrowed it from the French.   But however the use originated, it is such a gross violation of principle, that it ought to be reprobated and carefully avoided. What should we say to these phrases : He *was appeared* at an early hour.   They *were walked* half a mile.   The patient *was slept* well the last night.   These phrases are just as correct as *is perished, was arrived, were expired.*

A passage in the history of Herodotus which *has* manifestly *been written* in Italy.   [Was written.]—Mitford, sect. 11, note.

Buildings *have* all *been* anterior to the age to which they are commonly attributed.   [Were anterior.]—Id. ch. x, sect. 11, note.

Homer *has been* [was] far more conversant in military matters than Hesiod.—Mitford, vol. i, 140.

This mistake of the tense is evidently copied from the French, and I know of no author who has fallen into it, so frequently as Mitford.

It would seem that inquietude *was* [is] as natural to it as its fluidity. —Goldsmith's An. Nat., vol. i, p. 166.

If men were assured that the unknown event, death, *was* not the destruction of our faculties of perception and action.   [Is not.]—Butler's Analogy, ch. i, part 2.

I observed that love *constituted* [constitutes] the whole character of God.—Dwight's Theol., vol. i, 165.

Let us suppose a man convinced, notwithstanding the disorders of the world, that it *was* [is] under the direction of an infinitely perfect being.—Butler's Analogy : see part 2, ch. v, and ch. viii.

We might have expected that other sort of persons *should* have been chosen. [Would.] Three other instances occur in the same sentence. Id. part 2, ch. iii.

Agabus—signified by the spirit that there *should* [would] be a great dearth throughout all the world. Acts xi, 28. The like fault occurs in Hebrews viii, 4, 7 ; John xiii, 11 ; and in several other passages of the common version.

Upon the knight's asking him who *preached to-morrow.*—Addison's Spect., No. 106.

God never suffers the plain and faithful *denunciation* of his Gospel to be altogether fruitless.—Milner, ch. x.

*Denunciation* is here most improperly used for *annunciation*, or preaching.

### *Attain* for *obtain.*

If he finds—that he can not deserve regard or can not *attain* it. [Obtain.]—Rambler, No. 2.

Some previous knowledge must be *attained.* [Obtained.]—Id. No. 57.

I was not likely ever to *attain* them. [Obtain.]—Id. No. 197.

Every thing future is to be estimated, by a wise man, in proportion to the probability of obtaining it, and its value when *attained.* [Obtained.]—Id. No. 20.

To the rich I would tell of inexhaustible treasures, and the sure method to *attain* them. [Obtain.]—Id. No. 30.

Property is a kind of good which may be more easily *attained.* [Obtained.]—*Robert Hall*, vol. i, pp. 32, 35.

Freedom was *attained.* [Obtained.]—Id. vol. ii, p. 46.

If he may deviate a little to *attain* the see of Winchester. [Obtain.]— Id. vol. ii, p. 64.

After Augustus had *attained* the peaceable possession of the whole empire. [Obtained.]—Henry's Britain, vol. i, p. 17.

It is now a part of your plans for future life, to begin the great work of *attaining* his approbation. [Obtaining.]—Dwight's Theol., vol. i, p. 118.

This improper use of *attain* originated probably in a mistake respecting its etymology. Bailey, Ash, and Johnson, all refer the word to the Latin *attineo.* This is a palpable error : it is from *attingo*, and the true sense is to *reach* or *come to*, and hence the word should always be followed by *to*, as it is in the common version' of the Scriptures. We *obtain* land by purchase ; we *obtain* a sum of money by borrowing ; but we do not *attain* them. The correct use of *attain* may be seen in Gen. xlvii, 9 ; Ps. cxxxix, 6 ; Prov. i, 5.*

---

* We need not be surprised at the mistakes of authors, when we consider the superficial knowledge of those who compile grammars. The most popular English grammar of modern days was compiled by a man who had no acquaintance with our mother tongue, and who had not the classical attainments which are indispensable qualifications for the admission of freshmen in our colleges.

### ETYMOLOGY.[*]

The only English author who has, to my knowledge, made any important improvement in etymological inquiries, within a century past, is John Horne Tooke. We are indebted to this author for some useful discoveries, or illustrations, of the origin of words. Many of his etymologies are new and correct. But for want of discovering the radical meaning of words, and of the principles of derivation, and from his want of more extended researches, he hastily adopted great errors. For example, he says *right* signifies what is *ordered.* To arrive at this conclusion, he begins with the radical verb *rego*, *rectum;* then resorts to the compound *dirigo, directum ;* and from this he deduces the sense of *direct*, to order.

All this is as unnatural as it is erroneous. *Right*, Latin *rectus*, is *straight*, from the radical sense of *rego*, to rule, which is to *strain, stretch ;* and *straight* is the physical sense, whence we have the moral sense of *rectitude* and righteousness. The opposite sense of *wrong* is from *wring*, to twist or pervert ; so *iniquity* from inequality.

Tooke says that *truth* means simply what is *trowed*, thought, or supposed ; and hence there is nothing but *truth* in the world. Here he mistakes the radical sense ; for *true* is what is *fast, firm*, and *truth* is firmness. Had Tooke consulted the Swedish and Danish languages, he would have discovered his mistake.

Any person who wishes to see how utterly ignorant Tooke was of the radical sense of many words, and of the process of derivation, may satisfy his mind by examining his explanations of the proposition *for*, which are a tissue of mistakes from beginning to end.

In proof of the low state of etymological knowledge in Great Britain, I will advert to Richardson's Dictionary.

Richardson, or his publisher, in a prospectus of his dictionary, has attacked me without provocation, and in violation of all the rules of courtesy. He charges me with " abjuring the assistance of Skinner and Vossius, and the learned elders of lexicography." This charge is too general to be correct. I used Skinner, when his work could be of any assistance to me ; and I abjured Vossius, only when I found his etymologies so utterly incorrect as to be worse than useless.

The prospectus adds : " There is a display of oriental reading in his preliminary essays, which, as introductory to a dictionary of the English language, seems as appropriate and useful, as a reference to the code of Gentoo laws to decide a question of English inheritance." This representation proves the author to be utterly ignorant of the connection between the oriental languages, and their descendants in the west of Europe. For want of the knowledge which I have employed, the author has fallen into egregious mistakes.

The prospectus further asserts, that " Dr. Webster was entirely unacquainted with our old authors." This is untrue ; I had been for forty

---

[*] It is worthy of remark, that men may learn to read and speak a language perfectly, without having much knowledge of the etymology of words. This is a distinct subject, and the acquisition of any tolerable knowledge of it requires a distinct course of study.

years acquainted with some of the best of the old authors ; but I never found any use in consulting them, except in illustrating three or four words. And I go further and affirm, that scarcely one of the early writers, anterior to the age of Spenser, is worth reading, except for gratifying the curiosity of an antiquary. I took a better course ; I applied myself to examine our mother-tongue, in the Anglo-Saxon authors, and from them derived essential benefit.

The following examples will show what title the author has to impeach my labors and my dictionary.

*Abet*, Saxon *betan*, the author says is applied to inciting, causing to *beat* or become *better*.—[From Skinner.]

Now let us substitute *beat* for *abet*, in the examples which Richardson gives to illustrate his definitions.

> It may not be,
> And you that do *beat* [abet] him in this kind,
> Cherish rebellion, and are rebels all.—*Shaks.*

> But let the *beaters* [abettors] of the panther's crime
> Learn to make fairer wars another time.—*Dryden.*

That which demands to be next considered is happiness ; as being in itself most considerable ; as *beating* [abetting] the cause of truth.— Wollaston.

These examples prove the author's explanation not only to be false, but ridiculous. This is not all ; the author omits a most material circumstance in the definition—the application or appropriation of the word to the act of *encouraging or supporting a crime*.

This defect of explaining the *appropriate* use of words, a most necessary part of definition, runs through the whole work.

*Able*, the author, from Tooke, refers to the Gothic *abal*, strength. This is a mistake ; it has no connection with *abal*, any more than it has with *bell* or *bowl*.

The passage from Wiclif, which the author cites, might have taught the author the error of his etymology. " Vessels of wrath the *able into deeth*." The passage is in Romans ix, 22, and in our version, it is rendered, vessels of wrath *fitted* to destruction. Wiclif understood the word, which is from the Latin *habilis*, through the Norman. The original signification of *able* is *fit*, *suitable*, *adapted*, without any particular reference to *strength*. All the uses of the word, implying *strength*, are derivative or secondary.

*Arsenic*, the author from Vossius deduces from the Greek *arsen*, a male, so called from its masculine force in destroying man. This is a mistake, and a ridiculous one too. The word is of oriental origin. The Greeks borrowed the word from the east.

*Algebra*, the author from Menage refers to the Arabic *algiabaral*, rei redintegratio, the restoration of any thing. This is not true ; it is of Arabic origin and easily explained, as it is in my dictionary.

*Camphor*, the author spells *camphire*, which is wrong. He says Vossius thinks it is from the Hebrew ; but it seems Richardson knows nothing about its origin. Yet the word presents no difficulty. See the origin and explanation in my dictionary.

*Almanac.* This word Wachter and Menage pronounce to be of unsettled origin ; and Richardson gives no explanation, although nothing is better settled than its origin. See my dictionary.

Now here are *four words* from the oriental languages, of which the author appears to know nothing, and a knowledge of which the author thinks as little useful, as a code of Gentoo laws to decide a question of English inheritance.

*Allow.* This word Richardson informs us Menage refers to the Latin *allaudare ;* but Wachter to the German *lauben* [erlauben,] Anglo-Saxon *lyban,* to permit. Now if the author had been well acquainted with English law language and history, he would not have committed such a mistake ; for in that language, *allowance* is *allocatio.*

*Attain,* the author refers to the French *attaindre,* Latin *attineo.* But there is no French *attaindre ;* the word intended is *atteindre ;* this however is not from the Latin *attineo,* but from *attingo.* In this reference Johnson and all the English lexicographers are erroneous.

*Attract,* the Latin *attraho,* the author from Vossius, supposes to be from *trans* and *vehere,* quasi *travehere.* How can men of a moderate share of learning make such blunders ? The Latin *traho* is the English *draw.*

*Beau.* The author thinks the plural of this word, *beaux,* may have been corrupted into *bucks.* Was there ever such a combination of ignorance and stupidity ! There is no more connection between *beaux* and *bucks* than between *booby* and *bandit,* or between *garden* and *gingerbread.* *Beaux* is the plural of *beau,* and this is a contraction of the Latin *bellus.*

*Cause* gives the " elders of lexicography" no little trouble. Richardson tells us that " Some think it is so called *a chao,* because *chaos* was the first *cause* of all things : [what, before the Deity ?] Others from the Greek χαυσις, heat or burning, because a *cause* is that which kindles and inflames us to action. Some *a cavendo,* because it is that *quæ cavet,* that any thing should be done or not be done. Some *a casu* quod contigit, accidit. Vossius is in favor of *caiso,* seu *quaiso,* as the ancients wrote for *quæso.*"

It is difficult to imagine that more nonsense could be crowded into so small a compass. Neither Richardson, nor any of his elders of lexicography, appears to have had the least knowledge of the Welsh language, in which is found the original Celtic word from which the Latins had *causa.* The Welsh word denotes an agent or impelling force.

In consequence of not understanding the primary sense, Richardson's definition is erroneous, and little better than nonsense from beginning to end.

*Conge.* The author tells us that Menage, Skinner, and Du Cange, agree that this word is from the Latin *commeatus.* The process is thus stated : Italian *commiato, comiato, comjato, congedo.* French thus : *commeatus, commiatus, comjatus, conge.* Now we might as well derive *dog* from *doctissimus,* thus : *doctissimus, doctisse, docte, dog.*

This word presents not the least difficulty to one versed in the Latin, Italian, and Celtic languages. It is from the Italian *congedo,* leave, permission, from *congedare,* to give leave, from the Latin *concedo.*

*Council* and *counsel* Richardson unites, considering both as from one source ; whereas they have not the remotest connection in origin.

*Deny*, the French *denier*, Latin *denego*, Richardson supposes to be from *de ne agere*, be it not, let it not be. A tyro of fourteen years of age ought to be ashamed of such a supposition. The word is from the French and Latin as above ; but the principal verb *nego*, has its root in the Welsh *nacu*, Swedish *neka*, to deny, hence the English *nay*.

*Floor.* Skinner suggests that this word may have been derived from the practice, in the spring, of sprinkling floors with *flowers*. Miserable guessing ! *Floor* is a word which originally signified the earth or its surface, for the earth was the first floor of men, as it is still of the peasantry in many countries. This word is valuable, as it is found in the Basque or Cantabrian language of Spain ; in the Welsh and Irish ; in the Saxon, Dutch, English, and German. In the latter, the word is *flur*, still signifying a field or level ground, as well as *floor*. It is thus that etymology illustrates history and proves the common origin of nations. Of this result, Richardson appears not to have the least conception.

*Diamond* is said by all the etymologists, (and Richardson adopts their opinion,) to be formed from the Greek α privative and δαμαω to subdue ; quod nulla vi domabilis. Now if Richardson had looked into the Welsh, he would have seen at once that this word has no more connection with those Greek words, than the word *gem* has with *toad-stool*. See *Adamant* in my dictionary.

*Argue* is deduced from the Greek αργος, clear, manifest. But this is not the meaning of αργος ; this word signifies white ; that is, vacant, as any man may see by its derivatives. Yet the author, from this mistake, proceeds to give a wrong interpretation of the verb. The primary sense of the Latin *arguo* is to *strive, twist, struggle* in debate ; hence its derivative senses, smart, witty, jangling, &c. ; senses which can not be deduced from *clearness, openness*.

*Aver* is deduced from the Latin *vereor*, to fear. Then *aver, vereor,* and *fear*, are from one source. Was ever such blundering before admitted into books ?

*Avoid* is deduced from the Latin *vacuus, vacus, vocus*. This is all mistake, and ridiculous mistake too, for the words have different radical elements.

*Clear*, Richardson deduces from the Latin *calo*, to call ; and from the practice in games of proclaiming the victorious. He then proceeds to explain the word, in conformity with this opinion, and gives a series of palpable mistakes.

*Dispatch*, Richardson from Menage forms from *despedire*, that is, *expedire*. So Skinner. Expedire, dicitur qui pedem retentum liberat. [Donatus.] Then to *dispatch* is to *release the detained foot*. What blundering ! These men *make* a Latin word to answer their purpose ; and make one with wrong radical letters ; for they seem not to know that *tch* in English almost always represent a palatal letter *c* or *k*. See *latch* and *match*, in my dictionary. When they have made *despedire*, they commit another enormity, and suppose it to coincide with *expedire ;* and this has a *d* instead of a *c* in the radix, which they suppose to be *pes, pedis*. Such absurdities hardly deserve exposure.

*Furl*, says Richardson, is probably a contraction of *furdle* or *fardle*. Now how easily might the author have turned to a French dictionary, and discovered the true original in the French *ferler !*

*Gallant* furnishes the theme of a long story, and of ridiculous conjectures, but at length it is supposed that the word is from the Saxon
compound, *ge ælan*, to kindle. Nothing is more obvious to a man who
understands the primary ideas of words. *Gallant* is from the radix of
*gallus*, a cock, and Welsh *gallu*, to be able, the primary sense of
which is to strain, and push forward, giving the sense of strength and
boldness.

*Glory* is supposed to be from the Greek γλωσσα, the tongue, from a
conjectured connection between *glory* and *fame*. No; *glory* is from
the common radix of *clear*, and its primary sense is brightness, or
shining.

*Glib* is referred to the Saxon *ge hleapan*, to run or leap. How easy
would it have been to advert to the Latin *glaber*, a word of the same
elements!

*Gridiron* is referred to the French *griller*, a word of different rad-
icals. Had Richardson consulted the Welsh, he would have found the
real origin in the Welsh *greadian*, to heat, to roast.

*Hogshead* is referred to a Dutch compound word signifying a *measure*, and to *hold*. How strange it is, that neither Richardson nor one
of his authorities should discover that the word, in four different languages on the continent, signifies *oxhead !*

Richardson cites Vossius, as deciding that the word *father* is from the
infantile cry, *pa, pa*. Miserable conjecture ! It seems incredible that
any respectable man could indulge such puerility. The word signifies
indeed *genitor*, but such a signification could not have proceeded from
such a babyish source.

It has been the misfortune of all the European etymologists whose
works I have consulted, to be led into errors, in assigning words to their
originals, by a resemblance of words in orthography and pronunciation ; while they have overlooked or never discovered the natural connection between physical actions and properties ; nor the customary associations from which derived words proceed. Hence they often
imagine affinities derived from sounds merely, or from the most trivial
circumstances. Thus, for example, the word *floor* is conjectured to
have had its origin in the practice of sprinkling *floors* with *flowers*.
There is a resemblance in orthography and sound between these words ;
but when or where has such a practice existed ? And if it ever existed, is it supposable that men had no *floors* till they adopted such a
practice ?

Now it is very possible, and perhaps probable, that these two words
proceeded from one radix ; for the Latin *floris* has for its primary signification, the action of *spreading*, the opening of a bud ; and the primary sense of *floor* is that which is spread, or extended. Then a
rational etymologist determines that these words, if connected in origin,
unite in this signification.

From this ignorance of the manner in which men were led to form
words, or what may be called the philosophy of language, have proceeded a great part of all the mistakes which have brought the study of
etymology into disrepute.

The evil of assigning words to a wrong origin, is not confined to the
department of etymology ; it has often led authors, and none more fre-

quently than Richardson, in erroneous explanations. Thus Richardson deduces the word *lad* from the Saxon *lædan*, to lead ; and hence infers that the primary sense is, one *led* or educated to manly virtues. This opinion he has from Junius. Now it so happens that *lad* is not a Saxon word ; we have it from the Welsh. If Junius and Richardson had become acquainted with the manner of deriving words from their originals, they would never have adopted such a conjecture. The words which signify *lad, child,* and the like, are usually derived from the sense of production ; that is, *issue ;* what is brought forth.

*Baron,* Richardson assigns to the Gothic *bairgan,* which he renders to *defend,* and hence infers that the primary sense is, an *armed, defenseful,* or *powerful man.* Here the author is inaccurate in rendering the word *bairgan,* to defend ; the primary sense is to *keep* or *save,* and if it ever signifies to *defend,* this is a secondary or consequential sense. The sense of the word *baron* has not the least reference to *defense.* It is from the root of the Latin *vir,* and this is from the same radix as *virco,* to grow, to be strong ; *vis, viris,* force, whence *virtus,* bravery. But the Gothic *bairgan* belongs to a different family.

From a like mistake, the author assigns to *bargain,* the sense of an agreement, a contract, *confirmed, strengthened, ratified, assured.* But these ideas do not enter into the meaning of *bargain.*

Richardson gives the opinion of Junius, that the word *auger* is from the Saxon *ecg,* Dutch *egge,* edge ; and hence infers that the meaning of *auger* is an *edge-tool.* But the word is fully explained in the Saxon, in which it signifies a *nave-tool* or *nave-borer ;* its original use being to bore the naves of wheels.

Under the word *country,* the author, after stating the opinions of several writers respecting its origin, adds : " May it not owe its origin to the Anglo-Saxon *cunnan,* to bear ?" [he should have written *cennan.*] From this origin he infers that the word may have for its primary sense, the land of one's father, like the Latin *patria.* How could he overlook the Latin *conterraneus,* and the Italian *contrada ? Country* is land adjacent or near to a city.

The author errs in another respect. He brings together all the words of a family ; and to effect a regular, consistent plan of this kind, he ought to have placed the word, which is radical or primary in English, at the head of the family. But he has frequently deviated from this order. Thus he sets *able,* a verb, at the head of the family ; when the *adjective* is the primary word. Indeed *able,* a verb, hardly deserves a place in the list. So he places *author,* a verb, at the head of a family, when the *noun* is the primary word ; and as a verb is not used nor well authorized. So he sets at the head of the family, *anchor,* a verb ; *augur,* a verb ; *disease,* a verb ; when the noun is the word from which the verb and all the derived words proceed. These and many similar examples are all wrong, and tend to mislead the learner.

Richardson retains the old method of noting the accented syllable, and places the mark of accent, in all cases, on the vowel ; a method adopted probably at first from the Greek. Thus he accents *ha'bit, te'nor,* which would naturally lead an inquirer to pronounce as in *fa'vor, fe'ver.* This old rule has been discarded by orthoepists, for more than half a century. By placing the mark of accent after the vowel when long, as above, and after a consonant, when the preceding vowel is short, thus, *hab'it, ten'or*—we direct the learner to correct pronunciation. This is one of the most convenient modes of teaching pronunciation, and the more valuable, as it extends to a great proportion of all the accented syllables in the language.

Richardson, in a preliminary essay, undertakes to explain the origin of languages. His theory is, that each letter was the sign of a separate, distinct meaning; being in fact the sign of a word previously familiar in speech. It would be easy to overthrow this visionary and conjectural theory; but this is not the place.

The author adopts the opinion of Horne Tooke, that the *noun* is the origin of all other words, or was the part of speech first formed. Now it is not possible to know, in all cases, which word, of a family, the *noun* or the *verb*, was first formed; both being written in the same manner.

But one fact is undeniable, that in all languages of which I have any knowledge, by far the greatest part of nouns are *derived words*, and mostly derived from known verbs. *Motion, action*, is, beyond all controversy, the principal source of words; being the physical object which at first most powerfully impressed the human mind. But some objects may have received names, without reference to action. While therefore it can not be denied that, in some instances, a noun may have been the original word, it is demonstrably certain that most nouns are derived words; and that the theory of Horne Tooke is erroneous.

But no fault of Richardson's dictionary is of so much importance as the defect of precise definitions. This defect is so general as to render the work, in a great degree, useless to the young student.

It is not merely the want of discrimination in signification, that injures the value of the work; it is also the *omission* of many important definitions. Thus under *abate, abatement*, there is the omission of the senses of the word in law and in horsemanship; under *account, accountant* is not defined; *acceptance*, in law and commerce, is omitted; *advance, advances*, in a commercial sense, are omitted.

Some of the most common and useful words are wholly omitted; as *abeyance, admiralty, advowson, charter-party.* And what is worse than all, the omission of all the terms in the sciences, which modern improvements have introduced, is the omission of what is most wanted by students at the present period.

The Rev. J. Bosworth has published an octavo dictionary of the Anglo-Saxon language, with explanations of words in modern English. This seems to be an abridgment of Lye's dictionary, in two volumes folio, in which the explanations of words are in Latin. Bosworth's dictionary is a valuable work, though it does not contain the Mœso-Gothic words, which are in Lye's book, and the examples for illustration or authority are not numerous.

Bosworth gives the etymology of very few Saxon words; but here and there he gives his opinion. One instance will be selected for examination. This is respecting the origin of the Saxon *sacu*, which is the modern *sake.* The word in Saxon signifies *strife, contention, suit* or *cause in court.*

Of this word Bosworth remarks, that its " derivation has been a stumbling block for nearly all etymologists." Adelung considers it as the intensive of the German *sage*, a saying. Bosworth then mentions other words that appear to be analogous; *ding*, in German, is a *thing*, a court, but originally altercation, caviling. The Latin *causa*, he says, is derived from *causari*, which is a mistake; the derivation is the other way, and the original word is to be sought in the Welsh.

Bosworth then tells us that the Latin *res* belongs to the root of the German *rede*, speech, *recht*, right, *raushen*, to rush; all which is mistake, and so are other remarks which I omit.

But after all, the author has not even approached the truth. The Saxon *sacu*, English *sake*, is from the same radix as the English *seek*, Saxon *secan*, Latin *sequor*, French *essayer*, whence *essay*. The primary sense of all these words, is to *strive, seek* for, *follow, make efforts to obtain*. Hence its application to causes in court, and as *sacu* is a *suit* in law, so we have *suit* from the Latin *sequor*, through the French; both from one radix.

It is absolutely astonishing to see how little etymology is understood in Europe.

The latest English writer who has attempted the derivation of words is W. T. Brande, a professor of chimistry, who has edited a dictionary of science, literature and arts, which has just arrived in this country.

The word *chemistry*, this author says, is probably derived from the Coptic root *chems* or *hhems*, obscure or secret. The German word *geheim* is apparently of the same origin.

Where this writer found his Coptic word, I do not know; but *chimistry* is derived from an Arabic verb, signifying to conceal, and the word signifies truly the *secret art*. But what has this word to do with the German *geheim*, which is a compound of the common prefix *ge* and *heim*, home; whence *heimlich*, close, private, secret. Surely the author can have very little knowledge of German, or he would not have made such a mistake.

*Fee*, emolument, this author says, is derived from the Anglo-Saxon word signifying money, or from the French *foi*, faith. But the Anglo-Saxon word *feah* signifies cattle, used in trade instead of money. How could the author suppose the word to be from *foi*, faith? How little do writers know of the principles of etymology, when they suppose the word *fee*, an emolument, can have any connection with *faith*.

*Man*, the author refers to the Latin *humanus* or *mens*. How wild must be such a conjecture. The fact is directly the reverse. *Man* is the original word from which *humanus* is formed, but it has certainly no connection with *mens*, mind.

*Orchard*, the author refers to the Greek *orchatos*, a row of trees. But *orchard* has no connection with the Greek; it is a Saxon compound of *ort* and *geard*, a *wort yard*, an inclosure for *worts*, herbs. The latter and true derivation proves that the word was not originally a collection for trees, but of herbs.

*Ordeal* this author derives from the German *urtheil*, the same word differently written. He might as well have derived *urtheil* from *ordeal*, for this would be equally true.

But the most remarkable mistake of Brande, is his spelling of *taffrail* for *tafferel*, and explaining it as a *rail*—"the uppermost *rail* of a ship's stern." The word is from the Dutch, and signifies a *table*, or little table, from the Latin *tabula;* so called from its flat surface. The author has taken the vulgar corrupt pronunciation, and from that made the word signify a *rail*, when in truth it has no such signification. It is probable the word was introduced when the sterns of vessels were formed in a manner somewhat different from the present mode ; but it never had any reference to *rail*.

Shall we never be free from popular errors and vain conjectures! When will men cease to write on subjects which they do not understand ? How respectable does Brande appear when he writes on science, and how he lowers himself when he leaves his proper sphere !

Let us then turn our attention to Germany, where we may find the most profound philological scholars in Europe. But in the department of etymology, we find the Germans still in darkness. Take the following examples from Gesenius, in proof of this assertion.

Gesenius, like the English lexicographers, says, that the Hebrew *ben*, a son, comes from the idea of *building*, that is, of *begetting;* for the verb *banah* signifies to *build*, and sons are metaphorically said to *build up a family*. But it seems never to have occurred to these lexicographers that the offspring of beasts, named from this verb, can not be said to *build up a family;* and what is more to the purpose, the word *beni*, sparks of fire, in Job v, 7, can not with any propriety be deduced from the sense of *building up*. The truth undoubtedly is, lexicographers have overlooked the true primary sense, which is to *throw, thrust, set, lay*. This is the common signification of *building ;* that is, to throw down, set, lay ; in other words, to *found*. It so happens, that this very Hebrew verb is probably retained in modern languages, Irish *bun, bunait*, foundation ; Latin *fundo*. *Building* up, *erection*, is a secondary or consequential sense. From the primary sense however, the sense of son, the young of beasts, and sparks of fire are directly deducible ; they are *issues*, things *sent, thrown* or *thrust out*. This is usually the sense of children or offspring, as it is of branches of trees.

Again, the Hebrew *bara*, to create, Gesenius supposes to express primarily the sense of *cutting, carving, planing, polishing*, from the general sense of the elements *Br*, to separate. But the Hebrew word is the English *bear*, the sense of which is, to *bring forth ;* and this is its signification in the first verse in the Bible. In the beginning God *brought forth* or *produced* the heavens and the earth ; brought them into visible existence, from things not seen, as it is expressed in Hebrews xi, 3.

The Hebrew word *barak* Gesenius supposes to signify primarily to *break down*, to express kneeling. But the verb signifies to *bless*, to *curse*, and in Arabic, in addition to these meanings, it signifies to *rain violently*. Now these senses can not all proceed from *breaking down*. The primary sense is to drive, to throw out, expel ; for this is the usual sense of *speaking*, in all its forms. We have a familiar example of this fact in the Latin *appello*, to call, from *pello*, to drive. So also in *ejaculation*. This fact resolves all difficulty in regard to the opposite senses of the word, to *bless* and to *curse ;* these being different applications of the same action ; a *forcible utterance of the voice.* This also accounts for the Arabic signification, to *rain* violently, which is a *pouring* out from the clouds.

The Latin language retains this identical word in *precor,* applied to *praying* and *imprecating evil.* The Greek has also *bracho,* to sound, and *brecho,* to rain, from the same source, and hence the English, to *bray.*

But a more important mistake in the Hebrew lexicons is, to make the Hebrew *kafar* or *kofar* to be the origin of the English *cover,* and to give that explanation of the word in various passages of the Scriptures. The English word *cover* is from the Latin *co-operio,* through the Italian and French ; and it certainly has no more relation to the Hebrew word, than the English word *plate* has to *pin-cushion.*

Under this Hebrew word is one which signifies a *village,* and this, says Gesenius, is from its *covering* the inhabitants. This is a mistake ; villages do not cover people ; the sense is, *detached, separate, distant ;* a remote place of residence.

From this verb in Arabic came the word *Caffer,* an inhabitant of the south of Africa. How can this word be derived from *covering ?* The truth is, the verb in all the Shemitic languages, signifies to *remove, drive away ;* hence to *reject, deny.* The *Caffers* in Africa were so named from their inhabiting distant villages, or more probably from their rejection of the Mohammedan religion.

### DEFINITION.

Many men of distinguished erudition in England have compiled dictionaries of our language. Of these Dr. Johnson's great work has the preference, particularly in the department of definition.

In one particular, all the English authors of dictionaries have erred ; this is, by following the plan pursued in *translating* dictionaries, in which a word in one language is rendered by a synonymous word in another. This is proper in *translations ;* but in *definitions,* in our own language, this manner of executing a work of this kind must be extremely imperfect. To say that a disease is a distemper, a malady, a disorder ; and a malady is a disease, a distemper, &c. does not answer the purpose of a dictionary by satisfying the inquirer.

In another particular, allied indeed to the foregoing, all the English compilers have been negligent ; they have failed to note the differences of words apparently synonymous. This neglect has given origin to books of synonyms.

All the English dictionaries are very defective in etymology. I have attempted to supply this defect in part, but much remains to be done.

Of imperfect or incorrect definitions, the following are examples.

*Averment,* the establishment of a thing by evidence.—Johnson from Bacon.

An offer of the *defendant* to justify an exception, and the act as well as the offer.—Johnson from Blount, Chalmers, &c. Jameson of Lincoln's Inn. Qu. is Jameson a lawyer ?

The first definition is not correct according to present usage, yet I have *nine* dictionaries before me in which it is copied or abridged into " establishment by evidence ;" four or five of these dictionaries are now used in schools. The second definition is incorrect. In pleading, an averment is made by *either party* to a suit.

*Amercement*, the pecuniary punishment of an offender, or a pecuniary fine.—Walker, Maunder, Sheridan, Jones, Jameson. A fine is a pecuniary punishment. Then what is the difference between *fine* and *amercement* ?

*Escheat*, to fall to the lord of the manor by forfeiture.—English Dictionaries. But in the United States there are no lords of manors.

*Administratrix*, she who administers in consequence of a will.—Johnson, Sheridan, Walker, Jones.

Directly the reverse ; an administratrix administers when there is *no will.*

*Adolescence*, the age succeeding childhood, and succeeded by puberty—that part of life in which the body has not reached its full perfection.—Johnson, Chalmers, Walker, Jones, Sheridan, Jameson, and school dictionaries.

This is incorrect, *adolescence* is the *growth* of a youth, and hence the *state* of growing. In these last words Bailey is more correct.

*Effervesce*, to generate heat by intestine motion.—Johnson, Chalmers, Walker, Jones, Sheridan, Ash, Bailey, Jameson, Maunder, and school dictionaries.

It never occurred to these authors, that *effervescence* is the extrication of an elastic vapor or fluid.

*Efflorescence*, production of flowers ; excrescences in the form of flowers.—Johnson, Chalmers, Jameson, and others.

Very incorrect or imperfect.

*Emigrate*, to remove from one place to another.

*Emigration*, change of habitation ; removal from one place to another.—Johnson, Chalmers, Walker, Sheridan, Jones, Ash, Maunder, Grimshaw, and school dictionaries.

So then, if a man removes from Boston to Salem, or from Broadway in New York to Pearl Street, he *emigrates.*

*Migrate*, to remove, to change place.—Maunder. To remove from one place to another ; to change residence.—Jameson.

This word is not in Johnson and most other dictionaries.

*Peculation*, robbery of the public ; theft of public money.—Johnson, Chalmers, Walker, Sheridan, Jones, Maunder, Jameson, Grimshaw, and other school dictionaries.

Peculation is neither robbery nor theft.

*Accomplice*, a partner, an associate.—Maunder.

A *partner* in *trade* or *manufactures*, is *not an accomplice.*

*Promise*, declaration of some benefit to be conferred.—Johnson, Chalmers, Sheridan, Walker, Jones, Jameson, Maunder, and school dictionaries.

A *prediction* may be a declaration of a benefit to be conferred, as well as a *promise.*

*Ship.* A large hollow building made to pass over the sea with sails.—Johnson, Chalmers, Sheridan, Walker, Jones, Jameson, and others.

*Sloop.* A small *ship*, commonly with only *two masts.*—Johnson.

*Sloop.* A small *ship.*—Walker, Sheridan, Jones.

*Sloop.* A small *ship*, commonly with only *one mast.*—Chalmers, Jameson.

*Brigantine*, [brig.] A light vessel, such as has been formerly used by corsairs or pirates.—Johnson, Sheridan, Walker, Ash, Jones. Jameson, [*brigandine.*]

Now what is a *ship*, a *sloop*, and a *brig* ? What is the difference between them ?

*Water.* A very fluid salt, volatile, and void of all savor and taste ; and it seems to consist of small, smooth, hard, porous, spherical particles of equal diameters, and of equal specific gravities, &c.—Johnson from Newton. These great men may be excused for such a definition of water, as they wrote before the late discoveries in regard to that fluid. But what excuse can be made for Chalmers, [from Todd,] and even for Jameson, for giving such a definition, at this late period ?

*Water.* One of the four elements.—Walker, Sheridan, Jones, Bailey, Ash, Maunder, and school dictionaries. One dictionary has it, a *fluid.* True, and so is blood a fluid ; and milk is a fluid.

*Cross-examine.* To examine witnesses by putting to them unexpected questions.—Maunder.

*Cross-examination.* The act of examining by questions apparently captious ; the faith of evidence in a court of justice.—Maunder.

I can not conceive where this compiler found, or how he could invent, such mistakes.

*Cui bono ? cui malo ?* To what good, to what evil will it tend ?—Maunder, Treasury of Knowledge.

*Cui bono ?* To what end or purpose ? To what good will it tend ?—Usage. (See Biblical Repository, Vol. I, p. 150 and 771.)

This is not all ; the phrase in this sense has become proverbial. But the sense of the words, among the Latins, was different. The true phrase is, " cui est bono," *to whom is it for good,* for whose benefit is it. *Cui* is not an adjective agreeing with *bono ;* but the phrase consists of two datives.

That errors may escape the best scholars, even when using the utmost care and diligence, is certain ; and knowing by experience how difficult it is to avoid mistakes, I would not severely censure the mistakes of other authors and compilers. But I would rebuke the negligence which copies such errors without examination, and continues to republish them age after age. Still more would I rebuke the arrogance of men who write or compile books on subjects of which they have a very superficial knowledge ; relying for truth and facts not on their own resources, but almost wholly on the authority of other men.

### INDUCTIVE GRAMMAR.

Of all the singular schemes for teaching the English language, which modern sciolists have invented, that of teaching grammar by *induction* and *production*, is perhaps the most extraordinary.

Induction signifies the act or process of deducing consequences from premises, principles, or propositions, admitted or proved to be true. But in the grammar of a language there are no premises which require certain consequences, or from which particular inferences are necessarily deducible. The formation of words and the application of them to the expression of ideas are *arbitrary* ; and of course the propriety of them depends wholly on *usage.*

James *is* a good boy. Ask the question, Why must *is* be used here, instead of *am* ? The only answer is, because it is the established usage. James *are* a good boy. Why is this sentence not good English ? Because it is not the usage.

The common practice in English is to form words in the plural number by adding *s* or *es.* Why is this correct ? Because it is the usage. But some nouns are deviations from this form ; as *men, oxen.* Why are these plurals good English ? Because it is the usage. But had these words been subject to the principle of induction, and the general usage been the premise, then the plural of these words would have been *mans, oxes.*

The preterit tense of most English verbs ends in *ed ;* as in *moved,* from *move.* If this rule were the premise, and other verbs were to be formed by induction, then the preterit of *write* would be *writed.* But *writed* is not the preterit ; it is not good English, for it is not the usage.

*He strikes* John, and John strikes *him.* Why must *he* precede *strikes* in the first clause ? Because it is the usage. Why must *him* follow *strikes* in the second clause ? Because it is the usage. These usages are arbitrary ; and when the language was formed, it would have been just as proper to make *him* the nominative, and *he* the objective case or word, as the reverse.

The scheme of *induction* and *production* in grammar is founded on mistake ; for neither one or the other has any thing to do in the construction of language. Common practice or usage constitutes a general rule, and it is convenient that this rule should embrace all like cases, or be as extensive as possible. But in adjusting words to such a rule, there is no *induction ;* for *induction* would render a conformity to the rule *necessary* in every case. Yet there is no such conformity, nor any occasion for it in the language.

Hence it follows that the proper mode of teaching grammar is the common mode ; to define or describe the several classes of words ; then state the general usage, as the rule of construction, and illustrate this by various examples ; and at last, specify the deviations from the common usage, as exceptions to the rule.

## CONCLUSION.

Such is the miserable state of English philology ; such was the language in which I was instructed ; and such, in a great measure, is the language in which children are now instructed. And why is it such ? Read what Bishop Lowth writes on the subject. " A grammatical study of our own language makes no part of the ordinary method of instruction, which we pass through in our childhood ; and it is very seldom we apply ourselves to it afterward. Yet the want of it will not be effectually supplied by any other advantages whatever. Much practice in the polite world, and a general acquaintance with the best authors, are good helps ; but alone will hardly be sufficient. We have writers, who have enjoyed these advantages in their full extent, and yet can not be recommended as models of an accurate style.  Much less then will what is commonly called learning serve the purpose ; that is, a critical knowledge of the ancient languages, and much reading of ancient authors.  The greatest critic and most able  grammarian of the last age, when he came to apply his  learning and  his  criticism to  an  English author, was frequently at a loss in  matters of  ordinary use  and common construction in  his own vernacular idiom.''—(Preface to Lowth's Grammar.)

These remarks are applicable to  the grammatical construction ; but similar  remarks may  be  applied  to  other departments  of  philology. The English language  has  not  been  fully investigated ; instruction in its forms and principles has been left to the  inferior  schools ; even the elements of the  language  have  not  been  understood  and  explained. Particular authors  have  occasionally made corrections in the orthography and accentuation  of  words ; but much of the character of the language has been  formed by popular usage, and subjected to  ignorance and caprice, rather than  to rules and system.   Most of the compilers of elementary books in England, as well as in this country, have been very superficially acquainted with their subjects, and all their works which I have seen are incorrect.

In etymology, if we except the derivation of words from the Greek and Latin, or from more modern languages, there is scarcely a respectable work  which has come under my observation.   In this  department of philology, I have  pursued a new course  and  explored a wide field ; the results are very interesting ; but I began the study late in life, with few books ; I had no model  to follow,  no guide to direct me, and no assistance.  My researches therefore  must be imperfect, and  much is left for future investigation.

In my edition of the Bible and in  books of my own composition, I have rejected words, which, by ill formation or wrong spelling, express nonsense or a perverted sense ; anomalous and  incorrect orthography has been rectified, and the more prominent  errors in grammatical construction have been corrected.

If the English nation, one of the *first* in promoting science, has been the *last* to improve their native language, let their descendants in America supply the defect.   This language is probably destined to be as extensively used as any on the globe, and to be one of the instruments of evangelizing the heathen world ; it is my earnest desire  therefore that the language may be purified, improved  and  rendered an ornament to our literature.

Whether this desire is ever to be  gratified ; whether my corrections are to be respected and introduced into use, or whether they are to be condemned and  treated with neglect, is a question yet to  be decided. If the literary portion of the English and  American nations treat this subject with indifference, and suffer the language to descend to posterity with all its deformities, it will be in vain for me or any other individual to attempt a reformation.   But my own books have been rendered as correct as my present knowledge enables me to make them ; it having been my determination that they shall not be disfigured with the obvious mistakes and  improprieties of common usage.   There is a dignity in truth and correctness which always deserves respect, and which seldom fails to conciliate approbation and favor.